CIVIL PROCEDURE

Examples and Explanations

CIVIL PROCEDURE

Examples and Explanations

Fourth Edition

Joseph W. Glannon

Professor of Law
Suffolk University Law School

ASPEN

PUBLISHERS

1185 Avenue of the Americas, New York, NY 10036
www.aspenpublishers.com

Permissions
Aspen Publishers
1185 Avenue of the Americas
New York, NY 10036

Printed in the United States of America.

ISBN 0-7355-1982-X

3 4 5 6 7 8 9 0

Library of Congress Cataloging-in-Publication Data

Glannon, Joseph W.
 Civil procedure: examples and explanations/Joseph W. Glannon—4th ed.
 p. cm.
 Includes index.
 ISBN 0-7355-1982-X
 1. Civil procedure—United States—Cases. 2. Civil procedure—United States—Problems, exercises, etc. I. Title.

KF8839 .G58 2001
347.73′5—dc21   2001022259

About Aspen Publishers

Aspen Publishers, headquartered in New York City, is a leading information provider for attorneys, business professionals, and law students. Written by preeminent authorities, our products consist of analytical and practical information covering both U.S. and international topics. We publish in the full range of formats, including updated manuals, books, periodicals, CDs, and online products.

Our proprietary content is complemented by 2,500 legal databases, containing over 11 million documents, available through our Loislaw division. Aspen Publishers also offers a wide range of topical legal and business databases linked to Loislaw's primary material. Our mission is to provide accurate, timely, and authoritative content in easily accessible formats, supported by unmatched customer care.

To order any Aspen Publishers title, go to *www.aspenpublishers.com* or call 1-800-638-8437.

To reinstate your manual update service, call 1-800-638-8437.

For more information on Loislaw products, go to *www.loislaw.com* or call 1-800-364-2512.

For Customer Care issues, e-mail *CustomerCare@aspenpublishers.com*; call 1-800-234-1660; or fax 1-800-901-9075.

Aspen Publishers
A Wolters Kluwer Company

I dedicate this book to my parents,
Edward and Helen Glannon.

Summary of Contents

Contents

Preface to Students

Everyone comes to law school with some idea of what a contract is or of the meaning of assault and battery, but who ever heard of supplemental jurisdiction, impleader, or res judicata? Abstract concepts such as these make civil procedure the most unfamiliar and intimidating of the basic law school courses.

However, civil procedure can also be fascinating if you can get by the initial strangeness. Many of the topics covered in the course appear baffling upon first acquaintance but begin to make sense when you see how they apply in particular cases and how they relate to other topics in the course. The goal of this book is to demystify civil procedure by providing concrete examples of procedural doctrines and rules in operation, together with full explanations of how these abstract concepts apply to each example.

Most case books contain major or representative cases but provide little discussion of what the cases mean or "what the law is" on a particular topic. I hope that you will find, as my students have, that the discussion in this book helps to tie the cases together into a coherent picture of the law. In addition, the opportunity to try your hand at the examples and then to compare your answers with mine will provide an incentive to analyze the examples and make that process more rewarding—perhaps even enjoyable.

Each chapter (except for the pleading chapters in Part Six) includes an introduction that gives a basic explanation of the relevant procedural concept followed by a series of examples. The "Explanations" section of each chapter presents my analysis of the examples in that chapter. The most effective way to use the book is to read each chapter when that topic is covered in your civil procedure course and to try to answer the questions yourself, based on my introductions and your reading for class. To keep yourself honest, write out your own analysis of each example, if only in a few sentences, before comparing it to mine. You may also want to review the chapter again after class coverage or discuss with your civil procedure professor any issues that you don't fully understand.

One of my principal frustrations as a first year law student was that the questions posed in the casebooks were too hard. (Many are still beyond me, even after teaching procedure for twenty years.) I think you will find that the examples in this book are geared to cover the basics as well as more sophisticated variations; you really will be able to answer many of them, and the explanations will help to deepen your understanding of the issues.

You certainly will want to use *Civil Procedure: Examples and Explanations* for reviewing your civil procedure course at the end of the year. My students have found that these chapters are an excellent way to test their understanding of each topic and to fill in any gaps in class discussion or case reading. The examples provide an efficient means of learning the material because they help you to actively apply the concepts. You will learn a lot more by doing that than by passively rereading cases. In addition, the process will give you a sense of mastery of the material. As the year progresses, you will find that your ability to analyze the examples improves markedly, and that this positive feedback will help you feel more confident about your analytical skills. Surely every first year law student will be thankful for that.

March 2001   *Joseph W. Glannon*

Acknowledgments

In addition to those who offered advice in the original creation of this book, and in earlier editions, I would like to express my appreciation to Professors Mary P. Twitchell, of Frederic G. Levin College of Law, University of Florida, and Denis F. McLaughlin of Seton Hall University School of Law, for reviewing parts of the manuscript.

As always, I appreciate the excellent support and advice provided by the editors at Aspen Law & Business, including Carol McGeeghan, Melody Davies, and Jessica Barmack. Thanks, too, to Carrie Obry and Leslie Anne Webber for their patient and professional assistance in editing the final manuscript.

Special Notice

For several frequently cited treatises I have used shortened versions after the initial citation to the work. These are as follows: Casad, Jurisdiction in Civil Actions (2d ed. 1991), cited as Casad; Friedenthal, Kane, and Miller, Civil Procedure (3rd ed. 1999), cited as Friedenthal, Kane, and Miller; James, Hazard, and Leubsdorf, Civil Procedure (4th ed. 1992), cited as James, Hazard, and Leubsdorf; Moore's Federal Practice, cited as Moore's; Wright, Federal Courts (5th ed. 1994), cited as Wright; and Wright and Miller, Federal Practice and Procedure, cited as Wright and Miller. (My apologies to supplementary co-authors of the Moore's and Wright and Miller treatises.) For multi-volume treatises (Moore's and Wright and Miller) the volume numbers have been retained before the authors' names.

CIVIL
PROCEDURE

Examples and Explanations

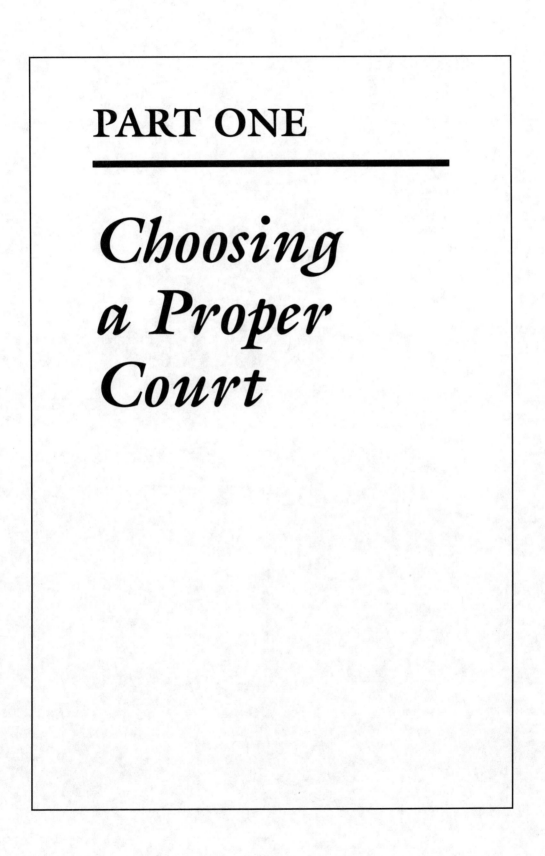

PART ONE

Choosing a Proper Court

1

Personal Jurisdiction: The Enigma of Minimum Contacts

Introduction

There is no place to start like the beginning, and the usual beginning for the defendant is the receipt of a summons from the court with an order to appear and defend a lawsuit. It is never a prospect that evokes much enthusiasm, but the reception is likely to be even chillier if the suit has been filed in a distant state. The defendant will want to know why on earth the plaintiff has chosen to sue in a court a thousand miles away and, perhaps more to the point, whether she *can* sue there. The answer to the second question lies shrouded in one of the foggiest realms of civil procedure, the doctrine of personal jurisdiction.

Ever since the landmark case of *Pennoyer v. Neff,* 95 U.S. 714 (1877), the Supreme Court has consistently held that plaintiffs are not free to bring suit wherever they choose. The fourteenth amendment to the United States Constitution forbids the states from "depriv[ing] any person of life, liberty or property, without due process of law." A state would violate this guarantee if its courts entered judgments against defendants without following a fair judicial procedure, and fair procedure includes not only such traditional elements as the right to counsel or to cross-examine witnesses, but also appropriate limits on the places where a defendant can be required to defend a lawsuit.

The Supreme Court has repeatedly attempted to define the appropriate limits on the power of state courts to "exercise personal jurisdiction over" defendants, that is, to require them to come into the state to defend lawsuits there. A number of bases for personal jurisdiction have evolved, including domicile, consent, physical presence, and the enigmatic "minimum contacts" standard. In many cases in which the defendant is not from the forum state (the state where suit is brought), the only basis for exercising personal jurisdiction over her will be the minimum contacts test developed in *International Shoe v. Washington*, 326 U.S. 310 (1945). This chapter focuses on the meaning of that test.

The Minimum Contacts Test

In *International Shoe,* the Supreme Court held that the courts of a state may exercise personal jurisdiction over a defendant if she has such minimum contacts with the state that it would be fair to require her to return and defend a lawsuit in that state. The Court did not elucidate this somewhat circular proposition by providing a list of what minimum contacts are sufficient, nor did it base the test on the number of contacts with the state. Instead, the Court suggested that whether jurisdiction is permissible depends on the "quality and nature" of the contacts with the state. 326 U.S. at 319. In some cases, the Court indicated, even a single contact will do, but not contacts that are "casual" or "isolated."

This language is too vague to provide much guidance in applying the minimum contacts test, but the rationale of *International Shoe* is more helpful. The *Shoe* Court suggested that a corporation that chooses to conduct activities within a state accepts (implicitly, of course) a reciprocal duty to answer for its in-state activities in the local courts. A defendant should understand that her activities within the state will have an impact there, that those activities may lead to controversies and lawsuits there, and that the state has a right to enforce the orderly conduct of affairs within its borders by adjudicating disputes that arise from such in-state activities. The defendant who deliberately chooses to take advantage of the "benefits and protections of the laws" (326 U.S. at 319) of a state will not be heard to cry "foul" when that state holds her to account in its courts for her in-state acts.

This rationale suggests an important limitation on minimum contacts jurisdiction. Because the court's power to exercise jurisdiction derives from the defendant's voluntary relation to the state, the power should be limited to cases arising out of that relation. *International Shoe* implies such a limitation, and subsequent cases have confirmed that minimum contacts jurisdiction is limited to claims arising from (or, perhaps, related to) the defendant's contacts with the forum state. In *Shoe,* for example, the corporation was held subject to personal jurisdiction in Washington for claims arising out of its shoe sales in that state, but the corporation could not have been required to defend a claim in Washington arising from shoe sales in Texas under a minimum contacts analysis. Sales in Texas are unrelated to Washington; the corporation would certainly not expect to be sued in Washington by a Texas shoe buyer, nor does the corporation take advantage of the benefits and protections of the laws of Washington by its activities in Texas. The analysis must always consider the relationship between the contacts that gave rise to the suit and the state where the suit is brought. Miscellaneous contacts are not minimum contacts. It is the contacts that spawned the lawsuit that are crucial to the minimum contacts analysis.

Specific and General Jurisdiction: The "Shoe Spectrum"

Although *International Shoe* is primarily viewed as a minimum contacts case, the opinion analyzes a broad spectrum of possible contacts with a state and their jurisdictional consequences. Figure 1-1 illustrates this spectrum of increasing contacts.

At one end of the "*Shoe* spectrum" are cases in which a defendant has no contact with the forum state. In such cases, *Shoe* indicates that the state has no authority to exercise personal jurisdiction over the defendant, unless she consents to it. "Casual" or "isolated" contacts (whatever they may be) are also insufficient to support jurisdiction. But other single acts, because of their "quality and nature," will support "specific in personam jurisdiction," that is, jurisdiction over claims arising out of that single act. See, e.g., *McGee v. International Ins. Co.*, 355 U.S. 220 (1957) (upholding jurisdiction over claim arising out of a single contract solicited in the state). Continuous but limited activity in the forum state, such as the ongoing business relationship in *Burger King Corp. v. Rudzewicz*, 471 U.S. 462 (1985), will also support "specific" jurisdiction, that is, jurisdiction over claims arising out of that continuous activity. In each of these categories of cases, the in-state activity is limited. In each, the defendant is only subject to jurisdiction for claims arising out of those "minimum contacts."

The *Shoe* opinion also suggests that if the defendant's forum contacts fall at the far right end of the spectrum, that is, the in-state contacts are very substantial, the defendant is subject to "general in personam jurisdiction." This means that the defendant may be sued in the state for any claim, even one completely unrelated to its in-state activities. Several cases since *International Shoe* affirm that general in personam jurisdiction is sometimes permissible (see *Helicopteros Nacionales de Colombia, S.A. v. Hall*, 466 U.S. 408 (1984); *Perkins v. Benguet Consolidated Mining Co.*, 342 U.S. 437 (1952)), but the Supreme Court has not clearly indicated where the line (marked "G" on Figure 1–1) lies between contacts that support general in personam jurisdiction and those that support only specific, minimum contacts jurisdiction.

Extent of Contacts	no contacts	casual or isolated	single act	continuous but limited		substantial or pervasive
Jurisdictional Consequences	no jurisdiction	no jurisdiction	specific jurisdiction	specific jurisdiction	G	general jurisdiction

Decreasing contacts

Increasing contacts

Figure 1-1: The *Shoe* Spectrum

General jurisdiction is apparently appropriate when the defendant's activities in the state are so substantial and continuous that she would expect to be subject to suit there on any claim and would suffer no inconvenience from defending there. See generally Friedenthal, Kane, and Miller, Civil Procedure §3.10 (3rd ed. 1999) (hereinafter cited as Friedenthal, Kane, and Miller).

Under general in personam jurisdiction analysis, for example, a major American oil company would be subject to personal jurisdiction in many, if not all states, regardless of whether the claim arose in the state where suit was brought. Companies that have such extensive activities, personnel, and facilities in a state may fairly be considered "at home" there and, therefore, subject to the burden of submitting generally to jurisdiction there.[1] This approach is analogous to general jurisdiction over individual defendants based on domicile in the state, which was approved in *Milliken v. Meyer,* 311 U.S. 457 (1940).[2]

Some Guidelines in Applying Minimum Contacts

Several important aspects of the minimum contacts test have been settled by cases since *International Shoe. First,* the minimum contacts test applies to individual as well as corporate defendants. See, e.g., *Kulko v. Superior Court,* 436 U.S. 84 (1978). This makes good sense, since individuals benefit from their voluntary in-state contacts just as corporations do and should likewise understand that those benefits may carry with them the burden of related litigation. *Second,* the limitations on personal jurisdiction found in long-arm statutes are distinct from the constitutional limit imposed by the minimum contacts test. See Chapter 2, which compares these two related concepts.

Third, it is clear that a defendant may have sufficient contacts *with* a state to support minimum contacts jurisdiction there even though she did not act *within* the state. If a defendant commits an act outside the state that she knows will cause harmful effects within the state, she will be subject to minimum contacts jurisdiction there for claims arising out of that act. In *Calder v. Jones,* 465 U.S. 783 (1984), for example, the defendant was held

---

1. Be careful not to confuse general in personam jurisdiction over a corporation with the corporation's state citizenship for diversity purposes under 28 U.S.C. §1332(c)(i). A corporation will almost certainly be subject to general in personam jurisdiction in the states where it is incorporated and has its principal place of business, but it may also be subject to general in personam jurisdiction in many additional states, as in the oil company example described above. General in personam jurisdiction is explored more fully in Chapter 9.

2. One Supreme Court opinion suggests in dicta that general in personam jurisdiction based on extensive in-state contact may only apply to corporations. *Burnham v. Superior Court of California,* 495 U.S. 604, 610, n.1 (1990). Whether or not this is true, the overwhelming majority of general in personam cases involve corporate defendants. Individuals' contacts with states other than their domicile are seldom so extensive as to support an argument for general in personam jurisdiction.

subject to personal jurisdiction in California for an allegedly defamatory article written in Florida, since the article was to be circulated in California, the plaintiff lived there, and the plaintiff's career was centered there. Similarly, if Healy, a Minnesota lawyer, calls a Missouri client on a regular basis to give her legal advice and bills the client for that advice, Healy derives benefits from conducting activities in Missouri. Even if she has never visited Missouri, she will have to answer there for a legal malpractice claim that arises from her deliberate business activity there.

Fourth, minimum contacts analysis focuses on the time when the defendant acted, not the time of the lawsuit. Even if Healy stopped representing her Missouri client a year before being sued and now has no contacts with Missouri, Healy is subject to jurisdiction in Missouri for claims arising from these prior contacts. Minimum contacts jurisdiction is based on the premise that parties who conduct activities in a state accept the risk that those activities will give rise to suits and understand that they may have to return to the state where the activity was conducted to defend such suits. This rationale applies whether or not the defendant is still acting in the state at the time the suit is actually filed. Compare jurisdiction based on service of process on the defendant within the state, which was reaffirmed in *Burnham v. Superior Court of California*, 495 U.S. 604 (1990). Jurisdiction based on in-state service only requires that the defendant be present in the state at the time that the summons and complaint are served upon her. In such cases, the defendant need not have had *any* contact with the state at the time of the events giving rise to the suit.

Purposeful Availment

The toughest problem in applying the minimum contacts test has been defining the "quality and nature" that makes a contact sufficient to support jurisdiction. Many cases have relied on the statement in *Hanson v. Denckla* that the defendant must have "purposely avail[ed] itself of the privilege of conducting activities within the forum State, thus invoking the benefits and protections of its laws." 357 U.S., 235, 253 (1958). This language emphasizes that the defendant must have made a deliberate choice to relate to the state in some meaningful way before she can be made to bear the burden of defending there. Unilateral contacts of the plaintiff or others will not do.

Although scholars have criticized this emphasis on the defendant's purposeful in-state contacts,[3] the Court has consistently required it. In *World-Wide Volkswagen v. Woodson*, 444 U.S. 286 (1980), for example, the Court concluded that the Audi dealer, Seaway, had not purposely availed itself of the opportunity to conduct activities in Oklahoma, although it could foresee

---

3. See, e.g., M. Weber, Purposeful Availment, 39 S.C.L. Rev. 815, 865-871 (1988).

that others would take its cars there. The dealer had not sold cars there, advertised there, cultivated Oklahoma customers, or deliberately focused on Oklahoma as a market. Thus, it had not sought any direct benefit from Oklahoma activities sufficient to require it to submit to jurisdiction there. In *Keeton v. Hustler Magazine, Inc.,* 465 U.S. 770, 780 (1984), by contrast, the defendant had purposely availed itself of the opportunity to engage in in-state activities, by distributing its magazines within the state. Those contacts supported jurisdiction even though the defendant's acts had greater impact in other states, and the plaintiff had few contacts with the forum state.

Much debate has swirled around application of this purposeful avail-ment requirement in cases where the defendant's goods reach the forum state through the so-called stream of commerce. This often happens in one of two ways. *First,* an out-of-state component manufacturer sells compo-nents to a manufacturer of a finished product outside the state. That manu-facturer then incorporates the component into a finished product and distributes the finished product into the forum state. *Asahi Metal Industry Co. v. Superior Court,* 480 U.S. 102 (1987), is an example of this situation. *Second,* a manufacturer sells finished products to a wholesaler outside the state, the wholesaler then resells to a retailer in the forum state, and the re-tailer resells to the consumer.[4] In these situations, the party at the beginning of the stream of commerce (the component maker in the first situation, and the manufacturer in the second) did not import the product into the forum state itself; it sold to others who did. The manufacturer or component maker may know that such resales take place in the state, may think it highly likely, or may not know or care about the ultimate destination of its product.

In *Asahi,* the Court split on the question of whether the mere act of sell-ing goods outside the forum state that will likely be imported into the forum state for resale suffices to support jurisdiction. Justice O'Connor's opinion, joined by three other Justices, rejected the premise that "mere awareness" that the stream of commerce may sweep goods into the state after they leave the defendant's hands suffices to satisfy "purposeful availment." O'Connor would require clearer evidence that the defendant seeks to serve the market in the particular state, such as designing the product for the market in that state or advertising there. 480 U.S. at 112-113. However, the concurring Justices in *Asahi* would find that sending goods into the stream of com-merce, at least in substantial quantities, constitutes "purposeful availment," whether or not the original maker knows that the goods will be sold in a par-ticular state or cultivates customers there. The rationale for this view is that the maker both foresees and benefits from such sales in other states, whether

---

4. A case may also involve both situations, that is, a component is sold to an out-of-state manufacturer, which then incorporates it into a product that is resold to a wholesaler, which imports it into the forum state, thus reaching the ultimate consumer.

it distributes them there directly or simply takes advantage of the fact that another entity conveniently does so in its place.

Since the *Asahi* Court split sharply on this issue, and since the membership of the Court has changed significantly since *Asahi* came down, it is difficult to say what "the law" is on stream-of-commerce cases today. Some courts continue to apply a fairly broad stream-of-commerce approach based on *World-Wide*, and take jurisdiction in cases that the O'Connor approach would not reach. See, e.g., *Ruston Gas Turbines, Inc. v. Donaldson Co., Inc.*, 9 F.3d 415 (5th Cir. 1993); *Barone v. Rich Bros. Interstate Display Fireworks*, 25 F.3d. 610 (8th Cir. 1994). Others appear to adopt the O'Connor view. See, e.g., *Lesnick v. Hollingsworth & Vose Co.*, 35 F.3d 939 (4th Cir. 1994). Many avoid lining up on either side by finding that jurisdiction would be proper (or lacking) under either approach. See, e.g., *Kernan v. Forbes Products Corp.*, 175 F.3d 236 (2nd Cir. 1999). This ambiguity is not very satisfying to an attorney who has to advise a client, or to a first year law student, but it is, as of this writing, the state of the law.[5] It *is* clear, however, that if the defendant's contacts satisfy Justice O'Connor's test they will support jurisdiction, since the other *Asahi* opinions would require a lesser showing.

Other Factors in the Jurisdictional Calculus

There is also a great deal of talk in the cases about factors other than the defendant's in-state contacts, such as the interest of the forum state in providing redress to its citizens, the interest of the plaintiff in obtaining relief in a convenient forum, the interest of the states in enforcing their substantive law or policy, and the extent of the inconvenience to the defendant if she is forced to defend away from home. The cases have repeatedly cited such factors in determining whether it would be fair to assert personal jurisdiction over the defendant. See *Keeton*, 465 U.S. at 775-780; *Burger King*, 471 U.S. at 476-477. However, *Burger King* suggests that, where the defendant has purposely directed activities to the forum state, jurisdiction is presumptively reasonable, and she will have to make a "compelling case" that other considerations make the exercise of jurisdiction unreasonable. *Burger King* at 477. In *Asahi*, on the other hand, the Court found such a case to be made: There, a clear majority of the justices concluded that, even if minimum contacts were established, it would be unreasonable to exercise jurisdiction on the unusual facts of that case.

While the plaintiff's interest, the forum state's interest, and other fairness issues enter the balance once minimum contacts are found, they are not sufficient to support jurisdiction if those contacts are not present. The defendant must first have purposely availed herself of the opportunity to conduct activities in the state. It is only when such deliberate contacts exist

---

5. For the author's prediction on this point, see infra example 11 and n.6.

between the defendant and the forum state (and in specific jurisdiction cases, when those contacts give rise to the claim) that other factors will be weighed in determining whether the exercise of jurisdiction would comport with "fair play and substantial justice."

Thus, although some principles are established in the minimum contacts area, the test still remains difficult to state and even more difficult to apply in close cases. Over the course of your lawyering life it will take on clearer meaning as you handle personal jurisdiction issues and begin to see how courts give flesh to the bare-bones test. The following examples will provide a start in that direction. In answering them, focus on the constitutional issue of minimum contacts only; do not worry about statutory problems under long-arm statutes. Also, assume that the contacts mentioned are the only contacts the defendant has with the forum state.

EXAMPLES

Opening Rounds

1.   Austin is a traveling salesman who lives in North Dakota and sells Fuller brushes in parts of North Dakota, South Dakota, and Minnesota. While en route to deliver brushes to a Minnesota customer, he is involved in an auto accident in Minnesota with Healy, a Minnesota citizen. He brings suit against Healy in North Dakota for his injuries in the accident. Does the court have personal jurisdiction over Healy?

2.   As a result of the same accident, Healy brings suit against Austin for her injuries. She sues in South Dakota. Does the court have jurisdiction over Austin based on minimum contacts?

3.   To be on the safe side, Healy also files suit against Austin in Minnesota. Does that court have personal jurisdiction over Austin based on minimum contacts?

A Parade of Perplexities

4.   *The Volkswagen.* Many of the most difficult personal jurisdiction cases involve commercial contacts, that is, contacts that arise out of business done in the state, either directly or indirectly, by a corporation acting outside the state. *World-Wide Volkswagen v. Woodson,* 444 U.S. 286 (1980) sets out the basic framework for analyzing these cases. The motorcade of hypotheticals that follows may help you to assess the importance of various contacts with the forum state.

Hudson, an Ohio citizen, buys a Volkswagen from Smoky Mountain VW, located on the east side of the Smoky Mountains in North Carolina, while she is on vacation in North Carolina. Shortly after she returns home, all four wheels fall off while she is driving, and Hudson is injured. Understandably upset, Hudson sues Smoky Mountain in an Ohio court for negligence. Does the Court have personal jurisdiction over the dealer?

5.   *The Chevy.* After Hudson leaves, Ford pulls into Smoky Mountain's lot with his engine belching smoke. His car is clearly a total loss, and he tells De Soto, the salesman, that he must have a car to get back home to Florida. De Soto sells him a (very) used Chevy. After crossing into Florida, Ford pushes the windshield wiper button, and the engine automatically ejects into the Everglades. Ford sues De Soto and Smoky Mountain in Florida. Is personal jurisdiction proper there?

6.   *The Maserati.* De Soto has an eye for fast cars. At the moment, he has a nice Maserati on the lot, with all the extras (engine, wheels, brakes). A customer tells him that a trucker buddy of his, Packard, from Pennsylvania, might be interested in buying the Maserati. De Soto calls Packard in Pennsylvania, extols the Maserati's virtues and encourages her to come in and test drive the car on her next delivery in North Carolina. Packard does stop to see the car, likes it, and buys it. She makes the mistake of towing it home, only to discover upon arrival that the engine, lights, carburetor, and exhaust system are missing. She sues De Soto in Pennsylvania. De Soto has no other contacts with Pennsylvania. Will the Pennsylvania court have personal jurisdiction over De Soto?

7.   *The Audi.* After lunch, Rambler comes in. Rambler lives across the border in Tennessee, where he read in a Tennessee paper Smoky Mountain's ad for a one-year-old Audi for $1,100. Because the Smoky Mountain dealership is located ten miles from the Tennessee border, it advertises frequently in Tennessee, as well as in North Carolina. Rambler visits the dealership, talks De Soto down to $1,025 and buys the car. He barely gets across the Tennessee line when the steering wheel comes off in his hand, and the body comes entirely loose from the frame of the car. Rambler sues Smoky Mountain in Tennessee. Does the court have personal jurisidiction over Smoky Mountain?

8.   Assume, on the facts of example 7, that Smoky Mountain only advertises occasionally in Tennessee and derives only 5 percent of its business ($20,000 of its annual gross sales of $400,000) from sales to Tennessee customers. The rest of its sales are in North Carolina. Rambler sees the ad and buys the Audi at Smoky Mountain's dealership; it breaks down in Tennessee on the way home. Can Rambler sue Smoky Mountain in Tennessee?

Sports Cars

9.   *The Ferrari.* You can't work all the time. When De Soto relaxes, he likes to go to the Georgia coast for some deep sea fishing. While drinking at a bar in the fishing lodge there, he gets to talking with Lenoir, another guest at the lodge. Lenoir asks De Soto about his work. The two get into a car lovers' debate over the relative merits of various sports cars. Before leaving the bar, Lenoir asks De Soto for his card.

Two months later, Lenoir visits Smoky Mountain and buys a jazzy looking Ferrari from De Soto. Imagine for yourself what happens to the Ferrari when Lenoir gets it back to Georgia. Lenoir sues De Soto in Georgia. Will the court have personal jurisdiction over De Soto?

Changing Cars in Midstream

10. *The Off-Road Vehicle.* Nippon Auto Unlimited is a Japanese corporation that manufactures off-road vehicles in Japan for sale worldwide. It sells substantial numbers of these vehicles in Japan to A-1 Wholesalers, Inc., a California dealer in off-road vehicles, which resells them in various Western states, including Nevada. Nippon sells an off-road vehicle to A-1, which then sells it to Fred's Recreational Emporium in Reno, Nevada. Fred's sells the off-road vehicle to Lincoln, who is injured (in Nevada) when the vehicle collapses while driving over a crack in the sidewalk. Lincoln sues Nippon in a state court in Nevada.

    a. Does the Nevada court have jurisdiction over Nippon?

    b. Would it have jurisdiction over A-1 if Lincoln sued it in Nevada?

11. Assume that A-1 bought the off-road vehicle from Atlanta Importers, Inc., a large importer of off-road vehicles in Atlanta, Georgia. A-1 has the off-road vehicles shipped to California and resells some to Fred's in Nevada, where Lincoln bought hers. Could Lincoln sue Atlanta Importers in Nevada?

12. *The Edsel.* Andretti is an Indiana race car driver whose hobby is collecting antique cars. He notices an ad in *Antique Auto,* a national magazine, for a mint condition Edsel for sale by a Michigan collector, Studebaker. He calls Studebaker, gets further information on the car, and decides to go up to look at it. While he is in Michigan, he and Studebaker discuss price but do not settle the deal. After Andretti returns to Indiana, he calls Studebaker back, agrees to his price, and arranges to pick up the car the following month. After buying the car and returning with it to Indiana, he discovers that it is a cleverly disguised Dodge Dart. He sues Studebaker in Indiana. Will the court dismiss for lack of personal jurisdiction?

13. Reconsider the case just described, involving Andretti's purchase of a car from Studebaker. However, assume that, instead of reading about the car in *Antique Auto,* Andretti dialed up Studebaker's "Hot Cars" website and learned of the Edsel through the Internet. He then called Studebaker, and the transaction unfolded as above in example 12. Could Andretti sue Studebaker in Indiana on his fraud claim arising out of the sale?

Fundamental (Un)truths

14. Every year, the following statements sprout like dandelions in civil procedure bluebooks. What is wrong with them?

    a. "Even if the defendant lacks minimum contacts with the state, the plaintiff may be able to get jurisdiction over him if he has taken advantage of the benefits and protections of the laws of the state."

b. "The defendant may be sued in the state because she has engaged in deliberate acts there and thus has minimum contacts sufficient to support personal jurisdiction."

EXPLANATIONS

Opening Rounds

1.   In this case Austin has sued Healy in a state in which Austin has contacts, but Healy has none. As far as the example tells us, Healy has never been there, has not formed any deliberate relationship to or performed acts within the state, and has done nothing to derive benefits from North Dakota. Consequently, she has no reason to expect to be sued there and has not impliedly swallowed that bitter pill in exchange for the benefits of in-state activity. She lacks minimum contacts with North Dakota and may not be sued there on this claim.

As this conclusion suggests, the personal jurisdiction rules are defendant-oriented: The plaintiff's contacts with the forum state will not do; the court must find some basis for forcing the defendant, the unwilling litigant, to appear before it. Conversely, if the defendant has minimum contacts with the forum state, it is irrelevant (at least, for personal jurisdiction purposes) that the plaintiff has none.

One might well ask why Austin should have to go to Healy instead of Healy coming to Austin. If someone will have to be inconvenienced by the suit, shouldn't it be the defendant rather than the injured plaintiff? On the other hand, the defendant may be completely blameless: Plaintiffs lose law suits as well as win them. If so, it seems unfair to add the insult of distant litigation to the injury of being sued in the first place. Perhaps more importantly, the defendant (unlike the plaintiff, who started the suit) has not chosen the forum and ought to have some veto power over unreasonable choices by the plaintiff.

2.   The South Dakota court will not have personal jurisdiction over Austin under the minimum contacts test. It is true that Austin has some contacts with South Dakota because he travels there to sell brushes. However, *International Shoe* does not hold that a defendant may be sued in a state simply because she has some contacts with that state. *Shoe* holds that a defendant may, by committing limited acts within a state, submit herself to jurisdiction for claims arising out of the in-state acts themselves. Here, Healy's claim is unrelated to Austin's brush sales in South Dakota. Austin had no reason to believe that he was submitting himself to the jurisdiction of the South Dakota courts for auto accidents in Minnesota by selling brushes in South Dakota. The situation would be different if the claim were for faulty brushes sold to a South Dakota customer. In that case, the claim would arise directly from Austin's voluntary contacts with the state, and jurisdiction would be proper.

However, Healy may still be able to sue Austin in South Dakota for the auto claim. Ever since *Pennoyer v. Neff,* 95 U.S. 714 (1877), it has been permissible to obtain personal jurisdiction over an individual defendant (that is, a person) by serving her with the summons in the state where suit is brought. The Supreme Court has reaffirmed that such "transient jurisdiction" is permissible, even if the defendant is only in the state briefly or for reasons unrelated to the litigation. *Burnham v. Superior Court of California,* 495 U.S. 604 (1990). Thus, if Healy is determined for one reason or another to sue in South Dakota, she may bring suit there and have the process server await Austin's next sales trip into the state.

3.   Healy has gotten it right by suing Austin in Minnesota. Austin's act of driving in Minnesota provides a minimum contacts basis for a suit against him there for injuries suffered in the accident. Motorists who use the roads of a state should realize that this purposeful activity in the forum subjects other drivers to serious risks, that people may be injured and may sue. It would be unfair to allow drivers to take advantage of Minnesota's highways but not to call them to account there for accidents they are involved in on those highways.

Even if causing the accident in Minnesota were Austin's only contact with the state, it would support specific in personam jurisdiction in this case. The "quality and nature" of this single, purposeful act, and the consequences that may predictably ensue from it, are so serious as to make it reasonable to force the driver to return to defend a suit that arises from the accident. This is true whether Austin causes an accident while in Minnesota on business or in Florida on vacation.

A Parade of Perplexities

4.   As the heading suggests, this case bears some resemblance to *World-Wide Volkswagen v. Woodson.* Here, as in *World-Wide,* the plaintiff purchased the car in one state and took it to another where she suffered injury from alleged defects in the car. As in *World-Wide,* the plaintiff sues where the injury is suffered, although the defendant acted in a distant state and is still in that state. And, as in *World-Wide,* the court will dismiss this case for lack of personal jurisdiction. Smoky Mountain (like Seaway in the *World-Wide* case) has committed no deliberate act that affiliates it with Ohio. It does not sell cars there, has not availed itself of the protection of Ohio's laws, and has no reason to expect that it will be sued there. Although it is foreseeable that the car will be driven though or end up in Ohio, it is equally foreseeable that it will go to many other states. A rule that such foreseeability establishes jurisdiction would essentially subject the seller of any portable product to nationwide jurisdiction, making "the chattel [product] his agent for service of process" (*World-Wide Volkswagen* at 296) wherever the buyer takes it.

5.   This case is somewhat stronger than Hudson's, since De Soto at least knew he was dealing with a Florida citizen who would use the Chevy in Florida. However, it is very doubtful that this knowledge is enough to support jurisdiction over De Soto or Smoky Mountain in Florida. Personal jurisdiction is the price defendants pay for deliberate efforts to derive benefits from or conduct activities in a state. These defendants did not solicit any business in Florida; they did not even solicit business from a Floridian. Ford rolled into the dealership under his own steam and initiated the transaction in North Carolina. It was only by chance that Ford told De Soto why he needed the car; it is reasonable to infer that it was irrelevant to De Soto that Ford planned to drive it to Florida. (A sale is a sale, right?) De Soto and his employer derived benefits from dealing with a Floridian in North Carolina, not from conducting business activities in Florida. Ford's Florida domicile is a unilateral contact of the plaintiff, not the defendant, with the forum state. See *Hanson v. Denckla*, 357 U.S. 235, 253 (1958); compare *Burger King*, 471 U.S. at 478-482, in which jurisdiction was upheld because the defendants had an on-going contractual relationship with a large Florida franchise, agreed that Florida law would govern the relationship, and regularly related to the Florida headquarters of the franchise regarding important aspects of their business.

It is true that the Supreme Court cases emphasize that the plaintiff's interest in a remedy and the forum state's interest in providing one are part of the personal jurisdiction calculus. See, e.g., *Asahi*, 480 U.S. at 113-115; *Keeton v. Hustler Magazine*, 465 U.S. at 775. However, before those factors can be weighed in favor of jurisdiction, the defendant must be shown to have appropriate purposeful contacts with the state asserting jurisdiction. *Burger King Corp. v. Rudzewicz*, 471 U.S. at 474-478. De Soto's relation to Florida on these facts appears too attenuated to support such a finding.

Nor is it sufficient that the defendants could anticipate that the car would be used in Florida. If that were sufficient to support jurisdiction, then the local store that sells a defective mountain climbing rope could be sued in any mountainous state, or a farmer who sells rancid tomatoes to railroad dining cars could be sued in any state the railroad serves. The Court has chosen a narrower view of personal jurisdiction, focusing on the scope of the activity of the seller, rather than the predictable area of use of the product by the buyer.

6.   Here, as in example 5, De Soto has consciously dealt with an out-of-stater, but here, unlike the earlier situation, he has voluntarily affiliated himself with the plaintiff's state. He not only anticipates that his acts will have consequences in the other state, but he has also deliberately set those events in motion by his own in-state act. De Soto voluntarily reached into Pennsylvania to conduct business with a Pennsylvanian. He made representations to Packard in Pennsylvania that encouraged her to come to North

Carolina to buy the car. He can reasonably anticipate that Packard will use the car extensively in Pennsylvania and likely suffer harm there from any defects in the car. De Soto should realize that his deliberate relationship with a Pennsylvanian, which he initiated by calling into that state, may lead to a lawsuit and that if a claim arises out of the sale, Packard will likely bring the suit in Pennsylvania. Thus, De Soto will be subject to personal jurisdiction in this action. His single contact with Pennsylvania is sufficient to support specific in personam jurisdiction (that is, jurisdiction for claims arising out of the contact itself), although it would not support jurisdiction for claims that did not arise out of the sale.

7.   In this case the dealership has reached into Tennessee to solicit business. It has attempted to draw customers from there into North Carolina, and in Rambler's case it succeeded. Although the actual sale took place in North Carolina, the claim arises directly out of deliberate efforts to serve the Tennessee market. Smoky Mountain can hardly plead unfairness or surprise when suits that arise from those efforts are brought in Tennessee. Even Justice O'Connor should have no problem upholding jurisdiction in this case, since the defendant has intentionally attempted to derive profits from dealing with Tennessee customers.

It is important that the dealership is the defendant here, instead of De Soto, because it is the dealership that solicited the business in Tennessee, not the salesman. It is unlikely that the dealership's contacts with Tennessee will be imputed to its employees. (Compare example 6, in which De Soto personally initiated contacts with the forum state.) Thus, if Rambler wanted to sue De Soto and Smoky Mountain together, he would probably have to bring suit in North Carolina.

8.   This hypo makes an important point. Personal jurisdiction is not based on the most contacts or the best contacts but on minimum contacts. Here, Smoky Mountain has a great deal more contact with North Carolina than it has with Tennessee, but the dealership has solicited business in Tennessee, and the claim arises out of its efforts to obtain that business. That is enough to support jurisdiction in Tennessee. Smoky Mountain will not be able to defeat jurisdiction there by arguing that it has more contacts with North Carolina.

A corollary of this point is that a defendant may be subject to minimum contacts jurisdiction in more than one state for a claim that arises from a transaction involving contacts with a number of states.

Sports Cars

9.   In my estimation, this is the kind of "casual" or "isolated" contact (*International Shoe,* 326 U.S. at 317) that is insufficient to subject the defendant to personal jurisdiction. Although De Soto did act in the state, he was not soliciting business and did not initiate the conversation for business

purposes. He gave Lenoir his card at Lenoir's request. He did not encourage Lenoir to go to North Carolina to buy a car. In the "but-for" sense, this contact did give rise to the claim Lenoir asserts, but it was not a purposeful act intended to take advantage of the benefits and protections of conducting activity in Georgia. De Soto would be justifiably upset if this off-hand interaction led to a suit in Georgia. He would hardly expect that to be the consequence of responding to a request for a business card, and jurisdictional doctrine is largely based on a common sense appraisal of what people should expect.

There is room for debate on this case, but it is doubtful that this constitutes deliberate in-state activity intended to exploit the local market or affect local citizens. In this regard, it is clearly distinguishable from the Maserati case, in which De Soto deliberately initiated a business contact with the in-state plaintiff, or *McGee v. International Ins. Co.*, 355 U.S. 220 (1957), in which the insurer reached into California by sending an offer there to reinsure a Californian.

Changing Cars in Midstream

10a. This is a relatively typical stream of commerce example, in which an out-of-state (in this case, out-of-country) manufacturer sells its product to a wholesaler outside the forum state, which then independently imports the product into the state for final sale to consumers. As in most cases, the original seller, Nippon, does not control the subsequent flow of the "stream." Nippon may or may not know that A-1 resells in Nevada, though it certainly could predict that it will. Doubtless, it hopes that A-1 will sell as widely as possible and profits from those sales regardless of what it knows about A-1's market area.

In the first edition of this book, written before *Asahi* was decided, I offered the following analysis of a similar example:

> *World-Wide Volkswagen* clearly supports jurisdiction over such out-of-state (or out-of-country) suppliers who deliver "products into the stream of commerce with the expectation that they will be purchased by consumers in the forum State." 444 U.S. at 298.
>
> Here, Nippon has purposely taken advantage of the benefits and protections of the laws of Nevada by importing cars to that state and deriving a profit from those sales. It cannot insulate itself from the jurisdictional consequences of that activity by using wholesalers to channel the goods into the state.

Since *Asahi*, however, it is not so clear that putting goods into the stream of commerce constitutes sufficient "purposeful availment" to support jurisdiction over Nippon in Nevada. Nippon has not done any of the things Justice O'Connor would require to cultivate the Nevada market. It neither markets directly there, nor advertises there, nor designs its goods for Nevada buyers. It just sells its product in Japan to a foreign whole-saler.

Arguably, this example is distinguishable from *Asahi*. The defendant there was a component maker, not a manufacturer of a final product. Also, it was a third-party defendant, not a direct defendant as here. More importantly, Nippon sold to an American buyer, while *Asahi* sold to a Taiwanese corporation. But it does not appear that these distinctions would make a difference to Justice O'Connor. Her position requires an active effort to serve the forum state market to support stream-of-commerce jurisdiction; Nippon merely sells its off-road vehicles to wholesalers in Japan. If O'Connor's view is "the law," or becomes the law, Nippon would apparently not be subject to jurisdiction in Nevada.

The concurring opinions in *Asahi* suggest that jurisdiction should be proper in this case, assuming that a reasonable quantity of Nippon's products are resold in Nevada, since Nippon predictably derives benefits from the ultimate sale of its goods in Nevada. Those benefits are the same, whether Nippon directs A-1 to sell in Nevada, knows that it does, suspects that it does, or deliberately avoids finding out. Arguably, that economic reality should support jurisdiction over Nippon, even though it does not control the means by which its product enters the forum state.

b. There is no question about jurisdiction over A-1 in Nevada on this claim. It imported the vehicle into the state, a purposeful contact, which directly gives rise to the claim.

11. The main difference here is that the defendant is an out-of-state corporation, not a corporation from another country. This might influence the second prong of the jurisdictional inquiry, the reasonableness of taking jurisdiction. Almost all the Justices considered it relevant to the fairness analysis that Asahi would be dragged into a foreign court halfway around the world. Here, unlike *Asahi*, the defendant, Atlanta Importers, has imported the product into the United States. Clearly, it is trying to serve the United States market.

It is not clear, however, that these distinctions would lead Justice O'Connor to a different conclusion on the issue of purposeful availment. Atlanta Importers has still sold a product to a buyer in Georgia, with no special knowledge or effort to serve the Nevada market where its buyer resold the product. If the O'Connor view would reject jurisdiction in cases like this, and if it becomes the position of the Court, this would be a very substantial change in the limits of jurisdiction in stream of commerce cases. (Compare *World-Wide*, 444 U.S. at 297-298 (reasonable to subject manufacturer to suit if it "serves, directly or indirectly, the market for its product" in the state)). Indeed, this reasoning could lead to a rejection of jurisdiction, even if Atlanta *manufactured* the off-road vehicles in Georgia but sold to wholesalers there for marketing in other states. See, e.g., *Lesnick v.*

Hollingsworth & Vose, 35 F.3d 939 (4th Cir. 1994) (maker of "micronite" filter not subject to jurisdiction in state where cigarettes incorporating filter sold).[6]

12. This is a close case indeed, perhaps too close to call. Studebaker does have a contact with Indiana: He advertised in a magazine circulated there with the express purpose of selling his Edsel. On the other hand, the magazine is a specialty publication circulated nationally. Studebaker was not specifically soliciting an Indiana buyer but was willing to sell to anyone, in or out of the state. Once Andretti learned of the car's availability, he took the initiative: He went to Michigan to see the car; he called back to make an offer; and he picked up the car in Michigan. Studebaker remained in Michigan and passively responded. It was irrelevant to him that Andretti was from Indiana. He may not even have known where Andretti was from.

I think this is a case in which the defendant does have a deliberate contact with the forum state, but the totality of the circumstances weighs against jurisdiction in Indiana. At least eight of the *Asahi* Justices agreed that, once a jurisdictionally significant contact with the forum state is found, the Court must consider whether it would be fair and reasonable under all the circumstances to take jurisdiction. 480 U.S. at 113-116. Given the lack of deliberate acts by Studebaker in Indiana, that all the negotiations took place at Andretti's initiative, and that Studebaker never left Michigan, it appears unreasonable to expect Studebaker to defend this claim in Indiana. Once again, compare example 6, in which the seller solicited the sale in the forum state.

13. Doubtless the Internet has changed a great many things, but it hasn't really changed the basic principles of personal jurisdiction. In this case, as in example 12, Studebaker has advertised the car but has not really reached in to Indiana specifically. The initiative came from Andretti and the transaction unfolded in Michigan. The court would likely conclude that the act of posting the car on a website accessible in Indiana (or anywhere else, for that matter) is like the advertisement in example 12, and insufficient to constitute purposeful availment by Studebaker. See, e.g., *Mink v. AAAA Development, LLC.,* 190 F.3d 333 (5th Cir. 1999) (website which constituted "passive advertisement" not sufficient to support jurisdiction).

---

6. If you want this author's view on how this will be resolved, it is that it won't be. The Court is likely to proceed on a case by case basis, and each will turn, as personal jurisdiction cases inevitably do, on its facts. If the Court ultimately requires more than placing goods into the stream, it is likely to require *very little more.* On the facts of this example the Court would likely recognize the economic reality that the very purpose of the importer is to serve the United States market, not just the Georgia market. Thus, the resale of its off-road vehicles in Nevada is consistent with Atlanta Importer's goals and expectations, and the company should be subject to jurisdiction there, even if it does not have the various in-state contacts referred to in the O'Connor plurality.

However, where the defendant engages more actively in in-state commerce over the Internet, jurisdiction will be found. If, for example, substantial negotiations take place between the defendant and the plaintiff in the forum state over the Internet, or products are sold into the forum state over the Internet, purposeful availment is likely to be found, just as it would be if the same contacts arose in person or by phone or fax. See, e.g., *Euromarket Designs Inc. v. Crate & Barrel Ltd.*, 96 F. Supp.2d 824 (N.D.Ill. 2000) (jurisdiction over defendant who conducted catalogue sales in Illinois over the Internet). Basically, it seems fair to say that analysis in Internet jurisdiction cases requires the same close examination of the defendant's specific contacts with the forum as in any other type of personal jurisdiction case.

Fundamental (Un)truths

14a. This statement implies that taking advantage of the benefits and protections of the laws of the state is an alternative basis for personal jurisdiction, independent of the minimum contacts test. On the contrary, the purpose for asking whether the defendant has taken advantage of the benefits and protections of the state's laws is to *evaluate* the defendant's contacts with the state, to ascertain whether they are of the "quality and nature" to support jurisdiction. If the defendant's in-state acts demonstrate a deliberate effort to take advantage of the benefits and protections of the forum state's laws, it is a fair inference that these acts satisfy the minimum contacts test, since minimum contacts jurisdiction is based on the defendant's deliberate decision to act in the forum state for her own purposes.

b. The problem with this statement is that it suggests that a defendant is subject to jurisdiction in a state for any claim if she has *some* contacts with the state. Not so. Conducting some activity in a state does not support such wide jurisdiction. Unless the contacts are so substantial as to pass that ambiguous "G" line in Figure 1–1, the defendant is only subject to jurisdiction for claims *related to the in-state contacts*.

Precision and clarity are the stock-in-trade of the law student as well as the lawyer. A few students who make statements like this on the exam have not really grasped the distinction between specific and general in personam jurisdiction. But most really mean to say, "The defendant may be sued in the state on this claim under the minimum contacts test because it has purposely conducted activities there, and the claim arises out of this purposeful contact." This second statement is not only a great deal more precise than the first, but it is accurate, while the other, as it stands, is not. It is differences like this that separate the daffodils from the dandelions in the Merry Month of May.

2

Statutory Limits on Personal Jurisdiction: The Reach and Grasp of the Long-Arm

Introduction

As Chapter 1 explains, the due process clause of the fourteenth amendment to the Constitution imposes fundamental limitations on the power of state courts to exercise personal jurisdiction over defendants in civil suits. Under that clause states may only assert jurisdiction over defendants who have established a significant relationship to the forum state, such as domicile, in-state presence, continuous and substantial business within the state, consent to suit in that state, or minimum contacts with the state that gave rise to the claim in suit. If the defendant is not subject to personal jurisdiction within the forum state on one of these limited bases, the court will be unable to adjudicate the plaintiff's claim.

However, even if it is constitutionally permissible for a court to exercise personal jurisdiction in a case, that court may still lack the power to call the defendant before it. The due process clause does not actually confer any jurisdiction on state courts; it only defines the outer bounds of permissible

Constitutional scope of jurisdiction
under the due process clause

Statutory power to exercise jurisdiction
under California Civil Procedure Code
§410.10 (same as constitutional scope)

Figure 2-1

jurisdictional power. That is, it says in the state legislatures: "When you authorize your courts to exercise jurisdiction, you may not go any further than this." It is up to the legislature of each state to actually grant the power to its courts to exercise personal jurisdiction, through jurisdictional statutes. Thus, every personal jurisdiction issue involves a two-step analysis. *First,* the court must ask whether there is a state statute that authorizes it to exercise personal jurisdiction under the circumstances of the case. *Second,* if there is, the court must ask whether it would be constitutional under the due process clause to do so.

State legislatures are free to grant their courts the power to exercise personal jurisdiction to the limits of the due process clause or to confer only part of the constitutionally permissible jurisdiction. In some states the legislature has granted the courts the full scope of personal jurisdiction permissible under the due process clause. California's statute, for example, authorizes its courts to exercise jurisdiction "on any basis not inconsistent with the Constitution of this state or of the United States." Cal. Civ. Proc. Code §410.10. In states with statutes like California's, the two inquiries are collapsed into one: If the court has the constitutional power to assert jurisdiction, it automatically has the statutory power to do so as well. Visually the relationship may be (somewhat simplistically) portrayed in Figure 2-1. One advantage of such expansive provisions is that they are "self-adjusting"; that is, if the courts reinterpret the due process clause to allow the exercise of personal jurisdiction in additional circumstances, these statutes automatically authorize the courts of the state to exercise jurisdiction in such cases. See K. Beyler, The Illinois Long-Arm Statute: Background, Meaning and Needed Repairs, 12 S. Ill. L.J. 293, 319, 320 (1988).

"Enumerated Act" Long-Arm Statutes

Other states, however, have not given their courts blanket authority to exercise personal jurisdiction to the limits of due process. Instead, these states have passed "long-arm" statutes, which authorize their courts to exercise jurisdiction over defendants based on specific types of contact with the forum state. Historically, these "enumerated act" long-arm statutes were passed in reaction to *International Shoe* and its progeny. See generally R. Casad, Jurisdiction in Civil Actions ¶4.01 (2d ed. 1991) (hereinafter cited as Casad). Once *International Shoe* and succeeding cases established that certain types of contacts were constitutionally sufficient bases for exercising personal jurisdiction over nonresidents, the states adopted long-arm statutes to authorize their courts to hear cases arising out of such contacts. Such enumerated act long-arm statutes frequently authorize state courts to exercise jurisdiction over cases arising out of contacts such as committing a tortious act within the state, transacting business in the state, or owning property in the state. A fairly typical provision is the Uniform Interstate and International Procedure Act, 13 U.L.A. 355 (West 1986), which has served as the model for the long-arm statutes of some 20 states. It is reproduced on p. 28 for use in the examples in this chapter.

Visually the relation of such statutes to the due process clause is represented by Figure 2-2. Such provisions convey a good deal of the jurisdiction authorized by the due process clause, but not necessarily all of it. Some areas remain (represented by the shaded area in the diagram) in which jurisdiction could be exercised, but the statute does not authorize it.

Students often ask why a state would enact an enumerated act long-arm when the California model is simpler and broader. One reason is historical: The first modern long-arm statute, the Illinois statute, used the enumerated act approach, and many states later used it as a model. Even if California's mellow approach is preferable in the abstract, many states are reluctant to tinker with statutes that have worked satisfactorily for years and have been construed repeatedly by their courts. In addition, the list of jurisdictionally sufficient acts in enumerated act long-arm statutes provides some guidance to nonresidents about the jurisdictional consequences of their choice to conduct particular activities in the state. Finally, some legislatures may not want to authorize jurisdiction in every case that barely passes constitutional

Constitutional scope of jurisdiction

Long-arm provisions granting parts of the constitutionally permissible jurisdiction

Figure 2-2

muster. The enumerated act statutes give courts some leeway to reject jurisdiction in cases having little connection to the state, without making constitutional pronouncements.[1]

Long-arm statutes take their colorful name from their primary purpose, which is to reach out of the state to call nonresident defendants back into the state to defend lawsuits.[2] Even though a defendant has left the forum state before he is sued (or in some cases has never been in the state at all), he may be required to defend a suit there under the *International Shoe* analysis if the suit arises out of his prior contacts with the forum. Legislatures tend to grant such long-arm jurisdiction liberally since it is usually invoked by plaintiffs who live in the state and prefer to sue at home.

Be careful, however, not to conclude that every assertion of jurisdiction under a long-arm statute is automatically constitutional simply because the statute purports to authorize it. In the area of personal jurisdiction, it is not always easy to tell what is and is not constitutional. Consequently, the reach of a state's long-arm statute may sometimes exceed its constitutional grasp. Suppose, for example, that an Iowa long-arm statute authorized its courts to take jurisdiction in all cases brought by resident plaintiffs. It would certainly be unconstitutional to apply such a statute to a case in which the Iowa plaintiff purchased goods from a Colorado defendant in Colorado. Assuming that the defendant has no other contacts with Iowa, there would be no constitutional authority to assert personal jurisdiction over the defendant, since the claim does not arise out of any minimum contacts with Iowa. This case falls within the "bulge" area in Figure 2-3, in which the statute authorizes jurisdiction (because the plaintiff is a resident), but it would exceed the limits of due process to exercise that jurisdiction.

However, the statute could be applied in other cases without violating due process. For example, if the case arose from a sale by the defendant to the plaintiff that took place in Iowa, the exercise of jurisdiction would be

---

1. A few states have taken the curious approach of *adding* a California-type, anything-constitutional-goes provision to their enumerated act statute. This seems calculated to confuse: Why specify enumerated acts which support jurisdiction, if everything else within due process limits does too? For a defense of this strategy, see K. Beyler, The Illinois Long-Arm Statute: Background, Meaning and Needed Repairs, 12 S. Ill. L.J. 293, 412-414 (1988).

2. Such statutes are usually unnecessary to obtain jurisdiction over in-state defendants. Individuals who are domiciled in the state are subject to personal jurisdiction on that basis. *Milliken v. Meyer*, 311 U.S. 457 (1940). Individuals present within the state may be personally served and are subject to jurisdiction under the ancient (but still viable) theory of *Pennoyer v. Neff*. In-state corporations are subject to jurisdiction on the basis of substantial and continuous activities in the forum state. See *International Shoe* at 318. In each of these cases, however, there must also be a statutory basis for the exercise of jurisdiction. See, e.g., Uniform Interstate and International Procedure Act §1.02 (jurisdiction based on domicile or incorporation in the forum state).

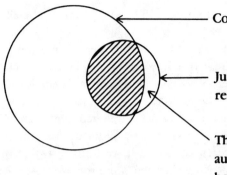

Constitutional scope of jurisdiction

Jurisdiction conferred by the resident plaintiff long-arm provision

The case described falls in this bulge authorized by the statute but beyond the bounds of the due process clause

Figure 2-3

constitutionally permissible because the defendant's voluntary contacts with Iowa gave rise to the claim. This case would fall in the shaded area on the diagram. In such cases, where the statute may be constitutional as applied to some cases but not all, the courts do not invalidate the statute entirely; they simply refuse to apply it to cases that fall outside the bounds of due process. Consequently, the statute remains in force and may be applied in other cases that are within due process limits.

All long-arm statutes that base personal jurisdiction on specific enumerated acts require that the claim sued upon arise out of the act itself. See, e.g., Uniform Interstate and International Procedure Act §1.03(b), infra p. 29. This limitation is rooted in the *International Shoe* analysis, which holds that limited in-state contacts only support jurisdiction over claims that arise from those contacts. See the "*Shoe* spectrum" at p. 6. By echoing that limitation in the long-arm statute itself, the legislature insures that the statute will not be used to reach cases beyond the constitutional bounds of due process.

Going to the Limits of Due Process

You will frequently read in the cases that an enumerated act long-arm statute is "intended to reach to the limits of due process." This is one of the most frequently misunderstood phrases in the civil procedure lexicon. Although innumerable cases broadly hold that the long-arm statute in question is intended to extend jurisdiction to the constitutional limits, this is *not* generally intended to mean that a statute like the Uniform Act occupies the entire constitutional field, as the California statute does. It would make little sense for the legislature to pass a statute enumerating specific contacts that support jurisdiction if it actually intended all minimum contacts to do so. Instead, this phrase is better interpreted to mean that the *specific categories* of jurisdiction conveyed by the long-arm statute are to be interpreted as liberally as the due process clause will allow.

For example, the phrase "transacting business" in a long-arm statute might be interpreted quite narrowly, to apply only in cases where the defendant has ongoing commercial activities and permanent employees within the state. Alternately it might be interpreted more broadly, to apply whenever the defendant enters into a single business transaction with an in-state party. If the statute is intended to go to the limits of due process, the court will interpret this language to reach all cases that are arguably within the statutory language and can be reached under the due process clause. See Casad at §4.01[1][b]; Moore's Federal Practice §108.60[3][a]. Since a single business transaction (depending on the facts) may be sufficient under due process analysis to give rise to personal jurisdiction over claims arising out of it, the statute should be broadly interpreted to reach such a case. In other words, the going-to-the-limits-of-due-process language commands liberal interpretation of the specific provisions of the long-arm statute; it does not fill in any interstices those provisions fail to cover.

Unfortunately, courts have not always grasped this distinction between broad interpretation of the enumerated acts and absorbing the whole constitutional sphere. Many decisions holding that the relevant long-arm is intended to "go to the limits of due process" really do mean, rightly or wrongly, that it fills all the shaded interstices in Figure 2-2.[3] Thus, if you are researching a case and find such language, it should set off a little alarm in the personal jurisdiction corner of your brain, stimulating some very careful reading of the cases under your long-arm statute to determine what the court really means to say.

In analyzing the following examples, consider first whether the applicable long-arm statute authorizes the court to exercise jurisdiction. Then consider whether it would be constitutional under the minimum contacts test for the court to exercise jurisdiction on the facts given. The Uniform Act, which is used in the examples, is set forth below.

UNIFORM INTERSTATE AND INTERNATIONAL PROCEDURE ACT

§1.03. [Personal Jurisdiction Based upon Conduct]

(a) A court may exercise personal jurisdiction over a person, who acts directly or by an agent, as to a [cause of action] [claim for relief] arising from the person's

---

3. For an example of the confusion such loose language has generated under one long-arm provision, see Comment, Georgia's Not-So-Long Arm Statute: Exposing the Myth, 6 Ga. St. L. Rev. 487 (1990).

(1) transacting any business in the state;

(2) contracting to supply services or things in this state;

(3) causing tortious injury by an act or omission in this state;

(4) causing tortious injury in this state by an act or omission outside this state if he regularly does or solicits business, or engages in any other persistent course of conduct, or derives substantial revenue from goods used or consumed or services rendered, in this state; [or]

(5) having an interest in, using, or possessing real property in this state[; or

(6) contracting to insure any person, property, or risk located within this state at the time of contracting].

(b) When jurisdiction over a person is based solely upon this section, only a [cause of action] [claim for relief] arising from acts enumerated in this section may be asserted against him.

EXAMPLES

Torts and the Long-Arm: Basic Cases

1. Hardy throws a pie at Fields while the two are making a movie in New York. Fields fails to see the joke and sues Hardy for assault in Pennsylvania, where Fields lives. Hardy has no other contacts with Pennsylvania.

  a. Could the Pennsylvania court assert jurisdiction over Hardy if the Uniform Act applied in Pennsylvania?

  b. Would it be constitutional for the court to do so?

2. Assume that Hardy, a comedian, performs two or three times a year at clubs in Pennsylvania. Fields sues him in Pennsylvania for the New York assault.

  a. Is jurisdiction proper under the Uniform Act?

  b. Would it be constitutional for the court to take jurisdiction?

3. While traveling to Pittsburgh for a performance, Hardy collides with Fields on Interstate 83 near Harrisburg. After the performance, Hardy returns to New York. Fields, fast losing his sense of humor, sues Hardy in Pennsylvania.

  a. May Fields do so under the Uniform Act?

  b. Would it be constitutional for the Pennsylvania court to take personal jurisdiction over Hardy?

4. West, in California, learns that Paramount Pictures plans to offer Fields a lucrative contract to make a movie in New York. She calls the producer in New York and tries to talk him out of it. During the conversation, she offers several vivid and distinctly uncomplimentary opinions concerning Fields's sense of humor. Fields is not amused; he sues West in New York for defamation.

  a. Does the Uniform Act authorize jurisdiction on these facts?

  b. Would it be constitutional for the New York court to exercise jurisdiction over West on this claim?

Torts and the Long-Arm: *Gray* Areas of Products Liability

5.   Chaplin manufactures stunt cars in Michigan for use in movie and television chase scenes. Paramount Pictures of Hollywood, California, a regular customer of Chaplin's, orders ten cars from Chaplin, which are shipped to California. Paramount takes one of the cars to Colorado, where it is used to film a cliff-hanging scene in Rocky Mountain Park. Brice, the star of the show, is injured when the brakes fail at 14,000 feet. Brice sues Chaplin in Colorado.

    a. Would jurisdiction be authorized by a long-arm statute that allowed jurisdiction for claims "arising out of a tortious act committed in this state"?

    b. Would long-arm jurisdiction be proper under the Uniform Act if it applied in Colorado?

    c. Would it be constitutional for the Colorado court to exercise jurisdiction over Chaplin in this action?

6.   Assume the same facts as example 5, except that the accident took place on location in Hollywood.

    a. Would jurisdiction be proper under the Uniform Act if it applied in California (instead of California's anything-constitutional-goes version quoted at p. 24)?

    b. Would it be constitutional for the California court to exercise personal jurisdiction on these facts?

7.   In this same case against Chaplin in California, Brice also sues Gleason Brake Corporation, the Michigan manufacturer of the brakes in the stunt car.

    a. Would the Uniform Act authorize jurisdiction if it were applicable in California?

    b. Would it be constitutional to require Gleason to defend this action in California?

Famous Foibles

8.   The following dandelion sprouts all too frequently in student answers to personal jurisdiction questions involving out-of-state acts and in-state torts:

> If the defendant does not have minimum contacts with the state, he may still be required to defend a suit there under the state's long-arm statute if the court concludes that the tort takes place where the plaintiff's injury occurs rather than where the defendant's negligent act took place.

> What is wrong with this analysis?

Transacting and Contracting

9.   Chaplin sells ten stunt cars to Paramount in California. Paramount sues Chaplin for breach of contract and breach of warranty after one of the cars

repeatedly breaks down during filming in Hollywood. Assume that suit is brought in California and that the Uniform Act applies. (Assume for purposes of examples 9 and 10 that breach of warranty is not a tort action.)

    a. Does the Uniform Act authorize jurisdiction over the suit?

    b. Does the court have power to hear the suit under the due process clause?

10. Chaplin manufactures stunt cars and sells them to a distributor, Indestructible Auto, Inc. in Salt Lake City, Utah; Indestructible in turn sells the cars to movie studios. Indestructible sells ten of Chaplin's specials to Paramount in California. Paramount sues Chaplin in California for breach of warranty after three of the cars break down repeatedly during filming.

    a. Is jurisdiction proper under the Uniform Act?

    b. Is jurisdiction permissible under due process analysis?

Statutory Restraint, and . . .

11. An agent for International Insurance Company calls Skelton in North Carolina and offers him a deal on some life insurance. Skelton agrees, fills out the policy application, and sends in his premium. He then moves to California and dies three weeks later. His mother sues in California to collect the proceeds of the policy. International Insurance has no other business in California.

    a. Would there be jurisdiction over this case under the Uniform Act?

    b. Would it be constitutional to sue International Insurance Company in California on these facts?

. . . Constitutional Constraints

12. Meadows, a mechanic, repairs a tire for Van Dyke, a tourist, at a service station in Indiana. As Van Dyke drives through Pennsylvania, the tire falls off the rim, causing an accident. Van Dyke, convinced that Meadows failed to secure the tire properly, wants to sue her in Pennsylvania. His lawyer looks up the Pennsylvania long-arm statute and finds 42 Pa. C.S.A. s. 5322(a)(4), which authorizes jurisdiction over a defendant for "causing harm or tortious injury in this Commonwealth by an act or omission outside this Commonwealth."

    a. Does s. 5322(a)(4) authorize suit against Meadows in this case?

    b. Would it be constitutional for the court to exercise jurisdiction over Meadows?

EXPLANATIONS

Torts and the Long-Arm: Basic Cases

1.   Long-arm jurisdiction: No   Constitutional power: No

    a. The Uniform Act does not provide statutory authority for Fields to sue Hardy in Pennsylvania. Although §§1.03(a)(3) and 1.03(a)(4) of the

Uniform Act authorize jurisdiction in tort cases, neither applies in the circumstances of this case. Subsection 1.03(a)(3) authorizes jurisdiction over claims arising out of tortious injuries caused by an act or omission in the state (meaning the state where the suit is brought). This subsection does not apply because Hardy's act took place in New York. Subsection 1.03(a)(4) allows the plaintiff to sue in Pennsylvania if he suffered tortious injury in Pennsylvania from an out-of-state act and if the defendant does business in the state or derives revenues from goods used or consumed in the state. This doesn't help Fields either. *First*, any injury he suffered took place in New York, where the assault occurred. *Second*, the example states that Hardy does not do business in Pennsylvania or have any other contacts with the state. No matter how liberally interpreted, the long-arm is too short to reach this case.

b. Had the statute purported to confer jurisdiction over this case, its reach would have exceeded its constitutional grasp. Although Fields has minimum contacts with Pennsylvania, Hardy does not. Nor do the facts suggest any other basis for personal jurisdiction, such as consent or domicile. Field's domicile in Pennsylvania is irrelevant; it is the defendant who is being forced into the state to defend. The plaintiff's unilateral contacts with the forum do not create a constitutional basis for requiring the defendant to defend there. *Hanson v. Denckla*, 357 U.S. 235 (1958).

2.   Long-arm jurisdiction: No   Constitutional power: No

a. Hardy's occasional forays into Pennsylvania do not lead to a different result from example 1. Subsection (a)(3) of the Uniform Act still doesn't apply because the tortious act took place in New York. Nor does subsection (a)(4) reach this case because the injury also occurred in New York. Even if the injury could be construed to take place in Pennsylvania, it is doubtful that the proviso in (a)(4) could be met. Such sporadic performances in Pennsylvania probably do not amount to "regularly do[ing] business" in the state or "deriving substantial revenue from . . . services rendered" in the state.

Fields might argue that Hardy has "transacted business" (Uniform Act §1.03(a)(1)) in Pennsylvania by his performances there. Indeed he has, but this is insufficient to subject him to personal jurisdiction for Fields's New York tort claim. The Uniform Act and all long-arm provisions limit jurisdiction based on specific contacts to claims *arising out of* the contacts. Indeed, this point is so fundamental that the Act says it twice, in the first sentence of §1.03(a) and in §1.03(b) as well. Hardy could be sued in Pennsylvania under §1.03(a)(1) for a breach of contract claim resulting from his performances there, but not for an unrelated claim arising in New York.

b. In this case, Hardy has contacts with Pennsylvania, but the claim doesn't arise from them. As the "*Shoe* Spectrum" on p. 6 illustrates, when the defendant's contacts with the state are limited, he is only subject to "specific in personam jurisdiction," that is, jurisdiction for claims that arise out of those in-state contacts. It is because of this constitutional limitation that long-arm statutes also restrict jurisdiction to claims arising from the listed contacts. Otherwise, their reach would frequently exceed their constitutional grasp in cases like this one.

3.   Long-arm jurisdiction: Yes   Constitutional power: Yes

a. In this case, Fields gets the last laugh. The case is clearly covered by subsection (a)(3) of the Uniform Act because Fields' suit arises from Hardy's tortious act (the negligent driving) in Pennsylvania. An argument might also be made, since Hardy was driving to a performance, that the claim arose out of Hardy's transacting business in Pennsylvania (subsection (a)(1)). It is certainly possible for a defendant's acts to satisfy more than one provision of a long-arm statute, as illustrated by the intersecting circles in Figure 2-2. The argument is dubious here, however, since the claim is for a tort to a person not involved in Hardy's in-state business. In any event, it is unnecessary, since subsection (a)(3) squarely applies.

b. Courts have consistently held that committing a tortious act within the state is a minimum contact of the "quality and nature" that gives rise to personal jurisdiction. Because the claim arises out of this in-state act, jurisdiction is proper under the minimum contacts test. The fact that Hardy left the state before suit was brought does not preclude jurisdiction. *International Shoe* premises jurisdiction on the in-state contacts that gave rise to the claim, not presence at the time of suit.

4.   Long-arm jurisdiction: Maybe   Constitutional power: Yes

a. Assuming that West has no other contacts with New York, the only likely basis for jurisdiction is subsection (a)(3) of the Uniform Act. The problem, of course, is that that section requires that the tortious injury result from an "act or omission in this state," yet West has not entered New York. In *Gray v. American Radiator and Standard Sanitary Corp.*, 176 N.E.2d 761 (Ill. 1961), the Illinois Supreme Court stretched to conclude that a "tortious act" took place where a negligently constructed product caused an injury. The Uniform Act precludes this extravagant interpretation by specifying that the act or omission that causes the injury, not the injury itself, must take place in the state. See §1.03(a)(3). Indeed, provisions like §1.03(a)(3) and (a)(4), which distinguish between in-state tortious acts and out-of-state tortious acts causing in-state injuries, were drafted to clarify the statutory ambiguity discussed in *Gray*.

However, a strong argument can be made that West *did* commit the tortious act in New York. West has deliberately projected her voice into the state via the telephone wires for the purpose of making the defamatory statement to a person in that state. (Compare *Gray*, in which the tortious act was done entirely in Ohio, but the harm was suffered after the water heater was shipped into Illinois.) Some courts have concluded in such cases that the act takes place where the statements are heard, rather than where they are uttered. Other courts have concluded that the act takes place where the actor acts, not where the statement is heard. These latter courts view such cases as out-of-state act/in-state injury cases and refuse to take jurisdiction unless the defendant has engaged in business or other persistent activity in the state under subsection (a)(4). See generally Casad at ¶7.07[1][b].

This is a good example of a case in which interpreting the long-arm statute to "go to the limits of due process" makes a difference. If this is the governing rule of interpretation, the court should interpret the "act or omission within this state" language as broadly as due process allows and conclude that the act took place in New York.

b. West's act is deliberately aimed at causing harm to Fields in New York. Such an act, undertaken with the intent to injure the plaintiff in New York and involving direct contact with the producer there, constitutes a voluntary affiliation with the forum of the "quality and nature" to support jurisdiction under the due process clause. West can hardly claim surprise when the harm she intended eventuates where she intended it, and Fields sues her there. See *Calder v. Jones,* 465 U.S. 783, 788 (1984); compare *Wilson v. Belin,* 20 F.3d 644 (5th Cir. 1994), cert. denied 513 U.S. 930 (1994) (no jurisdiction over defendants who *were called by* reporter from the forum state and made allegedly defamatory statements about the plaintiff that were then published in the state).

Torts and the Long-Arm: *Gray* Areas of Products Liability

5.   Long-arm jurisdiction: (a) Possibly   (b) No Constitutional power: No

a. The long-arm statute quoted here is similar to the Illinois statute interpreted in *Gray v. American Radiator and Standard Sanitary Corp.,* 176 N.E.2d 761 (Ill. 1961). In *Gray* the court interpreted this language to apply if the *plaintiff's injury* occurred in the state, even though the defendant's negligence occurred elsewhere. 176 N.E.2d at 763. However, other courts have refused to accept this strained interpretation. See *Feathers v. McLucas,* 209 N.E.2d 68, 79 (N.Y. 1965), in which the court concluded that the *Gray* interpretation "disregards [the statute's] plain language and exceeds the bounds of sound statutory interpretation" and that the phrase only applies to cases in which the defendant's tortious conduct took place in the state. Thus, whether Chaplin is subject to jurisdiction under this long-arm provision depends on the court's willingness to stretch the language as the court did in *Gray.*

b. The Uniform Act does not reach this case. Subsection (3) does not apply; it focuses specifically on the place where the defendant's negligent act (here the negligent manufacture) took place, which was Michigan in this case. Subsection (4) does not apply either. Although Chaplin may have caused tortious injury within the state by his out-of-state act, there is no indication that the additional requirement of regular in-state conduct or profits is met.

c. The only contact Chaplin has with Colorado in this case is that the motion picture company took one of his stunt cars from California to Colorado to make a movie, and the brakes failed there. Like the Volkswagen in *World-Wide Volkswagen v. Woodson*, the car reached Colorado by the unilateral act of a third party, not as the result of any deliberate contact by Chaplin with Colorado. Although it may be foreseeable that Paramount will use the car to make chase scenes in the Rockies, this foreseeability is not a sufficient basis for exercising jurisdiction over Chaplin there. *World-Wide Volkswagen v. Woodson*, 444 U.S. 286, 295-296 (1980). It would exceed the limits of due process for the Colorado court to exercise jurisdiction over Chaplin wherever Paramount chooses to film movies. Thus, this is another example in the "bulge" area of Figure 2-3, in which the long-arm statute might be interpreted to authorize jurisdiction (under the *Gray* approach), but it would exceed the bounds of due process to exercise that jurisdiction.

6. Long-arm jurisdiction: Yes   Constitutional power: Yes

a. If Brice's accident takes place in California, subsection (4) will authorize jurisdiction. Chaplin has caused Brice's injuries in California by an out-of-state act. In addition, he apparently does business with Paramount in California on a regular basis. Note that subsection (4) includes two requirements: an in-state injury from an out-of-state act and an ongoing relationship to the state. The second requirement may be satisfied by one of several alternative showings: regular solicitation of business, regularly doing business, any other persistent course of conduct in the state, or deriving substantial revenue from goods or services used or consumed in the state.

It may also be possible to argue that Brice's claim in this case arises from Chaplin's "transacting business" in California, under §1.03(a)(1) of the Uniform Act. Although Brice's claim does not arise directly out of the transaction itself (as a claim by Paramount for defects in the cars would, for example), it does "arise out of" the sale of the cars in California in a more general sense. Some courts would uphold jurisdiction in these circumstances under §1.03(a)(1). See Casad at §4.02[1][b]. However, others have held that "transacting business" provisions like §1.03(a)(1) are intended to apply to business-related claims such as contract claims, so that a plaintiff such as Brice must satisfy subsection (a)(3) or (a)(4) in order to sue Chaplin on this tort claim in California. See, e.g., *Whitaker v. Krestmark of Alabama, Inc.*, 278 S.E.2d 116, 118 (Ga. App. 1981).

b. There is a constitutionally significant difference between this case and the last. Here, the brake failure and resulting injury is not the sole contact Chaplin has with the forum state. The presence of the car in California arose through deliberate efforts by Chaplin to serve the market for his product in California. This is a voluntary affiliation with the state that changes the "quality and nature" of Chaplin's in-state act of causing injury in California. The Supreme Court's stream-of-commerce analysis in

World-Wide Volkswagen and *Asahi* supports jurisdiction over out-of-state defendants in these circumstances on the theory that a defendant who persistently takes advantage of the opportunity to market its product in the state may fairly be called to account in the state if his product causes tortious injury there.

Even under Justice O'Connor's view in *Asahi,* jurisdiction would be proper in this case. Unlike the valve maker in *Asahi,* Chaplin in this example has deliberately shipped his cars—including the one that caused the injury—to California. Thus, there is no question of being subjected to jurisdiction due to the unilateral acts of a subsequent distributor. Chaplin has chosen to sell cars directly to California, and this purposeful conduct gives rise to the claim in suit.

7.   Long-arm jurisdiction: Maybe   Constitutional power: Maybe

a. The issue here is whether the component part manufacturer, who has dealt with the final manufacturer but has not directly done business or sold goods in California, can be required to defend there in a products liability case arising out of injury in California allegedly resulting from a defect in its product. Gleason is analogous to Titan Value company in *Gray.* Gleason caused tortious injury in California by an out-of-state act. It also derives substantial revenue from goods used or consumed in California, assuming that Chaplin, and perhaps others as well, sell a substantial number of cars in California made with Gleason brakes. Jurisdiction has generally been upheld over component part manufacturers in such circumstances, under §1.03(a)(4) of the Uniform Act, and perhaps §1.03(a)(1) as well.

It will not always follow that the component part manufacturer will fit subsection (4) just because the final manufacturer does. For example, if Chaplin sold only 50 cars in California, this may be enough to constitute doing or soliciting business there or deriving substantial revenue from goods sold there. The company that makes the windshield wipers, however, at $6 a pair does not derive substantial revenue from goods used or consumed in California if the only wipers that go there are on Chaplin's 50 stunt cars. If the wipers failed and caused the accident, Chaplin would be subject to jurisdiction under this language but the wiper manufacturer probably would not.

b. Prior to *Asahi,* a number of courts held it within the bounds of due process to exercise jurisdiction over an out-of-state component manufacturer in this type of case. These courts reasoned that a component maker who derives revenue from substantial sales of its product in a state should not be able to accept that benefit without submitting to jurisdiction when the product causes injury there. Some courts reached this conclusion even if the component maker was unaware that the finished product for which it provided parts was being resold in the forum state. See, e.g., *Bean Dredging Corp. v. Dredge Technology Corp.,* 744 F.2d 1081 (5th Cir. 1984).

However, as Chapter 1 indicates, *Asahi* has thrown some doubt on the question of whether component makers who do not direct their goods into a state or cultivate the market there are subject to personal jurisdiction if their product reaches the forum state through resale of the finished product and causes injury there. The O'Connor approach would require more to establish "purposeful availment." The other five Justices (several of whom have since left the Court) apparently would not. A distinction might be premised on the fact that the component maker is in Michigan rather than Japan, but this seems to go more to the second prong of the analysis (reasonableness once minimum contacts are shown) than to the issue of minimum contacts themselves.

Famous Foibles

8. Obviously, this reasoning is based on the idea that a "tortious act" provision in a long-arm statute confers jurisdiction if the injury to the plaintiff takes place in the state, even though the negligent act that led to the injury took place elsewhere. The fallacy in this foible is the conclusion that satisfying the terms of a long-arm statute is enough to obtain personal jurisdiction. This is never the case: The statutory analysis only determines whether the legislature has granted jurisdiction, not whether it would be constitutional to exercise it.

Suppose, for example, on the facts of *World-Wide* that Oklahoma had had a statute authorizing jurisdiction over a defendant who "commits a tortious act in the state"; and assume further that the Oklahoma courts interpreted it as the Illinois Supreme Court did in *Gray v. American Radiator,* to be satisfied if the plaintiff suffers injury in Oklahoma. On these assumptions, the long-arm statute would authorize jurisdiction over Seaway, the New York dealer, since its negligent act in New York caused injury in Oklahoma when the Audi blew up there. But the *World-Wide* court held that it was not constitutionally permissible for the Oklahoma court to take jurisdiction over Seaway on these facts, since Seaway had not purposely availed itself of the benefits of conducting activities in Oklahoma. No matter how Oklahoma interpreted the "tortious act" provision in its statute, it could not make such an exercise of jurisdiction constitutional.

Transacting and Contracting

9. Long-arm jurisdiction: Yes   Constitutional power: Yes

a. This claim squarely fits subsection (2) of the Uniform Act because it arises directly out of Chaplin's agreement to sell the allegedly defective car to Paramount in California. It would likely satisfy subsection (1) as well. Even if Chaplin does not have a business office in California, most courts would hold that he transacts business there by selling his product to a California buyer, at least where the sale is as substantial as this one.

b. The decision to sell goods to buyers in another state is a deliberate, profit-oriented contact with that state. When the sale is substantial (as here) or part of a series of such sales, the seller enjoys the benefits and protections of doing business in the state and may have a significant effect on the commerce of the state. In such cases, the seller should expect to defend suits there arising out of those business transactions with forum-state customers. See *Burger King,* 471 U.S. at 475-476.

10. Long-arm jurisdiction: Probably   Constitutional power: Unclear

a. Paramount might argue that several provisions of the Uniform Act apply but will probably have to fall back on §1.03(a)(1), the "transacting business" provision. Subsection 1.03(a)(2) was probably meant to apply to cases in which the defendant directly contracted to supply goods in the state, not stream of commerce cases like this one where a distributor resells the defendant's goods in the state. Section 1.03(a)(4), the tortious-act-outside/injury-inside-the-state provision probably can't be stretched to reach the case either: The claim is for failure of the goods to perform properly, not for personal injury or property damage.

However, many courts would conclude that Chaplin did "transact business" in California, albeit indirectly. Chaplin has delivered his goods into the stream of commerce. He may well know that they are destined for California or hope that they are. Where he profits from these resales in the state, it appears likely that the long-arm's "transacting business" language was intended to reach his conduct even though he used a distributor rather than sending the goods directly to California. See, e.g., *Stabilisierungsfonds Fur Wein v. Kaiser Stuhl Wine Distributors Pty. Ltd.,* 647 F.2d 200, 204-206 (D.C. Cir. 1981).

b. This is another stream of commerce case. It differs from *Asahi* and example 7 in that Chaplin is a final manufacturer rather than a component maker. But it is still indirect, as Chaplin sold his cars to Utah, and they were then resold into California. The reasoning of Justice O'Connor's opinion would seem to bar jurisdiction in both types of cases. Because of the split in the Court and the change in its composition, it is hard to say whether jurisdiction is proper in such cases, in which a predictable stream of commerce sweeps the defendant's goods into the state.

Note that, should the O'Connor view prevail, interpreting "transacting business" provisions to apply to defendants who indirectly sell their goods in the state would often exceed the bounds of due process. This example, then, would fall in the bulge area of Figure 2-3, in which the statute authorizes jurisdiction but it would exceed due process limits to assert that jurisdiction.

Statutory Restraint, and . . .

11. Long-arm jurisdiction No   Constitutional power: Probably Not

a. Subsection (a)(6) of the Uniform Act specifically addresses claims arising out of insurance contracts. That subsection limits jurisdiction to claims arising from contracts to insure risks present in the state at the time the insurance contract was made. Skelton was not present in California when the insurance contract was made, so this subsection doesn't apply.

One might argue — though it's a stretch — that the claim arises from International's "transacting business" in California. But the court is very unlikely to apply this general provision where subsection (a)(6) specifically addresses insurance cases and limits the claims that can be brought to those involving risks in the state at the time of contracting. That would allow cases through the back door that the legislature pretty clearly barred explicitly in s. (a)(6).

b. The drafters of the Uniform Act probably included the in-state-risk limit in s. (a)(6) because they thought the limit was necessary to avoid constitutional problems. On the facts of example 11 (an obvious twist on *McGee v. International Ins. Co.*, 355 U.S. 220 (1957)) the insurer really has no deliberate contacts with California: it simply entered into an insurance contract with a North Carolinian in North Carolina. Perhaps one could argue that Skelton's listing of a California beneficiary provides some contact with California, but it is a very tenuous one at best. Thus, allowing suit wherever the insured dies, or a beneficiary lives, would often allow jurisdiction in states where it would exceed constitutional bounds. Drafting the long-arm statute to apply only if the risk was in the forum state at the time of contracting limits jurisdiction to cases which will virtually always involve a sufficient, related contact to constitutionally support jurisdiction there. Thus, the restraint exercised by the drafters will avoid constitutional problems in applying the statute.

. . . Constitutional Constraints

Long-arm jurisdiction: Yes   Constitutional power: No

12a. Subsection 5322(a)(4) clearly authorizes jurisdiction over Van Dyke's case. It only requires that the defendant have acted outside the state and caused an injury within it. Meadows did just that when she repaired the tire in Indiana, leading to Van Dyke's injury in Pennsylvania.

Note that s. 5322(a)(4) does not require additional, on-going contacts with the state, such as deriving profits from goods sold in the state, or on-going solicitation of sales. Compare s. 1.03(a)(4) of the Uniform Act, which allows jurisdiction based on out-of-state acts that cause in-state injuries, but only if such additional contacts exist.

b. This provision of the Pennsylvania long-arm statute is living proof that legislatures do enact long-arm statutes whose reach, in many cases, exceeds their constitutional grasp. In this case, Meadows has no contacts with Pennsylvania that would support personal jurisdiction over her, but the statute allows jurisdiction solely on the ground that the *plaintiff's injury* occurred in Pennsylvania. *Worldwide Volkswagen* clearly rejects resulting in-state injury —

even foreseeable resulting injury—as a basis for minimum contacts jurisdiction. "Foreseeability of harm within the forum state must be accompanied by conduct directed at the forum state in order for the defendant to reasonably anticipate being haled into the state's courts. There is a critical difference between an act which has an effect in the forum and one directed at the forum itself." *Surgical Laser Technologies, Inc. v. C.R. Bard, Inc.*, 921 F. Supp. 281, 285 (E.D. Pa. 1996) (footnote omitted).

One consequence of such broad jurisdictional statutes is increased litigation over personal jurisdiction. Subsection 5322(a)(4) is a clear invitation to lawyers to file cases like Van Dyke's: after all, the statute says that you can! So plaintiffs do, and the courts end up dismissing these cases, after substantial litigation, on the ground that the exercise of jurisdiction, though authorized by s. 5322(a)(4), would be unconstitutional. See, e.g., *Santana Products, Inc. v. Bobrick Washroom Equipment,* 14 F. Supp.2d 710, 715-716 (M.D.Pa. 1998) (discussing cases rejecting, on constitutional grounds, jurisdiction over cases within the reach of s. 5322(a)(4)).

3

Seeking the Home Field Advantage: Challenges to Personal Jurisdiction

Introduction

Surely one of the most fundamental principles of civil procedure is that the courts of a state may not exercise judicial power over a defendant unless that defendant has, in one way or another, submitted to the jurisdiction of the courts of that state. A century of case law has given some specificity to this requirement. As Chapter 1 indicates, defendants may be subject to jurisdiction under the due process analysis on the basis of domicile in a state, in-state service of process, consent to jurisdiction, continuous or substantial in-state service of process, or as a result of "minimum contacts" with the forum state that give rise to a particular cause of action.

It is not always clear when a plaintiff sues a defendant in a particular state whether one of these bases for personal jurisdiction is met. Suppose, for example, that Wolfe, a North Carolina novelist, gives a newspaper interview in North Carolina in which he disparages Hemingway's writing abilities. Hemingway sues Wolfe in Oregon for libel. When Wolfe is served with the complaint, he may be unsure whether the Oregon court has the right to exercise jurisdiction over him. For example, he may not know whether the newspaper that interviewed him is circulated in Oregon or whether Hemingway has suffered any injury in Oregon as a result of the alleged libel. If Wolfe has no other connections with Oregon, he may well conclude that the courts of Oregon have no right to order him to appear and defend the suit in Oregon.

This chapter explores the options available to a defendant like Wolfe to present his objection to the exercise of personal jurisdiction over him by the courts of another state. Generally, these options involve a challenge either in the court in which the original action is brought (the rendering state) or in another state where enforcement of the original judgment is sought (the enforcing state).

Challenging Jurisdiction in the Rendering State ("Direct Attack")

The defendant's first option is to appear in the original action at the beginning of the suit and object to the court's exercise of jurisdiction over her. For example, Wolfe may decide to appear in the Oregon court and ask the court to dismiss the action for lack of personal jurisdiction. The procedure for doing this varies from state to state. In some states, the defendant who objects to jurisdiction files a "special appearance." Under a special appearance, the defendant is allowed to appear before the court at the beginning of the action for the sole purpose of challenging its power to exercise personal jurisdiction over her. If the defendant is careful to appear "specially," she may litigate the jurisdictional question without submitting to jurisdiction by the very act of appearing before the court.[1]

However, the defendant who files a special appearance must exercise extreme care not to raise any other issue: If she raises any objection or argument that the court can construe as a defense on the merits, the court may conclude that she has waived her jurisdictional objection. For example, in *Koplin v. Saul Lerner Co.*, 201 N.E.2d 763 (Ill. App. 1964), the defendant entered a special appearance to object to the court's jurisdiction and also moved to strike the complaint for vagueness. The court held that this hapless defendant, by raising the vagueness issue, had addressed an issue going to the merits, and thereby had submitted to the court's jurisdiction. The

---

1. Presumably, the plaintiff may not obtain personal jurisdiction over the defendant by serving him with process while he is in the state to make a special appearance, despite the holding in *Burnham v. Superior Court*, 494 U.S. 604 (1990) that personal service in the state suffices to support personal jurisdiction. Obtaining jurisdiction under *Burnham* while the defendant is in the state to object to jurisdiction would effectively make the special appearance or Rule 12 (b)(2) motion a dead letter.

pitfalls of making a successful special appearance are discussed in Casad ¶3.01[5][a].

A growing number of states have abandoned the common law special appearance device in favor of the more liberal approach to challenging personal jurisdiction used in federal courts. Under the Federal Rules, as under the special appearance, a defendant may appear before answering to the merits of the complaint and object to personal jurisdiction. Fed. R. Civ. P. 12(b)(2). However, under the Federal Rules approach, the defendant may also raise other objections at the same time, without waiving the objection to personal jurisdiction. For example, under Fed. R. Civ. P. 12(b), a defendant may move to dismiss for lack of personal jurisdiction and, at the same time, for failure to state a claim upon which relief can be granted (see Rule 12(b)(6). This second objection clearly goes to the merits of the suit; if a defendant did this in a state that adheres to the older special appearance rule, the court would hold that she had waived her objection to personal jurisdiction by bringing up matters going to the merits of the case.[2]

Thus, in the federal courts under Rule 12(b), and in the numerous state courts with similar rules, the defendant has a little more flexibility in raising the objection and is less likely to be tripped up by the procedural technicalities of doing so. But under either approach, the objection to jurisdiction must be raised immediately or be lost: A defendant who answers on the merits and later concludes that personal jurisdiction is lacking will have waived the objection by failing to raise it at the outset. See generally Chapter 18.

If Wolfe properly raises his objection in the rendering court, under either the special appearance approach or the Federal Rules approach (whichever applies in that state), the court will hold a hearing on the issue. If the court concludes that there is no basis to exercise jurisdiction over Wolfe, it will dismiss the suit. However, if the court concludes that it does have the power to exercise jurisdiction over him (at least for the claim asserted by Hemingway), it will proceed with the case.

In most states a defendant who challenges jurisdiction at the beginning of the suit and loses may proceed to defend the merits of the suit without waiving her objection to the court's jurisdictional ruling. If she loses the suit on the merits, she may appeal to an appellate court in the rendering state, claiming that the trial court's conclusion that it had personal jurisdiction was wrong. Friedenthal, Kane and Miller, 190-191 (3rd ed. 1999). This scenario is hardly palatable to Wolfe, of course, since it requires him to do

---

2. Under Fed. R. Civ. P. 12(b), the defendant may also raise the jurisdictional objection in her answer to the complaint, if she did not file a pre-answer motion. The crucial thing is to raise it immediately, either in the answer or a pre-answer motion. See Chapter 18. For an example in which the objection was raised in the answer, see the defendant's answer in the *Schulansky* case, infra p. 568.

exactly what he believes he should not have to do, defend the action in a state that (allegedly) lacks personal jurisdiction over him. However, it at least leaves him an avenue to correct the trial judge's mistake and to avoid being bound by a decision rendered by a court that lacks jurisdiction to render it.

Challenging Jurisdiction in the Enforcing Court ("Collateral Attack")

The second option for the defendant who objects to personal jurisdiction is to ignore the original suit entirely. If Wolfe is truly convinced that Oregon lacks personal jurisdiction over him, he may view the suit as mere harassment, an ineffective proceeding that can give rise to no binding judgment and that can therefore be ignored with impunity. If the Oregon court lacks personal jurisdiction over Wolfe, any judgment it enters in Hemingway's suit will be unenforceable anyway. If that's true, why bother to respond at all?

Procedurally, it is true that Wolfe has a right *not* to appear in Oregon if the Oregon court lacks jurisdiction over him for the claim asserted in the suit. However, this course poses a serious risk: If Wolfe fails to appear at all in Oregon, either to object to personal jurisdiction or to defend on the merits of the libel claim, the court will enter a default judgment for Hemingway — that is, a judgment that Wolfe is liable to Hemingway on the claims asserted in the complaint. If that judgment is enforceable, Wolfe will have lost his suit without ever having had a chance to defend it.

The usual method of enforcing money judgments against out-of-state defendants is for the plaintiff to take her judgment against the defendant to a state where the defendant lives or has property and seek a court order from the courts of that state authorizing the sheriff to sell the defendant's assets to satisfy the judgment. Hemingway, for example, may take his Oregon judgment to North Carolina, where Wolfe lives, and ask the court to authorize a judicial sale of Wolfe's house to pay off the judgment.

However, the North Carolina court will not automatically enforce the Oregon judgment. Hemingway must first obtain recognition of the Oregon judgment (called "domesticating the judgment," like finding a home for a wild animal) in one of two ways. The traditional procedure is to file a new action on the judgment in the enforcing state — North Carolina in this case — seeking a "judgment on the judgment." A good many states now provide an alternative statutory procedure for domesticating foreign[3] judgments. The judgment creditor (Hemingway in our example) simply registers a certified copy of the Oregon judgment in the North Carolina court,

---

3. The word "foreign" in this context refers to a judgment of another state, not that of another country.

eliminating the need to file a new suit there.[4] In states that have such a procedure, the judgment creditor may either file a traditional action on the judgment or use the registration procedure.

The Full Faith and Credit Clause of the United States Constitution (Article IV, §1) requires the courts of each state to honor the judgments of other states by entering judgments upon them and allowing out-of-state creditors like Hemingway to use court process to collect them. Once Hemingway obtains a judgment on the judgment (or under a registration statute, registers the judgment in the enforcing state), he may invoke North Carolina procedures for collecting it, including placing liens on Wolfe's assets in the state, forcing sale of those assets, or initiating court hearings to determine Wolfe's ability to pay.

There is, however, an important exception to a state's duty to give full faith and credit to a judgment of another state: The enforcing court may always inquire as to whether the rendering state had jurisdiction in the original action and refuse enforcement if it did not. See *Pennoyer v. Neff,* 95 U.S. 714, 732 (1877). For example, if the North Carolina court concludes after a hearing on the jurisdiction issue that the Oregon court had jurisdiction over Wolfe, the North Carolina court must enforce the Oregon default judgment by entering a North Carolina judgment on the original judgment and making its procedures for execution[5] of judgments available to Hemingway. However, if the North Carolina court concludes that the Oregon court did *not* have jurisdiction over Wolfe, it will refuse to honor the Oregon judgment, and Hemingway will not be able to levy on Wolfe's property in North Carolina.

Thus, if Wolfe ignores the Oregon proceeding, he will still have an opportunity to protect his property from being sold on execution in North Carolina. Even though a default judgment will be rendered in the original Oregon law suit, Wolfe may oppose enforcement of that judgment by asserting in the North Carolina enforcement action that the Oregon court lacked personal jurisdiction over him.[6] This is referred to as a "collateral attack" on the judgment because the defendant challenges the original court's jurisdiction in the enforcement action rather than directly in the original suit. Collateral

---

4. Most registration statutes are based on a model act, the Uniform Enforcement of Foreign Judgments Act (1964 Revised Act), 13 U.L.A. 152 (1986). There is also a federal statute authorizing registration of federal judgments in other federal districts. 28 U.S.C. §1963.

5. This grim sounding term refers to the various court procedures available for obtaining satisfaction of a judgment by seizure and sale of the defendant's assets. See generally Friedenthal, Kane and Miller, §15.7.

6. If Hemingway brings a suit to obtain a judgment on the original judgment, Wolfe can raise this objection as a defense to the enforcement suit. If Hemingway registers the judgment directly, Wolfe can raise the objection by a motion to vacate the registration. See Uniform Enforcement of Foreign Judgments Act §2, 13 U.L.A. at 154.

attack is clearly more convenient for Wolfe because he does not have to go to Oregon, something that from his point of view he shouldn't have to do. It also allows him to litigate the jurisdictional issue in his home state. While the issue of whether the Oregon court had jurisdiction over Wolfe will theoretically be the same in either state, it is at least possible that a North Carolina court will be more sympathetic to Wolfe's objection than the Oregon court would be.

However, this strategy poses a great risk for Wolfe. The Full Faith and Credit Clause allows Wolfe to question the rendering court's jurisdiction but not to reopen the merits of the underlying libel action. If the North Carolina court concludes that the Oregon court had jurisdiction over Wolfe, it will automatically enforce the Oregon default judgment. If Wolfe's original conclusion that the Oregon court lacks jurisdiction is wrong (and most conclusions in this area are only educated guesses), the default judgment will be valid and enforceable, in Oregon or any other state. The idea is that a defendant has the right to stay away if a court lacks jurisdiction but not if it has jurisdiction. In the latter situation, the defendant is deemed to have waived her defense on the merits by failing to appear. That is a very considerable price to pay to avoid contesting the jurisdictional issue in the plaintiff's chosen forum.

All this is complex enough, but one further wrinkle is also important. It is true that the Full Faith and Credit Clause allows defendants such as Wolfe to resist enforcement of another state's judgment on the ground that the rendering state never obtained personal jurisdiction over them. But there is an exception to this rule as well: A defendant may not challenge personal jurisdiction in the enforcement action if she has already done so in the original action. Suppose, for example, that Wolfe had appeared in the Oregon action and moved to dismiss for lack of personal jurisdiction. If the motion was denied, and Wolfe then defaulted on the merits, he could not renew his challenge to jurisdiction in an enforcement action in North Carolina because he had already litigated and lost on that issue. Once is enough; the rules of collateral estoppel provide that a party who has fully litigated an issue in one action may not relitigate it in another. See Chapter 26. Thus, Wolfe gets his choice to raise the objection in one court or the other but not to resurrect it after it has been fully litigated and decided.

While the explanation of these principles is lengthy, their application is fairly straightforward. The following examples should help. See also Figure 3-1, on p. 47, which illustrates the various possibilities. Please assume that all cases are brought in state court unless the example specifies otherwise. Also assume that the special appearance rule applies in Mississippi.[7]

---

7. Until 1982 Mississippi practice required defendants to raise objections to personal jurisdiction by special appearance. Mississippi now follows the Federal Rules model, which allows defendants to raise the objection by a pre-answer motion to dismiss or in their answer to the complaint. Miss. R. Civ. P. 12(b)(2). Assume in analyzing the examples that the special appearance rule still applies.

Defendant's Response to the Original Suit	Action in the Rendering Court	Action in the Enforcing Court
D appears, defends on merits, and loses	Enters judgment for P	Must enforce the rendering court's judgment, even if D challenges the rendering court's jurisdiction; D has waived his objection
D makes special appearance or 12(b)(2) motion; court agrees that it lacks jurisdiction	In most cases, dismisses action for lack of jurisdiction; in some, may order proper service to cure jurisdictional defect	If original suit dismissed, there will be no judgment to enforce. However, P may file a new suit in a court that has jurisdiction over the defendant
D makes special appearance or 12(b)(2) motion; court upholds jurisdiction; D defaults	Enters judgment for P	Must enforce judgment because D already litigated the rendering court's jurisdiction and lost
D loses on objection to jurisdiction; defends action on the merits; loses; appeals	In most states, appellate court may review decision that jurisdiction was proper; a few may treat defense on merits as a waiver of the jurisdictional objection	If jurisdiction upheld on appeal, or objection waived by defense on merits, must enforce the rendering court's judgment
D defaults, contests jurisdiction in enforcing court	Enters default judgment for P, unless lack of jurisdiction is clear from the complaint	Enforcing court may decide whether rendering court had jurisdiction; if it holds it did not, it refuses enforcement. If it holds that it did, it must enforce the judgment
D defaults, denies liability on the merits in the enforcing court	Enters default judgment for P, unless lack of jurisdiction is clear from the complaint	Enforces the judgment; full faith and credit clause precludes reexamination of merits, which are settled by default

Figure 3-1: Challenges to personal jurisdiction: some common scenarios

EXAMPLES

Novel Developments

1. Lewis publishes books in Ohio. He agrees to sell a thousand copies of *Brandywine, Ohio,* a popular novel, to Faulkner, a book wholesaler with offices in Mississippi. At Faulkner's request Lewis ships the books to Faulkner's Louisiana warehouse. Faulkner subsequently discovers that the books are damaged and sues Lewis in Mississippi to recover the price of the books. Lewis claims that the books were damaged later, while stored in Faulkner's warehouse. He also doubts that the Mississippi court has jurisdiction over him because all the negotiations took place in Ohio and the parties contemplated from the beginning that the books would be shipped to Louisiana.

Lewis makes a special appearance in Mississippi to contest the Mississippi court's jurisdiction over him. The court concludes after holding a hearing that it lacks jurisdiction. What will the court do?

2.   When first served with the complaint in *Faulkner v. Lewis,* Lewis is confident that he can win on the merits and therefore answers the complaint and defends the case on the merits. Just before trial, however, he gets nervous about the outcome and decides to move to dismiss for lack of personal jurisdiction. How will the court respond to the motion?

3.   Assume that Lewis decides to appear in the Mississippi action, despite his doubts that the court has jurisdiction over him. He files an answer, defends that action on the merits, and loses. Judgment is entered for Faulkner. Faulkner brings a suit on the judgment in Ohio, and Lewis opposes enforcement of the judgment on the ground that the Mississippi court lacked personal jurisdiction over him. What will the court do?

The Silent Treatment

4.   Lewis is convinced from the outset that the Mississippi court lacks jurisdiction over him. Consequently, he does not respond to the complaint, and a default judgment is entered for Faulkner, who then brings an action on the judgment in Ohio.

    a. Lewis defends the Ohio enforcement action on the ground that he is not liable for the damage because the books were damaged after delivery. Assuming that Lewis can prove this, what will the court do?

    b. Lewis defends the enforcement action on the ground that the Mississippi court never obtained personal jurisdiction over him. Assuming this is true, what will the court do?

    c. Lewis defends the enforcement action on the ground that the Mississippi court lacked jurisdiction over him. The Ohio court, however, concludes that the Mississippi court *did* have jurisdiction. What will the court do?

5.   Lewis appears specially in the original suit in Mississippi to challenge personal jurisdiction. The court holds that it has personal jurisdiction. Lewis, convinced that the court is wrong, defaults. Faulkner gets a default judgment and seeks enforcement in Ohio. Lewis defends on the ground that the Mississippi court lacked jurisdiction over him. What result?

6.   Assume that Faulkner's suit is brought in a state that follows the Federal Rules model. Lewis appears and moves to dismiss for failure to join an indispensable party. The motion is denied. He then moves to dismiss for lack of personal jurisdiction. How will the court rule?

The Plot Thickens

7.   Assume that Faulkner brings suit in Louisiana, the state where Lewis has agreed to deliver the books, and the Louisiana long-arm statute authorizes

personal jurisdiction over a nonresident defendant as to all claims arising out of "contracting to supply goods in the state." The Ohio long-arm statute, however, has no such provision, nor any other that would apply on the facts on the case. Lewis defaults in the Louisiana action. When Faulkner seeks to enforce his default judgment in Ohio, Lewis defends on the ground that the court lacked personal jurisdiction under the Ohio long-arm statute. Will his defense be upheld?

8. Assume that Lewis is sued in Mississippi and makes a special appearance to object to the court's exercise of personal jurisdiction over him. The court concludes that it has jurisdiction and therefore refuses to dismiss the case. Lewis, fearful lest he lose his right to defend on the merits, decides to defend the case on the merits in Mississippi and loses. May he appeal the trial court's initial decision that it had personal jurisdiction over him?

9. Lewis makes a special appearance in Mississippi to challenge personal jurisdiction and loses. He is frustrated; he knows that decision is wrong. He foresees the following scenario: litigating the merits, losing, appealing on jurisdiction, winning the appeal, the case being dismissed for lack of jurisdiction, and Faulkner starting over in Ohio (where he ought to have started anyway). Is there any way Lewis can short-circuit this procedural nightmare?

Double Trouble

10. Lewis defaults in Mississippi and challenges enforcement of the resulting default judgment in Ohio. The Ohio court refuses to enforce the Mississippi judgment, on the ground that the Mississippi court lacked personal jurisdiction over Lewis. Faulkner, convinced that the Ohio decision is wrong, brings another action on the judgment in Illinois, where Lewis owns other property subject to execution. What do you think the Illinois court will do?

Hostage Taking

11. Faulkner learns that Lewis has a summer cottage in Wisconsin and brings suit against Lewis on his book damage claim in a Wisconsin court.
   a. What will the court do if Lewis fails to appear and defend the action?
   b. If Faulkner gets a default judgment in his Wisconsin action on the book damage claim, what is he likely to do next?
   c. What is Lewis virtually forced to do to assert his objection to jurisdiction in this case?

EXPLANATIONS
Novel Developments

1. In most cases, the court will dismiss the case because it lacks the power to render a binding decision if it lacks personal jurisdiction over the defendant. Thus, by entering a special appearance (or a motion to dismiss in a state

that follows the Federal Rules model), Lewis will avoid litigating the merits in Mississippi without risking a default judgment that might be enforced in Ohio or some other state where Lewis has property.

In a few cases the court may agree with Lewis that it has not acquired jurisdiction over Lewis and yet still refuse to dismiss. For example, if the defendant is subject to jurisdiction in the forum state but has not been properly served with process, the court may simply order process to be served in an appropriate manner and then proceed. See Chapter 17 on the proper methods for service of process. In the most cases, however, the defendant's objection will not be to the method of service but the power of the court to exercise jurisdiction. This objection, if valid, will usually require dismissal.

2.   In this case Lewis has waived his objection to personal jurisdiction by appearing and defending on the merits without raising his jurisdictional challenge. In states that follow the special appearance rule, the defendant waives her jurisdictional objection unless she raises it immediately, before pleading to the merits. The states that follow the federal approach similarly provide that objections to personal jurisdiction are waived unless raised by motion before answering or in the initial answer to the complaint. See Fed. R. Civ. P. 12(g), (h). Thus, under either approach, objections to personal jurisdiction must be raised immediately, or they are waived. Lewis may not hold back on this defense and spring it on the plaintiff later if things go badly on the merits. The motion will be denied.

3.   The answer to this example follows from the last. Lewis has waived his jurisdictional objection by defending on the merits without objecting to jurisdiction and is barred from raising it later, either by direct attack in the Mississippi court or by collateral attack in the Ohio enforcement action. It is true that it is ordinarily open to the defendant to defend the enforcement suit on the ground that the original, rendering court lacked personal jurisdiction over her. Here, however, Lewis waived the objection by appearing on the merits in the initial action. The raise-it-or-lose-it rule forces Lewis to assert his objection to jurisdiction (or to default) *before* the court invests time in litigating the merits of the case in the Mississippi action. He may not sandbag the court and the plaintiff by holding back his jurisdictional objection, trying to win on the merits in the Mississippi court and then asserting the jurisdictional objection later in Ohio.

The Silent Treatment

4a. Lewis defaulted on the merits in Mississippi. That precludes him from litigating any of the underlying substantive issues that Faulkner had to prove to recover, such as whether the books were damaged and whether the damage resulted from Lewis's negligence. Even if Lewis can conclusively prove that the damage was not his fault, the Ohio court will not listen. The

Full Faith and Credit Clause prevents it from reexamining issues that have been settled—even by default—in another state's courts.

If this seems like a victory of form (or procedure) over substance, consider what would happen if the opposite were true. If defendants could litigate the merits in the enforcement action, they could simply ignore the plaintiff's original suit and have the substantive issues heard in the forum of the defendant's choice instead. The plaintiff's traditional right to choose the forum (subject, of course, to venue and jurisdictional restrictions) would be replaced by the defendant's right always to litigate at home.

b. In this hypo, Lewis exercised his prerogative to ignore the Mississippi action because he is convinced that the rendering court had no power to order him to appear there. He may raise the defense of lack of personal jurisdiction in the Ohio enforcement action since jurisdiction is the one issue that the enforcing court may consider before giving full faith and credit to the Mississippi judgment. If it is true that the Mississippi court lacked jurisdiction, the Ohio court will refuse to enter a judgment on the Mississippi judgment, Faulkner will be unable to collect on his default judgment, and Lewis will suffer no harm from it—except, of course, the anxiety over whether the Ohio court will agree with him on the jurisdictional question. If I were Lewis, I would prefer to litigate the jurisdictional issue in the Mississippi court, by filing a special appearance there, rather than risk losing the chance to litigate the merits entirely by staking all on the chance that the Ohio court will agree that the Mississippi court lacked jurisdiction over him.

c. As in example 4b, it is open to Lewis to challenge the personal jurisdiction of the original court in this enforcement action. However, if Faulkner proves that the Mississippi court had jurisdiction, the Ohio court is bound under the Full Faith and Credit Clause to enter judgment on the original judgment and order execution of it on Lewis's assets. Thus, by postponing his jurisdictional challenge, Lewis has abdicated his chance to defend the substance of the claim in either Mississippi or Ohio. This is an extreme price to pay for the convenience of litigating the jurisdictional issue in your home state. This price was paid, for example, in *McGee v. International Life Ins. Co.*, 355 U.S. 220 (1957), in which the insurer ignored the original California suit, and the California judgment was subsequently held enforceable in Texas.

5. Once again, Lewis has run afoul of the rules. He has already raised his challenge to jurisdiction in the initial action. One bite at the apple is all that he gets; he may not challenge jurisdiction in Mississippi, lose, and try again in the enforcing court in hopes of getting a more favorable reading from an Ohio judge. See *Baldwin v. Iowa State Traveling Men's Association*, 283 U.S. 522 (1931). The plaintiff should not have to prove twice that the first court had jurisdiction, nor should the defendant be allowed to keep raising the issue until she finds some court that agrees with her. If Lewis insists on challenging jurisdiction in Ohio, he must default in Mississippi to preserve his right to do so.

6.   Alas, poor Lewis. All these arbitrary rules and traps for the unwary. Here, he has fallen into another by misconstruing Rule 12. That rule, as well as state rules modeled on it, allows the defendant to raise the jurisdictional objection along with other objections but not to raise other objections first and then challenge the court's personal jurisdiction in a subsequent motion. Responding with other objections and defenses (such as failure to join an indispensable party, failure to state a claim, or denials on the merits) without raising the personal jurisdiction objection operates as a waiver of that objection. See Fed. R. Civ. P. 12(g), (h). The jurisdictional challenge must always be raised in the defendant's first response to the complaint. Lewis's motion will be denied.

The Plot Thickens

7.   This example raises two important points. First, the rendering court must have jurisdiction not only under the minimum contacts standard of *International Shoe* but also under the applicable long-arm statute. Thus, even if Lewis's contacts with Louisiana are sufficient to support jurisdiction under the constitutional standard, Lewis could still argue (in the original suit or the enforcement action) that the rendering court lacked jurisdiction under the applicable long-arm statute.

The second point is, what *is* the applicable long-arm statute? Ohio's, where enforcement is sought? Or Louisiana's, where the initial suit was brought? The relevant issue is whether the Louisiana court had the right to exercise jurisdiction over Lewis. Therefore, the Ohio court must ask whether the Louisiana long-arm statute authorized jurisdiction in Louisiana, not whether the Ohio statute would have allowed it if Faulkner had sued there. Lewis's defense fails again.

8.   As the introduction indicates, most states allow the defendant, after raising the jurisdictional objection and losing, to take the safer course of defending on the merits and then appealing the decision on jurisdiction.[8] This way, Lewis may still obtain appellate review of the decision on personal jurisdiction without abandoning his opportunity to defend the case on its merits. If he wins on the merits, he will be content and obviously will not appeal the decision on jurisdiction. If he loses on the merits, he may appeal the trial court's decision that he was subject to personal jurisdiction in Mississippi. If the Mississippi appellate court concludes that he was subject to jurisdiction, it will affirm the judgment. If, however, it concludes that he was not subject to jurisdiction in Mississippi, it will order the case dismissed, even though there has been a full trial on the merits.

---

8. Mississippi follows the majority rule. See *E. B. Kaiser Co. v. Ludlow*, 243 So. 2d 62, 66 (Miss. 1971).

A few states still follow the older, more formalistic rule that the defendant waives the jurisdictional objection by defending the case on the merits. The theory behind this approach is that it is inconsistent for the defendant to appear and litigate in that court and at the same time claim that the court lacks jurisdiction over her. If you object to jurisdiction, these courts hold, you should stick to your guns by refusing to litigate the merits and appeal solely on the jurisdictional issue. See Casad, §3.01[5][a][1] p. 3-55.

9. Clearly the most efficient course for Lewis would be to file an immediate appeal in the Mississippi appellate court, challenging the trial court's decision that it had jurisdiction. That way he could avoid going through a trial on the merits in Mississippi, assuming that the trial judge was wrong.

This strategy would not be open to Lewis in the federal courts. Ordinarily, parties in federal cases can only take appeals from final judgments of the district courts. 28 U.S.C. §1291. The Supreme Court has held that decisions upholding personal jurisdiction are "interlocutory" orders because they do not finally resolve the suit and are therefore not appealable until the end of the suit. See *Van Cauwenberghe v. Biard,* 486 U.S. 517, 526-527 (1988).

However, state practice varies considerably on this issue. Some states allow interlocutory appeals of orders upholding personal jurisdiction or appellate relief through some extraordinary method of review. A good example is *World-Wide Volkswagen v. Woodson,* 444 U.S. 286 (1980), in which the defendants sought a "writ of prohibition" from the Oklahoma Supreme Court to prohibit the trial judge from acting in excess of his jurisdiction. Some states even *require* the defendant to seek interlocutory review of these decisions, presumably on the rationale that early dismissal of cases in which jurisdiction is improper will save everyone the useless exercise of a trial destined to be nullified on appeal. See Casad at ¶6.01[5][c] at 6-26 n. 60. The lesson is to check carefully the applicable state practice to see whether you may or must take an immediate appeal.

Double Trouble

10. This is an interesting strategy on Faulkner's part. Because Court Number Two has held that Court Number One lacked jurisdiction, Faulkner tries Court Number Three, in hopes that it will disagree with Two and enforce One's judgment. It is reminiscent of Lewis's attempt in example 5 to have the enforcing court reexamine the jurisdictional issue already litigated and decided in the rendering court.

For the same reasons, it won't work. The issue of whether the original court had personal jurisdiction over Lewis was litigated and decided in Ohio. Under the principle of collateral estoppel Faulkner will be barred from relitigating the jurisdiction issue in Illinois or any other state. Note that the Illinois court, by refusing to reopen the jurisdiction issue, is not choosing between the two courts and deciding to honor the judgment of one over the other. Only the Ohio court decided the issue of jurisdiction over Lewis in the original action; the Mississippi court never did because Lewis defaulted. Thus, the Illinois court is honoring the holding of the one court that reached the jurisdictional issue. See Restatement (Second) of Judgments, §81, comm. b.

Hostage Taking

11a. Lewis may not be subject to personal jurisdiction in Wisconsin for this claim simply because he has a summer place in the state. See *Shaffer v. Heitner*, 433 US. 186, 208-209 (1977) (questioning jurisdiction based on presence of property unrelated to claim in suit). However, if Lewis defaults, the Wisconsin court is not likely to ever consider the point. It will likely assume that Faulkner has no defense to the action, enter a default judgment for Faulkner on the claim, and assess damages for the books.

b. Since Faulkner chose to sue in Wisconsin, presumably Wisconsin is a convenient forum for him to enforce his judgment as well. Very likely, he will do what Mitchell did in *Pennoyer v. Neff*: take out a writ of execution on the Wisconsin judgment and commence proceedings to have Lewis's summer house sold to satisfy the damage judgment.

c. Can you see that in this predictable scenario, Lewis's only realistic option is to appear and object to personal jurisdiction in Wisconsin when the suit is originally brought? If he does not, and Faulkner obtains a default judgment and executes the judgment against Lewis's property in Wisconsin, Lewis will naturally have to resist the sale of his cottage by appearing in Wisconsin to object. On what ground? The same ground, of course, that Neff asserted in *Pennoyer v. Neff*: that the Wisconsin court had no jurisdiction to render the judgment which Faulkner now seeks to execute.

So, he will have to go to Wisconsin one way or the other, either to object to personal jurisdiction at the outset or to contest the sale of his house on execution. However, if he waits and objects to the sale, he is out of luck if the court holds that it had personal jurisdiction to render the default judgment. There goes the house, and Lewis will never have had the chance to defend the book claim on the merits. By contrast, by appearing at the outset, he preserves his right to defend on the merits if the Wisconsin court concludes that it has jurisdiction over him.

Thus, the presence of the defendant's property in the state effectively forces him to make a direct attack on the court's jurisdiction in the rendering state. A defendant in Lewis's situation can't wait and make a collateral attack when Faulkner brings the judgment to his home state, because Faulkner never *will* bring it to Lewis's state; he can collect on it in Wisconsin.

4

Federal Questions and Federal Cases: Jurisdiction over Cases "Arising under" Federal Law

Introduction

Our first three chapters dealt with personal jurisdiction—the power of a court to require a defendant from outside the state to defend a lawsuit in that state. Now we turn to *subject matter jurisdiction,* a separate, additional requirement for a court to hear a case. Suppose, for example, that Engle wishes to sue her employer, Consolidated Packing Corporation, after she is fired from her job for reporting acts of fraud committed by Consolidated officers to federal authorities. She needs to choose a court which has personal jurisdiction over Consolidated for her claim, but she must also choose one which can hear the type of lawsuit she plans to file against Consolidated.

To understand the principles governing subject matter jurisdiction in American courts, we have to start with those courts themselves. The United States Constitution created a system of divided sovereignty, in which the states and the national or "federal" government share power. Not only is legislative power split between the two levels of government, but the judicial power is as well. Thus, in every state there is a state court system and a branch of the federal court system. Some cases must be brought in the state courts. Others (though not many) must be brought in federal court. And still others may be filed in either court system. The trick is to know which ones go where, and that depends on which court has "subject matter jurisdiction" over the case, that is, the power to hear the particular type of case the plaintiff plans to file.

Let's start with the reach of subject matter jurisdiction in the state courts. Every state defines the types of cases its courts may hear in its constitution or by statute (or both), and all states have conferred very broad subject matter jurisdiction on their courts. That isn't particularly surprising: Plaintiffs generally prefer to sue at home, so broad jurisdiction accommodates local citizens, who, after all, elect the legislators who write jurisdictional statutes. So it's a fair working principle that the state courts in every *state* have very broad jurisdiction to hear most types of cases. For example, the state courts will be able to hear garden variety tort and contract claims, property claims, divorce claims, cases involving wills and trusts, and claims under state statutes. Indeed, it is hard to think of a case arising under *state* law that could not be filed in some court within the state, and most cases do arise under state law.

While the state courts will be able to hear most claims, statutes vary as to *which* court within the state hears those claims. All states have a trial court of general subject matter jurisdiction that can hear common types of suits. This court may be called the superior court, the circuit court, the district court, or something else, depending on the state.[1] In addition, states usually establish specialized courts to hear some types of cases requiring particular expertise, such as probate courts, municipal courts, land courts, or housing courts; some of our thirstier western states even have water courts.

The state courts handle by far the greatest part of the judicial business. In 1998 an astounding 91,000,000 cases were filed in the courts of the fifty states,[2] while some 1,700,000 were filed in the federal courts.[3] The respective numbers of judges also convey a sense of the extent to which state courts carry the laboring judicial oar. The California state trial courts had about 1500 judges in 1999, while there were only about 170 federal judges (including magistrate judges) sitting in the federal district courts in California.[4]

---

1. For a list of the courts of general jurisdiction in each state, see D. Meador, American Courts 96-97 (West 1991).

2. B. Ostrom and N. Kauder, eds., Examining the Work of State Courts, 1998: A National Perspective from the Court Statistics Project, National Center for State Courts 1999, p. 7 (includes all types of filings).

3. The 1998 Year-End Report of the Federal Judiciary, 31 The Third Branch, No. 1, p. 5 (Jan. 1999) (including bankruptcy cases).

4. Want's Federal-State Court Directory (Washington D.C.: Want Pub. Co. 2000), pp. 28-35, 159.

The Source and Limits of Federal Subject Matter Jurisdiction

Unlike the state courts, which exercise very broad subject matter jurisdiction, the type of cases that federal courts can hear is extremely limited. The subject matter jurisdiction of federal courts is defined in Article III, s. 2 of the Constitution, which lists certain limited categories of cases federal courts may hear. Generally speaking, any case not on the Article III, s. 2 list must be brought in state court: the basic premise of the Constitution is that the federal government has the authority to exercise powers expressly or impliedly granted in the Constitution, but that all others—those not granted to the feds—are reserved to the states. U.S. Constitution, Amendment X.

A look at the Article III list reveals that it is a pretty limited list. The federal courts are authorized to hear cases between states, between citizens of different states, between citizens and aliens, cases involving foreign ministers and consuls, admiralty and maritime cases, cases arising under the federal Constitution and federal law, and a few other narrow categories of suits. In each of these types of cases, the Framers perceived an important national interest. In cases between states, between citizens of different states, and cases between citizens and aliens, for example, they foresaw a risk of prejudice against the outsider—generally, the defendant—in state court. Admiralty and maritime cases and those involving ministers and consuls involve international relations, as to which the nation should speak with one voice. Similarly, it makes sense that federal courts should be able to hear cases that involve the application and interpretation of federal law, both to protect it from unsympathetic construction by state courts and to allow definitive interpretation of federal law.

With this background, let's return to Engle's case. Several of the categories in Article III, section 2, might give a federal court constitutional authority to hear this case. Federal subject matter jurisdiction may be proper if Engle is "diverse" from (that is, a citizen of a different state than) Consolidated. Article III, s. 2 also provides federal courts the constitutional authority to hear Engle's case if it arises under a federal statute or under the federal Constitution. If her case doesn't fit into one of these two cubbyholes in Article III, s. 2, it appears that Engle will have to sue in state court: remember the general premise that if a power is not granted to the federal government under the Constitution, it remains with the states.

These two categories of federal subject matter jurisdiction—cases that arise under federal law and cases "between citizens of different states" (diversity cases)—are by far the most common types of civil cases filed in federal court. This chapter will focus on the first category, which I shall refer to as "arising-under jurisdiction." The next chapter will tackle diversity.

Jurisdiction over Cases Arising under Federal Law: The Problem

Article III, s. 2 authorizes federal courts to hear cases "arising under this Constitution, the Laws of the United States, and Treaties made, or which shall be made, under their Authority." This provision obviously authorizes federal courts to hear at least some claims which involve federal constitutional issues or federal statutes, but the trick is to determine which claims that grand phrase, "arising under" federal law, includes. Does it authorize federal jurisdiction over a case which involves federal law in any way, or some more limited set of cases? Here are some examples that illustrate the problem:

- Engle sues Consolidated under a federal "whistle-blower" statute, which authorizes an employee who is discharged or disciplined for reporting violation of federal regulations to obtain reinstatement and damages from her employer.
- Engle sues Consolidated for breach of contract, for firing her in the first year of a three-year contract. Consolidated answers the complaint, raising the defense that it was required to discharge Engle under a federal statute barring employment of illegal aliens.
- Engle sues Consolidated for bad faith discharge, a state tort claim which allows damages if the defendant discharges an employee for reasons which violate certain public policies. She claims that Consolidated fired her because she refused to engage in accounting practices which violate federal statutory accounting requirements for government contractors.
- Engle sues Consolidated for breach of contract, claiming that her contract was for three years, but Consolidated fired her after one. She claims that Consolidated hired her to administer a research program partially funded by grants from the federal government, but fired her for taking time off to stay home with a sick child.

Federal law lurks in each of these cases in one way or another. In the first case, Engle has actually brought suit under a federal statute. In the second, she sues on the state contract claim, but Consolidated has asserted a defense involving federal law. In the third example, plaintiff sues on a state law bad faith dismissal claim, but tries to establish the defendant's bad faith by showing that it required her to violate federal law. In the last, federal law is only vaguely relevant, if at all. Examples like these illustrate that the courts need to develop some working standards to determine when a case which somehow *involves* federal law will "arise under" federal law.

Jurisdiction over Cases Arising under Federal Law: The Constitutional Scope

The Supreme Court has long taken an expansive view of the "arising under" language in Article III, s. 2. In *Osborn v. Bank of the United States,* 22 U.S. 738 (1824), Chief Justice Marshall, who advocated a strong national government, held that a case arises under federal law — as that phrase is used in Article III, s. 2 — if

> the title or right set up by the party, may be defeated by one construction of the constitution or law of the United States, and sustained by the opposite construction. We think, then, that when a question to which the judicial power of the Union is extended by the constitution, forms an ingredient of the original cause, it is in the power of Congress to give [the lower federal courts] jurisdiction of that cause, although other questions of fact or law may be involved in it.

22 U.S. at 822-823.

Under the broad holding in *Osborn,* the federal court could clearly hear the first case above, since the federal statute is the source of the substantive right Engle claims. Jurisdiction under this "federal ingredient" approach would also extend to the second example case, in which Engle sues under state contract law, but Consolidated claims as a defense that it was required to discharge her under a federal statute. The validity of this defense will clearly be an "ingredient" of the case, although that ingredient is injected by the defendant, not the plaintiff.[5] The third case would arguably also come within this broad "ingredient" approach to arising-under jurisdiction. Although Engle has sued under state tort law, in order to prove her bad faith dismissal claim she will have to show that she was fired because of her refusal to violate federal regulations. Thus, *proving* her state law contract claim will require her to show that the accounting practices she refused to adopt would violate federal law.

The last case described above would not "arise under" federal law even under the broad test of *Osborn.* Presumably, for federal law to be an "ingredient" of a case, one of the parties in the case would have to rely on federal law to establish either a claim or a defense in the lawsuit, or at least raise a federal issue in proving her case. While there is some peripheral relationship to a federal program in the fourth example, neither Engle nor Consolidated would need to refer to federal law to litigate the case. If Engle sued under a federal parental leave act, the result would be different, but on the facts given

---

5. Chief Justice Marshall's reference in *Osborn* to "the original cause" means to the case itself, not, as under *Mottley,* only to the claims asserted by the plaintiff in that case. A federal issue raised by the defendant would suffice under this reading. See Wright, Federal Courts 5th ed. 1994, p. 102.

neither her claim nor the company's defense would require evidence about any proposition of federal law.

So, the bottom line is that the phrase "arising under" in Article III, s. 2 is very broadly construed. It is probably satisfied in any case in which a party seeks to rely on or establish a proposition of federal law in order to prove either a claim or a defense in the case. In *Osborn,* Chief Justice Marshall even opined that *any case* brought by the Bank of the United States would "arise under" federal law, since the Bank was incorporated under a federal statute. Thus, the Bank's very existence, and its right to sue or be sued, are an issue in any such case. This is a very broad—perhaps extravagantly broad—conception of the reach of the Framers' "arising under" language in Article III. The Court has never been called upon to accept or reject the outer reaches of Marshall's view, but it has reaffirmed that the "arising under" language in Article III is broad enough to apply if substantial issues of federal law are raised by any party to the case.

Jurisdiction over Cases Arising under Federal Law: The Need for Both Constitutional Power and Statutory Authority

Now comes the problem. The Court's decision in *Osborn* indicates that the constitutional reach of arising-under jurisdiction in Article III, s. 2 is broad. However, Article III *does not confer subject matter jurisdiction on the lower federal courts.* In fact, Article III does not even create lower federal courts; it authorizes Congress to do so. See Article III, s. 1 (judicial power "shall be vested in one Supreme Court, and in such inferior Courts as the Congress may from time to time ordain and establish"). Since Congress has the authority to create lower federal courts—or not to—it has long been held that it also has the authority to define their jurisdiction, within the outer bounds of possible cases described in Article III, s. 2. *Kline v. Burke Construction Co.,* 260 U.S. 226, 233-234 (1922). In other words, if Congress chooses to establish federal trial courts—like the federal district courts as they exist today— it may give them the authority to hear all the cases listed in Article III, s. 2. But it may also—as it has—authorize them to hear some, but not all, of the cases described in Article III, s. 2. It could authorize them to hear diversity cases but not cases arising under federal law, or cases between states but not cases between citizens of different states, or cases between citizens of different states only if an amount-in-controversy requirement is met.

> [F]ederal courts may assume only that portion of the Article III judicial power which Congress, by statute, entrusts to them. Simply stated, Congress may impart as much or as little of the judicial power as it deems appropriate and the Judiciary may not thereafter on its own motion recur to the Article III storehouse for additional jurisdiction.

When it comes to jurisdiction of the federal courts, truly, to para-
phrase the scripture, the Congress giveth, and the Congress taketh
away.

Senate Select Committee v. Nixon, 366 F. Supp. 51, 55 (D.D.C. 1973).

It follows from this basic fact that a lawyer seeking to file a lawsuit in
federal court must ask two questions in determining whether a suit may be
filed there. *First,* is this case one which constitutionally may be granted to the
federal courts, because the power for them to hear it is granted in Article III,
s. 2 of the Constitution? And *second,* if the case does fall into one of the categories in Article III, s. 2, has Congress actually conveyed jurisdiction over
this type of case in a federal statute?

There are many illustrations of cases within the federal judicial power
under Article III that Congress has *not* authorized federal courts to hear.
For example, for many years there was no broad grant of arising-under jurisdiction to the lower federal courts. Prior to 1875, there were narrow
statutes authorizing jurisdiction over cases arising under *particular* federal
laws, such as the federal revenue statutes or federal patent statutes, but there
was no broad grant of arising-under jurisdiction. It was only after the Civil
War, when Congress doubted the willingness of the state courts in the
southern states to enforce the new federal civil rights statutes, that it
granted broad jurisdiction over cases arising under federal law to the lower
federal courts.[6]

Today 28 U.S.C. s. 1331, the statute by which Congress bestows
arising-under jurisdiction on the federal district courts, authorizes jurisdiction over "cases arising under the Constitution, laws, or treaties of the
United States." Because the statute conveys the arising-under jurisdiction in
the same language used in Article III, s. 2, one might reasonably conclude
that Congress intended to grant the full reach of such jurisdiction to the federal district courts — to the broad extent of the Court's interpretation of the
"arising-under" language in *Osborn.* However, such a reasonable conclusion
would, perplexingly, be wrong.

Construing the Statutory Arising-under Grant: The Enigmatic Mottley Rule

Even though 28 U.S.C. s. 1331 grants jurisdiction in the same language as Article III, s. 2, the federal courts have interpreted the reach of the statute much

---

6. Another example is a case between a citizen of Minnesota and a citizen of Illinois
demanding $35,000 in damages. This is a case "between citizens of different states,"
so it is within the diversity jurisdiction authorized in Article III, s. 2. However, Congress has not seen fit to allow this diversity case into federal court: 28 U.S.C. s.
1332(a), the statute that confers diversity jurisdiction on the federal district courts,
limits that jurisdiction to cases in which more than $75,000 is in controversy.

more narrowly than the constitutional scope of arising-under jurisdiction. The cases consistently hold that s. 1331 only applies if *the plaintiff's claim* requires proof of federal law. The statute does not confer jurisdiction on the federal district courts over cases that involve federal law unless the federal issue is necessary to the proof of the plaintiff's claim.

Louisville & Nashville R.R. v. Mottley, 211 U.S. 149 (1908), illustrates the puzzling distinction between the meaning of "arising under" in Article III, s. 2 and the meaning of the same phrase in s. 1331. In *Mottley,* the plaintiffs were given lifetime passes for free travel on the railroad, in settlement of a claim for injuries the Mottleys had suffered in an accident. After honoring the passes for thirty-some years, the railroad refused to renew them, because Congress had passed a statute barring railroads from giving free transportation. The Mottleys sued to obtain their passes, and the railroad defended on the ground that the federal statute barred renewal. The Mottleys had two responses to this argument. *First,* they argued that the statute was prospective only: surely Congress must not have meant the statute to apply to passes granted by the railroad before its enactment. *Second,* argued the Mottleys, if the statute were interpreted to bar their passes, it would be unconstitutional under the Fifth Amendment to the United States Constitution, since it would deprive them of vested property rights without due process of law.

These were two substantial, hotly contested questions of federal law. A person of common sense would be justified in concluding that a case which raised them — which, indeed, turned on them — would "arise under" federal law. Indeed, the parties and the trial court thought so, for no one questioned the federal court's jurisdiction in the trial court. No party questioned it on appeal to the United States Supreme Court, either. Yet the Court raised the subject matter jurisdiction issue itself and concluded that the lower federal court had lacked jurisdiction to hear the Mottleys' case.

How can this be? The Court explained that, for a plaintiff to sue in federal court under the *statutory test* for arising-under jurisdiction, *she* must assert a claim that arises under federal law. The Mottleys' case did not: they had sued for breach of contract, a state law cause of action that did not require them to prove any proposition of federal law. They could establish their right to relief simply by proving that the railroad had agreed to renew the passes and then refused to do so. True, the railroad had given the federal statute as its reason for failing to renew the passes, and it was clear that they would rely on the statute as a defense in responding to the Mottleys' suit. However, the statute would naturally arise as a defense, not as an element of the Mottleys' case in chief. It was up to the Mottleys to state *their* claim in their complaint and to leave it to the railroad to raise whatever defenses it chose. And it was clear that the Mottleys' claim arose under state contract law, not federal law.

Note several things about this counterintuitive holding. *First,* it is clear that the case would come out differently if the Court interpreted the statute (now, 28 U.S.C. s. 1331) as broadly as it has interpreted Article III, s. 2 under *Osborn.* The federal statute was clearly an "ingredient" of the case; indeed, the irony of *Mottley* is that the only disputed issues in the case were issues of federal law. *Second,* under *Mottley,* it is not enough that the plaintiff refers to federal law in her complaint: there is little doubt that the Mottleys did refer to both federal issues in their pleadings. The problem was that they didn't have to; they could have stated a perfectly adequate claim for relief by alleging only contract, breach, and a demand for specific performance. Under *Mottley's* "well pleaded complaint" rule, the court, in deciding whether the case "arises under federal law" for purposes of s. 1331, asks whether the plaintiff would have to raise the federal issue in a complaint which includes the elements she needs to prove to establish her claim, and *only those elements.* Jurisdiction under 28. U.S.C. s. 1331 "must be determined from what necessarily appears in the plaintiff's statement of his own claim in the bill or declaration" (*Taylor v. Anderson,* 234 U.S. 74, 75-76 (1914)), not from any anticipated defenses the defendant might assert.

The *Mottley* case illustrates and applies the well-pleaded complaint rule, but provides the beleaguered student with precious little to explain its rationale. Why shouldn't a case that involves a genuine issue of federal law qualify for federal court jurisdiction, regardless of who raises the federal issue? Perhaps it should, yet the *Mottley* rule remains the law today, primarily because it furthers sensible judicial administration. Courts need to determine their jurisdiction from the outset; the *Mottley* rule allows the court to do so based solely on the plaintiff's case, before the defendant answers. If *Mottley* had been decided the other way, plaintiffs might invoke federal jurisdiction simply by referring in their complaints to defenses they expected the defendant to raise — or by speculating about ones the defendant could raise, simply to create federal subject matter jurisdiction. Under the well-pleaded complaint rule, the court is able to determine at the outset whether it has jurisdiction, based on the claims the plaintiff has asserted, without waiting for the defendant's answer.

An Early Question

1. Suppose that federal courts did not use the *Mottley* rule; instead, they upheld jurisdiction under 28 U.S.C. s. 1331 if either the plaintiff's complaint or the defendant's answer raised an issue of federal law. The Mottleys bring suit in federal court, demanding specific performance of their contract. You represent the railroad, which is considering raising several defenses to the Mottleys' claim, some based in federal law and some in state law. If you wanted to avoid federal court, what would you advise the railroad to do in answering the complaint?

Applying the Mottley *Rule: The Holmes "Creation Test"*

Justice Oliver Wendell Holmes suggested a test for determining when *Mottley's* well-pleaded complaint rule is met: he suggested that a suit arises "under the law that creates the cause of action." *American Well Works v. Layne*, 241 U.S. 257, 260 (1916). The Holmes test would find jurisdiction under s. 1331 if the source of the plaintiff's enforceable legal right against the defendant is federal law. In *Mottley*, the source of the plaintiffs' right to demand relief from the court was state contract law. The Mottleys could sue the railroad because the state common law of contracts allows courts to order specific performance where a party makes a contract and fails to perform its obligations. Since the "law that creates the cause of action" was state law, the claim did not "arise under" federal law within the meaning of 28 U.S.C. s. 1331.

By contrast, in our first example case, if Engle sues under the federal whistle-blower statute, the Holmes test is met. The reason that Engle can demand damages from Consolidated is that the federal statute bars employers from discharging or disciplining their employees for reporting violation of federal regulations, and authorizes such employees to sue for reinstatement or damages if the employer does so. Thus, the federal law is the direct source of Engle's right to sue. If it did not exist, she would not be able to sue (at least, not under federal law); because Congress created that right, she can.

Compare the third example case, in which Engle sues for bad faith discharge, a state law cause of action. This case fails the Holmes test, since Engle sues on a state law claim. Here, her right to relief is created by state tort law, the common law cause of action for bad faith discharge. However, to *recover* on her state law claim, Engle will have to *prove* a proposition of federal law: that the accounting practices she refused to engage in violated the federal statute, so that she was justified in refusing to engage in them. Arguably, this should be sufficient to support arising-under jurisdiction (since the plaintiff will have to establish a proposition of federal law in order to prevail). However, the Holmes test would presumably leave this one out.

One fair rule of thumb in this area (in which, unfortunately, most "rules" turn out to have exceptions) is that, if a case meets the Holmes test, it does "arise under" federal law for purposes of section 1331. "Mr. Justice Holmes' formula is more useful for inclusion than for the exclusion for which it was intended." *T. B. Harms v. Eliscu*, 339 F.2d 823, 827 (2nd Cir. 1964). The vast majority of cases brought under the arising-under jurisdiction fit neatly within the Holmes test, and consequently there is no question that the federal court has jurisdiction under 28 U.S.C. s. 1331. Here are two easy examples:

- The federal copyright statute, 17 U.S.C. s. 106, provides that authors have the exclusive right to perform or reproduce their original works.

The statute also authorizes injunctive relief against any person who uses copyrighted works without permission. 17 U.S.C. s. 502. Shakespeare writes a play about a prince. The Elizabethan Publishing Company gets hold of a copy and announces publication of the same play. Shakespeare sues for an injunction under 17 U.S.C. s. 502.

Here, the federal copyright statute both creates a federal substantive right—the right to exclusive use of original works—*and* authorizes him to sue for violation of that right. Thus, his suit clearly satisfies the Holmes test.

- The Eighth Amendment to the United States Constitution, which bars "cruel and unusual punishment," has been interpreted to require jailers to provide medical care for prisoners in their charge. Willson, a prisoner in a state prison, is taken violently ill, but the guards ignore his pleas for medical help, leading to serious complications. He sues under 42 U.S.C. s. 1983, which authorizes any person deprived of rights under the United States Constitution by state actors to sue for damages.

Here, the United States Constitution creates a substantive right—the right of a prisoner to be free of deliberate indifference to his serious medical needs—and a federal statute authorizes him to sue for damages for deprivation of that right. Again, there is no question that federal law is the source of Willson's claim and that jurisdiction would be proper under s. 1331.

These two examples are easy, because in each, federal law *both* creates the underlying substantive right the plaintiff seeks to enforce *and* authorizes plaintiffs to bring suit to enforce that substantive right. However, these two don't always go together. For example, in *Shoshone Mining Co. v. Rutter,* 177 U.S. 505 (1900), the plaintiff sued in federal court to establish title to a mining claim. A federal statute authorized claimants to mining claims in the western states to bring such suits to determine title to those claims, but provided that the merits of the ownership claim should be determined according to the local property customs or statutes in the state or territory where the property was located. In other words, the federal statute in *Shoshone Mining* authorized claimants to sue, but it did not establish federal law which would govern the substance of the claims adjudicated: these were to be governed by local law.

Whether *Shoshone Mining* satisfies the Holmes test depends on just what it means for federal law to "create the cause of action." Did Holmes mean that the right to sue—to go into court and seek a remedy—must be granted by a federal statute (which was true in *Shoshone Mining*) or that federal law must create the *substantive right* which is being enforced, or both? Unlike the two "easy examples" above, in *Shoshone Mining* federal law authorized parties to sue on mining claims, but did not "create the cause of action": local property law principles provided the governing substantive law for claims brought under the statute. On essentially this rationale, the Supreme Court concluded that the claimant's suit did not arise under federal law. "A statute authorizing an action to establish a right," the Court noted, "is very different from one which creates a right to be established." 177 U.S. at 510.[7] However, the Court did not clearly hold that federal law must create the underlying substantive right in order for a case to "arise under" federal law.

Beyond the Creation Test: State Law Claims Turning on a Substantial Federal Issue

In another set of cases, federal courts have upheld arising-under jurisdiction where federal law clearly does not create the right to sue, but the plaintiff, in order to establish her state law claim, must prove a proposition of federal law. An oft-cited example is *Smith v. Kansas City Title and Trust Company*, 255 U.S. 180 (1920). In *Smith*, the plaintiffs sued to enjoin Kansas City Title & Trust from investing in certain bonds issued by federal banks under the authority of a federal statute. The plaintiffs claimed that investing in the bonds would exceed the company's corporate powers, since it was only authorized to invest in valid securities, and the bonds at issue in the case were invalid because the federal statute authorizing them was unconstitutional.

The claim in *Smith* does not satisfy the Holmes test: the plaintiffs sued to enjoin the corporation from exceeding its powers under state corporation law, a state law claim (just as the Mottleys sued to enforce a contract in *Mottley*). However, the plaintiffs in *Smith* could not prove this state law claim without establishing a proposition of federal law: that the federal statute under which the bonds were issued was unconstitutional under the United States Constitution. The federal issue was embedded in the state law claim and essential to its resolution. The Supreme Court held that this claim satisfied arising-under jurisdiction, since "the controversy concerns the constitutional validity of an act of Congress which is directly drawn in question. The decision depends upon the determination of this issue." 255 U.S. at 201. Interestingly, the *Smith* Court did not attempt to reconcile its holding with Justice Holmes' "creation" test in *American Well Works*.

Later Supreme Court cases suggest that the *Smith* exception, or alternative, or whatever it is, is still a viable basis for finding jurisdiction under s. 1331. In *Franchise Tax Board v. Laborers' Vacation Trust*, 463 U.S. 1, 9 (1983), for example, the Court stated:

---

7. It is not hard to see why, as a policy matter, the Court may have drawn this distinction in *Shoshone Mining*. Otherwise, a myriad of local property claims in the western states, involving no federal interest or law, would have been swept into federal court under the arising-under jurisdiction.

It is well settled that Justice Holmes' test is more useful for describing the vast majority of cases that come within the district courts' original jurisdiction than it is for describing which cases are beyond district court jurisdiction. We have often held that a case "arose under" federal law where the vindication of a right under state law necessarily turned on some construction of federal law. *See, e.g., Smith v. Kansas City Title & Trust Co.*

Here is an example of a case which applies this substantial-federal-issue approach. In *Sweeney v. Abramovitz,* 449 F.Supp. 213 (D. Conn. 1978), Sweeney, a police officer, sued Abramovitz for malicious prosecution, based on Abramovitz's prior filing of a civil rights claim against Sweeney under the federal civil rights statute, 42 U.S.C. s. 1983. Malicious prosecution is a state law tort claim. In order to prove this state tort, the plaintiff must establish (among other elements) that the prior action was brought without probable cause. The court held that Sweeney's claim arose under federal law, because, in order to establish the no-probable-cause element of his claim, Sweeney would have to show that Abramovitz had no probable cause to believe, when he filed the earlier suit, that he had a claim under s. 1983:

> The meaning of s. 1983 and its application to the circumstances alleged in Abramovitz' original suit are essential ingredients of Sweeney's claim. Only if Abramovitz did not have probable cause to believe that the facts known to him established a cause of action under s. 1983 does Sweeney have a valid claim now. The meaning of s. 1983 is thus a "pivotal question of federal law". . . the resolution of which will be essential in determining whether Sweeney will have established a prima facie case.

449 F. Supp. at 215–216 (citation omitted). Note that, while cases like *Smith* and *Sweeney* go beyond Holmes' "creation" test, they are faithful to *Mottley's* well-pleaded complaint rule in a broader sense, since in determining jurisdiction, the court looks at what the *plaintiff* must establish as part of her case.

Under this "substantial federal issue" approach, Engle could argue that the federal court has subject matter jurisdiction over the third example case given on p. 58, in which Engle sues for bad faith discharge (a state law claim), but alleges that she was fired for refusing to violate federal accounting requirements. Although state tort law creates the right to sue, in order to prove her claim Engle would have to prove that she was fired for refusing to engage in conduct that violated federal law.

A Further Complication: Merrell Dow and the Relevance of Implied Federal Causes of Action to Arising-under Jurisdiction

While all this seems puzzling—and does puzzle judges, lawyers, and federal courts scholars as well—the basics are relatively clear. *First,* we know that jurisdiction under the arising-under statute must be based on the plaintiff's claim. And *second*, we know that a case will "arise under" federal law if it satisfies the Holmes test—at least, if it satisfies the Holmes test in both senses discussed above: that federal law creates the underlying substantive right plaintiff seeks to enforce and authorizes plaintiffs to go to court for a remedy. It's worth noting that these two principles probably resolve ninety-five percent of the cases. Usually, jurisdiction under s. 1331 is clear because the plaintiff sues under a federal statute—like the copyright statute—that both creates enforceable rights and authorizes injured parties to sue for violations of those rights. *Third*, where a federal statute authorizes suit, but only to enforce a state cause of action, the court may well conclude that arising-under jurisdiction does not exist, as the Supreme Court did in *Shoshone Mining*. It isn't clear that this will always be so, but situations in which the federal statute simply authorizes a remedy for a state-created right are likely to be problematic. *Last*, we have a twist—the *Smith* holding that a state cause of action can suffice, if proof of that cause of action requires proof of a proposition of federal law. Occasionally, a case may arise where a court will hold that arising-under jurisdiction is proper on this basis.

Things would be complex enough if we could just leave it at that. In fact, if you have not read *Merrell Dow Pharmaceuticals Inc. v. Thompson*, 478 U.S. 804 (1986), for your civil procedure class, I sincerely recommend that you *do* leave it at that: Skip the rest of this introduction and deal with the complexities raised by *Merrell Dow* at some hopefully distant time in the future.

Merrell Dow raised a problem which is the converse of *Shoshone Mining*. Remember that in *Shoshone Mining* federal law established the right to sue, but did not establish a federal substantive standard to govern the actual disposition of claims. Sometimes, the opposite situation arises: federal law creates a substantive right, but does not—or, at least, does not expressly—authorize plaintiffs to sue for violation of that right. Here are two examples:

- *Cannon v. University of Chicago*, 441 U.S. 677 (1979), involved Title IX of the Educational Amendments of 1972, amendments to a federal statute. Those amendments bar discrimination on the basis of sex in any educational program which receives federal funds. However, the amendments do not expressly provide that a person who is subjected to such discrimination may sue for damages. Thus, the statute creates a substantive right—to be free of sex discrimination in such educational programs—but it was unclear whether Congress also intended to create a right to sue for damages for deprivation of that right. The plaintiff sued—in federal court—alleging that she was a victim of discrimination barred by the Amendments, and claiming damages.

- *J. I. Case v. Borak*, 377 U.S. 426 (1964), involved s. 14(a) of the Securities Exchange Act of 1934, a federal statute that bars companies from soliciting proxies in any manner prohibited by the rules of the Securities and Exchange Commission. A stockholder sued, claiming that the defendant company had issued a false and misleading proxy statement, in violation of s. 14(a), and seeking damages suffered as a result. Here again, the federal statute created a substantive standard of conduct, but it was unclear whether Congress also intended to authorize persons claiming a violation of that standard to sue for resulting damages.

In cases like these, if a plaintiff sues to enforce the federal right created by the statute, despite the lack of an express authorization to sue, the court must decide whether there is *an implied private right of action,* or right to sue, to recover for violation of the federal right. Over the years, the Supreme Court has established standards for determining when an implied right of action exists. Basically, the inquiry involves a search for congressional intent. In *Cannon* and *Borak,* the Court concluded that Congress did intend to authorize a private right of action for damages; in other cases it has concluded that no private right of action was intended.

If the court concludes that a federal statute does impliedly authorize suits for damages, there is no problem concluding that federal jurisdiction exists under 28 U.S.C. s. 1331. Such cases are a slam dunk under the Holmes test, since federal law creates *both* the substantive claim that is being enforced and the right to sue for violations of that right—although by implication rather than expressly. However, the situation is more murky if the court concludes that the federal statute creates a federal right or standard, but does not authorize private suits for damages to enforce it.

That was the situation in *Merrell Dow.* The plaintiffs sued for damages allegedly caused by Bendectin, a drug manufactured by Merrell Dow. They asserted claims based on negligence, breach of warranty, and strict liability, all state law tort theories. However, one of their negligence theories was that Merrell Dow gave inadequate warnings of the risks of Bendectin, because the warnings did not meet the labeling requirements of the Federal Food, Drug, and Cosmetic Act (FDCA). Thus, the complaint alleged a state cause of action (negligence) but asserted that the plaintiffs could *prove* this state cause of action by showing a violation of the substantive standard governing warnings in the federal statute. In this sense, the case resembled *Smith v. Kansas City Title & Trust,* in which the plaintiffs brought a state law claim to enjoin the corporation from investing in bonds, but had to establish that those bonds were issued under an unconstitutional statute.

In *Merrell Dow,* however, there was a twist which led the Court to distinguish *Smith:* All parties agreed that Congress did not intend to create an implied right to sue for damages for violation of the FDCA. To allow the *Merrell Dow* plaintiffs to go to federal court and sue for damages, simply by alleging that failure to comply with the federal warnings statute constituted negligence under state law, would fly in the face of Congress's decision *not* to create a federal right to sue for damages for FDCA violations. It would effectively create a federal court remedy where Congress had decided not to do so. Consequently, the Court held that the reference to the FDCA in the state negligence claim was insufficient to create arising-under jurisdiction under s. 1331.

Thus, after *Merrell Dow*, it appears that a statute that creates a federal substantive right, but is held not to create a private right to sue to enforce that right, will not support arising-under jurisdiction under s. 1331. This suggests that federal law must usually "create the cause of action" in both senses of the Holmes test in order to support arising-under jurisdiction. It also brings into question the continuing viability of *Smith v. Kansas City Title & Trust*, since in *Smith* federal law did not create the right for the plaintiff to sue to enforce it.

Some cases have suggested that *Merrell Dow* virtually overrules *Smith*. See, e.g., *Seinfeld v. Austen*, 39 F.3d 761 (7th Cir. 1994). Others, however, conclude that, where there is a sufficiently important federal interest implicated, *Smith* still authorizes federal jurisdiction. These cases simply conclude that the federal issue was not "substantial" in the *Merrell Dow* situation. See, e.g., *Milan Express Co., Inc. v. Western Surety Co.*, 886 F.2d 783 (6th Cir. 1989); *Barbara v. New York Stock Exchange, Inc.*, 99 F.3d 49, 54 (2nd Cir. 1996); *Morris v. City of Hobart*, 39 F.3d 1105, 1111 (10th Cir. 1994). *Merrell Dow* lends some support to this latter view: the Court stated that presence of a federal issue in a state law claim does not "automatically" confer arising-under jurisdiction (478 U.S. at 813) and quoted language from *Gully v. First National Bank*, 299 U.S. 109 (1936), suggesting that the result will turn on how substantial and central the federal issue is to the case. See also 478 U.S. at 814 n. 12 (emphasizing the importance of the "nature of the federal interest" in determining whether arising-under jurisdiction is appropriate under *Smith*). *Merrell Dow* may have been driven as much by fear of a flood of state law claims in federal court as by ruthless logic; after all, even the Supreme Court has the right to make a pragmatic decision once in a while. Thus, there is no bright line rule reconciling *Smith* with *Merrell Dow*, but it is likely that a substantial federal issue which is central to a state law cause of action will still suffice to create arising-under jurisdiction.

All of this seems confusing, but at least the fundamentals are fairly clear. If you feel at sea, perhaps the following examples will provide a few beacons of light to guide you toward an understanding of the fundamentals. Assume in considering the examples that there is no basis other than arising-under jurisdiction for suing in federal court.

EXAMPLES

Charting the Waters

2.   Landry wishes to sue Deveaux for violation of the New Mexico Consumer Protection Act. Does her case arise under the "laws of the United States"?

3.   Costa is injured in an accident with Prior on Interstate 95. Prior is a trucker who is engaged in interstate commerce, transporting goods among the various states on the eastern seaboard. Costa claims that Prior was negligent, in that he fell asleep and swerved into her lane, causing the accident. Does the claim come within the arising-under jurisdiction authorized by 28 U.S.C. s. 1331?

4.   Gould, who works at an auto assembly plant, sues Rambler Company, his employer, for failure to pay him overtime as required by the Federal Fair Labor Standards Act. He claims that he is an employee of Rambler, that he worked more than forty hours per week for twenty-one weeks, and that he is entitled to time-and-a-half for his overtime hours during those weeks. Rambler answers the complaint, denying the allegation in Gould's complaint that he is an "employee" entitled to extra pay for overtime work. Rambler's position is that Gould is a manager, who does not meet the definition of "employee" in the Act and is not entitled to overtime pay.

   a. Rambler, after filing its answer, moves to dismiss for lack of subject matter jurisdiction, arguing that the court lacks jurisdiction because the Fair Labor Standards Act does not apply to Gould. What should the court do?

   b. Rambler moves for summary judgment, submitting with its motion affidavits of various corporate officers and a copy of Gould's job description, to prove that Gould's duties were managerial. Gould submits evidence of his own on the point, but the court concludes based on the supporting materials that Gould is, as a matter of law, a manager and not entitled to overtime under the Act. Should it dismiss for lack of jurisdiction or on the merits?

5.   Steinberg, the public relations manager for Pinnacle Engineering Company, is fired. He concludes that he was fired simply because the company wanted a younger person in his job and brings suit against Pinnacle under the Age Discrimination in Employment Act (ADEA), a federal statute that bars discharge or other discrimination in employment based on age. The statute expressly creates a right for employees to sue for damages for acts of age discrimination.

   Pinnacle admits that the ADEA governs its employees, and that Steinberg, who is 57, is protected under the statute. It defends on the ground that it fired him for incompetence (thank goodness, that remains a permissible basis for discharge!), not based on his age. Is the case properly brought in federal court under 28 U.S.C. s. 1331?

6.   Suppose that Steinberg is from Florida and sues both Pinnacle (a Florida corporation) and Swift, president of Pinnacle and a Florida citizen. His suit alleges that he was fired because of his age and demands damages under the ADEA. Can he bring the action in federal court?

Concurrents

7.   Steinberg's counsel brings suit against Pinnacle in state court on his ADEA claim. (The ADEA statute says nothing one way or another about where suit must be brought.) Pinnacle moves to dismiss the case, on the ground that the case must be brought in federal court, since it arises under federal law. What should the state court do?

8.   Pinnacle sues Steinberg for conversion (a state tort claim), for removing confidential company records when he cleared out his office after being fired. Steinberg counterclaims — that is, asserts a claim of his own against Pinnacle — demanding damages from them under the federal ADEA. Could the case be brought in (or removed to) federal court based on federal arising-under jurisdiction?

Stemming the Flood

9.   Senator Doe, fed up with the continual demands for more federal judges, concludes that the problem could be alleviated by adding an amount-in-controversy requirement to 28 U.S.C. s. 1331 (that is, a provision limiting federal court jurisdiction to arising-under cases in which a particular amount of money is in dispute). He asks you, his legislative counsel, for advice on whether a bill adding such a requirement to s. 1331 would be constitutional. What would you advise him?

10. Senator Jones, upset that the *Mottley* rule keeps many cases which involve important federal issues out of federal court, proposes to amend 28 U.S.C. s. 1331 to authorize federal jurisdiction if the plaintiff's complaint or the defendant's answer raises a substantial issue of federal law. He asks you whether it would be constitutional to expand arising-under jurisdiction in this way. What would you advise him?

11. Einstein, holder of a patent on a new computer technology, licenses the idea to Gates, an entrepreneur, under a contract which requires Gates to pay Einstein a license fee for every computer sold with the new technology. Gates makes the computers, sells them, and pays royalties to Einstein. However, Einstein claims that Gates has understated the number of units sold and therefore underpaid. He sues Gates in federal court. Does the court have jurisdiction over the case under 28 U.S.C. s. 1331?[8]

12. Suppose that, on the facts of the last example, Einstein sued Gates for breach of the licensing contract *and* for an injunction to prevent him from continuing to manufacture the computers, on the theory that making them without paying the proper royalty is an infringement of his patent rights.

---

8. Actually, there is a special statute conferring jurisdiction on federal courts for patent claims. 28 U.S.C. s. 1338. However, the issue of when a case "arises under" that statute is substantially similar to that under s. 1331.

Would asserting the claim for injunctive relief allow Einstein to sue in federal court?

Another Port in the Storm

13. Caprano is arrested by Quan, a police officer. Quan allegedly used excessive force in making the arrest, causing serious injury to Caprano. Bryan, Caprano's lawyer, believes that Judge Kane, the only federal judge sitting in the federal district where the claim arose, takes a very defense-oriented view of cases under 42 U.S.C. s. 1983, the federal civil rights statute. Consequently, Bryan decides to sue in state court and to assert only a state law battery claim. Quan tries to remove the case to federal court. (As we will see in a later chapter, a defendant can remove a case to federal court if it could have been brought there originally.) Quan is not diverse from Caprano, but she argues that the complaint arises under federal law, because use of excessive force in the course of arrest would constitute a violation of the Fourth Amendment, a claim arising under the United States Constitution. Is the case removable?

14. Suppose that you represent Engle in the third example case on p. 58, in which she sues for bad faith discharge and alleges that she was fired for refusing to violate federal accounting requirements. You want to sue Consolidated in federal court.

   a. Would the case fall within the Article III, s. 2 grant of jurisdiction over cases arising under federal law?
   b. Which of the cases discussed in the Introduction would provide the most support for an argument that Engle's cases satisfies the arising-under requirement in s. 1331?

15. Bell alleges that, while he was sleeping peacefully at home, federal agents burst into his house without a warrant, seized documents and other evidence, and arrested him without probable cause. These allegations, if true, would violate Bell's right under the Fourth Amendment to be free of unreasonable searches and seizures. However, while the Fourth Amendment right to be free of such conduct is clear, the federal courts had not decided at the time of Bell's suit whether a person alleging Fourth Amendment deprivations had a right to sue federal agents for damages for violation of those rights.[9] In other words, the case is like the implied-right-of-action cases discussed on p. 67-69, where a federal substantive right exists, but there is no explicit provision authorizing injured parties to bring private suits for violations of the right.

---

9. Quan's case in example 13 is different: 28 U.S.C. s. 1983 expressly authorizes claims for violations of constitutional rights by state actors (persons acting under color of the law of a state). But that statute does not authorize suits against federal agents, the defendants in Bell's case.

Bell sues the agents in federal court. He claims that the court should find an implied private right of action in the Constitution for plaintiffs subjected to such violations to sue for damages, in order to uphold and enforce Fourth Amendment rights. The agents move to dismiss the case for lack of subject matter jurisdiction, arguing that such an implied right to sue for damages for Fourth Amendment violations does not exist. Does the court have arising-under jurisdiction to hear the case?

Second Time Around

16. When the Supreme Court held that the lower federal court had lacked subject matter jurisdiction over the Mottleys' case, it ordered the case dismissed from federal court. The Mottleys still wanted their passes, so they started over in a Kentucky state court, which clearly had subject matter jurisdiction over their breach of contract case. That court heard the case, accepted the Mottleys rebuttal to the railroad's defense based on the Federal statute, and ordered the railroad to renew the passes. The railroad appealed to the Kentucky Court of Appeals, which affirmed the judgment. The railroad then appealed to the United States Supreme Court. Although it had held in its first *Mottley* decision that it lacked jurisdiction to hear the case, this time the Court took jurisdiction and decided the appeal. See 219 U.S. 467 (1911). How can it be that it lacked jurisdiction the first time, when the case was appealed from the lower federal court, but had it the second time?

EXPLANATIONS

An Early Question

1.   Naturally, you would advise the railroad, in answering the complaint, to assert only their state law defenses and then move to dismiss for lack of subject matter jurisdiction. Since neither the complaint nor the answer raised federal law issues, that motion would presumably be granted and the Mottleys would have to start over in state court. (Remember that state courts have very broad subject matter jurisdiction; there will be no problem with a state court hearing a state contract claim.)

Suppose the railroad took your advice, the federal suit was dismissed, and the Mottleys sued in state court. If, in answering the state court complaint, the railroad confined itself to state law defenses, the case would obviously remain in state court. But suppose it now raised its federal defenses? Should the case then be removed to federal court? If so, the rule could lead to delay in determining which court will hear the case. Or should the railroad be barred from raising federal issues, to punish its manipulative effort to avoid federal court? This could lead to disputes about the defendant's reason for failing to assert the federal defense earlier. If the railroad only raises state law defenses in state court, should it be barred from later raising federal defenses which it discovers in preparing for trial? Or should it be entitled to raise them, but the case then removed to federal court?

These are perhaps not insuperable problems, but they do illustrate that practical difficulties would arise if potential defenses were considered in determining jurisdiction.

Charting the Waters

2.   Perhaps this is belaboring the obvious, but let's just eliminate one source of confusion at the outset. The language "laws of the United States" refers to laws made by Congress, not to the laws of the various states. A New Mexico statute is a law of *one of the states of the United States,* not of the United States, that is, of the national government. Unless she is diverse from Deveaux, Landry will have to proceed in state court.

3.   In this case, there is some vague presence of federal law lurking on the periphery, since the accident takes place on an interstate highway and involves a defendant engaged in interstate commerce. But the claim clearly does not arise under federal law as that phrase is construed in 28 U.S.C. s. 1331. Costa's suit will be for negligence, a claim based in state tort law. She is not suing for violation of any interstate commerce regulation, just for negligence. Her "well pleaded complaint" will be entirely sufficient if it alleges the basic elements of a negligence claim: that Prior owed her a duty of due care, that he breached that duty, and that the breach caused her damages. Nor will Costa have to prove anything about federal law in order to establish her state law claim.

4a. The court should deny the motion. Gould has sued under a federal statute, claiming that he is entitled to benefits under that statute. There is no question that the Fair Labor Standards Act creates a federal right to overtime, and that Gould is claiming recovery under that federal right. Rambler's position is simply that Gould isn't actually entitled to overtime under the statute, because he doesn't qualify as an "employee." This is simply a denial on the merits of Gould's claim; it does not alter the fact that federal law creates the cause of action that Gould asserts.

There is a crucial difference between challenging jurisdiction on the ground that the plaintiff has not asserted a federal claim, on the one hand, and claiming that he can't *prove* the federal right he has *asserted,* on the other. Think of it this way: if the defendant could defeat federal jurisdiction simply by denying that the plaintiff is entitled to win on her federal claim, the federal court would seldom have any arising-under jurisdiction!

b. Here, the court has taken jurisdiction over the case, as it properly should, since Gould asserts a federal claim. However, after receiving evidence on the issue of whether Gould is an "employee" under the Fair Labor Standards Act, the court concludes as a matter of law that he is not and, therefore, cannot recover overtime under the statute. Thus, judgment should enter against him on the merits: Gould has asserted a claim under federal law and lost on it, but this does not change the fact that the court had jurisdiction to hear the case. Gould's failure to prove his federal claim does not mean that he failed to *assert* one sufficient to give the federal court arising-under jurisdiction.

5.   Applying the Holmes test to this case, there is no question that the case arises under federal law even within the narrow definition in 28 U.S.C. s. 1331. The ADEA creates Steinberg's right to be free of age discrimination and expressly provides that employees who suffer such discrimination may sue for damages. Steinberg can sue *because* the federal statute exists and says that he can. He relies on the statute as the source of his right to relief.

The irony of the example, of course, is that the parties will not be litigating any issues of federal law in this case. No one is challenging the applicability of the statute, or even whether it protects employees in Steinberg's position. The only dispute between the parties is whether he was fired because of his age or because he couldn't cut the mustard. While *Mottley* makes the well-pleaded complaint approach to arising-under jurisdiction appear too restrictive, examples like this suggest that the test is overinclusive: it brings into federal court large numbers of cases in which the parties are suing under federal law, but not *disputing about* federal law at all: they're only disagreeing about the facts.

On the other hand, a convincing case can be made that federal jurisdiction in such cases is entirely appropriate. Patient, sympathetic application of federal statutes to the facts of particular cases may be as important to effective implementation of national policy as the legal interpretation of those statutes by federal courts. Particularly where subtle, subjective issues like intent must be assessed in order to apply the statute, administration by federal judges may go a long way to ensure that congressional policy is implemented where it really counts — in individual cases.

6.   This example is meant to dispel one potential source of confusion about federal court jurisdiction. Here, the defendants are from the same state as the plaintiff, so there is no diversity of citizenship. However, the federal court still has subject matter jurisdiction over the case: Steinberg brings his suit under a federal statute, so the case "arises under federal law." A plaintiff can sue in federal court if his case falls into any category of federal subject matter jurisdiction; he doesn't have to sue under federal law *and* be diverse from the defendant. Thus, it is irrelevant that Steinberg is from the same state as the defendants.

Concurrents

7.   The issue posed by this example is whether a case which *may* be brought in federal court (because it arises under federal law) *must* be brought there.

Nothing in Article III states that the cases within the federal judicial power *must* be brought in federal court. Article III, s. 2 provides that the federal judicial power "shall extend to" the cases delineated in that section, but does not withdraw jurisdiction over such cases from the state courts. The general principle is that cases within the jurisdiction of the federal courts may also be brought in the state courts; the state and federal courts have "concurrent jurisdiction" over such cases. However, Congress may provide that particular types of cases within the federal subject matter jurisdiction must be brought in federal court. Wright, 5th ed. 287. For an example, see 28 U.S.C. s. 1338(a), which makes federal court jurisdiction exclusive in patent, plant variety, and copyright cases.

Since (the example indicates) the ADEA does not provide that ADEA suits must be brought in federal court, Steinberg's counsel may file the action in state court if she chooses. In fact, many cases arising under federal law are litigated in the state courts. In such cases, state judges routinely interpret and apply the provisions of federal statutes—just as they do in the myriad cases in which issues of federal law are raised as a defense.

8.   In this case Pinnacle sues on a state law claim, and Steinberg counterclaims—that is, he asserts a claim for damages against Pinnacle—arising under federal law. Under *Mottley,* the court will look at *the plaintiff's claim,* that is, Pinnacle's, to determine whether the case arises under federal law. Pinnacle's claim clearly does not, so the case does not fit within the arising-under jurisdiction.

The irony here is that if Steinberg had sued first on his ADEA claim, he could have sued in federal court, since his claim is based on the federal statute. If Pinnacle, as the defendant, counterclaimed for conversion, this would not defeat federal jurisdiction: Under *Mottley,* the court assesses jurisdiction based solely on the claim asserted by the plaintiff. By losing the race to the courthouse, Steinberg loses the federal forum.[10]

Stemming the Flood

9.   You should advise Senator Doe that there is nothing in the Constitution that would prevent Congress from limiting the arising-under jurisdiction of the federal district courts by introducing an amount-in-controversy requirement into s. 1331. As the Introduction indicates, the Supreme Court has held that Congress is free to grant the federal district courts less than the full scope of Article III jurisdiction. Article III defines the *outer bounds* of what they may be given, but does not require that all cases which could be granted to the lower federal courts must be. If Congress wishes to grant a part, but not all, of the arising-under jurisdiction, it may do so.

---

10. As we will see in a later chapter, Steinberg would not be able to remove the case to federal court based on the counterclaim either. See Chapter 7, ex. 12.

Historically, Congress has often made this choice. For example, for many years there was no general grant of jurisdiction over cases arising under federal law. There were narrow statutes granting federal courts the authority to hear particular types of federal claims, but no broad arising-under statute like s. 1331. Indeed, if you had been a devotee of federal jurisdiction for twenty years or so, you could advise Senator Doe that 28 U.S.C. s. 1331 actually *had included* an amount-in-controversy requirement until 1980.

10. This expansion of statutory arising-under jurisdiction would be constitutional. As the Introduction suggests, a case "arises under" federal law, as that phrase is used in Article III, s. 2, if federal law is an "ingredient" of the case. This is true whether the federal issue is raised by the plaintiff or the defendant. Thus, Senator Jones's amendment would authorize federal district courts to exercise more of the constitutionally permissible arising-under jurisdiction.

The American Law Institute proposed an amendment along these lines in 1969. An ALI study recommended that s. 1331 be changed to allow removal to federal court if "a substantial defense arising under the Constitution, laws, or treaties of the United States is properly asserted that, if sustained, would be dispositive of the action or of all counterclaims therein." American Law Institute, Study of the Division of Jurisdiction between State and Federal Courts, p. 25 (1969). However, Congress has never adopted even this modest expansion of the *Mottley* rule.

11. Einstein's case involves a contract dispute about a patented device, but it does not involve a question of patent law, or a claim under the patent laws. The "law that creates the cause of action" is state contract law, just as it was in the Mottleys' suit. Federal patent law is certainly tangentially involved in the action—if Einstein didn't have a patent on the device, Gates would presumably not have agreed to pay licensing fees. But the claim is a claim for breach of contract, not a claim for patent infringement. Einstein has a right to the money because Gates agreed to pay it, not because the device was patented. He would have the same right to royalties if Gates had agreed to pay them on a device that wasn't patented. Nor will Einstein have to establish a proposition of patent law in order to recover, as was the case in *Smith v. Kansas City Title & Trust Co.* Presumably, he could enforce the contract whether the patent was valid or not.

12. Bringing suit for an injunction probably would change the result. The contract claim still doesn't arise under federal law, but the claim for injunctive relief to stop the infringement does. In order to obtain the injunction against Gates, Einstein will have to prove that he holds a patent on the technology. If he proves that he holds the patent, and that Gates is selling the technology without permission (or, at least, in excess of his permission since he isn't paying the proper fees), patent law expressly allows the court to enter an injunction to prevent Gates' use of the technology. See 35 U.S.C. ss. 281,

283. Here, Einstein relies directly on federal patent law as the source of the substantive right he seeks to enforce, and it is clear (unlike in *Merrell Dow*) that federal patent law expressly creates the right to seek an injunction if the federal right is violated.

If this seems to put the power to "create federal jurisdiction" in the hands of Einstein's counsel, in a sense it does. The plaintiff is free to bring whatever colorable claims he has against the defendant. Here, Einstein has a right to enjoin Gates from using his technology without paying the license fee, and that right to an injunction is based on his federal patent right to control the sale of the technology. If he chooses to assert the injunction claim, his claim arises under federal law, and the federal court will have jurisdiction over it under 28 U.S.C. s. 1331 and 1338.[11]

Another Port in the Storm

13. In this case, Caprano has brought a state law claim for battery. She could not have sued in federal court, since battery is a state tort claim, and there is no diversity of citizenship between her and Quan. Consequently, Quan cannot remove to federal court, unless she can claim that the case "arises under" federal law because Caprano *could have* asserted a claim under federal law.

Federal jurisdiction generally turns on the claims the plaintiff actually asserts, not on those she could have asserted but didn't. Even though Caprano could have asserted a claim arising under federal law, she is entitled to choose the claims she wishes to bring. If, for tactical reasons, she is sufficiently anxious to avoid federal court and wishes to forgo her federal claim in order to do so, she may.[12]

14a. This case is within the *constitutional* grant of arising-under jurisdiction, as broadly interpreted by Chief Justice Marshall in *Osborn v. Bank of the*

---

11. The related contract claim could then be heard in federal court along with the federal claim, under "supplemental" jurisdiction, discussed in Chapter 15.

12. There is an exception to this. If the true nature of the plaintiff's claim is federal, she may not "artfully plead" it as a state law claim to avoid federal court. For example, in *Bright v. Bechtel Petroleum, Inc.*, 780 F.2d 766 (9th Cir. 1986), the plaintiff sued Bechtel, claiming that it had breached its contract with him by paying him less than his agreed salary. However, it was clear that the basis of Bright's claim was that Bechtel had withheld sums from his wages for federal taxes, and that this was illegal under the Internal Revenue Code. The court held that Bechtel's claim actually arose under federal tax law and upheld removal to federal court based on arising-under jurisdiction.

In a sense, this "artful pleading" exception to the principle that the plaintiff may avoid federal court by pleading only state claims is simply an application of *Smith v. Kansas City Title and Trust*. The plaintiff in *Bechtel* could not establish his breach of contract claim without establishing a proposition of federal law: that the IRS regulation requiring withholding was invalid under the federal tax laws.

United States. In *Osborn,* Chief Justice Marshall interpreted the constitutional scope of the arising-under jurisdiction to be met if federal law was an "ingredient" of the case. Here, the federal accounting statute is an integral part of Engle's claim, since she will have to establish that it barred the practices Consolidated fired her for refusing to employ. In Marshall's language, Engle's right will be "defeated by one construction of the . . . law of the United States, and sustained by the opposite construction."

b. Engle would rely on *Smith* as the basis for arising-under jurisdiction over her claim. Federal law does not create Engle's right to sue here: it is a state law claim for bad faith dismissal. But Engle intends to establish this state law claim by reference to federal law — the federal accounting statute which she refused to ignore. To premise federal jurisdiction on this federal-proof-of-a-state-law-claim argument, Engle will have to convince the court that *Smith* is still viable after *Merrell Dow,* and that the federal accounting standards are central to her case and sufficiently important to support federal jurisdiction.

The Fifth Circuit Court of Appeals confronted a closely analogous case in *Willy v. Coastal Corp.,* 855 F.2d 1160 (5th Cir. 1988). In *Willy,* the plaintiff, a lawyer, alleged that he was discharged for failing to engage in activities that would violate federal environmental laws. Like Engle's claim (and like the plaintiffs' in *Merrell Dow*), Willy's was based on state tort law, but he sought to prove it by reference to federal law. The *Willy* court's analysis suggested that arising-under jurisdiction might still be premised on the reasoning in Smith but, for several reasons, including the centrality of state law to Willy's claim, held that it could not hear his claim.

15. In this case, Bell has sued in federal court, claiming that there is an implied right, under the United States Constitution, to bring private suits for violation of Fourth Amendment rights. If Bell is right, his claim arises under federal law in both senses of the Holmes test: the substantive right he sues to enforce is created by federal law (the Fourth Amendment), and the Constitution also (impliedly) authorizes suits for damages for deprivation of that right. The twist, however, is that it is not clear that Bell is right that the Constitution impliedly creates a private right to sue for damages for such deprivations. He claims that this implied right to sue exists, but it might be a case like *Merrell Dow,* in which federal law creates a right, but does not authorize private suits to enforce the right. And the defendants challenge federal subject matter jurisdiction in Bell's case, arguing that, if there is no private right to sue for Fourth Amendment violations, then the case doesn't arise under federal law.

In *Bell v. Hood,* 327 U.S. 678 (1946), on which this example is based, the Supreme Court held that the federal court had subject matter jurisdiction over Bell's claim. Bell was *clearly asserting that he had a right to relief under federal law:* he alleged that the Constitution itself impliedly authorizes private suits for damages for Fourth Amendment violations. He might turn out to be wrong — the court might hold that there is no such private right of action — but Bell certainly claimed that a right to sue existed and based his federal suit upon it.

On these facts, the Supreme Court held that Bell's case met the statutory arising-under test, and the federal court should hear it. Bell clearly sought relief under federal law. Since Bell claimed a federal right, the federal court should determine whether that federal right existed.[13] If it is determined that the implied right to sue for damages that Bell claimed did not exist, then it should dismiss his claim *on the merits,* not for lack of subject matter jurisdiction. If it determined that there was a private right to sue for damages for Fourth Amendment violations, it would proceed to decide the facts.

On remand in *Bell,* the federal court took jurisdiction over Bell's claim, but held as a matter of law that the Constitution did not authorize private suits for damages for Fourth Amendment violations. Consequently, it dismissed Bell's claim for failure to state a compensable claim, not for lack of jurisdiction. *Bell v. Hood,* 71 F.Supp. 813 (1947). Ironically, some years later the Supreme Court held that there is an implied right to sue for damages for Fourth Amendment violations. *Bivens v. Six Unknown Names Agents of the Federal Bureau of Narcotics,* 403 U.S. 388 (1971).

Bell is not inconsistent with *Merrell Dow.* In *Merrell Dow,* federal law created a substantive standard, but it was clear that federal law did not authorize private suits to enforce that right. In *Bell,* federal law created the substantive standard, and the plaintiff claimed that it authorized private suits to enforce that standard as well. The question of whether a private right of action to sue under the Fourth Amendment exists is a federal question raised by Bell's complaint. If the plaintiff in *Merrell Dow* had alleged that the Federal Food, Drug and Cosmetic Act impliedly authorized suits for violations of federal warning requirements (and the argument were not clearly foreclosed by the precedents), that case would have arisen under federal law too.

Second Time Around

16. The subsequent history of the *Mottley* case nicely illustrates the difference between the statutory and constitutional scope of the arising-under jurisdiction. Under Chief Justice Marshall's expansive interpretation of the constitutional scope in *Osborn,* a federal court — either the federal trial court or the Supreme Court — could take jurisdiction if federal law formed an "ingredient" of the case. Surely, the railroad's federal statutory defense would meet this constitutional test for jurisdiction. But because the Court interpreted the statute which conveyed jurisdiction to the federal trial court — the predecessor of s. 1331 — to require *the plaintiff* to rely on federal law, it held that the federal trial court had lacked subject matter jurisdiction under the

---

13. Indeed, what could be more appropriate than a federal court determining whether such an implied right to sue for federal constitutional violations exists? If the court in *Bell* had held that it lacked subject matter jurisdiction, the existence of the federal right Bell claimed would have had to be decided by a state court.

statute. Since the trial court lacked jurisdiction, its judgment was of no effect, and the Court could not review it.

The situation was different when the case came to the Supreme Court on appeal from the Kentucky state courts. Those courts certainly had jurisdiction over the case, a common law claim for breach of contract. And the statute which conveyed arising-under jurisdiction to *the Supreme Court* on appeal was worded more broadly than s. 1331. It read much like 28 U.S.C. s. 1257, which currently authorizes Supreme Court review of state court judgments

> where the validity of a treaty or statute of the United States is drawn in question . . . or where any title, right, privilege, or immunity is specially set up or claimed under the Constitution or the treaties or statutes of . . . the United States.

Clearly, the railroad in *Mottley* "claimed an immunity" under a statute of the United States; in addition, the Mottleys' claim that the statute was unconstitutional "drew into question" the validity of that statute. So the jurisdiction provision just quoted authorized Supreme Court review. And clearly, it makes sense for Congress to authorize Supreme Court review in cases involving federal defenses. If it did not, state court interpretations of federal law in cases like *Mottley* would never be subject to review or correction in the United States Supreme Court.

5

Diversity Jurisdiction: When Does Multiplicity Constitute Diversity?

Introduction

A major premise underlying our Constitution is that the states function quite well in most respects and that federal interference should be confined to those areas where there is a special need for national policy. For example, in 1787, when the Constitution was drafted, every state already had its own system of courts. The framers of the Constitution saw no need to abolish those courts in favor of federal courts administered by the national government. Instead, they authorized the creation of a separate federal court system (see U.S. Const. Art. III, §1), but they only authorized those courts to hear limited categories of cases that, for one reason or another, involved a particular national interest. U.S. Const. Art. III, §2. Jurisdiction of all other cases was left to the courts of the states.

One of the major categories of cases that the framers authorized federal courts to hear is the so-called diversity jurisdiction, described in Article III, §2, as cases "between citizens of different states." In diversity cases, as in some others enumerated in Article III, §2, the subject matter jurisdiction of the federal courts is defined by who the parties to the suit are, rather than the subject matter of the underlying dispute.[1] The plaintiff in a diversity case may seek recovery on a battery theory, a fraud claim, a right created by state statute, or any other state law cause of action. So long as he sues a diverse defendant and the claim is for more than $75,000, the federal court will have subject matter jurisdiction on the basis of diversity.

The framers' apparent reason for singling out diversity cases for federal jurisdiction was a fear that out-of-state citizens would suffer prejudice if they were forced to litigate against local citizens in the local state courts. That rationale has long been disputed by the scholars,[2] and repeated efforts have been made to abolish diversity jurisdiction. For example, the 1990 report of the Federal Courts Study Committee recommended abolishing diversity jurisdiction in all but a few unusual types of cases. Report of the Federal Courts Study Committee (April 2, 1990) pp. 38-42. However, reports of its death, in the words of Sam Clemens, have been greatly exaggerated.

Although Article III authorizes jurisdiction over diversity cases, it does not directly confer the diversity jurisdiction, or any other category of jurisdiction, on the lower federal courts. Rather, it authorizes Congress to create lower federal courts and to confer jurisdiction upon them to hear the types of cases enumerated in Article III, §2. This important additional requirement is succinctly explained in Judge Sirica's Watergate opinion:

> [F]ederal courts may assume only that portion of the Article III judicial power which Congress, by statute, entrusts to them. Simply stated, Congress may impart as much or as little of the judicial power as it deems appropriate and the Judiciary may not thereafter on its own motion recur to the Article III storehouse for additional jurisdiction. When it comes to jurisdiction of the federal courts, truly, to paraphrase the scripture, the Congress giveth, and the Congress taketh away.[3]

Thus, a plaintiff invoking federal jurisdiction must always be prepared to show that his case is not only within the constitutional bounds of Article III, §2, but has also been granted to the federal district courts by Congress in a statute.

In the case of diversity jurisdiction, Congress has granted to the federal courts some, but not all, of the Article III diversity jurisdiction. First, the statutory grant in 28 U.S.C. §1332 is narrower than Article III, §2, in that it includes an amount-in-controversy requirement, while Article III authorizes

---

1. Other examples in Article III that authorize jurisdiction based on the nature of the parties include cases to which the United States is a party; cases involving ambassadors, ministers, and foreign citizens; and cases between states.

2. For a review of the debate, see Wright, Federal Courts §23 (5th ed. 1994) (hereinafter cited as Wright).

3. *Senate Select Committee v. Nixon*, 366 F. Supp. 51, 55 (D.D.C. 1973).

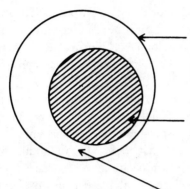

Scope of possible diversity jurisdiction under Article III, §2 ("the Article III storehouse")

Scope of the diversity jurisdiction conferred by Congress in 28 U.S.C. §1332

In this area lie cases in which some parties are diverse, but there is not complete diversity. Also cases in which diversity is complete but the amount-in-controversy requirement is not met.

Figure 5-1

jurisdiction over *all* diversity cases, regardless of the sum in dispute. Second, Chief Justice Marshall held in *Strawbridge v. Curtiss,* 7 U.S. 267 (1806) that a case is not within the statutory grant of diversity jurisdiction unless there is "complete diversity" between the parties, that is, all plaintiffs in a suit are from different states than all defendants at the time suit is brought. It is now clear, however, that Article III, §2, allows diversity jurisdiction as long as *some* opposing parties to the action are diverse. *State Farm Fire & Casualty v. Tashire,* 386 U.S. 523 (1967). As with arising-under jurisdiction, the *statutory* grant of diversity jurisdiction has historically been narrower than the *constitutional* grant of jurisdiction. See Figure 5-1. Consequently, many cases within the "Article III storehouse" may not be brought in federal court as diversity cases.

The Meaning of State Citizenship

Constitutions establish grand principles but seldom explain exactly how to apply them. In the area of diversity jurisdiction, for example, it has been left to the courts to determine what it means to be "citizens of different states." For natural persons (that is, human beings), the courts have equated state citizenship for diversity purposes with the common law concept of domicile. A person's domicile is usually defined as the state where he has taken up residence with the intent to reside indefinitely. Under this definition, residence is not equivalent to domicile; having a residence in the state is necessary but not sufficient to establish a domicile for diversity purposes. If Hawes owns houses in both Missouri and Wyoming and spends a good deal of time in both states, he will still have only one domicile. Which state it is depends on his subjective intent—sometimes almost impossible to ascertain—to make one particular state his "home." See Wright at 162.

The major problem in applying the domicile concept is determining what it means to "intend to stay indefinitely" in a state. It is not necessary to make an irrevocable commitment to stay in a place "permanently" to establish intent under the domicile test. That would be an unduly stringent requirement; few of us make such a firm decision about what we will do in the long term. Rather, "indefinitely" means that a person's presence in the state is open-ended: That is, he has no definite intent to leave to make a home elsewhere. This test can be met, even though a person expects that he probably *will* move on at some point, so long as he has no definite plans to do so at a particular time or upon the occurrence of a particular event. A person who is not committed to leaving is thought to be "at home" even though, like all of us, he may choose to leave at some time in the future.

For example, if Hawes quits his job and moves to Florida in hopes of finding a good job, he establishes a new domicile, even though he may leave if the job market proves unpromising. However, if Hawes goes to Florida for a few months as an undercover agent for the FBI, with the intent to return to his home in Missouri when the case is closed, he remains domiciled in Missouri, even if the exact length of time it will take to crack the case is unknown. Although the exact date of his departure from Florida is unknown, Hawes does not intend to stay "indefinitely" but rather to leave upon the occurrence of a particular event.

In addition, subjective intent to stay indefinitely is necessary but not sufficient: It must coincide with physical presence within the new domicile. Even if Hawes firmly intends to move to Florida after he retires next month, he does not acquire a domicile there until he physically arrives there to stay. Until then, he keeps his last domicile.

Corporate Citizenship for Diversity Purposes

Although it is hardly a foregone conclusion from the language of Article III and §1332, corporations have long been held to be "citizens" authorized to invoke the diversity jurisdiction. Until 1958 they were held to be citizens of the state in which they were incorporated, regardless of where they actually conducted their daily business activity. In 1958 Congress enacted 28 U.S.C. §1332(c), which provides a statutory definition of the state citizenship of corporations for diversity purposes. Under §1332(c)(1) corporations are now citizens for diversity purposes of both the state where their principal place of business is located and the state in which they are incorporated. Consequently, if an opposing party is a citizen of either of those states, diversity does not exist.

The "principal place of business" provision in §1332(c)(1) has also created some interpretive problems. Most corporations carry on their business totally or predominantly in one state, so there is no problem in ascertaining their principal place of business for diversity purposes. In other cases, however, particularly cases involving very large corporations whose business involves commerce or transportation among numerous states, it is difficult to point definitively to one state as the corporation's principal place of business. If there is a definable center of the productive activities of the corporation, that is, the manufacturing or other profit-making activity that the corporation is engaged in, most courts tend to choose that state. The term "place of business," after all, connotes the place where you do what you exist to do, and the term "principal" suggests the place where you do the most of it. This is sometimes referred to as the "place of operations" or the "bulk of the corporate activity" test. The asserted rationale for diversity jurisdiction, to avoid prejudice against "outsiders," supports the use of this test: The corporation will most likely be perceived as "local" where it employs the most people, conducts the most activities, and has the most interaction with the public. See generally Wright and Miller §3625.[4]

However, the day-to-day activities of some corporations may be so dispersed as to make it artificial to characterize one state as the center of their productive activities. For example, it may be difficult to say that the productive activity of an insurance company that insures risks in many states or an airline that flies to destinations in many states is centered in any one of those states. In cases involving such widely dispersed corporate activities, courts have sometimes looked to the so-called "nerve center" of the corporation, the corporate headquarters or home office from which its activities are coordinated, to determine the principal place of business. See, e.g., *Egan v. American Airlines, Inc.*, 211 F. Supp. 292 (E.D.N.Y. 1962).[5]

In analyzing the following examples assume that all actions are brought in federal court, that the amount-in-controversy requirement is met in each case, and (unless otherwise specified) that each case is based on state law.

EXAMPLES

The Basic Diversity Requirements

1. Is there diversity between the parties in the following cases?
    a. Marlowe, from California, sues Archer, from California, in a federal district court in Illinois.

---

4. On the other hand, this logic suggests that corporations should *not* be deemed citizens of their state of incorporation, if, as is often true, they conduct no activities in that state. But, of course, under §1332(c)(1), they are.

5. Like so many procedural issues, however, this one is not entirely settled. The Seventh Circuit uses the nerve center test alone to establish a corporation's principal place of business. *Wisconsin Knife Works v. National Metal Crafters*, 781 F.2d 1280, 1282-1283 (7th Cir. 1986).

    b. Carella, from New York, sues Marlowe (California) and Archer (California).

    c. Carella (New York) sues Marlowe (California) and McGee, a Floridian, in a federal district court in California.

    d. Carella (New York), McGee (Florida), and Spenser (Massachusetts) sue Marlowe (California), Archer (California), and Meyer (New York).

    e. Marlowe (California) sues Carella (New York) and Marple, an Englishwoman.

    f. Same facts as (e), except that Marple, still an Englishwoman, lives in California.

2.   Marlowe (California) sues Archer (California) in federal court in California for damages under a federal firearms control statute. May the court hear the case?

3.   Marlowe (California) sues Carella (New York) for breach of contract in state court. Can he do this?

4.   Marlowe (California) sues McGee (Florida) and Archer (California). Marlowe's claim against McGee is for defamation, a state law claim. His claim against Archer arises from the same incident but is based on federal law. Will the federal court have jurisdiction?

5.   Marlowe (California) sues McGee (Florida) in federal court for libel. A month later he amends his complaint to add a libel claim against Archer, a California citizen who co-authored the offending article. Will the federal court have jurisdiction over the action?

Homes Away from Home

6.   Carella (New York) collides with McGee (Florida) during a car chase in New York City. Carella is disabled in the accident, retires to Florida, and sues McGee in a federal district court in Florida. Is the suit proper?

7.   Meyer, a New Yorker, decides to move to Arizona. He buys an Audi from Isola Volkswagen, a New York dealership incorporated in New York, and sets off with his family for Arizona. While driving through Oklahoma, he is involved in an accident and hospitalized.

    a. Two months later, while still in the hospital, Meyer files a negligence suit against Isola in an Oklahoma federal court. Does the court have diversity jurisdiction?

    b. While in the hospital, Meyer receives an offer to stay in Oklahoma and work as a detective for an oil company. He accepts and several months after beginning work sues Isola in federal court. Is the suit proper?

    c. Meyer is released from the hospital after six months. The company he planned to join in Arizona has rescinded its job offer since he was unable to start work when it needed him. He still has six months of rehabilitation ahead of him in Oklahoma. After that, he plans to begin looking for a job as a detective in the oil industry, wherever one turns up. Is he diverse from Isola?

Corporate Diversity

8. Carella (New York) sues Underworld, Inc., incorporated in Delaware, doing business in every state, with its principal place of business in Florida. Suit is brought in the federal district court for the Northern District of Florida. Does the court have jurisdiction?

9. McGee (Florida) sues Underworld in a New York federal court. Is there diversity jurisdiction?

10. Marlowe (California) sues Gamblers International, Inc., a corporation incorporated in Nevada. Gamblers has two casinos: one very large casino in Reno, Nevada, which grosses $40 million per year, and another casino in California, which does $35 million in business each year. The corporate offices are in Reno. Is there diversity jurisdiction in Marlowe's suit?

11. Prior to the 1958 amendment that provided for dual citizenship of corporations for diversity purposes, corporations were considered citizens of their state of incorporation only. Did the amendment expand or contract corporate access to federal court?

The Amount-in-Controversy Requirement

As stated above, Article III, §2, broadly grants federal court jurisdiction over cases "between citizens of different states" without any requirement that a particular amount be in dispute between the parties. But Congress has always chosen to keep minor diversity cases out of the federal courts by providing that such cases can only be brought there if the amount in controversy exceeds a given figure. The figure started out at $500 in 1789, and has been periodically increased in pursuit of inflation. For thirty years, from 1958 to 1988, the amount was required to exceed $10,000. From 1988-1996, it was $50,000. In 1996, it was raised again to $75,000.

Courts face an awkward problem in applying the amount-in-controversy requirement, particularly in cases that involve intangible damages such as pain and suffering, emotional distress, loss of goodwill in a business, or punitive damages. There is no objective yardstick for lawyers to use in predicting the amount a jury will assess for such damages, or for juries to use in awarding them. Thus, it is difficult to determine at the outset of a case whether the recovery will meet the amount requirement.

Indeed, a plaintiff may legitimately seek more then $75,000 and recover nothing: The jury may conclude that the defendant was not regligent or that some defense to the claim is established. Thus it is impossible to know what value the jury will put on plaintiff's claim, or whether they will find for him at all, until the case is tried. How is the court to determine its power to hear the case without hearing the case?

This paradox has been resolved by the very sensible rule in *St. Paul Mercury Indemnity Co. v. Red Cab Co.*, 303 U.S. 283 (1938), which holds that a plaintiff's good faith claim for more than the amount required controls, unless it "appear[s] to a legal certainty that the claim is really for less. . . ." 303 U.S. at 288-289. This means that the court must find the amount-in-controversy requirement met unless it is quite clear that there is no way the recovery will reach $75,000.01. The *St. Paul Mercury* rule is heavily weighted toward the plaintiff. Where the plaintiff might get more or might get less, the amount-in-controversy requirement is deemed satisfied. Where he will probably get less, but just might get more, it is deemed satisfied. It is only where the judge, looking at the pleaded facts, concludes "to a legal certainty" that the plaintiff could only be awarded less that the amount-in-controversy requirement is not met.

This rule makes sense because Congress has not provided that jurisdiction exists only where the plaintiff *recovers* more than $75,000. The requirement is that more than $75,000 be *in controversy*. Where there is legitimate debate as to whether the jury might return a verdict above that amount, the Congressional mandate is satisfied. However, while the *St. Paul Mercury* rule makes sense, it is ineffective at keeping many types of diversity cases involving intangible damages out of federal court. Because intangible damages are hard to value, it will seldom be possible to conclude that there is no way the plaintiff will recover more than the amount required.

A second interpretive problem raised by the amount-in-controversy requirement is how to measure the amount in cases involving multiple claims or parties. Here are the traditional rules governing "aggregation of damages" to meet the amount-in-controversy requirement (after which I offer a caveat): Under the traditional approach, a single plaintiff may aggregate any claims he has against a single defendant to reach the required sum. However, he cannot add claims he has against different defendants to reach the magic number. Nor may he add his own claim to that of another plaintiff. Except in rare cases involving "common undivided interests" (such as joint owners of property), each plaintiff must have a colorable claim for more than $75,000 against each defendant. A useful way to look at such multiple party cases is to ask, "if each plaintiff alone were suing each defendant alone, would he satisfy the amount-in-controversy requirement?" For a full (but skeptical) discussion of the traditional aggregation rules, see Wright at 209-216.

Now, the caveat: Since the passage of 28 U.S.C. §1367, dealing with supplemental jurisdiction in the federal district courts, some cases have held that these traditional aggregation rules have been superceded by the supplemental jurisdiction statute. These courts have concluded that, so long as *one plaintiff* satisfies the amount-in-controversy requirement, other plaintiffs may add their claims under supplemental jurisdiction. See, e.g., *In re Abbott Laboratories,* 51 F.3d 524 (5th Cir. 1995) affirmed by an equally divided court, 529 U.S. 333 (2000) (upholding jurisdiction over class members in a class action where representative plaintiff satisfied the amount-in-controversy requirement); *Patterson Enterprises, Inc. v. Bridgestone/Firestone, Inc.,* 812 F. Supp. 1152, 1154-1155 (D. Kan. 1993) (holding that §1367 also changes the aggregation rules in non-class action cases); compare *Henkel v. ITT Bowest Corp.,* 872 F. Supp. 872, 876-879 (D. Kan. 1994) (disagreeing with *Patterson Enterprises*). The roots of this controversy will be more apparent after you have studied supplemental jurisdiction. See Chapter 15.

At this writing, the majority of courts appear to view the traditional rules as still in force, but you should be aware that the issue remains unsettled. *However,* even if the *Abbott Labs* view is accepted, it remains clear that *at least one plaintiff* must satisfy the amount requirement before the court can take supplemental jurisdiction over other parties' claims. If each plaintiff's claim is for less than $75,000.01, their claims cannot be aggregated to meet the amount requirement.

The following examples will help you to apply the aggregation rules, if not to appreciate them. Assume in analyzing them that the traditional rules apply.

EXAMPLES

Aggravation of Damages

12. Is the amount-in-controversy requirement met in each of the following cases? (Assume that diversity is otherwise proper and that there is no common undivided interest involved in the suit.)

   a. Hammer sues Holmes for $70,000 for his personal injuries suffered in an auto accident and for $15,000 for damage to his car in the same accident.

   b. Hammer sues Holmes to recover $60,000 on a loan he made to Holmes and for $50,000 for an unrelated libel.

   c. Hammer sues Holmes for $60,000 for damages suffered in an accident. In the same action, Marlowe, who was a passenger in Hammer's car, sues Holmes for $25,000 for his injuries.

   d. Hammer sues Holmes for $80,000 for his injuries in the accident. In the same suit, Marlowe, the passenger in Hammer's car, sues for $25,000.

   e. Hammer sues Holmes for $80,000 for injuries suffered in an auto accident. He also sues Dr. Watson, claiming that Watson negligently treated his injuries, causing $20,000 in additional damages.

Adding Insult to Injury

f. McGee sues Spenser for causing $50,000 worth of damage to McGee's houseboat. His complaint contains two counts. Count One seeks $50,000 from Spenser for negligently ramming the boat while docking in Fort Lauderdale. Count Two seeks $50,000 from Spenser on the theory that he intentionally damaged the boat.

g. McGee's $100,000 houseboat is destroyed in a collision with boats piloted by Spenser and Carella. He claims that either Spenser, Carella, or both, were negligent and sues them both to recover for the damage to the boat.

h. McGee sues Spenser for $60,000 for intentionally injuring his boat and for $50,000 in punitive damages.

Another Famous Foible

13. Here is another dandelion from the bluebook garden. What is wrong with it?

> The plaintiff's claim must be dismissed for failure to meet the amount-in-controversy requirement unless it appears to a legal certainty that he will recover more than seventy-five thousand dollars.

EXPLANATIONS

The Basic Diversity Requirements

1a. Marlowe and Archer are both from California. You can't get any less diverse than this, under any definition of diversity. The fact that Marlowe has sued in an Illinois federal court is irrelevant. No matter which district he chooses, the parties are from the same state. Don't be thrown off the track by the fact that the suit is brought in a third state. For diversity purposes (unlike personal jurisdiction purposes), the crucial question is where the opposing parties live, not where they sue.

b. This is a proper diversity case even though both defendants are from California. The *Strawbridge* rule requires that all defendants must be from different states than all plaintiffs; parties on the same side of the "v" may be co-citizens. While this might not satisfy one's intuitive notion of "complete diversity," it is diverse enough to satisfy Chief Justice Marshall and §1332.

c. This is the completest of all possible diversities because all parties are from different states. It is therefore a proper diversity case. Once again, the place of suit is irrelevant to the diversity analysis. Carella's choice of the defendant's home state does not destroy diversity, just as the choice of forum could not create it in example 1a.

d. There is no diversity jurisdiction here. While there are diverse citizens on both sides of the "v," there are also New Yorkers on both sides, which violates the *Strawbridge* rule. This is an ironic result: Why should a New York state court jury be any less prejudiced against Marlowe and Archer, simply because Meyer has been sued as well? Indeed, might not the jury shift the blame from the in-state defendant to the out-of-state defendants? It is easy to poke holes in the *Strawbridge* rule in cases like this; indeed, Chief Justice Marshall is said to have regretted the decision himself. Wright at 156.[6] But any effort to amend the diversity statute to revise the *Strawbridge* rule would probably lead to an expansion of diversity jurisdiction. In an age when diversity is in disrepute such an amendment is unlikely.

Note the various ways in which the plaintiffs could restructure this suit to use the federal courts. All three plaintiffs could sue Marlowe and Archer, or McGee and Spenser could sue all three defendants. In either case, diversity would exist, but some part of the controversy would have to be heard separately in state court.

e. This is a suit between diverse citizens with an additional party who is an alien (a harsh-sounding term for a person who is a citizen or subject of another country). Article III, §2, does not specifically provide for this kind of case, but it does separately authorize jurisdiction over cases between citizens of different states and cases between citizens and aliens ("between a State, or the Citizens thereof, and foreign States, Citizens or Subjects"). It is a fair inference that a combination of the two is also proper. Congress has expressly authorized jurisdiction in such cases in 28 U.S.C. §1332(a)(3).

f. Marple is an alien whether she is currently living in California or England. She cannot become a state citizen without first becoming a United States citizen. Thus, even if she is domiciled in California, this is a proper diversity case.[7] See, e.g., *Mas v. Perry*, 489 F.2d 1396 (5th Cir. 1974). For an interesting variation on this case, see *Twentieth Century-Fox Film Corp. v. Taylor*, 239 F. Supp. 913 (S.D.N.Y. 1965), in which Elizabeth Taylor was sued for various claims arising out of the filming of the movie "Cleopatra." Although Taylor was an American citizen at the time suit was filed, she was domiciled abroad. Consequently, she was not subject to suit in federal court under the diversity statute since she was not a citizen of any state, nor was she an alien since she had not relinquished her American citizenship. Id. at 914 n.2.

2. This example is meant to dispel one potential source of confusion. It is only necessary to have one basis of federal jurisdiction to sue in federal court. Here, Marlowe's suit is brought under a federal statute. It is a case "arising

---

6. On the other hand, this application of the rule is not entirely irrational. Carella could not sue Meyer in federal court alone, since they are both from New York. Why should he be able to do so simply by joining other defendants who are diverse?

7. However, §1332 treats an alien "admitted to the United States for permanent residence" as a citizen of the state where he is domiciled. See the last paragraph of 28 U.S.C. §1332(a).

under federal law," a separate basis for federal subject matter jurisdiction authorized by Article III and 28 U.S.C. §1331. It is therefore irrelevant that the parties are from the same state, since diversity is not needed to support federal jurisdiction.

3.   This example illustrates a point already raised in the last chapter: that a case within the federal court's jurisdiction may usually be filed in a state court instead. Marlowe's is a proper diversity case, so he could have filed it in federal court. But state courts have jurisdiction over contracts cases too. Under the principle of concurrent jurisdiction, Marlowe may file this case in state court if he wishes. (However, as we will see in Chapter 7, Carella may have a right to "remove" it to federal court if Marlowe does file in state court.)

4.   This suit is proper even though Archer and Marlowe are both from California. Marlowe has a federal claim against Archer, a separate basis for suing him in federal court. Thus, he is not relying on diversity between himself and Archer as a basis for jurisdiction. In determining diversity, you can disregard parties who are properly before the federal court on another basis and focus on the part of the case for which diversity is the source of jurisdiction. *Kauth v. Hartford Ins. Co. of Illinois.* 852 F.2d 951 (7th Cir. 1988). Because Marlowe is diverse from McGee, his claim against him is proper, so there is a basis for jurisdiction over all claims in the case.

Put another way, it is clear on these facts that Marlowe could sue McGee and Archer in separate actions in federal court, one based on federal question jurisdiction and the other on diversity. It would hardly make sense to allow him to do that, but not to allow him to sue them in a combined action.

5.   This looks like an obvious ploy to invoke federal jurisdiction for a case that fails the *Strawbridge* test. Marlowe sues a diverse defendant, gets into federal court, and then adds the non-diverse defendant by amendings his complaint. The federal court will probably either refuse to allow the amendment or dismiss this action for lack of diversity jurisdiction, since Marlowe's amendment has "destroyed diversity" by adding a party from his home state. Even though the court had jurisdiction over the action as originally filed, it must dismiss once the nondiverse party is added. Otherwise, the plaintiff would be able to gain access to federal court by suing diverse parties in the initial action and adding home-state defendants later on. See *Owen Equipment & Erection Co. v. Kroger,* 437 U.S. 365 (1978).

Homes Away from Home

6.   Although the parties were diverse at the time of the incident that gave rise to Carella's claim, they are not diverse at the time of the suit: Carella has apparently changed his domicile by retiring to Florida. Although it is unclear from the statute, courts have held that the magic date for determining

diversity is the date of filing suit. *Hawes v. Club Equestre El Comandante,* 598 F.2d 698, 701 (1st Cir. 1979). If the parties are not diverse on that date, there is no jurisdiction. If they are, it does not matter that they were from the same state when the claim arose. The fact that the accident took place in New York does not affect the analysis; the place of the underlying events in suit, like the place where the plaintiff brings the action, is irrelevant to the determination of diversity.

7a. You may recognize this hypo as a slightly modified version of the facts in *World-Wide Volkswagen v. Woodson,* 444 U.S. 286 (1980). The case could not be properly brought as a diversity case, since Meyer is still a New Yorker. Even though he intends to settle in Arizona and has left New York, perhaps never to return, he has not yet established a domicile in Arizona. To do so, he must physically arrive in the state with the intent to remain indefinitely.

Nor may Meyer argue that he is domiciled in Oklahoma, based on his two-month stay there. He has arrived there and established a residence of sorts,[8] but as far as we know, he has not changed his intent to go on to live in Arizona. Residence in Oklahoma without the necessary intent is just as ineffective to create a new domicile as intent to live in Arizona without residence there. Until the two coincide in a new state, Robinson remains a New York domiciliary.

Some authorities offer a looser test for establishing a domicile. In *Sadat v. Mertes,* 615 F.2d 1176 (7th Cir. 1980), for example, the court held that a person must "be physically present at the location and intend to make that place his home for the time at least" to establish a new domicile. This test would probably yield a different result in this example, since presumably Mayer intends to make Oklahoma his home "for the time at least" — until he gets out of the hospital. However, this test raises problems if taken literally. If Hawes goes to Florida for four months to conduct an investigation, he intends to remain in Florida "for the time at least," but it hardly seems likely that even the *Sadat* court would find him domiciled in Florida.

b. A frequent mistake in applying the domicile rule is to conclude that intent and residence must coincide when a person originally arrives in the state. That is not so; as long as the two coincide at some time while he is there, a new domicile is established. In this case, Meyer does not intend to stay in Oklahoma when he arrives but forms that intent later, while residing there. When he does form that intent, Oklahoma becomes his domicile.

---

8. Establishing a residence for domicile purposes need not entail purchasing a house or leasing an apartment. Even an overnight stay in a hotel or a night spent in the family camper may suffice. See Restatement (Second) of Conflicts of Law §12, illustration 2; cf. *T. P. Laboratories v. Huge,* 197 F. Supp. 860, 863 (D. Md. 1961). Some authorities state the requirement as one of "physical presence" rather than residence. See, e.g., *Holmes v. Sopuch,* 639 F.2d 431, 433 (8th Cir. 1981).

Restatement (Second) of Conflicts of Law §15, illustration 2 (1971). Consequently, this is a proper diversity case.

c. This is a difficult case. Meyer has not made any commitment to stay in Oklahoma after he finishes rehabilitation; nor does he have a reason any longer to go on to Arizona; nor is he likely to return to New York (they don't drill an awful lot of oil there, last I heard. Nor can you argue that he is in Oklahoma for a definite period of time, the six-month rehabilitation period. He will definitely be there for *at least* six months, but he is not definitely there for *only* six months. He may stay until Armageddon for all we know.

Of course, the rule is that you don't lose your old domicile until you acquire a new one. But I would conclude that Meyer has acquired domicile in Oklahoma. He might stay in Oklahoma—where they clearly do have oil wells—or he might go elsewhere. While he's not irrevocably committed to staying, he's not committed to leaving either. Meyer's plans are "indefinite."

A generation of civil procedure students have done battle with me over examples like this, resisting the idea that a person can be domiciled in a state where they have so little commitment or expectation of remaining. Many argue that Meyer remains domiciled in New York, since he is not committed to staying in Oklahoma; but I say he is domiciled in the state where he currently resides unless he is committed to going somewhere else. Meyer was committed to leaving in example 7a, but that isn't true here.

Corporate Diversity

8.   Diversity jurisdiction is proper here, since Carella is not from either Underworld's state of incorporation or the state where it has its principal place of business. The fact that Underworld does business in New York, the plaintiff's home state, does not affect diversity as long as New York is not Underworld's principal place of business. Distinguish personal jurisdiction over the corporation, which may be established (in appropriate cases) in a state where the corporation does business, even though it does a great deal more business in other states. See Chapter 1, example 8.

9.   There is no diversity jurisdiction here because the plaintiff is a citizen of the state in which Underworld has its principal place of business. McGee may not claim diversity on the ground that he is from Florida and Underworld from Delaware: Underworld is *also* from Florida under §1332(c)(1). Neither the corporation nor the opposing party can pick and choose between these two states in order to establish diversity. The corporation is from both states, and therefore, complete diversity is lacking.

10. In this case, the defendant has very large facilities in two states, both of which might ordinarily be deemed "principal" places of business. While it may seem artificial to designate either as more "principal" than the other,

§1332(c)(1) has been consistently interpreted to mean that a corporation can have only one principal place of business for diversity purposes. See 28 U.S.C. §1332(c)(1) ("*the* state where it has its principal place of business") (emphasis supplied). Thus, the court will have to choose California or Nevada; because the corporate headquarters and the larger casino are both in Nevada, the court will likely conclude that Gamblers' principal place of business is Nevada. Thus, it will be a citizen of Nevada on this basis as well as on the basis of its incorporation there and will be diverse from Marlowe. (In many cases, as in this one, corporations will be citizens of only one state under §1332(c)(1) because they are incorporated in the state where their principal place of business is located.)

11. The amendment restricted corporate access to the federal courts by increasing the number of cases in which corporations share the same state citizenship with opposing parties. For example, a mining corporation might incorporate in Delaware for tax or legal reasons, but do all its mining business in Colorado. Under the earlier interpretation, it was diverse from a Colorado citizen and could invoke federal jurisdiction even though, in day-to-day reality, it functioned as a local Colorado corporation. Under §1332(c)(1), however, that corporation is deemed a citizen of Colorado as well as a citizen of Delaware and confined to the state courts in suits against Colorado citizens.

Aggravation of Damages

12a. Hammer may aggregate any claims he has against Holmes, a single defendant, to reach the required jurisdictional amount. Because the two claims combined exceed $75,000, the amount-in-controversy requirement is met.

b. Aggregation is proper because the plaintiff may aggregate his claims against a single defendant even if, as here, the two claims are totally unrelated.

c. Both of these claims will be dismissed. Just as Hammer is barred from aggregating claims against separate defendants, he may not aggregate his claims with those of another plaintiff to reach the $75,000-plus threshold. When you look separately at each plaintiff's claim against Holmes, neither satisfies the amount-in-controversy requirement. Nor will §1367, the supplemental jurisdiction statute, change the result. If it affects these rules at all, it only does so where *one* plaintiff satisfies the amount requirement.

d. Under the traditional aggregation rules, Hammer's claim is proper, since his claim exceeds $75,000, but Marlowe's is not. Marlowe is not allowed, under the traditional approach, to piggyback his claim onto Hammer's, by arguing that there is $105,000 in controversy. He could only sue with Hammer if he could have sued alone in federal court, and here he could not since his claim is for less than the required amount.

In *Zahn v. International Paper Co.,* 414 U.S. 291 (1973), the Supreme Court applied this principle to a class action. In *Zahn,* the representative plaintiffs sought more than the jurisdictional amount, but many members of the class they sought to represent did not. The Court applied the traditional aggregation rule, holding that any class member whose claim did not reach the jurisdictional amount had to be dismissed.

As the introduction indicates, 28 U.S.C. §1367, the supplemental jurisdiction statute, has thrown this issue into some doubt, both in the class action context and in the traditional case like our example. Some courts have held that, where one plaintiff meets the amount requirement, the court may take supplemental jurisdiction over other claims that do not. In *Lindsay v. Kvortek,* 865 F. Supp. 264 (W.D. Pa. 1994), for example, an accident victim sued for injuries that satisfied the amount requirement, but his daughter sought recovery in the same action for injuries that did not. The court held that it had jurisdiction over the daughter's claim under 28 U.S.C. §1367. Accord: *Sayre v. Potts,* 32 F. Supp. 2d 881 (S.D.W.V. 1999). Other courts, however, have held that the traditional rules still apply. Stay tuned.

Civil procedure enthusiasts (not to mention litigants) thought we would get some clarification on this issue, after ten years of ambiguity, when the Supreme Court agreed to review *In re Abbott Laboratories,* 51 F.3d 524 (5th Cir. 1995), which held that 28 U.S.C. s. 1367 has changed the rule in *Zahn* (and probably the rule traditionally applied to this example as well). Alas, the Court affirmed the decision "by an equally divided court," without writing an opinion (or two opinions). Thus, it is still unclear whether s. 1367 has changed the traditional aggregation rules. Congress could save judges and litigants a lot of trouble and expense if it would just clarify the point by statute, but it hasn't done so.

e. Hammer's claim against Holmes is fine, but his suit against Watson fails, since Hammer does not seek more than $75,000.01 from Watson. Under the traditional aggregation rules, he cannot add his claim against one defendant to his claim against a different defendant to meet the amount requirement. Each must independently meet the requirement.

Adding Insult to Injury

f. If you thought carefully about this case, you should have concluded as a matter of common sense that the amount-in-controversy requirement is not met. The rule that the plaintiff may aggregate his claims against a single defendant applies to claims for *separate losses,* such as those asserted in example 12b, not to demands for the same damages based on different theories. McGee has only suffered $50,000 in damages; that is what he is suing to recover. Granted, he has two possible theories of relief, but he will clearly not recover $50,000 on each theory. Spenser could not have been negligent *and* intentionally caused the damage. If McGee wins at all, he will win on only one theory and will only recover the amount of his loss.

Indeed, even in cases where a plaintiff might recover on both theories, he will not be awarded more than his actual damages, absent a claim for punitive damages. For example, McGee might sue a truck dealer for breach of contract and breach of implied warranty to recover for a truck worth $50,000 less than he paid for it. Even if the court finds for McGee on both counts, he will still recover only the $50,000 he has lost; no court will give him double damages simply because he advances two theories for the same relief.

g. In this case McGee is claiming that one or both defendants' negligence contributed to cause the loss of his boat. If only Spenser was at fault, McGee would recover the entire $100,000 from him. If Carella caused the collision, McGee would recover the $100,000 loss from him. If they are both found negligent, the law in many states would allow McGee to collect the full $100,000 from either, assuming McGee was not negligent himself. Thus, since either defendant might be liable for the entire $100,000, the amount-in-controversy requirement is satisfied against each. Of course, either might be absolved completely, but as long as each *might* by liable for more than the jurisdictional amount, the requirement is met.

h. Here, McGee's actual damages are $60,000, but he may recover more than his actual damages if the governing law allows recovery of punitive damages. If the state allows punitive damages in the kind of action McGee brings, the amount requirement is likely met. Under *St. Paul Mercury,* the plaintiff's demand controls, unless it appears to be a legal certainty that he could not recover the jurisdictional amount. It is extremely difficult to say for sure that McGee will not recover $15,000.01 in punitive damages, since punitive damages turn on a jury's subjective assessment of the extremity of the defendant's conduct and, at the time the defendant challenges the sufficiency of the amount sought, the court will have little familiarity with the underlying facts of the case.

However, if relevant state law bars punitive damages, the amount-in-controversy requirement will not be met, and the case will be dismissed, since the only allowable damages do not exceed $75,000.

Another Famous Foible

13. This too-frequent misstatement of the *St. Paul Mercury* rule exactly reverses its meaning: It requires the plaintiff to prove that he *will* recover more than $75,000 to satisfy the amount-in-controversy requirement and stay in federal court. On the contrary, the rule gives the plaintiff every benefit of the doubt: If, looking at the pleaded facts, it appears that the plaintiff *might* recover more than $75,000, the requirement is met. It is only where it is clear to a legal certainty that the plaintiff *definitely will not* recover that much on the claim he has asserted that the court dismisses for failure to meet the monetary threshold.

6

Personal and Subject Matter Jurisdiction Compared: The First Two Rings

Introduction

Much of the civil procedure course is devoted to the fundamental issue of choosing the proper court in which to bring a lawsuit. As we have already seen, there is quite a choice: Each of the 50 states has its own court system, not to mention the District of Columbia and other territories. In addition, there is a separate system of federal courts, established and administered by the federal government but geographically located throughout the United States. Thus, in any particular state there will be both the local state courts and one or more "branches" or districts of the federal court system.

The plaintiff is not free to choose indiscriminately among the various federal and state courts in the 50 states. There are three basic requirements that limit the proper courts for any lawsuit. *First* is the need to find a court that can exercise personal jurisdiction over the defendant. *Second,* not all courts can hear all types of cases: The plaintiff must choose a court that has "subject matter jurisdiction" over the kind of case she wishes to litigate.

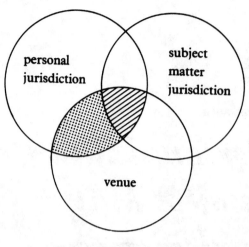

Figure 6-1

Third, the chosen forum must be a proper "venue" under the applicable venue statute. I call these the three rings of civil procedure and visualize them as in Figure 6-1.[1] As a rule, courts can only hear those cases that satisfy all three rings (the shaded area in the diagram). Frequently, a case will satisfy one or two of these prerequisites but fail the third. For example, the plaintiff may have chosen a court that has personal jurisdiction over the defendant and is a proper venue under the relevant venue statute (see the dotted area in the diagram), but the court will still have to dismiss the action if the third ring, subject matter jurisdiction, is not met.

This chapter compares the first two rings, personal and subject matter jurisdiction. The reasons for these two limitations on the right to bring an action are quite different, yet the concepts used to define them are sometimes confusingly similar. It is worth getting the distinctions clear in your mind before wading too deeply into the procedural morass.

Basic Distinctions

Personal jurisdiction, as Chapter 1 explains, is a geographical limitation on the places where a plaintiff may choose to sue a defendant for a particular claim. It is intended, as a matter of basic fairness, to prevent a plaintiff from suing a nonresident defendant in a state unless that defendant has established a relationship to that state that would reasonably lead her to anticipate being sued there.

Personal jurisdiction turns in each case on the relationship between the defendant and the state where suit is brought. Consequently, it may be

---

1. I am indebted to the late Professor Abram Chayes, of Harvard Law School, my own civil procedure teacher, for this helpful diagram.

proper to bring a particular action in one state but not in another. For example, if Gable sues Leigh, a Texan, for assault arising out of threats Leigh made at a Hollywood movie opening, it would be unreasonable to force Leigh to defend the action in Minnesota. She has (presumably) no minimum contacts with Minnesota, did not make the threats in Minnesota, and has no reason to expect this suit to be brought there. However, she could be sued in California for this claim, since she has relevant contacts with California: She made the threats there and can expect them to injure Gable there.

Similarly, the courts of a single state may have jurisdiction over one suit between particular litigants but not over another between the same parties, if the second suit is unrelated to that state. Although Gable's first assault action could not be brought in Minnesota, he would be able to sue Leigh there for another assault if Leigh repeats her threatening statements at a Minneapolis opening. Thus, the answer depends in every case on the defendant's contacts with the state where the suit has been brought.

Subject matter jurisdiction, by contrast, concerns the court's authority to hear generic types of cases. All state court systems have a set of trial courts with very broad subject matter jurisdiction. These courts (sometimes confusingly referred to as courts of "general jurisdiction") have subject matter jurisdiction over a wide range of suits, such as torts, contracts, property, and other common types of disputes. These state courts of broad subject matter jurisdiction have different names in different states. In California they are called the Superior Courts; in Pennsylvania, the Courts of Common Pleas; in New York, perversely, they are called the Supreme Courts. In addition, a state may create specialized courts to hear certain types of claims, such as landlord/tenant cases (housing courts) or family and inheritance matters (probate courts).

The subject matter jurisdiction of the *federal* courts, by contrast, is much more limited than that of the state courts. The federal courts were not created to displace the preexisting state systems, but only to provide a federal forum for specific categories of cases of national concern. The federal courts have jurisdiction over cases arising under federal law, cases between citizens of different states (the so-called diversity jurisdiction), and other more limited categories of cases. United States Constitution, Article III, §2. By contrast, they have no jurisdiction over most common types of suits, such as tort suits, contract actions, or actions seeking recovery under state statutes (unless the parties are diverse or some other narrow category of federal jurisdiction applies).

Unlike personal jurisdiction, the subject matter jurisdiction of a court does not usually depend on the location of the particular court the plaintiff chooses. For example, if a case arises under federal law, any federal district court will have subject matter jurisdiction over it. Since Article III, §2, and 28 U.S.C. §1331 authorize "the [federal] district courts" to hear cases arising under the laws of the United States, they all have jurisdiction over such cases. For example, if subject matter jurisdiction were the only limit on a plaintiff's right to sue, she could bring a case arising under federal law in any federal district court in the country.

Sources of Confusion

A number of factors conspire to make these differing concepts difficult to sort out. First, although Article III, §2, of the Constitution confers jurisdiction over various categories of cases on federal courts, it does not withdraw jurisdiction over those cases from the state courts. The state courts have "concurrent jurisdiction" over cases within the federal judicial power unless Congress has made federal court jurisdiction exclusive for a particular type of claim. Wright and Miller, §3527, p. 245. Thus, a state court may hear many claims arising under federal law, such as federal civil rights cases, even though the plaintiff would have the option to bring the action in federal court as well. By contrast, the federal courts do not have concurrent jurisdiction over state law actions (unless the parties are diverse); they may only hear those cases specifically provided for in Article III of the Constitution and jurisdictional statutes passed by Congress.

The framers of the Constitution made the situation particularly confusing by creating the diversity jurisdiction, in Article III, §2, which authorizes the federal courts to hear cases between citizens of different states. In most situations, subject matter jurisdiction is defined by the nature of the controversy (such as housing cases, probate cases, or tax cases), but here the framers chose to confer upon federal courts the power to hear cases on the basis of where the parties are from. Despite this focus on the domicile of the parties, this is *not* personal jurisdiction; it does not focus on the geographical relationship of the events giving rise to the suit to the state where suit is brought but broadly grants subject matter jurisdiction to *any* federal court, no matter where located, so long as the case is between citizens of different states. For example, if Flynn, from Oregon, sues Peck, from Maryland, for a breach of contract arising in Montana, the case is a proper diversity case (assuming the amount in controversy exceeds $75,000). Any federal district court will have subject matter jurisdiction over it, though many will not have personal jurisdiction over Peck.

Another potential source of confusion arises from the fact that the concept of domicile is relevant to both personal and subject matter jurisdiction. A natural person (that is, a human being type defendant) is subject to *personal jurisdiction* in the state where she is domiciled, the last state where she has established a residence with the intent to reside indefinitely. See Restatement (Second) of Conflicts of Law §27 (1971). An individual's state citizenship for purposes of determining *diversity jurisdiction* is also determined by this same domicile concept. But in applying the concept to determine personal jurisdiction, the court will ask whether the defendant's domicile is in the state where suit is brought. When invoking this concept to determine subject matter jurisdiction based on diversity, the court will simply compare the plaintiff's domicile to the defendant's to make sure they differ.

Yet another piece of terminology that breeds confusion is the concept of "general jurisdiction," which is used in connection with both personal and subject matter jurisdiction. The basic trial courts of each state, for example, are said to exercise "general jurisdiction." This means that they have very broad *subject matter jurisdiction* over many types of suits, unless the type of dispute has been delegated to a specialized state court or is within those few categories of cases in which Congress has made federal subject matter jurisdiction exclusive. By contrast, when used in the *personal jurisdiction* context, "general jurisdiction" refers to the authority of a state's courts to hear any claim against a particular defendant, whether or not it is related to the defendant's in-state contacts. Such general in personam jurisdiction may be based on domicile in the state or substantial and continuous in-state business activities. See Chapter 1, pp. 5-7.

Personal Jurisdiction in the Federal Courts

For the purposes of this chapter, it is necessary to touch briefly on a problem that puzzles lawyers as well as law students — the reach of personal jurisdiction in the federal courts. As a matter of *constitutional power*, the federal courts' power to exercise personal jurisdiction is not limited by the fourteenth amendment due process clause: That amendment, by its terms, only applies to the *states,* not to the federal government. However, the fifth amendment imposes its own limits on the power of federal courts to exercise personal jurisdiction. L. Teply & R. Whitten, Civil Procedure, (2d ed. 2000) 300.

Under fourteenth amendment analysis, state courts may only exercise personal jurisdiction over parties who have formed a relationship to that state. By contrast, under the fifth amendment a defendant need only have an appropriate relationship to the United States — such as being found or domiciled in the United States or having minimum contacts here that give rise to the claim — in order to be subject to personal jurisdiction in a federal court. Thus, it is generally held that Congress has the power to authorize federal courts to exercise nationwide jurisdiction, that is, to require parties with contacts anywhere in the United States to respond to suits brought in any federal district court. See generally R. Casad, Personal Jurisdiction in Federal Question Cases, 70 Tex. L. Rev. 1589, 1599-1606 (1992).[2]

---

2. A frequent argument in support of this conclusion is that Congress did not have to create separate federal courts in each state. It might have created regional courts or a single court located at the seat of the federal government. Had Congress taken this course, it would obviously have been necessary to authorize such a court to exercise broad jurisdiction over defendants from all over the country. Since such nationwide jurisdiction might well have been necessary, it would be incongruous to hold that it is constitutionally impermissible. See, e.g., *Briggs v. Goodwin,* 569

In some types of actions Congress *has* authorized nationwide jurisdiction in the federal courts through special jurisdictional provisions governing particular types of actions. An example is 28 U.S.C. §2361, which authorizes nationwide service in interpleader actions. Unless such a special provision applies, however, the authority for federal courts to serve process outside the state where they sit is restricted by the Federal Rules of Civil Procedure. Under Fed. R. Civ. P. 4(k)(1)(A), a federal court is authorized to exercise jurisdiction over a defendant "who could be subjected to the jurisdiction of a court of general jurisdiction in the state in which the district court is located." In other words, the federal court may exercise personal jurisdiction only to the extent it could be exercised by the courts of the state in which the federal court sits. Thus, if Gable sues Leigh in federal court in California, and Congress has not authorized broader jurisdiction for the type of suit involved, the court will only exercise personal jurisdiction over Leigh if the California courts could do so under the California long-arm statute and the due process clause of the *fourteenth* amendment.

This is really a very sensible rule. By generally confining the reach of personal jurisdiction in the federal court to that of the state courts of the same state, the Rules eliminate a potential ground for "forum-shopping" based on purely procedural considerations. As indicated above, in many cases plaintiffs will have a choice of state or federal court because both systems have subject matter jurisdiction over the suit. If the reach of personal jurisdiction were generally broader in federal court, plaintiffs would frequently choose to bring suit there for this reason alone, even though state court would otherwise be a more appropriate forum.

The following examples should help you sort out these related concepts. Assume in all cases that the relevant long-arm statute authorizes exercise of all constitutionally permissible jurisdiction. See the California statute supra p. 24.

EXAMPLES

Distinctions and Differences

1.   Stewart, a California citizen, wishes to sue Cagney, also a Californian, for battery, to recover for injuries he suffered in a fight between them on a Los Angeles street. Stewart prefers to sue Cagney in California.

F.2d 1, 8-10 (1st Cir. 1977), rev'd on other grounds sub nom. *Stafford v. Briggs,* 444 U.S. 527 (1980).

There may be limits to this; some courts have held that the Fifth Amendment, like the Fourteenth, includes a basic fairness requirement which may restrict the places where defendants can be required to defend a federal action. See, e.g., *Peay v. BellSouth Medical Assistance Plan,* 205 F.3d 1206m, 1211-1213 (10th Cir. 2000). Even if so, however, it will probably be the unusual case where a court would reject jurisdiction on this basis. Id. at 1212-1213.

    a. Would a California state court have personal jurisdiction over Cagney?

    b. Would a California federal court have personal jurisdiction over Cagney?

    c. Would a California state court have subject matter jurisdiction over the action?

    d. Would a California federal court have subject matter jurisdiction over the action?

2.   Assume that Cagney is from New York and that he attacked Stewart while visiting California to make a movie. Stewart, a California citizen, prefers to sue Cagney in California.

    a. Would the California state court have personal jurisdiction over Cagney?

    b. Would the California federal court have personal jurisdiction over Cagney?

    c. Would a California state court have subject matter jurisdiction over the action?

    d. Would a California federal court have subject matter jurisdiction over the action?

3.   On the facts of example 2, could Stewart have sued Cagney in either a state or federal court in New York?

4.   On the facts of example 2, could Stewart have sued Cagney in either a state or federal court in Nevada?

Variations

5.   One more variation on the facts of example 2: Assume that after the Los Angeles battery but before Stewart brings suit, Cagney moves to California.

    a. May Stewart sue him in federal court in California?

    b. May Stewart sue him in a New York state court?

6.   Colbert sues Hepburn in the federal district court for the Southern District of California for breach of a contract to star in a movie. Both parties are domiciled in New York, the contract was entered into there, and the movie was to be made there. However, Colbert prefers to sue in California, where she is currently working, and also prefers to sue in federal court. Hepburn, who is currently working in Arizona, does not object to the California court hearing the case. May it do so?

7.   Colbert, a New Yorker, sues Kojak for a violation of her federal civil rights. Suit is brought under 42 U.S.C. §1983, the federal statute that authorizes suits for such violations. The claim arises out of an unlawful arrest that took place in New York. Kojak is also domiciled in New York.

    a. May Colbert bring the suit in a New York state court?

    b. May she bring the suit in a California federal court?

    c. Assume, on the same facts, that Colbert is from California. Could she bring the action in a California federal court?

8.   May Colbert sue Hepburn in a New York state court for violation of a copyright she holds on a book about the golden age of the movies? See 28 U.S.C. §1338(a).

EXPLANATIONS
Distinctions and Differences

1a.   The California state court will have personal jurisdiction over Cagney on several bases. First, the California court may exercise personal jurisdiction over Cagney on the basis of his California domicile. Domicile in the forum state has been held an adequate basis for asserting personal jurisdiction, even if the claim sued upon did not arise in the state. *Milliken v. Meyer,* 311 U.S. 457 (1940). A person who has chosen the state as his domicile may fairly be said to have submitted himself generally to the judicial power of that state's courts, as a quid pro quo for enjoying the benefits and protections of living within the state.

In addition, Cagney has (allegedly) committed an in-state tortious act by assaulting Stewart in California. Virtually every state's long-arm statute authorizes personal jurisdiction over defendants for claims arising out of torts committed within the state, and this assertion of jurisdiction is clearly constitutional under *International Shoe.* Where Cagney has entered the state and consciously committed an act intended to harm Stewart in California, it is both fair and foreseeable to require him to respond to a California suit arising out of those in-state acts. See Chapter 2, example 3.

b.   As stated in the introduction, the federal district courts' reach of personal jurisdiction is restricted in most cases to that of the courts of the state. Under Fed. R. Civ. P. 4(k)(1)(A), the federal court first looks to the statutes or court rules governing personal jurisdiction in the state where the federal court sits. For example, the Idaho federal court will look to the Idaho long-arm statute. If the statute authorizes the assertion of jurisdiction and such an exercise of jurisdiction would not exceed the fourteenth amendment due process limits on *state* court jurisdiction, then the federal court will have personal jurisdiction. Similarly, the California federal court will look to the California jurisdiction statutes as well as the constitutional limits on state court jurisdiction. Since the California state court will have personal jurisdiction over Cagney, the federal court will too.

One interesting consequence of this rule is that the reach of personal jurisdiction may vary from one federal court to another because each exercises jurisdiction to the extent permitted in the state in which it sits, and the reach of long-arm statutes varies from state to state.

c.   Every state court system has a set of courts that has broad subject matter jurisdiction over state law claims, including battery claims. These courts of "general jurisdiction" are the workhorses of the state court systems, the basic trial courts for most types of claims. In California they are called the superior courts, and their jurisdiction includes tort claims such as the battery alleged in *Stewart v. Cagney*. Note that the analysis here for subject matter jurisdiction focuses on the nature of the case Stewart is asserting, rather than the relationship of the underlying events to the state of California, as in the personal jurisdiction analysis.

d. The California federal district court will not have subject matter jurisdiction over this case. The federal courts are not courts of general jurisdiction, but are limited to the types of cases listed in Article III, §2, and the federal statutes, such as 28 U.S.C. §§1331 and 1332, which confer this subject matter jurisdiction on the federal courts. Because nothing in Article III grants federal courts jurisdiction over battery cases, Stewart's suit may not be properly brought in federal court.

It is true that cases involving state claims, such as battery, negligence, or breach of contract may be brought in federal court if there is diversity between the parties. The framers, in their wisdom, saw fit to allow even cases based on state theories of recovery to be brought in federal court, if the parties are from different states. But here they are not, so there is no basis for federal subject matter jurisdiction. Only the California state court has both personal and subject matter jurisdiction over Stewart's suit; if venue is also proper, it may proceed to hear the case.

2a. On these facts Cagney is not subject to personal jurisdiction in California on the basis of his domicile, but the minimum contacts analysis in example 1a remains unchanged. Cagney has still committed a tortious act in California, which is likely to injure Stewart there. He will be subject to specific in personam jurisdiction there for suits arising out of this in-state conduct. Even though it may be extremely inconvenient for Cagney to return to California to defend the action, under due process analysis the California court may require him to do so.

b. As suggested above, the federal court under Fed. R. Civ. P. 4(k)(1)(A) will exercise personal jurisdiction to the same extent as the state court. Since the California state court may require Cagney to return and defend, the federal court may as well.

c. The answer here is the same as example 1c: The California superior court is a court of general subject matter jurisdiction that may hear tort claims. Thus, as in example 1, the California state court satisfies both rings; if venue is proper, it may hear this case.

d. It is still true, as in example 1d, that the federal courts have no subject matter jurisdiction over battery cases because nothing in Article III bestows jurisdiction over common law tort claims on the federal courts. However, Article III, §2, does authorize federal courts to hear cases between citizens of different states, regardless of the nature of the underlying dispute between them, and Congress has conferred that jurisdiction on the federal district courts in 28 U.S.C. §1332, subject to the amount-in-controversy requirement. Because Cagney and Stewart are diverse in this example, the federal court has subject matter jurisdiction over the suit between them if

Stewart seeks more than $75,000 in damages. So here, too, the two rings intersect: Stewart may choose a California state or federal court for this suit, assuming he can satisfy the third ring, venue, in both courts.

3.   Stewart may sue Cagney in state or federal court in New York. Here, there is no minimum contacts basis for personal jurisdiction, but Cagney is subject to personal jurisdiction there because New York is his domicile. When jurisdiction is based on domicile it is irrelevant that the cause of action did not arise there. Thus, the state courts in New York may exercise personal jurisdiction over him, and a New York federal court may do so as well, under Fed. R. Civ. P. 4(k)(1)(A).

Subject matter jurisdiction is also proper in the state or federal court in New York. The state trial courts of New York, the inaptly named supreme courts, have broad subject matter jurisdiction, including battery cases. That does not mean "battery cases arising in New York," but battery cases *as a class*. Thus, it does not matter for subject matter jurisdiction purposes that this battery took place in California.

The federal district court in New York also has subject matter jurisdiction based on diversity since Stewart and Cagney are still diverse. Note that Cagney's New York domicile is essential to establish a basis for personal jurisdiction over him in this case. For subject matter jurisdiction, however, he need only be domiciled in some state other than California. The fact that he happens to be domiciled in the state where suit is brought is not essential for establishing diversity. Forty-eight other states would do as well.

4.   If Stewart sues in Nevada, the subject matter analysis is the same as example 3. Nevada's trial level courts (called district courts) have broad subject matter jurisdiction, including tort claims. Further, the federal district court in Nevada will have diversity jurisdiction over this case; Stewart and Cagney are just as diverse there as they are anywhere else.

The personal jurisdiction analysis differs, however, because Cagney has no minimum contacts with Nevada that gave rise to this claim, and he is not domiciled there. Absent consent or service of process on Cagney in Nevada, neither the Nevada state court nor the federal court sitting in that state will have the power to require Cagney to come to Nevada to defend this particular suit. Here, Stewart will come up at least one ring short.

Note, in particular, that the existence of diversity here does not substitute for personal jurisdiction; diversity is a separate requirement for a separate purpose. To rephrase the old song, you *can* have one without the other.

Variations

5a.   Personal jurisdiction would be proper in this case based on minimum contacts analysis and Rule 4(k)(1)(A), but subject matter jurisdiction is not. Cagney and Stewart were diverse at the time of the events giving rise to the suit. However, as a result of Cagney's move, they are no longer diverse when suit is brought. Because the relevant date for determining diversity is the date suit is filed (*Smith v. Sperling*, 354 U.S. 91, 93 n.1 (1957)), there is no diversity. Nor is there a federal claim or other basis for federal subject matter jurisdiction.

b. The New York state court would have subject matter jurisdiction since it has broad jurisdiction over common law claims, but personal jurisdiction is not proper. The claim arises out of events that took place in California. Because the claim is unrelated to New York, the only possible basis for personal jurisdiction is Cagney's domicile. Cagney was domiciled in New York at the time of the assault but is not at the time of suit.

The rationale for allowing a state to exercise personal jurisdiction on the basis of domicile is that a party living in the state is so integrally related to the state that it is fair to require him to appear in its courts. *Milliken v. Meyer*, 311 U.S. at 463. In addition, it is unlikely to be inconvenient to defend in the state of one's domicile. This rationale suggests that domicile jurisdiction should require domicile at the time of suit, not at the time of the events that led to the suit. See *Nicholas v. Inglimo*, 421 N.E.2d 1014, 1016-1017 (Ill. App. 1981) (taking this view). Assuming the New York court takes this approach, it will dismiss for lack of personal jurisdiction over Cagney.

Minimum contacts (specific in personam) jurisdiction provides an interesting contrast. Cagney could be required to return to defend a California suit arising out of the assault there, even if he has had no contact with California since then. The rationale underlying minimum contacts jurisdiction is that performing certain acts in a state carries with it predictable consequences, including a duty to return to defend those acts in court. The defendant cannot avoid those consequences by subsequently avoiding the state. If he could, minimum contacts jurisdiction would be meaningless.

6.   This example highlights an important distinction between personal and subject matter jurisdiction. The California court lacks any basis for personal jurisdiction over Hepburn on this claim, which arose in New York. However, personal jurisdiction is deemed a privilege of the defendant, which will be waived if she fails to assert it. *Rauch v. Day & Night Manufacturing Corp.*, 576 F.2d 697, 701 (6th Cir. 1978). Consequently, a court that lacks personal jurisdiction may still hear the case if the defendant does not object. Because Hepburn is willing to litigate the claim in California, she will presumably waive her objection by failing to raise it. See Fed. R. Civ. P. 12(b)(2), (g), (h).

However, the California federal court also lacks subject matter jurisdiction over this action. Nothing in Article III, §2, or the federal jurisdictional statutes gives the federal courts jurisdiction over state contract claims between nondiverse citizens. Hepburn's willingness to have the federal court hear the case is irrelevant: The parties cannot confer subject matter jurisdiction on the court. Subject matter jurisdiction allocates governmental power among different tribunals. That allocation is made by the Constitution and Congress, not by the parties. Consequently, even if neither party objects to the federal court hearing the case, it will refuse to do so. See Fed. R. Civ. P. 12(h)(3).

7a. This suit is proper in state court in New York. Personal jurisdiction is satisfied because the claim arises out of alleged deprivation of rights taking place in New York. Under the minimum contacts test, Kojak could fairly be required to defend a suit arising out of these in-state acts in a New York court. In addition, he is subject to personal jurisdiction in New York on the basis of his domicile in the state.

Subject matter jurisdiction is also proper in the New York state court, even though this is a case arising under federal law. As a rule, the general trial courts of each state have subject matter jurisdiction over almost any kind of case, unless it has been exclusively delegated to a specialized state court or (for some cases within the federal subject matter jurisdiction) to the federal courts. Even though federal civil rights cases arise under federal law and are therefore properly brought in federal court under 28 U.S.C. §1331, Congress has not made federal jurisdiction over such cases exclusive. Consequently, the state courts also have jurisdiction to hear such claims.

b. Because the case arises under federal law, the California federal court will have subject matter jurisdiction. 28 U.S.C. §1331. However, the federal court will not exercise personal jurisdiction if the California state court could not do so. Fed. R. Civ. P. 4(k)(1)(A). Here, the claim does not arise out of any contacts with the state of California. The California courts therefore lack personal jurisdiction over Kojak (absent some other basis such as in-state service or consent), since there are no "minimum contacts" among the claim, Kojak, and the forum state.

c. Moving Colbert's domicile to California creates some distinctions from the prior case, but distinctions without any relevant difference. Colbert's California domicile would be an adequate basis for personal jurisdiction over *her,* were she the defendant, but it does not alter the due process requirement that the defendant, the party being unwillingly haled before the court, must have minimum contacts with the state that is doing so. Kojak lacks any such contacts, at least for this claim. Personal jurisdiction is therefore lacking.

The other difference here is that the parties in this case are diverse. This gives the court an alternative source of subject matter jurisdiction (which is unnecessary, since it is a federal-question case anyway), but it is irrelevant to personal jurisdiction. Innumerable first-year exam answers not withstanding, diversity is *not* a substitute for personal jurisdiction.

8. Although the general rule is that the federal and state courts have concurrent jurisdiction over cases arising under federal law, Congress may make federal court jurisdiction over cases within Article III exclusive. Wright and Miller §3527, p. 241-242. It has done so for copyright cases, presumably because of the specialized nature of these suits and the national scope of the protection conferred by the copyright laws. See 28 U.S.C. §1338(a). Consequently, the state court lacks subject matter jurisdiction over this case.

7

Second-Guessing the Plaintiff's Choice of Forum: Removal

Introduction

The traditional rule in American courts has been, and largely, still is, that the plaintiff chooses the forum in which to bring a suit, subject to the limitations of personal jurisdiction, subject matter jurisdiction, and venue. He may choose the geographical place of suit by suing in the courts of the state he prefers. And, assuming proper subject matter jurisdiction, he may also choose the court system in which to litigate by starting the action in either a federal or state court.[1] In this respect, and in others, it is said that "the plaintiff is master of his claim."

Removal is an exception to this rule, however. The federal removal statutes allow the defendant, after the plaintiff has chosen a state court, to "second-guess" that choice by "removing" some types of cases from the state court to a federal court. Once properly removed the case becomes a federal case, and the state court loses jurisdiction over it. Both pretrial litigation and trial will take place in the federal court.

The rationale for removal is that defendants as well as plaintiffs should have the option to choose federal court for cases within the federal jurisdiction — that jurisdiction is intended to protect both parties, and therefore,

---

1. As Chapter 6 explains, the state and federal courts will frequently both have subject matter jurisdiction over a case. See pp. 103-104.

both parties should have access to it. If a federal court is particularly qualified to decide cases arising under federal law, then a defendant should be able to ask it to do so, just as a plaintiff may. Similarly, if an out-of-state defendant may suffer prejudice from litigating in a state court, he should have the same right as an out-of-state plaintiff to avoid that prejudice by invoking federal diversity jurisdiction.

A natural corollary of this rationale is that removal jurisdiction should be available to the defendant only in cases that the plaintiff could have commenced in federal court. Removal is not meant to expand federal jurisdiction but merely to make it available to defendants. Therefore, 28 U.S.C. §1441(a) only authorizes removal of state court actions "of which the district courts of the United States have original jurisdiction." If the plaintiff could not have chosen to bring the action in federal court initially, the defendant cannot remove it. For example, if Oakley sues Cody, a fellow Kansan, on a state law contract claim, she could not sue in federal court, since there is neither diversity nor a federal question. Consequently, if she sues Cody in state court, her action against Cody will not be removable. By contrast, if she sued Cody in state court under a federal age discrimination statute, or if they were citizens of different states, Cody could remove because Oakley could have chosen to sue him on that claim in federal court.

A caution is in order here, however. While it is generally true that a defendant cannot remove a case if the federal court would not have had original jurisdiction over it, some cases are not removable *even though* the plaintiff could have brought them in federal court originally. In particular, 28 U.S.C. §1441(b) provides that a diversity case is only removable if "none of the parties in interest properly joined and served as defendants is a citizen of the State in which such action is brought." In other words, if a defendant is sued in his home state, he may not remove on the basis of diversity. If Pike, from Nevada, sues Cody, from Kansas, on a state law claim in Kansas state court, Cody cannot remove. The rationale for this exception is that Cody has no need to be protected from local prejudice, since he is from the forum state.

Interestingly, there is no explicit authority in the Constitution for snatching cases out of the hands of state courts by removal to federal court. Yet the First Congress provided for removal in the Judiciary Act of 1789, and it has been with us in one form or another ever since. The courts have consistently upheld the constitutionality of the removal procedure. See Wright at 223. Because removal only applies to cases that could have been brought *originally* in federal court, there seems little constitutional distinction between allowing the plaintiff to choose the federal court in a case within the federal court's jurisdiction and allowing the defendant to do so by removing a state court action.[2]

---

2. However, §1441(c), the enigmatic provision for removal of "separate and independent" claims, may be an exception to this principle. See L. Teply and R. Whitten, *Civil Procedure,* 2d ed. 2000, 153-154 (questioning constitutionality of §1441(c)).

Traditionally, removal jurisdiction depended not only on the scope of original federal jurisdiction, but also on the jurisdiction of the state court from which it was removed. The federal court's removal jurisdiction was said to be "derivative" (Wright at 226) of the state court's. Thus, removal jurisdiction was only proper if the removed case was properly before the state court to begin with. For example, if Butterfield brought a patent infringement action in state court, it could not be removed because the federal courts have exclusive jurisdiction over patent cases. 28 U.S.C. §1338(a). Thus, because only the federal court had jurisdiction, it had to dismiss the case when it was removed to federal court! However, if Butterfield was not too bewildered to press on (and if the statute of limitations had not passed), he could bring an *original* action on the patent claim in federal court.

This long-standing but impractical rule was changed by statute in 1986. Congress added §1441(e) to the removal statute, which provides that the federal court is not precluded from hearing the case simply because the state court lacked jurisdiction over it. Thus, a case like Butterfield's would now be removable, despite the fact that the state court had no power to hear his patent claim. Clearly, however, §1441 (e) does not change the requirement that the case be within *federal* jurisdiction to be removable. Section 1441(a) still requires that.

Even if a state court case satisfies the jurisdictional requirements for removal, there are drastic limits as to which court it may be removed *to*. You can't remove to another state court or to a state court in a different state. You can't remove to a federal court in another state or even in another district in the same state. There is only one lonely court that can host a removed action: the federal district court "for the district and division embracing the place where such action is pending [in the state court]." 28 U.S.C. §1441(a). For example, Figure 7-1 shows the configuration of the four federal districts in Texas. Each federal district spans a number of counties. Cases filed in any county within that district will be removed to that district. If Pike sued Cody in the District Court for Lipscomb County (the Texas *state* court of general jurisdiction, even though it is confusingly called a "district" court), the action would be removed to the federal district court for the Northern District of Texas. If he sued in Dimmit County, it would be removed to the Western District of Texas, and so on.[3] Thus, removal only partially displaces the plaintiff's choice of forum: He still gets to choose the state where the action will be litigated, even if he ends up in federal court in that state due to removal by the defendant.

---

3. Of course, the federal court may well sit in a city some distance from the place where the state court action was filed. For example, the Texas District Court for Lipscomb County sits in Lipscomb, Texas. If Cody removes his case from that court to the Northern District of Texas, however, court hearings will take place in Amarillo, where the Amarillo Division of the federal court for the Northern District sits, some 130 *miles* from Lipscomb.

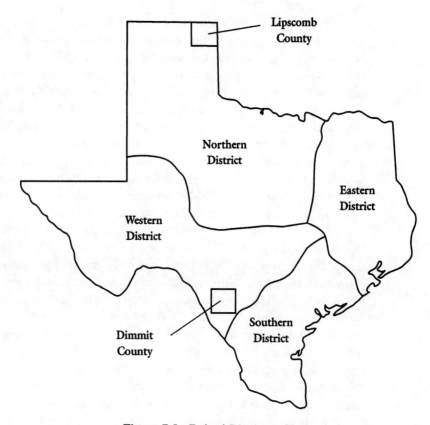

Figure 7-1: Federal Districts — Texas

The usual federal venue rules do not apply in removed actions. A case that is removable must be removed to the "district and division embracing the place where such action is pending" (§1441(a)), even if that federal district would not have been a proper venue under 28 U.S.C. §1391 if the case had been brought there initially. In the *Schulansky* case (see Part Six), for example, Ronan may only remove to the District of Massachusetts because the Plymouth County Superior Court, where the suit was initiated, falls within that district. Even if the District of Massachusetts would not have been a proper venue if Schulansky started her suit in federal court, it is the proper district when Ronan removes it on these facts.

It may be helpful to compare removal under §1441 with transfer of venue under 28 U.S.C. §1404(a). Section 1404(a) provides for geographical transfer from one district court within the federal system to another in a different state or district. See Jones's motion to transfer venue from the District of Massachusetts to the District of New Hampshire in the Schulansky case, infra Chapter 33. Removal, by contrast, authorizes transfer from the state court system to the federal court system within the same state. Transfer displaces the plaintiff's geographical choice for litigation, while removal displaces the plaintiff's choice of the state court system in favor of a federal court within the same geographical area. As the Schulansky papers suggest, it may be possible to use both devices in a single suit. For a case that was removed and then transferred (and then dismissed for forum non conveniens!), see *Piper Aircraft Co. v. Reyno*, 454 U.S. 235 (1981).

The general removal statute applies to cases, not claims: When the defendant properly removes a suit to federal court, the defendant's entire suit is removed, including not only the specific claim that gives rise to removal jurisdiction, but also any related claims that the federal court has the power to hear under supplemental jurisdiction. Suppose, for example, that Colter sues Bridger (a citizen of the same state) for violation of Colter's federal civil rights (a claim based on federal law, which state courts as well as federal courts may hear) and asserts a claim for relief on a state law battery theory as well. If Bridger removes, the federal court acquires jurisdiction of the entire action, including the civil rights claim that provides the basis for federal court jurisdiction and the supplemental state law claim. Neither the plaintiff nor the defendant can dissect a single case and send only parts of it to the federal forum.[4] In addition, remember that removal is a one-way street: A defendant who is properly sued in federal court cannot remove to state court.

After removal, a case proceeds in federal court under the Federal Rules. See Fed. R. Civ. P. 81(c). Essentially, that court picks up the ball in mid-air and continues to juggle it. The state court complaint and answer (if one has been filed before removal) will be filed with the notice of removal. 28 U.S.C. §1446(a). See the notice of removal in *Schulansky v. Ronan*, infra p. 557. The court may order the parties to file discovery material and other filings from the state court in the federal court for use in the action. 28 U.S.C. §1447(b). If the state court has entered any orders prior to removal, such as a preliminary injunction or a protective order concerning discovery, those orders remain in effect in the federal court, unless modified by the federal judge. 28 U.S.C. §1450. It's a little like the Red Sox being whisked out of Fenway Park to Dodger Stadium in the second inning and being told to just finish the game under the National League rules.

The following examples illustrate the substantive limits on removal jurisdiction. The second set of examples deals with removal procedure. For purposes of this chapter, I have stubbornly ignored the murky mysteries of §1441(c), dealing with removal of certain "separate and independent"

---

4. However, the federal court may, in its discretion, remand or dismiss supplemental state law claims in appropriate cases. See 28 U.S.C. §1367(c); *United Mine Workers v. Gibbs*, 383 U.S. 715, 726-727 (1966); *Carnegie-Mellon University v. Cohill*, 484 U.S. 343 (1988).

claims. You should do the same in analyzing the examples. Also, where it is relevant, assume that the amount-in-controversy requirement is met.

EXAMPLES

The Power to Remove

1.   Earp, from Kansas, sues Dillon, also a Kansan, in a state court in Kansas. His claim is based on violation of the federal civil rights law. May Dillon remove?

2.   Suppose Earp (still from Kansas) sues Carson, from Colorado, in the Colorado state court on a state law assault claim. May Carson remove?

3.   Assume the same facts as example 2, but Earp sues a second defendant, Hickok, as well. Hickok is from Missouri. Can the defendants remove?

4.   Consider the same facts again, with another twist: Earp, from Kansas, sues Carson (Colorado) and Hickok (Missouri) on the assault claims in a Kansas state court. Can the defendants remove?

5.   Chester, from Iowa, sues Carson, a Coloradan, and James, a Kansan, in Kansas state court on a federal civil rights claim.
     a. May the defendants remove?
     b. If so, to which court or courts?

6.   Recall that old chestnut case, *Louisville and Nashville R.R. v. Mottley,* 219 U.S. 467 (1911), in which the Supreme Court dismissed for lack of subject matter jurisdiction because the federal question in the case arose as a defense. Suppose that the plaintiffs in that case sued the (nondiverse) railroad in the state court for breach of contract. Ten days later the railroad answered, raising the defense that the federal statute precludes it from renewing the Mottleys' passes. Ten days after answering, the railroad removes the case to federal court. Is removal proper?

Some Refinements

7.   Suppose, on the facts of example 4, that Carson wants to remove, but Hickok likes the state court. Can Carson remove the case? See 28 U.S.C. §1441(a).

8.   Earp sues James, a fellow Kansan, on a state law assault claim. Six months later Earp's lawyer decides, on the basis of his further knowledge of the case gleaned from discovery, that Earp also has a claim against James for a federal civil rights violation arising out of the same facts. Earp amends to assert the federal claim. May James now remove?

9.   Earp, a Kansan, sues Bean, a Texan, on a state law abuse-of-process claim in an Iowa state court. Bean removes to federal court. Subsequently, Earp amends to add James, a fellow Kansan, as a second defendant. Should the federal court remand the case to state court?

10. On the facts of example 9, suppose that Earp (Kansas) has claims against Bean (Texas) and James (Kansas) for abuse of process. Earp deliberately decides to sue them jointly in a single action in state court in order to avoid removal to federal court. Is this permissible? Will it work?

11. Suppose, on the facts of example 9, that Earp sues Bean in state court. Anticipating removal, Earp seeks only $70,000 in damages, leaving out a demand for consequential damages worth $8,000. May Bean remove?

12. James sues Earp, his fellow Kansan, on an assault claim. Earp counterclaims for damages for violation of his federal civil rights, arising out of the same encounter. (See Fed. R. Civ. P. 13(a).) Does §1441 allow James to remove?

Unlucky Number 13

13. Dillon (a Kansan) sues Greeley (a New Yorker) for $90,000 for breach of contract. Dillon claims that he had contracted with Greeley to allow Greeley to manufacture electrical circuits upon which Dillon held a patent. In return, Greeley agreed to pay Dillon royalties but has failed to do so. Dillon also claims that Greeley, by making the circuits covered by his patent, has committed patent infringement. Suit is brought in state court in Kansas. Greeley removes.

    a. If the suit had been brought prior to 1986, how would this case have been resolved?

    b. How would it be resolved under current removal law?

The Procedure for Removal

The procedure for removal, set forth in §1446, is relatively straightforward. The defendant (or defendants) must file a notice of removal in the appropriate federal district court, together with all pleadings, process, and other papers on file in the state action. 28 U.S.C. §1446(a). The notice must be filed within 30 days of receiving the plaintiff's pleading in the state suit. 28 U.S.C. §1446(b). Once the notice is filed and the state court is notified, the state court loses control of the case automatically. It may not proceed with discovery, try the case, or issue orders to the parties. 28 U.S.C. §1446(d). The *Schulansky* case in Part Six provides a full example of the removal process. See Chapter 30.

    Although the state court loses power over the case once it has been removed, the removal decision is not irrevocable. If the plaintiff contends that the case is not within the federal court's subject matter jurisdiction, or that the defendant has not properly followed the requirements of removal procedure, his recourse is to move in the federal court to remand the case back to state court. If the basis for the motion is failure to comply with the procedural requirements (such as failure of all defendants to join in the notice, or failure to remove within the thirty day period), the remand motion must be made within thirty days after removal, or the objection is waived. 28 U.S.C. §1447(c). A motion to remand on the basis of lack of subject matter jurisdiction, however, may be made at any time prior to final judgment in the case. Id.

This procedure, under which removal takes place automatically, prevents any confusion as to which court has jurisdiction to proceed: Even if the federal court has no jurisdiction, the state court loses power to proceed. That way, the decision as to whether the federal court has jurisdiction over the case will be made, quite properly, by the federal court when the plaintiff challenges its jurisdiction by moving to remand. If that court lacks jurisdiction, it will remand the case to the state court, which will once more pick up the ball and run with it.

In many cases, the right to remove will not be clear from the face of the complaint. For example, most states do not require the plaintiff to allege the citizenship of the parties because state court jurisdiction does not depend upon it. Compare Fed. R. Civ P. 8(a)(1); see p. 545. Thus, a defendant who claims the right to remove on the ground of diversity may have to ascertain the citizenship of the plaintiff and allege in his notice of removal that diversity exists. Section 1446(a) explicitly allows the removing defendant to allege in the notice of removal any facts necessary to demonstrate the grounds for removing the suit.

EXAMPLES

Some Technicalities

14. Chester, an Iowa citizen, sues Holiday, of Kansas, for malpractice in a leg operation. Suit is brought in an Iowa state court. His complaint does not state a dollar demand for relief (some states don't require it; others don't even allow it). Holiday wants to remove. Can he?

15. Long Branch Saloons, a corporation, sues Holiday (a Kansan) in Nebraska to collect $60,000 rent due on Holiday's offices above its Dodge City, Kansas, saloon. The state court complaint makes no allegation about Long Branch's principal place of business. Several months later Holiday discovers, much to his surprise, that the Long Branch saloon in Dodge City is the smallest of three such establishments run by Long Branch. Its principal place of business and state of incorporation is Colorado. Holiday removes on the basis of diversity. Can he do so?

16. Assume that James sues Earp, and Earp removes the suit within 30 days. However, James disputes the right to remove since he claims that his action is based on state law rather than federal law.

   a. James moves in the state court to have the case remanded for lack of removal jurisdiction. The court agrees that removal was improper. What should it do?

   b. James moves for remand in the federal court. That court agrees that removal was improper. What should it do?

17. Masterson (Nebraska) sues Hickok (Missouri), Earp (Kansas), and Bean (Texas) for assault, arising out of a fight at a corral. He serves the complaint and summons on Hickok on June 1 and Earp on June 15. As of June 25 Bean has not yet been served. If Earp wants to remove, what should he do?

18. Assume on the facts of example 17 that Earp and Hickok remove the case on June 27. On July 12 Bean is served. If he prefers state court, does he have any recourse? Should he?

Hoist with his Own Petard

19. Masterson sues Hickok, Earp and Bean in state court. The defendants file a notice of removal in federal district court. Six weeks later, Masterson's counsel examines the docket and determines that the notice of removal was filed on the thirty-third day after service of the complaint. He moves to re-mand the case on the ground that the case was not removed within the thirty-day period for removal in 28 U.S.C. s. 1446(b). What should the court do?

A Final, Fundamental Point

20. Chester (Iowa) sues Holiday (Kansas) in an Iowa state court. Holiday removes. Three days later Holiday moves to dismiss the case, on the ground that the court lacks personal jurisdiction over him. Is this motion permissible?

EXPLANATIONS

The Power to Remove

1. Earp has asserted a right to relief under federal law. Had he chosen to do so, he could have commenced this case in federal court under 28 U.S.C. §1331. Thus, the case satisfies the requirement of §1441(a) that the federal courts have original jurisdiction over the action (or, more accurately, *would* have had original jurisdiction over it had it been brought in federal court).

However, §1441(b) must also be considered since it places some further restrictions on removal jurisdiction. That section does not restrict removal of Earp's suit. It provides that cases "founded on a claim or right arising under the Constitution, treaties or laws of the United States shall be removable without regard to the citizenship or residence of the parties." Since Earp's claim is based on a federal question, it is irrelevant that the parties are not diverse and that there is an in-state defendant in the action. Removal is proper.

2. This is a straightforward diversity case. A federal district court would have original jurisdiction over the case, but this illustrates the situation in which the federal courts' removal jurisdiction is narrower than their original jurisdiction. Section 1441(b) provides that actions based on diversity ("[a]ny

other such action") cannot be removed if any defendant is from the forum state. Under this provision Carson is barred from removing this case.

The logic behind this limitation is that diversity jurisdiction was intended to protect out-of-state parties from local prejudice, so there is no need to extend it to cases where suit is brought in the defendant's home state. Of course, that rationale would support a similar restriction on *original* diversity jurisdiction in the plaintiff's home state, but there is no such restriction. Logic has its limits.

3.   This example makes one narrow point: §1441(b) precludes removal of a diversity case if *any* defendant is from the state where the state court action is brought ("only if none of the parties . . ."). Carson is still in the case; ergo, no removal. Here again, Earp could have initiated the action in federal court as a diversity action in Colorado or elsewhere, but removal is narrower.

4.   Moving the case back to Kansas changes the result. The case is still within the federal court's diversity jurisdiction, but now no defendant is from the forum state, so they may remove under §1441(b). Note that this configuration, with the Kansas plaintiff using the Kansas state courts to recover from two non-Kansas defendants, presents the strongest risk of prejudice to the defendants and therefore is the best candidate for removal jurisdiction.

5a.   This case, like that in example 1, is a federal question case and is still removable as such. Here, however, there is also diversity of citizenship, a separate basis for federal jurisdiction. The interpretive problem raised is whether it is removable "without regard to the citizenship or residence of the parties" (§1441(b)) where there is *both* a claim under federal law and diversity. If not, removal would be barred due to the presence of an in-state defendant, James. The answer is "yes"; the case may be removed because it is just as squarely founded on a claim under federal law when there *is* diversity as when there is *not*.

b.   Carson would clearly prefer to remove to the Colorado district court, to get the benefit of the home forum. However, removal is not meant to give the defendant a geographical choice of forum, only a choice to use the federal court system. The action can only be removed to the federal district court for the District of Kansas. If there were more than one federal district in Kansas (as there is in Texas, for example), the defendants could only remove the case to the district in which the state court where Chester brought suit is located.

6.   On the facts given here, there is no original federal jurisdiction because it is a state law claim between nondiverse parties. Of course, when the railroad answers the complaint in the state court, raising the federal statute as a defense, it becomes clear that a federal issue exists in the case. However, that does not make it a case that "arises under" the laws of the United States. Jurisdiction is determined by looking at the plaintiff's complaint, to

determine if he seeks recovery under federal law. See Chapter 4, pp. 61-63. The Mottleys did not. The only difference between this hypo and *Mottley* is that in the hypo we *know* the railroad relies on a federal defense at the time when removal is sought. But it is a defense, nonetheless, and it does not convert the Mottleys' contract action into a federal question case. Because the federal issue does not arise on the face of the well-pleaded complaint, there is no original federal jurisdiction. Since there is no original jurisdiction, the case cannot be removed.

A number of commentators have suggested that this rule, like *Mottley* itself, makes little sense because the assertion of the federal defense clearly indicates that the case involves federal issues. See, e.g., American Law Institute, Study of the Division of Jurisdiction Between State and Federal Courts §1312(a)(2) and accompanying commentary (1969) (suggesting legislation to authorize removal in such cases).

Some Refinements

7. The answer to this example depends on the meaning of §1441(a), which provides that the "defendant or defendants" may remove. Although it is not a foregone conclusion from the language of the statute, the courts have held that the alternative reference to the "defendants" means that, in a multi-defendant case, all defendants must agree to remove. See *Chicago, Rock Island & Pacific Railway Co. v. Martin,* 178 U.S. 245 (1900); *Tri-Cities Newspapers, Inc. v. Tri-Cities Printing Pressman and Assistants' Local 349,* 427 F.2d 325, 326-327 (5th Cir. 1970). Since Hickok will not agree, Carson will be stuck in state court, even though he may be subject to prejudice as an out-of-stater. While this is a reasonable interpretation of the statute, it prevents removal in cases in which the policy underlying diversity jurisdiction would support it.

8. Again, removal jurisdiction turns on original jurisdiction. In this example, there was no original federal jurisdiction over the case when it was filed; the claim was based on state law and was between nondiverse parties. However, once Earp amends to assert a federal claim, the case looks different. Earp is now relying on federal law as a basis for relief. If the case had been brought in this amended form initially, it would have been removable as a federal question case with a supplemental state law claim.

The removal statute specifically provides for removal in cases like this, when the case becomes removable after the filing of the original complaint. See 28 U.S.C. §1446(b), second paragraph, which gives the defendant 30 days from the amendment to file a notice of removal. This approach is clearly necessary; otherwise plaintiffs could avoid removal by suing in state court on a state law theory alone and later amending to assert their federal claims.

Once Earp's case is removed, both the federal claim and the related state assault claim will be heard in the federal court. If the combined action had been brought originally in federal court, the court could have heard the state law claim under principles of supplemental jurisdiction. See Chapter 15, example 1. Consequently, the court may also do so in a removed action.

9.   Whatever answer you come up with for this example is troubling. By adding a Kansas defendant after removal, Earp has "destroyed diversity." If he had started this case in federal court and later added James, the court would have dismissed for lack of subject matter jurisdiction. *Owen Equipment & Erection Co v. Kroger*, 437 U.S. 365, 373-374 (1978). On the other hand, if Earp can win a remand by this device after Bean removes, it allows Earp to defeat the right to removal by his subsequent choice of defendants, a choice he was not inclined to make until the defendant invoked the removal jurisdiction.

Because the addition of the nondiverse party destroys the basis for subject matter jurisdiction, the court will have to remand the case if it allows the amendment. In some cases, when the amendment was apparently offered for the sole purpose of defeating removal, courts have simply refused to allow the amendment, thus preserving diversity jurisdiction. *Boyd v. Diebold, Inc.*, 97 F.R.D. 720, 722-723 (E.D. Mich. 1983). In other cases, however, in which the nondiverse party was added in good faith for independent reasons (such as efficiency or belated discovery of a claim against the added party), courts have allowed the amendment and then remanded the case to state court under 28 U.S.C. §1447(c). See, e.g., *McIntyre v. Codman & Shurtleff, Inc.*, 103 F.R.D. 619, 621-623 (S.D.N.Y. 1984). In 1988 Congress codified this practice by adopting 28 U.S.C. §1447(e), which authorizes the court to refuse the amendment or allow it and remand the case.

10.   There is nothing improper in Earp's choice here. It will work, so long as he really has colorable claims against both defendants. The joinder rules in most states allow Earp to choose to sue the defendants together. The fact that he has exercised that option in part to secure his preferred state forum is a permissible form of "forum shopping." However, were he to assert a frivolous claim against James for the sole purpose of avoiding removal, he would violate the procedural rules governing pleadings, as well as his professional responsibility as an officer of the court. In such a case, Bean could remove on the basis of diversity and argue to the federal court that James should be disregarded, since no meaningful claim is asserted against him.

11.   Here again Earp has structured his lawsuit to prevent removal by seeking damages that do not satisfy the amount-in-controversy requirement of §1332. This is permissible, even if Earp could have sought higher damages. If Earp is willing to pay the price—foregoing his other $8,000 claim—to buy a state forum, he may do so. *St. Paul Indemnity Co. v. Red Cab Co.*, 303 U.S. 283, 294-295 (1938).

12.   The issue here is whether a plaintiff can remove. James could not have started in federal court because he had no basis upon which to invoke federal jurisdiction. However, if Earp had started the litigation by suing on the civil

rights claim first, James could have removed. Shouldn't James have the same right to remove, whether as the original defendant or as the "defendant" on the counterclaim? The Supreme Court says no, as a matter of statutory interpretation. Section 1441(a) authorizes removal by the "defendant or defendants." In *Shamrock Oil and Gas Corp. v. Sheets,* 313 U.S. 100 (1941), the Court concluded that only the original defendant satisfies this language, so that a plaintiff may not remove under the statute.

Unlucky Number 13

13a. Even before 1986, this case would have been removable in part. Dillon's first claim is for breach of contract. True, it is a claim for breach of a contract involving a patent, but the source of the claim is still state contract law. See *Schwartzkopf Development Corp. v. Ti-Coating, Inc.,* 800 F.2d 240, 244 (Fed. Cir. 1986) (contracts for patent royalties have consistently been held to arise under state contract law). Since the parties are diverse and the amount in controversy requirement is met, this part of the case is removable.

However, the related claim for patent infringement was barred (before 1986) by the "derivative" jurisdiction doctrine. Since Congress has made federal jurisdiction exclusive in patent cases (28 U.S.C. §1338(a)), the state court in which the claim was brought lacked jurisdiction, and the federal court could not acquire jurisdiction of the infringement claim on removal. The federal court would have to dismiss it. Then, presumably, Dillon would have moved to amend the contract action (now in federal court) to add a claim for patent infringement.

b. As the Introduction states, Congress has jettisoned the derivative jurisdiction rule by adding §1441(e), which provides that the federal court acquires jurisdiction on removal even if the state court where the case was brought lacked the power to hear it. Under §1441(e) the patent claim would be proper in the federal court, so both could proceed. Even if there were no diversity between the parties, there would be supplemental jurisdiction over the contract claim (see Chapter 15), so the federal court would have jurisdiction over the entire action.

Some Technicalities

14. The problem for Holiday here is that removal turns on original federal jurisdiction, in this case, diversity jurisdiction. The federal court only has diversity jurisdiction if more than $75,000 is in dispute, but the court can't tell from the complaint whether this prerequisite is met, and Holiday must remove within 30 days or waive his right to do so. Section 1446(a) allows the defendant in situations like this to include in his notice of removal any further allegations that are necessary to demonstrate his right to remove. Thus,

Holiday could allege in the notice that Chester's claim might support damages in excess of $75,000. Such allegations are subject to the same ethical standards as the allegations in pleadings. See §1446(a) (incorporating by reference the pleading standard in Fed. R. Civ. P. 11).

15. The smart aleck answer to this question is "yes": You can always remove, even if you have no valid ground, by filing a notice of removal, which automatically removes the action whether it is within federal jurisdiction or not. But of course it will be remanded on the plaintiff's motion if that jurisdiction is lacking.

The more meaningful answer is that Holiday's motion comes too late. If a case is removable as originally filed, the notice of removal must be filed within 30 days after the complaint is served on the defendant. 28 U.S.C. §1446(b). Although there is no way to know it from the original pleadings, this case was removable from the beginning. The system puts the burden on the defendant to *find out* if the case is within the removal jurisdiction within the 30 day period, at least where the relevant facts can be ascertained fairly easily. Holiday's plea — "But I didn't realize we were diverse!" — will probably fall on deaf ears.

This principle may not apply to the amount in controversy requirement, however. It is sometimes difficult for a defendant, at the outset of a case, to determine how much is in controversy, if the plaintiff does not allege an amount in controversy in the complaint. Consequently, some courts have held that the period for removal in such cases does not commence until the defendant receives actual notice that the required jurisdictional amount is in dispute. See, e.g., *Chapman v. Powermatic, Inc.,* 969 F.2d 160 (5th Cir. 1992).

16a. Although the state court is convinced that it alone has jurisdiction over the case, it can do nothing to help Earp. Once the case is removed, the state court loses all power over it, even if it was improperly removed. 28 U.S.C. §1446(d). The court should advise Earp to lodge his objection in the proper forum, the federal court.

b. Here, Earp has followed the proper procedure for objecting to removal: a motion in the federal court to remand the action to the state court. See 28 U.S.C. §1447(c). The federal court will hear the motion and resolve any factual issues necessary to determine its jurisdiction. If it concludes that jurisdiction is lacking, it will remand the case to state court. Note that it does not *dismiss* the case, but *remands* it. The plaintiff does not have to refile, pay a new fee, or worry about the statute of limitations, since the original suit continues its wobbly way in the state court.

17. The problem here is that §1441(a) has been interpreted to require all defendants to join in the notice of removal. See example 7. Bean has not even been informed of the suit yet. Do the other defendants have to find Bean, tell him the bad news, and convince him to join in removing the case?

Although it is not entirely clear from the statute, the cases hold that only the defendants actually served need join in the removal. See 28 U.S.C.

§1441(b) (referring to "parties in interest properly joined and served as defendants"); 14C Wright & Miller, §3731 p. 274.

18. If all defendants are served at the same time, each will have the power to prevent removal by refusing to join in the removal. In this case, however, Bean finds himself in federal court without having had the chance to forestall removal by refusing to agree to it. However, Bean may still prevent the case from being heard in federal court by moving to remand on the ground that he does not consent to removal. Cf. *Hutchins v. Priddy*, 103 F. Supp. 601, 607 (W. D. Mo. 1952) (subsequently served defendant may move to remand to state court).

Hoist with his Own Petard

19. The court should deny the motion. Masterson has fallen afoul of the *separate* thirty day period for the plaintiff to seek remand for nonjurisdictional defects in the removal. Under 28 U.S.C. s. 1447(c), a motion to remand "on the basis of any defect other than lack of subject matter jurisdiction" must be made within thirty days after the notice of removal is filed in the federal court. Because late filing of the notice of removal is a procedural defect, not a defect in subject matter jurisdiction, Masterson's failure to move to remand within thirty days waives the objection. *Wisconsin Dep't. of Corrections v. Schacht*, 524 U.S. 381, 392 (1998).

A Final, Fundamental Point

20. The motion is proper. Holiday does not waive his objection to personal jurisdiction just because he prefers to litigate in federal court. Indeed, he may have removed precisely because he believes that a federal judge will take a more objective view of the jurisdiction question. Removal does not affect Holiday's right to raise any objections or defenses he may have; it only changes the court in which they will be presented. On the other hand, had Holiday waived his personal jurisdiction objection by answering in state court before removal without raising the jurisdiction objection (compare Fed. R. Civ. P. 12(b), (g), (h)), removal would not revive it.

8

Proper Venue in Federal Courts: A Rough Measure Of Convenience

Introduction

Earlier chapters have considered personal and subject matter jurisdiction, two crucial restrictions on the forums in which a lawsuit may be brought. Frequently, these "first two rings" will dramatically limit the plaintiff's choice of forum. For example, if Jones comes to Alabama, Smith's home state, and is injured there in a collision with Smith, Jones will likely be able to obtain personal jurisdiction over Smith only in Alabama.

However, personal and subject matter jurisdiction will not always limit the plaintiff's choice of forum so significantly. Suppose, for example, that Smith travels a great deal in her work, so that she could be personally served with process in other states. Under *Burnham v. Superior Court of California*, 495 U.S. 604 (1990), such personal service in another state — say Illinois or Oregon — would suffice to support jurisdiction in that state. And, because Smith and Jones are diverse, the federal district courts in every state would have subject matter jurisdiction. Even if they were not diverse, the broad subject matter jurisdiction of the *state* courts in every state would support jurisdiction over this ordinary tort case. Thus, if only the first two "rings" limited Jones's choice of courts, she might well be able to sue Smith in any state in the United States, quite possibly in either federal or state court in each one.

Venue rules are meant to further restrict the places where the plaintiff may choose to bring suit, to assure that suits are tried in a place that bears some sensible relationship to the claims asserted or to the parties to the action. Such venue rules form a third "ring," apart from and in addition to personal and subject matter jurisdiction, which must be satisfied (or waived) if a court is to hear a particular case. Every court system, state or federal, has venue rules, generally established by statute. State court venue provisions often provide that cases must be brought in the county where one of the parties resides or does business, where the claim arose, or where property in dispute is located. Friedenthal, Kane and Miller at §2.15.

The Basic Federal Venue Provisions

To provide an example of how venue provisions work, this chapter will focus on 28 U.S.C. §1391, the federal venue statute. Sections (a) and (b) of §1391 provide the basic options for venue in most federal cases. Section 1391(c) defines the "residence" of corporate defendants for purposes of applying sections (a) and (b) to cases involving corporations.

Section 1391(a), which governs venue in diversity cases, authorizes venue in

> (1) a judicial district where any defendant resides, if all defendants reside in the same state,
> (2) a judicial district in which a substantial part of the events or omissions giving rise to the claim occurred, or a substantial part of property that is the subject of the action is situated, or
> (3) a judicial district in which any defendant is subject to personal jurisdiction at the time the action is commenced, if there is no district in which the action may otherwise be brought.

All other cases ("a civil action wherein jurisdiction is not founded solely on diversity of citizenship") are governed by §1391(b), which provides that such cases may be brought in

> (1) a judicial district where any defendant resides, if all defendants reside in the same state,
> (2) a judicial district in which a substantial part of the events or omissions giving rise to the claim occurred, or a substantial part of property that is the subject of the action is situated, or
> (3) a judicial district in which any defendant may be found, if there is no district in which the action may otherwise be brought.

If you compare §1391(a) and (b), you will see that subsections (1) and (2) are the same in both sections. Subsection (b)(3) differs slightly from subsection (a)(3), but, as is explained below, both are very limited "fallback" provisions, which only apply in the rare case when no district is a proper venue under subsection (1) or (2).

Wouldn't it be nice if Congress would tidy up this statute, by collapsing sections (a) and (b) into a single provision, thus removing one small aggravation from the lives of bewildered first-year law students? Yes, it would be nice, but Congress hasn't, and probably won't, so let's analyze the two sections in tandem, starting with the identical provisions in subsections (a)(1) and (b)(1).

Venue Based on Individual "Residence"

Both §§1391(a)(1) and (b)(1) authorize venue in a judicial district where any defendant resides, *if they all reside in one state*. First, note that these provisions focus on judicial districts, not on states. Suppose, for example, that Sherman sues Stuart, from the Western District of Virginia, and Lee, from the Eastern District of Virginia, in a diversity case. Venue would be proper in either district, because both are from the state and §1391(a)(1) authorizes jurisdiction in such cases in any district in which a defendant resides. The same would be true if the case arose under federal law, since §1391(b)(1) parallels §1391(a)(1).

However, if Stuart was from the Southern District of California and Lee from the Central District of California, suit would not be proper in the Northern District of California under either §1391(a)(1) or (b)(1) since no defendant is from that district. This focus on districts contrasts with personal jurisdiction doctrine: A person who is subject to personal jurisdiction in a state is subject to jurisdiction *anywhere* in that state.

As in other areas of civil procedure, the venue provisions in §1391 include ambiguous terms that have required judicial interpretation. For example, the term "reside" spawned contradictory holdings under earlier versions of the venue statute. Some courts held that an individual defendant "resided" only in the state of her domicile. Others, however, concluded that a person could "reside" for venue purposes in several districts if she maintained residences in more than one, even though she could only have one domicile for diversity purposes. The weight of authority appears to equate an individual's "residence" for venue purposes with domicile (see, e.g., *Lee v. Hunt*, 410 F. Supp. 329, 332 (M.D. La. 1976)), but the issue is not clearly resolved.[1]

Assuming that an individual defendant's "residence" under §1391 is her "domicile," she will be deemed to reside only in the district where she actually lives. If Greeley lives in Manhattan, she will "reside" only in the Southern District of New York for venue purposes, even though the state of New York has three other federal districts.

---

1. Professor Wright suggests that the drafters used the term "reside" instead of "domicile" because the venue statute restricts suit to the *district* in which the party is domiciled; Congress used "reside" to avoid awkward references to parties as "citizens" or "domiciliaries" of a district. Wright, 5th ed. at 263.

Venue Based on Events or Omissions Giving Rise to the Claim

Prior to 1990, §§1391(a) and (b) authorized venue in the judicial district "where the claim arose." This created interpretive problems in cases involving activities in a number of states. For example, an action for violation of the federal tradmark laws might involve: 1) a decision made in one state to market the goods in violation of the trademark; 2) sales of the goods by the defendant in several states; and 3) harm to the plaintiff's business in other states where it manufactured goods or had its headquarters. The Supreme Court never established a single test for where a claim "arose" in such cases.

In 1990, Congress amended §1391 to substitute the current language in §§1391(a)(2) and (b)(2) for the "where-the-claim-arose" formula. Under these new subsections, venue is proper in a judicial district in which "a substantial part of the events or omissions giving rise to the claim occurred, or a substantial part of property that is the subject of the action is situated." Although there will certainly be close questions as to what constitutes a "substantial part" of the relevant events, these provisions will often authorize venue for a particular suit in several districts. In the trademark example above, this language would presumably authorize venue in the district where the decision to market the infringing product was made and in any district where the product was sold. See *Pilates, Inc. v. Pilates Institute, Inc.*, 891 F. Supp. 175, 182-183 (S.D.N.Y. 1995). In a products liability case, this language would likely authorize venue in both the district where the product was manufactured and the district where it caused injury. This is a perfectly sensible result. The purpose of this venue provision is to assure a relation between the underlying events that are litigated and the place where the case is tried. Such a relation will exist in each of the districts where significant events involved in the case took place.

The "Fallback" Provisions in Section 1391

Both §1391(a) and §1391(b) contain a third subsection, which authorizes an additional basis for venue in certain cases. Section 1391(a)(3) authorizes venue in "a judicial district in which any defendant is subject to personal jurisdiction at the time the action is commenced, if there is no district in which the action may otherwise be brought." Section 1391(b)(3) authorizes venue in "a judicial district in which any defendant may be found, if there is no district in which the action may otherwise be brought." These two subsections are similar, but not the same: (a)(3) allows venue in a district where any defendant is subject to personal jurisdiction, while (b)(3) authorizes venue in a district where any defendant may be "found."

It is unclear what it means for a defendant to be "found" in a district. An individual defendant is probably "found" in a district if she is served with process there, but something less, such as being subject to personal jurisdiction in the district, may also suffice. Nor is it clear how a corporate defendant may be "found" in a district, or whether it is "found" in any district where it would be subject to personal jurisdiction for the plaintiff's claim. The quirks and quiddities of these provisions are more readily explained as historical accidents than as logical distinctions.

One thing, however, *is* clear, and luckily it is the most important thing: Both of these subsections are "fallback" provisions that only apply if there is *no* district, *anywhere in the United States,* which would be a proper venue under either of the first two subsections. Let's consider an example to illustrate the point: Suppose that Stuart, from California, brings a diversity action against Sheridan, from Colorado, and Hooker, from Ohio, for an accident that took place in Illinois. No district will be a proper venue under §1391(a)(1) because the defendants do not reside in a single state. However, there will be at least one proper venue under §1391(a)(2): the district within Illinois in which the accident occurred, since a substantial part of the events giving rise to the suit took place in that district. Because there is a proper venue under one of the first two subsections, Stuart cannot invoke §1391(a)(3).

If Stuart's accident had taken place in Canada, he could try to lay venue under subsection (3), since on these facts there would be no proper venue under either §1391(a)(1) or (a)(2). However, to find a proper venue under subsection (3), he would have to find a district in which either Sheridan or Hooker was subject to personal jurisdiction.[2]

Three Other Important Points

Three other aspects of venue analysis should be noted. First, venue, like personal jurisdiction, is considered a personal privilege of the defendant, which may be waived. See *Neirbo Co. v. Bethlehem Shipbuilding Corp.,* 308 U.S. 165, 168 (1939). Under the Federal Rules of Civil Procedure, the defendant waives her objection to venue by failing to raise it when she responds to the plaintiff's complaint. See Fed. R. Civ. P. 12(b), (g), (h); Chapter 18, pp. 315-316. Parties may even agree in advance to a particular venue for suits that may arise between them. Many contracts contain such "forum selection clauses," and these have generally been held enforceable in the federal courts, even if they lay venue in a district that

---

2. Presumably, this means a district in which a defendant is subject to personal jurisdiction *for this claim*. It hardly seems likely that Congress meant to authorize venue in a district simply because a defendant could be sued there for some unrelated claim.

would not be proper under §1391. See *Carnival Cruise Lines, Inc. v. Shute*, 498 U.S. 807 (1991) (upholding forum selection clause in absence of showing of unfairness).

Second, §§1391(a) and (b) are general venue provisions that apply to diversity and other federal cases "except as otherwise provided by law." An important caveat is in order based on this exception: Specialized venue provisions govern many types of claims that appear to be covered by §§1391(a) and (b). For example, one would reasonably conclude from §1391(b) that patent infringement claims, which arise under federal law, may be brought wherever the defendant resides or wherever events giving rise to the claim occurred. Not so; lurking elsewhere in the Code is 28 U.S.C. §1400(b), which restricts venue in patent infringement actions to the district where the defendant resides or where she committed acts of infringement *and* has a regular and established place of business. Special venue provisions also govern copyright suits, interpleader actions, and actions against federal officials. See generally 15 Wright and Miller §§3810-3825. There is no way to guard against such pitfalls other than a careful search of the statutes prior to bringing suit.[3]

Finally, you should be aware of another exception to the general venue statute for so-called "local actions." From the early days of the common law, courts have treated certain actions relating to interests in land as "local actions," which must be prosecuted in the county or district in which the land is located. See generally L. Teply and R. Whitten, Civil Procedure 312-319 (2d ed. 2000). Although there is no explicit exception in §1391 for such cases, the federal courts continue to distinguish between "transitory actions" (the vast majority of suits that are not "local" and may be brought in any venue that is proper under the statute) and local actions, which still must be brought in the district where the land is located.

Although these federal venue provisions seem daunting at first, they basically require in most cases that the defendants must be sued in a district where they reside or where important events relevant to the suit took place. In at least a rough way, these provisions assure some reasonable connection between the court where suit may be brought and the suit itself. The first set of examples below considers venue in cases involving individual defendants. Then, after an introductory discussion of §1391(c), a second set deals with venue in cases brought against corporate defendants. In considering the examples, assume that all actions are brought in federal court, that the

---

3. Similar traps for the unwary may await the state court plaintiff. In Massachusetts, for example, there is a general venue statute, Mass. Gen. L. ch. 223, §1, analogous to 28 U.S.C. §1391, but an ancient venue statute provides that an action in replevin "shall be brought in the county where the goods or beasts are detained." Mass. Gen. L. ch. 223, §4.

amount-in-controversy requirement is met where it is relevant, and that no special venue statute or local action rule applies.

EXAMPLES

The Basic Venue Provisions

1. Grant, who lives in the Northern District of Ohio, sues Lee, who lives in the Eastern District of Virginia and has his architectural office there, for breach of a contract to design a building. Grant claims that Lee agreed, after extensive negotiations in the Northern District of Ohio, to design a building to be built in Nashville, in the Middle District of Tennessee. Subsequently, however, Lee refused to follow through on the contract. In which of the following districts would venue be proper?
    a. The Eastern District of Virginia?
    b. The Western District of Virginia?
    c. The Middle District of Tennessee?
    d. The Northern District of Ohio?

2. Grant sues Lee and Stuart, Lee's partner who lives in the Western District of Virginia. What venues in Virginia are proper?

3. Assume that Grant sues Lee and Longstreet (from the District of South Carolina) for breach of contract. Longstreet, an engineer, had represented to Lee (in a conversation that took place at Longstreet's Charleston, South Carolina, office) that he would do the mechanical engineering on the building for a certain price but then backed out. Lee then recalculated the cost of doing the job with the higher engineering costs and decided to renege on his contract with Grant. In which of the following districts would venue be proper?
    a. The Eastern District of Virginia?
    b. The Western District of Virginia?
    c. The Middle District of Tennessee?
    d. The Northern District of Ohio?

4. On the facts of example 3, assume that Grant also asserts a federal question claim against Lee. How would this affect the available venues?

5. Assume that venue is improper in Grant's case against Lee, but Lee does not raise an objection. May the judge dismiss the case sua sponte (on her own initiative, without a request to do so by the parties)?

Fallback Fallout

6. Reconsider the example in the Introduction, in which Stuart, from California, wants to bring a diversity action against Sheridan, from Colorado, and Hooker, from Ohio, for an accident that took place in Canada. Assume that Hooker lives in the Northern District of Ohio, and Stuart sues Hooker and Sheridan in that district. Is venue proper?

Venue in Cases Involving Corporations

Although the basic venue statutes can be seriously confusing, the real topper is 28 U.S.C. §1391(c), concerning venue in cases involving corporate defendants:

> For purposes of venue under this chapter, a defendant that is a corporation shall be deemed to reside in any judicial district in which it is subject to personal jurisdiction at the time the action is commenced. In a State which has more than one judicial district and in which a defendant that is a corporation is subject to personal jurisdiction at the time an action is commenced, such corporation shall be deemed to reside in any district in that State within which its contacts would be sufficient to subject it to personal jurisdiction if that district were a separate State, and if there is no such district the corporation shall be deemed to reside in the district within which it has the most significant contacts.

This is formidable language, but on closer examination it is not really as bad as it seems.

First, to clear away a little underbrush, note that §1391(c) applies only to corporate defendants. It says nothing about cases in which corporations bring suit as plaintiffs. Because §1391(c) does not apply, venue in such cases is governed by the basic venue provisions in §§1391(a) and (b).

Second, it is crucial to understand that §1391(c) is not a separate, exclusive provision governing venue in cases against corporations. All it does is define corporate "residence" for purposes of applying §§1391(a)(1) and (b)(1). Thus, it is proper to lay venue in a case against a corporation, for example, in a district where a substantial part of the events giving rise to the claim took place, under §§1391(a)(2) or (b)(2). Section 1391(c) is irrelevant in applying these subsections because venue under those provisions does not depend on where the corporation "resides."

If, however, the plaintiff wants to lay venue in the district where a corporate defendant "resides," under either §§1391(a)(1) or (b)(1), she must look to §1391(c) to determine where the corporation resides. Section 1391(c) defines corporate "residence" as any district in which the corporation is subject to personal jurisdiction. Suppose, for example, that Mead sues Jackson Corporation for breach of a contract that the parties made and performed in South Carolina (which only has one district, the District of South Carolina). If Mead bases venue on Jackson's residence under §1391(a)(1), he must refer to §1391(c) to determine where Jackson "resides." Under that section, it "resides" in the District of South Carolina because it would be subject to personal jurisdiction there based on the contacts of negotiating and performing the contract in South Carolina.

Jackson may also "reside" in other districts under §1391(c). For example, if it is incorporated in Delaware, the District of Delaware would be a proper venue, since corporations are subject to general in personam jurisdiction in the state where they are incorporated. Or, if Jackson has extensive production facilities in the District of Maryland, it will be subject to general in personam jurisdiction there (see Chapter 1, pp. 5-7), and thus "resides" there as well under §1391(c). Consequently, it may be sued in those districts in a diversity case under §1391(a)(1).

The more confusing part of the new §1391(c) is the second sentence, which applies this concept of corporate "residence" to states with more than one judicial district.

> In a state which has more than one judicial district and in which a defendant that is a corporation is subject to personal jurisdiction at the time an action is commenced, such corporation shall be deemed to reside in any district in that State within which its contacts would be sufficient to subject it to personal jurisdiction if that district were a separate state. . . .

Suppose, for example, that Jackson Corporation negotiated and breached the contract with Mead in Richmond, Virginia, but has no other contacts with Virginia. As Figure 8-1 shows, Virginia is divided into an Eastern District and a Western District, and Richmond is in the Eastern District of Virginia. Under §§1391(a)(1) and (c), venue would be proper in the Eastern District of Virginia: If the Eastern District were a separate state, Jackson's contacts in that district—negotiating and breaching the contract with Mead—would support personal jurisdiction there for this lawsuit under the minimum contacts test. Consequently, Jackson "resides" there under §§1391(a)(1) and (c). However, there would not be jurisdiction over Jackson in the Western District, if it were a separate state, since the corporation has no contacts in the Western District. Therefore, the Western District would not be a proper venue under §§1391(a)(1) and (c).

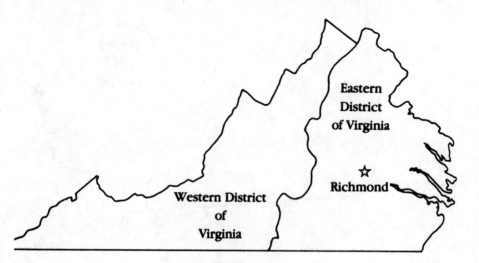

Figure 8-1

Now, suppose that Jackson has a permanent production facility in Atlanta, Georgia, but no other contacts with Georgia. As Figure 8-2 shows, Georgia has three districts. Jackson would be subject to personal jurisdiction in the Northern District of Georgia since, if that district were treated as a separate state, Jackson's Atlanta facility would support general in personam jurisdiction over it there. Thus, Jackson "resides" there under §1391(a)(1) and the Northern District is a proper venue. However, because Jackson has no contacts in the Middle or the Southern District of Georgia, venue would not be proper in either of those districts under §§1391(a)(1) and (c). Got that?!

Figure 8-2

EXAMPLES

Applying §1391(c)

7.   Mead, who lives and works in the Northern District of Ohio, sues Dixie Corporation for a libelous statement made about him by an officer of the corporation. Dixie is incorporated in Maryland and has large factories in Atlanta, Georgia (in the Northern District of Georgia), and Nashville, Tennessee (in the Middle District of Tennessee). The statement about Mead was made in Philadelphia, in the Eastern District of Pennsylvania. As a result of the statement, Mead was fired from his job.

   If Mead sues Dixie, which of the following districts would be proper venues?
   a. The District of Maryland?
   b. The Middle District of Tennessee?
   c. The Southern District of Georgia?
   d. The Eastern District of Pennsylvania?
   e. The Northern District of Ohio?

8.   On the same facts, suppose Mead sues both Dixie and Calhoun, the officer who made the statement. Calhoun lives in Atlanta. Which of the following districts is a proper venue?
   a. The Northern District of Georgia?
   b. The Southern District of Georgia?
   c. The Eastern District of Pennsylvania?
   d. The Middle District of Tennessee?

9.   Suppose that Dixie Corporation sues Mead for a violation of the federal trademark laws, arising from Mead's distribution throughout Ohio of products bearing the Dixie logo. What venues are proper? (Ohio has two districts, the Northern and Southern.)

10. Consider the facts of *World-Wide Volkswagen Corp. v. Woodson*, 444 U.S. 286 (1980), in which the Robinsons were injured when an Audi they bought from Seaway in New York exploded while driving across Oklahoma. Assuming that Seaway is a New York corporation doing business only in the Northern District of New York, and that the Robinsons sued Seaway based on diversity, can you think of a district in which venue would be proper but personal jurisdiction would not?

Unlucky Number Eleven

11. Sumner, from Massachusetts, sues Davis, from Louisiana, in Massachusetts Superior Court, for an allegedly libelous statement Davis made in Louisiana. He bases venue on a statute authorizing venue in the county where the plaintiff resides. He gets jurisdiction over Davis by serving him with process in Massachusetts while he is there at a convention. Davis removes to the federal

district court for the District of Massachusetts, and then files a motion to dismiss for improper venue, claiming that the District of Massachusetts is not a proper venue under §1391. Should the motion be granted?

EXPLANATIONS

The Basic Venue Provisions

1a.   Because this is a diversity case, §1391(a) prescribes the proper venues. Under §1391(a)(1) the Eastern District of Virginia is proper, since "a defendant" resides there and all defendants (Lee only) are from the same state. The Eastern District of Virginia would presumably be a proper venue under §1391(a)(2) as well, on the ground that Lee's "omission" to design the building took place there.

b.   The Western District of Virginia is not a proper venue under §1391(a), since Lee doesn't "reside" there and none of the relevant events took place there. It is true that the concept of "residence" in the venue statute is generally equated with domicile and that Lee is domiciled in the *state* of Virginia. But for venue purposes, the term "reside" refers to the district within the state in which Lee actually has his domicile, that is, where he actually lives.

The Western District of Virginia is not a proper venue under §1391(a)(3), even though Lee would be subject to personal jurisdiction there based on his domicile in the state. Section 1391(a)(3) does not apply to this case, since it is a fallback provision that only applies if there is "no district where the action may otherwise be brought." Here, there are several other proper venues for Grant's suit, so §1391(a)(3) is irrelevant.

c.   The only potential basis for venue in the Middle District of Tennessee is that the building was to be constructed there. Lee might be subject to venue in that district if he was to render services at the site during construction, since he "omitted" (see §1391(a)(2)) to render those services there. However, if he was solely to provide design services in Virginia, this provision would not support venue in the Middle District of Tennessee.

d.   The Northern District of Ohio may be a proper venue under §1391(a)(2) on the ground that "a substantial part of the events or omissions giving rise to the claim occurred" there. The courts will have to decide whether the negotiations that took place in the Northern District "gave rise to the claim." Arguably, the claim arose from the failure to follow through on the agreement rather than the contract formation. However, given the purpose of venue provisions — to site the litigation in a place with a substantial connection to the case — the court may well take the more flexible view of this phrase and conclude that venue is proper where the parties negotiated the contract.

2.   On these facts either district in Virginia is a proper venue under §1391(a)(1), since all defendants reside in the same state and one of the defendants ("any defendant") resides in each district.

3a. This is also a diversity case, so §1391(a) applies. Subsection (1) authorizes venue in a judicial district where any defendant resides, if they all reside in the same state. Here, they don't, so §1391(a)(1) is no help.

But how about §1391(a)(2), which makes a district a proper venue if "a substantial part of the events or omissions giving rise to the claim" occurred there? If Lee did his recalculations and decided to back out of the deal at his office in the Eastern District, this language in §1391(a)(2) is apparently satisfied, even though Longstreet was not involved in that "event." Of course, there would still have to be personal jurisdiction over Longstreet in Virginia, under the three-ring analysis, before suit could be brought against him there.

b. Venue is not proper in the Western District of Virginia. All defendants are not from the same state, so §1391(a)(1) does not apply. Nor does §1391(a)(2) apply, since none of the relevant events took place there. Finally, §1391(a)(3) does not apply, since there will be at least one proper venue under §1391(a)(2).

c. Once again, venue would only be proper in the Middle District of Tennessee if Lee omitted to render substantial services there. If he did, venue is proper there under §1391(a)(2), even though it was *Lee's* omission, not Longstreet's, that took place there: The standard in §1391(a)(2) apparently focuses on the events or omissions giving rise to the claim, not the acts or omissions of each individual defendant. But see *Kaplan v. Reed*, 28 F. Supp. 2d 1191 (D. Colo. 1998) (venue improper under s. 1391(b)(2) as to those defendants who did not engage in "events" in the forum district). Here again, however, Grant would have problems with personal jurisdiction over Longstreet.

d. The Northern District of Ohio would probably be a proper venue under §1391(a)(2), based on the extensive negotiations between Grant and Lee there. Note again that, even though venue is proper there, Grant will probably not be able to satisfy the personal jurisdiction "ring" as to Longstreet in Ohio, since Longstreet dealt only with Lee, and did so in Virginia rather than Ohio.

4. Because Grant has asserted a federal claim against one of the defendants, the case is "not founded solely on diversity of citizenship." Consequently, §1391(b) applies rather than §1391(a). However, this doesn't provide any additional venue options in this case. Subsections (1) and (2) are the same in sections (a) and (b), and §1391(b)(3), which authorizes venue in a district where any defendant may be "found," does not apply because there are other districts that are proper venues under the first two subdivisions of §1391(b). This "catch-all" provision, like §1391(a)(3), is apparently included to assure that there will be *some* proper venue in federal question cases, even if the events giving rise to the claim took place outside the United States. It does not apply unless no federal district is a proper venue under subsection (1) or subsection (2).

5.   Several cases have held that it is improper for the court to dismiss an action sua sponte for improper venue, since venue is a privilege of the defendant, which she may waive. See, e.g., *Concession Consultants, Inc. v. Mirisch*, 355 F.2d 369, 371 (2d Cir. 1966); see also 15 Wright and Miller at §3826 (p. 257). However, the court ought to have some control over inappropriate venue choices even if the parties are satisfied. The purpose of venue statutes is not only to prevent inconvenience to defendants, but also to allocate judicial business to courts with some connection to the case. See *Gulf Oil Corp. v. Gilbert*, 330 U.S. 501, 508-509 (1947) (listing various private interests and public interests that may make a court an inappropriate venue). The public interest may suggest that a particular venue is inappropriate even if the parties are willing to litigate there. However, this public interest may be protected by 28 U.S.C. §1404(a), which authorizes a court to transfer cases to other districts when justice so requires.

Fallback Fallout

6.   In this case, venue cannot be based on s. 1391(a)(1), since the defendants do not reside in the same state. Nor is s. 1391(a)(2) satisfied in any judicial district, since the events giving rise to the suit did not take place in any judicial district in the county. Thus, it is appropriate to look to the "fallback" provision, s. 1391(a)(3), which authorizes venue in a district where "any defendant is subject to personal jurisdiction at the time the action is commenced, if there is no district in which the action may otherwise be brought." This "fallback" venue provision is satisfied, since Hooker is subject to personal jurisdiction in Ohio.

This satisfies the venue requirement, but of course Stuart still faces the problem that Sheridan is *not* subject to personal jurisdiction in Ohio. Proper venue is a separate, additional requirement along with personal jurisdiction. If, however, Sheridan waived her objection to personal jurisdiction or was served with process while in Ohio, the suit could proceed.

Applying §1391(c)

7a. This is a diversity case, so venue is governed by §1391(a). Under that section, venue is proper in a district where the defendant resides (§1391(a)(1)) or in a district where events giving rise to the claim took place. Section 1391(a)(2). A corporation's "residence" is defined by §1391(c) to include any district in which it would be subject to personal jurisdiction. Because corporations are subject to general in personam jurisdiction in the state where they are incorporated, Dixie would be subject to jurisdiction in the District of Maryland (which encompasses the entire state of Maryland). Thus, it is a proper venue.

Note that this analysis makes the District of Maryland a proper venue even though the case does not arise out of events that took place there. But

venue provisions often lay venue where the defendant has important connections, such as a residence or a place of business, even if the claim arose
somewhere else. Thus, it is not anomalous that the place of incorporation is
a proper venue under §1391(c).

b. Once again, venue will be proper under §1391(a)(1) if Dixie "resides" in the Middle District of Tennessee. And again, §1391(c) provides
that Dixie resides in any district in which its contacts would subject it to personal jurisdiction. Here, Dixie is probably subject to general in personam jurisdiction in the district based on its large factory there. Thus, the Middle
District of Tennessee is a proper venue.

c. Dixie does not "reside" in the Southern District of Georgia under
§1391(c). True, Dixie is probably subject to personal jurisdiction throughout Georgia because of its large factory in Atlanta. But, under §1391(c),
Dixie is only deemed to "reside" in those districts within a state in which its
contacts would support jurisdiction if the district were a state. Thus, since
Georgia is a multi-district state, we must look at the contacts Dixie has with
each district, not at its contacts with the state as a whole. Here, Dixie has no
contacts with the Southern District of Georgia. If that district were a state,
Dixie would not be subject to personal jurisdiction in it for this claim. Thus,
it does not "reside" there under §1391(c), even though it has substantial and
continuous contacts with another district within the state.

d. The Eastern District of Pennsylvania is a proper venue on several
grounds. First, venue is proper there under §1391(a)(2), since a substantial
part of the events giving rise to the claim took place there. Second, venue is
proper under §1391(a)(1), since the corporation "resides" (so says §1391(c))
in any district where its contacts would support personal jurisdiction. Here,
Dixie would be subject to personal jurisdiction in the Eastern District of
Pennsylvania because its officer made the libelous statement there.

e. It is not clear whether the Northern District of Ohio is a proper
venue under s. 1391(a)(2). Although the venue statute used to allow venue
in a diversity case in the district where the plaintiff resides, it no longer does,
so Mead's residence in the Northern District won't support venue. The
other possible basis is that "a substantial part of the events or omissions giving rise to the claim" took place in the district, since Mead lost his job there
because of the statements. This will be an important interpretive question
under §1391(a)(2): whether a district in which the plaintiff sustains damages
as a result of the defendant's acts qualifies as "a judicial district in which a
substantial part of the events or omissions giving rise to the claim occurred."
28 U.S.C. §1391(a)(2). It seems likely that the courts will hold that a district where the plaintiff suffers substantial injury from the defendant's acts
satisfies this language.

8a. Section 1391(a)(1) authorizes venue where any defendant resides, if
they both reside in the same state. Calhoun resides in Georgia, as does Dixie,
as "residence" is defined for corporations in §1391(c). Thus, any district in

Georgia in which either defendant resides is a proper venue. Because they both "reside" in the Northern District of Georgia, that is a proper venue.

b. Although both defendants "reside" in Georgia, neither resides in the Southern District of Georgia. Consequently, it is not a proper venue under §1391(a)(1).

c. The Eastern District of Pennsylvania is a proper venue under §1391(a)(2), since a substantial part of the events giving rise to the claim took place there. Again, note that §1391(c) is irrelevant to this analysis, since it only defines the term "reside" for purposes of §1391(a)(1).

d. Here's one where the drafting of the statute may have gone awry. If you read s. 1391(a)(1) literally, venue would be proper in the Middle District of Tennessee: That section allows venue in a district where any defendant resides, if they both reside in the same state. Dixie and Calhoun do reside in the same state: they both reside in the Northern District of Georgia. So, venue is proper in a district where either resides. Dixie "resides" in the Middle District of Tennessee, under s. 1391(c), because it would be subject to personal jurisdiction there. So, the Middle District of Tennessee is a proper venue under s. 1391(a)(1)!

While this textual logic is unimpeachable, the evident purpose of s. 1391(a)(1) is to authorize venue in the state where both defendants reside — Georgia in this example. In light of this purpose, it seems likely that the courts won't read the statute literally, but confine venue to the state where both defendants reside. For a case rejecting this "clever" argument, see *Di Filippo v. Sherenian*, 1996 U.S. Dist. Lexis 1372.

9.   In this case Dixie is the plaintiff, so section 1391(c) does not apply. In addition, the claim is not based "solely on diversity," so §1391(b) applies. Venue is proper where Mead resides, in the Northern District, or in the districts where a substantial part of the events giving rise to the claim took place. Because the goods were distributed throughout Ohio, this would include both the Northern and the Southern districts.

By the way, trademark cases deal with a fairly specialized type of federal issue; perhaps Congress has seen fit to provide a specialized venue statute for them, as it has for copyrights and patents. In practice, you should be ever so careful to take a look for this. I took a quick look and didn't find a specialized venue statute for trademark cases, so I guess §1391 applies. If you bring a trademark case, look more carefully than I did.

10.   This one is easy. Venue would be proper in the district within Oklahoma in which the accident occurred, under §1391(a)(2), since a "substantial part of the events giving rise to the claim" took place there. But the Supreme Court held in *World-Wide* that the Oklahoma court did not have personal jurisdiction over Seaway. Of course, without jurisdiction over Seaway, the plaintiffs will take little advantage from the fact that another ring, venue, is satisfied.

Unlucky Number Eleven

11. The motion should be denied. Sumner brought suit in state court and chose one which was a proper venue under state law. Removal allows Davis to get the case out of the state court and into federal court, but it does not provide a means of avoiding trial in a state where suit was properly brought under the state rules.

Put another way, 28 U.S.C. s. 1391, the federal venue statute, does not apply to cases removed to federal court: it only applies to cases *commenced* in federal court. The proper "venue" for a removed action is "the district court of the United States for the district and division embracing the place where such [state court] action is pending." 28 U.S.C. s. 1441(a). Thus, the proper venue for Sumner's removed action is the District of Massachusetts and only the District of Massachusetts.

If defendants could do what Davis has tried to do here, it would give them a powerful means of avoiding trial in a state where they had properly been sued under state venue rules. Removal is meant to provide a federal forum only, not a means of avoiding the state in which the plaintiff has permissibly chosen to litigate.[4]

---

4. Once the case is in federal court, Davis could move for a change of venue under 28 U.S.C. §1404(a), and try to avoid Sumner's forum choice that way. However, this option is not radically different from his right to move in the state court for a forum non conveniens dismissal.

9

Choosing a Proper Court: The Three Rings Reconsidered

Introduction

A major purpose of this book is to introduce procedural concepts, such as personal jurisdiction, subject matter jurisdiction, and venue, and to illustrate their operation through a variety of examples. However, an equally important goal is to help you to see the interrelatedness of things, to explore how these procedural doctrines interact to form a rather elegant system for adjudication of law suits. This chapter reconsiders the three rings analyzed in earlier chapters in order to emphasize how these separate constraints operate together to circumscribe the plaintiff's choice of a proper forum.

As a preliminary matter it is important to reemphasize that all three of these prerequisites must be satisfied in order to bring suit in a particular forum. It is no answer to an objection to personal jurisdiction that diversity (or some other basis for subject matter jurisdiction) is present or that the venue provisions of 28 U.S.C. §1391 are satisfied. Each of the three doctrines has a different legal source, serves a distinct purpose, and employs a different standard. The limits on federal subject matter jurisdiction are found in Article III, §2, of the Constitution, which authorizes federal jurisdiction over certain limited types of cases. Personal jurisdiction, on the other hand, arises from due process limitations in the fourteenth amendment and limits the power of states to require out-of-state defendants to defend suits in their courts. The third ring, venue, does not have a constitutional source: It is a statutory limit that imposes separate constraints on the place of trial to protect parties from inconvenient litigation.

While the three rings are distinct, the potential for confusing them is great because the standards that govern personal jurisdiction, subject matter jurisdiction, and venue are closely related. For example, the concept of domicile may be relevant to analysis of all three rings. Courts use domicile to determine the state citizenship of individuals (that is, natural persons) under 28 U.S.C. §1332(a)(1), the basic diversity provision. Domicile in the forum state is also a proper basis for exercising personal jurisdiction over an individual defendant. *Milliken v. Meyer,* 311 U.S. 457 (1940). Finally, domicile is relevant (with a twist) to venue because most courts have held that an individual "resides" under the venue statute in the judicial district where he is domiciled. Wright at 263. (The "twist" is that venue is only proper in the particular district within the state in which the individual has his domicile, not in the entire state.)

The concept of domicile, in the traditional common law sense of a place of residence where one intends to remain indefinitely, does not apply to corporations because they cannot have intent in the same sense that individuals do. However, the analogous doctrines of corporate citizenship or presence within the state are also relevant to all three rings. For the purpose of establishing subject matter jurisdiction on the basis of diversity, a corporation is deemed to be a "citizen" of the state of its principal place of business, as well as the state where it is incorporated. 28 U.S.C. §1332(c)(1). To establish personal jurisdiction over corporations, however, the courts invoke the separate but confusingly similar concept of general in personam jurisdiction. Under general in personam jurisdiction analysis, a corporation is subject to personal jurisdiction in states in which it conducts substantial and continuous business activities. See Chapter 1, pp. 5-7. The state in which a corporation is incorporated and the state of its principal place of business would almost certainly satisfy this standard, but other states may satisfy it as well.

For example, a major airline would be subject to general in personam jurisdiction in many states, due to the volume of flights it operates from those states and the facilities and employees it maintains there. Yet only one state will be its "principal place of business" for diversity purposes under 28 U.S.C. §1332(c)(1). Thus, both of these related inquiries consider the amount of business activity in the state, but the two standards do differ, and the states that meet the standards will overlap but may not be exactly the same.

Venue in suits against corporations requires yet another related analysis. Under 28 U.S.C. §1391(a)(1) or (b)(1), venue will lie in any judicial district in which a defendant "resides," if all defendants reside in the same state. For individuals, residence for venue purposes is generally equated with domicile, but, as explained above, corporations do not have a domicile in the common law sense of the term. Instead, corporate "residence" for venue purposes is defined in the venue statute. 28 U.S.C. §1391(c). Under §1391(c), a corporate defendant resides for venue purposes in any judicial district in which its contacts would suffice to support personal jurisdiction.

Thus, corporate activity or presence in the district is relevant to determining venue in cases against corporate defendants, just as it is relevant to determining their state citizenship for diversity purposes and their amenability to personal jurisdiction. However, a much smaller quantum of corporate activity will satisfy the venue requirement than is needed to establish a corporation's "principal place of business" for diversity purposes, or "substantial and continuous activities" for general in personam jurisdiction. Under §1391(a)(1) and (c), for example, a district would be a proper venue based on a single act by a corporate employee in the district, if that act gave rise to the claim. Such a single act would support personal jurisdiction over the corporation for that claim, and therefore, under §1391(c), the corporation would "reside" in that district for purposes of the venue statute.

Relation of the Claim to the Forum

Another understandable source of confusion in applying the three-ring analysis is the fact that one of the rings may require a relationship between the state in which the suit is brought and the claim the plaintiff asserts, while that relationship is irrelevant to applying the other rings. Suppose, for example, that Santini, a California high-wire artist, sues Robinson Shows, Inc., a Virginia corporation with its principal place of business in Virginia. If Santini sues Robinson Shows in an Alabama federal court for a negligence claim that arose in Missouri, it is irrelevant to diversity analysis that the claim did not arise in Alabama. Diversity jurisdiction turns on a comparison of the citizenship of the parties, not on the relationship between the parties or the claim and the forum state. So long as the parties are from different states (and the amount-in-controversy requirement is met) diversity is satisfied.

Similarly, the fact that Santini's claim did not arise in Alabama may be irrelevant to the venue and personal jurisdiction analysis. If the circus does sufficient business in Alabama, it will be subject to general in personam jurisdiction there. And, if that is true, venue will be proper in the Alabama district where the business activity takes place, under 28 U.S.C. §1391(a)(1) and (c), even though the claim does not arise out of the business done in that district. For example, if Robinson does extensive business in the Southern District of Alabama, that activity would support general in personam jurisdiction over Robinson, if the Southern District were a state, even though Santini's claim did not arise there. This suffices to make that district a proper venue under §1391(a)(1) and (c).

Because venue in cases against corporations is proper where the corporation is subject to personal jurisdiction, under §1391(c), it should follow that wherever a corporation is subject to personal jurisdiction will also be a proper venue. Not quite true, unfortunately. *First,* of course, it would not suffice that it was subject to personal jurisdiction on some other claim unrelated to the case before the court. *Second,* the combination of §1391(a)(1) [or (b)(1)] and (c) authorizes venue only in the particular districts within a state where the defendant has contacts. So a corporate defendant may be subject to personal jurisdiction in a state, but some districts in that state may still be improper venues. In Santini's case, for example, the Northern District of Alabama would not be a proper venue, if Robinson Shows has no contacts in that district, even though it is subject to personal jurisdiction in Alabama.

The subtlety of these interrelations suggest that they were deliberately designed to intimidate first-year law students. However, the situation is not really so bad once you have worked with the related doctrines in the context of specific facts. The following examples will help you sort out the various rings. Assume, unless the example specifies otherwise, that the relevant long-arm statute is like California's (see supra p. 24), which authorizes the exercise of all constitutionally permissible jurisdiction and that all suits are brought in federal court.

EXAMPLES

Into the Rings

1. Barnum, a citizen of Maine, sues Ringling Brothers, Inc. for injuries suffered when Kelly, a Ringling Brothers' clown, fails to secure the door on a lion cage while the train is refueling in Bangor, Maine, and Leo, a trained lion, escapes. Ringling Brothers is incorporated in Wisconsin with its principal place of business in Manhattan, in the Southern District of New York. The circus has its winter quarters in Florida, has permanent facilities for training performers in the Northern District of Ohio, and performs for two or three weeks each year in every state on the eastern seaboard.[1]

    a. Could the suit be brought in federal district court in Maine? (Maine has only one judicial district.)

    b. Could the suit be brought in the Northern District of New York? (New York has Southern, Northern, Eastern, and Western Districts.)

    c. Could the suit be brought in any federal district court in Ohio?

    d. Could the suit be brought in any federal district court in New Jersey?

2. Barnum sues Ringling Brothers and Kelly, the clown who let the lion escape from the train. Kelly is domiciled in Florida.

    a. May Barnum sue in federal district court in Maine?

    b. May he sue in a Florida federal district court?

    c. May he sue in the Southern District of New York?

---

1. For those whose geography is rusty, the eastern seaboard states include Maine, New Hampshire, Massachusetts, Connecticut, Rhode Island, New York, New Jersey, Delaware, Maryland, Virginia, North Carolina, South Carolina, Georgia, and Florida.

3. Barnum sues Ringling Brothers and Kelly in the Eastern District of Pennsylvania for the injuries Barnum suffered in Maine. Barnum serves the summons and complaint on Kelly and on T. Thumb, General Manager of Ringling Brothers, while the circus train is stopped just west of Philadelphia to feed the animals. Is the suit proper under the three rings?

Juggling Acts

4. Suppose the circus sues Kelly, from Florida, and Rice, a Vermont citizen, for allowing Leo to escape. The circus alleges that Rice was negligent in failing to lock the cage when the train left Rutland, Vermont, and that Kelly was negligent in failing to check the lock when the train stopped to refuel in Bangor. The suit is brought in Maine.
   a. Will the Maine federal district court have subject matter jurisdiction over the action?
   b. Will the court have personal jurisdiction over the parties?
   c. Is Maine a proper venue?

5. Beatty, an Arizona citizen, sues the Bailey Circus Corporation for an injury suffered when Elmer, a willing but occasionally clumsy elephant, fell on him while Beatty was watching a circus performance in Phoenix, Arizona. When the accident occurred, in 1998, Bailey was incorporated in Delaware with its principal (and only) place of business in Phoenix. Since 1998, however, the circus has prospered. As of 2000, when suit was brought, its principal place of business was California, although it still performed extensively in Arizona as well. May Beatty bring suit in federal court in California?

Procedural Acrobatics

6. In 2000, Beatty sues the Bailey Circus and Stenk, Elmer's trainer, for the circus accident. Suit is brought in the New Mexico District Court for Guadaloupe County, the *state* court of general jurisdiction in New Mexico. Stenk is from New Mexico. Assume that the relevant New Mexico venue statute authorizes venue in the county where any defendant resides and that Stenk resides in Guadaloupe County.
   a. Is the suit properly before the state court?
   b. May the defendants remove to federal court?

A Two-Ring Circus

7. A representative of Ringling Brothers visits Adler, a retired clown who lives in Cedar Rapids, Iowa, in the Northern District of Iowa. The agent explains that the circus wishes to get Adler's permission to use a famous poster of Adler in promoting the circus, for a small royalty. Adler agrees. Ringling Brothers uses the picture in advertising in New York but does not pay Adler. Adler decides to sue Ringling Brothers for breach of contract and federal

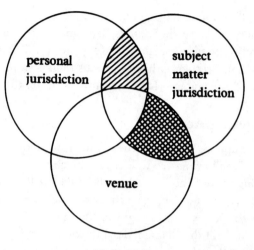

Figure 9-1

copyright infringement. (Assume, contrary to fact, that the general venue statute applies to copyright claims.)

    a. Can you think of a court or courts that would fall in the shaded area of Figure 9–1, that is, in which personal jurisdiction and subject matter jurisdiction are satisfied but venue is not? (The relevant facts concerning Ringling Brothers' business activities are found in example 1.)

    b. Assume that the contract involved was made in New York while Adler was visiting there, rather than in Iowa. Can you think of a court or courts that would fall in the hatched area of Figure 9-1, in which venue and subject matter jurisdiction are proper, but the court would not have personal jurisdiction over Ringling Brothers?

EXPLANATIONS

Into the Rings

1a. As pointed out in the Introduction, the suit may only be brought in those federal courts that satisfy all three rings of the analysis for choosing a proper court. There is clearly no problem with subject matter jurisdiction. Barnum is a Maine citizen, and Ringling Brothers is a citizen of Wisconsin (where it is incorporated) and New York (where it has its principal place of business) under 28 U.S.C. §1332(c)(1). As long as Barnum's claim is for more than $75,000 the requirements for federal subject matter jurisdiction based on diversity are met. The fact that Barnum is a citizen of the state where suit was brought is irrelevant to the diversity analysis; diversity is satisfied as long as he and Ringling Brothers are citizens of different states, regardless of which states those are.

    The Maine court will also have personal jurisdiction over Ringling Brothers in this action. The claim arises out of a negligent act by its employee, which took place in the state and caused injury in the state. The defendant's negligent in-state conduct is sufficient to support specific in personam jurisdiction under the minimum contacts test, that is, jurisdiction over a claim such as Barnum's, which arises out of the in-state act itself.

Venue is also proper in Maine. Venue in diversity cases is governed by 28 U.S.C. §1391(a), which authorizes laying venue in the district where the defendants reside (§1391(a)(1)) or where a substantial part of the events giving rise to the claim took place (§1391(a)(2)). Venue is proper in the District of Maine under either §1391(a)(1) or (a)(2). Venue would be proper under §1391(a)(1) on the ground that Ringling Brothers "resides" in Maine for venue purposes. Under 28 U.S.C. §1391(c) a corporate defendant "resides" in every district in which it is subject to personal jurisdiction. Because the circus is subject to minimum contacts jurisdiction in the District of Maine for this claim, it "resides" there under 28 U.S.C. §1391(c). Venue is also proper under §1391(a)(2), since a substantial part of the events giving rise to the claim took place in the district.

b. This case could not be brought in the Northern District of New York. The analysis of the court's subject matter jurisdiction is exactly the same as in example la. A diversity case is a diversity case is a diversity case: If the parties are from different states and the amount-in-controversy requirement is satisfied, any federal court will have subject matter jurisdiction on the basis of diversity.

Personal jurisdiction over Ringling Brothers is proper in New York because it has its principal place of business there, which in virtually every case will establish the type of substantial and continuous contacts necessary to support general in personam jurisdiction over a corporation. Be careful, however, to distinguish this personal jurisdiction analysis from the diversity analysis. For personal jurisdiction, the question is whether Ringling Brothers' activities in the state are so substantial and continuous as to make it fair to subject it to personal jurisdiction for any claim. By contrast, whether the corporation is a citizen of the state for diversity purposes turns on whether that state is the *one* state in which the corporation's business activities are centered under the various tests for determining a corporation's principal place of business. See Chapter 5, pp. 86-87.

Venue in Barnum's suit is analyzed under §1391(a), since it is a diversity case. Under §§1391(a)(1) and (c), Ringling Brothers "resides" in any New York district in which its contacts would suffice to subject it to personal jurisdiction. Once again, the analysis of the rings is similar but a little bit different. Since Ringling Brothers has contacts at its corporate offices in Manhattan, in the Southern District of New York, which would support personal jurisdiction over it (even for this claim, which arose elsewhere), venue would be proper in that district. However, the facts do not suggest that it has any contacts in the Northern District that would support jurisdiction over it there, nor did any events giving rise to the claim take place there. Nor does §1391(a)(3) apply, since it is a "fallback" provision that only applies if there is no other proper venue for the action. Since there is no basis for laying venue in the Northern District, the action may not be brought there; it comes up one ring short.

c. Suit would be proper in the Northern District of Ohio in Barnum's case. Subject matter jurisdiction is no problem since, as indicated above, the parties are just as diverse if suit is brought in Ohio as they are if suit is brought anywhere else. Note that Ringling Brothers is not a "citizen" of Ohio for diversity purposes even though it has substantial business activities there that would subject it to general in personam jurisdiction in that state.

General in personam jurisdiction would probably be proper over Ringling Brothers in Ohio because they have a substantial, continuous presence in the state, due to their permanent training facility there. Presumably, they own or rent property there and have regular employees in the state, contacts that frequently support general in personam jurisdiction.

Venue would also be proper in the Northern District of Ohio under §§1391(a)(1) and (c), since Ringling Brothers' contacts there, the permanent training facility, would suffice to subject it to general in personam jurisdiction there.

Even if Barnum has filed suit in a forum where all three rings intersect, it is still not certain that the suit will be heard there. The court has the power under 28 U.S.C. §1404(a) to transfer cases "for the convenience of parties and witnesses, in the interest of justice," including cases in which the plaintiff has properly chosen that court under the three-ring analysis. If Barnum brings suit in Ohio, the circus will have a good argument for transfer of venue under 28 U.S.C. §1404(a), since Barnum's claim did not arise in Ohio and the defendant's activities in the forum, though substantial, are completely unrelated to the claim before the court.

d. In this example, there is no basis for personal jurisdiction over Ringling Brothers in New Jersey for this claim. The claim does not arise out of any contacts of the defendant with New Jersey, so minimum contacts jurisdiction is not appropriate under *International Shoe*. Further, the two- or three-week tour that the circus makes in the state is unlikely to satisfy the substantial-and-continuous-contact requirement for general in personam jurisdiction. Since there is no basis for personal jurisdiction over Ringling Brothers, §§1391(a)(1) and (c) would not support venue there either. Nor would §1391(a)(2), since none of the events giving rise to this claim took place there.

2a. This suit may properly be brought in Maine. Complete diversity is present: Barnum is a citizen of Maine; Kelly is a citizen of Florida; and Ringling Brothers is a citizen of New York and Wisconsin. Personal jurisdiction is proper over both defendants under minimum contacts analysis, based on Kelly's negligent act of allowing Leo to get loose. This is a minimum contact of Kelly personally, since she actually performed the negligent act in the state.

It is also a minimum contact of the corporation because Kelly's negligence occurred in the course of her work for the circus, and the contacts of the corporation's agents while acting on its behalf will be attributed to the corporation.

Venue is also proper under §1391(a)(2), since a substantial part of the events giving rise to the claim took place in Maine. Note that §1391(a)(1) does *not* apply because Kelly does not "reside" in Maine, even though Ringling Brothers does under §§1391(a)(1) and (c) combined. Nor does §1391(a)(3), the "fallback" provision, apply, since there are other proper venues under §1391(a)(1) and (a)(2).

b. Barnum will also have the option to sue in at least one district in Florida under the three-ring analysis. Diversity is still present; here again it is irrelevant to diversity analysis that one of the parties (Kelly) is from the forum state. Personal jurisdiction is also likely to be proper over both defendants in Florida. Kelly is subject to jurisdiction there because she is domiciled there, and the circus is probably subject to general in personam jurisdiction there since it has its permanent winter quarters in Florida.

Venue is also proper. Under 28 U.S.C. §1391(a)(1) venue is proper in the district where any defendant resides if they all reside in the same state. For venue purposes, Kelly "resides" in the district within the state where she actually lives. See Chapter 8, p. 131. If Kelly's home is in the Northern District of Florida, for example, she "resides" there for venue purposes but not in the Southern District. Ringling Brothers resides, under §§1391(a)(1) and (c), in whichever district its winter quarters is in, since this extensive and permanent contact would support general in personam jurisdiction. On these facts, venue would be proper in either the district where Kelly lives or the district in which Ringling Brothers' winter quarters are located. See §1391(a)(1) (the district "where any defendant resides, if all defendants reside in the same State"). If these are the same district, only that district will be a proper venue.

c. Suit will not be proper in the Southern District of New York because personal jurisdiction could not be asserted over Kelly in New York, under either minimum contacts analysis or general in personam analysis. Venue would also be a problem, since Kelly does not reside there and none of the events giving rise to the claim took place there.

3.   The diversity analysis is unchanged here, but personal jurisdiction and venue are improper. Barnum may obtain "transient" personal jurisdiction over Kelly by serving her with process while she is passing through the state. *Burnham v. Superior Court of California*, 495 U.S. 604 (1990). But this "gotcha" theory, based on physical presence within the state, applies to individual, warm-body defendants, not to corporations: They are not necessarily "in" the state just because someone who works for them is. Because the claim arose in Maine, and the facts do not suggest any basis for general in personam jurisdiction over Ringling Brothers in Pennsylvania, the personal jurisdiction ring is not satisfied.

Nor is venue proper under §1391(a). Neither defendant resides there, and none of the events giving rise to the suit took place there. Nor does §1391(a)(3) apply, since there are other districts in which venue is proper under §1391(a)(1) or (a)(2).

Juggling Acts

4a. The Maine federal court, like any federal court, will have subject matter jurisdiction in this case, since there is complete diversity. Of course, the amount-in-controversy requirement will have to be met, but my guess is that more than $75,000 goes into your basic trained lion. If Leo falls in love with a moose and never returns, the circus might recover more than that amount; that's all that's needed to meet the amount requirement.

b. Personal jurisdiction presents a more difficult issue. Since neither defendant is domiciled in Maine, the circus will have to rely on specific jurisdiction, based on minimum contacts analysis. Kelly is clearly subject to jurisdiction in Maine under the *International Shoe* analysis because the claim arose from her negligent act (actually, her omission) in Maine. However, Rice's alleged negligence took place in Vermont, and it is doubtful that the mere foreseeability that the door would swing open in another state is sufficient to support jurisdiction over Rice there. Compare Chapter 1, example 4. Absent personal service in Maine or consent by Rice, the court will not have personal jurisdiction over her.

c. Once again, this case should be analyzed under §1391(a), since it is based on diversity. The District of Maine would be a proper venue in this action under §1391(a)(2), since a substantial part of the events or omissions giving rise to the claim took place in Maine. It would not be proper under §1391(a)(1), since neither defendant resides in Maine; and §1391(a)(3) does not apply, since there is a proper venue under one of the other subsections. (Of course, the fact that venue is proper is not enough to allow the court to hear the case, since it lacks personal jurisdiction over Rice.)

5.   The interesting aspect of this example is that none of the three rings would have been satisfied if Beatty had brought suit immediately after the injury. The parties were not diverse at the time of the accident, but became diverse by the time suit was brought, due to the change in Bailey's principal place of business. It is settled that diversity jurisdiction turns on the state citizenship of the parties when the suit is filed. See Chapter 5, example 6. Diversity jurisdiction is therefore proper in this case if the amount in controversy exceeds $75,000. In a case as weighty as this, that sounds likely.

Similarly, Bailey would not have been subject to personal jurisdiction in California in 1998 for this claim. Because the claim arose in Arizona, Bailey was not (and still is not) subject to specific jurisdiction in California for this claim. Nor was Bailey subject to general in personam jurisdiction in California in 1998. Bailey had no contacts with California then; its continuous and substantial business in California has all developed since 1998. May it be sued there based on general in personam jurisdiction at the time suit is filed, even if it was not subject to such jurisdiction at the time the claim arose?

Logically, it should not matter that the corporation was not subject to general in personam jurisdiction in California when the claim arose. No one was trying to assert jurisdiction over it then. The rationale underlying general in personam jurisdiction is that extensive corporate presence within the state reduces the inconvenience of litigation and affiliates the corporation with the state in such a substantial way as to make it fair to sue it there for any claim. If that presence exists at the time the suit is brought, the rationale for subjecting the corporation to jurisdiction is satisfied. In addition, any inconvenience to the corporation from litigating in the state occurs when the litigation takes place, and at that time Bailey had a substantial presence in the forum state.

If this personal jurisdiction analysis is right, then venue will also be proper in those federal districts within California where Bailey does substantial business. Looking at those districts as though they were states, the contacts there would support general in personam jurisdiction over Bailey, even though the claim arose elsewhere; consequently Bailey "resides" in those districts under §1391(a)(1) and (c).

Procedural Acrobatics

6a. This chapter deals primarily with the choice of a proper *federal* forum. The same three rings must also be satisfied if suit is brought in state court, but the standards for meeting those tests differ in a state suit. All states have a trial court that exercises broad subject matter jurisdiction over most types of claims, including negligence claims. In New Mexico, these courts of general jurisdiction are called district courts. They have subject matter jurisdiction over garden variety tort claims such as Beatty's, as well as a broad range of other common law and statutory causes of action. There is no need to consider the state citizenship of the parties, since the diversity requirements of 28 U.S.C. §1332 apply to subject matter jurisdiction of the federal courts, not that of the state courts.

Venue analysis also differs in state court actions. Each state has its own statutes defining proper venue for claims brought in its courts, which may vary considerably from the federal venue provisions. Here, the New Mexico statute is satisfied if Stenk "resides" (whatever that may mean under the New Mexico statute) in the county where the suit is filed. By contrast, venue would not be proper in this example under 28 U.S.C. §1391, since the circus has no contacts there and the events giving rise to the claim took place elsewhere.

Personal jurisdiction analysis, however, is likely to be the same whether the suit is brought in state or federal court. As indicated in Chapter 6, in most cases the federal courts exercise personal jurisdiction only to the extent that it would be exercised by the state courts of the state in which they sit, under Fed. R. Civ. P. 4(k)(1). See pp. 105-106. In this case, jurisdiction would be proper over Stenk, on the basis of her New Mexico domicile, but not over Bailey, since the claim did not arise in New Mexico and the facts do not indicate that Bailey would be subject to general in personam jurisdiction there.

b. By now you may wish you had run away and joined the circus instead of going to law school. Taming lions or swallowing swords might not be a bad alternative.

The personal jurisdiction analysis will not be affected by the defendant's decision to remove, since both courts usually apply the same statutory and constitutional standards for exercising personal jurisdiction, unless a federal statute authorizes the federal courts to exercise broader jurisdiction. Fed. R. Civ. P. 4(k)(1). The defendants do not waive their right to object to personal jurisdiction by removing to federal court. See Chapter 7, example 20. Thus, Bailey could seek dimissal on this ground in the federal court after removal.

Venue and subject matter jurisdiction, however, require further analysis. Venue would not be proper under §1391 because all defendants do not reside in New Mexico, and the events giving rise to the claim did not take place there. *However,* the usual federal venue provisions do not apply in removed actions. For removed cases, the applicable provision is 28 U.S.C. §1441(a), which requires that the case must be removed to the district and division embracing the place where the state action was brought. See *Polizzi v. Cowles Magazines,* 345 U.S. 663, 665 (1953). Thus, as long as the defendants remove to the federal district that includes Guadaloupe County, venue will not be a problem.

The subject matter jurisdiction analysis requires a two-level inquiry. First, the removal statute requires that the case have been within the original subject matter jurisdiction of the federal court. 28 U.S.C. §1441(a). Assuming that suit was brought after Bailey moved its principal place of business to California, that requirement would be met, based on diversity. However, even if a case satisfies the basic diversity requirements, §1441(b) bars removal if any defendant is a citizen of the forum state. So, the short version of this long-winded answer is that the case cannot be removed, since Stenk is a citizen of New Mexico.

A Two-Ring Circus

7a. It appears that the Southern District of Iowa falls in this area. Federal subject matter jurisdiction would be proper if the suit was brought in that district, as in any other: Adler asserts a claim under the federal copyright laws, and supplemental jurisdiction will apply to his related breach of contract claim. (The court would also have independent jurisdiction over the contract claim on diversity grounds.) Personal jurisdiction is likely to be upheld in any

Iowa court since the claim results, at least indirectly, from Ringling Brothers' deliberate contact in going to Iowa to make the royalty agreement with Adler. This would likely suffice for specific in personam jurisdiction under the *International Shoe* minimum contacts test.

However, venue would not be proper in the Southern District of Iowa. This case is not founded solely on diversity, so the analysis must be under §1391(b). Ringling Brothers does not "reside" in the Southern District under §§1391(b)(1) and (c) because it has no contacts there if the district is viewed as a state, nor did a substantial part of the events giving rise to the claim take place there. Nor does §1391(b)(3) apply. That section authorizes venue where any defendant may be "found." Even if this language is equated with "subject to personal jurisdiction" (which Ringling Brothers would be, under minimum contacts analysis), §1391(b)(3), like (a)(3), is a "fallback" provision that only applies if there is no district in which venue would otherwise be proper. Here, there are other districts in which venue is proper under §1391(b)(1) and (2), so the third subsection does not apply.

There could be numerous other districts that fall in this area as well. In any state where the circus does enough business to support general in personam jurisdiction, the diversity and personal jurisdiction rings will be satisfied. However, if the circus does business in some districts of those states but not others, venue will only be proper in those districts where it does business. (Got that?)

b. The Northern District of Iowa might fall into this area on the diagram, depending on the interpretation of §1391(b)(2). Subject matter jurisdiction is proper based on the federal question and supplemental jurisdiction. Venue may be proper under §1391(b)(2) since the claim arises in part from an "omission" — Ringling Brothers' failure to pay Adler the agreed royalties — which arguably took place in the Northern District of Iowa. However, it is doubtful that the circus would be subject to personal jurisdiction in Iowa if the agreement was made in New York and the circus's only contact with Iowa was the failure to send the royalty checks to Adler there.

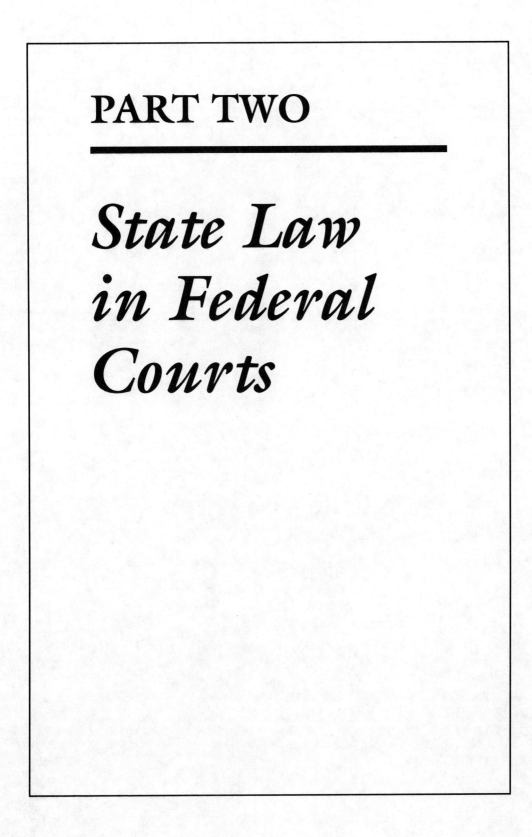

PART TWO

State Law in Federal Courts

10

Easy Erie: *The Law of Rome and Athens*

A Personal Fantasy

It is December, and the pace of the first year of law school is picking up. Glannon sits numbly in Civil Procedure class. The professor is droning on, quite learnedly. Subject: the *Erie* doctrine. Glannon cowers as unobtrusively as possible in the middle of the class. All around him, students listen intently, with apparent comprehension. Glannon understands nothing.

Suddenly, the Archangel Gabriel appears, hovering resplendent above the class. No one else takes notice; the discussion moves on obliviously. Pointing a star-studded scepter at the object of his visit, Gabriel speaks. "Glannon," he declaims, "listen well, for you, *you* shall be called upon to explain the *Erie* doctrine to a future generation of students."

Astonished by the apparition and appalled at his message, Glannon streaks from the room. After a long convalescence and many setbacks, he takes a job watering flowers in a nursery.

Introduction

Believe me, if old Gabe had really put in an appearance back then, I would surely have given the nursery job some serious thought. But even if I had stoically accepted the archangel's charge, I would never have contemplated calling anything about the *Erie* doctrine "easy." I certainly found it impenetrable then, and there is much about it that remains a mystery to me today. However, some aspects of *Erie* really are fairly straightforward, and, luckily, those

163

are the aspects that it is particularly important for you to understand. This chapter deals with these comprehensible aspects of *Erie*.

The whole problem is really the framers' fault. They decided to craft a federal form of government, in which most power would remain with the states, but certain limited powers would be delegated to the new national government. They spent a summer thinking about what legislative powers the national government really had to have and set them forth in Article I, §8 of the Constitution. All other powers, anything they hadn't mentioned (or by fair implication "necessary and proper" to the exercise of these "delegated" powers), "are reserved to the States respectively, or to the people." U.S. Const., amend. X.

At the same time, the framers adopted Article III of the Constitution, which authorizes the creation of federal courts and defines their jurisdiction. In defining the federal judicial power, they authorized federal courts to hear claims that arise under federal law ("cases arising under this Constitution, the Laws of the United States, or Treaties made, or which shall be made, under their Authority"). Thus, when Congress makes law under its delegated powers in Article I, §8, and cases arise in which plaintiffs seek recovery under those laws, the federal courts have jurisdiction.

However, the framers went further in Article III. They also created the diversity jurisdiction, which authorizes federal courts to hear cases that do not involve federal law at all. In fact, by definition a diversity case does not arise under federal law. If Plato, from Montana, sues Lucan, from South Dakota, for violation of the federal patent laws, the parties are diverse; but it is not a diversity case, since the claim arises under federal law. Plato's right to recover is created by federal law, a law Congress had the power to pass because the power to regulate patents is delegated to the federal government under Article I, §8. This is a federal question case; it is irrelevant that the parties are from different states.

On the other hand, if Plato's claim is for breach of contract, the federal court will have jurisdiction (if the amount in controversy is sufficient) based on diversity of citizenship. However, the substantive law that governs the claim cannot be created by Congress, since it has no delegated power to create a general law of contracts. The federal court has *judicial* power to hear the case, even though there is no federal *legislative* power to create the governing law. The question addressed in *Erie*—and in its infamous predecessor, *Swift v. Tyson*, 41 U.S. 1 (1842)—was what law should be applied in this anomalous situation.

The Rule of Swift v. Tyson

There was no real reason why this had to be such a problem. The First Congress had considered the issue in 1789 and passed a statute to deal with it.

The Rules of Decision Act, 1 Stat. 92 (1789), provides:

> The laws of the several states, except where the constitution, treaties
> or statutes of the United States shall otherwise require or provide,
> shall be regarded as rules of decision in trials at common law in the
> courts of the United States, in cases where they apply.

The Rules of Decision Act (referred to herein as "the RDA") is still in force today, little changed from the original of 200 years ago. See 28 U.S.C. §1652.

Much controversy could have been avoided if the Supreme Court had simply interpreted the RDA differently in 1842, when Justice Story decided *Swift v. Tyson*. In *Swift,* the plaintiff, Swift, brought a federal diversity suit to collect on a bill of exchange. The bill had been given by Tyson to a third party, Norton, who endorsed it over to Swift in New York. As consideration for the bill, Swift had cancelled an antecedent debt owed him by Norton. Swift, a "holder in due course," was entitled to collect on the bill if he had given "a valuable consideration" for it. The less than earth-shaking issue in the case was whether Swift's cancellation of Norton's pre-existing debt constituted such consideration. 41 U.S. at 14-16.

Tyson, the defendant, argued that the RDA required the court to apply New York law to determine the validity of consideration, since the case involved a bill executed in New York and no federal statute applied. Under New York case law, Tyson contended, such consideration was insufficient. Justice Story doubted that the New York cases were so clear, but concluded that it didn't matter anyway. The RDA, he concluded, did not require the federal court to follow New York's view of this question of general commercial law. In Story's view, the phrase "the laws of the several states" in the RDA referred only to the statutes and certain established local usages of the state, not to judicial decisions interpreting general principles of common law.

If the federal court did not have to apply the common law decisions of the state in a diversity case, what law should it apply? In Story's view, the federal court should examine all the common law authorities — including cases from the state in which it sat, from other states, from federal courts, English courts, and the views of respected commentators — to ascertain the proper rule. The federal judge's job, Story believed, was the same as that of any other common law judge: to choose the right rule of consideration, rather than to follow a rule that some other judge deemed to be the right one.

The Philosophical Underpinnings of Swift

It is not hard to see behind this conclusion a fundamental premise about the nature of law. The law, declared Justice Story, cannot be one thing in Rome and another in Athens. 41 U.S. at 19. The law is the Law, a body of absolute "right" rules, existing apart from a particular place, time, or judge. Under this "natural law" view (said to derive from Blackstone,[1] but doubtless more fundamentally from the Greek philosophers), the task of every judge was to look to all the available evidence to ascertain the ideal "right" rule on any common law question, such as the proper consideration for a contract or true duty owed to a trespasser on a railroad right of way:

> *Swift v. Tyson* rests on the philosophic premise that a court—specifically a state court—does not *make* the law but merely *finds* or declares the law, and so its decisions simply constitute evidence of what the law is, which another court is free to reject in favor of better evidence to be found elsewhere.

R. Jackson, The Rise and Fall of *Swift v. Tyson*, 24 A.B.A.J. 609, 612 (1938). In the lofty search for this "transcendental body of law,"[2] it is hardly surprising that one judge seeking the true rule of adequate consideration should not feel bound by a prior judge's perceptions. All looked to the same sources in their efforts to approximate the ideal outcome. The language of the pre-*Erie* opinions nicely reflects this premise. In *Swift*, for example, Story speaks of "the true result of the commercial law upon the question now before us." 41 U.S. at 19. In *Black & White Taxicab Co. v. Brown & Yellow Taxicab Co.*, 276 U.S. 518 (1928), the high-water mark of the *Swift* doctrine, the majority speaks of "the discovery" of common law principles and of looking to past cases as "evidence of the existing applicable rule." 276 U.S. at 529-530.

This natural law view ran into some problems along the way. *First,* it was clear that the law *could* be one thing in Rome and another in Athens, if the legislature so declared it. If the New York legislature passed a statute declaring that railroads owed a duty of due care to trespassers, that became the law of New York. There was no question that the RDA required the federal diversity court to apply that law to New York cases. If Pennsylvania passed a statute declaring that the railroad need only avoid wilful or wanton negligence, the federal court sitting in diversity would have to apply that rule in a Pennsylvania case. The federal courts under *Swift* also followed many so-called local usages, such as established state common law rules concerning interests in land, for reasons of stability and predictability of titles.

Second, the *Swift* rule created potential for manipulation of the sort upheld in *Black & White Taxicab Co. v. Brown & Yellow Taxicab Co.*, 276 U.S. 518 (1928). In that case, the Brown & Yellow Taxicab Company sought to enforce a contract with the railroad, providing it the exclusive right to pick up and discharge passengers at a train station in Kentucky. Aware that the

---

1. W. Castro, The *Erie* Doctrine and the Structure of Constitutional Revolutions, 62 Tul. L. Rev. 907, 913 (1988).

2. *Black & White Taxicab Co. v. Brown & Yellow Taxicab Co.*, 276 U.S. 518, 533 (1928) (Holmes, J., dissenting).

Kentucky state courts did not enforce such contracts, Brown & Yellow reincorporated in Tennessee, thus creating diversity between it and the defendant, Black & White. It then brought suit in *federal* court—in Kentucky, no less—to enjoin Black & White from interfering with its contract. The Kentucky federal court held, as other federal cases had, that the true rule was that the monopoly contract was enforceable, and enjoined the defendant from interfering with it. The Supreme Court upheld the decision on the ground that the federal court had the authority under *Swift* to reach its own conclusion on the common law issue of whether such exclusive contracts should be enforced. Thus, by invoking diversity jurisdiction, the plaintiff was able to choose a substantive rule of law which upheld rather than barred the contract.

The Legal Realist Attack on Swift

Justice Oliver Wendell Holmes wrote a marvelous dissent in *Black & White Taxicab*, in which he attacked *Swift's* basic philosophical premise about the nature of law. *Swift*, he wrote, was based on

> the impression that there is one august corpus, to understand which clearly is the only task of any Court concerned. If there were such a transcendental body of law outside of any particular State but obligatory within it unless and until changed by statute, the Courts of the United States might be right in using their independent judgment as to what it was. But there is no such body of law. The fallacy and illusion that I think exist consist in supposing that there is this outside thing to be found.

276 U.S. at 533.

If there is no "august corpus" of true rules of law, just what is the law anyway? The law, declares Holmes, is a set of rules laid down by those with the power to do so, to govern behavior in a given place at a given time:

> Law is a word used with many meanings, but law in the sense in which courts speak of it today does not exist without some definite authority behind it. The common law so far as it is enforced in a State, whether called common law or not, is not the common law generally but the law of that State existing by the authority of that State.

Id. For Holmes, the rule that a railroad owes a duty of due care to a trespasser—or doesn't—derives its force not from its inherent "rightness," but from the fact that the authorities empowered to make such a rule have made it. The law *can* be one thing in Rome and another in Athens because the people who make Roman laws are different from those who make the Athenian laws. Since Athens is a different place, with different conditions and problems, its lawmakers may well choose different rules than the Romans do. And later Athenian lawmakers may choose different rules than their predecessors. Each rule may be "right" in the sense that it is appropriate to its time and place, but it is not "right" because it is the one true rule for all time on a particular issue.[3]

If this "legal realist" view of the judge's role is correct, what should a federal judge do in a case like *Black & White*? According to Holmes, he should ask what body has the authority to make rules governing the enforcement of contracts. The answer to that question is usually the states, since the Constitution delegates no general law-making authority over contracts to the legislative or judicial branches of the federal government. Whether the state speaks through its legislature or through its "other voice" (its courts), it must be heeded because it is the body with the authority to create the applicable law under our constitutional distribution of powers.

The Erie *Decision*

Justice Holmes died in 1935, so it fell to Justice Brandeis to sound the death knell for *Swift*. It was doubtless a task Holmes would have relished, since the Court in *Erie* dramatically repudiated the 100-year tradition represented by *Swift*.

The facts of the case were simple: Tompkins lost an arm when hit by a projection from an Erie Railroad train while walking on a pathway along the tracks. His injury was quite likely the result of negligence; however, there was no evidence that the railroad's employees had acted wilfully or wantonly in creating the danger, which was the standard for recovery under Pennsylvania law.[4] The federal district court, relying on *Swift*, concluded that it was not bound by the Pennsylvania decision and instead followed federal decisions, which held that railroads owed a duty of due care to users of lateral pathways along the track. Tompkins recovered in federal district court, though he would have lost if the case had been brought in state court.

Interestingly, no party argued that *Swift* should be overruled: The defendant in *Erie* argued instead that the federal court should have followed the Pennsylvania rule because it was a matter of "local usage" rather than general common law. I. Younger, What Happened in *Erie*, 56 Tex. L. Rev. 1011, 1025-1026 (1978). The *Erie* Court, however, dramatically rephrased the issue: "The question for decision is whether the oft-challenged doctrine of *Swift v. Tyson* shall now be disapproved." 304 U.S. at 69 (footnote omitted). To its own question, the Court answered "yes" for a number of reasons.

---

3. Holmes's language in *Black & White*, like that of the natural law judges, reflects his premise. He speaks of state courts "establishing," "declaring," or "adopting" rules of law, "say[ing] . . . that thus the law is and shall be." 276 U.S. at 534-535. His is not the language of discovery, but of creation.

4. All involved assumed that, if state law applied at all, Pennsylvania law would apply.

First, Swift had failed to achieve one of the main goals of its supporters. It was hoped that the gradual accumulation of "general common law" decisions by eminent federal judges would induce state judges to recognize the "rightness" of those decisions and fall into line, leading to broad uniformity in the common law throughout the nation. But state judges had the temerity to believe that they too could examine the "evidence" and "discover" true principles for themselves. Rather than docilely following federal cases, the state judges persisted in taking their own views. The result was a multiplicity of rules on recurrent issues, not only from different state courts, but also from federal and state courts within a single state.

Second, Justice Brandeis concluded, the federal practice of making common law had led to grave discrimination in the administration of justice. As *Black & White Taxicab* illustrates, it allowed an out-of-state plaintiff to choose a different rule of substantive law because he could choose federal court. While a local taxicab company would have to sue in a Kentucky state court, which would refuse to enforce exclusive contracts, a diverse plaintiff could go to federal court and get a more favorable outcome. Ironically, while diversity was created to prevent prejudice against out-of-staters — to assure a "level playing field" as they said in the 1980s — *Swift* had introduced discrimination in favor of the out-of-stater.[5]

Third, and most fundamentally, Justice Brandeis declared the *Swift* doctrine unconstitutional, since it authorized federal judges to "make" law in areas in which the federal government has no delegated powers. *Erie* emphatically adopts Holmes's view that, in choosing its rules of decision, the federal court must look to the body with the authority to make those rules. When it comes to common law matters not within the delegated powers, that body is the state, whether it speaks by statute or judicial decision. Thus, ignoring state common law rules invades rights reserved to the states under our federal system of divided powers:

---

5. Arguably, there is no discrimination here between the parties to the case. After all, defendants get a choice of forum too: They can remove cases from state to federal court. But this is not true of in-state defendants. 28 U.S.C. §1441(b). Thus, in *Black & White,* if the Kentucky rule had been more favorable to the plaintiff than the "federal common law" rule, Brown & Yellow could have sued in state court, and the defendant would have been stuck in state court. In addition, when the diverse plaintiff chooses federal court initially, the defendant is stuck with it, since there is no such thing as removal to state court. In *Black & White,* for example, the out-of-state plaintiff sued in federal court because the federal rule was more favorable, and the defendant was stuck with that court and that rule.

Finally, there is another type of discrimination here, between out-of-state plaintiffs and in-state plaintiffs with similar claims against local citizens. A Kentucky taxi company who sued Black & White on a similar claim would not have had the same opportunity that Brown & Yellow had to choose the applicable law by choosing the "right" court.

> Notwithstanding the great names which may be cited in favor of the [*Swift*] doctrine . . . there stands, as a perpetual protest against its repetition, the constitution of the United States, which recognizes and preserves the autonomy and independence of the states, — independence in their legislative and independence in their judicial departments. Supervision over either the legislative or the judicial action of the states is in no case permissible except as to matters by the constitution specifically authorized or delegated to the United States.

Erie, 304 U.S. at 78-79, quoting from *Baltimore & Ohio R. Co. v. Baugh,* 149 U.S. 368; 401 (1893) (Field, J., dissenting).

I suggested earlier that Justice Story could have avoided the entire problem by interpreting the RDA a little differently. That act requires the federal courts to apply "the laws of the several States," unless the federal Constitution, treaties, or statutes require otherwise. If Story had concluded that the phrase "the laws of the several States" includes state common law decisions, the federal courts would have been required *by the RDA itself* to apply those decisions, and lofty questions of constitutional power to do otherwise would have been avoided. He didn't interpret it that way. In *Erie,* however, Justice Brandeis concluded that it would be unconstitutional to interpret it any other way. It was Justice Story's interpretation of the act, not the act itself, that the court rejected in *Erie.*[6]

What's Easy about Erie

Whatever its fascination may be as a triumph of legal realism or a constitutional landmark, the central command of *Erie* is basic. In diversity cases federal courts must apply the law that would be applied by the courts of the state in which they sit. They are not free to decide for themselves the "right" rule of consideration, the duty that a railroad owes to a trespasser, or the enforceability of exclusive contracts. Rather than create "general common law," their job in a diversity case is to *apply* state common law. In those broad areas where the law is largely judge-made, such as contracts, torts, probate, and property, state law reigns supreme because "there can be no other law." *Hanna v. Plumer,* 380 U.S. 460, 472 (1965).

In 97 percent of the cases, this *is* easy. Lawyers and federal courts apply *Erie* every day without the slightest difficulty because all parties recognize that state law provides the governing rules of decision and there is little

---

6. Not everyone agrees, even after sixty years, that *Erie* is the best solution to the problem of state law in diversity cases. See, e.g., J. Coor, Thoughts on the Vitality of *Erie,* 41 Am. U. L. Rev. 1087 (1992), which rebuts Justice Brandeis's arguments for overruling *Swift,* argues that *Erie* has raised more problems than it has solved, and advocates returning to *Swift.*

question as to what the state law is. There's been a lot of fuss about some fringe cases—we'll fuss over them ourselves in the next chapter—but in the overwhelming number of diversity cases *Erie* functions simply and effectively to determine the applicable principles of substantive law.

The following examples consider the basic mechanics of applying the *Erie* doctrine. In analyzing them, assume, unless otherwise specified, that all actions are brought in federal court on the basis of diversity. After the initial examples, we will consider a related question: How does a judge determine what the law of the state actually is?

EXAMPLES

When in Rome . . .

1.   Plato was injured in an accident in Minnesota when his car collided with those of Solon and Ovid. He sued Solon and recovered $200,000 in damages, which Solon paid. Solon then sued Ovid for contribution, that is, to get a judgment that Ovid, as a joint tortfeasor, must reimburse Solon for half of the damages he paid to Plato. The contribution action was brought in federal court in Minnesota.

At the time of Solon's contribution suit, the law on contribution was in a state of flux throughout the United States. Most courts refused to order contribution between joint tortfeasors. A few courts, however, had adopted the opposite view, that a tortfeasor who had paid the plaintiff could require other negligent parties to pay their share of the loss. Several states had adopted statutes authorizing contribution. Minnesota had no statute on point, but its courts had followed the minority rule, allowing contribution.

   a. How should the federal district court decide the issue of Solon's right to contribution, if the case arose prior to *Erie?*
   b. How should the court decide the issue after *Erie?*

2.   Assume that Solon's contribution action arose in 1925, before *Erie* was decided, and that most *federal* courts that had considered the issue had concluded that contribution should be allowed between joint tortfeasors. However, Judge Quintus, the federal trial judge in Solon's action for contribution, agreed with the reasoning of the courts that deny contribution. What should he do?

3.   Assume that, prior to Solon's contribution action, Minnesota had passed a statute that authorized contribution among joint tortfeasors.

   a. How should the federal district court decide the contribution question, if the case arose before *Erie?*
   b. How should the court decide the issue after *Erie?*

4.   Assume that Minnesota had a statute authorizing contribution among joint tortfeasors. Most states with contribution statutes had held that they are not intended to allow a party who acted wilfully or wantonly to seek

contribution. However, assume that the Minnesota Supreme Court had construed the Minnesota statute to authorize a tortfeasor to seek contribution even if her conduct was wilful or wanton. If Solon seeks contribution, and Ovid argues that the statute does not authorize it because Solon's conduct was wilful or wanton, how should Judge Quintus rule if

    a. the case arose prior to *Erie*?

    b. the case arose after *Erie*?

History Repeats Itself

5.   Assume that Harry Tompkins III is walking on a lateral pathway along the tracks of the Erie Railroad in Pennsylvania in 1999. He is injured when hit by something projecting from a passing train. He sues the Erie Railroad in federal court under the Federal Interstate Railway Act, which (we will assume) authorizes suits for damages arising from railroad accidents. He also asserts a claim against the Erie for common law negligence. On the negligence claim, the railroad raises the defense that Pennsylvania law does not allow trespassers on the right of way to recover damages, absent wilful or wanton negligence, but Tompkins argues that the court should apply the "more modern" due care standard to the negligence claim. What should Judge Quintus do, and why?

Ascertaining State Law

Because *Erie* requires federal courts to apply state law in diversity cases, federal judges obviously must decide what the state law is. In many cases that is easy because the issue has been clearly decided by the state's highest court. If there is a recent case from the Pennsylvania Supreme Court holding that railroads are only liable to trespassers for wilful or wanton conduct, the federal court knows its course and will dismiss a future Tompkins's case if there is no evidence of such aggravated fault. Similarly, if the Kentucky decisions consistently refuse to enforce exclusive contracts like that in *Black & White*, the federal court in Kentucky will also refuse to enforce them.

    Many cases, however, are not so squarely resolved by the case law. For example, there may be older cases from the Pennsylvania Supreme Court requiring wilful conduct but recent tort cases in related areas that suggest a trend to expand duties in tort cases generally. Or perhaps the Kentucky courts have refused to enforce exclusive contracts, but those cases are distinguishable because they involved matters of particular public interest. Or there may be no state supreme court case on the point, but there may be one from an intermediate appellate court. Or perhaps no appellate court from the state has decided the question in dispute, but a trial judge has. Or going one step further, perhaps there is absolutely no decision on point, though there are decisions on analogous tort issues.

The early post-*Erie* cases suggested that the federal court, in deciding what state law is, should follow any existing state precedent, without making creative predictions about how that precedent might be treated in a future case. In *West v. American Tel. & Tel. Co.*, 311 U.S. 223 (1940), for example, the Court held that, where there was no decision on point from the state supreme court, a decision of the state's intermediate appellate court was binding, "even though [the federal district court] may think that the state Supreme Court may establish a different rule in some future litigation." 311 U.S. at 238. The furthest extension of this approach came in *Fidelity Trust Co. v. Field*, 311 U.S. 169 (1940), in which the Supreme Court required the federal court to follow two trial court decisions on a question of New Jersey law, in the absence of any appellate cases on point, even though no other New Jersey judge would have been bound by those decisions. This led Judge Frank of the Second Circuit to complain that the federal judge was to woodenly follow existing state cases like a "ventriloquist's dummy." *Richardson v. Commissioner*, 126 F.2d 562, 567 (2d Cir. 1942).

The Supreme Court has since suggested, however, that federal judges have more flexibility in determining state law under *Erie*. In *Commissioner v. Bosch*, 387 U.S. 456, 465 (1967), the Court held that a federal court construing state law should give "proper regard" to decisions of trial and intermediate appellate courts, but that its job is to apply the law as announced, or as it *would be announced*, by the state's highest court. Thus, the federal judge must predict how the issue before it would be decided by the state supreme court if that court decided the issue today. In making that prediction, the judge may look to all available data, including decisions from the state's lower courts, developing trends in the area of law that cast doubt on the earlier decisions, and dicta or legislative developments that weaken (or reaffirm) the existing precedents. The judge is not free to make up state law, but he is entitled to make an educated judgment on what rule the state supreme court would apply to the case *today*, rather than merely parroting what the rule was when the last case on point was decided. See generally Moores §124. 22[3].

The federal court may have an additional option in determining state law. Some states have "certification" procedures, which allow a federal court faced with a thorny state law issue to certify the issue to the state supreme court. See, e.g., Kan. Stat. Ann. §§60-3201 to 60-3212; W. Va. Code §§51-1A-1 to 51-1-12. When the federal judge certifies the issue, a statement of the issue and the relevant facts is sent to the state court. The case then goes into the regular appellate pipeline: The parties brief and argue the issue before the state court as though it were a regular appeal from a lower state court. Ultimately, the state supreme court issues an opinion, much like that on any other appeal, resolving the issue. Then, armed with the answer to their question, the parties return to the *federal* court and pick up the litigation there.

While certification assures an accurate reading of state law (assuming the state court accepts the certification), a mere description illustrates why it can only solve the problem of ascertaining state law in a small percentage of cases. It is a lengthy and expensive diversion from the federal litigation. In addition, it creates the anomalous situation of federal courts determining the state supreme court's workload. For this latter reason, certification statutes usually give the state supreme court the power to accept or refuse the certification. Only those cases that the federal court chooses to certify and the state court accepts will lead to authoritative pronouncements of state law.[7]

. . . Do As the Romans Do

6. Assume that the Minnesota Supreme Court, in *Aristotle v. Caesar*, a 1952 decision, refused to allow contribution between joint tortfeasors, reasoning that each tortfeasor who caused the plaintiff's injury may justly be made to pay the entire damages and that the legislature is the proper body to change this basic tort principle if it is dissatisfied with the common law no-contribution approach. In 1999, the issue comes before the Minnesota Court of Appeals, the state intermediate appellate court, in a new case, *Justinian v. Lycurgus*. It reviews the broad changes in many areas of tort law since 1952, including the very wide adoption by other states of the right of contribution. On balance, it concludes that if the state supreme court reconsidered the issue it would likely overrule *Aristotle* and allow contribution.

  a. What should the Minnesota Court of Appeals do in *Justinian v. Lycurgus*?

  b. Assume that, shortly *before* the midlevel appeals court's decision in *Justinian*, Solon brings an action against Ovid for contribution in federal court. Judge Quintus, the federal judge, reviews the 1952 *Aristotle* opinion, as well as the broad trend of tort law decisions in Minnesota, and concludes (as did the Court of Appeals in *Justinian*) that the Minnesota Supreme Court would overrule *Aristotle*. How should Judge Quintus rule on Solon's claim for contribution?

  c. Suppose that Solon sues Ovid for contribution in federal court after the Minnesota Court of Appeals (the intermediate state court) had predicted in *Justinian* that the Minnesota Supreme Court would overrule *Aristotle*. However, Judge Quintus, who is handling the *Solon* case, does not agree with the Court of Appeals' prediction. What should he do?

---

7. Despite the complications it introduces, some recent federal cases have shown a renewed interest in using certification "to avoid making unnecessary *Erie* 'guesses.'" See, *Mosher v. Speedstar Div. of AMCA Intl., Inc.*, 52 F.3d 913, 916 (11th Cir. 1995) (certifying unresolved state issue to the Florida Supreme Court despite fact that issue had been resolved by the federal district court).

d. If you represented Solon in the contribution action against Ovid, would you file suit in federal court or state court?

Role Reversal

7.   Justinian is held liable to Draco in a negligence action and sues Charondas in a Minnesota state court for contribution as a joint tortfeasor. Judge Ulpian, the state trial judge, prior to ruling on the right to contribution, researches the law on contribution and finds that there is no Minnesota case addressing the right to contribution between joint tortfeasors. However, in *Solon v. Ovid* (a diversity case applying Minnesota law), the Federal Court of Appeals for the Eighth Circuit had concluded that the Minnesota Supreme Court, if it considered the question, would allow contribution. How should Judge Ulpian rule?

8.   Assume that Justinian's contribution action is brought in the federal district court for the District of Minnesota. Judge Quintus, the federal district court judge, must decide whether Minnesota would allow contribution. His research uncovers *Solon v. Ovid* from the Eighth Circuit (which hears appeals from the District of Minnesota). How should Judge Quintus decide the contribution question?

Preempted Predictions

9.   Lucian sues Caesar for contribution in the federal district court for the District of Minnesota. At the time, it is unclear from the cases whether Minnesota recognizes a right to contribution among joint tortfeasors or not; the Minnesota Supreme Court has never decided the issue. Judge Quintus, the federal district judge, reviews the state law precedents in related areas and predicts that the Minnesota Supreme Court would not allow contribution. Consequently, he refuses to order contribution in Lucian's case, and enters a judgment dismissing it.

   Eighteen months later, the Minnesota Supreme Court takes review in a case raising the issue of the right to contribution, and holds that Minnesota law recognizes a right to contribution among tortfeasors. Now, Lucian moves for relief from judgment under Fed. R. Civ. P. 60(b) in his federal contribution suit against Caesar, asking Judge Quintus to reopen the case and order contribution, since it is now clear that he had guessed wrong about the right to contribution under Minnesota law. What should Judge Quintus do?

High Fidelity

10. The State of Illinois has not one, but five intermediate appellate courts. Each handles appeals from a separate geographical area of the state. See Figure 10-1. A case tried in Washington County, for example, in the Fifth District, would be appealed to the Fifth Judicial District of the Illinois Appellate Court. A case tried in Cook County goes on appeal to the First

Figure 10-1: Judicial Districts of Illinois Appellate Court. Reprinted with permission from Forster-Long, Inc. *The American Bench,* 10th ed. 1999 p. 811.

Judicial District. (In fact, Cook County is the only county in the First District because Chicago is located there and creates as much judicial business as many other counties put together.)

Assume that Gaius sues Draco in Cook County Circuit Court (the Illinois trial court of general jurisdiction) for contribution as a joint tortfeasor. Assume further that the Illinois Supreme Court has never decided whether contribution is available between tortfeasors. The Fourth and Second Districts of the Illinois Appellate Court have held that it is, but the First District has held that it is not.

   a. What rule should the state trial judge in *Gaius v. Draco* follow?

   b. Now, assume that the *Gaius* case is brought in Cook County but is removed to the federal district court for the Northern District of Illinois, which includes Cook County. What rule should the federal district judge apply?

EXPLANATIONS

When in Rome . . .

1a. If this case arose under the *Swift* regime, the federal judge would not be bound by the Minnesota decisions on the right to contribution. *Swift* authorized federal judges to make independent judgments as to what the proper rule should be on issues of "general common law." Contribution was a question of tort law, which had long been governed by the common law decisions of courts rather than by statute. Thus, the judge was not bound to follow the Minnesota decisions, even though, had the suit been brought in a Minnesota state court, contribution would have been allowed.

Nor would he have been bound by the majority position of the other states: The rule was not necessarily "right" because it was more widely followed. The judge would look to all the cases and authorities, assess their reasoning, and reach the decision that, in his judgment, represented the proper rule on the issue.

b. After *Erie,* the judge would clearly be bound to follow the Minnesota rule, even though it is a judge-made common law rule rather than a statute. *Erie* held that the RDA requires federal courts to apply state law in diversity cases, whether judge-made or statutory, rather than following their own perception of the best rule. The rationale of *Erie* is that the grant of jurisdiction over diversity cases in Article III is not a grant of authority to displace state substantive rules of decision, but only to apply those rules in a federal, presumably neutral forum. Since only the state has the general power to make law on tort issues like the right of contribution among joint tortfeasors, the federal court must apply the state's law rather than creating its own law.

Note that the court must apply the Minnesota rule, not the rule that the majority of states would choose. Where the case is governed by Minnesota law, the issue is not how most state courts would rule, but how the Minnesota courts would.

2.   This is an interesting dilemma for the judge under *Swift.* He was not bound by the state decisions—either those of Minnesota or of other states—but was he bound by the trend in the federal cases? One of the arguments for the *Swift* doctrine was that eventually uniform common law rules would evolve as a body of "general common law" decisions on similar issues accumulated. But the basic rationale of *Swift* is that each judge looks to the common law sources to reach an independent judgment as to the proper rule. Presumably, if a judge did that and concluded that the majority of his federal colleagues had reached the wrong result, he should not follow them any more than state judges who had missed the mark. Thus, he should not be bound by decisions from other federal district courts either. Although such decisions might be persuasive (just as the Minnesota decisions might be) he would make an independent judgment as to the proper contribution rule.

3a.   In this case the state rule is the same as in the previous examples, but it has been established by statute rather than by judicial decision. Even under *Swift* it was consistently held that the RDA required federal courts to apply state statutes in diversity cases. Moore's §124 App.01[2]. Thus, the federal court had to apply the state rule if the legislature made it but was free to ignore it if the state supreme court did.

b. *Erie* held that the RDA must be interpreted to require federal courts to apply state common law decisions in diversity cases. It did not in any way impair the long-established view that the act required federal courts to apply state statutes in divesity cases. Indeed, under *Erie* this is not only the proper interpretation of the RDA, but the only permissible one. Since there is no general federal power to enact laws governing contribution among joint tortfeasors, state law must govern because "there can be no other law." *Hanna v. Plumer,* 380 U.S. 460, 472 (1965). Thus, after *Erie,* as before, the court would apply the Minnesota statute.

4a.   Here, there is a state statute on point, and the issue is the proper interpretation of it. Minnesota courts construe their statute one way, though other states construe similar provisions differently. Under *Swift,* the federal court had to follow state statutes in diversity cases, but did the federal court have to follow state court cases construing the meaning of those statutes?

Even under the *Swift* regime, the federal courts generally recognized that the issue in a case like this was what the Minnesota contribution statute meant, not what the "best" interpretation of similar statutes was. Most cases under *Swift* recognized that the Minnesota courts were the proper body to determine the meaning of the Minnesota statute, and therefore would follow the state cases interpreting it. Moore's Federal Practice, §124 App.01[2].

Ironically, however, some cases, particularly earlier ones, even refused to follow state courts' interpretations of their own state statutes. See R. Jackson, The Rise and Fall of *Swift v. Tyson,* 24 A.B.A.J. 609, 611-613 (1938). This seems even more of an affront to the state courts than the basic doctrine of *Swift:* It is one thing for the federal courts to take an independent view of what the common law rule of contribution *should be.* It is quite another for them to ignore the Minnesota court's conclusion as to what their own state statute *actually says.*

b. Under *Erie,* the federal court clearly should apply the Minnesota court's interpretation of the statute. The source of the applicable law is the state, since the question is not within the federal legislative authority. The federal diversity court must therefore follow the law of the state, as laid down in the statute and construed by the state court. This follows as a matter of *Erie* policy as well as constitutional division of powers: If the federal court were free to construe the statute differently, parties could invoke the diversity jurisdiction to get a more favorable substantive result, just as they did under *Swift.*

History Repeats Itself

5.   Strictly speaking, this case does not raise an *Erie* problem at all. The case is a federal question case rather than a diversity case, since Tompkins III has sued under the Federal Interstate Railway Act. However, as plaintiffs are wont to do, Tompkins has asserted a state law negligence claim as well.

The state negligence claim would be properly before the federal court under supplemental jurisdiction, which authorizes a federal court to entertain related state claims that arise from the same facts as a federal claim. See 28 U.S.C. §1367; Chapter 15. However, supplemental jurisdiction is another example of a situation—like diversity—in which federal courts have jurisdiction to hear state claims but no power to create the governing law. Here, as in diversity cases under *Erie,* the court's job is to apply state law to the supplemental claim, not to make up its own rule. Thus, Judge Quintus should have his law clerk research Pennsylvania law to determine whether it requires a showing of wilful or wanton negligence. If it does, he must apply that rule to the supplemental claim.

Obviously, the court would apply federal law to the interpretation of the Federal Interstate Railway Act claim. It may "make" law on that claim if necessary to decide the case, but it would have to follow state law, or predict it, on the state negligence claim. Thus, in many federal cases that are *not* diversity cases the court must indulge in the same exercise of guessing at the content of state law that is required in diversity cases under *Erie*. Even if the foes of diversity jurisdiction ultimately achieve its repeal, ascertaining and applying state law will still be necessary in every case involving supplemental state law claims.

. . . Do As the Romans Do

6a. The Minnesota Court of Appeals is a mid-level appellate court, bound by the decisions of the highest court of the state. *Aristotle v. Caesar* is such a case, and it is directly on point. An intermediate appellate court would almost certainly consider itself bound by *Aristotle*. The role of the lower courts is to follow the law established by the highest court of the state, not to speculate about how that court might change it in the future. Unless *Aristotle* had been utterly eviscerated and effectively overruled by more recent Minnesota Supreme Court decisions, the Minnesota Court of Appeals would feel bound to follow *Aristotle* and deny contribution. The Court of Appeals might well write an opinion encouraging the state supreme court to review the case and change the law, but it cannot do so itself.

b. In this case, the only Minnesota Supreme Court case on point denies contribution, but Judge Quintus (like the Court of Appeals in the previous example) has strong grounds to believe, in light of other tort law developments, that the state supreme court would adopt a more liberal approach on this issue if it came before that court today.

The federal judge's role in a diversity case is to predict how the case would ultimately be decided if it wended its wobbly way through the state system and reached the highest court of the state. Judge Quintus may be very circumspect about predicting that *Aristotle* would be overruled, but if he is firmly convinced that the Minnesota Supreme Court would approve contribution today he should apply that rule.

c. The only difference in this scenario is that Judge Quintus, when he rules, has the benefit of the intermediate appellate court's prediction of what the state supreme court will do. That is certainly useful data in determining what the highest court would say; indeed it is highly persuasive. But it is not absolutely dispositive. The federal judge's role is to predict what the Minnesota Supreme Court would do, not to follow what the Court of Appeals thinks the supreme court would do. See, e.g., *Dimidowich v. Bell & Howell,* 803 F.2d 1473, 1482 (9th Cir. 1986) (intermediate court decisions are data to be followed unless the court is convinced by other persuasive data that the state's highest court would decide otherwise). If Judge Quintus is convinced from his general review of the law in the area that the Minnesota Supreme Court would continue to follow *Aristotle,* he must do so.

d. If you had strong arguments that the Minnesota Supreme Court would change the rule, you might well file this case in federal court. In the state trial court you would likely lose on a motion to dismiss, since *Aristotle* is mandatory precedent, which the state trial judge must follow. Even if the case goes to the state Court of Appeals, you would still lose under *Aristotle,* since the intermediate appellate court will consider itself bound by that decision. Only if the Minnesota Supreme Court takes the case (a matter vested in its discretion, which is sparingly exercised)[8] will you have a chance of winning.

In federal court, on the other hand, if the trial judge is convinced that the state supreme court would adopt contribution, he may allow the case to go forward. This will keep the case alive. Maybe it will settle. If it goes up on appeal, the federal Court of Appeals will not be bound by *Aristotle,* if convinced it is a derelict waiting to be interred by its creator. Federal judges are not anxious to disregard state supreme court decisions, but they can do it upon strong evidence, and sometimes it is pretty clear that the law will change.

The irony here is that the federal judge's freedom to predict what the law *will be,* rather than woodenly applying what it has been, opens up a narrow opportunity for diversity plaintiffs to choose more favorable substantive law despite *Erie.* Theoretically the ultimate result would be the same because the Minnesota Supreme Court, if the case got up there, would do what the federal court predicts it would. But, as a practical matter, the case probably won't get there. The result in state court is likely to be dictated by the (perhaps outdated) *Aristotle* case but might not be in federal court.

Perhaps because of this disparity some federal courts have expressed considerable reluctance to recognize new state law rights in diversity cases. See, e.g., *Tritle v. Crown Airways, Inc.,* 928 F.2d 81, 84-85 (4th Cir. 1991).

---

8. Cf. *Abbott Laboratories v. Granite State Ins. Co.,* 573 F. Supp. 193, 198 & 198 n.5 (N.D. Ill. 1983), in which Judge Shadur argues that the chance of getting the Illinois Supreme Court's view on an issue of Illinois law is miniscule. For 1982, he notes, 706,893 cases were disposed of in the Illinois trial courts, but the Illinois Supreme Court only wrote 199 opinions.

These courts reason that the plaintiff who seeks recognition of new rights under state law should sue in state court:

> We have warned, time and again, that litigants who reject a state fo-rum in order to bring suit in federal court under diversity jurisdiction cannot expect that new [state-law] trails will be blazed.

Carlton v. Worcester Ins. Co., 923 F.2d 1, 3 (1st Cir. 1991) (quoting from *Ryan v. Royal Ins. Co.*, 916 F.2d 731, 744 (1st Cir. 1990); cf. *Spector Motor Service, Inc. v. Walsh*, 139 F.2d 809, 823 (2d Cir.) (Hand, J., dissenting), va-cated 323 U.S. 101 (1944) (warning lower courts against "embrac[ing] the exhilarating opportunity of anticipating a doctrine which may be in the womb of time, but whose birth is distant").

Role Reversal

7.   Judge Ulpian should rule any way he wants to: He is not bound by the Eighth Circuit's conclusion that Minnesota law allows contribution. The Eighth Circuit under *Erie* cannot make the law of Minnesota, it can only predict what the Minnesota courts will do or follow what they have done. Minnesota judges are not bound by federal judges' predictions about Minnesota law, even federal appellate judges.

Although not bound by the Eighth Circuit's decision, Judge Ulpian is likely to give the opinion in *Solon v. Ovid* serious consideration in deciding Justinian's case. A panel of three august federal judges has looked at Minnesota tort law and concluded that the Minnesota Supreme Court would allow contribution. Judge Ulpian may not be bound to follow that conclu-sion, but he may well be persuaded by a well-reasoned opinion by judges who, though they do not make Minnesota law, are fully conversant with it. Put another way, *Solon v. Ovid* is persuasive authority, though not mandatory.

8.   Federal district courts are normally bound to follow the precedents of their supervisory court of appeals. Certainly, if the Eighth Circuit Court of Appeals decided an issue of federal law, Judge Quintus would be bound to follow it. That's what the whole system of mandatory prece-dent means. However, in diversity cases, federal courts do not make the law, they just guess at it. Should the federal district judge be bound by the Eighth Circuit's guess as to what the Minnesota Supreme Court would do?

As a practical matter, if Judge Quintus makes a different guess, the los-ing party will appeal, and the Eighth Circuit will overrule him based on its *own* guess announced in the *Solon* case. So it makes sense for the district court judge to follow the Eighth Circuit's conclusion even though the Eighth Circuit does not "make" Minnesota law.

Suppose, however, that after *Solon* the Minnesota Supreme Court de-cided several cases in related areas that suggest that they would *not* change the rule on contribution. At this point, Judge Quintus may be convinced that the Eighth Circuit would no longer make the same prediction on Minnesota law that it did in *Solon* because the evidence as to what Minnesota law "is" has changed. In such cases, where the court is convinced that later developments render the federal appeals court's prediction obsolete, it may disregard it. See, e.g., *Scadron v. City of Des Plaines*, 734 F. Supp. 1437, 1451-1452 (N.D. Ill. 1990).

Preempted Predictions

9.   In this example, Judge Quintus did his best to ascertain what Minnesota's rule on contribution was, but his prediction on the matter simply turned out to be wrong. Once that becomes clear, should a party like Lucian be able to undo the judgment Quintus rendered 18 months before and proceed with his contribution action? A ruling that he may do so would arguably further the policies of *Erie*, since it would facilitate having the case come out the same way in federal court that it would in state court. But it would severely hamper another procedural value, the ability of litigants to rely on the finality of judgments.

Several federal courts of appeals have confronted this problem. In *DeWeerth v. Baldinger*, 38 F.3d 1266 (2d Cir. 1994), the Second Circuit refused to reopen a diversity case, even though the federal judgment was based on an interpretation of state law that was later held wrong by New York's highest court:

> The very nature of diversity jurisdiction leaves open the possibility that a state court will subsequently disagree with a federal court's interpretation of state law. However, this aspect of our dual justice system does not mean that all diversity judgments are subject to revision once a state court later addresses the litigated issues. Such a rule would be tantamount to holding that the doctrine of finality does not apply to diversity judgments . . .

38 F.3d at 1273-1274. The Seventh Circuit similarly refused to reopen a diversity judgment in *McGeshick v. Choicair*, 72 F.3d 62 (7th Cir. 1995), though the court left open the possibility that "extraordinary circumstances" might support a different result. Accord: *Batts v. Tow-Motor Forklift Co.*, 66 F.3d 743 (5th Cir. 1995).

These decisions, while obviously frustrating to the losing party, make sense. Ordinarily, if a judgment is entered and no appeal is taken, parties can rely on the fact that the case is over. If a diversity case could be reopened whenever the state court clarified state law down the line, the case would only be *provisionally* over. The parties would not be able to rely on the judgment, since it might be reconsidered at some indefinite future time. As has been said in another context, "sometimes it is more important that a judgment be stable than it be correct." Friedenthal, Kane and Miller 3d ed. 1999 at 636. This is probably one of those situations.

The risk of an erroneous prediction of state law is inherent in diversity jurisdiction after *Erie*. It is probably best to recognize that and let the chips fall where they may.

High Fidelity

10a. The Illinois Supreme Court has held that the trial courts within each judicial district must follow the rule established by the appellate court for that district, even though other appellate courts of equal stature have ruled otherwise. See *People v. Thorpe*, 367 N.E.2d 960, 963 (Ill. App. 2d 1977). Consequently, the judge in *Gaius v. Draco* must follow the holding of the First District that contribution is not allowed between joint tortfeasors.

Under this approach, if there is a split among the districts of the Illinois Appellate Court, the "law" of Illinois will differ from one part of the state to another until the Illinois Supreme Court takes a case on further review and resolves the split in the appellate decisions.

b. The *Erie* doctrine requires the federal judge to follow the law of the state, but in this case, the "law" of the state differs, depending on which judicial district the case is filed in. What should the federal judge do?

There are several possible answers in this situation. One, perhaps the most obvious in light of the earlier examples, is to predict how the Illinois Supreme Court would rule on the issue. The federal court's job, after all, is to predict what "the law" of Illinois is, not the law of the First Appellate District or the Third.

. . . Or is it? Judge Shadur of the Northern District of Illinois has consistently ruled otherwise. He argues that the federal judge's job is to assure that the suit comes out the same way in federal court that it would in state court. See, e.g., *Abbott Laboratories v. Granite State Ins. Co.*, 573 F. Supp. 193, 196-200 (N.D. Ill. 1983). Allowing Gaius to avoid the First District's non-contribution rule by going to federal court, Judge Shadur argues, will undermine the *Erie* goal of uniformity and encourage choice of the federal court to obtain a "better rule of law." Consequently, he concludes that the federal district court must follow the rulings of the Illinois Appellate Court for the district in which the case was filed.

Most courts, however, have followed the "Supreme Court predictive approach," which asks how the state supreme court would decide the issue if the case got up that far. See *Outsource Intern: Inc. v. Barton*, 192 F.3d 662, 674 (7th Cir. 1999) (Posner, C. J. dissenting) (suggesting that Circuit Court should "put the contending district judges out of their misery" by definitively adopting the predictive approach). Judge Shadur finds this rule unrealistic, because few cases *do* get that far: For most parties "the law" is the rule of the appellate court for their judicial district. Thus, he argues, the "Supreme Court predictive approach" will often yield a result quite different from the one the parties would obtain in state court. See *Abbott Laboratories* at 198 & 198 n.5. For a good review of this problem, and the arguments both ways, see B. Mattis & B. Mattis, *Erie* and Florida Law Conflict at the Crossroads: The Constitutional Need for Statewide Stare Decisis, 18 Nova L. Rev. 1333, 1365-1376 (1994).

Like example 6, this example demonstrates that, despite the command of *Erie,* it is very difficult to assure absolute uniformity in treatment within the two court systems.

11

Eerie Erie: *The Substance/Substance Distinction*

Introduction

As "Easy *Erie*" suggests, the *Erie* doctrine is applied without substantial difficulty in most diversity cases. *Erie* and the Rules of Decision Act (RDA) require the federal court to apply state law, and the court does. It uses the state rules governing the standard of care to a trespasser, enforceability of contracts, the validity of wills and property transfers, and myriad other state rules of law, whether pronounced by statute or by common law.

It sounds easy, and often it is easy. But not always. Lurking behind the majestic and simple truths of the *Erie* case were some complex implications, which, if not foreseen by the *Erie* justices, have certainly bedeviled their successors. These implications are so subtle and important to our ideas of federalism that they have fascinated law professors as well. Consequently, while they play a relatively minor part in the daily administration of diversity jurisdiction, they figure prominently—too prominently, perhaps—in the first-year Civil Procedure course.

The most puzzling problem, of course, has been determining which issues are governed by the command of *Erie*. Clearly, *Erie* requires federal courts to apply state law to issues upon which there is no federal law-making power. For example, neither Congress nor the federal courts have any authority to establish the standard of care generally owed to trespassers. Thus, the RDA, as interpreted in *Erie,* requires the federal court to apply state law on this "substantive" issue. But it is doubtful that the Court ever thought that *Erie*'s command would require federal courts to follow state law on clearly *procedural* issues in diversity cases.

The Emergence of the Problem

It didn't take long for the substance/procedure problem implicit in *Erie* to begin to emerge. The very next term the Court decided *Cities Service Oil Co. v. Dunlap*, 308 U.S. 208 (1939), which raised an issue much closer to the line between substance and procedure than the tort issue in *Erie:* which party had the burden of proof on a question of title to land. Texas law placed the burden of proof on validity of title on the party challenging the title, but federal procedure placed it on the party who brought suit, in this case the holder of the record title. The federal Court of Appeals concluded that *Erie* did not require use of the state rule, since the issue was "a matter of practice or procedure and not a matter of substantive law." 101 F.2d 314, 316 (1939). However, the Supreme Court reversed, holding that the burden of proof issue "relates to a substantial right" so that *Erie* mandated application of state law. 308 U.S. at 212.

The *Dunlap* decision must have sent shock waves through the legal community. The decision suggested that *Erie* required diversity courts to defer to state law not only on "substantive" rules but also on matters of procedure that related to the enforcement of state rights. If the federal court had to apply state law on burden of proof in a diversity case, why not on the time for filing a complaint, the right to amend, or the admissibility of evidence? At its most extreme, this would mean that federal courts would have to abandon the Federal Rules of Civil Procedure in diversity cases and apply instead the entire *procedural* law of the state in which they sat. Federal courts would then operate under a dual system of procedure: the Federal Rules in federal question, admiralty, and other types of cases within federal subject matter jurisdiction, but state procedural law when jurisdiction was based on diversity.[1]

The next major post-*Erie* case did little to allay these concerns. In *Guaranty Trust Co. v. York*, 326 U.S. 99 (1945), the issue was whether a federal diversity court must apply the state statute of limitations to a claim, or whether it was free to apply its own more flexible "laches" doctrine to the case. The court, speaking through Justice Frankfurter, refused to distinguish

---

1. This prospect was enormously ironic because up until 1938 federal courts *had* followed state procedural rules in all cases. The Federal Rules of Civil Procedure took effect in 1938, the same year that *Erie* was decided. Prior to 1938 the Conformity Act of 1872 provided that federal courts should follow the procedural rules of the state in which they sat. Thus, under the Conformity Act the procedural rules differed from one federal court to another because each applied the procedure of the state in which it sat. The Federal Rules introduced a uniform, independent set of federal procedural rules for the first time . . . and the progeny of *Erie* promptly threatened to destroy it.

Erie on the basis that it involved state "substantive" law while *York* involved "procedure." Instead, the Court held that the state limitations statute must be applied, in order to implement the "policy" of *Erie* that

> in all cases where a federal court is exercising jurisdiction solely because of the diversity of citizenship of the parties, the outcome of the litigation in the federal court should be substantially the same, so far as legal rules determine the outcome of a litigation, as it would be if tried in a State court.

326 U.S. at 109. If following a federal practice that differed from state procedure might "significantly affect the result of a litigation" (id.), the court must apply the state rule instead, to prevent diverse parties from gaining unfair advantages simply because they can choose federal court. In *York*, this "outcome-determinative" test dictated use of the state limitations statute, since the claim was barred under that statute but might have been allowed to proceed under the federal laches doctrine.

In retrospect, it is clear that *York* and *Cities Service Oil* extended the *Erie* doctrine well beyond the area where application of state law was compelled by the United States Constitution. *Erie* required the lower federal court to apply the state duty of care because neither the federal courts nor Congress has constitutional authority to create rules of tort law.[2] However, *York* and *Cities Service Oil* involved situations in which there *was* federal authority to create a separate rule for the federal courts. The Constitution grants Congress the power to establish lower federal courts (Article I, s. 8; Article III s. 1), and to make laws "necessary and proper" for exercising that power. Article I, s. 8. Thus, there is constitutional authority to make federal procedural rules, even for diversity cases, presumably including the authority to provide a federal limitations period in a case like *York*, or a burden of proof rule for a case like *Cities Service Oil*. Despite this federal authority, *York's* outcome determinative test required federal courts to apply state law, *as a matter of policy, not constitutional compulsion*, where using a separate federal rule could lead to a different outcome. Although the Court in *York* could have applied the separate federal laches rule, it concluded that uniformity of outcomes in state and federal court was more important than following a separate federal rule whenever it constitutionally could. Where *Erie* had commanded, "follow state tort law, because 'there can be no other law,'"[3] *York* pronounced, "follow state law, even where

---

2. This is often, but not always, true. Various constitutional provisions may support federal power to enact tort legislation in some circumstances. For example, the interstate commerce power in Article I, §8, would doubtless support federal legislation dealing with products liability claims. And scholars have argued that Congress could have enacted a standard of care governing the *Erie* facts under the interstate commerce power because of its impact on interstate transportation. See, e.g., 19 Wright and Miller §4505 at 63-64.

3. *Hanna v. Plumer,* 380 U.S. 460, 472 (1965).

there can be federal law, if it will further the policy of uniform outcomes in diversity cases."

However, this uniformity policy clearly could have a drastic impact on federal procedure in diversity cases. Suppose that state law allows 30 days to answer a complaint and federal law only allows 20. If Clinton files suit in federal court, and Fisk answers on the twenty-fifth day, that difference could be outcome determinative. If Clinton serves Fisk by leaving the summons and complaint at his last and usual place of abode (see Fed. R. Civ. P. 4 (e)(2)), but state law requires personal delivery to Fisk, that difference may be outcome determinative. If federal law allows Clinton to amend his pleadings to add new claims after the limitations period passes, but state law does not, that also may be outcome determinative. At its broadest, *York* would mandate use of the state rule in each of these cases, although there is federal constitutional authority to establish a different rule. If so, it should be clear that there would not be much left of the Federal Rules of Civil Procedure in diversity cases.

The Pendulum Swings Back . . . a Little

Next in this intimidating line of post-*Erie* decisions is *Byrd v. Blue Ridge Rural Electrical Cooperative, Inc.*, 356 U.S. 525 (1958). The *Erie* issue in *Byrd* was whether the judge or the jury should determine the plaintiff's status as an "employee" of the defendant. State law left the question to the judge, but the practice in federal court was to send such issues to the jury.

Although *Byrd* is often viewed as a departure from *York*, the *Byrd* Court actually reaffirmed the holdings of both *Erie* and *York*. First, the Court reiterated that federal courts must honor the "definition of state-created rights and obligations by the state courts." 356 U.S. at 535. This is the constitutional prong of the *Erie* doctrine, exemplified by *Erie* itself, in which the rule at issue involved clearly "substantive" law — duty of care to a trespasser — which the Constitution reserves to the states. In this category of cases, *Byrd* reaffirms, the federal court must follow state law because it has no power to create a separate federal rule. In *Byrd*, however, the South Carolina rule authorizing the judge to decide "employee" status was *not* "bound up with the definition of the rights and obligations of the parties," but "merely a form and mode of enforcing" the compensation scheme. 356 U.S. at 536. Thus, the issue was a matter of procedure as to which the federal court was not constitutionally compelled to apply the state practice.

Having determined that *Erie's* constitutional analysis did not require the federal court to apply South Carolina's rule, Justice Brennan next considered whether *York* did. He acknowledged that *York* evinced a "broader policy" than *Erie*, requiring federal courts to follow state practices even of "form and mode" (as opposed to clearly substantive law) if ignoring them would substantially affect the outcome of the litigation. 356 U.S. at 536. Thus, *Byrd* reaffirmed that, under *York*, federal courts should apply outcome-determinative state law even on procedural issues as to which there is federal constitutional authority to make its own rule. Brennan even conceded that, absent other considerations, the outcome determinative test would very likely require the court to apply state law to the judge-jury issue before it in *Byrd*. 356 U.S. at 537.

However, Justice Brennan went on to hold that, in deciding whether to follow state law in matters of "form and mode" (that is, the area in which the court follows state law as a matter of policy rather than constitutional command), the federal court must consider not only the *York* policy of uniform outcomes in diversity cases, but also any countervailing federal policies that arise from the federal court's status as an independent judicial system. In *Byrd*, the constitutional right to jury trial under the seventh amendment to the Constitution was at least tangentially implicated in making the choice between judge and jury. Given the importance of that right in the administration of federal courts, Justice Brennan concluded that the *Erie* policy of maximizing uniformity of outcome should yield to the federal policy of broad availability of jury trial. 356 U.S. at 538-539. The state of *Erie* analysis after *Byrd* is illustrated by Figure 11-1.

Because *Byrd* reaffirmed that state rules of form and mode should usually be applied if they might prove outcome determinative, it still appeared after *Byrd* that state procedural rules would often supersede the Federal Rules of Civil Procedure in diversity cases. It remained for the Warren Court to rescue the Rules in *Hanna v. Plumer*, 380 U.S. 460 (1965).

Nature of issue	Federal Court should
Matters of clearly substantive law ("bound up with the rights and obligations" created by state law)	apply state law (*Erie*)
Matters of "form and mode" (procedure) where applying separate rule would likely affect the outcome	apply state law (*York*)
Matters of "form and mode" (procedure) where applying separate rule would likely affect the outcome, but there are important federal countervailing considerations	apply federal law (*Byrd*)
Matters of "form and mode" (procedure) where applying separate federal rule is unlikely to affect outcome	apply federal law

Figure 11-1: *Erie* Analysis after *Byrd*

The Rules Rescued: Hanna v. Plumer

The issue in *Hanna,* like many of these post-*Erie* cases, was less than titillating. The plaintiff served process on the defendant, the executor of a Massachusetts estate, by leaving the summons and complaint at his home with "a person of suitable age and discretion," as required by Fed. R. Civ. P. 4(d)(1).[4] However, a Massachusetts statute required in-hand service upon the executor. Mass. Gen. L. ch. 197, §9. While the issue was dull, the stakes were high: If service was valid, the case would go forward. If it was not, it would have to be dismissed, since the executor had not been served within the limitations period. Validity of service turned, of course, on whether the federal court was required to apply the state service rule instead of Rule 4(d)(1).

The defendant made a seemingly airtight argument for application of the state rule: *York* says "use state law if doing so will affect the outcome." I win immediately if the state statute is applied, since service was not made within the limitations period. But the case goes forward if service was valid under the Federal Rule. Certainly, that difference is outcome determinative, so the state rule must be applied.

The argument was a good one, but Chief Justice Warren found several reasons for rejecting it. In the first part of the opinion (which I will call *Hanna* Part 1) he analyzed the conflict between the two service rules under a modified outcome-determinative test. Whether a federal procedure is outcome determinative, Warren concluded, must be viewed in light of the policies underlying *Erie,* to prevent forum shopping and inequitable administration of the laws. Not every difference between state and federal rules leads to those problems. It is very doubtful, for example, that a plaintiff would choose federal court over state court simply to avoid serving the defendant in person, since the effort required to do so is only marginally greater than that required to serve under the federal rule. Nor is the minor difference in litigation effort between "last and usual" service and in-hand service sufficient to be viewed as "inequitable administration of the laws." Thus, the Court concluded, the outcome-determinative test, viewed in light of the aims of the *Erie* doctrine, did not require the federal court to substitute the state rule for its own.

Hanna *Part 2: A Distinct Analysis for Federal Rules Conflicts*

The major *Erie* cases, before *Hanna,* involved conflicts between federal judicial practices (that is, informal practices of federal judges not required by federal statute or Federal Rule) and state law. For example, *Erie* involved the

---

4. See now Fed. R. Civ. P. 4(e)(2).

practice of federal judges of "making" common law on tort issues, despite differing state common law. *York* involved the federal judicial practice of applying the laches doctrine, rather than state statutory limitations periods. *Byrd* involved the choice by federal judges, not commanded by statute or Rule, to send certain issues to the jury, which were determined by the judge under corresponding state practice. Thus, the Court in these cases had no occasion to decide whether the standard for deferring to state law in a diversity case would be the same if the state law conflicted with a formal Federal Rule of Civil Procedure.

In *Hanna* Part 1, the Court analyzed the service issue before it *as though* it involved the typical "relatively unguided *Erie* choice" between an uncodified federal judicial practice and state law. It concluded that such conflicts should be addressed under a "modified outcome-determinative test" based on avoidance of forum shopping and inequitable administration of the laws. However, in the second part of *Hanna,* the Court noted that the service provision at issue (Rule 4(d)(1)) was a Federal Rule of Civil Procedure, recommended by the Advisory Committee on the Civil Rules, officially promulgated by the Supreme Court under the Rules Enabling Act (see 28 U.S.C. §2072, hereinafter referred to as the REA), and implicitly endorsed by Congress. In *Hanna* Part 2, the Court established an entirely different analysis for cases in which an official Federal Rule of Civil Procedure conflicts with state law.

The REA was enacted in 1934 and is still in effect. The first section of the REA authorizes the Supreme Court to "prescribe general rules of practice and procedure" for the federal courts.[5] Pursuant to this authority, an advisory committee appointed by the Supreme Court drafted the Federal Rules (and continues to revise them periodically). They were then promulgated by the Supreme Court and, as required by the REA (28 U.S.C. §2074), submitted to Congress for review before taking effect.

Thus, there is both constitutional and statutory authority for the adoption of the Federal Rules. In *Hanna,* the Court held that Article III and the Necessary and Proper Clause provide broad *constitutional* authority to

> make rules governing the practice and pleading in [federal] courts, which in turn includes a power to regulate matters which, though falling within the uncertain area between substance and procedure, are rationally capable of classification as either.

---

5. The relevant provisions of the REA, as it presently reads, are as follows:

> §2072. (a) The Supreme Court shall have the power to prescribe general rules of practice and procedure and rules of evidence for cases in the United States district courts (including proceedings before magistrates thereof) and courts of appeals.
>
> (b) Such rules shall not abridge, enlarge, or modify any substantive right. . . .

380 U.S. at 472. This language suggests, as some have concluded, that Congress and the Court have broad constitutional authority to promulgate any rule that is "arguably procedural."[6]

The first section of the REA also provides broad *statutory* authority to promulgate "general rules of practice and procedure." In *Hanna* the court endorsed an equally broad construction of this statutory grant:

> The test must be whether a rule really regulates procedure — the judicial process for enforcing rights and duties recognized by substantive law and for justly administering remedy and redress for disregard or infraction of them.

Hanna, 380 U.S. at 464 (quoting from *Sibbach v. Wilson*, 312 U.S. 1, 14 (1941)). Like *Hanna*'s broad definition of the constitutional grant, this somewhat tautological definition suggests that the Court has the authority under the REA to adopt any Federal Rule that is "arguably procedural." And, for what it is worth, Congress's acquiescence in the rules (by failing to intercept them after they are promulgated and submitted for review) provides a little extra dose of credibility. To invalidate one of the Rules, the Court would have to conclude that the Advisory Committee, the Supreme Court, and Congress had all erred in their judgment that the rule could validly be applied in federal court.

Given *Hanna*'s very broad construction of the federal constitutional and statutory authority to promulgate the Federal Rules, a party who argues that a Federal Rule is invalid because it is not "procedural" faces a very steep uphill battle. Suppose, for example, that the Court adopted a formal Federal Rule providing that the plaintiff shall bear the burden of proof in establishing title to property (the issue analyzed in *Cities Service Oil*). This rule, which governs the method of proof at trial of a civil case, is "arguably procedural." While it might not pass a *York* outcome determination test (perhaps even as modified by *Hanna*, Part I), it would survive scrutiny under the first subsection of the REA.

But wait! The second subsection of the REA (28 U.S.C. s. 2072(b)) opens another avenue of attack: It provides that "[s]uch rules shall not abridge, enlarge, or modify any substantive right." Thus, alas, the elusive substance/procedure distinction also emerges in assessing the validity of Federal Rules under the REA. A Rule, though "procedural" under the first subsection of the REA, is invalid under the second if it impinges on "substantive rights."

Well, this is a little eerie: A federal judicial practice may not be applied in a diversity case, under *Hanna* Part 1, if it is "substantive" in the sense that it fails the modified outcome-determinative test. And a formal Federal Rule may not be applied if it impinges on "substantive" rights under the

---

6. See *Hanna*, 380 U.S. at 476 (Harlan, J., concurring) (describing the majority's test for validity as "arguably procedural, *ergo* constitutional").

second subsection of the REA. However, "substance" must mean something different in the Federal Rules context than it does under the outcome-determinative test (hence the enigmatic title of the chapter) or there would be no need for separate analyses under *Hanna* Part 1 and *Hanna* Part 2.

A Framework for Analysis

Although cases since *Hanna* have fine-tuned the analysis somewhat, *Erie*, *York*, *Byrd*, and *Hanna* provide the basic framework for determining when the federal court must defer to state law. What follows are some basic ground rules that should help you identify the proper arguments to make in such cases.

There are four basic types of federal provisions that may conflict with state law. *First*, a federal constitutional provision might mandate a federal court procedure that differs from state law (as, for example, requiring a unanimous jury verdict, even though state law would allow a majority verdict). *Second*, a federal statute may govern federal practice but conflict with state law. An example might be a statute that requires federal courts to enforce arbitration agreements, even though the courts of a state would not. *Third*, a formal Federal Rule of Civil Procedure may conflict with state law, such as the conflicting service provisions in *Hanna*. *Last*, federal judges may develop judicial practices, that is, procedures applied as a matter of common practice not embodied in a Federal Rule or statute, which differ from state law (the situation discussed in *Hanna* Part 1). For example, federal judges may, as a matter of accepted judicial practice, comment to the jury on the evidence or allow alternate jurors to deliberate on cases or allow juries to decide certain issues, even though state practice is different. Each of these categories of conflicts requires a slightly different analysis.[7]

A. Conflicts between a Federal Constitutional Provision and State Law

The United States Constitution is the "supreme Law of the Land." U.S. Const., Article VI, ¶2. Its provisions apply even if they conflict with state law, *substantive or procedural*, because we all agreed to that, by proxy, back in 1789, without any "ifs," "ands," "buts," or "outcome-determinative" modifiers. If the constitution mandates a practice different from state law, the constitutional requirement prevails. For example, if the seventh amendment

---

7. This discussion, and my understanding of the entire *Erie* doctrine, owes much to the fine article by Westen and Lehman, Is There Life for *Erie* After the Death of Diversity, 78 Mich. L. Rev. 311 (1980). I highly recommend it to those who want to explore these issues further.

requires unanimous jury verdicts (an issue still unclear at this writing), the federal court would apply that requirement in a diversity case even though state practice allowed majority verdicts, as some do. Indeed, if the Constitution were amended to bar trespassers from recovering from railroads, that provision would *also* trump state law, even though it establishes a clearly substantive rule.

B. Conflicts between a Federal Statute and State Law

Federal statutes are also the supreme Law of the Land, if they are valid. So, if the conflict is between a federal statute and state law, the issue is whether Congress had the authority to enact the federal statute. *Hanna* holds that Congress has the constitutional authority to enact statutes governing procedure in the federal courts if, "while falling in the uncertain area between substance and procedure, [they] are rationally capable of classification as either." *Hanna,* 380 U.S. at 472. The duty-to-trespassers rule in *Erie* would fail this test, but most statutes related to the litigation process will not. If this "arguably procedural" test is met, the statute must be applied if it conflicts with state practice because Congress has the authority to enact the statute, and valid federal statutes are the "supreme Law of the Land" even if they conflict with state law. U.S. Const., Article VI, ¶2.

In *Stewart Organization, Inc. v. Ricoh Corp.,* 487 U.S. 22 (1988), the Supreme Court upheld application of 28 U.S.C. §1404 (a), the federal statute governing transfer of cases between federal district courts, on this reasoning. In *Stewart* the Court found a state practice refusing to enforce forum selection clauses in conflict with §1404(a), which calls for case-by-case discretion in deciding whether to transfer a case. Since the question of which federal court should hear a particular case is "arguably procedural," the Court concluded that Congress has the power to enact §1404(a). Thus, the statute is valid and applies in federal court even if the state court would apply a different rule.

C. Conflicts between a Federal Rule and State Law

If a Federal Rule of Civil Procedure conflicts with state law, the Federal Rule applies if it is valid. *Hanna* Part 2. Congress has the constitutional power to authorize the Supreme Court to adopt a Federal Rule, *Hanna* concludes, if the Rule is "rationally capable of classification" as a procedural regulation. And the first section of the REA authorizes the Court to adopt the rule if it is procedural under the similarly broad definition in *Sibbach,* that is, it "really regulates procedure—the judicial process for enforcing rights and duties recognized by substantive law and for justly administering remedy and redress for disregard or infraction of them." Virtually all Federal Rules will satisfy these broad tests. So the Federal Rules are valid, unless they "abridge, enlarge, or modify" a substantive right under the second subsection of the REA. (This exception is discussed further at pp. 196-197.)

D. Conflicts between a Federal Judicial Practice and State Law

Federal judges have to run their courtrooms. That means they often make rulings resolving recurring issues that arise in the day-to-day administration of justice but are not addressed by the Constitution, federal statutes, or Federal Rules. Under *Erie* itself, such federal judicial practices are invalid if they purport to establish rules of primary behavior (like the duty to trespassers rule in *Erie*), which there is no federal constitutional power to make. In other cases, where the practice relates to the conduct of litigation (so that there is federal authority to make a separate rule), *Hanna* Part 1 indicates that a diversity court should still choose the state rule if the difference between it and the federal practice could prove "outcome determinative," in the sense that following a separate federal practice could lead to forum shopping or inequitable administration of the laws. Whether the difference leads to those evils may be problematic in a particular case, but at least it is fairly clear that the argument should be framed under *Hanna* Part 1.

Problems in Applying the Hanna Analyses

The principles above provide a framework for analyzing these eerie *Erie* problems. However, they do not answer the really hard questions which arise in working through the analysis. Here are some sticky parts:

* When is there a direct conflict between a federal statute or Rule and state law?

There is no need to choose between a Federal Rule or federal statute and state law unless there is a "direct conflict" between them, but it is not clear when such a conflict exists. Some cases have avoided displacing state law by reading the Federal Rule narrowly to avoid a conflict. In *Walker v. Armco Steel Corp.*, 446 U.S. 740 (1980), for example, the issue was whether the plaintiff had to file suit or serve process on the defendant within the limitations period. The plaintiff filed suit within the limitations period, but did not serve the defendant with the summons and complaint until well after. The Supreme Court avoided a difficult *Hanna* Part 2 clash by holding that Federal Rule 3, which provides that a suit is commenced by filing, is not intended to govern when the limitations period is tolled: It only prescribes the point for calculating various time requirements under the Federal Rules (such as the time for filing an answer, taking depositions, or sending interrogatories.

Similarly, the court in *Gasperini v. Center for Humanities, Inc.,* 518 U.S. 415 (1996), found no conflict between Federal Rule 59, which specifies that new trials may be granted in federal court for "the reasons for which new trials have heretofore been granted in actions at law in the courts of the United States," and a state statute which set a specific, stringent standard for review of damage awards. By contrast, the Court found a conflict between a state costs statute that required a penalty for certain appeals and Federal Rule 38, which gives appellate courts discretion to award costs for frivolous appeals. *Burlington Northern R.R. Co. v. Woods,* 480 U.S. 1 (1987).

These decisions don't provide consistent guidance. The easy cases will be those where the federal provision (whether a federal statute or a Federal Rule) and the state provision are directly contradictory. If a federal statute required unanimous verdicts and state law provided for majority verdicts, the two would require contradictory procedures and could not coexist. Probably, a conflict will also be found where federal law provides a discretionary standard to govern an issue, but state law requires a particular outcome, as was true in *Burlington Northern.* Beyond that, a conflict will likely be found where the relevant federal provision was meant to "occupy the field," or where applying the state rule would demonstrably impair the operation of the cognate federal provision.

- When does a Federal Rule, which is constitutionally valid and "procedural" under the first subsection of the REA, violate the second subsection because it "abridges, enlarges, or modifies substantive rights?

This is a real toughie. A short answer is "seldom;" very few cases have invalidated a Federal Rule under this subsection of the REA. The Federal Rule will have to have a substantial impact on a state policy unrelated to litigation to be declared invalid under the second paragraph of the REA, given the heavy presumption of validity created by *Hanna.* The Court in *Burlington Northern R.R. Co. v. Woods,* 480 U.S. 1, 8 (1986), held that procedural rules which "incidentally" affect substantive rights are permissible under the second sentence of the REA, and rather casually concluded that Federal Rule of Appellate Procedure 38 passes muster because it "affects only the process of enforcing litigants' rights and not the rights themselves." 480 U.S. at 5, 8.

Various tests have been proposed to determine when a federal rule impermissibly trenches on "substantive" rights to this extent. One commentator suggests that a right is "substantive" in the REA sense if it is "granted for one or more nonprocedural reasons, for some purpose or purposes not having to do with the fairness or efficiency of the litigation process."[8] A House Report on amendments to the REA suggests that a Rule would interfere with substantive rights if it involved "lawmaking choices that necessarily and obviously require consideration of policies extrinsic to the business of the courts."[9]

---

8. J. Ely, The Irrepressible Myth of Erie, 87 Harv. L. Rev. 693, 725 (1974).
9. House of Representatives Report 99-422 (1985) p. 22.

A few illustrative cases may give a sense of the type of provision likely to pass muster — or not — under the second subsection of the REA. Doubtless, a Federal Rule barring trespassers from recovering damages would be struck down as substantive, or a provision barring enforcement of monopoly contracts. These examples govern primary rights outside the courtroom (though, of course, they must be enforced within one). On the other end of the spectrum, courts have applied Rule 42(a), which allows bifurcating a trial (for example, trying the liability and damages issues separately) in diversity cases even though state law requires a single trial.[10] Another case applied Federal Rule 32(a)(3), limiting use of depositions at trial in a diversity case in lieu of a more liberal state rule.[11] These examples deal directly with the administration of litigation in the courtroom, are not tied to any particular type of case, and do not necessarily favor one party over another. In between are the closer cases. For example, the right to claim the attorney-client privilege to avoid giving certain testimony is invoked in a courtroom, but clearly affects primary behavior — the communications between lawyer and client — outside the courtroom as well. Similarly, the right of a prevailing party to recover attorneys' fees in certain cases is administered in court, but has a substantial impact on the protection of the rights claimed in those cases. Very likely, a Federal Rule which contradicted state law in either of these two examples, though they deal with issues "arguably procedural," would be held invalid under the second subsection of the REA.

- What differences are sufficient to lead to "inequitable administration of the laws" under *Hanna* Part 1?

Here again, the cases provide a framework for analysis but little clarity as to how the court will apply the relevant concepts. *Hanna* Part 1's modified outcome determinative test is certainly narrower than *York's*, which required use of state law any time the difference could be outcome determinative. But it evidently requires more deference to state law than the second section of the REA, which bars Federal Rules which abridge, enlarge, or modify substantive rights. Some practices will pass muster if the Court and Congress formally require them, but not if federal judges simply adopt them as a matter of practice.

For example, *Walker* held that the state practice of tolling the limitations period upon service must prevail over a contrary federal judicial practice, but suggested that this difference would be upheld if the tolling-on-commencement rule were embodied in a formal Federal Rule, despite the effect on outcome. 446 U.S. at 753. Thus there is a tough "substance/substance distinction" between the analysis under *Hanna* Part 1

---

10. See, e.g., *Oulds v. Principal Mut. Life Ins. Co.,* 6 F.3d 1431, 1435-1436 (10th Cir. 1993).
11. *Frechette v. Welch,* 621 F.2d 11, 14 (1st Cir. 1980).

and *Hanna* Part 2. Probably such "inequitable administration" will be found where using the federal approach instead of the state rule would open up a significant difference in litigation opportunity, viewed not after the fact but prospectively.

- What is the current status of *Byrd?*

In *Gasperini v. Center for Humanities, Inc.,* 518 U.S. 415 (1996), the Supreme Court resurrected *Byrd* after several decades of neglect. The analysis in *Gasperini* is somewhat opaque — not all that legal academics had hoped for from Justice Ginsburg, a former civil procedure professor. But it is clear that the Court analyzed the case as a *Hanna* Part I conflict, and that it approved *Byrd's* emphasis on the importance of the federal interests as a factor in making the "relatively unguided *Erie* choice" required under *Hanna* Part I. Thus, where a federal statute or rule is not directly implicated, so that the choice between state and federal law involves the broader *Erie* policy of uniformity, *Byrd's* admonition to weigh important federal policies against that uniformity policy remains a factor in the analysis.

This introduction may not help you all that much in "answering" hard *Erie* problems. But hopefully the discussion and the following examples will provide a framework for analyzing these problems, so that you will understand which branch of the decision tree the court is likely to venture out upon and recognize the appropriate precedents to rely upon in arguing your client's position.

EXAMPLES

Collisions and Close Calls

1. Assume that Colorado's comparative negligence statute provides that the plaintiff's recovery in a negligence case is to be reduced in proportion to his own negligence but that the plaintiff may not recover at all if his negligence was "as great as" the defendant's. The statute also specifies that the jury shall be instructed that the plaintiff will not recover if his negligence is as great as (or greater than) the defendant's.[12] The evident purpose of this provision is to let the jury know that, if they find the plaintiff 50 percent or more at fault, he will take nothing.

Morgan brings a diversity suit against Harriman in federal court for negligently causing a motor vehicle accident. The Colorado statute applies, but no one thinks to request the instruction on the effect of plaintiff's negligence. The jury is not so instructed and returns a finding that Morgan was 60 percent at fault. The judge enters judgment against Morgan, and he

---

12. The Colorado comparative negligence statute contained such a provision for some years, but it has since been repealed. See Colo. Rev. Stat. §13-21-111(4), as amended by 1975 Colo. Sess. Laws 570, §1; repealed by 1986 Colo. Sess. Laws 679, §5.

appeals, claiming a right to a new trial because the jury was not instructed in accordance with the statute.

The Colorado courts hold that a plaintiff in these circumstances is entitled to a new trial (at which the required instruction is given), even if he did not request the instruction. However, Fed. R. Civ. P. 51 provides that "[n]o party shall assign as error the giving or the failure to give an instruction unless that party objects thereto before the jury retires to consider its verdict. . . ." Harriman argues that Rule 51 applies, while Morgan argues that *Erie* principles require the court to follow Colorado law and order a new trial.

   a. How would this issue be resolved under Justice Frankfurter's analysis in *York?*
   b. How do you think it would come out after *Byrd,* but before *Hanna?*
   c. If the case arose after *Hanna,* should the issue be analyzed under *Hanna* Part 1 or Part 2?
   d. How would the issue be resolved under *Hanna* Part 2?
   e. How would it come out if there were no Federal Rule on point, but federal judges followed a judicial practice of refusing to review errors that were not objected to below?

2.   Morgan sues Harriman for negligence in federal court. The relevant state negligence law recognizes contributory negligence of the plaintiff as a complete defense and provides that the plaintiff bears the burden of proving that he was not negligent. Morgan argues, however, that the defendant should bear the burden of proving that he (Morgan) *was* negligent because Fed. R. Civ. P. 8(c) requires defendants to plead contributory negligence as an "affirmative defense." How should the court rule?

3.   Assume that the *York* case arose immediately after *Hanna v. Plumer* was decided. How would the issue in *York* be decided under the principles of *Hanna?*

4.   Assume that the judges in courts of the state of Aroostook, as a matter of judicial practice, give the jury instructions in writing, but that the federal judicial practice is to read the instructions to the jury without giving them a copy. Underwood sues Drew for negligence in federal court. Because jurisdiction is based on diversity, Aroostook law governs the underlying negligence claim. Must the federal judge instruct the jury in writing?

The Ultimate Test

5.   Assume that the Aroostook legislature has enacted a statute authorizing its supreme court to promulgate rules of procedure for the Aroostook courts, and it has adopted Aroos. R. Civ. P. 49(c), which requires the judge to give the jury a written copy of the instructions. Assume further that federal judges, as a matter of judicial practice, instruct the jury orally. Underwood sues Drew for negligence in the federal court. Aroostook law again governs the underlying negligence claim. Must the federal judge instruct the jury in writing?

Switching Tracks

6.   Clinton brings a diversity suit in federal court against Fisk for negligence. To prove Fisk's negligence, Clinton offers two days of testimony by an eminent (and expensive) expert on accident reconstruction. Clinton wins at trial, and moves to collect as "costs" a $10,000 fee he paid to the expert to review the facts, perform experiments, and prepare for trial. The relevant federal statute, 28 U.S.C §1920, provides that the prevailing party may recover certain limited types of costs of suit from the losing party. These costs include a $30-per-day attendance fee for witnesses who testify at trial, but include no provision for recovering an expert's fee for preparing for trial. By contrast, a state statute provides that the prevailing party in a negligence case may recover the full costs of retaining expert witnesses.

    a. Is there a conflict between the federal and state statutes?

    b. How should the judge rule on the motion?

7.   The State of Aroostook, concerned by skyrocketing medical malpractice insurance premiums, passes a statute limiting recovery for intangible damages (such as pain, suffering, and emotional distress) in malpractice cases. The statute provides that recovery for intangible injuries from any incident shall not exceed $250,000 and that such damages shall be determined by the judge. Morgan sues Dr. Drew in federal court for medical malpractice. The trial judge concludes that, under the seventh amendment, the jury must determine the intangible damages in federal court and that it need not apply the cap in the Aroostook statute. The jury returns a verdict for Morgan, which includes $400,000 for pain and suffering.

    Dr. Drew appeals, arguing that the federal court should have followed the Aroostook statute, since its jurisdiction is based on diversity. Thus, the $250,000 cap on damages should apply, and the judge rather than the jury should assess the damages for intangible injuries. Morgan argues that the verdict should be upheld, since the seventh amendment mandates jury trial of factual issues such as the amount of the damages — which it does. How should the court rule?

The Late Train

8.   Morgan sues Harriman but discovers after the passage of the limitations period that it was actually Gould who was driving the car that hit him, not Harriman. He seeks to amend his complaint to name Gould as a defendant. The relevant state law does not allow amendments to add a defendant who was not sued and served within the limitations period. Assume that Federal Rule 15(c), however, allows a plaintiff to amend the complaint to add a party if the party: 1) received notice of the action within the limitations period; and 2) knew that, "but for a mistake concerning the identity of the proper party," the action would have been against him. Assume that Gould was aware of the suit within the limitations period and that he was actually the

intended defendant. Morgan argues that, since the requirements of Rule 15(c) are satisfied, the amendment should be allowed. Should the court allow the amendment?

9. Assume that the same version of Federal Rule 15(c) applies, but the state in which Morgan brings his action has a statute that provides:

> In any civil action, the court may, at any time, allow an amendment adding or changing a party, and allow any other amendment in matter of form or substance which may enable the plaintiff to sustain the action for the cause or recovery for which the action was intended to be brought. Such an amendment shall relate back to the time of the original pleading.[13]

After the passage of the limitations period, Morgan makes a motion in the federal action to name Gould as a defendant. Assume that Gould had no prior notice that Morgan intended to sue him. What rule should the court apply?

EXPLANATIONS
Collisions and Close Calls

1a. In *York*, Justice Frankfurter concluded that federal courts should follow state rules if the difference between the state and the federal rules could be "outcome determinative." If *York*'s outcome-determinative test were applied to this example, there appears little doubt that the court would have to defer to state law. If the federal court sticks with its rule, Morgan loses because the appellate court will not consider the error. But if the federal court applies the Colorado approach, Morgan will get a new trial. At the new trial, the jury will be told the effect of finding Morgan more at fault and may well find him less faulty (say, perhaps, 49 percent?). Of course, we can't say Morgan will definitely win if he gets the new trial, just as the *York* court could not say for sure that the plaintiffs there would win if they were allowed to proceed to trial. However, applying the federal rule could make a difference, so the *York* test would require use of the state rule.

b. The court in *Byrd* reaffirmed that the federal courts *must* follow state rules that define the "rights and obligations" of the parties. 356 U.S. at 535. This presumably refers to those clearly "substantive" rights, which (as *Erie* declared) the federal government has no authority to create. This matter of instructing the jury, however, seems more like a "matter of form and mode" for the conduct of the litigation itself, as to which there is federal authority to apply a separate rule. *Byrd* reaffirmed that the federal court should generally defer to state rules even in matters of "form and mode," if they are likely to be outcome determinative, in order to implement the policy of uniformity pronounced in *Erie* and reaffirmed in *York*. 356 U.S. at 536-537. Thus,

---

13. This statute is an edited version of a Massachusetts statute. Mass. Gen. L. ch. 231, §51.

unless affirmative countervailing considerations require application of the federal rule, *Byrd* would also support application of the state practice in this case.

A problem with the *Byrd* analysis is that it does not specify what federal policies will outweigh the *Erie/York* policy of assuring that diversity cases come out the same in state and federal court. Here, the federal objection rule is meant to assure that objections are presented to the trial court so they can be considered and resolved there, thus reducing errors and appeals. That is certainly a meaningful policy, aimed at increasing accuracy and efficiency of federal trials, but it is probably not such an overriding "countervailing consideration" as to outweigh *Erie's* policy of uniformity. It certainly isn't as lofty a concern as the constitutional right to jury trial implicated in *Byrd*.

c. As the introduction states, where there is a direct conflict between a state rule or statute and a Federal Rule of Civil Procedure, the court must analyze the problem under *Hanna* Part 2. Here the Colorado practice (ordering a new trial even if no instruction was requested) and Fed. R. Civ. P. 51 (barring reversal if no objection is made) are clearly incompatible. The court will affirm the verdict for the defendant if it follows the Federal Rule but will reverse if it follows state law. Thus, there is a direct conflict, and the REA analysis of *Hanna* Part 2 applies.

d. There can be little doubt about the Court's authority to promulgate Rule 51. On the constitutional level, it is "rationally capable of classification" as procedural, since it governs the process of instructing the jury at trial and reviewing those instructions on appeal. It also passes muster under the similar test of "procedurality" under the first subsection of the REA, since it relates to "the judicial process for enforcing rights and duties recognized by substantive law. . . ." Thus, it is valid unless it "abridge[s], enlarge[s], or modif[ies]" substantive rights: The second subsection of the REA prohibits enacting rules — even procedural rules — that alter substantive rights.

As discussed in the introduction, it is at this stage that the analysis becomes murky. Professor Ely would ask whether the statute was enacted for any "nonprocedural" reason. Interestingly, the Colorado provision involved here was not found in Colorado's procedural code, but was part of the comparative negligence statute itself, suggesting a "nonprocedural" purpose. While it governs behavior in the courtroom, it is evidently aimed at affecting the substantive outcome of suits: More plaintiffs will win if juries know that they must be less than 50 percent at fault to recover.

Despite this argument, the case on which this example is based concluded (relying on Ely's article!) that following Rule 51 would not transgress the restriction in the second paragraph of the REA:

> This effect [denying review of the failure to give the instruction] however, is not an enlargement, abridgment or modification of the comparative negligence doctrine, which is the substantive rule of law at issue. It is rather a procedural directive, aimed at augmenting the fairness and efficiency of the litigation process in federal court.

Platis v. Stockwell, 630 F.2d 1202, 1206 (7th Cir. 1980). This reasoning, of course, is circular: The Rule does not abridge substantive rights because it is procedural. However, despite the Ely test, my sense is that most courts would reach the same conclusion, based on the heavy presumption of validity that *Hanna* accords to the Federal Rules, the fact that the Rule governs trial procedure, and the fact that the plaintiff can avoid any abridgement of the "right" involved by the simple expedient of asking for the instruction.

   e. If the refusal to grant a new trial in the absence of an objection were a matter of federal judicial practice, rather than a Federal Rule, the analysis would proceed under *Hanna* Part 1. This may be an example of a rule that would be "substantive" under *Hanna* Part I although it does not affect "substantive" rights under *Hanna* Part 2. Under *Hanna* Part 1, the question would be whether the twin aims of *Erie* would be compromised by allowing the federal courts to ignore the state statute in favor of their usual practice. It is very clear that using the federal practice instead of the state statute would *not* lead to forum shopping. Any plaintiff who knows about the jury instruction rule would have no need to base his forum choice on the difference: He would simply be sure to ask for the instruction in either court, so the difference would make no difference!

   However, it would arguably be "inequitable administration of the laws" for the federal court to refuse a new trial where a state court would be bound to grant one. Compare *Walker v. Armco,* in which the Court concluded that it would foster inequitable administration of the laws to allow a suit to go forward in federal court that would be barred in state court.[14]

2. The first issue here is whether there is a direct conflict between the state practice requiring the plaintiff to prove that he is free of negligence and Fed. R. Civ. P. 8(c). If there is such a conflict, the court must consider whether Rule 8(c) is valid under the REA. It certainly is "procedural" under the first sentence of the REA, since it regulates the process of proof at trial. However, it is a tough question whether the Rule would "abridge, enlarge, or modify" a substantive right under the second paragraph of the REA. The burden of proof can have a profound impact on the case, particularly where one or both

---

14. Many differences look "inequitable" if viewed retrospectively, but not if viewed prospectively. The difference here, for example, hardly seems inequitable when viewed at the outset of the litigation: Any inequity can be avoided by careful trial planning. But looking back, after the plaintiff has failed to seek the instruction, the difference is crucial to his case.

   The Court in *Hanna* Part 1 appeared to call for a prospective analysis. It emphasized that the prospective burden to comply with the two rules was not very different, though the plaintiff could no longer comply with the state rule at all at the time of the appeal. However, in *Walker* the Court appeared to revert to a retrospective approach, relying on the fact that the plaintiff would lose if the state rule applied but might win if allowed to proceed in federal court. 446 U.S. at 753.

of the parties is unable to produce evidence (as, for example, when one of two drivers is killed in the accident).

In *Palmer v. Hoffman,* 318 U.S. 109 (1943), the Supreme Court nicely avoided tackling this REA issue by concluding that there is no direct conflict between Rule 8(c) and state burden of proof rules. The *Palmer* Court concluded that Rule 8(c) only addresses who must *plead* contributory negligence, not who bears the burden of proof on it. Based on this cramped reading of the Rule, the Court concluded that there was no conflict with state law, since federal law said nothing about who bore the burden of proof. Consequently, the state rule applied. As in *Walker v. Armco,* the Court construed the Rule narrowly to avoid a hard problem under the second section of the REA.

3.   *York* involved a conflict between a state statute and a federal judicial practice, not a Federal Rule or federal statute. Thus, it presents the "relatively unguided" *Erie* choice analyzed in *Hanna* Part 1. The Court would have to consider whether allowing federal courts to use their own limitations principles would lead to forum shopping or inequitable administration of the laws.

Very likely, ignoring the state limitations period in federal court would encourage both of these "twin evils." Clearly, a plaintiff whose claim was barred under the state statute would shop for the federal forum if the claim might not be barred under federal limitations principles. And, as the Court concluded in analogous circumstances in *Walker,* allowing such dramatic disparity in results would be inequitable:

> There is simply no reason why, in the absence of a controlling federal rule, an action based on state law which concededly would be barred in the state courts by the state statute of limitations should proceed through litigation to judgment in federal court solely because of the fortuity that there is diversity of citizenship between the litigants.

446 U.S. at 753.

4.   This case should be analyzed under *Hanna* Part 1, since the conflict is between a judge-made federal practice and state practice. The issue is whether the difference between written instructions and oral instructions will trigger the "twin evils" of forum shopping and inequitable administration of the laws. Neither seems at all likely from such a relatively minor discrepancy between state and federal practice. *First,* it is unlikely that a litigant would choose federal court based on this procedural difference; if he wants to make sure that the jury clearly understands a particular instruction, he can ask the federal judge to instruct on it clearly and emphasize it in closing argument, rather than make the choice of forum turn on it.

Nor is there a substantial inequity in allowing this discrepancy between the administration of diversity cases in federal court and similar cases in state court. For one thing, it is not at all clear that it favors one litigant over the other, or (if it does) which one it will be in any particular case. Further, as suggested, any anticipated problem can probably be alleviated by careful argument to the jury. Thus, the federal court should apply this simple "housekeeping rule" despite contrary state practice, since doing so will not foster the "twin evils" discussed in *Hanna* Part 1.

The Ultimate Test

5.   If this example did not throw you off the track, you are well on your way to understanding the *Erie* doctrine. The analysis here is so straightforward that it's almost impossible to get it right.

In all of these cases, *it is the nature of the federal provision, not the competing state provision,* that determines the analysis. The issue is when *federal law,* whether made by the framers, Congress, the Supreme Court, or federal judicial practice, is valid and therefore applies in federal court. If the federal provision is valid it prevails over a contrary state provision, whether found in the state constitution, a state statute or rule, or a state judicial practice.

A federal judicial practice is valid federal law if it governs the litigation process and passes the *Hanna* Part 1 test. The oral instruction rule here is valid, since the difference between the federal practice of giving oral instructions to the jury and the state written-instruction rule is unlikely to lead to forum shopping or inequitable administration of the laws. Consequently, the federal court may follow its own practice despite contrary state law. See example 4. It does not matter that the state provision is found in a formal Rule. The question is not whether a "higher" form of law (such as a constitutional provision, statute, or Rule) prevails over a "lower" one (such as a judicial practice). The question is whether the federal provision, from whatever source derived, is valid and applicable.

On the same analysis, a Federal Rule that passes muster under the constitutional and statutory analysis of *Hanna* Part 2 is valid federal law, which will apply despite a conflicting state provision, even if the state provision is found in a state constitution or statute. This is because federal law, made with the authority to make it, is the "supreme Law of the Land." See *Hanna* Part 2, in which the Court held that the Federal Rule prevailed over a state statute. See also *Hanna* Part 1, where the Court stated that the federal last-and-usual service provision would prevail over the state statute, even if it was a matter of judicial practice rather than a formal rule. 380 U.S. at 466-469.

Switching Tracks

6a.   Clinton will probably argue that the two statutes are not in conflict. The federal statute only addresses the costs for a witness's testimony at trial; since it says nothing about fees for experts' preparation time, the matter is not covered by the federal statute, there is no direct conflict, and the issue should be analyzed under *Hanna* Part 1. This argument makes some sense, but was rejected by the Supreme Court. In *Crawford Fitting Co. v. J. T. Gibbons, Inc.*, 482 U.S. 437 (1987), the Court held that the statute, by specifying those items that may be recovered as costs, implicitly rejects taxing others, such as the expert's preparation fee. See 482 U.S. at 441-443 (§§1920 and 1821 "comprehensively addressed" the taxation of fees for litigant's witnesses, barring further fees for expert witnesses). Since the state statute allows full reimbursement for expert witness expenses, while the federal statute only authorizes minimal attendance fees,[15] the two are in direct conflict.

b. Assuming that there is a direct conflict between the state and federal statutes, the federal statute governs if it is constitutional, because the Constitution provides that federal statutes are the "supreme Law of the Land." U.S. Const., Article VI.

The Court's discussion in *Hanna* certainly supports the conclusion that these cost statutes are constitutional under Article III and the Necessary and Proper Clause. *Hanna* concludes that Congress has power under those provisions to "regulate matters which, though falling within the uncertain area between substance and procedure, are rationally capable of classification as either." 380 U.S. at 472. A statute specifying which expenses in the conduct of a lawsuit may be collected by the winning party can rationally be classified as procedural. Thus, Congress had the power to enact this statute, and the statute applies despite the contrary state law.

Note that the second paragraph of the REA is irrelevant to this analysis. That provision limits *the Supreme Court's rule-making authority*, not Congress's own power to enact procedural statutes. Only the Constitution limits that, and the constitutional authority (so says *Hanna*) is broad enough to encompass a statute of this sort, since it can rationally be classified as addressing a procedural issue.

7.   Interestingly, the analysis of this example doesn't have much to do with *Byrd*. In *Byrd* the "influence" of the seventh amendment lurked in the background, but it appears that it did not directly *require* that the jury decide the question. Here, by contrast, the seventh amendment directly conflicts with the state statute. That statute requires the judge to make the factual finding as to the amount of the intangible damages, while the seventh amendment requires factual questions such as the amount of damages to be decided by the jury in federal court.

Because there is a direct conflict between the federal constitutional provision and the state statute, the analysis follows from the Court's discussion in Part 2 of *Hanna*. That analysis makes clear that if a federal statute or rule is valid and covers the issue, the federal court must apply it. A fortiori, if a federal constitutional provision applies, it will control despite a contrary state

---

15. After *Crawford*, Congress enacted 42 U.S.C. s. 1988(c) which authorizes award of expert witness fees in civil rights cases.

statute or practice. U.S. Const., Article VI, §2. Thus, since the assessment of Morgan's damages is an issue of fact, it must be decided by the jury if suit is brought in federal court.[16]

However, the type and measure of damages recoverable in a tort case is a classically "substantive" issue, in the basic *Erie* sense. States are free to expand, define, or eliminate tort causes of action. See *Martinez v. California*, 444 U.S. 277, 282 (1980). The Aroostook legislature could eliminate recovery for intangible damages entirely; it may also establish a cap on such damages instead. By doing so, the statute creates a state law "right" (or, better phrased, partial *immunity*), which must be honored under the command of *Erie* to follow state law on issues where the states have the authority to create it. Cf. *Gasperini v. Center for Humanities, Inc.*, 518 U.S. 415, 416 (1996) (state standard for reviewing size of verdict "substantive" under *Erie* analysis). Thus, the $250,000 limit on damages for intangible injuries will apply in Morgan's federal action. The judge should enter judgment on the jury's verdict but reduce the amount for intangible damages to $250,000.

The Late Train

8.   This is a direct conflict case: State law would bar the amendment, but Gould could be brought in if the version of Fed. R. Civ. P. 15(c) given in the example applies. Because the conflict is between a formal federal rule and a state practice, the analysis comes under *Hanna* Part 2. There appears to be little doubt that Rule 15(c) is within the "arguably procedural" arena, so that Congress may authorize federal courts to apply their own rules. There is also little doubt that it passes muster under the first subsection of the REA, since it regulates the "judicial process for enforcing rights and duties recognized by substantive law. . . ."

The battleground in this case will be under the limiting language of the second subsection of the REA. Does the rule, which extends the right to sue a party beyond the limitations period, "abridge, enlarge, or modify" a substantive right? There is a nice analysis of this conflict in Westen and Lehman's article, 78 Mich. L. Rev. at 363-364. They argue that the "substantive" purpose of a limitation period is to provide notice to the defendant within the limitations period. Because the federal rule in the example only allows the amendment if the defendant has such notice and is aware that he is the intended target of the suit, this substantive purpose is not "abridged" and Rule 15(c) is valid. There is some difference in the state and federal approaches, but it is not sufficiently substantial to violate the REA limitation concerning

---

16. The seventh amendment does not apply to the courts of the states. However, most state constitutions include a similar guarantee of jury trial. The statute hypothesized here might be unconstitutional under the Aroostook constitution but is still useful for illustration purposes.

substantive rights. In effect, there is a difference, but it does not significantly trench upon the policy underlying the state's approach, so (the authors conclude) it is a tolerable difference. See 19 Wright and Miller §4509, at 272-275 for a similar analysis.

9.   There is also a direct conflict between the statute and the Rule in this case: The amendment may be allowed under the state rule but would not be permissible under the version of Fed. R. Civ. P. 15(c) described in example 8, since Gould had no notice within the limitations period that anyone intended to sue him. Thus, a *Hanna* Part 2 analysis is again in order.

In this case there is a dramatic difference between the state statute and the Federal Rule. In example 8 the state rule required notice within the limitations period, and the Federal Rule, while slightly more liberal, did too. Here, however, the state rule is much more indulgent than the Federal Rule. It allows Morgan to amend to sue a person who had no notice of the action within the limitations period, so long as he sued *somebody* before that period expired. Thus, Morgan's possibilities are a great deal broader under the state statute than under the federal version.

On the constitutional level, the analysis is the same as in example 8. The federal government has authority to regulate procedure in the federal courts, including matters like this, which, while within the "uncertain area between substance and procedure," can rationally be classified as procedural. Further, the first section of the REA authorizes the rule, since it regulates court procedure.

The problem, again, is that nasty second subsection of the REA, and this time it is a much more substantial problem. There is a dramatic difference between the reach of Rule 15(c) (as set forth in the example) and the state statute. The policy behind the state statute is to maximize litigants' ability to assert causes of action, at the expense of the policy of repose behind limitations periods. Rule 15(c) draws a very different balance between these policies. This is an example, I think, where the difference so affects the right to recover that it would abridge state substantive rights to apply the federal rule. Cf. *Marshall v. Mulrenin*, 508 F.2d 39 (1st Cir. 1974) (reaching this conclusion under an earlier version of this statute); see also 19 Wright and Miller at 278-288.

For many years Rule 15(c) contained the provisions stated in example 8. However, in 1991 the Court amended Rule 15 to provide that an amendment will also relate back if it would relate back under state law. Fed. R. Civ. P. 15(c)(1). Evidently the rulemakers were concerned about the validity of Rule 15(c) under the second subsection of the REA and therefore amended it to conform to state law in cases such as this. The current version of Rule 15(c) would expressly authorize Morgan's amendment, so the potential problem under the second subsection is avoided.[17]

---

17. However, the amended version of Rule 15 says nothing about the situation illustrated by example 8, in which the state practice is more restrictive than the federal relation back rule.

12

Erie *and State Choice of Law: Vertical Uniformity and Horizontal Chaos*

Introduction

Chapter 10 suggests that the whole *Erie* problem was the framers' fault, for creating a federal form of government. See p. 164. But that isn't really true. *Another* part of the problem is the colonists' fault because they settled in separate colonies. Those colonies developed more or less independently for 150 years before they became states and retain a great deal of autonomy under our constitution. This autonomy—from each other as well as from federal control—has some very interesting consequences for our judicial system.

A fundamental consequence, not generally appreciated, is that "the law" governing many types of claims can differ from state to state. The law of torts, for example, can be, and often is, one thing in Rome, Wisconsin, and another in Athens, Ohio. As "Easy *Erie*" explains, there is no general federal authority to "make" common law in areas such as tort law, so each state has to make its own. Also, there is nothing in the Constitution or in nature that says Wisconsin has to make the same tort law that Ohio does. Very frequently they don't, so that a tort case might come out differently if it were decided under Ohio law than it would if it were decided under Wisconsin law. The same is true in many other areas, such as commercial law, probate, contracts, and property. In this respect, the states are a little like independent countries, each of which has the authority to develop its own rules of law to apply to its own cases.

This phenomenon, that the 50 states may have 50 different rules on the duty of care to a trespasser, or the enforcement of exclusive contracts, is in itself surprising but tolerable. It is part of the price we pay for having a system of divided sovereignty, in which the states retain the power to make law in the many areas not delegated to the federal government. But this doctrine of state autonomy has a very unruly stepchild, the problem of "choice of law," which bedevils state courts as well as federal ones. This chapter explores the interaction of *Erie's* state law mandate with the curious quagmire[*] known as choice of law.

The Dismal Swamp: The Problem of Choosing the Proper State Law

The problem of choice of law is exactly what the phrase suggests, the need to choose a body of substantive law to apply to the dispute before the court. The *Erie* case itself involved a choice of law problem, since the Supreme Court had to determine whether federal courts in diversity cases were free to choose "federal common law" or were required to follow state law. But choice of law problems also arise when the plaintiff sues in *state* court, and the state court must choose whether to apply its own law to the claim or the law of another state.

The answer may appear obvious: The court should apply its *own* law, that is, the law of the state where the suit is brought. If Pogo sues Albert in Ohio for injuries suffered in a boat collision, the Ohio court should apply Ohio law. If he sues in Wisconsin, that court should apply Wisconsin law. Adopting this as the universal choice of law rule would have one great advantage: Everyone would know what law would be applied in each court, and there would be no litigation over choice of law.

Despite the simplicity of this choice of law rule, courts have not opted to apply their own substantive law in all cases, for several reasons. *First,* this approach would obviously encourage plaintiffs like Pogo to "forum shop" by suing in the state with the "best" (that is, the most Pogo-oriented) tort law. Suppose, for example, that Wisconsin applies contributory negligence, which would bar recovery if Pogo was negligent in any degree, but Ohio applies

---

[*]The "quagmire" and "dismal swamp" metaphors are from Prosser's famous quotation, see p. 212.

comparative negligence, which would allow him to recover but would reduce that recovery to account for his negligence. If Ohio always applied its own law, and Pogo was 10 percent at fault, he could sue in Ohio and recover 90 percent of his damages. However, if he brought the suit in Wisconsin, he would get nothing.[1] That's a big difference. If Ohio's courts always chose to apply Ohio law, Ohio could become a magnet for tort cases that had no relation to that state or had more significant connections with other states.

In addition, as a matter of policy, it seems unwise to decide a controversy under a substantive rule completely foreign to the events in dispute. If Pogo lived in Wisconsin, the accident took place in Wisconsin, and Albert is a Wisconsin citizen, it would make little sense to apply Ohio law to the case, even if, for one reason or another, Pogo could sue in Ohio. The events and the parties had substantial connections to Wisconsin, but none at all to Ohio. At the time of acting, the parties had no expectation that Ohio law would determine the legal consequences of their conduct. In addition, Ohio has little interest in regulating or compensating this occurrence, but Wisconsin does. Pogo's choice of an Ohio court looks like a blatant attempt to avoid application of Wisconsin's contributory negligence rule to a Wisconsin accident between Wisconsin citizens. In such cases, where the case has little connection to the forum state but strong connections to another, many states would choose to apply the substantive law of the other state.

Similarly, suppose that Schulansky, from Massachusetts, goes to New Hampshire to meet with Ronan, a New Hampshire contractor. They negotiate there for the construction of an addition to her vacation home in Alton, New Hampshire, and enter into an agreement there for the work. If Schulansky has a problem with the quality of the work and sues Ronan in Massachusetts, the court would likely decide that the dispute has such significant ties to New Hampshire, and so few to Massachusetts, that it ought to be decided under New Hampshire contract law. Again, the result may be that a court in one state hears the suit but chooses to apply the substantive law of another.

Intellectual Quicksand: Approaches to Choice of Law

If courts do not always apply the law of the state in which they sit, they need to develop "choice of law" rules for deciding when they will choose the law of another state instead. They have done so, and the resulting rules are indeed a quagmire:

---

1. Whether Pogo *can* sue in Ohio (or Wisconsin, or Idaho, or any other state) depends on the three ring analysis explored in Part One. Often, Pogo will be able to satisfy the rings in a number of states, potentially giving him a choice of substantive tort rules as well as forums.

The realm of the conflict of laws is a dismal swamp, filled with quaking quagmires, and inhabited by learned but eccentric professors who theorize about mysterious matters in a strange and incomprehensible jargon. The ordinary court, or a lawyer, is quite lost when engulfed and entangled in it.

W. Prosser, Interstate Publication, 51 Mich. L. Rev. 959, 971 (1953).

Stated less poetically, the various approaches that courts use for choosing the proper law in cases with connections to several states are complicated and in flux. The rules used to be fairly mechanical, based on "objective" connections between the claim and the state. See W. Richman and W. Reynolds, Understanding Conflict of Laws, pp. 167-185 (2d ed. 1993) (describing the "vested rights" principles of the First Restatement of Conflicts of Laws). Under the First Restatement approach, tort cases were usually determined under the law of the place of injury, contracts cases under the law of the place of making, and property cases under the law of the place where the property was located. It wasn't quite that neat, but that was the general idea. Under this approach Pogo's case would be decided under Wisconsin law (where the injury occurred), and Schulansky's under New Hampshire law (where, on the facts given above, the contract was made).

However, many courts have concluded that the First Restatement principles are too mechanical to yield satisfying solutions to choice of law problems. Led primarily by conflicts scholars, they have attempted to formulate choice of law rules that are more responsive to underlying policy considerations. One "modern" approach to conflicts of law weighs the interests of each affected state in applying its law to the case. See Richman and Reynolds at 212-225 (describing the "interest analysis" approach to conflicts). Suppose that Churchy and Howland, two Florida neighbors, decide to take a canoe trip in the Okefenokee Swamp, just over the Georgia border. A half mile into Georgia, the canoe swamps due to poor maintenance, causing serious injuries to Howland, who is hospitalized in Florida and permanently disabled. The First Restatement would require the court to apply the "lex loci delicti," the law of the place where the injury occurred, which is Georgia. However, a court that applies an "interest analysis" approach to conflicts might conclude that Florida has a greater interest in the case than Georgia, since the parties are domiciled there, the injured plaintiff was treated there, and the negligent maintenance, which caused the accident, took place there. Thus, "interest analysis" might lead the court to apply Florida law.

Another current approach to conflicts problems is to apply the law of the state with the "most significant relationship" to the case, in light of various policy considerations, including the expectations of the parties, the policy interests of the states with connections to the case, uniformity in enforcement, and others. See Richman and Reynolds at 199-212 (describing the approach of the Second Restatement of Conflict of Laws to torts, contracts and property issues). There are also other approaches and variations on all of them.[2] It is not crucial for our purposes to understand these theories, but rather to realize that *different approaches exist,* that they may lead the court in one state to choose different substantive law than another would apply to the same case, and that the selection of the applicable law will depend on the choice of law approach of the court in which the suit is filed.

Quirks in the Quagmire: Federal Courts Choosing State Law

The situation is made even more complicated by the fact that the plaintiff often has the choice not only of state courts in different states, but also federal courts in each of those states. Suppose, for example, that Pogo becomes an Ohio citizen and sues Albert, from Wisconsin, for his injuries in the Wisconsin accident. Because the parties are diverse, Pogo may choose federal court and chooses the federal district court in Ohio. What law should that court apply? Clearly, the answer under *Erie* is "state law," since it is a diversity case. That is not the whole answer, however, because there are several states whose law might apply. Should the federal court choose Ohio law or Wisconsin law?

Three years after *Erie,* the Supreme Court addressed this question in *Klaxon v. Stentor Manufacturing Co.,* 313 U.S. 487 (1941). In *Klaxon,* the Court held that the policy underlying *Erie* mandates the application of the forum state's choice of law rules as well as its substantive law:

> We are of opinion that the prohibition declared in *Erie R. Co. v. Tompkins,* 304 U.S. 64, against such independent determinations by the federal courts, extends to the field of conflicts of laws. The conflict of laws rules to be applied by the federal court in Delaware must conform to those prevailing in Delaware's state courts. Otherwise, the accident of diversity of citizenship would constantly disturb equal administration of justice in coordinate state and federal courts sitting side by side.

313 U.S. at 496 (footnote omitted). Under *Klaxon,* the federal court must do whatever the state court within that state would do. If an Ohio state judge would apply Ohio law to Pogo's case, so must the federal judge if the case is brought in an Ohio federal district court. If the Ohio state judge would choose Wisconsin law, the federal judge in Ohio must do so as well.

The *Klaxon* rule makes a certain amount of sense, as a matter of policy. *Erie* teaches that plaintiffs should not obtain an advantage due to the "accident of diversity" that they would not have in state court. If the state court would apply Ohio tort law to Pogo's case, but the federal court were free to choose Wisconsin's, the case could still come out differently simply because

---

2. See *Ferens v. John Deere Co.,* 494 U.S. 516, 538 (1990) (Scalia, J., dissenting) (variety in state approaches to choice of law "has become kaleidoscopic"). Take the course in conflicts of laws if you want to delve into these mysteries. It is a fascinating area and useful background for law practice.

Pogo was able to invoke diversity jurisdiction. In the words of Judge Magruder, if federal diversity courts could follow their own choice of law rules, "the ghost of *Swift v. Tyson* . . . still walks abroad, somewhat shrunken in size, but capable of much mischief." *Sampson v. Channell,* 110 F.2d 754, 761 (1st Cir. 1940). The *Klaxon* rule puts the ghost to rest, since the federal court must again do whatever the state court would.

Klaxon has been met with some skepticism by the scholars. Although *Erie* clearly requires diversity courts to apply state law, it is certainly arguable that it is both constitutional and appropriate for a federal court to choose *which state's law* to apply in diversity cases. Choice of law involves the relations among the states, and the framers might well have considered that a federal diversity court should be available to litigants as a neutral decision-maker in choosing the proper body of state law. See, e.g., H. Hart, The Relations Between State and Federal Law, 54 Colum. L. Rev. 489, 514-515 (1954) (arguing that *Klaxon* impedes development of conflicts law and promotes forum shopping).

Whatever the merits of these arguments may be, the Supreme Court continues to adhere to the *Klaxon* rule. The issue was raised again in *Day & Zimmerman v. Challoner,* 423 U.S. 3 (1975), a case involving strict liability claims for serious injuries to military personnel in Cambodia during the Vietnam War. The *Klaxon* approach required application of the Texas conflicts of law rule to the case, which in turn would lead to application of Cambodian law, since that was the place where the injury took place. However, Cambodian law did not recognize strict liability, so choosing its law would end the plaintiff's case. Despite these implications, the Supreme Court unanimously reaffirmed *Klaxon* in a brief per curiam opinion.[3]

Because *Klaxon* requires the federal court in a diversity case to apply the conflicts law that would be applied by the courts of the state in which it sits, the combination of *Klaxon* and *Erie* produces substantial "vertical uniformity" between the state and federal courts within each state. However, a side effect of the two decisions is to destroy "horizontal uniformity" among the federal courts in different states. If Ohio would apply Ohio's comparative negligence principle to Pogo's accident, and Michigan would apply Michigan's contributory negligence law, the federal court in Ohio will apply a different rule than the federal court in Michigan would. Thus, *Erie* has not ended the game of forum shopping for a more favorable substantive law, it has just changed the rules of that game. Instead of choosing between federal and

---

3. *Challoner* is a nice example of a situation in which interest analysis would yield a different result than the place-of-the-injury rule. The plaintiffs in *Challoner* were American servicemen: The defendant was an American corporation; and the shell that caused the injury was manufactured in Texas. As the Fifth Circuit pointed out in its opinion (reversed on other grounds by the Supreme Court), Cambodia had no interest in enforcing its fault requirement under the circumstances, while Texas had a substantial interest in applying its strict liability policy to the claim. See 512 F.2d at 80.

state court to obtain more favorable substantive law, plaintiffs may get the same result by choosing between federal courts in different states or between state courts in different states.

The following examples illustrate the effect of *Erie* and *Klaxon* on the law applied to the facts of the *Erie* case. Assume that all example cases arise after *Erie* and *Klaxon* were decided and that each case is based on diversity. After these examples, we will wade a little further into the quagmire by considering the implications of transfer of venue under 28 U.S.C. §1404(a).

EXAMPLES

Wading In

1.   The unfortunate Harry Tompkins, Jr., a Pennsylvania citizen, is injured while walking on a track along the Erie Railroad near Hughestown, Pennsylvania. Evidently he was hit by an object, perhaps a door, projecting from the side of the train. He brings suit against the Erie Railroad, a New York corporation with its principal place of business in New York.

Assume that, under Pennsylvania law, a trespasser like Tompkins is only entitled to recover if the railroad's conduct was wilful and wanton. New York law, on the other hand, holds railroads to a duty of due care to trespassers on a frequently used pathway along the tracks. Assume further that the Pennsylvania choice of law rule requires the court to apply the law of the place of the injury (lex loci delicti) in tort cases, and that the New York choice of law rule is the same.

   a. If Tompkins sues in a state court in Pennsylvania, what standard of care rule should the court apply?
   b. If Tompkins sues in a federal court in Pennsylvania, what standard of care rule should the court apply?
   c. If Tompkins sues in a state court in New York, what standard of care rule should the court apply?
   d. If Tompkins sues in a federal court in New York, what standard of care rule should the court apply?

2.   On the same basic facts, assume that Pennsylvania tort law requires a showing of wilful and wanton conduct under the circumstances, and that it applies the place-of-the-injury choice of law rule. However, New York applies a due care standard to trespassers in Tompkins, Jr.'s position, and New York's choice of law rule involves a balancing of interests, which would lead to the application of New York law on the facts of Tompkins's case.

   a. If Tompkins sues in a state court in Pennsylvania, what standard of care rule should the court apply?
   b. If Tompkins sues in a federal court in Pennsylvania, what standard of care rule should the court apply?
   c. If Tompkins sues in a state court in New York, what standard of care rule should the court apply?

d. If Tompkins sues in a federal court in New York, what standard of care rule should the court apply?

3.   Tompkins, Jr., is injured near Hughestown and two weeks after the accident is transferred to a hospital in West Virginia. His wife moves to West Virginia to be near him. He is released three months later, is bedridden for nine more months, and does not recover fully for over two years. Mr. and Mrs. Tompkins decide to stay in West Virginia, and they bring a diversity suit against the Erie Railroad in federal court there. Mr. Tompkins seeks recovery for his injuries, and Mrs. Tompkins seeks recovery for loss of consortium, that is, for the interference with her relationship to her husband during the time he was incapacitated due to the injury. See *Hopson v. St. Mary's Hospital,* 408 A.2d 260 (1979) (loss of consortium includes the "'constellation of companionship, dependence, reliance, affection, sharing and aid'" which flows from marriage) (quoting from W. Prosser, Handbook of The Law of Torts, 881-882 (4th ed. 1971). Assume that Pennsylvania law allows such claims, but West Virginia law does not. Assume also that West Virginia applies the place-of-the-injury choice of law rule in tort cases.

a. What state's tort law should the federal court apply to Mrs. Tompkins's claim?

b. If the judge is unsure which law to apply, to which state court should she certify the issue?

A Quagmire Quandary

4.   Tompkins is injured near Hughestown, Pennsylvania, and decides to sue the Erie Railroad. He consults Webster, a local lawyer. Webster would like to sue "at home," of course, as most lawyers would. However, she is aware that Pennsylvania law requires wilful and wanton conduct in cases like this, and that a Pennsylvania court would apply its own law to the case, under the lex loci rule.

In preparation for filing suit, Webster researches New York law on the duty of care to trespassers. She finds no case directly on point. Some older cases applied the wilful/wanton standard in analogous circumstances, but more recent New York cases have "modernized" some related doctrines of landowner liability.

Webster also researches New York conflicts of law doctrine, and finds (we will assume) that New York used to follow the mechanical conflicts rules of the First Restatement. A recent case rejected the First Restatement's approach to *contract* cases in favor of interest analysis, but no case has arisen asking the court to abandon the First Restatement's place-of-the-injury rule for tort cases. In short, it looks like change may be coming both in New York conflicts law for torts cases and in New York tort law, but it hasn't arrived yet, and may not arrive at all.

a. Should Webster sue in New York or Pennsylvania?

b. Should she choose state or federal court?

The Procedure/Procedure Distinction

5.   Assume that New York would choose Pennsylvania tort law in the Tompkins case under the place-of-the-injury approach. Webster decides to sue in *state* court in New York. She sues the Erie Railroad Company and also Hepzibah, the conductor in charge of the train that hit Tompkins. Webster learns that Hepzibah lives with her mother in Queens, New York, and serves process on Hepzibah by delivering the summons and complaint to her mother at the house. Hepzibah moves to dismiss for improper service, on the ground that New York law requires service in hand upon her personally. Assume that New York law does indeed require in-hand service but that leaving it at the house with Hepzibah's mother would suffice under Pennsylvania law.

    a. How should the court decide the motion?

    b. If Webster had sued in federal court in New York, how would that court have ruled? See Fed. R. Civ. P. 4(e).

6.   Two-and-a-half years after his accident, Tompkins goes to see Webster. Assume that the statute of limitations on tort claims in New York is four years, but that it is two in Pennsylvania. Assume further that New York choice of law rules would lead to the application of Pennsylvania tort law to the case. Webster files a diversity suit in federal district court in New York against the Erie Railroad. The Erie brings a motion for summary judgment on the ground that the claim is barred due to passage of the limitations period. What should the federal court do?

Totally Swamped: The Impact of Transfer

All of this is exquisitely complex. So let's make matters worse by considering another procedural wrinkle, transfer of venue under 28 U.S.C. §1404(a). Because the basic federal venue rules provide a wide choice of venues (see Chapter 8), the plaintiff will often have the right to bring suit in courts that have little connection to the events in suit. Section 1404(a) provides federal courts with the discretionary authority to transfer a case to another federal district "for the convenience of parties and witnesses, and in the interest of justice," where the plaintiff has chosen one district but it makes more sense to litigate the case in a different district.[4] If a case is based on diversity, and

---

4. The factors to be considered in deciding whether a transfer is appropriate include the private interests of the parties, such as their residences, access to sources of proof, ability to subpoena witnesses, the need for a view of premises involved in the litigation, whether a judgment can be enforced in the forum, and others. There are also systemic interests involved, including appropriate distribution of cases among the federal districts, local decision of local cases, distribution of the burden of jury service, and the trial court's familiarity with the applicable law. See *Gulf Oil Corp. v. Gilbert*, 330 U.S. 501, 508-509 (1947).

if the judge transfers it to another district, even more elaborate complications arise in determining the applicable law.

An example may help to explain the problem. In *Van Dusen v. Barrack,* 276 U.S. 612 (1964), the plaintiffs were the personal representatives of passengers who died when an airplane crashed upon takeoff from a Boston airport, en route to Philadelphia. They brought a diversity action in federal district court in Pennsylvania against the airline, the manufacturer of the plane, and other defendants. The defendants moved for transfer to the District of Massachusetts under §1404(a).

There were some good practical reasons for the court to grant the motion. The site of the accident and many witnesses and documents were in Massachusetts. In addition, other actions arising from the crash had been filed there; if the Pennsylvania suits were transferred, they could be consolidated with those and litigated more efficiently, which is presumably "in the interest of justice."

However, the defendants' motion may have been motivated less by these practical factors than by several significant substantive differences between the wrongful death statutes of Massachusetts and Pennsylvania. The Massachusetts statute limited damages to $20,000 per decedent, while Pennsylvania law did not. Liability under the Massachusetts statute turned on the culpability of the defendant (so that even the $20,000 figure was limited to egregious conduct), while Pennsylvania law viewed wrongful death damages as purely compensatory. Because of these differences, recovery under Pennsylvania law might be substantial in each case, while recovery under Massachusetts law might not even equal the expenses of litigation.

In *Van Dusen* much turned, then, on what law the Massachusetts federal court (called the "transferee court") would apply if the case were bounced up there. If the defendants could convince the Pennsylvania federal court to transfer, and the transferee court applied Massachusetts law, *they could forum shop too.* After the plaintiffs chose a federal court in Pennsylvania, to have the case decided under Pennsylvania's more favorable wrongful death statute,[5] the defendants could trump that choice with a strategic coup of their own, by seeking transfer to a court that would apply the stingy Massachusetts wrongful death remedy.

The Supreme Court refused to take the gambit. In *Van Dusen* the Court held that a transfer of venue under §1404(a) should effect a change of court but not a change of law. That is, the transferee court should apply the law that the transferor court would have applied if the case had not been transferred. On the *Van Dusen* facts, if the case were transferred to the Massachusetts court, that court should choose whatever law the Pennsylvania federal court would have

---

5. This assumes, of course, that the Pennsylvania courts would have applied Pennsylvania law, while the Massachusetts courts (and therefore the Massachusetts federal court, if bound to do the same) would have applied Massachusetts law to the case. It is entirely possible, under current choice of law principles, that this would have happened on the *Van Dusen* facts.

applied (based on *Klaxon's* mandate to mimic a Pennsylvania state court), because the plaintiffs had the right to file suit there and had done so. Put a bit more cynically, the transferee court should honor the plaintiffs' forum-shopping choice, rather than allowing the defendants to displace it through transfer.

The combination of *Erie, Klaxon,* and *Van Dusen* places the federal judge in a transferred case in a position wondrous to contemplate. Under *Van Dusen* and *Klaxon,* she must determine what the choice of law rules of the transferor state are, and what state's law the courts of the transferor state would have chosen under that choice of law rule. Then, under *Erie,* she must determine what the substantive law of *that* state is and apply it. As Judge Friendly wryly observed in a related context:

> Our principal task, in this diversity of citizenship case, is to determine what the New York courts would think the California courts would think on an issue about which neither has thought.

Nolan v. Transocean Airlines, Inc., 276 F.2d 280, 281 (2nd Cir. 1960). The following examples illustrate some of the complexities engendered by the combination of *Erie, Klaxon,* and *Van Dusen.*

EXAMPLES

Games People Play

7. Assume for the purposes of this example the same facts concerning Tompkins, Jr.'s accident. Tompkins goes to see Webster two-and-a-half years after the accident, inquiring about suing the railroad and wishing to sue at home. Webster researches the law and learns that Pennsylvania tort law would allow Tompkins to recover on a showing of simple negligence, but New York law would require him to prove wilful or wanton conduct. She also learns that New York applies the place-of-the-injury choice of law rule to tort cases. Last, she finds that Pennsylvania has a two-year limitations period for tort claims, but that New York's limitations period for tort claims is four years.

    a. Tompkins brings suit in state court in New York. The Erie Railroad moves to transfer the case to Pennsylvania, arguing that the accident took place there, the plaintiff and all the witnesses are there, and that Pennsylvania law will apply, so it makes more sense to litigate the case in Pennsylvania. What will the court do?

    b. Tompkins sues in federal court in the Southern District of New York, based on diversity. The Erie Railroad then moves to transfer the case to the Middle District of Pennsylvania, in which Hughestown is located. If the court grants the motion, what law will be applied to the limitations question and to the merits?

    c. Suppose that Tompkins sues in the Southern District of New York, and then *he* moves to transfer to the Middle District of Pennsylvania. If the court grants the motion, what law will apply to the limitations question and to the merits?

EXPLANATIONS

Wading In

1a. This case has some connections to both New York and Pennsylvania, since it involves a New York corporation and a Pennsylvania citizen, and the accident occurred in Pennsylvania. In such cases a court must choose which state's law to apply. Pennsylvania's choice of law principles (the example assumes) require its courts to apply the law of the place of the injury in tort cases, so the Pennsylvania state court will apply Pennsylvania law to this case. Tompkins will lose unless he can prove wilful and wanton conduct.

b. If this case is brought in federal court in Pennsylvania, the federal district judge must, under *Klaxon,* apply Pennsylvania choice of law rules to determine the applicable tort standard. She must first decide which state's tort law Pennsylvania courts would apply, and then she must decide what the law of the chosen state is on the tort issue. Here, because Pennsylvania applies the place-of-the-injury choice of law rule to tort cases, the federal judge must do so as well. Under Pennsylvania's place-of-the-injury approach, she will select Pennsylvania tort law, since the accident took place there. Under Pennsylvania law (the example assumes) the railroad is only liable for wilful or wanton conduct toward a trespasser, and the federal court must apply this standard. *Klaxon* assures "vertical uniformity" within Pennsylvania, because Tompkins, Jr., will be stuck with the same rule in Pennsylvania federal court that would apply in the state court.

c. If Tompkins sues in a state court in New York, that court must use its choice of law rules to determine what state's substantive law to apply. Since New York applies the place-of-the-injury choice of law rule (the example assumes), New York will apply the tort law of Pennsylvania to this case. Since Pennsylvania law requires a showing of wilful and wanton conduct to recover, the New York state court will do so as well. Even though a plaintiff injured in a similar accident in New York would be entitled to recover on a showing of simple negligence, the "lex loci" choice of law rule means that the New York court will apply another state's law to the case.

An interesting consequence of this scenario is that the New York state court will end up doing the same kind of exercise that federal courts do in diversity cases, making their best guess at the content of another state's substantive law. New York courts cannot "make" Pennsylvania tort law, so when they choose to apply Pennsylvania tort law to a case, they have to engage in an *Erie*-type analysis of what the Pennsylvania law is on the point.[6]

d. The federal judge in New York must apply the same choice of law rule that a state court in New York would apply. Since the state court would look

---

6. It would be interesting to know whether state courts use the same kind of predictive approach in this context that the federal courts use under *Erie* or whether they try to act like a trial court of the other state in following any binding precedent on point.

to Pennsylvania law, the New York federal judge must do so as well. Thus, the combination of Klaxon, New York choice of law doctrine and Pennsylvania tort law again leads to application of the wilful/wanton rule.

In this example the case comes out the same way in all four courts because the choice of law principles in all four courts point to application of the same state's law. If all states used the same choice of law rules, all cases would theoretically be decided under the same substantive law no matter where suit was brought, since the choice of law rules would always direct the court — whatever court it was — to the same law.[7] That would eliminate forum shopping for more favorable substantive law.

The First Restatement rules aspired to this legal nirvana, but exceptions and idiosyncratic application made uniformity elusive. The more recent approaches, because they are based on judgmental balancing of interests and policies unique to each case, are less likely to lead courts in different states to apply the same state's law. Consequently, they create greater opportunities for forum shopping. However, because modern choice of law "rules" involve an ambiguous (one might even say, slushy) balancing of policy considerations, it is also harder to predict what state's law the forum court will choose. Thus, plaintiffs can only *try* to forum shop; they may end up mired in a different state's law because the court drew the balance differently than they predicted.

2a. The Pennsylvania state court judge will apply Pennsylvania choice of law doctrine, which points to Pennsylvania tort law. As in example 1a, the result is application of the wilful/wanton rule.

b. The Pennsylvania federal judge, under *Klaxon,* will also choose Pennsylvania's wilful/wanton rule, as in example 1b.

c. The New York state judge will apply New York's balancing of interests approach to conflicts law, which leads (the example assumes) to the conclusion that New York tort law should apply to the case. This is a realistic possibility under modern choice of law principles. A number of factors, such as the residence of the parties at the time of the accident, the interests promoted by application of a particular tort principle, the place of the negligence that led to the accident, and the place in which the effect of the injuries is felt, might lead a court to apply its own law even though the accident took place in another state.[8]

If New York does choose its own law in this case, Tompkins will be able to recover by showing that the railroad was negligent, even though he would have to show wilful or wanton conduct in a Pennsylvania court. He will have exactly the choice of two different substantive rules that the Court decried in *Erie.* However, the result arises because *different states* apply different tort

---

7. Unless, of course, the choice of law rule was to always apply forum law.

8. See, e.g., *Challoner,* discussed in note 3.

law, not because the results differ between the state and federal courts within the same state, as was true under *Swift*.

d. Once again, *Klaxon* requires the New York federal judge to achieve "vertical uniformity" by applying the same law that the New York state judge would. Therefore, the federal judge will apply the New York simple negligence rule. "Horizontal" uniformity is lost because the New York federal court applies different law than the Pennsylvania federal court would. Compare example 2b. The Court in *Klaxon* acknowledged that its decision would destroy horizontal uniformity among the federal courts:

> Whatever lack of uniformity this may produce between federal courts in different states is attributable to our federal system, which leaves to a state, within the limits permitted by the Constitution, the right to pursue local policies diverging from those of its neighbors.

313 U.S. at 496. The different results in these examples are illustrated in Figure 12-1. Note that in each scenario, there is "vertical uniformity" between the federal court and the state court in which the federal court sits—both will apply the same law to the case. However, in example 2 this vertical uniformity leads to horizontal disuniformity: The federal courts in Pennsylvania and New York apply different standards of care to the case because the state courts of those states would too.

3a. *Klaxon* requires the West Virginia federal court to apply the choice of law approach of West Virginia courts, which is the lex loci delicti (place-of-the-injury) rule. The problem, however, is in determining whether

	Pennsylvania	New York
Example 1		
State Court:	Chooses Pa. law, wilful/wanton rule applies	Chooses Pa. law, wilful/wanton rule applies
	↕	↕
Federal Court:	Chooses Pa. law, wilful/wanton rule applies	Chooses Pa. law, wilful/wanton rule applies
Example 2		
State Court:	Chooses Pa. law, wilful/wanton rule applies	Chooses N.Y. law, negligence rule applies
	↕	↕
Federal Court:	Chooses Pa. law, wilful/wanton rule applies	Chooses N.Y. law, negligence rule applies

Figure 12-1: Choice of Courts and Choice of Law

Mrs. Tompkins's consortium injury took place in Pennsylvania, where her husband was injured, or in West Virginia, where they lived during most of the time that her relationship with him was impaired by his injury. Or did part of her "injury" take place in Pennsylvania (where she suffered two weeks of consortium losses) and part in West Virginia?

The First Restatement had a mechanical solution for this problem. Under Section 377 the court looked to "the state where the last event necessary to make the actor liable for the alleged tort takes place." Presumably, this would be Pennsylvania, since the Erie Railroad became liable to Mrs. Tompkins as soon as she started to suffer consortium losses. If West Virginia followed the First Restatement approach, the federal court would do so as well, and apply Pennsylvania tort law to her loss of consortium claim. But it is hardly self-evident that the law of Pennsylvania *should* govern this injury, which primarily affects Mrs. Tompkins in another state. Such rigidities led to a revolt against the First Restatement, which is still going on.

b. The ambiguity here is not as to the content of the tort law of either state, but rather as to how a West Virginia court would identify the "place of the injury" in applying its choice of law rule. Because the federal judge in West Virginia must apply the place-of-the-injury rules as the West Virginia court would, it should certify the issue to the West Virginia Supreme Court, if it has a certification procedure.

Suppose that the judge were unsure whether West Virginia's choice of law rule would point to Pennsylvania law *and* whether Pennsylvania tort law allowed recovery for loss of consortium. Presumably, the judge would have to certify the choice of law issue to the West Virginia court and (if it determined that Pennsylvania law should apply) then the substantive law issue to the Pennsylvania court!

A Quagmire Quandary

4a. This is a quandary indeed. Several important strategic considerations point to suing at home: The witnesses will likely be available in Pennsylvania; it is convenient for Tompkins; and it is convenient for Webster. It is *not* so convenient for the Erie Railroad, which will have to hire local counsel and monitor litigation in another state. However, the wilful/wanton rule looms as a serious stumbling block to recovery, and one certainty in the case is that the wilful/wanton rule will apply if Webster sues in Pennsylvania.

On the other hand, suing in New York is inconvenient for Tompkins, who wants to sue at home and wants Webster to do it. In addition, important witnesses may be beyond the subpoena power of the New York court. Yet suing in New York has some important potential advantages. If the court decides to apply New York law, and if New York tort law would allow recovery based on simple negligence, Tompkins's case looks a good deal stronger on the merits. Naturally, Tompkins has a strong interest in the merits.

This is a difficult tactical decision because the advantage New York offers turns on several contingencies. *First,* Webster must convince the New York court that the lex loci delicti rule has effectively been overruled by recent New York choice of law decisions adopting interest analysis for contract cases, so that it should apply interest analysis to tort cases as well. *Second,* if the court applies interest analysis to the case, Webster must also demonstrate that that approach supports application of New York law to this accident. Just because the court applies a different choice of law *rule* does not necessarily mean it will choose the law of New York. The court might assess the interests of the parties and the states involved and conclude that they weigh in favor of Pennsylvania law anyway. *Last,* if she convinces the New York court to look to New York law, she must still convince that court that New York tort law now allows recovery based on simple negligence.

All of this is a little chaotic, isn't it? It is hard to give up the home forum on the speculative chance that all those decisions will go your way in a distant court. These contingencies will certainly act as a check on forum shopping in many cases. Webster's decision will turn on how strong her arguments are on these legal issues and, conversely, how weak her case would be if she sued in Pennsylvania and had to meet the wilful/wanton standard.

b. If Webster does choose to sue in New York, she might be well advised to choose a federal court in New York. If New York law — both tort law and conflicts law — is in the process of change, the federal court may have more flexibility to anticipate those changes than the state trial court would. Presumably, the federal diversity court must apply New York conflicts law in the same way it would apply New York substantive law; that is, it must ask what the state's highest court would do if the issue were before it today. If the case law strongly suggests that the highest court would no longer apply the place-of-the-injury rule, the federal court may be more willing to reject it than a state trial court, which will feel bound by the highest court's past precedents unless they are clearly eviscerated by later holdings. See Chapter 10, example 6d.

The Procedure/Procedure Distinction

5a. This example raises the issue of whether the New York court, when it chooses the law of another state, must apply the whole law of the other state, including matters of procedure. Sound familiar? It is akin to the dilemma explored in "Eerie *Erie*," as to when the federal court must select state law and when it may apply its own procedures. In the "horizontal" choice of law context, as in the *Erie* context, things get dicey because, generally speaking, state courts apply their own procedural law even if they have chosen the substantive law of another state under their choice of law rules. Moores, §124.30 [4].

It isn't hard to see why this dichotomy has long been accepted in the horizontal choice of law context. Just as federal diversity courts would have to abandon the Federal Rules entirely if *Erie* required them to exactly imitate the state court, the New York court would have a very difficult task if, once it chose to apply Pennsylvania tort law, it *also* had to apply Pennsylvania procedural law. The problem would be even worse than the federal judge's under *Erie*. Since New York courts might choose the law of many different states in different cases, the New York judge would have to learn the procedural quirks of many states. Effectively, she would be forced to run her courtroom under 50 different procedural systems instead of one. See G. Gelfand and H. Abrams, Putting *Erie* On the Right Track, 49 U. Pitt. L. Rev. 937, 963 (1988). That is insupportable; to avoid it, the substance/procedure distinction has emerged in conflicts of law doctrine as it has under *Erie*. Thus, the New York court would require compliance with its in-hand service of process rule, even though Pennsylvania would not.

b. If Webster sued in federal court in New York, the court would deny the motion to dismiss. While Erie mandates application of state law in diversity cases, it does not require wholesale abandonment of federal procedure. Where a valid Federal Rule covers an issue, it may be applied in a federal diversity case despite contrary procedure in the state court. *Hanna v. Plumer,* 360 U.S. 460 (1965). Here, Fed. R. Civ. P. 4(e)(2) clearly provides that leaving the papers at Hepzibah's home with a person residing therein is sufficient. The federal court need not ask (under *Erie*) what New York law would require, nor must it ask (under *Klaxon*) whether New York would look to Pennsylvania law. It may apply the Federal Rule.

6.   You don't know enough to "answer" this example, but you do know enough to see the quizzical problem it poses. The case is in federal court. Under *Erie,* the judge must look to state law on "substantive" issues — "substantive," that is, in the *Erie* sense of the term. In *Guaranty Trust Co. v. York,* the Supreme Court concluded that the state limitations period for a claim was "substantive" for *Erie* purposes, so that state law applied. So, the judge has to apply the state limitations period.

That much is easy, but only gets us part of the way. There remains the question as to *which* limitations period should be applied, New York's or Pennsylvania's? Well, that's easy too: *Klaxon* requires the federal court to do what the New York court would do. That turns on whether a New York court would apply the Pennsylvania limitations period or its own longer one.

If the issue is "substantive" (see *Guaranty Trust Co. v. York*), presumably the New York court would apply the Pennsylvania limitations period. Unfortunately, it very well might not. The line between substance and procedure has been drawn differently in the horizontal choice of law cases than it has in the vertical choice of law cases under *Erie*. Limitations periods are an example. While the statute of limitations issue is "substantive" for *Erie* purposes, many courts still apply their own limitations law to a case even if their conflicts of law rules mandate application of the substantive law of another state. See *Sun Oil Co. v. Wortman*, 486 U.S. 717 (1988) (approving application of Kansas limitations period to claim even though Kansas lacked sufficient connections to the case to apply its own substantive law); Richman and Reynolds at 264-265 (stating and criticizing this approach). Thus, New York might apply its limitations period to the claim, because it is "procedural" for choice of law purposes, while the federal court would be required to make the same choice because it is "substantive" for *Erie* purposes![9]

Games People Play

7a. The one thing that the New York state court will *not* do is transfer the case. A New York state court has no authority to send a case to a Pennsylvania court; these are different, autonomous court systems, which decide for themselves which cases they will hear.[10] The situation is different in federal court, because all federal courts are "branches" of the same federal court system and are required under §1404(a) to entertain cases transferred from other branches of the same system.

That leaves the state court with several options. It could dismiss under "forum non conveniens." The forum non conveniens doctrine is based on a premise similar to §1404(a), that sometimes cases that are properly filed under the three ring analysis still logically belong somewhere else. Under forum non conveniens, which is recognized in many states, the court may dismiss a case where the interests of justice indicate that it should be litigated elsewhere.[11]

If the court dismisses Tompkins's case he will lose: If he refiled in Pennsylvania, the Erie Railroad would plead the two-year statute of limitations as a complete defense. That prospect is likely to convince the New York court

---

9. Another area that has been subject to this schizophrenic classification is burden of proof. See *Sampson v. Channell*, 110 F.2d 754 (1st Cir. 1940), in which the First Circuit held that *Erie* required a federal court to apply state law on the issue of burden of proof. However, it chose to apply the burden of proof rule of the state in which suit was brought (Massachusetts) rather than the rule of the state where the accident had occurred (Maine). The court concluded that the Massachusetts court would have viewed burden of proof as "procedural" for horizontal choice of law purposes, and therefore applied its own rule. Consequently, the court held (anticipating *Klaxon*) that the federal court should do the same.

10. There is a model state statute, the Uniform Transfer of Litigation Act, which, if adopted, would allow such transfers between state courts. However, as of September 2000, no state had adopted this model act.

11. The doctrine is also applied in the federal courts when the appropriate forum is in another country. Just as a New York court cannot order a Pennsylvania court to hear a case, a United States court cannot order a court in another country to do so. If, therefore, the case clearly should be litigated in another country, the federal court's only option is to dismiss under forum non conveniens.

not to dismiss for forum non conveniens. So the court is likely to take the alternative course of entertaining the action. If, as a good many courts do, New York applied its own limitations statute (see example 6), Tompkins would get the benefit of the four-year limitations period and—since New York looks to Pennsylvania tort law under the place-of-the-injury choice of law rule—the simple negligence standard of care.

b. Tompkins gets a pretty good result under the first scenario, but he would still have to go to New York to litigate. Maybe he can do better by suing in federal court in New York. Since the federal court under *Klaxon* must act like the New York state court, it will apply New York's longer limitations period (see example 6) and Pennsylvania's simple negligence rule. In addition, if the federal court transfers the case to the Middle District of Pennsylvania under §1404(a), he will get the best of both worlds. The suit will be litigated in Pennsylvania, and, under *Van Dusen*, the court will apply New York limitations law and Pennsylvania tort law.

In the forum-shopping business, this is the highest form of art: The plaintiff shops for New York law on some issues and Pennsylvania law on others . . . maybe it should be called "issue shopping." In this case there will be a good argument for transfer, since the accident took place in Pennsylvania, most of the witnesses are likely to be there, Tompkins is there, and Pennsylvania law will apply to the case.

Even this scenario is chancy, however. The railroad may not move to transfer, since it is from New York and will have the advantage of litigating at home. Even if it does, the court may deny the motion.

c. This is the ultimate in chutzpah: Tompkins sues in New York and then asks the court to send the case to his home forum, taking the New York statute of limitations—but not New York tort law—with it. *Van Dusen* was not quite this egregious, since the defendants sought the transfer.

The scholars had predicted that the Supreme Court would discourage this game by holding that the law of the *transferee* forum would apply if the plaintiff sought transfer. In Tompkins's case, that would mean that the Pennsylvania court would apply its own two-year limitations period (which would mean, in turn, that Tompkins wouldn't seek the transfer). However, in *Ferens v. John Deere Co.,* 494 U.S. 516 (1990), the Supreme Court perplexed the prognosticators by holding (by a 5-4 majority) that the *Van Dusen* rule applies even where the plaintiff seeks transfer. The reasons are complicated, and the arguments on both sides of the issue are close. Read the case if you can. The bottom line, however, is that Tompkins could sue in the inconvenient forum, get back into Pennsylvania, obtain the benefit of Pennsylvania tort law, and invoke the longer New York limitations period.

If this isn't chaos, it certainly is a peculiar form of order.

PART THREE

The Scope of the Action

13

Sculpting the Lawsuit: The Basic Rules of Joinder

Introduction

A great deal of time is spent during the first year of law school analyzing decided cases, doing postmortems on past lawsuits. But every lawsuit also has a beginning, and at the beginning someone must make important tactical decisions about the scope of the lawsuit, that is, whom to sue and which claims to assert. The traditional rule in American courts has been, and largely still is, that "the plaintiff is master of his claim," that it is up to the plaintiff (or his lawyer) to decide who the parties to the suit will be and which claims will be asserted in the action.

An example may help to frame the problem. Assume that Wright is the main contractor on a construction job. The electrical subcontractor is Edison Electric. While driving an Edison truck to the construction site, Edison's site manager, Volt, collides with Wright's cement truck, as well as with a private vehicle driven by Ellsworth. All three drivers are injured, and the two trucks are heavily damaged.

If Volt decides to bring suit against Wright to recover for his injuries, he will have to decide whether to sue alone or to bring a combined action along with Edison Electric, which will seek to recover for the damage to its truck. Ellsworth may also wish to join as a plaintiff to recover for her personal injuries and property damage. Alternatively, Volt may wish to sue both Wright and Ellsworth on the theory that each was negligent or, for whatever reason, to sue one tortfeasor but not the other.

231

Volt's options as to which defendants he may sue and which potential plaintiffs he decides to sue with are defined by the rules of "joinder of parties." In the federal courts, initial joinder of parties is governed by Fed. R. Civ. P. 20(a), which authorizes plaintiffs to sue together if (1) they assert claims arising out of the same transaction or occurrence (or series of transactions or occurrences); and (2) their claims against the defendant or defendants will involve a common question of law or fact. In Volt's suit, for example, Volt and Edison may join as plaintiffs because their claims arise out of the same accident, and the factual issue of whose negligence caused the accident is common to both their claims.

Similarly, Rule 20 allows the plaintiff to sue multiple defendants in a single action if the same criteria are met. Volt could sue Ellsworth and Wright as codefendants in the same action, since he claims relief from each arising from the same accident and there will be a common question as to whose negligence caused the accident. Here are some configurations that would be permissible under the rule:

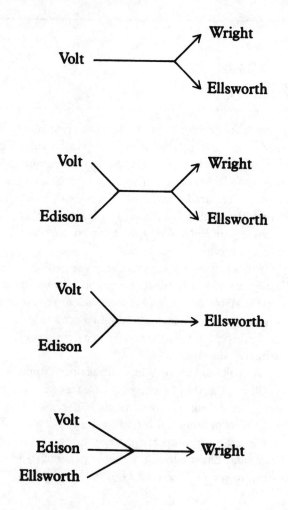

It makes good sense to allow parties to join as plaintiffs or to sue defendants jointly in a single action if the criteria in Rule 20(a) are met. When a number of claims involve a single transaction or occurrence, and the same issue or issues will have to be litigated to resolve each claim, it is more efficient to litigate those issues once in a combined action, rather than repeatedly in separate suits. In addition, resolving those issues in a single action avoids the possibility of inconsistent judgments on the same issue. For example, if Volt sues Ellsworth and recovers, but Edison sues Ellsworth and loses, the two juries must have disagreed on whether Ellsworth was negligent (barring any contributory negligence defense). Such inconsistent results reflect unfavorably on the judicial system and are best avoided where possible. If Volt's and Edison's claims are tried together there will be no inconsistent verdicts, since there will be only one finding on Ellsworth's negligence.

Interestingly, however, Rule 20(a) does not *require* parties to be joined whenever the criteria in the rule are met. At least initially, the joinder decision is left to the plaintiffs. If they choose to sue some but not all defendants in one action, they may sue the others in a separate action or never sue them at all. If they choose not to join in a suit by other plaintiffs against the defendant, they remain free to pursue their own claims in separate suits.

An Early but Sensible Question

1.   Since it promotes efficiency and consistency to litigate related claims such as Volt's and Edison's together, why doesn't Rule 20(a) require joinder of parties where the two criteria in the rule are met?

Counterclaims and Cross-Claims

You should be careful to distinguish Rule 20, which governs joinder of *parties,* from Rules 18 and 13, which authorize parties, once they are properly joined in a law suit, to assert additional *claims* against opposing parties. Rule 13 authorizes a defending party in a suit to assert claims back against a party who has claimed against him. Such counterclaims come in two shapes, compulsory (Rule 13(a)) and permissive (Rule 13(b)). If the defending party's counterclaim arises from the same transaction or occurrence as the claim against him, it is compulsory, which essentially means that he must assert it in the original action or lose it. For example, if Volt sues Ellsworth for his injuries arising out of the accident and Ellsworth suffered injuries in the same accident, which she attributes to Volt's negligence, Rule 13(a) requires Ellsworth to assert her claim for these injuries in Volt's action. This rule makes sense; it forces parties who are already adversaries to litigate all claims arising from the same set of facts in a single action.

Another Impromptu Question

2.   Under Rule 20(a), the parties are never forced to bring parties into a particular suit. Rule 13(a), by contrast, compels a party to assert some claims at a time and place not of his choosing. Why did the rulemakers choose to force parties to assert compulsory counterclaims?

Defending parties may also assert counterclaims that are completely unrelated to the original claim under Rule 13(b). This cannot be justified on efficiency grounds, since (by definition) a permissive counterclaim will involve different events from the main claim, and the court will almost certainly order separate trial of the permissive counterclaim. See Rule 42(b). But the rule at least allows a defendant, once brought before the court, to settle all his claims against his opponent without having to file a separate lawsuit.

Yet another type of claim is addressed in Rule 13(g), which provides for assertion of *cross-claims* arising out of the same transaction or occurrence as the main claim. A cross-claim is a claim asserted by one party against a co-party; that is, someone on the same side of the "v" as the claimant. Suppose that Volt sues Wright and Ellsworth for injuries suffered in the accident. If Wright suffered injuries as well and believes that the accident was Ellsworth's fault, she may cross-claim against Ellsworth for her injuries. This is called a cross-claim rather than a counterclaim because it is asserted by one defendant against a codefendant, not against an opposing party. The configuration would look like this:

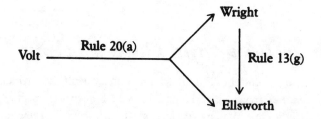

(Volt joins Wright and Ellsworth as defendants under Rule 20(a); Wright cross-claims against Ellsworth under Rule 13(g)).

Here again, allowing assertion of these claims in the main action promotes efficiency and consistency because the same underlying facts will be litigated on the main claim and on the cross-claim. Yet here again, the rule makes joinder optional, leaving Wright free to sue separately on her claim against Ellsworth if she prefers to do so.

The various joinder rules may also work in tandem. For example, the counterclaim rules, Rules 13(a) and (b), both authorize "a pleading" to assert a claim against an "opposing party." Once again the rulemakers have chosen the language of the rule with care. This language authorizes any defending party—not just an original defendant—to assert counterclaims against a party who has claimed against him. In the last diagram, once Wright cross-claims against Ellsworth, she becomes an "opposing party" on Wright's cross-claim. Rule 13 applies to any claim she may have against Wright. If she has a claim against Wright for her injuries in the collision, she must assert it as a compulsory counterclaim once Wright has asserted a claim against her. If she has any unrelated claims against Wright, she may assert them, but is not required to, under Rule 13(b).

Joinder of Claims under Rule 18(a)

Rule 18(a) is the last and broadest of the basic joinder rules. Unequivocally, it provides that a party seeking relief from an opposing party may join with his original claim any additional claims he has against that opposing party. Suppose, for example, that Volt exchanges words with Wright after the accident and a fight ensues. Rule 18(a) allows Volt to assert his claim for assault in the same action with the negligence claim. It would also allow Volt to add a completely unrelated claim against Wright for libel, trespass, or anything else. Unlike Rule 20(a), there is no common transaction or occurrence

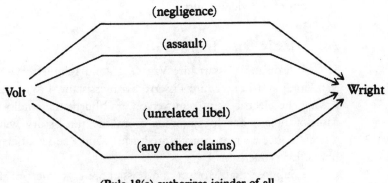

(Rule 18(a) authorizes joinder of all
these claims, related and unrelated)

requirement in Rule 18(a).

Rule 18(a), like Rule 13, authorizes "a pleader" to assert as many claims as he has against an opponent. This applies not only to the original plaintiff, but also to any party seeking relief against another party, whether on a counterclaim, a cross-claim, or a third-party claim. Suppose, for example, that Volt sues Ellsworth and Wright for negligence, based on the collision at the construction site, and Ellsworth cross-claims against Wright for her damages arising out of the accident. Rule 18 authorizes Ellsworth, as a party seeking relief, to add on any claim, related or unrelated, that she may have against Wright:

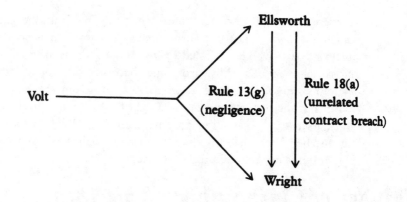

Note that Ellsworth could not have asserted this unrelated contract claim as a cross-claim if it were the only claim she had against Wright: Rule 13(g) only allows cross-claims that arise out of the same transaction or occurrence as the main claim. However, once Ellsworth asserts a proper cross-claim against Wright, Rule 18(a) kicks in, allowing her to add on totally unrelated claims as well.

In puzzling out the following examples, start by identifying the party asserting the claim as a plaintiff or defendant and then consider, given the particular posture of the claim, which of the rules applies. Assume that all suits are brought in federal court.

An Artistic Disaster

3.   Morisot and Cassatt hire Van Gogh and Renoir to paint their studio. Van Gogh and Renoir hire Pissarro as an assistant. Pissarro goes for coffee, leaving the electric paint remover on, and burns the studio to the ground. Morisot breaks her leg jumping from the third-story window, three of Cassatt's priceless masterpieces are burned, and Renoir suffers second-degree burns. Everyone is mad.

    a. Suppose that Morisot and Cassatt are co-owners of the studio. May they join as plaintiffs to sue Pissarro for the damages to the studio from the fire?

    b. Suppose that Cassatt owns the studio on her own. May she and Morisot join as plaintiffs to sue Pissarro for his negligence, if Cassatt seeks recovery for damage to the building and Morisot seeks damages for her broken leg?

    c. Assume that Van Gogh and Renoir are liable for the negligence of Pissarro under the law of respondeat superior, if he acted in the scope of his employment in leaving the heat gun on. May Morisot sue Van Gogh, Renoir, and Pissarro in a single action to recover for her broken leg?

    d. Could Cassatt sue Van Gogh and Renoir for breach of contract for burning down her studio in the process of painting it, and Morisot

join as a coplaintiff, asserting a negligence claim against the same defendants for the injury to her leg?

e. Change the facts a little: Assume that either Pissarro or Gauguin, another employee, left the paint remover on, and Cassatt is unsure
which it was. Can she sue them both under Rule 20(a)?

f. If Cassatt sues Renoir for breach of contract, may Renoir assert
claims against Pissarro and Van Gogh in the same suit for negligently
causing his injuries? (In considering this example, compare Rule
20(a) with Rule 14(a).)

4.   If Cassatt chooses to sue Renoir alone, may she assert both negligence
and breach of contract claims against Renoir for her losses in the fire?

5.   If Cassatt sues Renoir and Van Gogh for breach of contract, do the rules
authorize her to add a claim against Renoir for breach of a separate contract
to paint her house in another village?

6.   Cassatt sues Renoir for breach of the studio painting contract. Later, after losing on that claim, she sues Renoir for a previous breach of the unrelated contract to paint her house. Can she do that?

The Tables Turned

7.   Assume that Morisot owned the studio and contracted with Renoir and
Van Gogh to paint it. Morisot sues Renoir and Pissarro for negligence and
breach of contract as a result of the studio fire. Renoir asserts a claim against
Morisot in the same action for payments due for part of the painting that had
been completed before the building burned. Is Renoir's claim properly
joined?

8.   Following up on the last example, assume that Renoir also has a claim
against Morisot for injuries suffered in an auto accident two months after the
fire but before the suit was commenced. Can he assert this claim as well?

9.   Suppose on the same facts that the only counterclaim Renoir had against
Morisot was for the unrelated auto accident. Could he assert it in this action?

10.   If Morisot sues Renoir for her fire losses, may Renoir assert his claim
against Morisot for breach of the studio painting contract and also bring in
Cassatt (a co-signer of the contract) as a codefendant on that claim?

Acting at Cross-Purposes

11.   Suppose that Cassatt sues Renoir, Van Gogh, and Pissarro jointly. She
seeks recovery from Pissarro for his negligence and from Renoir and Van
Gogh as Pissarro's employers, under the doctrine of respondeat superior.
Renoir wishes to assert a claim against Pissarro for indemnification (that is,
reimbursement for any damages he — Renoir — must pay if he is found liable
to Cassatt) since it was Pissarro's negligence that actually caused the damage
to the studio.

a. May Renoir assert this claim against Pissarro in the same suit?

b. Why is this claim *not* a counterclaim?

12. On the facts of example 11, could Renoir assert a claim against Pissarro for his own injuries suffered in the fire?

13. If Cassatt sues Renoir and Van Gogh for their negligence in burning the studio, may Renoir assert a claim against Van Gogh for his failure to pay him half of the money they earned on another paint job?

14. Another variation: Suppose that Cassatt sues Renoir and Van Gogh, and Renoir wishes to assert claims against Van Gogh for his own injuries due to the fire *and* for the money owed him for the other paint job. May he do so?

15. Assume that Van Gogh and Renoir do not agree as to who was negligent in causing the fire. Van Gogh claims that it was Renoir's negligent instructions to Pissarro that caused the blaze. Renoir claims that Van Gogh failed to cut the power to the paint remover when Pissarro left for his break. When Cassatt sues Van Gogh and Renoir, Renoir cross-claims against Van Gogh for indemnification for any damages he must pay Cassatt on the main claim. May Van Gogh assert a claim against Renoir for injuries he suffered in the fire?

Last Impressions

16. One final example to make a particular point. Suppose Morisot (from Massachusetts) sues Renoir (from Maine) and Van Gogh (from Massachusetts) for their negligence in burning down the studio. Is the suit proper?

EXPLANATIONS

An Early but Sensible Question

1.   While it would serve several goals of our procedural system to force all parties to join in a single action if their claims arise out of the same events, it would raise other serious procedural difficulties. Suppose that Volt and Ellsworth want to sue in federal court, but Edison prefers the state court? Suppose that Volt prefers to sue in Maine, but the others prefer New Hampshire? What if Edison wants to bring suit immediately, but Volt prefers to attempt a settlement first? Will Volt's lawyer represent all parties, or will each have her own lawyer? Who will plan litigation strategy? What if they can't agree? Suppose that some of the potential plaintiffs are also potential defendants: Who will decide which side of the "v" to put them on?

  In addition to these possible differences of opinion as to tactical choices, the jurisdictional problems would be even more serious. The right to join parties under the Federal Rules does not confer subject matter jurisdiction on the court. Fed. R. Civ. P. 82. For example, suppose that Volt is from Maine, Ellsworth from New Hampshire, and Wright, the intended defendant, from Maine. If Volt and Ellsworth were forced to sue together, the suit could not be brought in federal court because there would not be complete diversity. Under the permissive language of Rule 20(a), if Ellsworth prefers federal court she may preserve the option to sue there by *not* joining as a coplaintiff with Volt. Alternatively, assume that Volt wishes to sue Wright, from Maine, and Ellsworth, from New Hampshire, for damages that took place in a Pennsylvania accident. Under Rule 20(a), which allows Volt to sue each defendant separately, he will at least be able to sue Wright at home in Maine because the Maine court will have personal jurisdiction over Wright on the basis of her domicile. If Volt were forced to join both defendants, he would have to sue in Pennsylvania, the one state where he could obtain personal jurisdiction over both defendants.

Obviously, a compulsory joinder rule would raise a host of procedural problems, which could undermine rather than further the goal of efficiency. The federal rulemakers chose to stick with the old adage that "the plaintiff is master of his claim," rather than to create a whole new set of procedural complexities.[1] However, despite these problems, the time-honored principle of plaintiff autonomy has had its critics. In this era of scarce judicial resources and managerial judging, broader suggestions for limiting plaintiff autonomy have also been floated. Professor Richard Freer, for example, suggests that the court should play a greater role in determining the scope of party joinder. See R. Freer, Avoiding Duplicative Litigation: Rethinking Plaintiff Autonomy and the Court's Role in Defining the Litigation Unit, 50 U. Pitt. L. Rev. 809 (1989). "A plaintiff is entitled to due process, but has no right to sole possession of center stage; we need to tell the prima donna of the legal world that she must work with some co-stars." Id. at 819.

For some years New Jersey experimented with a doctrine which rejected Rule 20(a)'s plaintiff autonomy rule. Under New Jersey's "entire controversy" doctrine, a plaintiff who brought suit on a transaction or occurrence was required to join all parties who might be liable to him for that transaction or occurrence in the action, or lose his claims against the omitted parties. See *Cogdell v. Hospital Center at Orange,* 560 A.2d 1169 (N.J.1989). The premise of the doctrine was that parties have an obligation to facilitate efficient resolution of cases, and that joining all defendants in the first action would facilitate that goal. In practice, however, the rule led to confusion as to when parties had to be joined. It also led to assertion of questionable claims simply to prevent forfeiting those claims by operation of the rule. New Jersey recently abandoned the entire controversy doctrine in favor of a more modest requirement that plaintiffs notify the court of potential claims against other parties, and allowing the court to order such parties joined in some

---

1. One exception, however, is Fed. R. Civ. P. 19, which requires joinder of certain persons under limited circumstances.

circumstances. See New Jersey Rules 4:5-1, 4:29-1, 4:30A as amended through July 10, 1998.

Another Impromptu Question

2.   Although forcing joinder of parties raises many problems, most of these do not apply to the joinder of an additional *claim* between parties who are already properly before the court. The subject matter jurisdiction problems referred to in the analysis of example 1 will not arise in the compulsory counterclaim situation because there is usually supplemental jurisdiction over compulsory counterclaims. See Chapter 15, example 4. Nor will personal jurisdiction bar assertion of the claim: The plaintiff, by initiating suit, submits to jurisdiction for counterclaims arising out of the transaction or occurrence that is the subject of his claim. 6 Wright and Miller at §1416. Nor does compulsory joinder of the counterclaim pose uncertainties as to who must be joined since no new parties are brought into the suit by the assertion of the counterclaim.

The only substantial argument against making counterclaims compulsory is that it violates the longstanding common law principle that the plaintiff (or, in this case, the defendant) is master of his claim, free to choose where and when to assert any claim he may have. The federal rule makers evidently concluded that this was insufficient to outweigh the obvious advantage of litigating the same facts and issues between the same parties in a single action. Some state rulemakers have weighed these policies differently, however, and refused to make any counterclaims compulsory. See Friedenthal, Kane, and Miller at 358 n.15 (1999).

An Artistic Disaster

3a.   This is the simplest example of parties who wish to join as coplaintiffs in a single lawsuit. Rule 20(a) allows it, so long as they are asserting claims arising out of the same transaction or occurrence and their claims will involve at least one common question of law or fact. These criteria are met here because Morisot and Cassatt both seek relief arising out of the fire and both claims involve a common question of fact, whether Pissarro was negligent.[2]

b.   The only difference between this example and the last is that the two plaintiffs seek compensation for different injuries. However, that does not affect their right to sue together. Rule 20(a) does not require that the plaintiffs seek recovery for exactly the same injuries or on a joint interest. In fact, the rule specifically provides that any one plaintiff "need not be interested in obtaining . . . all the relief demanded." It only requires that the underlying transaction or occurrence be the same and that the two plaintiffs' claims

---

2. Indeed, as joint owners they may even be required to join as plaintiffs, under Fed. R. Civ. P. 19.

share a common question of law or fact. Those criteria are met here, and joinder is proper under the rule.

This result is appropriate, given the efficiency and consistency goals of Rule 20(a). As long as the claims will require resolution of common issues, joint litigation in a single suit will save time for the parties, the witnesses, and the court.

c. Rule 20(a) applies not only to plaintiffs bringing suit together, but also to one or more plaintiffs bringing suit against multiple defendants. Here, Morisot seeks relief from all three defendants on claims arising out of the same fire, and her right to recover on each claim will require litigation of the common negligence issue. Joinder is proper.

d. This example involves multiple plaintiffs and defendants. While Rule 20(a) does not explicitly authorize suit by multiple plaintiffs against multiple defendants, it does authorize suits by multiple plaintiffs and (in the subsequent sentence) against multiple defendants. It is a fair inference that both types of joinder may be used in the same suit. It is proper, therefore, for some or all of the potential plaintiffs to join to sue all of the potential defendants or to sue selected defendants.

The other difference in this example is that the two plaintiffs are proceeding on different theories: Cassatt for breach of contract and Morisot for negligence. Compare example 3b, in which the plaintiffs proceeded on the same theory but for different damages. Nothing in Rule 20(a) requires the plaintiffs to proceed on the same theories in order for joinder to be proper. The idea behind the joinder rule is that there is efficiency and consistency to be gained from litigating the same facts in a single action. These goals are served by joinder criteria that allow a single action even though the plaintiffs are proceeding on different theories.

However, the criteria of Rule 20(a) must still be met. In this case the "same transaction or occurrence" test clearly is met since all claims arise out of the fire. The "common question of law or fact" requirement will likely be met as well: Both Morisot and Cassatt will have to prove that Pissarro's acts caused the fire in order to recover from Van Gogh and Renoir on their respective theories. So long as some such common question exists, joinder is proper, even though many issues (for example, the damages suffered by each plaintiff) will be different.

e. In this example, one of the defendants—but not both—will be liable to Cassatt. However, she may still sue them as codefendants under Rule 20(a). She has a legitimate claim against each of them, though she will presumably only win against one or the other. Her claims against both defendants arise from the fire, and they both involve the common question of who caused it. Where these two requirements are met, Rule 20(a) expressly allows joinder, even though relief is sought against the defendants "in the alternative."

f. In this case, it is the defendant who has joined multiple parties in the action, not the plaintiff:

The general language of the second sentence of Rule 20(a), if read in isolation, might be interpreted to allow a defendant to join new parties as "defendants" in the original action. However, a look at Rule 14(a) indicates that this type of situation, a defendant bringing new parties into the suit (whom the plaintiff did not choose to sue), is separately dealt with in that rule, which allows joinder only in much more limited circumstances than Rule 20(a). See Chapter 14. The Rule 14(a) requirements for impleading Pissarro and Van Gogh would not be met on these facts.

By contrast, Rule 20(a) only applies to joinder of parties by the original plaintiffs. The rulemakers' meticulous language confirms this: Rule 20(a) speaks specifically of "plaintiffs" and "defendants" rather than "parties claiming a right to relief" or similarly general language. Compare Rules 18 and 13, which are deliberately phrased more generally in order to apply more broadly.

4.   This example is typical of the myriad cases in which a plaintiff asserts a number of claims against a single defendant for the same injuries but bases those claims on different theories of relief. The question here is joinder of claims, not parties, since Cassatt is seeking relief from a single party on two separate claims. Rule 18(a) establishes a refreshingly broad rule for joinder of claims: Once Cassatt decides to sue Renoir, she may join whatever claims she has against Renoir in the suit. Thus, joinder of the negligence and contract claims is proper. It would also be proper if they were totally unrelated.

5.   The answer to this question involves application of both Rules 20 and 18. Rule 20 allows Cassatt to sue Renoir and Van Gogh together for breach of the studio-painting contract. Compare example 3c. Rule 18 allows Cassatt, once she has properly asserted a claim against Renoir, to assert her unrelated contract claim against Renoir as well, even though it arises out of a completely separate incident. Visually, the case looks like this:

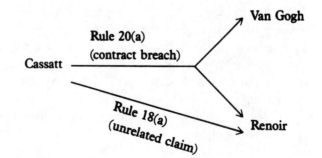

This compound effect of the rules is confusing. It seems to contradict the limitations on joinder established in Rule 20(a), since it allows Cassatt to inject into the case a claim that is completely unrelated to the transaction or occurrence that gave rise to the joint claim she has against the two defendants. After all, if she sued Van Gogh on the studio claim, she could not add Renoir on the unrelated claim under Rule 20(a), could she?

That is true, but the Rules take the position that once you *have* properly gotten the two of them into court, you may add any claims you have against either defendant, related or unrelated. Presumably, the theory is that once the parties become proper adversaries in a lawsuit they ought at least to have the opportunity to resolve all their differences in one suit.

6.   This example is meant to emphasize one point about Rule 18(a): It is permissive. Cassatt may assert unrelated claims against Renoir under Rule 18(a) but is not obligated to do so. Thus, she could bring separate actions against Renoir on these two unrelated contract claims in whatever order she chooses.

One note of caution should be added. While Rule 18 may not force a plaintiff to join all his claims against a defendant in a single action, the rules of res judicata will (at least under federal res judicata principles) if the claims arise out of a single transaction or occurrence. If Morisot has claims for breach of contract and negligence against Renoir and both arise from the studio fire, these would constitute a single "claim" for res judicata purposes that must be litigated in one action, despite the permissive language of Rule 18(a). See Chapter 25, which compares the joinder rules with the principles of res judicata, especially example 2, which specifically addresses the Rule 18 issue. However, because the two claims asserted here are completely unrelated, separate suits will be permissible under res judicata analysis as well as under Rule 18(a).

The Tables Turned

7.   Morisot's joinder of Renoir and Pissarro as codefendants is proper here under Rule 20(a). Renoir's claim against Morisot is a counterclaim under Rule 13(a), that is, a claim by a defending party against the party suing him. Not only do the rules authorize Renoir to assert this claim, they require him to do so. Rule 13(a) provides that a defending party's pleading "shall" state as a counterclaim any claim he has that arises out of the same transaction or occurrence as the main claim. Here, Renoir's claim arises out of the performance of the same paint job that gave rise to Morisot's claims. It is therefore a compulsory counterclaim under Rule 13(a).

8.   Rule 13 provides for the assertion of both compulsory (13(a)) and permissive (13(b)) counterclaims. In this example, Renoir has properly asserted one of each: the compulsory claim against Morisot based on the painting contract and the permissive counterclaim arising out of his auto accident with Morisot. The difference between the two is the source of the claim: The contract claim, which arises out of the same transaction as the original claim, is compulsory, while the claim arising from unrelated events is permissive.

9.   Yes, Renoir is free to assert his unrelated counterclaim, even though it is the only claim he has against Morisot. Rule 13(b) authorizes the assertion of unrelated counterclaims without restriction.

This may seem illogical. Why drag claims into the lawsuit that will have no factual relation to the main claim? It hardly seems likely to promote efficiency to join the painting contract claim with the auto accident claim, which will present completely different factual and legal issues. The rules allow joinder of such claims, however, on the theory that a defendant, once forced into court by the plaintiff, at least ought to have the option to settle all disputes with that plaintiff in a single action. That way, the defendant can save the cost of filing a new action and serving process again, and perhaps lower the cost of discovery as well. Also, in terms of fairness, Rule 13(b) gives defendants the same broad authority to join unrelated claims that plaintiffs have under Rule 18(a). If a single trial does not make sense, the court may order a separate trial of the unrelated counterclaim. Fed. R. Civ. P. 42(b).

10.   Here Renoir asserts a counterclaim against Morisot and wants to add Cassatt as an additional party to the counterclaim. Although the plaintiff is ordinarily "master of his claim," to include or exclude possible parties, this is a situation where the defendant also gets some control over the parties. Under Rule 13(h), Renoir is authorized to bring in an additional party on the counterclaim, so long as his claims against the added party and the original plaintiff meet the requirements of Rule 20(a), that is, both claims arise out of the same transaction or occurrence and share a common question of law or fact. These prerequisites are met here, so the joinder of Cassatt as an additional party to the counterclaim against Morisot is proper.

Acting at Cross-Purposes

11a. This is the first example in which one defendant seeks to recover against a codefendant. Rule 13(g) authorizes assertion of such "cross-claims" if they arise out of the same transaction or occurrence as the original claim. Renoir's claim qualifies because it arises out of the fire.

b.   Be careful to distinguish cross-claims from counterclaims. Counterclaims are asserted against a party who has asserted a claim against you. Cross-claims are asserted against a coparty, that is, a party to the action who is on the same side of the "v" as the cross-claimant. Renoir's claim is not a counterclaim since Renoir is not claiming against Cassatt, who sued him, but against Pissarro, his codefendant.

12.   This is also a valid cross-claim under Rule 13(g). It differs from the last example because the cross-claimant here seeks recovery for his own injuries, not indemnification for damages he may have to pay the plaintiff. Either type of claim is permissible so long as it arises out of the transaction or occurrence that gave rise to the main claim. The second sentence of Rule 13(g) specifically allows cross-claims for indemnification, such as Renoir asserted in example 11.

But the broad language of the first sentence clearly authorizes any cross-claim that arises from the same underlying events as the main claim in the action.

13. This attempt at joinder is improper. As already stated, Rule 13(g) requires that the cross-claim arise out of the same transaction or occurrence as the main claim; this completely unrelated claim is therefore improper. Under the efficiency rationale of the joinder rules, this result is appropriate. There will be little efficiency gained from litigating the unrelated claim in this suit because it involves a completely separate transaction. In addition, litigating these claims separately poses no risk of inconsistent judgments because the judgments rendered on them will not involve the same issues.

14. After the last example, you may be somewhat frustrated by the answer to this one: Joinder of both claims is proper here. Renoir's claim for his own injuries is a proper cross-claim (as in example 12). And, once a proper cross-claim has been asserted against Van Gogh, Renoir may add on any other claims he has against Van Gogh, under Rule 18(a).

It is crucial to understand the differing role of Rule 18(a) in these two cases. Although Rule 18(a) appears on its face to authorize any party to assert any claim he has against an opposing party, the rule actually requires a party to assert one claim that is proper under the other joinder rules before he can add others to it under Rule 18(a). Thus, once Renoir has properly asserted a cross-claim against Van Gogh under Rule 13(g), he may add others under Rule 18(a). Similarly, if Renoir asserted a third-party claim against Pissarro under Rule 14(a), he could add others under Rule 18(a). But Rule 18(a) is not a general hunting license to assert any claim against any party; if it were, all the other rules discussed in this chapter would be unnecessary.

Admittedly, it does not seem logical to allow Renoir to assert the unrelated claim if he asserts a related one (as here), but not if he asserts it alone (as in example 13). Yet, that is just what the Rules do. The apparent rationale is that once Renoir and Van Gogh become adversaries by the assertion of a proper cross-claim, they might just as well resolve all their differences in a single suit. Once again, the court has the discretion to order a separate trial of the unrelated claim if there is no efficiency to be gained from joint litigation.

15. Not only may Van Gogh assert this claim, he *must* do so under Rule 13(a). When Renoir claims against him, Van Gogh becomes an "opposing party" subject to the counterclaim rules of 13(a) and (b). Visually the case looks like this:

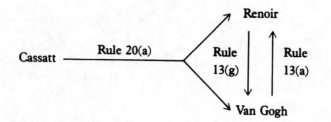

Remember that the counterclaim rules are written in general language to apply to all defending parties, not just original defendants. Since Renoir had made Van Gogh an opposing party by asserting a cross-claim against him, and Van Gogh's claim against Renoir arises out of the same transaction or occurrence as Renoir's cross-claim, it is a compulsory counterclaim. It must be asserted in this action or lost.

Last Impressionists

16. The point of this example is so important that I have devoted an entire chapter to it. See Chapter 16, which explores the distinction between "power" (subject matter jurisdiction) and "permission" to join claims under the Rules. The problem here is that Morisot has properly joined Van Gogh and Renoir as codefendants under Rule 20(a), but the court lacks subject matter jurisdiction because there is neither complete diversity nor a federal claim. The joinder rules *do not provide a basis for subject matter jurisdiction;* they only govern who may properly be made parties when all jurisdictional rules are satisfied. Thus, this case is not properly before the court, even though the joinder rules authorize joinder.

14

Into the Labyrinth: Joinder of Parties under Rule 14

Introduction

A persistent civil procedure theme explored in the earlier chapters is the right of the plaintiff or plaintiffs to sculpt the lawsuit by their choice of the forum and their initial decisions to join parties as plaintiffs or defendants. An equally persistent theme, however, is the various ways in which the plaintiff's well-laid plans may go awry. For example, she may end up in a different court if the defendant removes or seeks a change of venue; or she may end up *defending* a claim if another party asserts a cross-claim or counterclaim against her.

Rule 14 provides another example of the complexities that await the unwary plaintiff who disregards Dickens's famous advice.[1] Rule 14 gives a defendant a limited right to *implead* (that is, bring into the suit) new parties against whom she has claims related to the main action. Under the rule the defendant may bring in a person not yet a party to the suit who may be liable to her, the defendant, for all or part of any recovery the plaintiff obtains on the main claim.

In many tort cases third parties are impleaded for *contribution*, that is, to obtain a judgment that the third party is liable to pay the main defendant part of the damages she is ordered to pay the plaintiff. For example, suppose

---

1. "Suffer any indignity that can be done you rather than come [to the courts of chancery]." Charles Dickens, Bleak House 7 (Norton ed. 1977).

that Napoleon sues Wellington for negligently injuring him during a polo match. Wellington claims that Robespierre, riding a third horse, was also negligent. Under the rules of contribution among joint tortfeasors, Wellington would be entitled to recover from Robespierre part of any damages Wellington pays Napoleon,[2] if he can prove that Robespierre was also negligent. On these facts Wellington may implead Robespierre under Rule 14 since he may be liable to Wellington for part of any damages that Wellington is ordered to pay Napoleon. The case looks like this:

Napoleon ⟶ Wellington (defendant/third-party plaintiff)

Rule 14(a)

Robespierre (third-party defendant)

In other cases the defendant may claim that the third party is liable to her for all damages that she may have to pay the plaintiff. For example, consider Ronan Construction's third-party complaint against Jones in the *Schulansky* case. Ronan's last claim for relief (see infra p. 586) alleges that, if it is liable to Schulansky for the damage to the house caused by Jones's backhoe work and pays for that damage, it should be reimbursed by Jones. Under tort law, this is generally true: Ronan, as the general contractor, would be liable for the negligence of a subcontractor but, if the subcontractor's negligence caused the harm, would have a right of full indemnification from the negligent subcontractor. On this theory, Ronan may implead Jones to recover "all" of its liability to Schulansky.

Another common example of a proper impleader claim is a claim for indemnity against an insurer. In Napoleon's case against Wellington, for example, suppose that Wellington has liability insurance with Lloyds of London, but Lloyds denies that the policy covers the claim. Wellington may implead Lloyds under Rule 14(a), seeking indemnity for any judgment Napoleon recovers against him. In both these examples, the defendant seeks to pass on all of his liability, not just a part as in the contribution example. This also satisfies the requirement in Rule 14 that the impleaded party may be liable to the defendant for "all or part" of the plaintiff's claim against the defendant.

---

2. In some jurisdictions, Wellington would recover half of the judgment from Robespierre. In others, the extent of Robespierre's liability for contribution would depend on the percentage of negligence the jury attributed to him in causing Napoleon's injury. See Glannon, The Law of Torts: Examples and Explanations 469 (2d ed. 2000).

It is crucial to distinguish these cases from situations in which the defendant contends that another person is liable directly to the plaintiff but not to her. Suppose that Wellington's polo match took place in a jurisdiction that did not allow contribution between joint tortfeasors. In that case Robespierre might still be liable to Napoleon directly, but Wellington could not implead him because Robespierre would not be liable to Wellington at all. He can't offer up Robespierre as an alternate defendant to Napoleon, saying, "Here, Napoleon, you sued me, but you really should have sued us both, so here's Robespierre; go at him." That would allow the defendant to dictate to the plaintiff whom to sue where, in defiance of the conventional doctrine that the plaintiff is master of her claim.

To further illustrate this point, assume that a police officer assaults Dillinger in the course of arresting him for robbery. Dillinger sues Officer Hayes, a six-foot-two, red-headed policeman, for the assault. Hayes claims mistaken identity: It was actually Officer Kelly, another six-foot redhead, who arrested Dillinger. Hayes cannot implead Kelly. He has no claim that Kelly is liable to him. Either one or the other assaulted Dillinger; one or the other will be solely liable to him. Hayes contends of course that Dillinger should have sued Kelly instead of him, but this gives him no right to substitute another defendant or to add one under Rule 14. That rule does not allow defendants to suggest new targets for the plaintiff. Rather, it allows defendants to bring in targets of their own if they may be able to pass on liability to the impleaded party.[3]

It follows from this central requirement of Rule 14 that the third-party defendant's liability will depend on the outcome of the main claim. If Napoleon does not recover from Wellington, Wellington will have no right of contribution against Robespierre. Robespierre can hardly be asked to contribute if Wellington doesn't have to pay; nor would Lloyds be liable to indemnify Wellington unless Wellington has to pay a judgment; nor Jones to pay Ronan if Schulansky loses on the main claim. The impleaded party may escape liability by defeating either the plaintiff's original claim or the defendant's derivative claim against her. Consequently, the rule allows her to assert defenses to both. See Rule 14(a), fourth sentence (defenses to third-party claim) and fifth sentence (defenses to the plaintiff's claim against the original defendant).

---

3. At one time Rule 14 did allow defendants to add new parties who might be liable directly to the plaintiff. That provision created serious problems that led to the elimination of this option:

> [I]n some cases plaintiff declined to press his claim against the third-party defendant and could not be compelled to amend his complaint in order to do so. When that occurred, the third-party action would have to be dropped since no one had alleged a claim against the third-party defendant. In other cases, an amendment to assert a direct claim against the third-party defendant, if allowed, would have destroyed diversity of citizenship as the basis of federal jurisdiction. For these reasons the rule was amended in 1948 to eliminate defendant's right to implead persons directly liable to plaintiff.

6 Wright and Miller at 287-288.

The impleader claim is treated like an original suit for pleading, service, and other purposes. The defendant, as "third-party plaintiff," must file a third-party complaint against the impleaded "third-party defendant." The complaint must comply with the pleading requirements of Rules 8 through 11 and must be served under Rule 4 (see ch. 32, p. 584, for an example of a third-party complaint in the *Schulansky* case). The third-party defendant must respond under Rule 12 and has the same options to answer or move to dismiss. The third-party defendant may also file counterclaims against the third-party plaintiff and may implead further parties under Rule 14. That rule also allows the plaintiff and the third-party defendant to assert claims against each other if they arise out of the same transaction or occurrence as the main claim. See Rule 14, sixth and seventh sentences.

Under Rule 14 the defendant may implead a third party within ten days of answering the complaint, without obtaining leave of court. This automatic impleader provision suggests that the court must hear the third-party claim if it is filed within the ten-day period. However, the cases establish that it is always within the court's discretion to refuse to entertain the impleader claim. See generally 3 Moore's at ¶14.20. Factors favoring impleader include the efficiency of hearing the related claims together and avoidance of repeated suits or inconsistent judgments. Factors suggesting denial of impleader include undue delay in seeking it, complication of the issues in the main action, and potential prejudice to the plaintiff from impleading a sympathetic third party. In some cases the court may be able to address these concerns by allowing the impleader but separating the main suit and the third-party suit for trial. See Rule 14, eighth sentence; 6 Wright and Miller at §1443.

Two further points should be mentioned concerning the relation of impleader claims to the three-ring analysis in the earlier chapters. First, impleading a third-party defendant does not affect the court's jurisdiction over the original claim. Suppose, for example, that Napoleon is from Maine, Wellington from Connecticut, and Robespierre from Maine:

The original case between Napoleon and Wellington is a proper diversity case. Wellington's decision to implead Robespierre does not affect the court's jurisdiction over the original claim, even though Robespierre is from

Maine.[4] However, there must still be a basis for subject matter jurisdiction over the impleader claim. Here, there may be diversity jurisdiction, if the amount-in-controversy requirement is met, since Wellington and Robespierre are from different states. If there isn't, there will usually be "supplemental jurisdiction" over a proper impleader claim, under 28 U.S.C. s. 1367(a). See Chapter 15, example 7.

Second, the third party is also disregarded in determining whether venue is proper. For example, the case in the illustration could properly be brought in the District of Connecticut, where Wellington resides, under 28 U.S.C. §1391(a)(1), despite the fact that the third-party defendant resides in Maine, not Connecticut. 6 Wright and Miller at §1445, pp. 348-352. Here too, if the third-party defendant's residence were considered in applying the venue statute, defendants would be able to defeat federal jurisdiction in many cases in which the plaintiff had properly invoked it, simply by impleading defendants from the right (that is, the wrong) states.

The examples below may help to dispel some of the darkness that engulfs this murky rule. In considering them, assume that all cases are brought in federal court and that subject matter jurisdiction is proper in each case. In addition, focus on whether the claim would satisfy the requirements of Rule 14, not whether the court (assuming the rule is satisfied) would exercise its discretion to hear the impleader claim.

EXAMPLES

Pleaders and Impleaders

1. Ali sues Bellefonds, the engineer on a canal construction project, for negligence arising out of faulty engineering calculations in planning the canal. May Bellefonds implead Le Pere, another engineer whom he claims was also negligent in making the calculations?

2. Ali sues Bellefonds for his faulty engineering calculations. Bellefonds impleads Le Pere, alleging that it was actually Le Pere who did the calculations. Is the impleader proper?

3. France sues DeLesseps, a general contractor, for faulty canal construction. DeLesseps claims that if there was a breach it was actually the fault of Said, the subcontractor he hired to do the dredging work on the canal, and that Said should therefore bear the loss. Can he implead Said?

4. Suppose that DeLesseps is unclear as to whether the defective construction work resulted from Said's dredging work or faulty concrete work done by another subcontractor, Ismail. May he implead both?

---

4. If the citizenship of the third party did affect jurisdiction over the initial claim, it would allow defendants to manipulate jurisdiction by impleading third-party defendants to destroy diversity.

5.   Assume that France sues DeLesseps on the canal contract, and Delesseps wishes to recover from Said, his subcontractor, for certain camels Said took away when he left the job. May he implead Said?

6.   In the same contract action, could DeLesseps implead Said and assert both the indemnification claim described in example 3 and the camel-trover claim in example 5?

7.   France sues DeLesseps for the faulty canal construction. DeLesseps does not implead Said. France recovers a judgment from DeLesseps and DeLesseps pays the damages. May he now sue Said for indemnification?

Heads of the Hydra

8.   Suppose that DeLesseps is sued by France for breach of the canal contract. He impleads Said for faulty subcontract work, and Said wants to assert a claim against France for intentional interference with his subcontract with DeLesseps. May he do so?

9.   Note that the language of the Rule (always so carefully chosen by the Solomons of civil procedure) does not call Said's claim against France in the last example a counterclaim. Why isn't it a counterclaim?

10. Think of three ways in which a counterclaim could insinuate itself into this suit.

11. Assume that DeLesseps impleads Said for indemnification on the theory that his faulty dredging work caused the contract breach. Said claims that his insurer, Cairo Casualty and Indemnity Co., has a duty to pay any damages resulting from his breach. May Said assert a claim against Cairo in the same action?

12. If Said is impleaded, may France assert a claim against Said for shoddy construction on an unrelated job Said did for France?

Another Unlucky Number 13

13. Assume that France is from California, DeLesseps from Texas, and Said from Arizona. The canal work was done in Colorado. France sues DeLesseps in Texas, and DeLesseps impleads Said. Is the impleader proper?

14. Suppose that DeLesseps counterclaims against France, to collect the contract price for the canal work. May France implead Disraeli, who cosigned the contract along with France and is, therefore, also contractually bound to pay DeLesseps for the contract work?

A Last Brainteaser for the Rules Enthusiast

15. Along the same general lines as the earlier examples, assume that France sues DeLesseps, who then impleads Said. Said wishes to assert a claim against France for interference with his contract with DeLesseps. He also claims that Porte (an agent of France not yet party to the suit) took part

in the intentional interference. Can Said add Porte as an additional party to his interference-with-contract claim against France? Visually the hypo looks like this:

EXPLANATIONS

Pleaders and Impleaders

1. Here, Bellefonds seeks to implead Le Pere, not yet a party to the suit, to recover part of any judgment Ali recovers from Bellefonds. Assuming that the relevant state law authorizes contribution among joint tortfeasors, this is a proper impleader claim. Le Pere is a new party who "is or may be liable to the third-party plaintiff [Bellefonds] for all or part of the plaintiff's claim against [Bellefonds]." If Bellefonds is found liable to Ali and Le Pere is also found negligent, Bellefonds will be entitled to recover from Le Pere part of the damages Bellefonds pays Ali. Note that at the time he impleads Le Pere, it is not clear that Le Pere will be liable to contribute. That depends on whether Bellefonds is found negligent, whether Le Pere is found negligent, and whether Bellefonds pays more than his share of the judgment. But the rule only requires that Le Pere "may" be liable to Bellefonds; Le Pere's liability need not follow automatically from Bellefonds's, nor must Bellefonds have already been adjudged liable before he can implead Le Pere.

2. As stated in the introduction, impleader under Rule 14 cannot be used to foist alternate defendants on the plaintiff. Ali chose to sue Bellefonds, not Le Pere. If Bellefonds didn't do the faulty calculations, Ali will lose his suit against him. Maybe Ali will then sue Le Pere or maybe he won't. That is his choice. But Bellefonds may not bring Le Pere in on the mere allegation that Le Pere is liable to Ali. Bellefonds may only implead Le Pere to recover from him all or part of the damages Bellefonds must pay Ali. If liability is an either/or proposition, Bellefonds has no such claim against Le Pere, and impleader should be denied.

Ali could have chosen to join Bellefonds and Le Pere as codefendants under Rule 20(a). See Chapter 13, pp. 232-233. Alternatively, Bellefonds may defend against Ali's claim on the ground that Le Pere was the offending party instead of him. But he can't use Rule 14 as a backdoor means of forcing Ali to sue Le Pere, which Rule 20(a) allows, but does not require, Ali to do.

3. This is a proper impleader claim. DeLesseps, as the general contractor, will be liable to France if the work does not meet the contract specifications, even though it was a subcontractor's negligence that caused the breach. However, DeLesseps will surely have a contractual right under his separate contract with Said (and probably a right under negligence law as well) to indemnity for damages caused by Said's faulty subcontract work. Thus, Said "may be liable to the third-party plaintiff [DeLesseps] for all . . . of the plaintiff's claim against [DeLesseps]," and DeLesseps may properly implead Said under the first sentence of Rule 14(a).

4. In this case DeLesseps is unclear as to whether he should be indemnified by one subcontractor or the other or both. Although the rule is not explicit on the point, there is no reason why a defendant should have to limit his impleader claims to one third party when several may be liable to him. As long as the provisions of Rule 14 are satisfied, a defendant may implead multiple third-party defendants, claiming either joint or alternate liability.

5. This is not a proper impleader claim. Here, DeLesseps has a claim against Said, arising out of the same transaction (the construction of the canal) as the main claim, but Said's liability to DeLesseps is not derivative of the main suit. DeLesseps has a totally independent claim against Said, which he could assert whether France wins or loses on the main claim or never sues at all.

It might make sense to design the rules of procedure to allow the defendant to expand the lawsuit in this way, but it would certainly introduce many tangential claims sharing few witnesses or factual or legal issues with the main claim. That would be the case here, since the claim for the missing camels is clearly distinct from the faulty construction claim. The rule-makers decided to confine the defendant's options more narrowly, by use of the "may be liable to the third-party plaintiff for all or part of the plaintiff's claim" language.[5] But see, with some perplexity, the following example.

6. Curiously, despite the previous answer, Rule 18(a) expressly allows DeLesseps, once he has forced Said into the suit on a proper impleader claim, to add on this independent claim. Presumably the rationale for this is that

---

5. There is nothing inevitable about the strict limit Federal Rule 14 imposes on impleader claims. Some state rules are much more liberal. See, e.g., Pa. St. Ann. §.2252(a), which authorizes a defendant to join a party who "may be

> (1) solely liable on the plaintiff's cause of action, or
> (2) liable over to the joining party on the plaintiff's cause of action, or
> (3) jointly or severally liable with the joining party on the plaintiff's cause of action, or
> (4) liable to the joining party on any cause of action arising out of the transaction or occurrence or series of transactions or occurrences upon which the plaintiff's cause of action is based."

Subsection (4) clearly would allow DeLesseps' camel claim in example 5.

once the third-party defendant is in the case the Rules might as well allow the defendant to settle all her differences with the third-party defendant in a single action. Visually the suit looks like this:

However, Rule 18(a) alone does not allow DeLesseps to bring Said into the suit. To do that, DeLesseps must first assert a claim complying with Rule 14. Rule 18 only allows him to add related (or unrelated) claims once he has properly impleaded Said under Rule 14.

7.   This example makes a single important point, that a defendant is not forced to implead a third party under Rule 14, even if the third party may be liable to reimburse the defendant for all or part of the plaintiff's claim. The rule says the defendant "may" implead a third party, which clearly implies that he has a choice. If DeLesseps chooses not to, he will not be barred from suing Said in a separate action to recover indemnification for the judgment he paid.

A mandatory impleader rule might make sense, from an efficiency perspective. However, it would cause problems if the third party was not subject to personal jurisdiction, and it would override the deference that the system has traditionally paid to DeLesseps's choice of when and where to sue Said. In an era of scarce judicial resources, the system may move toward mandatory joinder in situations like this, but has not yet arrived there.

Heads of the Hydra

8.   In this example, Said has been properly impleaded and seeks to assert a related claim against the original plaintiff. The sixth sentence of Rule 14(a) explicitly authorizes Said to do so. The suit now looks like this:

But Said cannot assert any claim he has against France. Under Rule 14(a), his claims against the plaintiff are limited to those that arise out of the same transaction or occurrence as the main claim. Assuming the court takes a reasonably broad view of that test, this claim will satisfy it.

9.   A counterclaim is defined in both Rules 13(a) and (b) as a claim against an "opposing party." Before Said asserts a claim against France they are not opposing parties. France has a claim against DeLesseps, not Said. Although France and Said are locked in the same litigious dance, they are not yet partners.

10. Counterclaims may be asserted by any defending party against her opponent. Rule 13(a). Obviously, DeLesseps may have some counterclaims against France. Said, once impleaded, may assert counterclaims against DeLesseps. See Rule 14(a), fourth sentence. Indeed, Said *must* assert them if they satisfy the Rule 13(a) test for compulsory counterclaims. For example, he may have a claim against DeLesseps for the subcontract price for his services. This claim arises out of the same transaction as De-Lesseps's claim against him and must be asserted in the impleader action under Rule 13(a).

Finally, once Said has asserted a claim against France, they become opposing parties as well. If France has any claim against Said arising from the canal construction, he must assert it. If he has any other claim against Said, he may assert it as well under Rule 13(b). Thus, hydra-like,[6] the suit may grow:

11. Said may indeed implead Cairo under Rule 14(a). The ninth sentence of that rule allows the third-party defendant to assert such telescoping third-party claims against further parties, so long as the Rule 14(a) standard for impleader ("is or may be liable to the [fourth party plaintiff] for all or part" of the third-party plaintiff's claim against him) is met. The suit now looks like this:

---

6. The hydra, a Greek beast, was reputed to sprout two heads for each lopped off by its unfortunate adversary.

Imagine the title of Cairo's answer to this claim: "Fourth-Party Defendant's Answer to the Third-Party Defendant/Fourth-Party Plaintiff's Fourth-Party Complaint"![7]

12. France's claim here does not arise out of the same transaction or occurrence as the main claim. The seventh sentence of Rule 14 authorizes joinder of claims the plaintiff has against the third-party defendant if those claims satisfy the same transaction or occurrence test. By implication, the rule excludes unrelated claims, so this one fails. As well it should; there has to be some limit to the introduction of unrelated matters into the action, lest it become completely unmanageable.

Another Unlucky Number 13

13. The fact that you were given the states for each party should have tipped you off that there is some jurisdictional problem here. It can't be diversity: As the Introduction points out, the third party's citizenship is irrelevant to determining diversity, and besides, there is complete diversity anyway. It can't be venue either: The third party is also disregarded in determining proper venue. Here, at least one district in Texas is a proper venue, since DeLesseps resides there, although Said, the third-party defendant, does not.

It must be personal jurisdiction. Indeed it is, or may be. *Whenever* a party is brought into a suit, whether as an original defendant, a third-party defendant, an additional party to a counterclaim, or whatever, the court must have the power to require that party to appear and defend in that state. Said's due process rights would be as clearly abridged if he were forced to defend a third-party action in a forum with which he lacks contacts as if he

---

7. For a case taking these antics to the sixth power, see *Bevemet Metais, Ltd. v. Gallie Corp.,* 3 F.R.D. 352 (S.D.N.Y. 1942).

were forced into such a court as the original defendant. If Said objects to personal jurisdiction, the court will have to consider whether Said has minimum contacts with Texas or is subject to personal jurisdiction there for this claim on some other basis. Compare Jones's motion to dismiss in *Schulansky v. Ronan*, Chapter 33.

14. This is an example of a plaintiff, now a defendant on a counterclaim, impleading a party who may be liable to her (the plaintiff) for all or part of a judgment the counterclaiming defendant obtains from her. Since Disraeli is a co-obligor on the contract, France may be entitled to pass on to him part of the contract price. Thus, impleading Disraeli is explicitly authorized by Rule 14(b).

A Last Brain Teaser for the Rules Enthusiast

15. At some point the hydra must be stopped, and it appears that the Rules draw a limit here. Rule 14(a), sixth sentence, allows the third-party defendant to assert claims against the plaintiff if they arise out of the underlying dispute. That sentence makes no mention of adding additional parties. (Compare Rule 13(h), which expressly allows adding parties to counterclaims and cross-claims.) Nor does Rule 20(a) apply here; that rule only applies to the joinder of original defendants. For these more abstruse variants you have to find explicit authority in one of the other joinder rules, and it appears that by providing no such authority the rules stop short of allowing this claim.

15

Jurisdictional Fellow Travelers: Supplemental Jurisdiction

Introduction

The preceding chapters on the federal joinder rules describe a highly flexible system that liberally allows parties to expand the litigation by joining claims in a single action. However, permission under the joinder rules to assert a claim, while necessary, is not sufficient to allow the court to hear it: From early on, we have seen that the court must always have subject matter jurisdiction over a claim if it is to proceed. As you have already read — and you will hear it repeated ad nauseum for the rest of your professional life — the subject matter jurisdiction of the federal courts is limited to the categories of cases enumerated in Article III, §2, of the Constitution.

These two principles, broad joinder under the Rules of Civil Procedure and the need for subject matter jurisdiction over every claim, are on something of a collision course. Frequently, the rules will authorize joinder of claims over which there is no independent basis of subject matter jurisdiction. Such cases pose a dilemma for the courts: The efficiency goals of the Rules favor inclusion of related claims, but the ineluctable need for subject matter jurisdiction appears to bar the court from hearing them.

Examples of the Problem

The problem can arise in a number of contexts. The simplest is the case in which the plaintiff asserts two claims against a nondiverse defendant, one arising under federal law and one under state law. Assume, for example, that Byron brings suit in federal court against Rossetti (a fellow resident of Wisconsin) for violation of a federal age discrimination statute and also claims that the dismissal constitutes a breach of contract. Visually, the case is illustrated as follows:

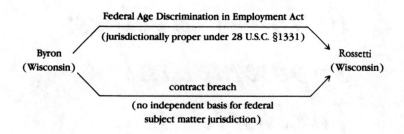

Clearly, these claims are properly joined under Rule 18(a). Also, the court clearly has jurisdiction over the federal law claim. But nothing in Article III authorizes jurisdiction over the breach of contract claim: The parties are not diverse, and the claim does not arise under federal law. If Byron sued solely on the contract claim, the federal court would have to dismiss it. Yet the efficiency and consistency goals of the Rules favor hearing Byron's two claims together, since they involve the same occurrence — the dismissal. Doubtless, the witnesses will be the same on both claims, and much of the same evidence will be relevant to both claims. If the federal court is to litigate this case, it would surely be desirable for it to hear the *whole* case, including the federal claim and the related state law claim.

Here is another example: Byron brings his dismissal action against Rossetti under the federal statute, and Rossetti counterclaims against Byron for assault, claiming that at the time of the firing Byron threatened to kill her for firing him. The case now looks like this:

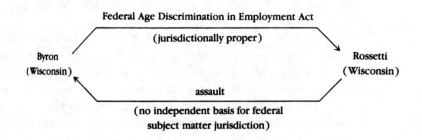

This is a compulsory counterclaim under Rule 13(a), since it arises from the same occurrence as Byron's claim. However, it is again a state law claim between parties from the same state. If Rossetti sued Byron on this claim alone, the federal court would not have the power to hear it, since nothing in Article III, §2, or the United States Code gives the federal district courts subject matter jurisdiction over state law claims between parties from the same state.

One more frequent example: Burns, from Wyoming, sues Cowper, from Utah, for injuries suffered in an auto accident. Cowper impleads a third driver, Hunt (also from Utah) under Rule 14(a), claiming that Hunt was also negligent and is therefore liable to him for contribution:

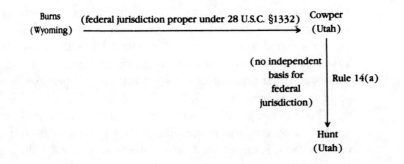

Again, this is proper under the Rules; and again, the existence of common issues argues for allowing the third-party claim to be heard with the main claim. But, once again, there is no independent basis for subject matter jurisdiction: Cowper's claim is a state law claim between two citizens of the same state.

Essential History, Part I: Pendent Jurisdiction

Historically, two doctrines evolved to support jurisdiction over such related claims in federal court. The first, *pendent jurisdiction*, involved the configuration in the first diagram above, in which the plaintiff asserted a jurisdictionally proper claim against a nondiverse party and added on a related state law claim. In *United Mine Workers v. Gibbs*, 383 U.S. 715 (1966), the Supreme Court established guidelines for the exercise of jurisdiction over such "pendent" claims.

In *Gibbs* the plaintiff asserted a federal claim against the defendant under the Labor Management Relations Act and a second claim under state law for interference with contractual relations. Both claims were based on the same dispute, concerning the opening of a particular mine. Because there was no diversity between the parties in *Gibbs* and the interference claim arose under state law, there was no independent basis for subject matter jurisdiction over the interference claim. Yet the *Gibbs* Court held that the federal court had pendent jurisdiction over the state law claim because it was joined with the federal labor law claim.

The Court rationalized this conclusion on the ground that Article III grants jurisdiction over entire "cases," not just over particular claims or issues in a case. If a case includes a claim that is jurisdictionally proper under Article III, the argument goes, the court has constitutional power to hear the *entire dispute* between the parties, not just the claim that is expressly provided for in Article III, §2. Thus, so long as the plaintiff asserts a proper claim based on federal law, diversity, or some other federal ground, the federal court has the power — at least the *constitutional* power — to hear other claims arising out of the same "common nucleus of operative facts."[1] In *Gibbs,* for example, the case was properly before the federal court because the plaintiff asserted a claim under the federal labor laws. The constitutional "case," however, was broader than the federal claim, encompassing all of Gibbs's claims arising out of the same nucleus of operative facts, the opening of the new mine.

This holding in *Gibbs,* that a "case" includes not simply the plaintiff's jurisdictionally sufficient claims, but all claims that arise from the same set of historical facts, is one of the Court's most sensible and enduring procedural decisions. Further, it is consistent with the intent of the framers, who would hardly have contemplated that the federal courts would be required to dissect a single dispute and limit their jurisdiction to certain strands of a logically interrelated set of claims. The language of Article III, §2, after all, speaks in terms of "cases" and "controversies," not of individual theories or causes of action.

While the *Gibbs* Court concluded that the federal courts had the *power* to hear claims that arose from the same nucleus of facts as the jurisdictionally proper claim, it did not *require* the federal court to entertain the related claims. Wisely, the Court provided a second step in the analysis: Once the judge ascertains that he has power to hear the related claim, because it is part of the same "case," he must then determine whether it makes sense to exercise that jurisdiction. See *Gibbs* at 726-727. This discretionary decision depends on a variety of factors in each case, such as whether the state law claim predominates, whether it would require the court to decide sensitive or novel issues of state law, whether hearing the claims together might confuse

---

1. Chief Justice Marshall is a little more explicit on the point in *Osborn v. Bank of the United States,* 22 U.S. 738 (1824):

> [W]hen a question to which the judicial power of the Union is extended by the constitution, forms an ingredient of the original cause, it is in the power of congress to give the [federal courts]...jurisdiction of that cause, although other questions of fact or of law may be involved in it.

the jury, and whether the federal issues are resolved early in the case, leaving only a state law claim for decision. These factors might lead the court to conclude that; while it had power under the first part of *Gibbs* to entertain the pendent claim, it should refuse, in its discretion, to do so. If it does decline jurisdiction over the state law claims, and therefore dismisses them, they may then be brought in a separate suit in state court.

Essential History, Part II: Ancillary Jurisdiction

The courts evolved a similar approach, under the rubric of *ancillary jurisdiction*, to deal with cases like those in the last two diagrams above, in which related claims were asserted by defendants or other additional parties after the initial complaint. In *Moore v. New York Cotton Exchange*, 270 U.S. 593 (1926), the plaintiff sued the defendant under the federal antitrust laws, and the defendant asserted a compulsory counterclaim against the plaintiff under state law. The Court upheld jurisdiction over the state law counterclaim, even though the parties were not diverse and there was no other basis for independent federal jurisdiction over the counterclaim. The Court's discussion in *Moore* is terse, but it did emphasize that the counterclaim (like all compulsory counterclaims) arose out of the same transaction as the main claim. Thus, the decision appears to turn, as did *Gibbs,* on the conclusion that the close connection between the original, jurisdictionally proper claim and the added claim made them part of a single "constitutional case."

From the seed of the *Moore* case, courts extended ancillary jurisdiction to many claims asserted by defending parties that bore a "logical relationship" to the main claim. Third-party claims like that in the figure on p. 261 were consistently held ancillary, since they are by definition "logically related" to the main claim: The third-party plaintiff can only recover from the third-party defendant if the plaintiff recovers from the third-party plaintiff. Fed. R. Civ. P. 14. On a similar rationale, ancillary jurisdiction was extended to cross-claims under Rule 13(g) and to intervention as of right under Rule 24(a). But the same logic dictated denial of ancillary jurisdiction for permissive counterclaims. By definition, such claims arose from different events (see Rule 13(b)) and therefore lacked a close logical relation to the main claim. See generally Friedenthal, Kane, and Miller 3rd at §2.12, pp. 65-67.

Essential History, Part III: Statutory Limits on Jurisdiction

All of this was complex enough, but the Court multiplied these woes in three major cases by introducing a more sophisticated analysis of the limits of such supplemental jurisdiction. In *Aldinger v. Howard,* 427 U.S. 1(1976), *Owen Equipment & Erection Co. v. Kroger,* 437 U.S. 365 (1978), and *Finley v. United States,* 490 U.S. 545 (1989), the court reiterated the basic principle that federal jurisdiction is not only limited by the Constitution but also must be conveyed to the federal district courts by Congress in a jurisdictional statute. (Recall Judge Sirica's well-phrased comments on the "Article III storehouse," supra p. 60.)

In *Aldinger* the plaintiff was dismissed from her county job and brought suit against Howard and other individual defendants under a federal statute, 42 U.S.C. §1983. She also asserted a state law claim based on the same incident, against Spokane County. The case looked like this:

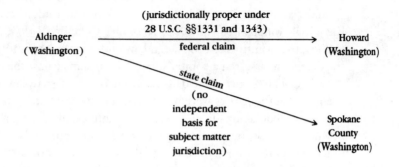

This was an attempt to exercise "pendent party" jurisdiction, that is, to add a jurisdictionally insufficient claim against one defendant to a jurisdictionally proper claim against the other. The claim against Howard was proper, since Aldinger asserted a right to relief under §1983, a federal statute. Jurisdiction was proper under 28 U.S.C. §1331 and under 28 U.S.C. §1343, a separate statute providing for jurisdiction in civil rights cases. However, the claim against the county was based on state law and, thus, not jurisdictionally proper in itself. *Aldinger* at 5. The Court concluded that even though the claim could be viewed as part of a single constitutional case under the first part of *Gibbs,* allowing a state law claim against the county would be inconsistent with the apparent intent of Congress to bar federal civil rights claims under §1983 against counties.[2] Thus, there was no *statutory* grant of jurisdiction over the pendent party claim.

The second case, *Kroger,* involved an interesting twist on the established types of supplemental jurisdiction. In *Kroger,* the plaintiff sued the Okla-

---

2. At the time *Aldinger* was decided, counties were not considered "persons" subject to suit under §1983. *Monroe v. Pape,* 365 U.S.167, 187-191 (1961). After *Aldinger* was decided, however, the Supreme Court overruled this aspect of *Monroe.* See *Monell v. Department of Social Services,* 436 U.S. 658, 690-691 (1978).

homa Public Power District (OPPD), a diverse defendant, which then impleaded Owen, a corporation. Owen, it turned out, was not diverse from either original party. The plaintiff, Kroger, then asserted a direct claim against Owen, as Rule 14(a) allows. The configuration of the parties was as follows:

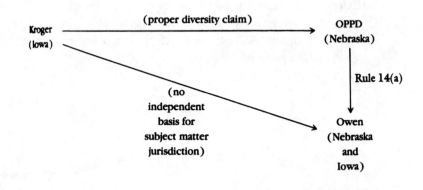

The issue posed was whether the court had jurisdiction over Kroger's claim against Owen.

The *Kroger* Court assumed, under the constitutional analysis in *Gibbs*, that Kroger's claim against Owen was part of the same "constitutional case" as the main claim against OPPD, since it arose out of the same accident. 437 U.S. at 371 n.10. However, the Court went on to consider whether the relevant jurisdictional *statute*, 28 U.S.C. §1332, indicated congressional intent to grant federal courts ancillary jurisdiction over a related claim asserted by the plaintiff against a nondiverse third-party defendant. The Court held that extending ancillary jurisdiction to this claim would be inconsistent with the long-standing interpretation of §1332, requiring complete diversity between the parties. Since Mrs. Kroger could not have sued OPPD and Owen together originally, it would ignore the statutory limits on jurisdiction to allow her to do the same thing indirectly after Owen was brought in as a third-party defendant.

However, the *Kroger* Court's discussion suggested that ancillary jurisdiction could be exercised over compulsory counterclaims, cross-claims, and third-party claims. The opinion implied, for example, that OPPD's claim against Owen would be ancillary, even though it also abridges the complete diversity requirement. The court emphasized the difference between the claim of a defending party, brought in against its will, and a plaintiff, who presumably had the choice to sue all parties jointly in state court. 437 U.S. at 375-377.

The third important background case, *Finley v. United States,* involved pendent party jurisdiction. The plaintiff, Finley, sued the United States under the Federal Tort Claims Act (FTCA). Jurisdiction over this claim was proper under Article III, §2, because the United States was a party. It was also authorized by 28 U.S.C. §1346(b), which gives the federal district courts exclusive jurisdiction[3] over claims against the United States under the FTCA. However, Finley also asserted state law claims against other defendants in the action. There was no diversity between the plaintiff and these defendants; instead she asked the court to take jurisdiction over them on the basis of "pendent party" jurisdiction. The configuration of the parties looked much like that in *Aldinger,* in which the court had previously refused to allow pendent party jurisdiction:

Although the pendent party claims in *Finley* arose from the same nucleus of facts as the jurisdictionally proper claim against the United States, the *Finley* Court reiterated that jurisdiction must be granted not only by Article III, but also by statute. The Court found no indication in §1346(b) that Congress meant to convey jurisdiction over any claims other than those against the United States. Consequently, it held that the district court had no jurisdiction over the pendent party claims. As the Court acknowledged, this meant that Mrs. Finley would have to bring two lawsuits, one in federal court against the United States and a second state court action against the other defendants. But that, the court opined, was not a reason to ignore the statutory limits on the federal court's subject matter jurisdiction. 490 U.S. at 555-556.

After *Finley* it appeared that pendent and ancillary jurisdiction had converged into a single doctrine, which required a three-part analysis.

First, the court had to consider whether there was a constitutional basis for the exercise of jurisdiction over the related but jurisdictionally insufficient claim. This analysis, set forth in the first part of *Gibbs,* turned on whether the plaintiff had asserted a substantial claim within the federal court's jurisdiction and whether the state law claim was part of the same "constitutional case" because it arose from the same "nucleus of operative facts."

---

3. "Exclusive" jurisdiction means that *only* the federal court can hear such claims. Thus, Mrs. Finley had no chance to bring her claim against the United States in state court, which clearly could have heard her state law claims against the other defendants.

Second, if the court could constitutionally assert jurisdiction over the entire case, including the state law claims, it would analyze the congressional intent behind the statute that granted jurisdiction over the proper federal claim. If the statute or its legislative history suggested that Congress had "expressly or by implication negated" (*Aldinger* at 18) jurisdiction over the related, jurisdictionally insufficient claim, it could not hear it. If, on the other hand, there was evidence of congressional intent to confer broad jurisdiction over the entire "case," including the added claims, then the court at least had power to entertain all the claims in the case.

Third, if the added claims passed the first two parts of the test so that the court had jurisdictional power to hear them, the court then decided whether it should exercise that jurisdiction, based on the various discretionary factors discussed in *Gibbs.*

A Stroke of the Pen

All of this case law is now history, albeit very important history. In 1990 Congress enacted 28 U.S.C. §1367, which for the first time provides a statutory basis for "supplemental jurisdiction" in the federal courts. With a stroke of the pen, Congress has substantially clarified the authority of the federal courts to entertain claims that are related to proper federal claims, but are not jurisdictionally proper in themselves.

Let's take §1367 one section at a time. Section 1367(a) provides:

> Except as otherwise provided in subsections (b) and (c) or as expressly provided otherwise by Federal statute, in any civil action of which the district courts have original jurisdiction, the district courts shall have supplemental jurisdiction over all other claims that are so related to claims in the action within such original jurisdiction that they form part of the same case or controversy under Article III of the United States Constitution. Such supplemental jurisdiction shall include claims that involve the joinder or intervention of additional parties.

Under this section, if the plaintiff brings a proper federal claim or diversity claim, so that the federal court has "original jurisdiction," the court may hear all the claims that are part of the same "case or controversy under Article III...." While the section does not explicitly define what claims come within a single case or controversy, this phrase has been held to have the same meaning in §1367 that it was given in *United Mine Workers v. Gibbs. Chicago, v. Int'l College of Surgeons,* 522 U.S. 156, 165-166 (1997). Congress was aware of the widespread use of the *Gibbs* test for a single "constitutional case" in pendent and ancillary jurisdiction cases. Since it chose the same concept in defining the limits of supplemental jurisdiction, the natural inference is that it meant to adopt the same standard. See 13B Wright and Miller §3567.3 [2000 Supp.] (§1367 "ratifies and incorporates" the constitutional analysis in *Gibbs*). Thus, it appears that the section (with certain exceptions discussed below) authorizes the courts to hear all claims that arise out of the same nucleus of operative facts as the proper federal claim. This includes additional claims asserted by the plaintiff, but also those asserted by other parties as well, such as cross-claims and counterclaims.

If *Gibbs* already defined a single constitutional case in those terms, why did Congress pass the statute? Well, in *Aldinger, Kroger,* and *Finley,* the Supreme Court emphasized that it was not enough that the court has constitutional power to hear the related claim. These cases required statutory authority to exercise that jurisdiction as well. This opened up a complex second level of analysis: The court had to look at many different jurisdictional statutes, most of which showed little evidence one way or the other about the intent to allow related state law claims, and divine Congress's intent. Where there was no evidence of intent to allow the related claims, *Finley* strongly suggested that pendent or ancillary jurisdiction could not be exercised, thus severely undermining the efficiency goals of the broad joinder rules.

By enacting §1367, Congress responded to *Finley* (decided the previous year) by *providing the necessary statutory authority to hear the related claims.* The Court in its recent cases had said, "Congress, we can't exercise jurisdiction, even if it would be proper under Article III, unless you give it to us as well." And Congress responded by saying, "Okay, federal courts, you say we have to give you jurisdiction over the related claims, so here it is." The authority Congress gave is very broad indeed, reaching in most situations to the outer bounds of the "constitutional case" before the court. For future cases, the statute, not the "essential history" cases reviewed above, provides the governing law. For example, the exercises of pendent party jurisdiction held improper in *Finley* and *Aldinger* would be upheld under §1367. See 28 U.S.C. §1367(a) (last sentence).

Limits on Supplemental Jurisdiction: Section 1367(b)

While Congress granted supplemental jurisdiction in very broad terms in §1367(a), it hedged a little in §1367(b). That section provides that supplemental jurisdiction shall not extend to certain claims by plaintiffs in diversity cases, specifically

> ...claims by plaintiffs against persons made parties under Rule 14, 19, 20, or 24 of the Federal Rules of Civil Procedure, or over claims by persons proposed to be joined as plaintiffs under Rule 19 of such rules, or seeking to intervene as plaintiffs under Rule 24 of such rules, when exercising supplemental jurisdiction over such claims would be inconsistent with the jurisdictional requirements of section 1332.

This provision must also be read in light of the "essential history" reviewed above. Section 1367(b) obviously responds to *Kroger,* in which the Supreme Court rejected jurisdiction over Mrs. Kroger's claim because it contradicted the complete diversity requirements of §1332. In §1367(b), the drafters tried to catalogue various joinder possibilities under the Rules that would allow the plaintiff to circumvent the limits of the *Strawbridge* rule, and specified that supplemental jurisdiction would not extend to joinder in those circumstances if it allowed an end run around those limits.[4] The scholars have suggested that the drafters—some other scholars—did a clumsy job here,[5] but their basic idea in drafting §1367(b) was to preserve the limits on ancillary jurisdiction suggested in *Kroger.*

Finally, in §1367(c), Congress codified the second holding in *Gibbs,* which gave the trial court discretion to decline to exercise pendent jurisdiction. Section 1367(c) authorizes the court to decline jurisdiction over supplemental claims for any of four reasons, similar to but not quite the same as those discussed in the second half of the *Gibbs* opinion.

An Attempted Synthesis

The *Aldinger/Kroger/Finley* trilogy suggested that pendent and ancillary jurisdiction were coalescing into a single doctrine. Congress has confirmed this by adopting a single term, "supplemental jurisdiction," to describe claims that would previously have been classified as either pendent or ancillary. Such supplemental jurisdiction under §1367 still requires a three-part analysis:

First, the court must determine whether there is *constitutional power* under Article III, §2, to hear the supplemental claim. This analysis has nothing to do with §1367: Congress cannot determine by statute what claims the Constitution authorizes a court to hear. The analysis must still stem from *Gibbs,* which held that the constitutional power to hear the related claim exists if there is a proper claim within the jurisdiction of the federal court and the related claim arises from the same nucleus of operative facts. This level of the analysis is no different now than it was before §1367 was enacted.

Second, the court must determine whether there is a *statutory grant* of jurisdiction over the related claim. Now, such a grant is provided in most cases by §1367 itself. Because §1367(a) grants jurisdiction over all related claims that are part of the same "case," the answer to the statutory question will be much simpler than it was under *Kroger* and *Finley.* The court need not analyze a variety of jurisdictional statutes (like §§1343 and 1346(b)), which contain little evidence of an intent one way or the other concerning related claims. Statutory authority is broadly granted for all types of cases un-

---

4. In several respects, §1367(b) restricts jurisdiction previously available under case law. For example, prior to the new statute, claims by intervenors as of right under Fed. R. Civ. P. 24(a) were considered ancillary, even if the intervenor destroyed complete diversity. This anomaly has been eliminated by §1367(b), which bars claims by plaintiff intervenors in diversity cases.

5. See, e.g., R. Freer, Compounding Confusion and Hampering Diversity: Life after *Finley* and the Supplemental Jurisdiction Statute, 40 Emory L.J. 445 (1991).

der §1367(a) if the *Gibbs* constitutional test is met. However, under §1367(b), certain claims in diversity cases, which would contradict the limits on jurisdiction in §1332, are excepted.

Third, Congress has codified the second half of the *Gibbs* analysis in §1367(c). Once the court determines that it has constitutional and statutory authority to hear the related claims, it must decide, based on the various discretionary factors in that section, whether to do so.

To properly analyze the following examples, it would help to read *Gibbs, Kroger,* and *Finley,* as well as §1367 and this Introduction. It will also help to draw quick diagrams of the configuration of the parties and claims in the examples. Then consider whether the constitutional test of *Gibbs* and the statutory requirements in §1367 are met. (Disregard for the moment the third, discretionary prong of the analysis.) Assume that all cases are brought in federal court.

EXAMPLES

Simple Addition

1.   Keats, from Minnesota, is arrested by Shelley, a Minnesota police officer, for disturbing the peace. During the arrest, Shelley forcibly restrains Keats, and Keats resists. Keats claims that Shelley used excessive force in making the arrest and sues Shelley under the federal civil rights statute, 42 U.S.C. §1983. Keats also seeks to recover from Shelley on a state law claim for battery based on the scuffle that took place during the arrest.

    a. Does the court have constitutional power to hear the battery claim?

    b. Does the court have statutory authority to hear the battery claim?

    c. Assume that the court concluded that it lacked power to hear the battery claim. What should it do with the §1983 claim?

    d. Assume that the court declined in its discretion to hear Keats's battery claim. What would happen to the §1983 claim?

    e. Assume for this example only that there were no statutory authority to exercise supplemental jurisdiction. What would Keats have to do in order to recover on both of his claims?

2.   Apparently there was some prior history to the Keats/Shelley altercation. Shelley owed Keats $500 at the time of arrest as payment for work that Keats had done on his house. Keats was upset because he had not been paid and tempers flared, leading to the arrest. Keats therefore asserts a third claim for the debt in his action against Shelley. Does the court have the power to hear it?

3.   Browning, Blake, and Wordsworth are involved in a three-car collision on Route 192, near Dayton, Ohio. Browning, a New Yorker, sues Blake and Wordsworth, both from Ohio, for $80,000 for her personal injuries. Blake asserts a cross-claim against Wordsworth for his own injuries

arising from the same collision. Does the court have jurisdiction over the cross-claim?

4. Suppose, on the facts of example 3, that Blake (Ohio) asserts a counterclaim against Browning (New York) for $35,000 for his injuries. Does the court have jurisdiction to hear the counterclaim?

5. May Blake assert a $25,000 counterclaim in the accident case against Browning for Browning's trespass on Blake's property four months prior to the accident?

Important Example, Requiring Thought

6. Please reconsider example 3, in which Browning sued Blake and Wordsworth for her injuries in an auto accident. In that case could Blake (Ohio) assert a counterclaim against Browning (New York) for an unrelated infringement of a patent Blake holds? Assume that the counterclaim is for $30,000 in damages.

7. Suppose that Browning (New York) sues Blake (Ohio) for her injuries from the collision, and Blake impleads Wordsworth (Ohio) for contribution if he is found liable to Browning
   a. Is there independent subject matter jurisdiction over the impleader claim?
   b. Is there supplemental jurisdiction over it?

Complex Equations

8. If Blake (Ohio) impleads Wordsworth (Ohio), and Browning, the New York plaintiff, then asserts a claim directly against Wordsworth, will the court have the power to hear it?

9. Blake (Ohio) impleads Wordsworth (Ohio) as a third-party defendant, and Wordsworth asserts a claim against Browning, the New York plaintiff, for $25,000 for his own injuries in the accident.
   a. Will the court have supplemental jurisdiction over the claim?
   b. Assume that, after Wordsworth asserts his claim against Browning, Browning then asserts a claim against Wordsworth for $15,000 for property damage to her car in the same accident. Will the court have supplemental jurisdiction over the claim?

10. Browning, from New York, sues Blake, from Ohio, for $100,000 as a result of her injuries in the auto accident. Coleridge, a New York passenger in Browning's car, joins as a plaintiff, seeking $25,000 for his injuries.
   a. Does the court have the constitutional power to hear Coleridge's claim?
   b. Is there supplemental jurisdiction over it under §1367?

11. Assume that Browning sues Blake for $60,000, and Coleridge joins with him to assert a claim for $40,000. Does the court have jurisdiction over the case?

12. Byron (Wisconsin) sues Rossetti (Wisconsin) for patent infringement, arising out of Rossetti's manufacture of inverse roto-turnbuckles on which Byron claims he holds a patent. Byron also asserts a claim against Hunt, a former employee and Wisconsin citizen, for breach of contract, for assisting Rossetti in making the devices.

    a. Is there supplemental jurisdiction over Byron's claim against Hunt under §1367?

    b. Does the court have the constitutional power to hear Byron's claim against Hunt?

EXPLANATIONS
Simple Addition

1a. This is a straightforward example in which the plaintiff asserts a federal question claim and a related state law claim against the same defendant. It is exactly analogous to *Gibbs,* and clearly satisfies *Gibbs's* criteria for a single constitutional case: The plaintiff has asserted a proper claim under federal law (the §1983 claim), and the state law battery claim arises out of the same "nucleus of operative facts," the scuffle during the arrest. Thus, there is constitutional power to hear the battery claim.

    b. Before Congress enacted §1367, the court would have had to analyze the statute granting jurisdiction over §1983 claims to determine whether Congress intended to allow pendent claims in §1983 cases. Now, however, Congress has answered that question in §1367: If the federal claim and the related claim are part of the "same case or controversy under Article III," the court has supplemental jurisdiction to hear the related claim. Because the "same case or controversy" requirement in §1367(a) means essentially the same thing as a single "constitutional case" under *Gibbs,* the court has supplemental jurisdiction, since the battery claim arises from the same nucleus of operative facts as the §1983 claim. Nor does §1367(b) bar this claim; that subsection only applies to cases based solely on diversity.

    c. If the court lacked jurisdiction over the related state law claim, it would have to dismiss it. But it could not dismiss the federal claim: The court has jurisdiction over that claim, and (absent some extraordinary situations not discussed here, such as federal abstention) it has a duty to exercise that jurisdiction by hearing and deciding the §1983 claim.

    d. The same result follows if the court concludes that it has jurisdiction over the battery claim but declines to hear the claim as a matter of discretion under §1367(c). Keats is still entitled to a federal forum on his federal claim even though the related state claim will be heard in state court. If the court dismisses the state law claim, Keats may end up litigating the same facts in state and federal court at the same time.

   e. If there were no statutory authority to hear related state claims, Keats
would not be able to join his battery claim in the federal suit. He would then
have two choices. He could bring two lawsuits, one in federal court on the
§1983 claim and the other in state court on the battery claim. Alternatively,
he could bring a single action in state court seeking relief on both claims,
since state courts have concurrent jurisdiction over federal claims unless
Congress makes federal jurisdiction exclusive. If he chose the latter course,
the state court would decide Keats's §1983 claim, and, of course, it would
decide his state law claim as well.

   These alternatives for Keats illustrate the importance of supplemental
jurisdiction. Without it, a plaintiff like Keats would have a strong incentive to sue in state court in order to have his entire case resolved in one
proceeding. Many federal law cases would be heard in state rather than
federal courts, even though a primary purpose of federal courts is to ex-
pound and develop federal law. Thus, supplemental jurisdiction assures
that plaintiffs in Keats's position who prefer the federal forum will have full
access to it.

2.   This example fails at the first level of the analysis, the same-constitutional-
case requirement established in *Gibbs*. Under *Gibbs*, jurisdictionally insufficient claims are part of the same case (and therefore within the Article III
grant of federal jurisdiction) if they arise out of the same nucleus of operative facts as the federal claim. Here, the assault claim does arise out of the
same set of facts, but the debt claim does not. Although there may be a
causal relationship between the debt and the eventual arrest and assault, it is
probably too attenuated to make them part of the same nucleus of facts.

3.   This case, illustrated below, involves a cross-claim by a defending party
against another defendant arising out of the events that gave rise to the original claim. There is no independent basis of federal jurisdiction, since both
parties to the cross-claim are from Ohio.

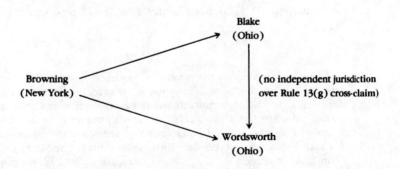

Prior to §1367 the courts routinely took "ancillary" jurisdiction over cross-
claims. Because a cross-claim must arise out of the same transaction or occurrence as the main claim (see Rule 13(g)), it was considered part of the

same constitutional case.[6] And, because cross-claims are asserted by a defendant, "hauled into court against his will," *Kroger* suggested that they would not be barred even if they abridged the complete diversity requirement of §1332. 437 U.S. at 376.

Now, a statutory basis for supplemental jurisdiction over Blake's cross-claim is provided by §1367(a), which authorizes the court to hear all related claims that arise from the same set of facts. Since Blake's claim arises from the same accident as the proper diversity claim, this requirement is met.

Although §1367(b) limits the broad reach of supplemental jurisdiction in diversity cases, that subsection only bars certain claims by plaintiffs in diversity cases. Here a defendant asserts the related claim, so §1367(b) does not apply.

4.   This is the classic ancillary jurisdiction situation addressed in *Moore v. New York Cotton Exchange*, 270 U.S. 593 (1926). Blake's counterclaim is compulsory because it arises from the same accident as the main claim. Yet the court lacks independent jurisdiction over it because it is based on state law and does not satisfy the amount-in-controversy requirement.

Under the *Gibbs* analysis, the court has constitutional power to hear the added claim since it arises out of the same incident as the main claim. Further, the court has statutory authority to hear the claim because §1367(a) authorizes supplemental jurisdiction over all claims that meet the *Gibbs* standard. The exceptions in §1367(b) do not apply, since the claim is not asserted by the plaintiff.

5.   There is no independent basis for subject matter jurisdiction over the counterclaim in this case, since it does not meet the amount-in-controversy requirement of 28 U.S.C. §1332(a). Further, because this permissive counterclaim does not arise out of the same events as the main claim, there is no basis for supplemental jurisdiction over it. It founders on the *Gibbs* constitutional analysis, which only allows the court to hear related claims that arise from the same nucleus of operative facts as the main claim. Consequently, there is no basis under Article III to append it to the other claim.

---

6. It is not clear whether the reach of a "common nucleus of operative facts" is exactly the same as the "same transaction or occurrence test" used in the federal joinder rules. One scholar suggests that since the transaction or occurrence test was well established when *Gibbs* was decided, the court must have meant something different — and probably broader — when it formulated the common nucleus test in *Gibbs*. See Matasar, A Pendent and Ancillary Jurisdiction Primer: The Scope and Limits of Supplemental Jurisdiction, 17 U.C. Davis L. Rev. 103, 130 (1983). It is probably safe to assume that the *Gibbs* test is satisfied if the related state claim arises out of the same transaction or occurrence as the federal claim but that it might also be satisfied in some more loosely related situations. See generally 16 Moores Federal Practice §106.25. Compare the formulation used in the earlier ancillary jurisdiction cases, which required only a "logical relationship" between the two claims.

Since this claim fails at the constitutional level of analysis, there is no need to consider whether §1367 provides a statutory basis for jurisdiction over the claim. However, it clearly does not: Section 1367 defines the statutory reach of supplemental jurisdiction by the same test as the outer reach of constitutional authority under *Gibbs*. Because the constitutional test is not met, the statutory test isn't either.

Important Example, Requiring Thought

6. This example isn't that hard, but is is very important. This case is like example 5, except for one crucial difference. In this case there *is* an independent ground for jurisdiction over the counterclaim. While the court could not take supplemental jurisdiction over the claim under §1367 (because it is not part of the same case or controversy as the main claim) it has *original* jurisdiction over the patent claim since it arises under the federal patent laws. 28 U.S.C. §1338. Blake could have sued Browning separately on this claim in federal court, and the court would have had jurisdiction. Thus, there is no need to invoke supplemental jurisdiction here based on a relationship to Blake's diversity claim.

7a. The point here is fundamental, but by no means obvious. The impleaded third party, Wordsworth, is diverse from the plaintiff but not from the defendant who impleaded him. Whom do you count in measuring diversity over the third-party claim?

The third-party action by Blake against Wordsworth must be viewed separately for purposes of determining subject mater jurisdiction over it. If the court would not have jurisdiction over this claim as a separate suit, it lacks independent jurisdiction when it is brought as a third-party claim as well. Since Blake and Wordsworth are from the same state, there is no independent ground for jurisdiction over the impleader claim. The fact that Wordsworth is diverse from Browning avails him not. Conversely, if Wordsworth were from New York there would be independent subject matter jurisdiction over the impleader claim even though he was *not* diverse from the plaintiff.

b. This claim is analogous to the Power District's third-party claim against Owen in *Kroger*, in which the Power District impleaded Owen as a third-party defendant for contribution. Impleader claims must arise from the same set of facts as the main claim to satisfy the requirements of Fed. R. Civ. P. 14. Thus, they will meet the common nucleus test of *Gibbs* and the statutory test of §1367(a) for supplemental jurisdiction.

Section 1367(b) does not prevent the court from exercising supplemental jurisdiction here. That section bars some "claims against persons made parties under Rule 14(a)," but only such claims *brought by plaintiffs*. This claim is not asserted by the plaintiff, so the general supplemental jurisdiction authority under §1367(a) applies.

Complex Equations

8.   If you diagrammed this case, you will have noticed that it is the same configuration as *Kroger*, with the plaintiff asserting a claim against the third-party defendant. Although it arises from the same set of facts (and therefore satisfies the *Gibbs* constitutional test), *Kroger* clearly held that there was no ancillary jurisdiction over such a claim in a diversity case. And Congress took the same position in §1367(b), which bars supplemental jurisdiction over claims brought by plaintiffs against parties brought in under Rule 14.

However, in this case there may be *independent* subject matter jurisdiction over the claim. The plaintiff and the third-party defendant here are diverse; if Browning's claim is for more than $75,000 the court will have jurisdiction over it without regard to supplemental jurisdiction.

9a.   This configuration, the reverse of *Kroger*, is a claim by the third-party defendant against the plaintiff. There is no independent jurisdiction over the claim because the amount-in-controversy requirement is not satisfied. But it is part of the same "constitutional case," since the claim arises from the same accident as the main diversity claim. Consequently, the court has both constitutional power to hear the claim under *Gibbs* and supplemental jurisdiction over it under §1367(a), unless it is excepted by §1367(b). Since Wordsworth is a defendant, §1367(b) does not apply. Ironically, supplemental jurisdiction is proper here, even though it was not in example 8 when the plaintiff asserted the claim.

b.   Of course this had to be the next example. Here, the third party has claimed against the plaintiff, and that makes the plaintiff a defending party who must assert any counterclaim he has arising out of the same incident. Fed. R. Civ. P. 13(a). The case looks like this:

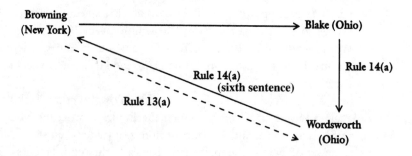

Since Browning's claim arises from the original accident, it is a compulsory counterclaim, and also satisfies the single "constitutional case" test of *Gibbs* and the basic §1367(a) test for supplemental jurisdiction. Thus, the court has jurisdiction unless it is barred by the exception in §1367(b).

This is an interesting one: Section 1367(b) bars "claims by plaintiffs against persons made parties under Rule 14." Browning's claim is against

Wordsworth, who was made a party under Rule 14 when Blake impleaded him. So the claim appears to fall within the §1367(b) exception. This makes little sense: Rule 13(a) requires Browning to assert the claim, and much efficiency will be gained by hearing it in the federal action. Yet the plain language of §1367(b) precludes the court from hearing it. Perhaps the courts will blink at the language to achieve a more sensible result.

However, at least one court has refused to do so in analogous circumstances, while clearly expressing the wish that it could. See *Guaranteed Systems, Inc. v. American National Can Co.*, 842 F. Supp. 855 (M.D.N.C. 1994) (where plaintiff sued on counterclaim, no supplemental jurisdiction over its impleader claim against a third party under §1367(b)). The court in *Guaranteed Systems* stated that, if it could, it would construe §1367(b) to allow jurisdiction, but that "such a construction would reach beyond the limits of Section 1367(b)." Id. at 857.

10a. In this case, there is complete diversity, but Coleridge's claim does not meet the amount-in-controversy requirement. That of course is irrelevant to satisfying the constitutional requirements for diversity jurisdiction: There is no amount-in-controversy requirement in Article III, §2. Since both plaintiffs are diverse from the defendants, there is proper diversity jurisdiction under Article III.

b. This example illustrates a situation in which the traditional rules regarding aggregation of damages in diversity cases may be changed by the supplemental jurisdiction statute. Under the traditional aggregation rules, each plaintiff has to meet the amount-in-controversy requirement independently in order to sue in federal court. See Chapter 5, pp. 90-91. A plaintiff in Coleridge's position could not add his $25,000 claim to Browning's $100,000 claim to meet the amount requirement in 28 U.S.C. s. 1332(a).

However, the supplemental jurisdiction statute arguably supports jurisdiction over Coleridge's claim. Certainly, it is part of the same "constitutional case" as Browning's, since it arises from the same accident. And the second sentence of s. 1367(a) expressly allows claims which involve additional parties. So the broad grant of supplemental jurisdiction applies.

The question, then, is whether s. 1367(b) withholds jurisdiction in this scenario. Section 1367(b) bars supplemental jurisdiction over "claims by plaintiffs against persons made parties under...Rule 20,"—that is, cases involving multiple defendants. But it doesn't bar jurisdiction in situations—such as this one—where multiple plaintiffs join under Rule 20 to sue a single defendant. Thus, while it appears that the drafters did not intend to change the traditional aggregation rules in diversity cases, they may have done so inadvertently, due to the lack of a specific exception for cases like this. Some cases under §1367 have held that, where one plaintiff satisfies the amount-in-controversy requirement, others who don't may now join as co-plaintiffs. See, e.g., *Patterson Enterprises, Inc. v. Bridgestone/Firestone, Inc.*, 812 F. Supp. 1152, 1153-1154 (D. Kan. 1993). Others, however, relying on the legislative history of §1367, have held that §1367 has not changed the traditional aggregation rules. See, e.g., *Meritcare, Inc. v. St. Paul Mercury Ins. Co.*, 166 F.3d 214 (3rd Cir. 1999).[7]

11. Section 1367(a) requires that the court have "original jurisdiction" over *some claim* in the case before supplemental jurisdiction can be invoked to add other claims. Here, neither Browning nor Coleridge has a claim sufficient to confer diversity jurisdiction on the court. Since there is no claim that is properly before the court on its own, there is nothing to add other claims *to* under §1367. Thus, even if the statute is held to change the aggregation rules in cases like the last example, there will be no jurisdiction over either claim in cases like this, where neither plaintiff meets the amount-in-controversy requirement.

12a. This "pendent party" case is closely analogous to *Finley*. The plaintiff asserts a proper federal claim against Rossetti. (In fact, Byron must take this claim to federal court since federal courts have exclusive jurisdiction over patent claims. 28 U.S.C. §1338(a).) Byron then seeks to add a state law claim against Hunt, a nondiverse party. There is no independent jurisdictional basis for this claim.

However, it appears clear that Congress intended to authorize supplemental jurisdiction over this type of claim. "Such supplemental jurisdiction shall include claims that involve the joinder or intervention of additional parties." 28 U.S.C. §1367(a). This language suggests that, if the court has jurisdiction based on a proper federal claim, the court's supplemental jurisdiction extends to claims by or against other parties, *even if the plaintiff has not asserted any jurisdictionally sufficient claim against the added party.* For example, this language seems to authorize jurisdiction on the facts of *Finley*.

This result does not "overrule" *Finley*. On the contrary, it responds to *Finley's* pronouncement that Congress must provide statutory authority for courts to exert jurisdiction to the reach of their constitutional power. Nor does the exception in §1367(b) apply, since §1367(b) does not apply to cases in which the jurisdictionally proper claim is a federal question claim.

The same result would apparently follow if Arnold, another plaintiff, joined with Byron to assert a state law claim for damages for the same acts. Even if there were no independent basis for federal jurisdiction, the quoted language would allow the added party to sue with Byron. Once again, §1367(b) would not apply since it is not a diversity case.

---

7. Indeed, wouldn't s. 1367(a), strictly interpreted, authorize jurisdiction over Coleridge's claim even if he were not diverse from Blake? The argument goes thus: Browning has a proper diversity claim against Blake; Coleridge's claim arises out of the same events, so jurisdiction is granted by the last sentence of s. 1367(a); s. 1367(b) does not apply, because Coleridge's claim is not one of the prohibited types of claims listed in that section. This interpretation, of course, would go the whole route and overrule *Strawbridge v. Curtiss*. See Moores, §106.45[2].

b. There is at least some question as to whether this expanded authority to hear related claims by different parties comes within the constitutional grant in Article III. *Gibbs* held that a related claim *by the same party* was part of the same constitutional case, but §1367 goes a step further by allowing a new party to be added to the claim because the plaintiff has asserted a jurisdictionally sufficient claim against someone else. In *Finley*, the Court "assumed without deciding that the constitutional criterion for pendent-party jurisdiction is analogous to the constitutional criterion for pendent claim jurisdiction." 490 U.S. at 549. But it clearly is more attenuated to conclude that a "constitutional case" includes jurisdictionally insufficient claims against a different party, against whom Byron has no jurisdictionally proper claim at all.

Certainly, the fact that Congress has purported to grant supplemental jurisdiction over added claims by different parties does not make it constitutional for the court to exercise that jurisdiction. On the other hand, numerous cases prior to the enactment of §1367 exercised "pendent party" jurisdiction (see 13B Wright and Miller §3567.2), and the Supreme Court, though it had opportunities to do so, never held it unconstitutional. So it is entirely possible that the Court will find pendent parties within the limits of a "constitutional case." But see *Elsaas v. County of Placer*, 35 F. Supp. 2d 757 (1999) (concluding, with reluctance, that pendent party jurisdiction is unconstitutional under Ninth Circuit precedents).

16

Jurisdiction vs. Joinder: The Difference between Power and Permission

Introduction

Concepts such as supplemental jurisdiction and joinder of parties are difficult enough to grapple with individually. Yet these doctrines do not exist in isolation; they interact to create a system[1] that lawyers must understand as a whole in order to litigate effectively. The real challenge (and fascination) of civil procedure is to try to see how the various pieces of the puzzle fit together into an interrelated, consistent framework for adjudication.

The preceding three chapters have separately analyzed the rules governing joinder of claims and parties, on the one hand, and the doctrine of supplemental jurisdiction on the other. However, a particular suit is proper only if both the joinder rules and the jurisdictional requirements are met. This chapter will explore the interrelations of these affiliated doctrines.

---

1. Some lawyers, those unfortunates who have never been captivated by the symmetry and logic of it, might call it a maze, a net, or a trap.

As the earlier chapters on joinder demonstrate, no party may assert a claim against another party in the federal courts unless one of the joinder rules—Rules 13, 14, 18, 20, or 24—authorizes assertion of that claim. However, the fact that the Rules authorize joinder of a particular claim is not sufficient to assure that the federal court may hear it. The court must also have a basis for exercising subject matter jurisdiction over the claim. The federal courts have only limited jurisdictional power; if there is no basis in Article III, §2, to hear a claim, "permission" to join a claim under the Rules cannot substitute for it.

An example may help. If Nimitz is injured in an auto accident involving two other drivers, Spruance and Halsey, Rule 20(a) allows him to sue them both in a single suit. Nimitz's claims against both arise out of a single occurrence and will both involve the common factual issue of whose negligence caused the accident. However, if Halsey and Nimitz are both from Texas, the suit will be dismissed for lack of subject matter jurisdiction since there is no complete diversity and the suit (a basic tort claim) does not arise under federal law.

This need for both power and permission follows from basic constitutional doctrine. All federal jurisdiction must be found in the "Article III store-house," and it is up to Congress to confer all or part of that jurisdiction on the lower federal courts. See Judge Sirica's comments, p. 60. The Federal Rules, on the other hand, are promulgated by the Supreme Court. While the Court has the power to make rules to assure the orderly conduct of business in the federal courts (see 28 U.S.C. §2072), it may not use its rule-making power to expand their jurisdiction. Thus, though the Court has broadly authorized joinder of claims and parties under the Federal Rules, the need for subject matter jurisdiction provides an implicit limitation on joinder in every case. The Court itself reaffirmed this limitation in Fed. R. Civ. P. 82, which provides in part that "[t]hese rules shall not be construed to extend or limit the jurisdiction of the United States district courts."

Although joinder cannot substitute for jurisdiction, it would often make life easier if it could. As we saw in the last chapter, there is a tension between the Rules, which encourage broad joinder of related claims to promote efficiency, and the strict Article III limits on federal court jurisdiction. In cases such as the Halsey example, it would make eminent good sense to hear the related claims together, since the witnesses and much of the evidence will be the same, the legal issues will overlap, and the plaintiff is the same in both claims. The joinder rules encourage and sometimes even require such sensible litigation practice, but good sense may be thwarted at times by the limitations on federal subject matter jurisdiction.

Similarly, in *Owen Equipment & Erection Co. v. Kroger,* 437 U.S. 365 (1978), joinder of Kroger's claim against Owen, the third-party defendant, was permissible under Rule 14. It certainly would have made sense to hear that claim in the same action with the main claim and the third-party claim:

The parties were all before the court already, much of the evidence would have been the same, and the judge was already familiar with the case. But the Court balked at extending ancillary jurisdiction to provide a basis for subject matter jurisdiction over the claim. Absolutes are absolutes, and subject matter jurisdiction is as absolute as you get in the civil procedure business.

In many cases supplemental jurisdiction under 28 U.S.C. §1367 *will* provide a jurisdictional base for additional claims. By granting broad authority to hear related claims, Congress acknowledged the good sense of allowing those related claims to be settled in a single action. In other cases, where supplemental jurisdiction does not authorize the additional claims, there may be an independent basis for subject matter jurisdiction. For example, in the *Kroger* case, if Kroger had been from Colorado, there would have been independent diversity jurisdiction over her claim against Owen. Since joinder was proper under Fed. R. Civ. P. 14(a), both power and permission would have been proper. Yet other cases may fall between the cracks, either for lack of jurisdiction or, conversely, because the joinder rules do not authorize assertion of the claim.

The examples below will help you grasp the distinction and the interrelations between these two problems. In analyzing these cases, assume that all are brought in federal court and that personal jurisdiction is proper.

EXAMPLES

Some Basics

1.   Nimitz, a citizen of Texas, sues Bradley, from Missouri, and Patton, from California. Nimitz claims that each defendant libeled him, though on different occasions. He claims $100,000 in damages from each. Is the case properly before the court?

2.   Nimitz (Texas) sues Bradley (Missouri) for the libel claim and an unrelated breach of contract. He seeks $55,000 in damages on the contract claim and $40,000 on the libel claim. Can the court entertain the claims?

3.   Nimitz (Texas) brings suit against Bradley (Missouri) and Clark, a Texas citizen. Nimitz asserts that the two defendants violated his federal civil rights by arresting him under an invalid warrant. Does the federal court have power and permission to hear the claims?

4.   Suppose that Nimitz (Texas) sued Clark (Texas) only on the federal civil rights claim and on a state law battery claim arising from the same arrest. Are power and permission both present?

Mixing Apples and Oranges

5.   Assume that Nimitz (Texas) sues Clark (Texas) and Bradley (Missouri). He asserts a federal civil rights claim against Clark for using excessive force

in the course of arresting him and a state law battery claim against Bradley, arising from the same arrest. Is the case properly before the court?

6. Suppose, on the facts of the last example, that Clark counterclaims against Nimitz for $90,000 due on a loan he made to Nimitz six months prior to the arrest. Does the court have both power and permission to hear the claim?

7. Instead of counterclaiming against Nimitz, Clark (Texas) cross-claims against Bradley (Missouri) to recover on a $90,000 loan to him. Is the claim properly before the court?

8. Nimitz (Texas) sues both Bradley (Missouri) and Gavin, also from Missouri, for violation of his federal civil rights. Could the federal court entertain a cross-claim by Bradley against Gavin, alleging that Gavin assaulted him (Bradley) in the course of the arrest?

A Few Mazes, Nets, or Traps

9. Halsey, a New Jersey citizen, brings a negligence action against MacArthur, from Arkansas, seeking $95,000 for injuries arising out of a boating accident. MacArthur impleads Spruance, from Arkansas, who was piloting a third boat involved in the collision. In his impleader complaint, MacArthur seeks contribution from Spruance on any damages he must pay Halsey for the boating injuries, as well as recovery for libel arising out of a newspaper article in which Spruance deprecated his leadership skills. Can a federal district court in Arkansas entertain the entire suit?

10. Suppose on the facts of example 9, that MacArthur (Arkansas) impleaded Spruance (Arkansas) for contribution, and Halsey, the New Jersey plaintiff, then asserted a $90,000 libel claim against Spruance. Is Halsey's claim against Spruance properly before the court?

11. Assume that Halsey (New Jersey) sues MacArthur (Arkansas) alone on his claim arising out of the boating accident, and MacArthur counterclaims against Halsey and Spruance (Arkansas) for his own injuries in the collision. Can the federal court hear the counterclaims?

12. Halsey (New Jersey) sues MacArthur (Arkansas) for his injuries in the accident, and Spruance (Arkansas) intervenes in the suit to assert a claim against MacArthur for his injuries. May the court hear Spruance's claim?

EXPLANATIONS

Some Basics

1. Power: Yes   Permission: No

This case in its present form would have to be dismissed. Jurisdiction is proper in the action since there is complete diversity and the amount in controversy exceeds $75,000 against each defendant. However, Nimitz's joinder of Patton and Bradley is improper under the joinder provisions of the Federal Rules. Rule 20(a), which governs joinder of multiple defendants, only authorizes joinder if the plaintiff's claims against both defendants arise out of the same transaction or occurrence. Nimitz alleges libel stemming from two separate incidents; although his theory of liability is the same against each, his claims are based on separate historical occurrences. Thus, joinder under the Rules is not satisfied, though jurisdiction is proper.

Although Nimitz's case can't be heard in its present form, it need not be dismissed in its entirety either. Under Fed. R. Civ. P. 21, the court may drop either Patton or Bradley from the action, eliminating the joinder problem. Nimitz will presumably then file a separate suit against the dropped defendant, perhaps in the same court, which will proceed independent of the original case.

2. Power: Yes   Permission: Yes

The court in this case has an adequate basis for joinder and jurisdiction. Rule 18(a) authorizes a single plaintiff to join any claims she has against an opposing party, regardless of whether they arise from a single transaction or occurrence. Rule 18(a) is the ultimate in permissiveness: Whatever claims you have, based on the same or separate historical events, may be joined, so long as the various claims are asserted against a single defendant.

Jurisdiction is also satisfied here because the parties are diverse, and the amount-in-controversy requirement is satisfied by aggregation of Nimitz's two claims against Bradley. A single plaintiff like Nimitz may aggregate claims—including totally unrelated claims—against a single defendant to meet the amount requirement, but not against multiple defendants. See Chapter 5, pp. 90-91.

3. Power: Yes   Permission: Yes

This case may properly be brought in federal court. Joinder is proper here, unlike in example 1, because the same transaction or occurrence requirement of Rule 20(a) is met; Nimitz seeks damages against both defendants based on the same underlying real-world event. The second requirement of Rule 20(a), that Nimitz's claims against the two defendants share a common question of law or fact, is also met since Nimitz must presumably prove many of the same facts (for example, the invalidity of the warrant) to prevail on both claims.

Jurisdiction is also satisfied in this suit since Nimitz asserts a federal claim against each defendant. 28 U.S.C. §1331. The lack of complete diversity is therefore irrelevant.

4. Power: Yes   Permission: Yes

This is an easy case. Rule 18(a) authorizes joinder of the two claims, even though they are based on different sources of law. It would similarly authorize joinder of any other claims that Nimitz's creative genius (tempered, of course, by the ethical constraints of Rule 11) might come up with, regardless of whether they arose from the arrest or any other incident.

Jurisdiction over the federal civil rights claim is proper under 28 U.S.C. §1331. Jurisdiction over the state law claim is also proper. This is a classic "pendent claim," a jurisdictionally insufficient claim that arises from the same nucleus of operative facts as the proper federal claim. Prior to the enactment of the supplemental jurisdiction statute it would have been proper (though discretionary) under *United Mine Workers v. Gibbs*. See Chapter 15, pp. 261-263. It is now authorized by §1367(a), since that statute authorizes the court to hear claims that are part of the same case or controversy as the jurisdictionally sufficient claim. See Chapter 15, example 1.

Mixing Apples and Oranges

5. Power: Yes   Permission: Yes

The problem here is clearly not on the joinder issue; Rule 20(a) authorizes joinder of these claims since they both arise out of the same arrest and will likely involve common questions of fact, such as which injuries were caused by Clark and which by Bradley.

Jurisdiction is more difficult. Jurisdiction is proper over Nimitz's claim against Clark because it arises under federal law. However, his claim against Bradley is based on state law; it must have a separate basis for federal jurisdiction. Nimitz and Bradley are diverse...but Nimitz and Clark are not. However, since there is a separate basis for jurisdiction over Clark, his citizenship need not be considered in measuring diversity, even though he is a party to the action. See Chapter 5, example 4. Consequently, Clark does not destroy diversity. If Nimitz seeks more than $75,000 from Bradley the suit is proper.

Even if there were no diversity between Nimitz and Bradley, the supplemental jurisdiction statute would provide a basis for jurisdiction over Nimitz's claim against Bradley. Section 1367(a) authorizes jurisdiction over claims that are part of the same case or controversy as the main claim, including such claims against additional parties. This provision would presumably apply here, authorizing supplemental jurisdiction over Nimitz's claim against Bradley, since it is part of the same "case" as his claim against Clark, which is properly before the federal court as a claim arising under federal law.[2] Prior to the enactment of §1367, this would have been referred to as "pendent party" jurisdiction and would have required a

---

2. The limit on such supplemental claims in §1367(b) does not apply, since the case is not "founded solely on §1332," the diversity statute.

complex analysis. See the discussion of "essential history" in Chapter 15, pp. 263-266.

6.   Power: No   Permission: Yes

Here, the federal court lacks power to hear the counterclaim, although the Rules grant permission to join it. Clark's counterclaim is permissive because it arises from a transaction unrelated to the main claim. Rule 13(b) authorizes (but does not require) Clark to assert it in this action.

However, there is no independent basis of subject matter jurisdiction over this claim because it is a state law claim between nondiverse parties. Clark would have to rely on supplemental jurisdiction to support this claim. As discussed in Chapter 15, however, the courts will apply the "common nucleus of operative fact" test in determining whether the added, state law claims are part of the same case or controversy as the jurisdictionally sufficient claim. Since the loan counterclaim does not arise out of the same nucleus of operative facts as the arrest claim, it is not part of the same case, so it fails both the *Gibbs* test and the similar "case or controversy" test for supplemental jurisdiction under §1367(a). Presumably, this will always be true of Rule 13(b) permissive counterclaims, since, by definition, they are unrelated to the main claim.

7.   Power: Yes   Permission: No

Clark will have to save this claim for another day as well. Jurisdictionally, the claim passes muster since there is diversity between Clark and Bradley (the opposing parties on the cross-claim) and the amount in controversy is sufficient. But the Rules don't authorize assertion of this claim in the Nimitz lawsuit: Rule 13(g) limits cross-claims to those arising out of the same transaction or occurrence as the main claim.

This result makes good sense. There is no relationship between the factual or legal issues relevant to the arrest claim and those relevant to the loan cross-claim and, therefore, no efficiency to be gained from allowing them to be heard in the same suit.

8.   Power: Yes   Permission: Yes

This is a nice contrast to example 7. Here, unlike example 7, joinder is proper under Rule 13(g), since the cross-claim arises out of the same incident as the main claim. There is no independent basis for subject matter jurisdiction, but jurisdiction is supplied by §1367(a), the supplemental jurisdiction statute, because the cross-claim arises out of the same nucleus of facts as the main claim.

Because cross-claims can only be asserted under Rule 13(g) if they arise from the same set of events as the main claim, they should always satisfy the test for supplemental jurisdiction. But see 28 U.S.C. §1367(b), which may sometimes deny supplemental jurisdiction to cross-claims brought by plaintiffs.

A Few Mazes, Nets, or Traps

9.   Power: In part   Permission: Yes

The Rules authorize joinder in this case, but jurisdiction is only proper over part of the case. First of all, I asked whether an *Arkansas* federal district court could hear the action. Really, this was just to blow a little smoke. Personal jurisdiction and venue are satisfied because both the defendant and third-party defendant are domiciled in Arkansas. *Milliken v. Meyer*, 311 U.S. 457 (1940); 28 U.S.C. §1391(a)(1). And the particular federal district in which the suit is brought is irrelevant to determination of subject matter jurisdiction. See Chapter 5, example 1a.

Joinder is proper in this action under Rules 14 and 18. MacArthur properly brought in Spruance under Rule 14(a), since he is seeking to recover from Spruance part of any damages that Halsey recovers from him, MacArthur. MacArthur's claim for contribution satisfies this requirement because he is asking Spruance to pay him half of any judgment Halsey wins, by way of "contribution" to the judgment. MacArthur's libel claim is also proper: Under Rule 18(a) MacArthur may assert any additional claims he has against Spruance, once he has asserted one claim against him that is proper under Rule 14(a). MacArthur could not have impleaded Spruance on the basis of the libel claim since it is an independent claim that does not satisfy the "may be liable to the third-party plaintiff for all or part of the plaintiff's claim" requirement of Rule 14(a). But once he impleads Spruance on a proper Rule 14(a) claim, he can pile on any claims he has against Spruance. See A. Greenbaum, Jacks or Better to Open: Limitations on Co-Party and Third-Party Joinder, 74 Minn. L. Rev. 507, 531-534 (1990).

So much for permission. The claims must also be analyzed individually as to jurisdictional power. There is supplemental jurisdiction over MacArthur's contribution claim against Spruance since it arises from the same nucleus of operative facts as Halsey's jurisdictionally sufficient claim against MacArthur. But supplemental jurisdiction does not extend to the libel claim since it is unrelated to the main claim and therefore not part of the same case or controversy under §1367(a). Nor is there an independent basis for subject matter jurisdiction since it is a state law claim between non-diverse parties.

10.   Power: Yes   Permission: No

This example involves a state law claim somewhat similar to Kroger's claim against Owen, the third-party defendant. Supplemental jurisdiction would not apply, but since the claim is between diverse parties and is for more than $75,000, it is within the court's independent diversity jurisdiction. (Always remember that supplemental jurisdiction is irrelevent where there is a direct basis for jurisdiction over a claim, as there is here.)

However, the Rules do not authorize joinder of this claim. Claims by plaintiffs against third-party defendants are authorized by Rule 14(a), which limits such claims to those arising from the same transaction or occurrence as the main claim. See Rule 14(a), seventh sentence. Halsey's claim is independent of the boating accident and therefore must be sued upon separately.

Curiously, if Halsey asserted a claim against Spruance for injuries arising from the boating accident, he could then pile on the unrelated libel claim under Rule 18(a). Jurisdiction and joinder would both be satisfied, and the court would be able to entertain the claim. However, it would likely be severed under Rule 21(b) and proceed effectively as a separate action anyway.

11. Power: Yes   Permission: Yes

Both joinder and jurisdiction are satisfied in this case. Joinder is proper under Rule 13(a) and (h); MacArthur has asserted a compulsory counterclaim against Halsey, and added Spruance (who destroys diversity) as an additional party to it, which is authorized by Rule 13(h). Visually the case looks like this:

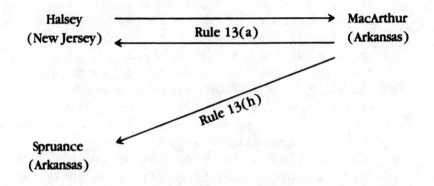

As to the power question, supplemental jurisdiction will provide a basis for jurisdiction. Section 1367(a) is apparently intended to reach these claims, since they arise from the same dispute over the boating accident. Even though MacArthur has added a new party to the compulsory counterclaim, §1367(a) expressly states that supplemental jurisdiction includes "claims that involve the joinder or intervention of additional parties." Further, the exceptions in §1367(b) do not apply, since the party asserting the added claims is not a plaintiff. Thus, even though complete diversity is lacking, the court may hear the counterclaims.

The irony here is that MacArthur may assert a counterclaim that he could not have asserted as an original claim: If he had sued Halsey and Spruance together, the case would have been dismissed for lack of diversity. While this result is ironic, it is not completely illogical. Prior to the enactment of §1367 the courts had given defendants hauled into court against their will broad opportunities to settle all claims arising out of the events that gave rise to the litigation. See *Kroger*, 437 U.S. at 375-377 (distinguishing jurisdictionally insufficient claims by defendants from Kroger's on this basis). In §1367,

Congress has preserved this defendant bias by barring claims by plaintiffs that are inconsistent with complete diversity, but allowing similar claims by defending parties.

12. Power: No   Permission: Yes

Permission to join Spruance's claim is provided here by Rule 24(b), which allows a party to seek intervention if her claim shares a question of fact or law with the main claim. Here, Spruance and Halsey will both seek to prove that MacArthur was negligent, thus satisfying the Rule 24(b) standard. Of course, Spruance would need to seek leave to intervene, since permissive intervention under Rule 24(b) is always at the discretion of the court.

However, Congress has barred supplemental jurisdiction over this claim in 28 U.S.C. §1367(b). That section bars supplemental jurisdiction over claims by persons "seeking to intervene as plaintiffs under Rule 24 of such rules, when exercising supplemental jurisdiction over such claims would be inconsistent with the jurisdictional requirements of section 1332." Allowing Spruance to intervene here would be inconsistent with the requirements of §1332, since it would allow a claim by one Arkansas citizen against another, based on state law. If Spruance were allowed to intervene in this case, it would allow him to evade the complete diversity requirement: Instead of suing with Halsey, which would be improper under *Strawbridge v. Curtiss*, 7 U.S. 267 (1806), he could simply allow Halsey to start the suit and then achieve the same result by intervening. Obviously, Congress adopted the view of the Supreme Court, expressed in *Kroger*, that, in an age when diversity is viewed with disfavor by many, supplemental jurisdiction should not provide a means of evading the complete diversity requirement.

This case presents a situation in which it would make good litigation sense to take jurisdiction. The claims arise out of the same nucleus of operative facts, thus satisfying the constitutional test for a single case. In terms of efficiency there is as much justification for hearing this claim as there is for hearing a third-party impleader claim, or MacArthur's counterclaim against Spruance in example 11. But without a statutory basis, the court can't exercise jurisdiction over the claim, and here Congress has quite deliberately withheld the authority to do so.

PART FOUR

Steps in the Litigation Process

17

The Bearer of Bad Tidings: Service of Process in the Federal Courts

Introduction

Some of the most profound protections of our constitutional system are astoundingly simple. "Due process of law" under the fourteenth amendment, for example, guarantees parties the basic right to notice of a court's intention to adjudicate their rights and an opportunity for those parties to be heard before the court proceeds to do so. "An elementary and fundamental requirement of due process in any proceeding which is to be accorded finality is notice reasonably calculated, under all the circumstances, to apprise interested parties of the pendency of the action and afford them an opportunity to present their objections." *Mullane v. Central Hanover Bank*, 339 U.S. 306, 311 (1950). In civil suits, this requirement is fulfilled through service of process.

The term *service of process* is often used to refer to the delivery to a party or witness of various court orders required by the relevant rules of law to be served upon him, including subpoenas, writs, and other orders that are entered in the course of litigation. However, in a stricter sense the term is used—as we will use it here—to refer to service of the initial notice to the defendant of the filing of a lawsuit against him. Service of this initial summons both notifies the defendant that he has been sued and informs him that the court intends to proceed to adjudicate his rights. The summons in the *Schulansky* case, for example (infra p. 550), specifically warns the defendants that they must respond to the plaintiff's complaint, or judgment by default will be entered against them.

All courts, state and federal, have elaborate provisions governing service of this initial notice to defendants. State service provisions may be found in statutes (see, e.g., N.Y. Civ. Prac. Law §§305-318) or in court rules (see, e.g., Mass. R. Civ. P. 4, set forth on pp. 300-301 for use in this chapter). This chapter explores the intricacies of Rule 4 of the Federal Rules of Civil Procedure, which governs service of process in the federal courts, as an example of service provisions.

Rule 4 specifies in detail what documents must be served on the defendant (Rule 4(c)(1)), the contents of the summons (Rule 4(a)), how the papers must be served (Rules 4(e)-(j)), when they must be served (Rule 4(m)), who must serve them (Rule 4(c)(2)), and how the requirement of service may be waived (Rule 4(d)). For example, if you look at Form 1 of the Federal Rules Forms, which follows the Federal Rules of Civil Procedure, you will see that the summons there complies with each of the requirements in Rule 4(a) as to the contents of the summons. It provides for the signature of the clerk and the seal of the court, identifies the court and the parties, provides the name of the plaintiff's attorney, states the time within which the defendant must respond, and that default judgment will enter against him if he fails to do so. Compare the summons in the *Schulansky* case (infra p. 544), drawn to comply with similar provisions as to form in Mass. R. Civ. P. 4(b).

The permissible methods of serving process on the defendant are found in Fed. R. Civ. P. 4(e)-(j). Under these provisions, the proper method of service depends on the type of defendant being served. For example, the methods for service on individual defendants differ from those for service on a corporation or on the United States. These provisions were extensively revised in 1993, and are now simpler to follow than before the amendments. The revision rearranged Rule 4 entirely. You should be very careful, in reading cases about service of process, to sort out whether the court is talking about apples, under the current version of the rule, or oranges, under an earlier version. The 1993 amendments made another important and sensible change in Rule 4: They eliminated separate provisions governing the methods for in-state and out-of-state service. Now, for example, Rule 4(e) governs service of process on an individual defendant, whether that defendant is being served in the state where the suit is pending or anywhere else in the country. However, the revised rule retains special provisions for service on both individuals (Rule 4(f)) and corporations (Rule 4(h)(2)) in other countries.

Methods of Service on Individual Defendants

Let's turn now to a description of the available methods for serving process on various categories of defendants. Rule 4 treats the methods for serving different types of defendants (such as individuals, corporations, the United States, and other governmental entities) in different subsections.

Fed. R. Civ. P. 4(e) governs service of process on an individual defendant, that is, a person. It provides five different methods for serving process on individual defendants in federal suits. The three traditional methods are found in Rule 4(e)(2), which authorizes service by personally delivering the summons and complaint to the defendant, or by leaving copies of the summons and the complaint at his dwelling house or usual place of abode with a person of suitable age and discretion residing therein, or by delivering the papers to an agent appointed by the defendant to receive service of process on his behalf.

Until 1983 service by personal delivery on a defendant had to be made by a United States marshal or a person specially designated by the court to serve process. This provision frequently led to delays in service or motions to the court for appointment of special process servers because the marshals were too busy with other duties to serve process promptly. Now, however, Rule 4(c)(2) provides that personal service may be made by any person who is over 18 years of age and not a party to the action. In most cases, plaintiff's counsel will hire a constable or professional process server to serve the papers.

The plaintiff's fourth option is to serve individual defendants under the provisions governing service on individuals in the courts of the state where the federal court sits. Fed. R. Civ. P. 4(e)(1). The plaintiff in an action in the federal district court in Massachusetts, for example, may use any methods for service of process on individuals that apply in the Massachusetts Superior Courts; that is, any of the methods provided in Mass. R. Civ. P. 4(d)(1) (see infra p. 300). If the suit were brought in federal court in Maine, the plaintiff would look to the service rules of the Maine courts. Note that service under the state rules pursuant to Rule 4(e)(1) is an *alternative* to service under the other methods provided in Rule 4(e)(2); the plaintiff may choose whichever he prefers.

Rule 4 also authorizes a fifth method of serving process on individual defendants who are served outside the state where the action is pending. Rule 4(e)(1) authorizes service "pursuant to the law of the state . . . in which service is effected," that is, the state where the defendant is actually being served. Suppose, for example, that Vaughan brings suit in the federal district court for the District of Massachusetts against Spenser, who lives in Maine, and wishes to serve process on Spenser there. Rule 4(e)(1) authorizes Vaughan to use any method for service on an individual defendant authorized by the *Maine* service rules, since that is the "state . . . in which service is effected [i.e., takes place]."

Methods of Service of Process on Corporations and Other Entities

Methods of service of process on corporations or other entities (such as partnerships or unincorporated associations) are specified in Rule 4(h). If the defendant is served anywhere in the United States ("in a judicial district of the United States"), Rule 4(h)(1) applies. If the defendant is served outside the United States ("in a place not within any judicial district of the United States"), Rule 4(h)(2) applies.

Under Rule 4(h)(1), the available methods parallel the methods for service on individuals under Rule 4(e). Service may be made by delivery of a copy of the summons and complaint to an officer, managing or general agent of the defendant, or to an agent authorized to receive service of process. Alternatively, service may be made by one of the methods prescribed in Rule 4(e)(1), which includes service by a method prescribed by the law of the state where the federal court sits *or* by a method prescribed by the law of the state in which process is to be served on the defendant. (Presumably, however, this means a method prescribed by the state's law for service *on a corporation;* it does not make methods for service on individuals under state law applicable to corporations.)

To illustrate these options, assume that Vaughan sues the Sidney Corporation, a corporation incorporated in Maine and conducting most of its business there, in the federal district court for the District of Massachusetts. Under Rule 4(h)(1), he could serve process on Sidney by delivering the papers to an officer, managing or general agent of Sidney, or an agent authorized to receive service of process for Sidney. Alternatively, he could serve Sidney under any of the provisions for serving process *on a corporation* available under the Massachusetts rules for service of process. He could also use any method available under the Maine rules for serving process on a corporation.

Waiver of Service of Process

Rule 4(d) also provides an alternative to the various methods of service of process described above. It authorizes the plaintiff to solicit a waiver of all these technicalities by sending the defendant the complaint, two copies of a notice of the action and a request that the defendant waive formal service of the summons and complaint upon him. The defendant is supposed to return the request, thus waiving formal service.

Rule 4(d) contains several provisions intended to give defendants an incentive to waive formal service. First, Rule 4(d)(2) creates a duty to avoid "unnecessary costs of serving the summons" by agreeing to waive service. Second, under the last sentence of Rule 4(d)(2), the court must impose the costs of service on a defendant who refuses to waive service without good cause. Third, Rule 4(d)(3) offers defendants a tempting reward for waiving service: It gives them 60 days, rather than the usual 20, to respond to the complaint. For busy defense counsel, this carrot may be more persuasive than the relatively mild threat of paying the costs of service if they refuse to waive it.

The Relation of Service of Process to Personal Jurisdiction

It is crucial to distinguish the concept of service of process from the related concept of personal jurisdiction. In many cases, particularly older cases, challenges to personal jurisdiction have been framed in terms of "insufficient service of process," although the actual basis of the defendant's objection was insufficient contact between the defendant and the state to support personal jurisdiction. In modern phraseology, a challenge to service of process (a motion to dismiss for insufficiency of service of process under Fed. R. Civ. P. 12(b)(5)) attacks the adequacy of the method used by the plaintiff to give the defendant notice of the action (the subject of this chapter), *not* the power of the court to exercise personal jurisdiction over him, which would be raised by a motion to dismiss for lack of personal jurisdiction under Fed. R. Civ. P. 12(b)(2).

It is not surprising that the *Pennoyer*-era cases blended the two concepts. When *Pennoyer* was decided, service of process on the defendant within the forum state was the predominant means of obtaining jurisdiction, as well as giving notice to the defendant of the suit. Thus, under *Pennoyer*, if service was not made properly (that is, delivered personally to the defendant within the state), personal jurisdiction was not obtained. The two requirements were thus frequently discussed as though they were interchangeable; but today the two are quite distinct, and either may be satisfied though the other is not.

For example, suppose that Drayton is injured in Utah when Lovelace, a vacationing Marylander, hits him on the street in Salt Lake City. He sues Lovelace in Utah and serves process on Lovelace by publishing notice of the suit in a Salt Lake City newspaper. On these facts, the Utah court would have the constitutional power to exercise personal jurisdiction over Lovelace, based on the in-state contact of causing tortious injury in the state. However, service would be improper, since in most cases publication is not a constitutionally adequate means of informing a defendant that he has been sued. In this example, a Rule 12(b)(2) motion would not be granted, but a Rule 12(b)(5) motion would. By contrast, if Drayton sued Lovelace in Alaska for the Salt Lake City accident, personal jurisdiction would be improper, assuming Lovelace has no contacts with Alaska. If Drayton served the summons and complaint on Lovelace by personal delivery to him (the best possible means of informing him of the suit), service would be proper under Fed. R.

Civ. P. 4(e)(2), but the court would not have personal jurisdiction over Lovelace. Thus, while historically intertwined, these two due process requirements are distinct, and should always be analyzed separately.

The Federal "Long-Arm Statute" in Rule 4

Most of Rule 4 deals with the mechanics of service, that is, how the defendant is actually informed that a lawsuit has been filed against him. However, Rule 4 also contains a "long-arm statute" for the federal courts. Rule 4(k), entitled "Territorial Limits of Effective Service," specifies when a federal court may assert personal jurisdiction over a defendant served under Rule 4. In this sense, it is like a state long-arm statute, by which a state legislature specifies the circumstances in which personal jurisdiction may be exercised by its courts.

When suit is brought in a federal court, just as when it is brought in a state court, two questions must be asked to determine whether that court can assert jurisdiction over the defendant. First, has the relevant legislature authorized the jurisdiction, and second, if it has, would it be constitutional for the court to exercise jurisdiction in the circumstances of the particular case? See Chapter 2, which analyzes state grants of jurisdiction in long-arm statutes, and the examples in that chapter, which compare the reach of long-arm statutes to constitutional limits on personal jurisdiction.

In federal suits, the first question, the legislative authority for federal courts to exercise personal jurisdiction, is addressed in Rule 4(k).[1] That rule provides that service of process "is effective to establish jurisdiction over the person of a defendant" in four circumstances. First, the federal court is authorized to assert jurisdiction if the courts of the state in which the federal court sits could assert jurisdiction over the defendant. Rule 4(k)(1)(A). In other words, if the *state* long-arm statute authorizes jurisdiction in the circumstances of the case, and it would be constitutional for the *state* court to assert jurisdiction under Fourteenth Amendment analysis, then the federal court may do so as well. In most cases, this subsection of Rule 4(k) will apply, because the other three subsections cover fairly limited situations. Under it, the reach of personal jurisdiction in a federal court is *the same as the reach of personal jurisdiction in the courts of the state in which it sits.* An Arizona federal court will exercise jurisdiction to the same extent that an Arizona state court would; a Michigan federal court will exercise jurisdiction to the same extent that a Michigan state court would; and so on.

In addition, Rule 4(k) authorizes federal courts to take jurisdiction in certain other limited situations, including impleaded parties served within

---

1. Although Rule 4 was promulgated by the Supreme Court rather than Congress, the Court promulgates the Rules under congressional authority in the Rules Enabling Act. Thus, Rule 4(k) is analogous to a legislative grant of the power to exercise personal jurisdiction.

100 miles of the courthouse (Rule 4(k)(1)(B)), parties subject to interpleader jurisdiction (Rule 4(k)(1)(C)), and in federal question cases, over parties who have sufficient contacts with the United States as a whole to constitutionally support jurisdiction, but whose contacts would not suffice to support personal jurisdiction in the courts of any state. Rule 4(k)(2). Last, service will support jurisdiction if some other federal statute provides that service suffices to support jurisdiction for a particular type of case. Rule 4(k)(1)(D).

As with state long-arm statutes, the fact that Rule 4(k) authorizes the assertion of jurisdiction will not always mean that it is constitutional to exercise it; the second prong of the analysis must always be considered as well. However, recall that the constitutional constraints on a *federal court's* exercise of personal jurisdiction are found in the Fifth Amendment due process clause, not in the Fourteenth Amendment. The Fifth Amendment has usually been held to require only that the defendant have minimum contacts with the *United States as a whole* to support jurisdiction, not with any particular state. See Chapter 6, pp. 105-106; see generally R. Casad, Personal Jurisdiction in Federal Question Cases, 70 Tex. L. Rev. 1589, 1599-1606 (1992). Thus, for example, taking jurisdiction under Rule 4(k)(2) over a defendant who has scattered contacts with a number of states may well be constitutional under the Fifth Amendment, even though the defendant has too few contacts in any one state to support personal jurisdiction under Fourteenth Amendment analysis.

Several other mechanical aspects of service should be mentioned. *First,* the person making service must make proof of service (often called "return of service") by promptly filing an affidavit with the court setting forth the manner in which service was made. Fed. R. Civ. P. 4(1). Proof of service is often inserted on the summons itself. See the Schulansky summons (infra p. 544), which contains a printed form for proof of service.

Second, Rule 4(m) specifies that service of process must be made within 120 days of filing the complaint, or the action may be dismissed. Earlier versions of Rule 4 did not specify a time limit for service, and in some cases service was upheld long after the complaint was filed, so long as there was no unreasonable delay on the plaintiff's part in attempting it. Under Rule 4(m), the court may (but does not have to) dismiss the action if the plaintiff fails to show "good cause" for failure to make service within the 120-day period. This time limit for service of the summons and complaint is separate from and in addition to the requirements of any applicable statute of limitations. The fact that an action is *filed* within the limitations period (which, in many cases, will satisfy the statute of limitations) does not affect this additional requirement in Rule 4(m) to *serve* the complaint within the 120-day period.

Third, as noted earlier, many other papers get "served" on parties and witnesses in law suits in addition to the original complaint. All motions, pleadings (other than the complaint), discovery requests, and other papers filed with the court must be served on each party to the action; all parties have a right to notice of subsequent filings in the case, as well as notice of the commencement of suit. However, virtually all such papers may be served under the more flexible provisions of Fed. R. Civ. P. 5, which authorizes service of papers subsequent to the complaint by mailing them to the party's attorney. See the certificate of service at the end of the answer in the *Schulansky* case, infra p. 572 and the accompanying note (p. 577). The complaint is singled out for special treatment because it is the first notice the defendant receives of the filing of the suit. If he does not receive this notice, he may never learn of the action at all. Once he *has* been properly informed of the suit, however, the law presumes that he will keep an eye on the docket and eventually learn of any paper that was served by mail under Rule 5 but, for one reason or another, never reached him.

In analyzing the following examples, assume that all actions are brought in the federal district court for the District of Massachusetts. Because Federal Rule 4 incorporates state provisions for service of process in some circumstances, you will have to consider the methods of service provided in Mass. R. Civ. P. 4, as well as those in Federal Rule 4. The relevant portions of Massachusetts Rule of Civil Procedure 4 are as follows:

> **(c) By Whom Served.** Except as otherwise permitted by paragraph (h) of this rule, service of all process shall be made by a sheriff, by his deputy, or by a special sheriff; by any other person duly authorized by law; by some person specially appointed by the court for that purpose; or in the case of service of process outside the Commonwealth, by an individual permitted to make service of process under the law of this Commonwealth or under the law of the place in which the service is to be made, or who is designated by a court of this Commonwealth. A subpoena may be served as provided in Rule 45. Notwithstanding the provisions of this paragraph (c), wherever in these rules service is permitted to be made by certified or registered mail, the mailing may be accomplished by the party or his attorney.
>
> **(d) Summons: Personal Service within the Commonwealth.** The summons and a copy of the complaint shall be served together. The plaintiff shall furnish the person making service with such copies as are necessary. Service shall be made as follows:
>
> (1) Upon an individual by delivering a copy of the summons and of the complaint to him personally; or by leaving copies thereof at his last and usual place of abode; or by delivering a copy of the summons and of the complaint to an agent authorized by appointment or by statute to receive service of process, provided that any further notice required by such statute be given. . . .
>
> (2) Upon a domestic corporation (public or private), a foreign corporation subject to suit within the Commonwealth, or an unincorporated association subject to suit within the Commonwealth under a

common name: by delivering a copy of the summons and of the complaint to an officer, to a managing or general agent, or to the person in charge of the business at the principal place of business thereof within the Commonwealth, if any; or by delivering such copies to any other agent authorized by appointment or by law to receive service of process, provided that any further notice required by law be given. . . .

(e) **Same: Personal Service outside the Commonwealth.** When any statute or law of the Commonwealth authorizes service of process outside the Commonwealth, the service shall be made by delivering a copy of the summons and of the complaint: (1) in any appropriate manner prescribed in subdivision (d) of this Rule; or (2) in the manner prescribed by the law of the place in which the service is made for service in that place in an action in any of its courts of general jurisdiction; or (3) by any form of mail addressed to the person to be served and requiring a signed receipt; or (4) as directed by the appropriate foreign authority in response to a letter rogatory; or (5) as directed by order of the court.

EXAMPLES

A Comedy of Errors

1.   Marvell brings a pro se[2] diversity action against Donne for breach of contract. He serves Donne by having a copy of the complaint delivered to Donne personally at his summer home on Cape Cod, in Hyannis, Massachusetts. Is service proper?

2.   The court upholds Donne's objection to the original service and orders Marvell to re-serve Donne properly. Marvell takes a copy of the complaint and summons, drives to Hyannis, and serves them personally on Donne. Donne moves again to dismiss for improper service of process. Why will the motion be granted?

3.   Disgusted with the whole process (no pun intended), Marvell retains Herbert to represent him. Herbert promptly serves process on Donne by having Marple, an investigator from his office, deliver copies of the summons and complaint to Donne in Hyannis. Donne is not there when the investigator arrives, so she pushes the papers under the front door. Donne renews his objection to the method of service. Is the objection valid?

4.   Herbert changes tactics and orders Marple to serve the summons on Donne at his year-round residence in Boston. Since the elusive Donne is not at home, Marple serves copies of the summons and complaint by leaving them with Donne's sister, who lives in Texas but is visiting Donne to run in the Boston Marathon. Though not to be found at home, Donne reappears faithfully in court to object once again to the manner of service. Has Herbert cured the defect?

---

2. A pro se action is one brought by a party who is not represented by a lawyer.

5.   If Donne is elusive, Herbert is tenacious. He sends the sheriff to Donne's house in Boston to serve the papers. As the sheriff knocks on the front door, Donne leaves by the back for a pressing appointment. The sheriff slips the papers under the front door and leaves. Is service finally proper?

6.   Assume that Herbert decides to try to get Donne to waive service instead of using the methods in the prior examples.

    a. How should he solicit the waiver of service from Donne?

    b. Suppose he follows the required waiver procedure, but receives no waiver back from Donne. What should he do next?

At Your Service

7.   Herrick sues Marlowe for personal injuries arising out of an accident while visiting Marlowe's truck repair garage in Revere, Massachusetts. The action is again brought in the federal district court for the District of Massachusetts. Herrick serves copies of the summons and complaint by having them delivered in hand to Daniel, Marlowe's service manager, at the garage. Is service proper?

8.   Herrick sues both Marlowe and Daniel for his injuries arising out of the accident at the shop. He serves the complaint by having his investigator, Poirot, deliver a copy of the complaint and summons to Marlowe at the shop. Is service proper?

9.   Herrick sues Marlowe in Massachusetts federal district court for the injuries suffered in the accident at the shop, and Marlowe decides to implead Daniel under Fed. R. Civ. P. 14, on the theory that Daniel, who actually caused the injury, should indemnify him for any judgment Herrick obtains in the main action. Marlowe serves the complaint on Daniel, under Fed. R. Civ. P. 5, by mailing a copy to him at his home in Boston. Is service proper?

10.   Assume that Marlowe has incorporated his business in Massachusetts, as Poetic Truck Repair, Inc., with himself as president. Herrick decides to sue the corporation for injuries he suffered on its premises.

    a. He serves the complaint by having Poirot take the papers to Marlowe's house and leave them there with Marlowe's wife. Is service proper?

    b. He serves the complaint by having Poirot deliver copies of the summons and complaint to Daniel at the shop. Is service proper on the corporation?

Process and Due Process

11.   As the introduction explains, service of process is a separate requirement from personal jurisdiction; the fact that service was properly made on the defendant does not mean that the court has the power to require the defendant to defend in the forum state. Conversely, the fact that it would be permissible,

under due process analysis, to require the defendant to defend the action in the forum state does not eliminate the need to provide adequate notice of the action. Consider whether the two requirements have been met in the cases below.

Davies sues the Holland Corporation, a corporation incorporated and doing business only in Florida, in federal district court for the District of Massachusetts, for injuries suffered in an accident in Florida. She serves process on Holland by mailing a copy of the summons and complaint, certified mail, return receipt requested, to Chapman, the president of Holland Corporation, at the corporate headquarters in Florida.

    a. Is service proper?

    b. Does the court have personal jurisdiction over Holland Corporation?

12. In the same case, Davies sues Holland Corporation in Massachusetts federal court and serves process on Chapman, Holland's president, while he is visiting his daughter in Boston.

    a. Is service proper?

    b. Does the court have personal jurisdiction over Holland Corporation?

13. Sidney, a New Hampshire contractor, does occasional business in the town of Pepperell, just over the border in Massachusetts. He builds a garage for Chapman in Pepperell and Chapman, unhappy with the work, sues Sidney in Massachusetts Superior Court. She serves process on Sidney by delivering a copy of the summons and complaint to the Pepperell town clerk under Mass. Gen. L. ch. 227, §5A, which provides that a person who does business in a city or town of the Commonwealth appoints the town clerk as his agent for service of process for suits arising out of that business.

    a. Is service proper?

    b. Does the court have personal jurisdiction over Holland Corporation?

14. Suppose that Chapman serves Sidney by having the sheriff slip the summons and complaint under the front door at his home in Peterborough, New Hampshire. Sidney's housekeeper picks the papers up along with the newspaper, and later absent-mindedly throws them out. Sidney does not learn of the suit and default judgment enters against him.

    a. Is the judgment valid?

    b. If you represented Sidney, what would you do?

Unlucky Number Fifteen

15. National Assurance Corporation, an insurer, brings an action under the federal interpleader act, 28 U.S.C. §1335, against a number of defendants, to determine who is entitled to the insurance proceeds on a building that was destroyed by fire in Atlanta, Georgia. The action is brought in the federal district court for the District of Massachusetts. A special service statute, 28 U.S.C. §2361, applies to actions under the interpleader act. It authorizes service of process anywhere in the nation in interpleader cases and provides

that service shall be "addressed to and served by the United States marshals for the respective districts where the claimants reside or may be found." National's counsel serves process on Drayton, a co-owner of the building and one of the defendants, by mailing the summons and complaint, certified mail, return receipt requested, to Drayton at his home in Louisiana. Drayton has no contacts with Massachusetts.

   a. Is service proper?
   b. Does the court have personal jurisdiction over Drayton Corporation?

EXPLANATIONS

A Comedy of Errors

1.   Service is improper because Marvell has only delivered a copy of the complaint itself. Rule 4(c)(1) requires both the summons and the complaint to be served on the defendant.

   This requirement makes sense. The complaint is simply the plaintiff's introductory pleading, stating the nature of the case and the relief sought. It is designed to inform the defendant of the events that gave rise to the plaintiff's claim and the nature of his claim. The summons, on the other hand, is an official court document, issued by the court and signed by the court clerk (see Fed. R. Civ. P. 4(a)), commanding the defendant to respond to the accompanying complaint and telling him the time within which it must be done. The Schulansky summons, for example, warns the defendant that "[y]ou are hereby summoned and required to serve . . . an answer to the complaint which is herewith served upon you." It is the court itself, not the plaintiff, that has the authority to compel the defendant to respond to the complaint, and it is the summons by which the court exercises that power.

2.   This time Marvell has served the right documents but has done it in the wrong manner. Presumably, he is proceeding under Fed. R. Civ. P. 4(e)(2), which authorizes service by delivering the papers to the defendant. However, Rule 4(c)(2) provides that service of process may be made by any person who is not a party and is not less than 18 years of age. Marvell is a party; the rule bars him from serving the summons and complaint himself, perhaps on the theory that such service might lead to immediate (but distinctly nonjudicial) settlement of the parties' differences.

3.   Technicalities, technicalities. Herbert has apparently relied again on Federal Rule 4(e)(2) but has not fulfilled the requirements of that subsection. *First,* it is doubtful that Donne's summer house constitutes his "dwelling house or usual place of abode"; it is apparently a vacation home. *Second,* the rule requires the process server to leave the summons and complaint with a person of suitable age and discretion residing therein. Herbert has clearly failed to meet this requirement.

Herbert might claim that service was proper under Mass. R. Civ. P. 4(d)(1). Remember that Fed. R. Civ. P. 4(e)(1) allows Marvell to serve Donne under the state service rules. Mass. R. Civ. P. 4(d)(1), unlike its federal counterpart, does not require that the summons and complaint be left with anyone. However, it does require them to be left at the "last and usual place of abode," which probably does not include a seasonal home. In addition, under the Massachusetts rule, service must be made by a sheriff or other official process server. Mass. R. Civ. P. 4(c). Service is therefore improper under either rule.

4.   It is difficult to fault Marple here, but Donne will probably win this round too. Here again, Herbert has apparently tried to comply with Rule 4(e)(2) of the Federal Rules. That rule allows him to leave the summons with a person other than the defendant but only if that person is of suitable age and discretion *and* resides at the defendant's dwelling house or usual place of abode. Presumably, Sister Donne has just flown in for the marathon and would not be held to "reside" at Donne's Boston home.

You well might ask, "How is Marple to know that Sister Donne doesn't live in the house?" Perhaps Sister will tell her if she asks; most people are fairly trusting and not expecting the process server. If not, Marple risks another motion to dismiss under Rule 12(b)(5) by serving in this manner.

Some cases have been more obedient to the spirit than the letter of the "then residing therein" requirement in Rule 4(e)(2). In *Churchill v. Barach*, 863 F. Supp. 1266, 1270-1271 (D. Nev. 1994), for example, the court found this requirement satisfied when service was made on a doorman in an apartment building who, though he regularly took messages and packages for residents, didn't live there.

5.   He who laughs last laughs best. Although Herbert's latest attempt is insufficient under Fed. R. Civ. P. 4(e)(2) (because not left with a person of suitable age, etc.), that is not his only option. Rule 4(e)(1) authorizes service under the Massachusetts provisions as well. Mass. R. Civ. P. 4(d)(1) allows service by leaving a copy of the summons and complaint at the defendant's last and usual place of abode. The state rule does not include a requirement that it be left with a family member or with any person at all. Thus, having the alternative of service under state law proves useful to effect service on an elusive defendant such as Donne.[3]

Service is proper here, unlike in example 4, because the papers were left at the defendant's last and usual place of abode, and they were served by the

---

3. While it is clear that leaving copies of the summons and complaint at the last and usual abode is sufficient under Mass. R. Civ. P. 4(d)(1), it is questionable whether such service is constitutionally sufficient in all cases. See *Greene v. Lindsey*, 456 U.S. 444, 452-456 (1982) (service in eviction proceeding by posting on door of apartment invalid under due process clause).

sheriff. The Massachusetts rule may be more liberal on the methods of delivery, but it is more restrictive on the issue of who delivers it. This is certainly appropriate if service is to be allowed without personal delivery. A sheriff or constable is a neutral party with a professional reputation to protect. His or her certification that service was actually made by leaving the papers at the last and usual place of abode is more trustworthy than that of a party or someone working for a party.

6a.   Federal Rule 4(d) sets forth the procedure for obtaining a waiver of service. Herbert should send a notice of the action addressed to Donne, with a request that Donne waive service of process. Rule 4(d)(2). The notice must identify the court in which suit has been filed, be accompanied by a copy of the complaint (Rule 4(d)(2)(C)) and must be sent by first class mail "or other reliable means." Rule 4(d)(2)(B). It must inform the defendant of the consequences of waiving service, and of not waiving service. Rule 4(d)(2)(D). It must also include the date on which the request is sent (Rule 4(d)(2)(E)), provide the defendant at least 30 days to respond (Rule 4(d)(2)(F)), and include an extra copy of the notice and request with a prepaid means of responding (such as an envelope with a stamp on it!). Forms sufficient to comply with Rule 4(d) are provided in the Appendix to the Rules. See Forms 1A and 1B.

   b.   Donne has a duty under Rule 4(d)(2) to "avoid unnecessary costs of serving the summons," but what if he doesn't do his duty? The clear implication of the rule is that Donne must then be served through one of the regular methods in Rule 4(e). The court may impose costs on Donne for his non-compliance (see Rule 4(d)(2), last sentence and Rule 4(d)(5)), but Donne still must be served in order to be properly brought before the court.

   In some states, the date for determining whether the statute of limitations has been satisfied runs from the date of *service on the defendant*, rather than the date of filing of the complaint. See, e.g., the infamous *Walker v. Armco*, 446 U.S. 740 (1980). Rule 4(d)(4) provides that, where the waiver procedure is used, service shall be deemed effected on the date of *filing* of the waiver of service (that is, filing with the court). Plaintiffs who file suit shortly before the expiration of the statute of limitations should not use the waiver procedure, since they may not receive it back for at least 30 days—or may not receive it at all—and *mailing* the waiver form does not toll the limitations period.

At Your Service

7.   Since nothing in this example indicates that Marlowe's business is incorporated, we will assume that he is doing business as an individual and that Herrick is suing him individually. Herrick's argument here must be that service is proper under Fed. R. Civ. P. 4(e)(2) because Daniel, as manager at

Marlowe's shop, is his agent for service of process. The argument fails, however, because 4(e)(2) (and its Massachusetts counterpart) only permit service on an agent "authorized by appointment or by law to receive service of process." Daniel may act generally for Marlowe in the shop, but this general authority to conduct his business is not the same as being specifically appointed to receive service of process.

This provision is meant to reach cases in which the defendant has specifically empowered another person to accept notice of suits. It does not apply to an employee who acts generally as the defendant's agent in the conduct of his business. See Moore's at §4.93. Specific appointments to accept process are sometimes made in contracts, where one of the parties seeks to insure that he will be able to sue the other in a particular state. See, e.g., *National Equipment Rental v. Szukhent,* 375 U.S. 311 (1964) (approving service on agent for service appointed in contract between the parties). They may also occur by operation of law. For example, Massachusetts law provides that a nonresident who does business in any Massachusetts city or town appoints the clerk of that city or town his agent for service of process in actions arising out of business conducted there. Mass. Gen. L. ch. 227, §5A. In such a case, service on the city clerk would satisfy the provision in Federal Rule 4(e)(2) for service on an agent "authorized . . . by law to receive service of process."

8.   This raises a fairly obvious issue but one that is not explicitly answered by the rule. Service is proper on Marlowe in this case, under Fed. R. Civ. P. 4(e)(2), but not on Daniel. Every defendant is entitled to direct notice of suits against him, under the provisions of Rule 4. Just as the law refuses to presume that a general agent of Marlowe would inform him of a suit, it also refuses to rely on one defendant to inform others (who, in many cases, he may not even know) that they have been sued. Each defendant is entitled to proper service under the Rules. Herrick will have to serve Daniel separately under one of the provisions of Rule 4.

9.   By now you may be wondering how these rules can be so intricate yet leave so many questions unanswered. In this case, the defendant has brought in a new party, who clearly must be informed of the suit. It appears that Rule 4 should apply since it governs service of summonses and complaints, and Rule 14(a) requires the impleading party to serve a summons and complaint on the third party. However, Rule 5(a) provides that "every pleading subsequent to the original complaint" shall be served on all parties, and Rule 5(b) authorizes such service by ordinary mail, which is insufficient under Rule 4.

While the Rules themselves are not explicit on the point, the policies that underlie service support the conclusion that the third-party complaint, like an original complaint, should be served under Rule 4. The purpose of Rule 4 is to insure adequate notice to parties who do not yet know that they have been sued. Rule 5, by contrast, is designed to provide a simple method for exchange of the many subsequent pleadings and papers that are filed in the case. It trades a little bit of certainty (under the stricter procedures of Rule 4) for a great deal of efficiency (under the ordinary mail provision of Rule 5). The rationale for doing so is that the defendant is already aware of the suit and, presumably, will stay in touch with subsequent developments. That rationale does not apply to the new third-party defendant; as to him, the third-party complaint is his first notice of the action, and he has the same right to notice of it under the due process clause as an original defendant. See *Adams Dairy Co. v. National Dairy Products Corp.*, 293 F. Supp. 1164, 1165 (W.D. Mo. 1968) (Rule 4 makes exclusive provision for service of all summonses and complaints, including third-party complaints). Moore's at §14.22.

10a. In this case, it appears that Herrick has used the Rule 4(e)(2) procedure for service of process on an individual, by leaving the papers at Marlowe's house with a person of suitable age and discretion residing therein. Unfortunately, he is not serving Marlowe as an individual defendant: Herrick is serving Marlowe as an officer of the corporation in order to effect service on *the corporation,* Poetic Truck Repair. It is certainly proper to serve the president of Poetic, under Rule 4(h)(1), but that rule says nothing about leaving the papers with someone else. It speaks of "delivering [the papers] to an officer . . . ," suggesting that they must be served directly on the officer to comply with the rule.

Herrick's attempted service on Poetic is also improper under Mass. Rule 4(d)(2), since it also requires personal delivery to the officer. In addition, under the Massachusetts service rules the papers must be delivered by an official process server. Mass. R. Civ. P. 4(c).

b. Service on corporations is governed by Rule 4(h)(1), which authorizes service on a "managing or general agent" of the corporation as well as various officers or appointed agents. Therefore, whether service on Daniel will suffice turns on whether his functions as service manager for Poetic make him a managing or general agent. This will depend on the specifics of Daniel's duties, but it is likely that he will satisfy this requirement. The rationale for allowing service on a general agent for a corporation is that an employee with general responsibilities is likely to realize the importance of the summons and complaint and inform the appropriate officers of the corporation of service. A service manager (again, no pun intended) for a business that solely does repair work is likely to have that kind of general responsibility and awareness.

Note that under Rule 4(h)(1) service on a managing agent is sufficient, although example 7 indicates that it is not under Rule 4(e). This distinction reflects the policy of the rule that when an individual is sued, service should be made on him personally (or on a member of his household) unless he has specifically consented to service on another on his behalf. A corporation, however, is not a flesh-and-blood defendant; it cannot be "personally" informed of the action. Instead, the Rule authorizes service on corporate employees sufficiently highly placed to make it probable that the corporate officers who must respond to the suit will learn of it.

Service on Poetic in this case might also be proper under Mass. R. Civ. P. 4(d)(2). Use of state procedure is proper for service on corporations as well as individuals: Federal Rule 4(h)(1) incorporates the provisions of Rule 4(e)(1), which allows service under state law. Mass. R. Civ. P. 4(d)(2) authorizes service on a domestic corporation by service on a managing or general agent, or on the person in charge of the corporate business at its principal place of business in the state. Depending on the particular facts, Daniel might well satisfy this provision. However, under the Massachusetts service rules, an official process server must serve the papers, which was not done in this case.

Process and Due Process

11. Service: Yes   Personal Jurisdiction: No

a. In this case service was properly made on Holland under the combination of Federal Rule 4 and the Massachusetts rules. Federal Rule 4(h)(1) authorizes use of the procedures available under Fed. R. Civ. P. 4(e)(1), which in turn authorizes service under the Massachusetts rules. Mass. Rule 4(e)(3) authorizes service on an out-of-state party by any form of mail requiring a signed receipt. (Mail service would also be proper if it were authorized by the Florida rules for service on corporate defendants.)

b. Personal jurisdiction is not proper in this case, since the defendant has no contacts with Massachusetts. It is not incorporated there, does not do business there (which might support general in personam jurisdiction), and the claim arises from contacts with Florida, not Massachusetts.

12. Service: Yes   Personal Jurisdiction: No

a. Here again, service is proper. Personal delivery of the summons and complaint to the president of the corporation is proper under Fed. R. Civ. P. 4(e)(2); it's hard to imagine a better way of letting Holland Corporation know it has been sued.

b. Personal jurisdiction is still not sufficient here. Although *Burnham v. Superior Court*, 495 U.S. 604 (1990), reaffirmed that service of process in the state confers jurisdiction over an *individual* defendant, it does not suggest that a corporation is subject to personal jurisdiction in a state simply because an officer is served while there for an unrelated purpose.

13. Service: No   Personal Jurisdiction: Yes

a. The answer to this one is a little bit tricky. Service here was proper in the sense that Federal Rule 4 authorized Chapman to serve process as she did. Rule 4(e)(2) authorizes service on an agent appointed by law to receive service, and the town clerk has been appointed by law — specifically, by Mass. Gen. L. ch. 227, §5A — to receive service on Sidney. However, compliance with the service rules is not enough to make service proper: It must also comply with the constitutional requirement in *Mullane v. Central Hanover Bank* that it be "reasonably calculated . . . to apprise interested parties of the pendency of the action . . ." 339 U.S. at 311. Simply delivering the papers to the town clerk will not satisfy that standard, since it provides no assurance of actual notice of the action to Sidney.

An earlier version of §5A was held invalid for failure to provide actual notice to the defendant. *Impoco v. Lauro,* 129 F. Supp. 543 (D. Mass. 1955). Subsequently, the following sentence was added to the statute: "When legal process against any such person is served upon such clerk, a copy of such process shall forthwith be sent by registered mail with a return receipt requested by the plaintiff to the defendant at his last known address." Under this provision the plaintiff must give the required notice by mail; if he does, service will be proper under Rule 4(e)(2) and constitutionally sufficient under *Mullane.*

b. Clearly, personal jurisdiction is not a problem in this case, since it arises from the defendant's contracting work done in the forum state. This would suffice to allow the Massachusetts court to assert jurisdiction under the "transacting business" provision of a long-arm statute and under *International Shoe.* Since the Massachusetts court could require Sidney to appear, the federal court in Massachusetts could do so as well, under Federal Rule 4(k)(1)(A).

14a. This is a tough question, which sometimes gets a tough answer. Here, Chapman has used a method of service that is authorized by Mass. R. Civ. P. 4(d)(1), and that is reasonably calculated to inform Sidney that he has been sued. However, it still went awry, and Sidney never found out about the case. Is the resulting judgment valid?

Most courts would hold that it is. Under *Mullane,* Chapman must use a method of service that is reasonably calculated actually to inform Sidney of the action. *Mullane* does not hold that the defendant must *actually find out about the suit* for notice to be adequate. See Restatement (Second) of Judgment, §2, comm. c. (where procedure used was reasonably likely to provide notice, valid judgment may be entered though the defendant does not actually learn of the action). Here, delivery to Sidney's home is sufficient under the *Mullane* standard, so the judgment is probably valid though Sidney never learned of it and therefore never had a chance to present his defense. (But see the next answer.)

b. If I were Sidney, I would move for relief from judgment under Rule 60(b). That rule gives a judge discretionary power to undo the finality of a judgment for various reasons, including "inadvertence, surprise, or excusable neglect" (Fed. R. Civ. P. 60(b)(1)) and "any other reason justifying relief from the judgment." Rule 60(b)(6). Although lack of actual notice may not render the judgment void, it certainly should satisfy the standard for reopening the case. The purpose of Rule 60(b) is to allow the court to relieve a party from the effect of a judgment—even a valid judgment—where fairness supports reopening the case. Sidney will have a good argument that this purpose would be served in his case, since he has never really had an opportunity to respond to the claim.

However, in some cases the equities might lead to denial of the motion for relief from judgment. Suppose, for example, that the suit involved an action to quiet title to land, that a judgment declaring Chapman the owner had entered, and the land had been sold to a third party after the judgment entered and a factory built on it. On those facts, allowing the judgment to be reopened would upset the legitimate expectations of third parties, and a judge might refuse to do it.

Unlucky Number Fifteen

15. Service: No   Personal Jurisdiction: Maybe

a. In this case, National's counsel has used a method of service that is proper under the Massachusetts rules for serving an individual outside the state. Ma. R. Civ. P. 4(e)(3). Ordinarily, this would be authorized by Fed. R. Civ. P. 4(e)(1), which allows use of state service methods. However, §4(e) begins with the loaded caveat, "except as otherwise provided by federal law." Here, federal law provides otherwise: It requires service by the federal marshals, for reasons unknown to me. If a federal statute mandates another method of service, the methods in Rule 4(e) do not apply.

b. Interestingly, personal jurisdiction may be proper here, even though Drayton has no contacts with Massachusetts. The court would *not* obtain personal jurisdiction through Rule 4(k)(1)(A), which allows a federal court to exercise jurisdiction if the local state court could. State court jurisdiction is limited by the Fourteenth Amendment due process clause, and it would be unconstitutional under the Fourteenth Amendment due process clause for a Massachusetts court to assert jurisdiction over Drayton, who has no contacts with Massachusetts.

However, Rule 4(k)(1)(C) allows the federal court to assert jurisdiction in interpleader cases without regard to the limits on the state court's jurisdiction. Because jurisdiction is being asserted by a federal court rather than a state court, the constitutional restriction on its exercise of personal jurisdiction is found in the Fifth Amendment due process clause, not in the Fourteenth Amendment. Most courts have held that, under the Fifth Amendment due process clause, a federal court may exercise personal jurisdiction over a defendant who has contacts *with the United States as a whole*. Drayton certainly has such contacts, based on his ownership of the building in Georgia and his residence in Louisiana.

On this rationale, the court might find jurisdiction over Drayton proper. But some federal courts have held that the Fifth Amendment due process clause also imposes a fairness limit on where a suit can be brought, similar to the limit on minimum contacts jurisdiction under *International Shoe*. See, e.g. *Peay v. Bellsouth Medical Assistance Plan*, 205 F.3d 1206

(10th Cir. 2000) ("where jurisdiction is invoked based on nationwide service of process, the Fifth Amendment requires the plaintiff's choice of forum to be fair and reasonable to the defendant"). A court which takes this view would probably not find that suit in Massachusetts, against a Louisiana citizen for a claim arising in Georgia, comports with this due process limit.

And you thought you wanted to be a litigator.

18

Getting Off Easy: The Motion to Dismiss

Introduction

The defendant usually responds to the plaintiff's complaint by filing an answer as provided in Fed. R. Civ. P. 12(a). (For an example, see the answer to the Schulansky complaint, Chapter 31) However, the rules provide a second option in limited circumstances: If the defendant has certain preliminary objections to the suit, she may avoid answering immediately by filing a motion to dismiss the complaint instead under Fed. R. Civ. P. 12(b). See Jones's motion to dismiss in the Schulansky case, infra p. 597.

Two important points about such "pre-answer motions" should be made at the outset. *First,* filing a pre-answer motion under Rule 12(b) is an *alternative* to answering the complaint. A defendant who moves to dismiss under Rule 12(b) need not answer the complaint until after the motion is decided. See Rule 12(a)(4). If she prevails on the motion, she may never have to answer. This can be a strong tactical advantage since filing an answer may require the defendant to admit damaging allegations in the complaint or undertake substantial factual investigation.

Second, filing a pre-answer motion is entirely optional. Defendants are not required to use it to raise the defenses listed in Rule 12(b); each may be raised in the answer instead. See Fed. R. Civ. P. 12(b), which provides that the listed defenses may, "at the option of the pleader," be raised by pre-answer motion. What, then, is the point of providing a separate device for raising these particular defenses?

Essentially, the Rules provide this device in order to short-circuit the usual litigation process in cases in which the defendant has a valid defense, evident from the outset, to the court proceeding with the case. These defenses are of two kinds. Some of the 12(b) defenses are immediately fatal to the plaintiff's case. For example, if the court lacks subject matter jurisdiction over the action (Rule 12(b)(1)), it has no power to render a valid judgment; it would be a useless charade for it to go any further with the action. The same is true if the court is not a proper venue (Rule 12(b)(3)) or lacks personal jurisdiction over the defendant (Rule 12(b)(2)). A defendant should not even be required to answer the allegations in the complaint if the case has been brought in the wrong court. To protect the defendant from such inappropriate suits, Rule 12(b) provides an avenue to secure immediate dismissal in cases where the court is powerless to do anything else.

Other defenses under Rule 12(b) raise defects in the procedure by which the plaintiff has initiated the action. The defense of insufficiency of service of process (Rule 12(b)(5)), for example, attacks the manner in which the complaint was served. Similarly, the Rule 12(b)(7) defense of failure to join an indispensable party asserts a defect in the scope of the suit as the plaintiff has framed it. Generally, these are curable defects that will not require dismissal of the suit but will have to be remedied before the case proceeds. If service of process was insufficient, for example, the court will order proper service of the complaint before proceeding. Similarly, if an indispensable party has not been joined, the court will not automatically dismiss the case but will order joinder of the indispensable party if feasible.[1] In these cases the Rule provides a mechanism to flush out preliminary problems and resolve them before getting into the substantive work of the lawsuit.

The 12(b)(6) dismissal, unlike the other pre-answer defenses, challenges the substantive merits of the complaint. The defendant who moves to dismiss "for failure to state a claim upon which relief can be granted" asserts that even if the plaintiff were to prove all the allegations in the complaint, she would still not be entitled to any relief. It hardly makes sense for the court to entertain the action and decide the facts if the law will not provide any relief to the plaintiff even if she proves everything alleged in the complaint. An example would be a suit for negligent infliction of emotional distress in a jurisdiction that does not recognize a right to recover for emotional distress unless the plaintiff also suffers physical injury. If physical injury is required, and the plaintiff cannot allege it, the court might just as well dismiss at the outset since the plaintiff will not be entitled to relief if she is allowed to proceed with the suit.

---

1. In some cases these defects may not be curable. For example, joinder of an indispensable party might destroy diversity, thus undermining the federal court's subject matter jurisdiction. In such cases the court may have to dismiss.

Although the 12(b)(6) motion is unique in attacking the substantive merits of the plaintiff's claim, it is akin to the "fatal" defenses under 12(b)(1), (2), and (3), in that it can lead to dismissal if it is upheld by the court. However, a plaintiff whose *complaint* has been dismissed under Rule 12(b)(6) will virtually always be given at least one opportunity to amend the complaint to state a compensable claim, before her *case* is dismissed.[2] If the plaintiff has grounds to plead all the elements of a proper claim, but had simply failed to include them all in the original complaint, she can amend the complaint to state a compensable claim once the defect is brought to her attention. (For example, a plaintiff who had suffered a physical injury, but had simply failed to allege it in her complaint for emotional distress, could amend to add an allegation of physical injury.) On the other hand, if the plaintiff is unable to amend to state a compensable claim because the facts do not support a necessary element of the claim, then the case will be dismissed. The Rule 12(b)(6) motion is explored in more detail in Chapter 21.

Waiver of Defenses under Rule 12

So much for the consequences of raising 12(b) defenses. The more puzzling aspect of the rule is the consequences of *not* raising them. Rules 12(g) and (h), which govern those consequences, appear Byzantine at first but are more easily understood once their rationale is clear. Essentially, those subsections of the rule, read together (very carefully), provide that four of the 12(b) defenses will be waived if not raised in the defendant's first response to the complaint. If the defendant objects to personal jurisdiction, venue, the form of the process, or the method of service of process, she must raise those defenses in the pre-answer motion or (if she does not make a pre-answer motion) in the answer. If she fails to raise one of these four "disfavored" defenses in her initial response, she has waived the omitted defense for all time.

This result, hard though it may be to extract from the language of these subsections, makes good sense. If the defendant has suffered any prejudice from these preliminary defects, she should become aware of it when the complaint is served upon her. For example, if the suit is filed in a state that has no personal jurisdiction over the defendant, she should be able to tell that from the caption of the complaint (indicating where the suit has been filed) and the facts alleged in it, which indicate what events gave rise to the claim. Thus, it is not unreasonable to put the burden upon the defendant to raise these defects

---

2. Some circuits hold that the plaintiff has an absolute right to amend under Fed. R. Civ. P. 15(a). See e.g., *Car Carriers, Inc. v. Ford Motor Co.*, 745 F.2d 1101, 1111 (7th Cir. 1984). Others allow such amendments as a matter of discretion. *Triplett v. Leflore County, Oklahoma*, 712 F.2d 444, 446 (10th Cir. 1983). See generally Moore's ¶15.07[2].

right away. If the rule did not require these objections to be raised immediately, the court and the parties might proceed to adjudicate the suit, only to learn down the road that the court had no right to do so. A defendant might even keep procedural objections in her back pocket and spring them on the court and the plaintiff later on if things go badly on the merits. To avoid such tactics and wasted judicial resources, the rule provides that the defendant must raise these defenses immediately or waive them by her failure to do so.[3]

An Early Question

1.   Presumably, if the complaint fails to state a clam upon which relief can be granted, the defendant should be able to tell that from the complaint alone. Why, then, did the rulemakers not provide that the Rule 12(b)(6) defense is also waived if it is left out of a pre-answer motion?

These rules may seem fussy and technical to you, but it is well worth your while to learn them now. Many a lawyer has re-read Rule 12 in a cold sweat to find out if she has unwittingly waived her client's rights. It is one thing to lose a case by doing the wrong thing, but it is all the more embarassing to lose it by doing nothing. Under Rule 12 the decision to do nothing is fraught with consequences for your client.

EXAMPLES

Traps for the Unwary

2.   David files a complaint for assault against Goliath. Goliath files a timely motion to dismiss for insufficient service of process. Several months later, the judge denies the motion to dismiss and so notifies the parties.
     May Goliath, after being notified of the denial of his motion:
     a. move to dismiss for lack of personal jurisdiction?
     b. answer, including the defense of lack of personal jurisdiction in the answer?
     c. move to dismiss for failure to state a claim upon which relief can be granted?
     d. answer, including the defense that the complaint fails to state a claim upon which relief can be granted in the answer?
     e. move for a more definite statement under Rule 12(e)?
     f. move to dismiss for lack of subject matter jurisdiction?

---

3. While a defending party waives "disfavored" defenses by failing to raise them properly under Rule 12, asserting those defenses under Rule 12 may not suffice to preserve them. The party must also press these defenses *after* raising them. See *Hamilton v. Atlas Turner, Inc.*, 197 F.3d 58 (2nd Cir. 1999) (although defendant asserted personal jurisdiction defense in its answer, it forfeited the defense by failing to press it over four years of litigation).

3.   After the court denies his motion to dismiss for insufficient service of process, Goliath answers the complaint. May he include in his answer:
   a. a defense of improper venue?
   b. a claim that the court lacks subject matter jurisdiction over the action?
   c. a defense that David has given him a signed release from liability on all claims arising out of the alleged assault?

4.   Suppose that Goliath decides to answer David's complaint instead of filing a Rule 12(b) motion to dismiss or any other pre-answer motion. May he include in his answer:
   a. a defense of insufficiency of service of process?
   b. a defense that the complaint fails to state a claim upon which relief can be granted?
   c. a motion for a more definite statement?
   d. a defense that the court lacks subject matter jurisdiction over the action?

5.   Assume that Goliath's first response to the complaint is to move for a more definite statement under Rule 12(e). The judge grants the motion and orders David to file a clearer complaint within ten days. David complies. After Goliath receives the more definite statement, may he:
   a. move to dismiss for insufficiency of service of process?
   b. move to dismiss for failure to state a claim upon which relief can be granted?
   c. answer, raising the defense of insufficiency of service of process?
   d. answer, raising the defense of failure to state a claim upon which relief can be granted?

6.   If Goliath responds to the complaint by moving to dismiss for insufficiency of service of process, may he move at the same time to dismiss for improper venue and lack of personal jurisdiction?

7.   What is the difference between the defense of insufficiency of service of process (Rule 12(b)(5)) and insufficiency of process (Rule 12(b)(4))?

8.   Goliath does not raise *any* objections by pre-answer motion. He simply answers the complaint, denying the substance of the plaintiff's claims. Three months later, he files a motion to dismiss for lack of personal jurisdiction. What will the court do?

Permutations

9.   Assume that Goliath answers the complaint and includes in his answer a counterclaim against David, seeking damages from David for calling him a bully. David contends that the counterclaim does not state a claim upon which relief can be granted. What should he do?

10. David files his claim for assault. Goliath moves to dismiss it under Rule 12(b)(3). While the motion is pending, David decides to amend his complaint to add a claim for battery. May he do so without leave of court?

(Consider the first sentence of Rule 15(a) and Rules 7(a) and 7(b) in analyzing this example.)

11. David sues Goliath in state court. Five days later Goliath files a notice of removal in the appropriate federal district court. Three days after that he files a Rule 12(b)(2) motion to dismiss for lack of personal jurisdiction in the federal court. Is the motion proper?

12. One more variation, and then we will banish David and Goliath back to antiquity. David sues for assault, and Goliath files an answer, denying that he intentionally assaulted David. Several months later he realizes that the court lacks personal jurisdiction over him and seeks to amend his answer, with leave of court under Rule 15(a), to raise this defense. May he do so?

A Useful but Audacious Exercise

13. Students always express frustration with Rule 12(g) and (h) on the ground that they are unreadable and hypertechnical legalisms. If you agree, try to rewrite those two subsections in clearer terms without changing their meaning.

EXPLANATIONS

An Early Question

1. It is true that a defendant should be able to tell that a complaint is legally insufficient from the complaint itself, so that it would be arguably justifiable for Rule 12 to provide for waiver of the Rule 12(b)(6) defense unless it is asserted immediately. However, the defense of failure to state a claim is a fundamental challenge to the merits of the plaintiff's claim. If the defendant really has committed no legal wrong, she should not be held to waive this basic defense by the mere failure to raise it at the beginning of the suit. If this were the rule, we would be back to the rigidities of the common law, which forced the parties to stick to their original pleadings even if subsequent investigation uncovered basic defenses or theories that went to the merits of the dispute. The four disfavored defenses are distinguishable since these involve procedural objections, which should be apparent to the defendant as soon as she receives the summons and complaint.

In addition, it may not always be easy to determine whether a complaint fails to state a claim at the outset. It may be clear enough in a case like my emotional distress hypo, but imagine a securities fraud case involving alleged violations of complex statutory filing and disclosure requirements. It might be very difficult to determine at the outset whether such a claim is legally sufficient. On balance, the system properly favors preservation of this basic objection over the efficiency gained from forcing defendants to raise it immediately.

Traps for the Unwary

2a. No. Rule 12(g) provides that a defendant who chooses to make a pre-answer motion must include in that motion all of the 12(b) defenses she has at the time. If she leaves an available defense out, Rule 12(g) bars her from making another pre-answer motion based on that objection. Here, Goliath must have known, if he received the complaint at all, that he was being ordered to appear before a court that might not have jurisdiction over him. Since the personal jurisdiction defense was "available" to him at the time he filed his first motion to dismiss, it could have been consolidated in the first motion. Rule 12(g), first sentence. Because Goliath omitted it, Rule 12(g) provides that he cannot make a second motion to dismiss on this ground.

This provision prevents the defendant from nickel and diming the plaintiff to death by repeated motions to dismiss on different grounds. Otherwise, Goliath might make three or four successive motions, each on a single ground, and unduly delay the proceedings.

b. No again. Here Goliath seeks to raise in his answer a defense that he could have included in his pre-answer motion. Rule 12(g) does not cover this; it only bars Goliath from making a second pre-answer motion on this ground. However, Rule 12(h)(1)(A) does prevent him from raising it because he made a pre-answer motion but omitted this defense from it. Goliath does not have to file a pre-answer motion to dismiss at all, but if he decides to, the combination of Rule 12(g) and (h) forces him to put all four of these defenses in the motion or waive the ones he omits.

Don't be fooled by Rule 12(h)(1)(B), which appears to imply that these four defenses can be raised in either the motion to dismiss or the answer. True, they may be raised in either response, but if a defendant makes a pre-answer motion, she can't raise some in the pre-answer motion and reserve others for the answer. Subsection (h)(1) provides that these defenses are waived if the defendant makes a pre-answer motion and leaves them out (Rule 12(h)(1)(A)); or answers instead, and leaves them out (Rule 12(h)(1)(B)). The rule does not authorize the defendant to leave some out of a motion and then insert them in her answer.

c. Probably not. Since Goliath has made a pre-answer motion to dismiss, Rule 12(g) requires him to include in that motion all 12(b) defenses "then available" to him. The second sentence of the rule states that he cannot make a new pre-answer motion based on such defenses.

This does not mean, however, that Goliath has waived his right to raise this defense entirely. As example 1 indicates, this objection is too fundamental to be subject to any rigid early waiver requirements. Rule 12(g) only prevents Goliath from *making another pre-answer motion* on this ground. Rule 12(h)(2) allows him to raise it in his answer or by another motion after pleading or at the trial on the merits.

I said above that Goliath would "probably not" be allowed to move to dismiss on this ground. It is possible that his objection to service of process was that no copy of the complaint was served on him. If that were the case he would not have known what the complaint alleged and could not have had grounds to dismiss under Rule 12(b)(6). On those facts Goliath *would* be able to file a second pre-answer motion raising this defense since the 12(b)(6) defense was not "available" to him when he filed the first one. The fact that the judge denied the first motion makes this unlikely, however.

d. Yes. The 12(b)(6) objection may be raised in the answer, even though it was omitted from an earlier pre-answer motion. Rule 12(h)(2) expressly provides that this defense may be raised "in any pleading permitted or ordered under Rule 7(a)." An answer is clearly permitted (indeed, required) by Rule 7(a).

e. Probably not. The motion for a more definite statement raises the defense that the complaint is so unclear that the responding party cannot frame a meaningful response to it. This defense is "available" to the pleader as soon as the complaint is served on her and therefore should have been raised in Goliath's first pre-answer motion. Note that the carefully chosen language of Rule 12(g) (referring to defenses or objections "that this rule [i.e., Rule 12 in its entirety] permits to be raised by motion") requires consolidation of this 12(e) defense as well as the various 12(b) defenses.

There is a possibility, as in example 1c, that Goliath never received a copy of the complaint. If so, then he could hardly be expected to know that it would be incomprehensible when he did get it. If this were the case, the defense would not have been available to Goliath when he filed his first pre-answer motion, and he would be allowed to file a second motion on this ground.

f. The language of 12(g) would support an argument that this motion is barred. Rule 12(g) provides that a party who makes a pre-answer motion must consolidate all 12(b) defenses in the first motion and may not make a further motion on any of these grounds "except as provided in subdivision 12(h)(2)." However, despite the puzzling lack of reference to it in Rule 12(g), Rule 12(h)(3) provides that the objection of lack of subject matter jurisdiction may be raised at any time. That subsection provides that "[w]henever" it appears, by "suggestion of the parties or otherwise," that subject matter jurisdiction is lacking, the court shall dismiss the action. Presumably, "whenever" includes before an answer but after a pre-answer motion, and presumably "suggestion of the parties" may be by a second pre-answer motion. Because no court can act beyond its subject matter competence, a court will dismiss whenever the lack of jurisdiction is called to its attention.

3a. No. As soon as the complaint was served on Goliath, he was in a position to object to venue. Here Goliath made a pre-answer motion, and Rule 12(g) required him to include his objection to venue in his pre-answer motion or waive it. Because he did not include it in his first response to the complaint, it is lost, waived, gone forever.

Actually, it may not always be that easy for defendants to determine from the complaint that they have an objection to venue or to personal or subject matter jurisdiction. It may not be possible to tell from the complaint, for example, whether a corporate defendant is subject to personal jurisdiction in a district for purposes of 28 U.S.C. §1391(c) or whether all defendants reside in the same state. See 28 U.S.C. §1391(a)(1),(b)(1). Yet the rule requires immediate assertion of the defense. Clearly, if there is doubt as to the propriety of venue the defense should be raised, subject to the ethical restraints on pleading in Rule 11. If more time is needed to investigate before responding, counsel may move for an extension of time to file a response under Fed. R. Civ. P. 6(b).

b. Yes. As previously stated in example 2, Rule 12(h)(3) authorizes either party to raise this defense at any time.

c. Yes. This is not one of the preliminary defenses singled out in Rule 12(b) for special treatment. It is an affirmative defense on the merits to the plaintiff's claim, which properly should be raised in the answer. Indeed, it could not be raised in a pre-answer motion even if Goliath wished to: Rule 12(b) provides that all Goliath's defenses, except the seven listed in Rule 12(b) itself, must be presented in the answer.[4] Since this defense may not be raised before answering, it is certainly appropriate to put it in the answer.

4a. Yes. Rule 12 does not require Goliath to raise his defense of improper service in a pre-answer motion. It only requires that *if he makes such a motion,* he include all his preliminary defenses in it. He may simply file an answer including this defense, and it will be considered by the court in the same manner as if it had been raised by pre-answer motion. (See the answer in the *Schulansky* case, infra p. 568, which asserts an objection to personal jurisdiction that could have been presented by pre-answer motion under Rule 12(b)(2) instead.) The real difference is a tactical one: If Goliath answers, he must respond to the substantive allegations in the complaint. He must make his admissions and denials under Rule 8(b), raise his affirmative defenses under Rule 8(c), and assert his counterclaims under Rule 13. If he moves to dismiss, he may avoid, at least temporarily, the need to answer the plaintiff's allegations.[5]

b. Yes. As in the previous answer, Goliath has a choice to raise this in the answer instead of by pre-answer motion. Indeed, he may raise it in the answer even if he omitted it from a pre-answer motion. See example 2d.

---

4. However, the defense of release could be raised by a motion for summary judgment even before answering. See Fed. R. Civ. P. 56(b), authorizing a defendant to move for summary judgment at any time.

5. Filing a Rule 12(b) pre-answer motion does not, however, suspend the litigation. For example, the parties may engage in discovery, even while a motion is pending challenging the court's authority to hear the case. See, e.g., *Hand Tool Corp. v. Corcoran Partners, LTD.,* 852 F.2d 936, 945 (7th Cir. 1988).

c. No. The purpose of the motion for a more definite statement is to provide the defendant with a sufficiently clear statement of the plaintiff's allegations so that the defendant can meaningfully respond to them, either by filing a pre-answer motion or by answering the complaint. Consequently, Rule 12(e) requires the defendant to make this motion "before interposing a responsive pleading."

d. Yes. Rule 12(b) allows this to be raised by motion but Rule 12(h)(3) makes clear that whether or not a pre-answer motion was made, this basic defense may be raised in the answer or at any other time as well.

5a. No. The defense of insufficiency of service challenges the manner in which the complaint and summons were served upon the defendant. Goliath should have been aware of any defects in the method of service as soon as the papers were served upon him, even if the complaint itself was indecipherable. Since the defense was available to him when he filed the motion for a more definite statement, he should have joined it in that motion. Rule 12(g), read very carefully, says so; Rule 12(h)(1)(A) says that the defense is now waived.

b. Yes. This defense was presumably not "available" to Goliath when he filed his motion for a more definite statement because he couldn't figure out what the plaintiff's complaint was alleging. It is only after Goliath receives the clearer complaint that he is able to ascertain whether the plaintiff's allegations state a claim. Because this defense was not previously available, Rule 12(g) does not preclude Goliath from subsequently asserting it in another pre-answer motion, despite the usual command of Rule 12(g) that all pre-answer defenses be raised together.

c. No. Goliath should have been aware of defects in the method of service at the time he was served with the complaint. This defense was available to him when he filed the earlier Rule 12(e) motion, and Goliath waived the defense by failing to raise it there.

d. Yes. *First,* this defense was not available at the time the first motion was made. See example 5b. *Second,* this defense can be raised, even if it was omitted from a pre-answer motion. Rule 12(h)(2).

6. I threw this question in to see if you would stick to your guns and answer "absolutely." The defendant is not required to stake his case on one of these defenses if others may also be available to him. Not only may he assert multiple objections in a pre-answer motion under Rule 12(b), he *must* do so to avoid waiving them. That is the purpose of Rule 12(g) and (h).

7. The Rule 12(b)(4) motion challenges the adequacy of the summons itself, the court document served on the defendant that orders her to respond to the complaint. Rule 4(a) details the requirements of a proper summons. (For an example of a summons, see Chapter 29, p. 544) A motion to dismiss under Rule 12(b)(4) might allege that some requirement of that rule was omitted, such as the clerk's signature or the court seal.

By contrast, the Rule 12(b)(5) motion for insufficiency of service of process challenges the manner in which the complaint and summons were delivered to the defendant. See Chapter 17 concerning proper methods of serving process in the federal courts. A Rule 12(b)(5) motion by Goliath might be based, for example, on the ground that it was not left at his cave with a person of suitable age and discretion (see Rule 4(e)(2)) but at a neighbor's instead.

8. The court will refuse to entertain the motion. Goliath has waived the personal jurisdiction defense by failing to raise it in his response to the complaint. The whole point of the complexities of Rule 12(g) and (h) is to provide for the automatic waiver of the four disfavored preliminary objections, unless they are brought forth in the first response to the complaint. Goliath did not include this defense in his answer (his first response to the complaint), and so it is waived by operation of the rule.

Permutations

9. Rule 12(b) governs not only an original defendant's options in responding to a complaint, but also those of other defending parties. See Rule 12(b), first sentence (referring to defenses to "any pleading, whether a claim, counterclaim, cross-claim or third-party claim"). Here, David, as a defending party on Goliath's counterclaim, has the same options for responding to the counterclaim that Goliath had in responding to the original complaint. David may present his defense of failure to state a claim by a pre-answer motion to dismiss or in his answer to the counterclaim, just as the original defendant may. The same would be true of a defendant responding to a cross-claim or a third-party complaint.

10. Rule 15(a) allows a party to amend her pleading once "as a matter of course"—that is, without leave of court—before her opponent files a responsive pleading. Is Goliath's motion to dismiss a responsive pleading? No. Rule 7(a) enumerates possible pleadings, including complaints, answers, and replies; motions are provided for in a separate subsection (7(b)). See *Car Carriers, Inc. v. Ford Motor Co.*, 745 F.2d 1101, 1111 (7th Cir. 1984). Since a motion is not a pleading, Goliath has not yet filed a responsive pleading, and David is free to amend once without the court's permission. Indeed, if the court is slow to decide the motion, this period for an amendment as of right may go on for some time.

11. In cases like this my students sometimes respond that Goliath has waived his right to object to personal jurisdiction because he did not include the objection in his first response to the complaint—the notice of removal. However, if you analyze Rules 12(g) and (h) carefully, you will conclude that Goliath's removal does not waive his right to object to personal jurisdiction. Rule 12(g) does not bar the motion, because Goliath has not made a previous

pre-answer motion. And Rule 12 (h)(1) does not bar the motion, because the objection was not left out of a previous Rule 12 motion or answer.

Filing a notice of removal simply moves the case from the state to the federal court; it does not affect the right to raise Rule 12(b) defenses by pre-answer motion once you get there. Once the case has been removed, the defendant must respond to the complaint by motion or answer. See Fed. R. Civ. P. 81(c), which provides that, after removing, the defendant shall "answer or present the other defenses or objections available under these rules . . ." (i.e., move to dismiss under Rule 12(b)) within a specified number of days.

12. Goliath's train of thought here is obvious. He has run afoul of the rule by failing to include the jurisdictional defense in his answer. Under Rule 12(h)(1), therefore, he has waived the personal jurisdiction defense. When Goliath realizes his oversight, he tries to get the defense into the answer by amendment under Rule 15, asking the court to accept the amendment and treat it as though it had been included in the original answer. (See Rule 15(c)(2), which provides that an amendment "relates back" to the date of the original pleading if certain requirements are met.)

If this worked, it would provide an easy end-run around the waiver provisions of Rule 12, at least if the judge granted the motion. It won't work though. Rule 12(h)(1)(B) provides that the defense is lost if it is left out of a pre-answer motion, a responsive pleading, "or an amendment thereof permitted by Rule 15(a) to be made as a matter of course."[6] As usual, the rule-makers thought about this possibility and impliedly rejected Goliath's tactic by limiting amendments to cure such omissions to those filed as a matter of course. Goliath only had 20 days to amend as a matter of right (Rule 15(a)); since several months have elapsed, he has waived his objection to personal jurisdiction. Even if the judge was willing to grant leave to amend, it would be inconsistent with the limitation in Rule 12(h)(1)(B) to allow the defendant to do so. *Morgan Guaranty Trust Co. of New York v. Blum*, 649 F.2d 342, 345 (5th Cir. 1981); 5A Wright and Miller §1391, p.752.

A Useful but Audacious Exercise

13. If you made a real effort to rewrite these subsections, you will have developed some grudging respect for the work of the rule-makers. Their version is elegant and precise, although difficult to understand without considerable study. Here is my rewrite; it may be clearer in some respects, but I still like their version better.

> **12(g).** A party who makes a motion under this rule may join with it any other motions authorized by this rule that the party then has available to him. If a party makes a pre-answer motion under this

---

6. Amendments as a matter of course may only be made to a responsive pleading within 20 days of filing the pleading. Fed. R. Civ. P. 15(a).

rule, he must include in it any defense then available to him under Rule 12 (b)(2), (3), (4), or (5), or 12(e). Any of these defenses is waived if it was available and omitted from a pre-answer motion.

12(h)(1). If a party does not make a pre-answer motion, he must include any defense he has under Rule 12(b)(2), (3), (4), or (5) in his responsive pleading or in an amendment to it permitted by Rule 15(a) as a matter of course. If he fails to do so, the omitted defenses are waived.

12(h)(2). A defense of failure to state a claim upon which relief can be granted or failure to join a party indispensable under Rule 19 may be raised by pre-answer motion under Rule 12(b). If omitted from a pre-answer motion, these defenses may be raised in any pleading permitted or ordered under Rule 7(a) or by a motion for judgment on the pleadings or at the trial on the merits.

12(h)(3). The defense of lack of subject matter jurisdiction may be raised in a pre-answer motion, in a responsive pleading, or at any time by suggestion of the parties or the court. Whenever it appears by suggestion of the parties or otherwise that the court lacks jurisdiction over the subject matter, the court shall dismiss the action.

My version sounds more like a civil procedure class than a provision of the Rules. In addition, if you read my version very carefully, you will find a few cases that aren't clearly dealt with.

19

The Scope of Discovery: The Rules Giveth, and the Rules Taketh Away

Introduction

The big news in civil procedure over the last century has been the demise of pleading and the rise of discovery. In the early common law, pleading played a central role in defining the issues and the factual contentions of the parties. Plaintiffs learned as much as they could about their cases before commencing suit, and then pleaded their cases based on their best guess as to what they would be able to prove. Once the pleadings were closed, the shape of the case was settled; it only remained to be seen whether the parties could prove what they had alleged.

Modern civil practice turns this approach on its head. Under our current notice pleading rules, the complaint and the answer provide a tentative view of the parties' positions, based on preliminary research and investigation. Once issue is joined, full development of the parties' positions evolves through the process of discovery, the court-mandated production of information from other parties and non-party witnesses. As discovery puts flesh on the bare-bones case presented in the pleadings, the parties may usually amend those pleadings to conform to their evolving understanding of the dispute.

The major tools of discovery include interrogatories under Fed. R. Civ. P. 33, requests for production of documents under Fed. R. Civ. P. 34, oral depositions under Fed. R. Civ. P. 30, and automatic disclosure under Rule 26(a). These tools are discussed in detail in the next chapter; this one addresses more general issues concerning the permissible scope of discovery under the Federal Rules of Civil Procedure.

Perhaps the most fundamental point about discovery is that it is conducted by the parties, not by the court. Interrogatories and requests for production are sent by counsel for the parties to each other, and responses are sent back by counsel. Depositions are scheduled and conducted by counsel. The judge is not present at the depositions, nor does she screen interrogatories and document requests before they are sent. She is there to assist in scheduling discovery and resolving disputes that arise during the exchange, but does not directly participate in the exchange herself.

However, the devices of discovery, established by court rule and enforceable by the court, give counsel for the parties powerful mechanisms for demanding the production of evidence from those who have it. It really is a remarkable system when you think about it. Through discovery requests, counsel may force opposing parties and other witnesses to give oral testimony on any issue in the case, and can force opponents to produce even the most damaging "smoking gun" documents lurking in their confidential files. There is nothing inevitable about this liberal approach to discovery. In civil law systems, the development of the case rests primarily in the hands of the judge. Even here, discovery is much more limited in criminal cases than it is under the civil rules.

The Rules Giveth: The Basic Test of Relevance

The rules of discovery are powerful not only because they compel the production of evidence, but also because of the broad scope of the evidence that must be produced. The scope of discovery is governed by Rule 26(b)(1):

> Parties may obtain discovery regarding any matter, not privileged, that is relevant to the claim or defense of any party, including the existence, description, nature, custody, condition, and location of any books, documents, or other tangible things and the identity and location of persons having knowledge of any discoverable matter. For good cause, the court may order discovery of any matter relevant to the subject matter involved in the action. Relevant information need not be admissible at the trial if the discovery appears reasonably calculated to lead to the discovery of admissible evidence.

This provision, which allows parties to obtain virtually any information relevant to the claims or defenses raised in the case, seems about as broad as it could be. Interestingly, however, until very recently the scope of discovery under Rule 26(b)(1) was even broader: Until 2000 the standard allowed discovery of "any matter, not privileged, relevant to the subject matter involved in the pending action." Under this broader language the Supreme Court had held that a party could

> discover any matter that bears on, or that reasonably could lead to other matter involved that could bear on, any issue that is or may be in the case. . . . Consistently with the notice pleading system established by the Rule, discovery is not limited to issues raised by the pleadings, for discovery itself is designed to help define and clarify the issues.

Oppenheimer Fund, Inc. v. Sanders, 437 U.S. 340, 351 & n. 12 (1978). The Advisory Committee on the Civil Rules recommended the somewhat narrower "relevant to the claim or defense of any party" language in an effort to rein in excessive discovery at the outer bounds of relevance. Under this revised provision, discovery will be limited to the issues framed by the parties' pleadings. However, it remains to be seen whether discovery will really be more restricted under the new standard; the new rule may be narrower than the anything-goes standard of the prior rule, but it is still extremely broad.[1]

While the presumptive reach of discovery is broad under Rule 26(b)(1), information is not automatically subject to production if it meets the broad relevance standard. Rule 26 provides that relevant information is discoverable unless "otherwise limited by the court." A party who receives a discovery request may seek a "protective order" from the court, under Rule 26(c), limiting discovery—even of information clearly within the relevance standard in Rule 26(b)(1)—"to protect a party or person from annoyance, embarrassment, oppression or undue burden or expense." Under Rule 26(c), the court may enter a protective order limiting discovery for various reasons, including the burden and expense of producing the information, the potential for revealing intimate facts which should remain private, the potential for use of discovery to annoy or intimidate an opponent, to protect proprietary business information, or for other reasons.

The Rules Taketh Away: Privilege Objections to Discovery

Although Rule 26 creates a broad presumption in favor of discovery of all relevant evidence, it also taketh away through several important exceptions to discovery. Rule 26(b)(1) itself limits discovery to information that is "not privileged." Courts have long recognized that some evidence, even though

---

1. Clearly, the rule makers *intended* the new standard to be more restrictive: The second sentence of the new rule allows the court to expand discovery to the reach of the old standard where necessary. There would be no point to this provision if there were no difference in the two standards.

relevant to litigation, should be protected from disclosure in a lawsuit. Despite the general principle that "the law is entitled to every person's evidence," courts have created privileges where some policy favoring confidentiality is judged to be more compelling than access to the evidence. "Their warrant is the protection of interests and relationships that, rightly or wrongly, are regarded as of sufficient social importance to justify some sacrifice of availability of evidence relevant to the administration of justice." McCormick on Evidence, 5th ed. 1999 §72, p. 114.

The classic example is the attorney-client privilege, which bars inquiry into communications between a client and her counsel in the course of legal representation. The rationale for the privilege is that effective representation requires full and frank communication between lawyer and client. See *Upjohn v. United States,* 449 U.S. 383, 389 (1981). Such communication will be inhibited if opposing counsel could essentially "listen in" on these communications by asking about them at trial — or in discovery. If Murrow sends an interrogatory to Pyle, asking him whether he admitted to his lawyer that he ran the red light at the time of the accident, Pyle's counsel may respond "The defendant objects to Interrogatory #7 on the ground that the requested information is protected by the attorney-client privilege." Although Pyle's conversations with his lawyer about the accident are relevant to Murrow's claim under the broad standard in Rule 26(b)(1), the policy of confidentiality underlying the attorney-client privilege is deemed to outweigh the opponent's need for this information.

A variety of other privileges are also recognized by the courts. For example, many states recognize a privilege for communications between priest and penitent, between doctor and patient, between psychotherapist and patient, and between husband and wife. In recent years, more exotic privileges have been claimed and sometimes recognized, such as a news reporter's privilege to keep sources confidential, a scholar's privilege to protect confidential sources, a teacher-pupil privilege, and others. See generally Haydock, Herr & Stempel, Fundamentals of Pretrial Litigation (3rd ed.) 1994 217-219. Such privileges may be created by state or federal common law or statute or — as in the case of the privilege against self-incrimination — in the U.S. Constitution. The important point for our purposes is not to analyze privileges in detail, but to recognize that courts may choose to protect information despite its relevance, and that where they do, the information need not be disclosed in discovery.

The Rules Taketh Away: "Work Product" Objections

A second major exception to the broad scope of discovery under Rule 26(b)(1) is the so-called work product privilege, which bars production of certain materials developed in anticipation of litigation. The work product privilege was recognized in *Hickman v. Taylor,* 329 U.S. 495 (1947), in which plaintiff's counsel in a wrongful death case sought discovery of defense counsel's notes of interviews with various witnesses to the tugboat sinking that caused the death. He also requested, through interrogatories, the substance of other interviews that Fortenbaugh (the defendant's lawyer) had conducted but had not written down. In other words, he wanted Fortenbaugh to write out his memory of the interviews in response to the interrogatories.

Fortenbaugh balked at producing either his written notes of the interviews or information on the interviews that had not been recorded. He argued that allowing this discovery would improperly interfere with the privacy of his trial preparation.

Some Early Questions

1a. Does the information sought in *Hickman* satisfy the general standard for discovery in Rule 26(b)(1)?

    b. Why couldn't Fortenbaugh raise the attorney-client privilege to avoid producing the requested materials?

    c. Two types of statements were sought in *Hickman*: those in writing, and the content of those that were taken orally. Which is more intrusive, and why?

    d. How could plaintiff's counsel have obtained the requested information without getting it from Fortenbaugh?

    e. Since the information was available by other means, why did plaintiff's counsel seek it from Fortenbaugh instead?

When *Hickman* was decided, Rule 26 provided no explicit basis for an exception to discovery for "trial preparation materials." However, the plaintiff's efforts to "secure the production of written statements and mental impressions contained in the files and the mind of the attorney . . ." (329 U.S. at 509) troubled the Supreme Court for several reasons. First, allowing such discovery would interfere with the confidentiality of trial preparation. Opposing counsel would be able to "psych out" her adversary's strategy by learning through discovery who she had interviewed and what issues she had pursued in those interviews. It would be very difficult to separate factual information in trial preparation materials from the thought processes of the lawyer who developed them; if such discovery were allowed, it could reveal much about an adversary's legal theories, evaluation of witnesses, and plans for trial and settlement. If such discovery were routinely allowed, lawyers would become reluctant to keep written records, an approach hardly calculated to improve the quality of representation.

Second, the court expressed concern that allowing discovery of trial preparation materials would allow lawyers to ride on their adversary's coattails in preparing for trial, by letting opposing counsel do all the work, and then obtaining the results through discovery. That might not be a good way to prepare for trial — indeed, it certainly would not be — but it would be a temptation that the system ought not to encourage. Third, the *Hickman* court expressed concern about the prospect of lawyers ending up as witnesses in their own cases if the statements they produced contradicted other testimony from the same witness.

Based on these concerns, the *Hickman* Court denied production of the requested information. However, the Court did not categorically bar production of all such "attorney work product." Instead, the Court indicated that written statements given by witnesses might be subject to discovery if the party seeking discovery made a sufficient showing of need for the material and inability to obtain it through other means. 329 U.S. at 511-512. At the same time, the Court expressed considerable doubt that an attorney's mental impressions or personal notes on a witness interview would ever be subject to discovery.

Some twenty years after *Hickman,* the federal rule makers partially codified the "work product" doctrine in Fed. R. Civ. P. 26(b)(3). That subsection provides that "documents and tangible things . . . prepared in anticipation of litigation by or for another party or by or for that other party's representative" can only be obtained in discovery if the requesting party demonstrates that she has substantial need for the materials and cannot obtain substantially equivalent information through other means without undue hardship. Rule 26(b)(3) further provides that, *even where such a showing is made,* the "mental impressions, conclusions, opinions or legal theories of an attorney" shall be protected from disclosure.

Thus, today, claims of "work product privilege" regarding documents or other tangible items are analyzed under Rule 26(b)(3). The rule creates three categories of "work product." First, as to documents prepared in anticipation of litigation that contains information that can reasonably be obtained through other means, discovery is barred. For example, on the facts of *Hickman,* where the witnesses involved were available for plaintiff's counsel to interview or depose herself, discovery of statements made by those witnesses to the defendant's counsel would be denied. Second, if the requesting party demonstrates that she has a substantial need for materials developed in anticipation of litigation, and that similar information cannot be obtained through other means without substantial hardship, the court may order production of the materials. Third, opposing counsel's thought process in preparing a case, such as legal theories or litigation strategy (often called "opinion work product"), cannot be discovered under the rule.[2]

---

2. Rule 26(b)(3) (second paragraph) also allows a party to obtain a statement made by that party concerning the events in suit at any time, without any showing of particular need.

The Rules Giveth and Taketh Away: Discovery of Experts

Most witnesses testify as to facts relevant to the action, such as who entered the intersection first, how many tons of sand were delivered to the worksite, or whether the defendant made harassing comments to the plaintiff. In many cases, however, parties also offer the testimony of "expert" witnesses on issues in the case. An expert witness is a person whose testimony, because of her specialized knowledge, skill, experience, training, or education, will assist the trier of fact in understanding the facts and reaching conclusions on the contested issues. Fed. R. Evid. 702.

An expert may be used to provide important background information to help the trier of fact understand the case, such as how a hip replacement operation is performed, the proper procedure for supporting a bridge, or the manner in which electronic fund transfers are accomplished between banks. Experts may also offer *opinions* on issues critical to the case. An epidemiologist may testify as to whether a chemical released by the defendant caused the plaintiff's illness. A psychiatrist may testify as to whether psychiatric care was provided in accordance with professional standards. A medical actuary may testify as to the likely cost of operations the plaintiff will require at various times in the future. Where the issues require experts to assist the jury, both sides will likely offer expert testimony.

In addition to such "testifying experts," parties often hire experts to help them understand the issues in a case, even though they do *not* plan to use experts as witnesses at trial (or plan to use a different expert at trial). In a complex construction case, for example, counsel might hire an experienced construction manager to help her understand the proper sequence of construction, the propriety of change orders demanded by the contractor, and whether materials used complied with the contract specifications. In a surgical malpractice case, counsel might retain a surgeon experienced in the type of procedure in issue, to analyze whether the procedure was performed properly and whether it caused the plaintiff's injury. In this chapter, I will refer to these experts as "non-testifying experts."

There is little doubt that the knowledge experts can provide about complex issues in a case is relevant to the claims or defenses in the case, so that their testimony is within the presumptive scope of discovery under Rule 26(b)(1). However, the Federal Rules (and similar state rules) contain special provisions restricting the right to obtain pre-trial discovery from other parties' expert witnesses. Under Federal Rule 26(a)(2), parties are required to disclose the names of their *testifying* experts at least 90 days before trial, together with a report concerning their opinions and the bases of those opinions, their qualifications, compensation, and other information. After disclosure, testifying experts may be deposed as well. Rule 26(b)(4)(A). This broad right under the Rules to discovery from testifying experts culminates a long trend toward liberal discovery based on the recognition that experts cannot be effectively cross-examined at trial without the opportunity to conduct discovery concerning their opinions and the bases for those opinions. See Wright and Miller §§2029-2031.1.

Non-testifying experts, however, are treated quite differently. Rule 26(a) does not require disclosure of the identity or opinions of non-testifying experts, and Rule 26(b)(4)(B) provides that a party may only seek discovery concerning non-testifying experts upon a showing of "exceptional circumstances." This protection echoes the similar protection for work product under Rule 26(b)(3)), and for similar reasons. Non-testifying experts are fully involved in the preparation of a case for trial, including educating counsel on the procedures and lore of a specialized profession, developing theories of recovery, sifting relevant testimony, producing exhibits, and preparing witnesses to testify. Allowing discovery from these crucial participants would allow counsel to delve deeply into her opponent's trial strategy, and would stultify open exchange between counsel and her own experts.

It is useful to analyze problems concerning the scope of discovery in much the same sequence as they are discussed in this introduction. That is, ask first whether the information is within the broad presumptive scope of discovery under Rule 26(b)(1), and then whether one of the exceptions to discovery of relevant information applies. In analyzing the following examples, assume that the Federal Rules apply.

EXAMPLES

The Rules Giveth: Relevance

2.   Liebling was injured using a pair of electric hedgeclippers manufactured by the Miller Manufacturing Company. He sues Miller, alleging that it negligently manufactured the hedgeclippers, by leaving a bare wire inside that caused an electric shock. During discovery, he sends a Rule 34 request for documents that includes a request for all written warnings provided with the clippers concerning risks that the clippers posed to users. Miller objects to this request on the ground that it is relevant to a negligent failure to warn or strict liability theory, and Liebling has only pleaded a different theory, that the hedgeclippers were negligently manufactured. Is the objection valid?

3.   When Liebling files suit, Miller Corp. responds by filing a motion to dismiss under Fed. R. Civ. P. 12(b)(2) for lack of personal jurisdiction.

   a. Liebling sends interrogatories to Miller inquiring about its business contacts with the forum state and the manner in which the offending clippers entered the state. Must Miller answer the interrogatories?

   b. Liebling sends interrogatories to Miller asking questions about the design of its hedgeclippers and complaints from consumers about injuries using them. Must Miller answer the interrogatories?

4.   Liebling sends interrogatories to Miller requesting information on any changes it had made to the design of its clippers "from the date of the accident to the present." Miller objects, on the ground that changes after the date of the accident are irrelevant to Liebling's claim, and would be inadmissible at trial under Fed. R. Evid. 407, which bars use of evidence that the defendant took "subsequent remedial measures" to improve the product after an accident to show that the product was negligently designed at the time of the accident.[3] Is the objection proper?

The Rules Giveth and Taketh Away: Balancing Relevance and Burden

5.   Liebling claims in his action that he has been disabled from performing his former job as a landscaper, and seeks damages for loss of earning capacity. Miller sends a request for production of documents to Liebling seeking his tax returns for the five years before the injury and the two years that have passed since the injury. Must Liebling produce them?

6.   Murrow Corporation brings an antitrust action against the Pyle Company, a menswear company that brought out a new line of shirts in 1999. Murrow claims that Pyle has engaged in illegal price fixing arrangements with various retailers concerning marketing of the shirts. Murrow sends a Rule 34 Request for Production of Documents, requesting all documents relating to pricing of the company's menswear products between 1989 and 2000. Pyle's counsel replies that it "objects to the Plaintiff's Request for Production on the ground that it is unduly burdensome and seeks information irrelevant to the claims or defenses in this case." Is the objection justified? If Murrow's counsel believes the objection is not justified, how should she proceed?

7.   Gellhorn sues Jones for sexual harassment, claiming that Jones harassed her over a period of months, and then fired her from her job as a waitress at a bar because she refused to engage in sexual conduct with him. Jones contends that he actually fired Gellhorn because she was using her job to pick up men at the bar.

During discovery, Jones's counsel sends interrogatories seeking the names of all men with whom Gellhorn has had sexual relations in the last five years.

    a. Does the information requested satisfy the relevance standard in Rule 26(b)(1)?

    b. How should Gellhorn's counsel respond to this interrogatory?

---

3. The rationale for this evidentiary rule is that, if such evidence could be used at trial, it would discourage parties from making changes that increase the safety of their products, for fear that such changes would be used to prove that they were negligent in the first place.

The Rules Taketh Away: Privilege

8.   Shirer sues Tubbs for injuries suffered in an accident. He claims that Tubbs was drunk at the time of the accident. Tubbs retains Severeid to represent him. At their first meeting, Tubbs says, "Look, you're my counsel and I'm entitled to speak with you in confidence. The fact is that I had been drinking at Fred's Bar and Grill for two hours before the accident, had seven beers, and was pretty well around the bend when I left Fred's. But you're not going to tell them that, are you? How do you think we should play this?"

Subsequently, Shirer sends interrogatories to Tubbs asking whether he had been drinking before the accident, if so where, and how many drinks he had had. What should Severeid do in responding to the interrogatories?

9.   At Tubbs's deposition, Shirer's counsel asks him, "Didn't you tell your lawyer that you had had seven beers before the accident?" Severeid objects based on the attorney-client privilege. Does the privilege apply?

10.   Suppose that at the deposition Severeid instructs Tubbs not to answer a question, on the basis of the attorney-client privilege. Shirer's counsel does not believe the information he has asked for is privileged, since he thinks that Severeid did not represent Tubbs at the time of the conversation. What should Shirer's counsel do?

11.   Consider again example 7, in which Gellhorn sues Jones for sexual harassment. Unfortunately, Gellhorn has no witnesses to Jones's alleged harassment, which took place in his office for obvious reasons. However, she knows that Jones is in psychotherapy, and from comments he made she believes that Jones has discussed his actions with his therapist. Gellhorn's counsel, while acknowledging that Jones's communications with his therapist are privileged, moves for an order granting discovery of the therapist's notes, arguing that, even though the records are privileged, the only way he can make a case against Jones is through access to them. How should the court rule?

The Rules Taketh Away: Work Product
Limits on Discovery

12.   Irwin Coal Company supplies coal to Mauldin Corporation's factory under a two-year contract. Early in the course of the contract, a dispute arises as to whether the coal Irwin is supplying meets the contract specifications, which require delivery of "first quality coal." Irwin delivers Grade AB coal, but Mauldin claims this does not constitute "first quality" coal. Mauldin threatens to refuse further deliveries if Irwin continues to deliver AB coal. Irwin counters by threatening to recall coal already en route if Irwin does not accept grade AB.

Irwin's president asks Crane, the sales representative who negotiated the contract with Mauldin, to write out in detail the sequence of negotiations leading to the contract, to determine whether Mauldin's position is justified.

Crane drafts a long memorandum detailing the negotiations and the various statements he made during three meetings with Mauldin employees. He attaches his personal notes of the meetings.

Later, Mauldin cancels the contract and Irwin sues to collect. Mauldin's counsel sends interrogatories to Irwin seeking all "notes, records, letters, memoranda, or other communications concerning the contract in issue."

    a. May Irwin invoke Rule 26(b)(3) to avoid producing Crane's memorandum?

    b. May it protect Crane's notes of his meetings with Mauldin employees under Rule 26(b)(3)?

13. Irwin sues Mauldin for breach of the coal contract. Assume that Hersey, the employee who negotiated the contract for Mauldin, has since moved to Abbu Dhabi and cannot be found, and that Hersey left no memos detailing the negotiations for the contract. Irwin's counsel sends an interrogatory to Mauldin's president asking him to "relate the substance of any interviews you and/or your counsel conducted with Hersey concerning the contract involved in this action." Mauldin's lawyer had in fact interviewed Hersey, though he did not record or take notes at the interview. Does Rule 26(b)(3) protect this information from discovery.

14. Assume that Mauldin's lawyer took extensive notes at his interview with Hersey. The notes include factual statements made by Hersey about the course of the negotiations, and evaluative comments concerning the credibility of Hersey's statements, other evidence that might contradict it, and problems with admissibility of the evidence. Irwin's interrogatories seek production of "any notes, memoranda, recordings, or other records of discussions with Hersey concerning the events in suit." Are the notes protected under Fed. R. Civ. P. 26(b)(3)? (Assume, for purposes of the example, that Mauldin's counsel did not object to the request on the basis of attorney-client privilege.)

15. Irwin sends an interrogatory to Mauldin asking whether, at the time of the negotiations for the contract, Hersey had given assurances to Irwin's employees during the negotiations that Grade AB coal would suffice under the contract. Hersey had admitted to Mauldin's counsel that he had said that Grade AB was satisfactory. Mauldin's counsel refuses to answer, on the ground that the information is protected by the "work product privilege." Does Rule 26(b)(3) apply?

The Rules Giveth and Taketh Away:
Discovery from Experts

16. Sherrod is injured in a plutonium mining accident and sues Gold Mining Company for his injuries. Bigart is a Ph.D. metallurgist with his own company who consults for Gold Mining Company, periodically testing the effects of stress on various metals used in shoring up its mine shafts, and

conducting tests of any supports involved in accidents. Before the accident, Bigart performed stress tests on several structural members that collapsed during the accident.

Sherrod sues Gold for his injuries and his counsel notices Bigart's deposition. Gold objects on the ground that he is a non-testifying expert who cannot be deposed absent "exceptional circumstances" under Rule 26(b)(4)(B). Is the objection valid?

17. In deciding whether to sue Gold, Sherrod's counsel contacts Dr. Mydans, a renowned expert on mine safety, to ask her for a preliminary opinion as to whether the methods used to shore up the mine were adequate. Mydans reviews the documents concerning the accident and indicates that she can find nothing wrong with the procedures used. Sherrod's counsel decides not to hire Mydans and looks elsewhere for an expert with a more congenial view.

Gold sends interrogatories to Sherrod seeking the names of all experts whom he or his counsel has consulted or retained. Must Sherrod reveal that he has consulted Mydans?

18. In addition to Sherrod, 23 other miners were injured in the accident. Gold, anticipating numerous cases, begins its litigation preparation shortly after the accident. Its counsel learns that there are only three known experts on the field of plutonium mining, one of whom is not well reputed. It hires the other two, one as a testifying expert and the other as a non-testifying expert.

Six months later Sherrod retains counsel, and she looks for an expert. Having unearthed the same three names, she contacts the two good experts, only to find that both have been sewed up by the opposition. What can she do about it?

EXPLANATIONS

An Early Question

1a. The statements requested in *Hickman* clearly satisfy the broad relevance standard in Rule 26(b)(1)—even the amended standard of 2000. All were from witnesses to the accident or to the subsequent repairs on the tug, and would have shed light on events in suit, such as how the accident happened or the decedent's injuries. Certainly, this would be relevant to the plaintiffs' claims for personal injury damages.

b. The attorney-client privilege did not apply, since the interviews did not involve confidential communications with Fortenbaugh's client, but rather discussions with non-party witnesses to the events. Even if the witnesses may have believed they were meeting with Fortenbaugh "in confidence," this belief would not protect their statements from court-ordered discovery.

c. It is one thing to seek written statements taken from a witness. It is quite another to conscript opposing counsel to write out the details of an oral interview with a witness. True, both would force a lawyer in Fortenbaugh's position to assist in developing her opponent's case, but the latter enlists him even more in that effort, since it requires him to recall what was said at an earlier interview and write it out for the plaintiff's benefit.

On the other hand, if Fortenbaugh were ordered to produce the substance of oral statements, he could at least protect his own mental evaluations of the testimony by producing only *factual* statements the witness had made. If he were forced to produce the notes he had taken on earlier interviews, he would be revealing both factual statements and his own interpretive or evaluative comments at the same time.

d. Plaintiff's counsel had an unusually comprehensive opportunity to learn the nature of the witnesses' testimony. First, they had all appeared and given testimony at a public hearing about the accident. See *Hickman,* 329 U.S. at 498. Second, plaintiff had inquired concerning the facts in interrogatories to Fortenbaugh's client. Any information about the accident gleaned from the witness interviews would have to be revealed in answering those interrogatories. Finally, plaintiff's counsel could presumably have called these witnesses for depositions under Fed. R. Civ. P. 30 and compelled them to testify fully about the events in suit.

e. Plaintiff's counsel claimed that he wanted the information only to cover all the bases — to make sure he hadn't missed anything in his own preparation. 329 U.S. at 513. However, he may not have been fully candid about his reasons for seeking the information from Fortenbaugh rather than by other means. He may have been trying to limit his expenses by getting these statements from the witnesses without the expense of deposing them or obtaining transcripts of the public hearing. In addition, he may have believed that these witnesses were likely to be more candid in speaking "off the record" to Fortenbaugh than they would be at a public hearing or a recorded deposition, and hoped to catch them in inconsistencies or revelations unavailable through these other avenues.

The Rules Giveth: Relevance

2. This is an interesting question, and it is rendered more interesting by the 2000 amendment to Rule 26(b)(1). That Rule now authorizes discovery of any information "relevant to the claim or defense of any party." If the word "claim" refers to the "claim" asserted in Liebling's complaint, there is a strong argument that this information is not discoverable. The "claim" in Liebling's complaint is for negligence in the manufacture of the hedgeclippers, not for failure to warn of the risks involved in using the clippers. Arguably, this is a different claim, not yet raised by any party, and therefore not within the scope of discovery.

In fact, isn't it likely that Liebling is seeking this information in order to ascertain whether there is a factual basis for adding a new "claim" for negligent failure to warn? At the time he filed the complaint, he may not have had enough facts to support a failure to warn claim, and therefore left that theory out of his complaint to avoid Rule 11 problems. Now he would like to use discovery to gather the information necessary to decide whether to amend the complaint to add a failure-to-warn claim. Under the new wording of Rule 26(b)(1), it appears that he may not be able to do so.

If the rule is interpreted to refer only to the "claims"—that is, the legal theories—already pleaded, counsel will be under great pressure to plead multiple theories, even if they have little or no evidentiary support for some of them. To obtain access to discovery on those theories under Rule 26(b)(1), counsel would have to plead them first. This could create considerable tension between the need for discovery to develop a case and the strictures in Rule 11 on unsupported pleadings.

Under the prior version of Rule 26(b)(1), this tension was avoided. The documents concerning warnings may not be relevant to negligent manufacture (the "claim" Liebling pleaded initially), but they would be discoverable under the standard in Rule 26(b)(1) prior to 2000, because they are relevant to the "subject matter involved in the pending action"—the hedgeclipper accident. Under that standard, Liebling was able to seek discovery of information relevant to the underlying litigation events even if he had not yet pleaded a "claim" for failure to warn.[4]

3a. Strictly speaking, Liebling's interrogatories are relevant to the court's jurisdiction, not to the merits of the personal injury claim itself or any substantive defense to it. However, it is not much of a stretch to argue that the information sought is relevant to Miller's jurisdictional "defense," and therefore within the scope of discovery under Rule 26(b)(1). Clearly, the jurisdiction question is relevant to whether the court can adjudicate Liebling's claim *at all*, and Liebling should be entitled to find out the jurisdictional facts so that he can litigate the motion. Consequently, courts generally held that jurisdictional issues were within the scope of discovery under the prior version of Rule 26(b)(1). See Moore's, s. 26.41[6]. It seems very likely that they will continue to do so.

b. Liebling's interrogatories are clearly within the scope of discovery under Rule 26(b)(1), since they seek information relevant to his claim that the hedgeclippers were negligently designed. Miller, however, may argue that it should not have to respond to these interrogatories at all, since it is not subject to the jurisdiction of the court where Liebling has filed suit.

Generally, the fact that a defendant raises a jurisdictional objection to an action does not suspend the right of parties to take discovery on the merits.

---

4. The amended version of Rule 26(b)(1) does give Liebling another option: He can make a motion for an order expanding the scope of discovery to the broader limits under the prior version of the rule. See Rule 26(b)(1), second sentence (authorizing the court, upon a showing of good cause, to allow discovery of any matter relevant to the subject matter of the action). However, it is doubtful that judges are going to be very enthusiastic about such motions. If the litigant's only ground for the motion is that she would like to see what she can find, the motion could be made in every case and looks like mere disagreement with the new rule rather than an individualized ground for a waiver in particular circumstances.

However, Miller could move for a protective order, asking the court to stay discovery on the merits of the claim until its jurisdictional objection has been resolved. Miller's position is that it should not have to litigate in the forum at all; it seems appropriate that, if the objection is substantial, discovery on the underlying personal injury claim should be suspended until the court determines whether it has the power to adjudicate the merits. The court might grant the stay, if it thinks the jurisdictional objection may prevail. However, if the jurisdictional facts are intertwined with the merits, or the court views the objection as dubious, it also might not.

4.   No, it is not proper, because discovery is not limited to information that would be admissible under the rules of evidence. Information "need not be admissible at trial" (Rule 26(b)(1)) to be discoverable, if it is relevant and "appears reasonably calculated to lead to the discovery of admissible evidence." Id. Here, evidence of changes in the design will certainly help Liebling to locate witnesses with information about the design, and may help her to prove that other designs could have avoided the danger. Thus, the evidence would assist Liebling in examining Miller's witnesses about the negligence issues, and is discoverable.

The Rules Giveth and Taketh Away:
Balancing Relevance and Burden

5.   Miller has a good case for obtaining information about Liebling's income through discovery. A major issue in the case is whether the accident has affected Liebling's earnings. His tax returns from before and after the accident are an excellent source of proof on that issue; thus, they are clearly relevant to Liebling's claim for damages.

Liebling, of course, will be reluctant to produce his tax returns, which contain much confidential information besides his income. However, there is no blanket "tax return privilege" that bars their production, and litigation often compels parties to share information that is otherwise private with opponents in the suit.

On the other hand, Miller's legitimate need for discovery can be accommodated while still protecting Liebling's privacy interest in his tax returns. To meet Liebling's claim of lost earning capacity, Miller needs to know Liebling's *earned income* prior to the accident. There is no need to produce his entire tax returns to provide this information to Miller: It is available from his wage statements or self-employment tax forms. Producing these will meet Miller's legitimate discovery needs while preserving the privacy of other aspects of Liebling's returns. See Wright and Miller §2019, p.308.

If Miller requests the returns themselves, Liebling's counsel will likely respond by offering the wage statements instead. Miller will likely acquiesce in this, because he probably won't be able to convince the court that he needs anything more.

6.   Pyle's objection here is to the breadth of the material requested. The suit relates to pricing of shirts, but the request is much broader, extending to all marketing documents concerning any of Pyle's products. In addition, the line of shirts at issue in the case only came out in 1999, while the request seeks documents going back to 1989. On the other hand, the test for discovery is broad, and it is arguable that Pyle's general pricing practices are relevant to Murrow's claim here. If Pyle has engaged in price fixing on other products, information concerning their methods may assist Murrow in proving that they did the same thing with their new shirts.

There is simply no bright line "yes or no" answer to the proper scope of discovery here. The documents become less relevant as we go further back in time and move to other lines of products, but are still of some relevance. This is the type of practical, ambiguous discovery dispute that counsel ideally work out during discovery. Perhaps they can agree to some limits on the time period, the products involved, or the method of identifying relevant documents to satisfy the plaintiff's discovery need without undue burden, expense, or intrusion on the defendant's business.

Both parties' lawyers have an incentive to work out such discovery disputes. Murrow's counsel wants to get the information, without the hassle of going to court to do so. Pyle's counsel, while he objects to the breadth of this request, doubtless realizes that some subset of the information is relevant and important. If Murrow files a motion to compel production of the documents, Pyle will be ordered to respond to some extent, and the judge will be irked if he takes up court time by inflexibly resisting production. In addition, Pyle's counsel will be seeking discovery too; if he digs in his heels on this one, he can expect corresponding resistance to his requests as well.

The rules now *require* the parties to attempt to resolve problems like this before seeking an order from the court compelling production of the information. Under Rule 37(a)(2)(B) the party moving to compel production must certify that he has "in good faith conferred or attempted to confer with the person or party failing to make the discovery in an effort to secure the information or material without court action." If the parties cannot resolve the issue, the court will have to decide. Since Pyle has refused to produce the documents, Murrow will have to seek an order from the court compelling production, or accept Pyle's refusal. If the information is likely to be marginal, Murrow may let the matter go, given the time and expense of the motion to compel. Or, Murrow's counsel may explore the issue in depositions, where the deponent must generally answer questions even if he deems them beyond the proper scope of discovery.[5]

If Murrow moves to compel and Pyle's objection is held insufficient, the court may award the costs of the motion (including Murrow's attorney's

---

5. See Fed. R. Civ. P. 30(c), which requires the witness to answer even if an objection is raised.

fees) to Murrow. Fed. R. Civ. P. 37(d). In a case where the objection is arguable, however, (as it probably is here), the court may refuse to do so, even if it orders production of some or most of the documents requested.

7a. Arguably, evidence of at least some of Gellhorn's past sexual conduct is relevant to Jones's defense that Gellhorn was using her position to "pick up" men at the bar. For example, if Gellhorn identifies her past sexual partners Jones might learn of men whom she had picked up at his bar, which would corroborate his version of the events in suit.

b. Gellhorn should respond by objecting to the interrogatory based on the private nature of the information sought, or moving for a protective order barring production of this information. Even if evidence is relevant, it is not necessarily discoverable: The court has a role to play in limiting discovery where disclosure may not be justified. Rule 26(c) allows the court to enter protective orders limiting discovery *even if* the requested information meets the broad relevance standard in Rule 26(b)(1). See also Rule 26(b), first sentence, which provides that relevant evidence is discoverable "unless otherwise limited by order of the court..."

Here, there is a strong argument that Gellhorn should not be compelled to produce such intimate information. In *Priest v. Rotary,* 98 F.R.D. 755, 761 (N.D. Cal. 1983), on which this example is loosely based, the court granted a protective order barring such inquiries, noting that "[d]iscovery of intimate aspects of plaintiffs' lives as well as those of their past and current friends and acquaintances, has the clear potential to discourage sexual harassment litigants from prosecuting lawsuits such as the instant one." Although intimate information must often be produced in discovery, the marginal value of the information requested here is outweighed by the intrusion on Gellhorn's privacy.

The Rules Taketh Away: Privilege

8. To say the least, Tubbs has placed Severeid in a very delicate position. He has told him facts that, if revealed in the litigation, will clearly hurt Tubbs's case. While he evidently assumed that the attorney-client privilege would protect his candid comments from disclosure, he is seriously mistaken about the limits of the privilege.

The attorney-client privilege only protects *the communications between lawyer and client themselves* from discovery. The privilege does *not* protect a party from responding to discovery of facts about the case just because those facts have been told to an attorney.

> The protection of the privilege extends only to *communications* and not to facts. A fact is one thing and a communication concerning that fact is an entirely different thing. The client cannot be compelled to answer the question "What did you say or write to the attorney?" but may not refuse to disclose any relevant fact within his knowledge

merely because he incorporated a statement of such fact into his communication to his attorney.[6]

A moment's thought makes it obvious that this distinction must be made: Otherwise, Tubbs could immunize everything he knows from discovery simply by telling those facts to his lawyer. Thus, in answering the interrogatories, Severeid cannot disregard facts he knows about the case, even though Tubbs told him those facts "in confidence." Although the factual responses to interrogatories are signed by the client, not the lawyer (see Rule 33(b)(2)), Severeid cannot facilitate perjury by filing answers that he knows to be untrue. A.B.A. Model Rules of Professional Conduct, 3.3(a)(4). The system is predicated on lawyers hewing to their ethical obligations, and, in the long run, you will fare better in the profession by taking those obligations seriously. Severeid will have to explain to Tubbs that (absent some *other* privilege, such as the Fifth Amendment privilege against self-incrimination) he must reveal what he has been told, or else withdraw from representing Tubbs.[7]

The irony here, of course, is that the attorney-client privilege purports to encourage full and open communication between lawyer and client. See, e.g., *Fisher v. United States,* 425 U.S. 391, 403 (1976) (purpose of privilege is to "encourage clients to make full disclosures to their attorneys"). But a client like Tubbs may feel sandbagged by the unexpected consequences of his candor. At the least, the example suggests that lawyers should explain to clients at the outset the limits on the protection the attorney-client privilege provides.

9.   The privilege is validly raised here. Tubbs's conversations with Severeid in the course of the representation are protected by the privilege, lest he be discouraged from consulting counsel. Thus, Shirer's counsel cannot inquire about what Tubbs told Severeid to determine whether he may have told him a different story than he told at some other time.

10. The party requesting information through discovery need not roll over and play dead just because opposing counsel objects to producing the information. The obvious first response is to ask opposing counsel the basis for the objection. Perhaps Severeid can be convinced that his objection is not well grounded under the circumstances. If not, the discussion will at least

---

6. *Upjohn v. United States,* 449 U.S. 383, 395-396 (1981) (quoting from *City of Philadelphia v. Westinghouse Electric Corp.,* 205 F. Supp. 830, 831 (E.D. Pa. 1962).

7. If this answer seems naive, there may be other sufficient reasons for facing the music in a situation like this rather than playing fast and loose with the facts. If Tubbs really was drinking at Fred's, one way or another this fact is likely to surface. If it does, and Tubbs has denied it under oath, his credibility with the jury on other issues in the case will suffer grievously.

Some lawyers suggest that you should make sure that this situation never arises, by signaling to the client one way or another what you don't want to hear. To the extent this is true, it is ironic, because such signals obviously undermine the professed goal of open communication between lawyer and client.

elicit the ground of the objection more specifically, so that Tubbs's counsel can decide whether to accept the objection or press for an answer. Rule 26(b)(5) requires a party claiming the privilege to "describe the nature of the documents, communications or things not produced or disclosed in a manner that, without revealing information itself privileged or protected, will enable other parties to assess the applicability of the privilege or protection".

If Tubbs's lawyer considers the information important, and is still convinced that it is not privileged, she will have to file a motion to compel Shirer to answer under Rule 37(a)(2). The court will then decide whether the privilege applies and, if it does not, order Shirer to respond.

11. Here, the psychotherapist/patient privilege applies to protect Jones's communications with his therapist from disclosure. But, argues Gellhorn, I *really need* the privileged material; without it I simply cannot make a case.

This is not strictly true, of course—Gellhorn can testify herself to the harassment in Jones's office, and that may suffice to make a prima facie case. But the evidence is obviously of great importance to her case. However, even if the testimony is essential, its importance will generally not override the claim of privilege. The creation of a privilege represents a judgment by a court or legislature that it is more important to protect the communication from disclosure than it is to give litigants access to it. Thus, absent some constitutional issue, a claim of privilege will usually prevail even if the information withheld is crucial. Compare, however, the more limited protection under Rule 26(b)(3) for trial preparation materials.

The Rules Taketh Away: Work Product Limits on Discovery

12a. Crane's memo is clearly relevant to Irwin's claim, so it is presumptively discoverable under Rule 26(b)(1). However, Irwin will argue that it is "work product" subject to the limits on discovery in Rule 26(b)(3).

There are several problems with Irwin's argument. First, Crane's memo was created by an Irwin employee for another Irwin employee; no lawyer was involved at all. (Compare *Hickman,* in which the materials involved were prepared by counsel for the defendant). Can it still be work product?

Yes it can; the rule expressly applies to documents or tangible things "prepared by or for another party" *or* by or for that party's representative (such as his lawyer). This makes sense; lawyers are not the only ones who prepare for trial; parties do too. The rule protects the privacy of their preparation as well as counsel's. Indeed, in many cases it will be hard to separate materials prepared for the party from those prepared for counsel. The rule protects them both.

However, there is a second problem with Irwin's work product claim. At the time Crane drafted his memo, no lawsuit was pending between the parties. They were involved in a dispute, but no one had threatened suit or retained counsel to file one. They were simply at odds on interpretation of a contract, a very common commercial occurrence. Thus, there is a very substantial question as to whether the memo was "prepared in anticipation of litigation" as Rule 26(b)(3) requires.

Materials certainly can be "prepared in anticipation of litigation" even if no suit has been filed. In many cases it will be clear that suit is imminent and the documents are for use in the case, so that the work product privilege will apply. In others, however, documents relating to a dispute will be prepared in the regular course of business (such as an accident report or investigation) or in order to *avoid* litigation. One test used in the cases protects materials under Rule 26(b)(3) if they are prepared "'because of the prospect of litigation.'" *United States v. Adlman,* 134 F.3d 1194, 1202 (2nd Cir. 1998) (quoting from Wright & Miller, s. 2024 at p. 343). This test would probably not apply to Crane's memo, which was evidently prepared to resolve the dispute with Mauldin rather than to prosecute a lawsuit. Another test found in the cases, whether the document was prepared "primarily or exclusively to assist in litigation" (see Moores's. 26.70[3][a]), is even more restrictive and would clearly not be met in this case.

b. It might be argued that every record a business creates these days is "in anticipation of" litigation: It certainly is common enough for commercial transactions to end up in court. But accepting this argument would allow the exception (work product protection from discovery under Rule 26(b)(3)) to swallow the rule (broad access to relevant information under Rule 26(b)(1)). Instead, Rule 26(b)(3) restricts work product protection to those documents prepared for use in litigation. Crane's notes of the meetings with Mauldin were created before the dispute concerning the terms of the contract arose, at a time when neither party contemplated litigation, and presumably for general record-keeping purposes. They are not protected under Rule 26(b)(3).

13. Actually, Rule 26(b)(3) does not apply here at all: that rule only applies to "documents and tangible things." Here, Irwin has asked Mauldin's lawyer to relate the substance of conversations which he had with Hersey, but never wrote down. Admittedly, these are "mental impressions" of the lawyer, which, if revealed, may disclose his legal theories or conclusions. They merit protection, but Rule 26(b)(3), read literally (or even liberally), doesn't provide that protection.

While Rule 26(b)(3) doesn't apply, the court would doubtless fall back on the common law protection of *Hickman* itself to bar the discovery Irwin has requested. Requiring Mauldin's counsel to reconstruct interviews with witnesses would raise all the concerns that troubled the *Hickman* Court. Rule 26(b)(3), because of its limitation to "documents and tangible things," only *partially* codifies *Hickman,* but the same concerns would very likely lead a court to protect attorney mental impressions (so-called "opinion work product") in other circumstances as well. See, e.g., *In re Sealed Case,* 856

F.2d 268, 273 (D.C.Cir 1988) (deposition questions that would have required attorney testimony on mental impressions of their witness interviews protected under *Hickman*).

14. The notes requested here are documents prepared in anticipation of trial, since Mauldin's counsel interviewed Hersey in preparing his defense of the contract claim. Thus, the notes enjoy qualified protection under Rule 26(b)(3). However, the court still might order production of at least parts of the notes on motion by Irwin's counsel. Rule 26(b)(3) creates a limited right to obtain trial preparation materials on a showing of substantial need and inability to obtain equivalent information through other means. That showing might well be made here, since Hersey's testimony will be crucial but cannot otherwise be obtained.

However, even if such a showing is made, the Rule protects Mauldin's counsel's "mental impressions, conclusions, opinions or legal theories" from discovery. His notes concerning admissibility of the evidence, Hersey's credibility, and other evidence in the case are all protected "opinion work product." If the court orders production of the notes on Hersey's testimony, it should allow Mauldin's counsel to produce a "redacted" version of the notes, with all this evaluative material stricken out.

This example asks you to assume that no attorney-client privilege objection was raised. If Mauldin's counsel did invoke the attorney-client privilege to bar discovery of the notes, the court would have to decide whether that privilege protects the communications from Hersey, an employee of Mauldin, to counsel representing the corporation — whether Hersey is "the client" where the corporation is the named defendant. This issue has given the courts a good deal of trouble, but the Supreme Court has suggested that in many cases communications from employees to corporate counsel will be protected. See *Upjohn v. United States,* 449 U.S. 383 (1981); see generally Haydock, Herr & Stempel, Fundamentals of Pretrial Litigation (3rd ed. 1994) 215-216.

15. In this example, Irwin has asked Mauldin a *factual question*, whether Hersey made a particular statement about Grade AB coal during the negotiations. Mauldin's counsel knows that he did, and his knowledge of that information is imputed to his client, since Mauldin's lawyer acts as its agent in conducting the litigation. Even though counsel knows this information as a result of his work in preparing for litigation, he still must reveal it. The work product doctrine does not protect *facts* from being discovered, even if they are learned through trial preparation. Virtually all the facts are learned that way.

Suppose, for example, that Mauldin's lawyer had discussed the case with various Mauldin employees, to determine who had information regarding the contract, and was then faced with an interrogatory asking for "the names of all persons with information relevant to the events in suit." He cannot protect such information under the work product privilege, even though his knowledge of the names of witnesses is a "mental impression" and was acquired in the course of trial preparation. The privilege protects documents produced in the course of case preparation, and opinions of counsel, but does not allow counsel to refuse proper discovery requests for factual knowledge about the issues.

The Rules Giveth and Taketh Away: Discovery from Experts

16. Gold's objection is not valid. While Bigart rendered specialized services for Gold, at the time he was not retained in anticipation of litigation. The facts indicate that he routinely performed such tests for Gold. Although Bigart is an "expert" in the sense that he has specialized information relevant to the case, his knowledge comes from his testing of the structural members in the ordinary course of his employment. As to this information, acquired prior to the litigation and for general business purposes, Bigart is a fact witness, not an expert hired to offer an opinion in a lawsuit, and is subject to full discovery.[8]

This is a very important distinction. In most complex cases there will be witnesses with specialized knowledge of the facts who are not experts in the litigation. For example, in a fraud case, a bank's systems analyst, who understands how transactions are processed through the computer system, can provide valuable testimony about how the system was programmed and the sequence of steps in completing a particular type of transaction. However, this is factual evidence about the case, which the expert acquired independent of the litigation in the normal course of business. Counsel is entitled to inquire into such information, whether the analyst is an "expert" or not. Similarly, General Motors doubtless has highly trained, "expert" employees who run its crash testing program. But the Rule 26 discovery limits on experts would not bar a plaintiff from deposing those employees about how the crash testing program is conducted or how the car in issue was designed to meet crashworthiness standards.

17. You can certainly see why Gold would like to have Mydan's name, and why Sherrod would prefer not to reveal it. If Gold finds out that Sherrod consulted Mydans, and that she offered an opinion that there was no negligence, it could hire Mydans and use her favorable testimony at trial. It probably could not elicit testimony that Sherrod had consulted her, but it might gain valuable insights into Sherrod's case from the questions he had asked Mydans during their meetings.

Rule 26(b)(4) addresses the testifying expert and the retained expert, but does not expressly deal with experts who were consulted but, for whatever reason, *not* retained to assist in preparing the case. However, the

---

8. Nor would Bigart's test results be protected as trial preparation materials under Rule 26(b)(3), since they were not prepared in anticipation of litigation, but as part of normal company quality control procedures.

Advisory Committee note to Rule 26(b)(4)(B) states that "the subdivision precludes discovery against experts who were informally consulted in preparation for trial but not retained or specially employed. . . . [A] party may on a proper showing require the other party to name experts retained or specially consulted, but not those informally consulted." Advisory Committee Note, 1970 amendments to Rule 26, Moores, §26 App. 05[2]. Thus, Sherrod is free to "expert shop" without fear that Gold will obtain the names of his rejected experts through discovery.

18. This is a "real world" litigation problem that Sherrod's counsel probably can't do much about. Nothing in the Rules bars Gold from hiring good experts, even if there aren't many of them. And the rules seriously limit Sherrod's ability to obtain discovery from Gold's experts. Absent "exceptional circumstances," Sherrod cannot get discovery from the retained expert at all (Rule 26(b)(4)(B)), and must wait until shortly before trial (under Rule 26(a)(2)) to depose the testifying expert.

This situation might constitute "exceptional circumstances" under Rule 26(b)(4)(B), allowing Sherrod to seek discovery from Gold's non-testifying expert. See Wright and Miller §2032, pp. 451-454 (such discovery may be proper where one party has "cornered the market" on experts). Even if Sherrod is allowed some discovery from Gold's retained expert, however, the fact remains that the best experts have been co-opted by the defense, leaving Sherrod to use the third stringer to make his own case.

20

Tools of the Trade: The Basic Methods of Discovery

Introduction

The last chapter considered broad conceptual issues raised by the right of discovery in civil litigation. This chapter addresses more practical, "how-to" issues that arise in using the rules of discovery to develop the facts of cases.

As the previous chapter indicates, modern procedure, unlike traditional practice, is premised on wide access to information possessed by adversaries and third parties *before* trial. Under the federal discovery rules, for example, parties may obtain almost all information in the other side's hands before the case is tried. Ideally, broad discovery makes trial a matter of clear, orderly presentation of evidence known to all litigants. It also encourages settlement by educating the parties about the strengths and weaknesses of their cases.

The discovery process is conducted by counsel for the parties with the court sitting as a referee to adjudicate disputes that arise during the exchange. Until recently, the process was driven entirely by discovery requests; that is, counsel had to ask for information or testimony; if they didn't ask for an item, they didn't get it. If an appropriate request was made, the opponent generally had to respond, but there was no provision for automatic exchange of information. This basic premise was changed by the 1993 amendments to the Federal Rules, which introduced some "automatic disclosure" requirements for the first time. Fed. R. Civ. P. 26(a). For the most part, however, discovery remains an antiphonal process, under which a litigant who wants information sends a request for discovery to her adversary, who either provides the necessary information or raises an objection to doing so.

The basic devices for seeking discovery in federal court are interrogatories under Fed. R. Civ. P. 33, requests for production of documents under Fed. R. Civ. P. 34, and oral depositions under Fed. R. Civ. P. 30. Each of these is discussed in turn below. Although state practice may differ, the federal rules provide a representative example of a discovery system.

Interrogatories

Interrogatories are probably the most frequently used form of discovery. Plainly put, they are questions propounded by one party to an opposing party, seeking information relevant to the issues in dispute. In practice, of course, they are not written by the parties; they are drafted by counsel for the requesting party, who is experienced at framing interrogatories to extract the required information as fully as possible.

The great advantage of interrogatories is that they are an inexpensive means of getting information from the other side. However, interrogatories are often less effective than one might expect. Although Rule 33(b)(1) requires the responding party to answer each interrogatory under oath (unless she has an objection), interrogatories are seldom answered spontaneously by regular people — the answers will be drafted by the opposing party's lawyer after consultation with the client. In an adversarial system, the answers are often crafted to reveal as little as possible, to avoid embarassing admissions, and to place the facts in a light favorable to the client.[1] Objections based on the discovery limits and privileges discussed in the previous chapter are also frequently raised. (See p. 377 for a set of interrogatories and responses in the *Schulansky* case, which illustrate both the use and the frustrations of interrogatories.)

Thus, interrogatories are probably most effective for obtaining basic background information, like the names and addresses of witnesses, the location and nature of records and other evidence, the names of treating physicians, itemization of bills, and similar information. They are also useful to force an opponent to specify the grounds of the general claims raised in a complaint or answer, through so-called "contention interrogatories." Many lawyers recommend using interrogatories early in the case, to help develop a plan for further discovery through document requests and depositions.

---

1. "[L]awyers who craft the responses [to interrogatories] seem to assume that it is their professional responsibility to be as stingy and self-serving in the answers they write as a strained view of the English language and the proper bounds of legal ethics permit." *McCormick-Morgan, Inc. v. Teledyne Ind. Inc.*, 134 F.R.D. 275 (N.D. Cal. 1991).

Requests for Production of Documents

Rule 34, the second common discovery rule, dramatically illustrates the Federal Rules' premise that litigation should be based on open access to all relevant information. It authorizes a party to require an opponent to produce designated documents or things in its control for inspection and copying. In essence, the rule requires the opponent to open her files, or at least cull through them for documents relevant to the issues in suit, and produce them for the other side to review in preparing for trial.

It is not hard to imagine how intrusive many litigants find this process, even if they have nothing to hide. Naturally, the client who *does* possess potentially damaging documents — as most litigants will in cases of any size — finds it even more objectionable. The lawyers are caught in the middle, between clients pressing to minimize exposure, and the Rules, which clearly mandate very broad production of documents. This can lead to great pressure on counsel to resist document requests. "The difficulties surrounding requests for documents can resemble those that might be encountered in a large library staffed by hostile librarians who respond to research queries only if asked precisely the right question." Yeazell, Civil Procedure, 5th ed. 2000 p. 502. Parties resist document requests by construing them narrowly and by liberally invoking the privileges and other objections discussed in the previous chapter. If such objections are asserted without a substantial basis, the responding party may be sanctioned under Rule 37. In many cases, however, the objections do not so clearly transgress permissible bounds as to court the risk of sanctions.

Because the receiving party need only produce documents that are within the scope of the request, parties serving requests for production under Rule 34 tend to draft them broadly to snare as much information as possible. Often, requests will be introduced by a tedious list of definitions, intended to assure that opposing counsel cannot construe the request narrowly to avoid revealing a critical document. Here, for example, is an introductory definition of the term "document" that might be routinely spewed out of a litigator's word processor to preface a Rule 34 request:

> The word "documents" means all writings of any kind, including the originals and all non-identical copies, whether different from the originals by reason of any notation made on such copies or otherwise, including without limitation, correspondence, memoranda, notes, diaries, statistics, letters, telegrams, minutes, contracts, reports, studies, checks, statements, receipts, returns, summaries, pamphlets, books, interoffice and intraoffice communications, notations of any sort of conversations, telephone calls, meetings, or other communications, bulletins, printed matter, computer printouts, teletypes, telefax, invoices, worksheets, all drafts, alterations, modifications, changes and amendments of any of the foregoing, graphic or oral records or representations of any kind, (including, without limitations, photographs, charts, graphs, microfiche,

microfilm, videotapes, recordings, motion pictures), and any electronic, mechanical or electric records or representations of any kind (including, without limitations, tapes, cassettes, discs, recordings, and computer memories).

R. Haydock and D. Herr, Production of Results under Rule 34, 5 Am. J. Trial Advoc. 253, 261-262 (1981). Lawyers draft dismal passages like this to make sure that the opposing party cannot avoid discovery by narrowly construing the request. For example, absent a definition of this sort, a request for "all documents concerning a meeting held on April 27, 1997, at company headquarters" might be construed not to extend to a tape recording of the meeting. However, it is debatable whether such tedious edicts actually do much to assure full discovery.[2]

Parties responding to Rule 34 requests sometimes offer to open their records as they are kept in the ordinary course of business for examination by the requesting party. See Fed. R. Civ. P. 34(b), third paragraph. This can often impose a greater burden on the requesting party to cull through the records than it would on the responding party. For example, it may be a great deal easier for Ace Corporation to review its records to locate "all documents relating to recall decisions for Ace roto-turnbuckles manufactured between January 1, 1988, and December 31, 1998," than it would be for the plaintiff, unschooled in Ace's business or its recordkeeping methods, to unearth such information from voluminous computer records or files organized under unknown methods. At a minimum, the responding party should indicate how the records are organized, what records respond to which requests, and any other information necessary to locate requested items. See also Fed. R. Civ. P. 33(d) (allowing party to respond similarly to interrogatories that require search of records).

Extensive Rule 34 requests often give rise to disputes over who is going to search for relevant documents—and who is going to pay for it. Ideally, counsel work these issues out between themselves, without resort to the judge, who invariably believes that she has better things to do with her time. The requesting party will usually pay the costs of the search initially, though these costs may be taxable to the losing party if the case goes to trial. The

---

2. An interrogatory is almost useless if not understandable on its own. Definitions and instructions often alter or expand the plain, ordinary meaning of the words in the question. If the words carried only their usual meanings definitions and instructions would be unnecessary. When definitions and instructions are used, an understanding of the questions requires a continual cross-reference to the definitions and instructions to be sure that the answer is responsive to the question. It gets much worse if the interrogatory will be used in court. The proponent of the question must state the question as written and clumsily explain to the court or jury any meanings that are apparent only from the definitions.

K. Berman, Q: Is This Any Way to Write an Interrogatory? A: You Bet It Is, 19 Litig. 42 (1993).

presumption is that virtually any document that fits the broad relevance standard of Rule 26(b)(1) must be produced. A party who objects will have the burden on a motion to compel production to convince the court that she has a good reason to refuse.

Rule 34 is not limited to requests for documents. It also authorizes inspection of tangible things, such as a car involved in the disputed accident or a urine sample alleged to have tested positive for drugs. Counsel can also inspect places under Rule 34, such as the assembly line where the plaintiff's accident took place, or even conduct tests on relevant items of evidence, such as stress tests on a metal girder involved in a platform collapse. See Rule 34(a) (authorizing production for testing and sampling as well as entry upon land for testing and other purposes).

Oral Depositions

The third common method of discovery is the oral deposition under Rule 30. A deposition is the taking of testimony from a witness under oath. Counsel for both parties sit down with the witness, and the attorney requesting the deposition questions the witness. Because the witness is sworn, her testimony is subject to the penalties for perjury. Fed. R. Civ. P. 30(c). The testimony is recorded, usually by a court stenographer.[3]

Such live testimony is, without doubt, the most effective means of obtaining detailed information from witnesses before trial. First, counsel gets to *see* the party or witness. There is nothing like looking the crucial witnesses in the eye to evaluate how effective they will be as trial witnesses. A deposition may well be counsel's only opportunity to do so prior to trial.

Second, because the witness is required to answer questions spontaneously, uncoached by counsel (at least, at the deposition itself), the deposition provides a much better preview of the witness's trial testimony than sanitized interrogatory answers can. Third, examining counsel can frame follow-up questions at a deposition based on previous answers, and explore in detail issues that arise during the examination. Fourth, the deposition gets the deponent "on the record," that is, it commits her to a detailed version of the relevant events. If the witness later changes her testimony, excerpts from the deposition can be used effectively to impeach that testimony.

The major drawback of the deposition is the time and expense of conducting it. Taking an effective deposition requires a full understanding of the case, including the legal issues, elements of proof, likely defenses, testimony of other witnesses, and the relevant documents *before* taking the deposition. Developing this understanding takes time. In addition, the deposition itself takes time, from several hours for a short deposition to several days or more

---

3. For a short excerpt from a deposition in the *Schulansky* case, see p. 617.

for an extensive one. The cost of the court reporter is also substantial. Reporters are usually paid by the page for providing transcripts of the deposition. Transcripts may cost as much as $3.00 per page; a deposition might run anywhere from seventy-five to several hundred pages or more. Thus, between the deposing lawyer's time, witness fees, and the reporter's fee, a short deposition could easily cost more than $500, and many will cost a good deal more than that.

Taking Depositions: Timing and Mechanics

Because counsel should have a thorough understanding of her case before taking depositions, the conventional wisdom is that they should come after interrogatories, which reveal general information and positions of the opponent, and after requests for documents, which produce the documents needed to examine the deponent effectively. In addition, because of their expense, it may be wise to postpone depositions until it is clear that trial is likely. Thus, depositions are frequently taken toward the end of the discovery phase.

However, taking an early deposition sometimes makes tactical sense. For example, counsel may wish to pin down an opponent to a version of the facts or a particular legal position before she (or her counsel) have conducted extensive discovery or educated themselves about the facts. A deponent's untutored, spontaneous testimony early in the case may be more damaging than it would be after she becomes familiar with contradictory evidence.

Rule 30 allows counsel to take the deposition of "any person, including a party." Thus, persons who are not parties, such as witnesses to the events in suit, treating physicians, or the custodians of relevant records, may be deposed. If the deponent is a party, counsel initiates the deposition by sending a notice of deposition to all parties in the action, stating the time and place of the deposition. Fed. R. Civ. P. 30(b). If the person to be deposed is not a party, she must also be "subpoenaed" for the deposition under Fed. R. Civ. P. 45. A subpoena is a court order to appear and give testimony. If deposing counsel wishes a non-party deponent to produce records or other tangible evidence for the deposition, she must serve a subpoena (now functioning as a "subpoena duces tecum" to command the production of the requested items) with the notice of deposition specifying the documents or things to be brought to the deposition.

As a practical matter, the time and place of depositions will usually be arranged informally between counsel. In most cases, they are taken at deposing counsel's office, unless there is reason, such as the location of voluminous files or physical evidence, to take a particular deposition elsewhere.

At the deposition, the witness is sworn, and may be examined by deposing counsel on any issues within the scope of discovery. Counsel representing the deponent may object to questions on a number of grounds, such as irrelevance. However, unlike at trial, the witness is usually required to answer the question even if she has an objection to it. See Fed. R. Civ. P. 30(c) (when objection is made, it shall be noted on the record but "the examination shall proceed, with the testimony taken subject to the objections").

This approach avoids many battles over arguably objectionable deposition questions. Most evidentiary objections are aimed at keeping evidence from being introduced at trial. Thus, answering objectionable questions in a deposition does not prejudice the objecting party as long as her counsel can still object to use of the evidence at trial. Ninety to ninety-five percent of cases don't go to trial, so these objections generally don't have to be resolved, saving a great deal of court time ruling on objections which ultimately don't have to be decided.[4]

However, where an objection is based on a *privilege* not to reveal information, such as the attorney-client privilege, counsel for the deponent may instruct her not to answer the question. Fed R. Civ. P. 30(d)(1). The whole point of a privilege is to protect information from disclosure *at all*, not just disclosure at trial. Obviously, the privilege would be eviscerated if the privileged testimony had to be revealed at deposition, even if its use at trial could still be contested later on.

At the deposition, counsel for the deponent, (and for other parties as well) have the right to cross-examine after deposing counsel has finished examining the deponent. Generally, there is little reason for counsel "defending the deposition" to cross-examine, since she can talk to her own witnesses privately. However, counsel may want to cross-examine at times to clarify statements made during the direct examination. For example, if the witness gives adverse testimony because she was confused by the question, or gives testimony that could be misinterpreted, it may be important to clarify it right away, rather than try to explain later at trial if the answer is used to impeach the witness.

Opposing counsel would also cross-examine fully if the deposition is a "trial deposition" rather than a "discovery deposition." A trial deposition is one that will be used at trial *in place of* the witness's live testimony. The evidence rules allow this if the witness cannot be subpoenaed to testify in the trial district or if the witness is unable to testify in person. Where the deposition may be so used, counsel taking the deposition will prepare and stage the deposition much differently than if it is simply to obtain the witness's story. And opposing counsel will want to cross-examine fully, since the deposition will provide her only opportunity to do so.

---

4. In practice, counsel usually stipulate at the beginning of the deposition that they will save all objections, except as to the form of the question or as to privilege, until the time of trial.

Physical or Mental Examinations and Requests to Admit

The Rules authorize two other important methods of discovery, the physical or mental examination under Rule 35 and request for admissions under Rule 36.

Under the Rules, parties are required to respond to most discovery requests without court intervention. Rule 35, which authorizes physical or mental examination of parties whose condition is at issue in the case, is an exception to this principle. Due to the intrusive nature of such examinations, parties must obtain a court order for a physical or mental exam, which will only be granted "for good cause shown." Fed. R. Civ. P. 35(a). The rule is most commonly invoked to allow the defendant to obtain an independent medical examination of the plaintiff in cases involving claims for physical injury. In almost all such cases, the fact that the plaintiff is claiming substantial injuries will justify an order for an exam. Because a physical will likely be ordered in such cases, the parties often arrange it without the required court order.

If a party does obtain an examination of another party under Rule 35, she must provide a copy of the independent examiner's report to the examined party if she requests it. Fed. R. Civ. P. 35(b)(1). In response, the party who has submitted to the exam must provide copies of any reports she has from her examining physician. Id. These reports will provide a preview of the medical testimony for both sides, as well as a basis for deposing each side's medical witnesses.

The request for admissions under Rule 36 is not really a discovery device at all, but a means of narrowing the scope of trial by eliminating uncontested issues. The rule authorizes a party seeking admission of certain facts to send a request to an opponent to admit those facts. The receiving party is required to admit or deny the truth of the statements, or raise an objection to the request. Admissions can be used to narrow the scope of proof at trial, since matters that are admitted are deemed established for purposes of the case. Fed. R. Civ. P. 36(b).

Unfortunately, it is not always possible to rely on admissions to remove issues from dispute. First, opponents will usually go as far as ethical constraints allow in refusing to admit damaging facts. In addition, if the admitting party has not thoroughly prepared for trial, she may learn later that she had grounds to contest facts previously admitted, and therefore move to withdraw the admissions. Judges will often grant such requests if the admitting party has good ground to contest the facts: Naturally they prefer to see cases resolved on the evidence rather than on mistaken concessions of counsel. Thus, the motion to withdraw admissions may be granted, leaving the opponent in the frustrating position of litigating an issue that her opponent had previously withdrawn from contention.[5]

The Wave of the Future? Automatic Disclosure

In 1993, the Supreme Court approved the most radical change in the discovery rules since they were promulgated in 1938. The 1993 amendments to Rule 26 introduced, for the first time, automatic disclosure requirements in civil actions. Under Rule 26(a)(1), parties are required, at the outset of the case and without a request from any other party, to disclose to other parties the names and addresses of persons with relevant information, copies or descriptions of relevant documents and tangible evidence, computations of damages with supporting documentation, and copies of insurance contracts covering the claims in suit.

Automatic disclosure was introduced to speed the process of discovery and reduce its cost. Most of this information would be exchanged under the usual discovery rules; thus, it seems to make sense to simply require its exchange at the outset. However, adoption of mandatory disclosure in 1993 was controversial, and views are still mixed about its value. Critics have suggested that it is difficult to determine exactly what must be disclosed, when disclosures must be supplemented, or what to do if the disclosures made are insufficient. Some have also suggested that the rule would raise ethical conflicts between counsel's duty to her client and to the court under the disclosure rules. See, e.g., Justice Scalia's dissenting statement from the promulgation of the 1993 rule amendments. U.S. Supreme Court Order, April 22, 1993, 146 F.R.D. 510-11.

However, the controversy surrounding disclosure seems to have abated somewhat. In the latest round of rule amendments, the rule makers decided to refine rather than abandon disclosure. Under Rule 26(a) as amended in 2000, disclosure is limited to discoverable information and witnesses the party "may use to support its claims or defenses." This formulation does not force a party to disclose damaging information — even though within the scope of discovery under Rule 26(b)(1) — if the party does not intend to present it at trial. This eliminates the awkward obligation created by the 1993 rule to automatically disclose unfavorable witnesses and information.[6] In addition, eight categories of cases in which discovery is infrequently used are now exempted from the disclosure requirement. The Rule also allows parties

---

5. Frequently, stipulations at the pre-trial conference provide a more effective means of removing issues from dispute. See Fed. R. Civ. P. 16(c)(3) (consideration should be given at pre-trial conference to obtaining admissions and stipulations).

6. It does not, of course, exempt such unfavorable information from discovery under the other discovery methods discussed in this chapter.

to agree to forgo automatic disclosure. Fed. R. Civ. P. 26(a)(1). Last, an important change in the amended rule makes disclosure mandatory in all federal districts; the original disclosure rule allowed districts to "opt out" of the experimental disclosure requirements.

Limiting disclosure to information "the disclosing party may use to support its claims or defenses" makes disclosure a good deal less controversial, since it is much narrower than the anything-relevant standard in the prior rule. However, this narrower standard also makes it clear that disclosure can never substitute for use of the other discovery tools: under the amended rule, it is only through interrogatories, document requests, and depositions that a party may obtain information *unfavorable* to the responding party.

Rule 26(a)(1) also includes other disclosure requirements, which have not been substantially altered by the 2000 amendments. As trial approaches parties must disclose the identity and reports of experts (Fed. R. Civ. P. 26(a)(2)), the names of witnesses to be called at trial, and documents and depositions each party expects to offer in evidence at trial. Fed. R. Civ. P. 26(a)(3). To facilitate disclosure, Rule 26(f) requires the parties to confer about disclosure and the subsequent course of discovery. Until this is done, parties are barred from traditional discovery by interrogatories, requests for documents, and depositions. Fed. R. Civ. P. 26(d).

Discovery: Court Supervision and Sanctions

Unfortunately, litigators who use the discovery rules every day almost inevitably begin to think about procedural issues like this: "The Rules require me to do *X,* but what will happen if I *don't* do *X?*" It's a dirty little secret that frequently the roof doesn't fall in if you fail to comply with the rules. Often, indeed, nothing happens.

The consequence of failure to comply with a request for discovery depends on your opponent. A refusal to provide requested discovery puts the ball in the requesting party's court. If the information is of marginal importance, she may not pursue it, or may make informal efforts to force compliance but not go beyond that. If the information is important, however, she will likely move for an order to compel discovery under Fed. R. Civ. P. 37.

Under Rule 37(a)(2), a party who believes an opponent has failed to comply with a proper discovery request must first confer informally with the opponent. This requirement, introduced by the 1993 discovery amendments, is obviously aimed at resolving these disputes whenever possible without resort to the court. If informal means don't resolve the matter, the requesting party must move to compel disclosure or discovery under Fed. R. Civ. P. 37(a)(2). If the motion is granted, the court may order the noncomplying party to pay the moving party's expenses and fees for the motion to compel. Fed. R. Civ. P. 37(a)(4). The court may also enter protective orders defining the scope of required discovery and barring unwarranted or harassing discovery. Fed. R. Civ. P. 37(a)(4)(C). If the court grants a motion to compel, but the party still does not respond adequately, Rule 37(b) authorizes a variety of sanctions, such as striking claims, taking disputed facts or claims as established (or barring the recalcitrant party from establishing them), excluding evidence, dismissing the action, or ordering payment of the fees and expenses caused by the refusal to comply.

Too often, parties deliberately drag their feet in the discovery process, leading to frustration, reciprocal stonewalling, and consequent discovery battles. While counsel for each party may believe that her position is supported by the rules, many discovery issues are ambiguous and complex. Going to court tends to absorb the parties' resources, irritate the judge, leave counsel feeling unsupported by the court, and yield compromise solutions that satisfy no one. Thus, while the threat of court sanctions lurks in the background, the vast bulk of discovery disputes are resolved (or left unresolved) by the parties. If it were any other way the system would break down very quickly.

The following examples explore the basic discovery devices, the tools of the modern litigator's trade.

EXAMPLES

Gone Fishin'

1. Alewife sues Dr. Perch for injuries allegedly caused by Perch's negligence in the course of back surgery. Her lawyer obtains a copy of the surgical notes that indicate that Trout, a nurse, assisted at the operation. She contacts Trout to interview him about the case, but Trout refuses to speak to her.
   a. Is Trout within his rights to refuse to speak with Alewife's lawyer?
   b. Since Trout refuses to cooperate, Alewife sends a set of interrogatories to him. Must Trout respond to the interrogatories?
   c. Advise Alewife as to how she can best obtain evidence from Trout.

2. You represent Dr. Perch. You have received a set of interrogatories for Perch to answer. Interrogatory #12 asks "State whether, prior to commencing the surgical incision in the operation in suit, you examined the x-rays of the plaintiff's back in her medical records."

In preparing answers to the interrogatories, you sit down with Dr. Perch and ask her whether she examined the x-rays prior to the surgery. She replies, "Well, between you and me, I didn't. It was a hectic morning, we had an emergency surgery right before hers, and I just didn't do it. I knew what had to be done anyway." As a medical malpractice defense lawyer, you know that this testimony will severely damage Perch's case, since any expert will testify that good medical practice requires full review of the x-rays prior to back surgery. How do you answer the interrogatory?

Refusing to Take the Bait

3.   Assume, on the facts of example 3, that Perch had examined the x-rays two days before surgery. Could you answer "yes" to interrogatory #12?

4.   In the same set of interrogatories, the plaintiff asks the names of every person who conducted any investigation of her surgical incident. Dr. Perch tells you that she thinks someone from the hospital did an investigation, but she has no idea who it was.
   a. How should you respond to the interrogatory?
   b. Suppose you represented the hospital as well. How should you respond?

5.   Assume that Dr. Perch is unaware that an investigation was conducted of the incident and answers the interrogatory in example 5 stating that there was none. Later, at the deposition of one of the nurses, Perch's counsel learns that the hospital did conduct an inquiry. Does she have a duty under Fed. R. Civ. P. 26(e)(2) to supplement or retract her earlier response to the interrogatory?

6.   Interrogatory #9 in Alewife's interrogatories to Dr. Perch asks her to state the substance of any discussions she has had with her counsel concerning the possible causes of Alewife's injury. As counsel for Perch, you conclude that this information is privileged. How should you respond?

7.   Salmon is injured when his hand is caught in a stamping machine manufactured by Puffer Corporation. He brings a product liability action against Puffer for his injuries. One of his interrogatories asks Puffer to list all complaints it has received over the past ten years concerning safety guards on any of its machines. The company, which manufactures some 20 types of machines, has a complaints file that is not broken down by product. Any one of the 4,000 or so complaints in the file could be responsive to the interrogatory.

Puffer responds to the interrogatory as follows: "The information requested in Interrogatory #7 is contained in the company's complaints file, located in its administrative offices at 731 Angel Drive, San Francisco, California, in the custody of Mr. Robert Guppy, Secretary of the Corporation. The records are organized by the year in which the complaint was filed. The records will be made available to plaintiff's counsel for inspection and copying at a mutually agreeable time to be arranged with Mr. Guppy."

Is Puffer's response proper? See Rule 33(d).

Keeping the Sharks at Bay

8.   Snapper is the plaintiff in a negligence suit against Blue based on an auto accident. Blue requests production under Rule 34 of "all medical records

pertaining to any treatment Snapper has received, from any medical provider or other health care professional, which the plaintiff alleges was required as a result of injuries suffered in the accident that is the subject of this action." Snapper responds that he does not have these medical records, which are retained by the doctors or hospitals that have treated him. Is this response proper?

9. Assume that you represent Sword, a company that has recently marketed a new line of shirts. Several competitors have complained to Sword that its pricing of the shirts may constitute price fixing, but have not threatened to sue. Should you advise the corporation to go through and destroy all documents that might contain damaging evidence relating to its pricing practices?

10. In Snapper's case against Blue, Snapper learns that the car Blue was driving was owned by Herring, and that Herring plans to junk the car because it was totalled in the accident. You, as Snapper's counsel, want to inspect and test it first. What should you do?

On the Hook

11. You are the newest associate in the firm of Capelin & Menhaden, which represents Blue in the accident case. A partner asks you to prepare all the necessary documents to bring in Minnow, the driver of a third car involved in the accident, for a deposition and to obtain any relevant documents Minnow may have. You never had to do that in law school.
    a. Where should you start in determining what documents to prepare?
    b. What documents should you prepare?
    c. Who should you send them to?
    d. How should they be served on the deponent?

12. On the appointed date, Minnow shows up for the deposition. (Hey, it really worked!) However, he does not bring counsel with him. Can the deposition proceed?

Lines of Inquiry

13. Assume that Snapper's counsel deposes Minnow early in the case. At the time, her theory of the case is that Blue was distracted by something in his car, and swerved, causing him to collide with Snapper's and Minnow's cars. Later, however, she learns from another witness that Minnow may have swerved before the accident, and wants to get Minnow's testimony on this. What should she do?

14. Gold sues Puffer Corporation in federal district court in South Dakota for sexual harassment by Tiger, her former supervisor at Puffer. She tells you that Shad, who worked with her at the time of the alleged harassment, will corroborate her testimony about various instances of harassment. Through

interrogatories, you learn that Shad left Puffer Corporation (which is located in South Dakota) a year ago for a job in Tucson, Arizona. You manage to trace her down and would like to depose her. How can you do that? Consider Rules 45(a)(2) and (b)(2).

15. To build the case against Puffer, Gold's counsel would like to depose whoever keeps the records and investigates complaints of harassment by supervisors at Puffer. However, she does not know who that person is. How should she proceed?

16. At Gold's deposition, Puffer's counsel asks her if she has ever been unfaithful to her husband. What should Gold's counsel do?

Exposure Disclosure

17. Assume that Gold's counsel does not depose Shad in Arizona, but she talks informally with her by phone several months after filing suit. She learns that Shad had secretly videotaped some of Tiger's offensive conduct with Gold, and is willing to produce the videotape for the trial and return to authenticate it. At a pre-trial conference pursuant to Fed. R. Civ. P. 16, Gold's counsel reveals that she will offer the testimony of Shad and the videotape. Tiger's counsel objects, on the ground that, while Gold had disclosed Shad's name under Fed. R. Civ. P. 26(a)(1), the existence of the videotape was not disclosed. He argues that Rule 37(c)(1) bars use of the evidence if proper disclosure was not made. Is the evidence barred? Consider Rule 26(c)(1).

EXPLANATIONS

Gone Fishin'

1a. It is generally true that "the law is entitled to every person's evidence," but that does not mean that private citizens have to provide information just because someone—even a party to a lawsuit or her lawyer—asks them for it. Very frequently, witnesses—particularly favorable witnesses—will cooperate with counsel, and it generally makes sense to ask them to give a statement voluntarily. However, a non-party witness is generally within her rights to tell you to get lost; if she does, some type of court-ordered discovery will be necessary to get her evidence.

b. Rule 33(a) authorizes serving interrogatories on "any party" to be answered "by the party served." The rule uses this language deliberately: It establishes a means for parties to the action to obtain information from other parties, but does not authorize sending interrogatories to non-party witnesses. Trout is not a party, has never been brought before the court, and is consequently not required to answer the interrogatories.

c. The only way to force Trout to give testimony is to subpoena him for a deposition: Rule 30(a) authorizes a party to take the deposition of "any person, including a party."

Although this clearly authorizes Alewife to take Trout's deposition, it may be frustrating to have to get Trout's story this way. For one thing, Trout may be put off by being served with a subpoena, which means he will come in reluctantly and perhaps predisposed against the deposing party. In addition, Trout might not have much relevant information once you get him there, so that the effort and expense of deposing him may turn out to be unproductive. It certainly would be nice if you could just sit down and talk with Trout, like two normal people, instead of going through all this formality. However, since witnesses like Trout need not cooperate, it will often be necessary to subpoena them to get them to talk to you at all. In other cases, it may be important to "get the witness on the record" by taking her deposition even if she is willing to talk informally.

2.   This is a tough one, isn't it? Your client appears to be a decent, hard-working professional. You represent her; she is *your client*. You know full well that answering "no" to this interrogatory will harm her defense. What do you do?

The rules, and an attorney's ethical obligations to the court, leave no doubt as to what you must do. Hard as it is in a system that is designed to be adversarial, you bite the bullet and tell the truth. As an officer of the court, an attorney cannot misrepresent the facts in litigation. See ABA Model Rules of Professional Conduct 3.3(a)(1) (1983).

But wait: The *factual responses* to interrogatories are signed by the client; the lawyer only signs as to the legal objections. Fed. R. Civ. P. 33(b)(2). If the client wants to put herself on the hook by giving false information, perhaps that is her problem?

Not under the rules of professional conduct. Interrogatories are to be answered "under oath." Fed. R. Civ. P. 33(b)(1). Obviously, the rule contemplates telling the truth, and lying under oath, in answering an interrogatory just as on the witness stand, constitutes the crime of perjury. No lawyer can assist or countenance such a fraud on the court by his client. ABA Model Rules of Professional Conduct 3.3(a)(4) (1983) (lawyer shall not offer evidence that the lawyer knows to be false).

So, Perch's counsel is in a box. One way out might be a quick settlement, before answering the interrogatories. There is no ethical restraint on settling a case that you think will go badly, nor is there any bar on settling while a discovery request is pending. Another is to answer truthfully, but add explanatory information that will cushion the effect of this admission, such as the fact that Perch had read the x-rays the day before, or been fully briefed by the assisting surgeon, or whatever.

Refusing to Take the Bait

3.   This is a very tempting way out of the dilemma above, isn't it? There is some ambiguity in the interrogatory, as there will be in many. By

liberally construing it to mean "at any time before surgery," you may be able to answer "yes" and mask the fact that Perch didn't check the x-rays that morning. Perhaps it will never come out that it was 48 hours before, rather than ten minutes.

A law professor might argue that the interrogatory clearly means "*immediately* prior to commencing the surgical incision," so that counsel here should answer "no." Many litigators, however, would seize on this ambiguity to answer "yes," based on the earlier review of the x-rays. It is, after all, an adversarial system. Perch's counsel would have to answer to Perch for being overly conscientious: Like most clients, Perch may malign the legal profession for cutting it close to the line but demand that her own counsel do just that at every opportunity. And, as a litigator, Perch's counsel may feel that her opponent deserves what she gets for poor drafting: She could easily have averted the problem by adding the simple phrase "and if so, when?"

It seems a pity that the judicial search for truth should foster such scholastic jousting. The system pays a large price for its adversarial premise.

4a. A party answering interrogatories has no duty to go out and conduct a detailed investigation of facts beyond her control in order to respond. James, Hazard & Leubsdorf, Civil Procedure (4th ed. 1992) 243. It is sufficient to respond with information you know or that is within your control. Here, for example, it would be proper to respond that "The defendant believes that an investigation was conducted by employees of the City General Hospital shortly after the surgery. The defendant does not know the names of the person or persons who conducted that investigation, other than Dr. Hilda Kildare, Chief of Surgery."

b. If the hospital were a defendant, and were asked this interrogatory, counsel clearly would have a duty in responding to provide information about the incident known by the hospital's employees, since information they possess is within the hospital's control. Thus, if the Chief of Surgery were answering the interrogatories on behalf of the hospital, she would have an obligation to find out which employees conducted the investigation and answer accordingly.

This provides an interesting contrast with deposition practice. If the Chief of Surgery were deposed, she would only answer from personal knowledge, or records she had brought with her. In responding to interrogatories, however, parties must conduct a reasonable investigation to provide facts within their control. See Haydock, Herr & Stempel, Fundamentals of Pretrial Litigation, 370 (3rd ed. 1994).

5. Rule 26(e)(2) provides that a party has a duty to supplement a discovery response that she later learns is incorrect or incomplete. However, Perch hasn't learned of it . . . her counsel has. Well, this puts too fine a gloss on the Rule. Perch's counsel acts as her agent in the discovery process: Whatever she learns will be imputed to Perch. Thus, if counsel learns that earlier

discovery responses are incomplete or inaccurate, she should send supplemental responses to correct them.

However, under Rule 26(e)(2) prior responses need only be supplemented if the information "has not otherwise been made known to the other parties during the discovery process or in writing." The example here indicates that the information came out in a deposition, which was doubtless attended (perhaps even conducted) by Alewife's counsel. Thus, Perch probably has no duty to supplement since the information was "made known" to Alewife's agent (*her* counsel) through the deposition.

6. Discussions between counsel and a party about possible causes of the injury would clearly fall within the attorney-client privilege. Such information does not have to be revealed, even if within the broad relevance standard in Rule 26(b)(1).

A party who believes that information requested is not subject to discovery may object to the interrogatory and state the specific ground for the objection. Fed. R. Civ. P. 33(b)(1), (4). Where an objection is interposed, the party need not answer. However, Fed. R. Civ. P. 26(b)(5) requires the objecting party to expressly claim the privilege and describe the nature of the documents or communications withheld. Perch's counsel might respond as follows: "The defendant refuses to answer Interrogatory #9 on the ground that it requires her to reveal the contents of discussions with her counsel concerning the cause of the injury in suit, which are protected from discovery by the attorney-client privilege."

Note that Perch's *counsel* signs the interrogatories as to any legal objections raised in the response. Fed. R. Civ. P. 33(b)(2). Obviously, it is counsel, not the client, who decides to raise legal objections such as privileges. The signature requirement reminds counsel, as the person raising the objection, that she stands behind that decision and takes the risk of sanctions if a motion to compel is granted.

7. Under Rule 33(d), a party may respond by specifying the records from which the relevant information can be ascertained and inviting the requesting party to conduct the search herself. However, you can't just say "come and get it"; the response must identify the nature and organization of the records sufficiently to allow the requesting party to "locate and identify, as readily as can the party served, the records from which the answer may be ascertained." Fed. R. Civ. P. 33(d).[7]

Rule 33(d) provides a tempting means for counsel to avoid a potentially burdensome discovery request. "Here, Salmon, you want it, you do it." However, the rule authorizes this response only in situations where the

---

7. "Here is the room, here is the pile, open the drawers and see all the files" will not do under Rule 33. R. Haydock, D. Herr & J. Stempel, Fundamentals of Pretrial Litigation (3rd ed. 1994), 357.

burden of extracting the information is "substantially the same" for both parties. In many cases, this will not be so, since the party keeping the records will be familiar with the content and organization of the records, and better positioned to retrieve specific items.

Even if the burden is substantially the same, Puffer still might not invoke Rule 33(d). It may not want Salmon mucking around in its files, for various good reasons. No large operation would want strangers, who don't know the system and don't ever have to find anything from it again, pawing around in ten years' worth of records. In addition, while culling through all those files may be burdensome, it will give Salmon's counsel a thorough education concerning complaints about the company's products, including much information that might not come to light if Puffer had searched the records for the exact items requested. Providing access to the records may also waive the attorney-client privilege as to the materials examined by an adversary. And, of course, such wholesale access may reveal other corporate skeletons that could come back to haunt Puffer later on.

Aside from all of this, Puffer, or its counsel, will eventually end up going through these records anyway: Even if it allows Salmon to search them, it will surely want to know what Salmon *found* about the product in order to prepare an effective defense. Consequently, in many cases the wiser course will be for the responding party to search the records itself rather than open them to opposing counsel.

Keeping the Sharks at Bay

8.   This is a bogus objection. Rule 34(a)(1) authorizes requests for production of documents "in the possession, custody or control of the party upon whom the request is served." Surely Snapper's medical records are within her "control"; as the patient, she is entitled to obtain them and should do so in response to the request, or send Blue's counsel a release allowing her to get them directly. An objection like this will only make Snapper's counsel look like an obstructionist in the eyes of the court. Reasonable cooperation is expected in discovery and this does not qualify. In many cases such obviously crucial records would be forwarded to the defense without any formal request.

9.   The first question here is whether Sword's counsel has an ethical obligation as an attorney not to advise the destruction of information that may be relevant to future litigation. She would have such an obligation if suit had been filed, or, perhaps if it were clearly impending. See, e.g., ABA Model Rules of Professional Conduct, 3.4(a) (1983) (lawyer shall not "unlawfully" obstruct another party's access to evidence); *Capellupo v. FMC Corp.*, 126 F.R.D. 545, 550-551 (D. Minn. 1989); *Alliance to End Repression v. Rochford*, 75 F.R.D. 438, 440 (N.D. Ill. 1976) (imposing sanctions for document destruction where suit was clearly

about to be filed).[8] However, there is no clear ethical bar on a preemptive policy of document destruction simply because documents might be relevant to some future lawsuit. See Note, Legal Ethics and the Destruction of Evidence, 88 Yale L.J. 1665, 1666-1674 (1979).

As a practical matter, however, advising Sword to destroy the documents may not be wise. If the organization is large, it may be hard to purge all copies of the unfavorable documents. Even if Sword manages to do so, it cannot purge the knowledge of these documents from its employees' memories. Unless those employees lie under oath, existence of the documents is likely to come out in depositions. At that point, the fact that they cannot be found looks very suspicious. Indeed, if asked, the employees who destroyed the documents would have to admit to doing it, which could be pretty devastating evidence at a future trial. At the same time, the substance of the documents will probably be pieced together from the witnesses anyway, so that destroying the documents may well turn out only to be counterproductive. For these reasons, playing it straight may well be the most practical as well as the most ethical approach.

10. If Herring were a party to the suit, Rule 34 would clearly authorize inspection and testing of the car. See Rule 34(a) (authorizing requests to a *party* to produce documents and tangible things for inspection, copying, or testing). However, since Herring has not been sued, he is not yet subject to the court's authority, and must be subpoenaed to produce the car. See Fed. R. Civ. P. 34(c), 45. Snapper would have to subpoena Herring under Rule 45(a)(1) to produce the car. Although Rule 45(a) now authorizes issuance of a subpoena solely to examine or test things, Snapper might decide to subpoena Herring for a deposition too, so that she can establish ownership and other relevant facts about the car from Herring at the time of the inspection.

On the Hook

11a. Students often resist the idea, but the *rules* really are the place to start in analyzing many procedural issues, especially those involving discovery. In this case, Rules 30 and 45 pretty much chart your course, describing the proper steps for "noticing" the deposition and subpoenaing the witness to appear.

b. Rule 30(b) provides that a notice of deposition must be served on the other parties to the action and specifies all the information that must be in it. The notice must state the time and place of taking the deposition, the name and address of each person to be examined (Fed. R. Civ. P. 30(b)(1)),

---

8. A party destroying evidence might also be subject in some situations to a suit for spoliation of evidence. See I. Johnston, Federal Courts' Authority to Impose Sanctions For Prelitigation or Pre-Order Spoliation of Evidence, 156 F.R.D. 313, 314 (1994).

and the method by which the examination will be recorded. Fed. R. Civ. P. 30(b)(2). If records are to be produced for inspection at the deposition, the notice must also specify the documents to be produced. Fed. R. Civ. P. 30(b)(1), (5). Figure 20-1 is an example of a notice of deposition that would meet the requirements of the rule.

Here, Minnow, the deponent, is not a party to the action. Thus, he is not yet under the court's authority, and must be ordered to appear and give evidence. A subpoena is a court order that commands a non-party to appear and produce evidence or give testimony. In practice the court in which the action is pending will issue blank subpoenas, signed by the court clerk, to attorneys. Fed. R. Civ. P. 45(a)(3). Counsel sending the subpoena will then fill in the details (names, places, documents requested, nature of the hearing or deposition, and so forth) and serve it on the deponent. Thus, while the court "issues" the subpoena, and may enforce compliance with it, the attorneys carry the laboring oar in filling it out and serving it. In most cases, the court will not even know that it has been served and may never have to know as long as discovery proceeds without incident.

The subpoena must include the name of the issuing court, the title of the action, the name of the court in which the case is pending, and the civil action number of the case, and it must command the person to whom it is directed to appear and give testimony. Rule 45(a)(1). If documents are requested, it must also command the deponent to produce the documents designated for inspection or copying. Id. The subpoena must also set forth in full the text of Rule 45(c) and (d), which explain the rights of witnesses and the means of raising objections to the subpoena. Since in many cases subpoenas are directed to persons who are not parties, and are not represented by counsel, this assures that the person subpoenaed will be informed of her rights and obligations in responding to it. Fed. R. Civ. P. 45(d). Figure 20-2 is an example of a subpoena drafted to comply with the requirements of Rule 45.

c. The subpoena must, of course, be sent to Minnow, the party to be deposed: It is the official command of the court to appear and give evidence. The notice of deposition should be sent to "every other party in the action." Rule 30(b)(1). Other parties are entitled to notice so that they can exercise their right to be present, object, and cross-examine at the deposition. In practice, both documents are routinely sent to all parties and to the deponent. Sending a copy of the subpoena to other counsel in the case indicates that the witness has been subpoenaed, as required by law.

d. A non-party who is subpoenaed to testify is not yet before the court, and may not even know that an action is pending. Service of the subpoena provides notice of her duty to respond and also asserts the court's jurisdiction over her. Thus, it is important that it be served in a manner likely to inform her of the obligations it imposes. Rule 45(b)(1) requires subpoenas to be served *in person* on the person to be deposed. This is even stricter than

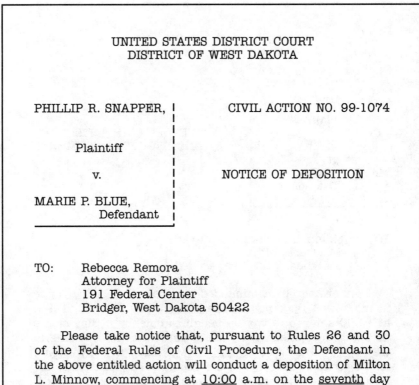

UNITED STATES DISTRICT COURT
DISTRICT OF WEST DAKOTA

PHILLIP R. SNAPPER, | CIVIL ACTION NO. 99-1074

          Plaintiff |

             v. | NOTICE OF DEPOSITION

MARIE P. BLUE, |
               Defendant |

TO: Rebecca Remora
        Attorney for Plaintiff
        191 Federal Center
        Bridger, West Dakota 50422

        Please take notice that, pursuant to Rules 26 and 30
of the Federal Rules of Civil Procedure, the Defendant in
the above entitled action will conduct a deposition of Milton
L. Minnow, commencing at 10:00 a.m. on the seventh day
of April, 1999, and continuing from that time until complete, at the law offices of Pollock & Hake, 3 First Avenue,
Badlands, West Dakota 60417.
        The deposition shall be by oral examination, with a
written record made thereof, before a notary public or
before some other officer authorized by law to administer
oaths. A copy of the designation of materials to be produced
by the witness at the deposition is attached.

Date: March 21, 1999

                              Frederick C. Pollock
                              Frederick C. Pollock
                              Pollock & Hake
                              3 First Avenue
                              Badlands, West Dakota 60417
                              (904) 522-9804

Figure 20-1

UNITED STATES DISTRICT COURT
DISTRICT OF WEST DAKOTA

PHILLIP R. SNAPPER,
    Plaintiff

v.

MARIE P. BLUE,
    Defendant

CIVIL ACTION NO. 99-1074

SUBPOENA TO TESTIFY
AND PRODUCE DOCUMENTS

TO: Milton L. Minnow
        84 Pleasant Street
        Badlands, West Dakota 60417

    You are hereby commanded to appear at <u>3 First Avenue</u> in the city of <u>Badlands</u> on the <u>seventh</u> day of <u>April, 1999</u>, at <u>10:00</u> a.m., to testify on behalf of <u>defendant Blue</u> at the taking of deposition in the above entitled action pending in the _____ District of <u>West Dakota,</u> and to bring with you for inspection and copying the documents (and things) described in the attachment to this subpoena entitled "Attachment to Subpoena Duces Tecum."

    This subpoena has been issued by the United States District Court for the _____ District of <u>West Dakota</u>. You must appear, give testimony, and produce all of the materials described in this subpoena and its attachments, for inspection and copying at the time and place set out in this subpoena. Your failure to do so may be punished as a contempt of court.

    [Here, the subpoena should set forth here the full text of Fed. R. Civ. P. 45(c) and (d).]

Date: <u>March 21, 1999</u>

Elizabeth Smith
_____
Clerk of Court

Harold Hake
_____
Harold R. Hake

Attorney for
Address:

Telephone:

<u>Marie P. Blue</u>
<u>3 First Avenue</u>
<u>Badlands, West Dakota 60417</u>
<u>(904) 522-9804</u>

Figure 20-2

the service provisions for complaints under Rule 4. And, as the new associate, don't forget that the subpoena must be served with the fees for a day's attendance and mileage to the place of deposition. Rule 45(b)(1).[9] The partner will be duly impressed if you present her with the subpoena, the notice of deposition, and the checks together. She will be correspondingly irked if you omit them. Without the checks, the subpoena could perhaps be ignored with impunity.

The notice of deposition, like virtually all papers exchanged among parties to the action, can be served on other parties to the action under Rule 5, which authorizes service by mail. Rule 5(b).

12. Persons subpoenaed for a deposition will frequently appear without counsel. There is no requirement that non-party witnesses be represented by counsel at a deposition. It is bad enough to have to give up a day of work to appear and be grilled by two humorless adversaries, without having to pay a lawyer for the privilege of doing so. The deposition can proceed.

Lines of Inquiry

13. Naturally, Snapper's counsel would like to depose Minnow again, but opposing counsel or the witness may well object to being called for a second deposition. Rule 30(a)(2)(b) now provides that, unless the parties agree that Minnow can be called again (the rule says nothing about Minnow's feelings on the matter!) Snapper's counsel must obtain leave of court to do so.

Counsel might avoid the strictures of this new provision by "suspending" depositions rather than terminating them. This technical distinction leaves counsel free to recall the witness at a later date to finish. However, they will still have to deal with opposing counsel if they do so without good cause. This suggests one reason for taking depositions late in the discovery process. After the facts and theories of recovery have been developed fairly clearly, counsel will be able to plan depositions to cover all the bases, avoiding the expense and disputes likely to arise from requests for a second deposition.

14. First, remember that Shad, as a non-party, is under no obligation to talk to Gold's counsel. Even if she is willing to, counsel may want to depose her

---

9. How do you know how much to make these checks out for? I spent a half hour in the library running this down. It turns out that 28 U.S.C. §1821 specifies the fees. The daily attendance fee is $40. 28 U.S.C. §1821(b). The mileage fee is more complicated. Section 1821(c)(2) states that the travel allowance if the deponent is to travel by private vehicle (and how do you know *that*?) is "equal to the mileage allowance which the Administrator of General Services has prescribed, pursuant to section 5704 of title 5, for official travel of employees of the Federal government. . . ." I didn't bother to try to run that down. As a practical matter, someone in your firm is likely to know the current rate. If you hang out your own shingle, this is only one of a multitude of minutiae calculated to drive the sole practitioner berserk.

anyway: If Shad is unavailable for trial in South Dakota, her deposition will be admissible instead. See Fed. R. Civ. P. 32(a)(3). Thus, she should be subpoenaed for a deposition. However, under Rule 45(a)(2) and (b)(2), a federal district court can only subpoena witnesses within that district or within 100 miles of the place within the district where the deposition is taken. This is intended to protect witnesses like Shad from having to travel long distances to be deposed. Thus, the West Dakota court will not be able to subpoena Shad for the deposition.

If Gold's counsel really needs Shad's testimony, then, he has several options. First, he can go to Arizona to depose her. An *Arizona* federal district court has the authority under Rule 45(a)(2) and (b)(2) to subpoena Shad to testify in Arizona, even though the *lawsuit* is pending in South Dakota. Thus, Gold's counsel could obtain a subpoena from the federal district court in Arizona and take the deposition there. See Friedenthal, Kane and Miller, 3rd ed. p. 411.

This isn't going to be cheap. Gold's counsel will have to fly down there to take the deposition. So will Puffer's counsel, if she chooses to attend. The clock is running and the expenses mounting for both sides. (Although Gold will not initially pay for Puffer's counsel to attend the deposition, if Puffer wins at trial some of this expense may be taxed to Gold as part of the costs of suit.)

There are some cheaper alternatives. If Shad would like to visit old friends, Gold might pay for her to fly back to South Dakota, thus saving both attorneys' travel time and one airfare. The rules also now authorize a deposition to be taken by telephone or other electronic means. Fed. R. Civ. P. 30(b)(7). Counsel could arrange to question Shad by telephone and have her answers videotaped in Arizona. Last, Rule 31 authorizes depositions on written questions. Under this rule, the witness is brought before an authorized officer (in practice a court reporter), and asked questions drafted by counsel. See Rule 31(a)(3). The witness's answers are recorded by the reporter and forwarded to counsel for the parties.

15. Gold could use interrogatories to learn who within the defendant's corporate structure has this information. Alternatively Rule 30(b)(6) allows her to send a notice of deposition to the defendant, describing the matters to be examined, and requesting that the defendant designate the person or persons best able to testify as to those matters. Gold will then depose that person on the matters specified.

16. Naturally, counsel should object, on the ground that Gold's marital fidelity is irrelevant to her harassment claim against Puffer. But what do you do when Puffer's counsel smugly quotes to you from Rule 30(c), which provides that objections at a deposition shall be noted, but the answers taken subject to the objection?

Well, that may be true as a general matter, but there must be some limit to counsel's ability to embarrass the deponent by wide-ranging inquiry into irrelevant matters. That limit is provided in Rule 30(d)(3), which authorizes a party to move to suspend or limit the scope of the deposition where "the examination is being conducted in bad faith, or in such manner as unreasonably to annoy, embarrass, or oppress the deponent or party . . ." See also Rule 30(d)(1), which authorizes defending counsel to instruct a deponent not to answer "to present a motion under paragraph (3)." Gold's counsel should instruct her not to answer and indicate her intent to make a Rule 30(d)(3) motion. At that point, Puffer's counsel will likely withdraw the question rather than try to justify this indefensible line of inquiry to the court.

Exposure Disclosure

17. Let's sort through the Rules to determine whether Gold has violated her disclosure obligations under the Rules. Rule 26(a)(1)(A) requires Gold, at the outset of the suit, to reveal the existence of witnesses with relevant evidence, but the example indicates that Gold did reveal Shad's name in its initial disclosure. Evidently, Puffer's lawyer never talked to Shad, or he tried to but she wouldn't, and counsel decided not to go to Arizona to depose her.

Rule 26(a)(1)(B) requires Gold to disclose "all documents, data compilations, and tangible things in [her] possession, custody or control" that are relevant to the disputed facts. A videotape doubtless qualifies as a "tangible thing," and this one certainly is relevant to the issues in dispute. But it was not in Gold's "possession, custody or control" at the time of the initial disclosure, so Gold did not violate her disclosure obligations by failing to disclose it initially. (She didn't even know about it back then.)

Did she have an obligation, when she learned of the videotape, to disclose it? Rule 26(e)(1) requires her to supplement her disclosure if she "learns that in some material respect the information disclosed is incomplete or incorrect and if the additional or corrective information has not otherwise been made known to the other parties during the discovery process or in writing." Does this apply? Gold has not learned that the information was incomplete when the initial disclosure *was made;* she did not have or know of the videotape then. Does this rule require her to supplement disclosure by updating the opposition on all documents and things she learns about after disclosure as she prepares her case?

There is a strong argument that Gold has a duty to reveal the existence of the tape under Rule 26(e)(1). Certainly, Gold's disclosure is "incomplete" in the sense that she now knows of an important document within the scope of Rule 26(a)(1) that she has not disclosed to Puffer. (She might argue that it is not within her "possession, custody or control," but a court would likely conclude that Shad's willingness to produce it brings it within Gold's "control.") To rest on the technical ground that disclosure was complete *when made* may ignore the spirit of the rules to provide full disclosure of such supporting documents.[10]

Even if Gold might make a colorable argument that she did not have to provide a supplemental disclosure of the tape, she would be well advised to disclose it. Rule 37(c)(1) gives the court the power—and perhaps the duty—to exclude evidence which had to be disclosed under the rules but was not. Shad's tape is such powerful evidence that it is better to be safe than sorry: Gold should bend over backwards to avoid any risk that it might be excluded at trial due to failure to disclose it.

A Practical Perspective: Sample Interrogatories, Answers, and Comments

It may be helpful after all this theory to see an actual set of interrogatories and responses. The sample that follows is based on the facts of *Schulansky v. Ronan,* the example case explored in more detail in Chapters 29 to 34.

The plaintiff in *Schulansky,* Deborah Schulansky, met with Richard Ronan, of Ronan Construction Company, to discuss putting an addition on her historic vacation house in Alton, New Hampshire. Allegedly, he represented to her that he was a specialist in such work. After some discussions, they signed a short agreement (the "proposal and estimate") and Ronan proceeded with the work. While the cellar was being excavated, Schulansky visited the site to check on the work. The house had an old foundation made of loose stones. While she was there she saw that Jones, the bulldozer operator, had dislodged some of the stones. She asked Ronan if the old foundation was adequate to support the addition, and he allegedly said it was, but that he would reinforce it with concrete if necessary. A major dispute in the case involves exactly what he had agreed to do to repair the old foundation (if anything) and whether Schulansky waived any agreement to rebuild it during their conversation at the job site.

After the work was mostly done, Schulansky visited again and noticed cracks in several rooms of the old part of the house. She had an engineer look at the house, and he concluded that the old foundation was settling, causing structural damage. After trying to get Ronan to address the problem, Schulansky sued Ronan and his company, Ronan Construction Company, for damages. (For more detail on the facts, see pp. 533-537 and 563-567.)

Figure 20-3 illustrates a set of interrogatories that Schulansky might serve on Ronan in the action. Figure 20-4 provides Ronan's responses. Some explanatory comments follow.

---

10. Rule 26(e)(2), governing supplementation of requests of documents, imposes a similar requirement to supplement where production of documents was "in some material respect incomplete or incorrect." Since this provision almost certainly applies to later acquired documents, it seems reasonable to conclude that Rule 26(e)(1) does as well.

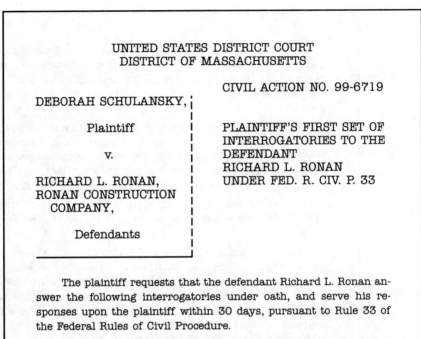

UNITED STATES DISTRICT COURT
DISTRICT OF MASSACHUSETTS

CIVIL ACTION NO. 99-6719

DEBORAH SCHULANSKY,

Plaintiff

v.

RICHARD L. RONAN,
RONAN CONSTRUCTION
COMPANY,

Defendants

PLAINTIFF'S FIRST SET OF
INTERROGATORIES TO THE
DEFENDANT
RICHARD L. RONAN
UNDER FED. R. CIV. P. 33

The plaintiff requests that the defendant Richard L. Ronan answer the following interrogatories under oath, and serve his responses upon the plaintiff within 30 days, pursuant to Rule 33 of the Federal Rules of Civil Procedure.

1. Please list each occasion on which you or anyone acting on behalf of you or Ronan Construction Company discussed the terms or performance of the contract in issue in this action with the plaintiff.

2. For each conversation identified in Interrogatory #1, please state in detail the substance of that conversation, stating in chronological order what was said by each of the parties.

3. Please identify the name and address of each person who was present during each and every conversation between yourself and the plaintiff, prior to, during, and after the execution of the contract at issue in this action.

4. Please identify the name and address of each person who has any knowledge of the facts concerning the negotiations, execution, or performance of the contract that is at issue in this action.

5. Please identify each and every document, letter, memorandum, or other record, whether in electronic or other form, of which you have knowledge, whether or not it is in your custody, possession, or control, which contains any information concerning the negotiations, execution, or performance of the contract in issue in this action.

6. Please identify each and every document, brochure, information sheet, advertisement, or other writing that describes the nature of the construction services offered by Ronan Construction Company, or its expertise or experience in restoring or working on historic properties.

Figure 20-3

7.   For each document identified in response to Interrogatory #5 and #6, please state whether such document is within your possession, custody, or control, and if not, state to the best of your knowledge who does have possession, custody, or control of such document.

8.   Please state whether any documents relating to the events alleged in this action have been lost or destroyed. If the answer is "yes," please state for each such document the nature and content of the document, the person creating the document, and the circumstances surrounding the loss or destruction of that document.

9.   Please list the names and addresses of all persons who performed any services related to the work that forms the basis of this action.

10. For each person identified in Interrogatory #9, please specify the nature of the services performed, the manner in which such person was compensated (whether by the job, hourly, weekly, or otherwise), the amount of compensation provided to such person for this job, whether a contract was entered into for the services rendered by such person, and the number of other jobs on which such person has rendered services for either of the defendants during the last two years.

11. Please identify each and every contract or other agreement, whether in writing or not, concerning the addition work that is the subject of this action, which either defendant entered into with the plaintiff, with Alton Jones, or with any other persons who rendered services on the contract that is the subject of this action.

12. Please identify, by giving the address of the property and the name and address of the owner, each and every structure in excess of 100 years old on which you or your company have rendered construction services during the last six years.

13. For each property identified in Interrogatory #12, please state whether any dispute arose concerning the terms or performance of the work, and if so, whether any legal action was threatened or initiated against you or Ronan Construction Company as a result of such dispute.

14. Please state whether either of the defendants has made an investigation into the allegations upon which the complaint in this action is based.

15. If the answer to Interrogatory #14 is "yes," please state for each such investigation
   a. the names and addresses of each person who has made such investigation;
   b. the dates of each such investigation;
   c. identify all reports, summaries, witness statements, photographs, estimates, opinions, or other documents, whether

in written or electronic form, that have been created as a result of such investigation, including any specifications or estimates of damages to the original house or addition at the Alton property.

16. Please describe, step by step, in detail and in chronological order, exactly what you or your servants or agents or subcontractors did to rebuild or reinforce the old part of the foundation exposed during the excavation for the addition that is the subject of this action, or to ascertain the sufficiency of that foundation to support the addition at issue in this action.

17. Please identify by name and address each person who was present during any part of the work that is the subject of Interrogatory #16.

18. Please state each and every fact upon which you rely in support of your contention in the Fourth Defense in your Answer to the complaint, alleging that the plaintiff waived performance of the contractual obligation to reinforce the foundation prior to construction of the addition.

19. Please state each and every fact upon which you rely in support of your contention in the Second Defense in your Answer that the defendants are not subject to personal jurisdiction in this action.

20. Please state each and every fact upon which you rely in support of your contention in the Third Defense in your Answer that the Proposal and Estimate for the work involved in this action constitutes the entire agreement of the parties and does not require reconstruction of the foundation.

21. Please state the name and address of each expert you expect to call to testify at the trial.

22. For each expert identified in Interrogatory #21, please specify
   a. his or her professional qualifications;
   b. the subjects upon which the expert is expected to testify;
   c. the substance of the opinion to which the expert is expected to testify;
   d. the grounds upon which the expert bases his or her opinion.

Deborah Schulansky
By her attorney
Phyllis Slater
Gomez, Robbins and Slater
322 Puritan Road
Plymouth, MA 02360
(508) 293-7024

UNITED STATES DISTRICT COURT
DISTRICT OF MASSACHUSETTS

CIVIL ACTION NO. 99-6719

DEBORAH SCHULANSKY,

Plaintiff

v.

RICHARD L. RONAN,
RONAN CONSTRUCTION
COMPANY,
Defendants

DEFENDANT'S ANSWERS TO
PLAINTIFF'S FIRST SET OF
INTERROGATORIES UNDER
FED. R. CIV. P. 33

The defendant Richard L. Ronan responds to the plaintiff's first set of interrogatories as follows:

1. Please list each occasion on which you or anyone acting on behalf of you or Ronan Construction Company discussed the terms or performance of the contract in issue in this action with the plaintiff.

Answer: I met with the plaintiff twice in early March of 1999 to discuss the work. She also visited the site in early May during the construction. She called me twice late in May to discuss alleged damage resulting from the work.

2. For each conversation identified in Interrogatory #1, please state in detail the substance of that conversation, stating in chronological order what was said by each of the parties.

Answer: At the first meeting, we discussed generally the nature of the work to be done, my experience on similar jobs, and when I would be able to do the work.

At the second meeting, we went over specifics concerning dimensions, materials, excavation, subcontracting electrical work, and landscaping. We agreed to a price and I agreed to send a Proposal and Estimate for Ms. Schulansky to sign. During the conversations in late May, the plaintiff expressed concern about some stress cracks in several rooms of the house. I explained that these cracks did not result from the addition work, but were there when we began the job. They result from settling over the two hundred odd years since the house was built.

3. Please identify the name and address of each person who was present during each and every conversation between yourself and the plaintiff, prior to, during, and after the execution of the contract at issue in this action.

Figure 20-4

<u>Answer:</u> Deborah Schulansky, 219 Parker Street, Plymouth, MA 02360, and Richard L. Ronan, 3 Carleton Drive, Nashua, NH 04125.

4. Please identify the name and address of each person who has any knowledge of the facts concerning the negotiations, execution, or performance of the contract that is at issue in this action.

<u>Answer:</u> Deborah Schulansky and Richard L. Ronan. As to performance, Arlen Jones, 14 Prescott Place, Canterbury, NH 03316; Marie Shepard, 62 Summer Street, Laconia, NH 03329; Renee Dufresne, 19 Third Ave, Nashua, NH 03325; and T. J. Argento, 414 Piper Lane, Nashua, NH 03327 (office address) as well.

5. Please identify each and every document, letter, memorandum, or other record, whether in electronic or other form, of which you have knowledge, whether or not it is in your custody, possession or control, that contains information concerning the negotiations, execution, or performance of the contract in issue in this action.

<u>Answer:</u> Proposal and estimate attached to plaintiff's complaint: letter agreement dated April 8, 1999, between Ronan Construction Company and Arlen Jones.

6. Please identify each and every document, brochure, information sheet, advertisement, or other writing that describes the nature of the construction services offered by Ronan Construction Company, or its expertise or experience in restoring or working on historic properties.

<u>Answer:</u> occasional advertisements in Manchester Union Leader, Old House Journal, Lowell Sun over the last three years. Specific dates not known.

7. For each document identified in response to Interrogatory #5, please state whether such document is within your possession, custody, or control, and if not, state to the best of your knowledge who does have possession, custody, or control of such document.

<u>Answer:</u> Advertising copy may be available from publisher of each paper specified in answer to Interrogatory #6.

8. Please state whether any documents relating to the events alleged in this action have been lost or destroyed. If the answer is "yes," please state for each such document the nature and content of the document, the person creating the document, and the circumstances surrounding the loss or destruction of that document.

<u>Answer:</u> None.

9. Please list the names and addresses of all persons who performed any services related to the work that forms the basis of this action.

<u>Answer:</u> Richard L. Ronan, Arlen Jones, Marie Shepard, Renee Dufresne. Also T. J. Argento (electrical contractor).

For addresses see response to Interrogatory #4.

10. For each person identified in Interrogatory #9, please specify the nature of the services performed, the manner in which such person was compensated (whether by the job, hourly, weekly, or otherwise), the amount of compensation provided to such person for this job, whether a contract was entered into for the services rendered by such person, and the number of other jobs on which such person has rendered services for either of the defendants during the last two years.

Answer: The defendant objects to this interrogatory as burdensome and calling for information that is irrelevant to the issues in suit. Without waiving this objection, the defendant responds that Arlen Jones conducted the excavation pursuant to a letter agreement dated April 8, 1999, for a fixed price of $3,000.

11. Please identify each and every contract or other agreement, whether in writing or not, concerning the addition work that is the subject of this action, which either defendant entered into with the plaintiff, with Alton Jones, or with any other persons who rendered services on the contract that is the subject of this action.

Answer: Proposal and estimate attached to plaintiff's complaint; letter agreement dated April 8, 1999, between Ronan Construction Company and Arlen Jones.

12. Please identify, by giving the address of the property and the name and address of the owner, each and every structure in excess of 100 years old on which you or your company have rendered construction services during the last six years.

Answer: The defendant objects to this interrogatory as burdensome and calling for irrelevant information beyond the proper bounds of discovery.

13. For each property identified in Interrogatory #12, please state whether any dispute arose concerning the terms or performance of the work, and if so, whether any legal action was threatened or initiated against either you or Ronan Construction Company as a result of such dispute.

Answer: The defendant objects to this interrogatory as burdensome and calling for irrelevant information beyond the proper bounds of discovery. Without waiving this objection, the defendant states that neither he nor Ronan Construction Company has been sued for any claim arising out of his construction business during the past six years.

14. Please state whether either of the defendants has made an investigation into the allegations upon which the complaint in this action is based.

Answer: Yes.

15. If the answer to Interrogatory #14 is "yes," please state for each such investigation

a. the names and addresses of each person who has made
such investigation.

<u>Answer:</u> Richard L. Ronan

b. the dates of each such investigation.

<u>Answer:</u> June 1, 1999.

c. identify all reports, summaries, witness statements, photographs, estimates, opinions or other documents, whether
in written or electronic form, that have been created as a
result of such investigation, including any specifications or
estimates of damages to the original house or addition at
the Alton property.

<u>Answer:</u> None.

16.   Please describe, step by step, in detail and in chronological order, exactly what you or your servants or agents or subcontractors
did to rebuild or reinforce the old part of the foundation exposed
during the excavation for the addition that is the subject of this action, or to ascertain the sufficiency of that foundation to support the
addition at issue in this action.

<u>Answer:</u> The rock foundation was solid and did not require any
reconstruction. At the plaintiff's request, we poured concrete
into several open spaces among the rocks during the work.

17.   Please identify by name and address each person who was
present during any part of the work that is the subject of Interrogatory #16.

<u>Answer:</u> Richard L. Ronan, Deborah Schulansky, Arlen Jones,
Marie Shepard, Renee Dufresne, T. J. Argento.

18.   Please state each and every fact upon which you rely in support of your contention in the Fourth Defense in your Answer to the
complaint, alleging that the plaintiff waived performance of the contractual obligation to reinforce the foundation prior to construction
of the addition.

<u>Answer:</u> When the plaintiff visited the site on April 17, 1999,
the foundation was exposed and she asked whether it was sufficient. I said it was, but I would fill in any holes in the foundation with concrete. She agreed that this would be satisfactory.

19.   Please state each and every fact upon which you rely in support of your contention in the Second Defense in your Answer that
the defendants are not subject to personal jurisdiction in this action.

<u>Answer:</u> This action arises out of work done in New Hampshire.
The defendant Richard L. Ronan is domiciled in New Hampshire
and has not been served with process in Massachusetts. Ronan
Construction Company is a New Hampshire corporation with offices in New Hampshire. None of the services rendered under

the agreement in suit were rendered in Massachusetts, nor has either defendant consented to suit in Massachusetts on this claim.

20. Please state each and every fact upon which you rely in support of your contention in the Third Defense in your Answer that the Proposal and Estimate for the work involved in this action constitutes the entire agreement of the parties and does not require reconstruction of the foundation.

<u>Answer:</u> The parties signed the Proposal and Estimate, which includes all the terms of the contract between them. There was no other agreement requiring reconstruction of the foundation nor does the written contract require it.

21. Please state the name and address of each expert you expect to call to testify at the trial.

<u>Answer:</u> The defendant will make disclosure of its expert witnesses in accordance with Fed. R. Civ. P. 26(a) (2) at least 90 days prior to the anticipated date of trial.

22. For each expert identified in Interrogatory #21, please specify
   a. his or her professional qualifications;
   b. the subjects upon which the expert is expected to testify;
   c. the substance of the opinion to which the expert is expected to testify;
   d. the grounds upon which the expert bases his or her opinion.

<u>Answer:</u> The defendant will make disclosure of its expert witnesses in accordance with Fed. R. Civ. P. 26(a) (2) at least 90 days prior to the anticipated date of trial.

Signed Under the Penalties of Perjury This <u>21st</u> Day of <u>November</u> 2000.

_____
Richard L. Ronan

Signed as to objections

_____
Arthur Ackerman
Ackerman, Sloan & Cariotis
59 State Street
Boston, MA 02114
(617) 228-6301

Comments on the *Schulansky* Interrogatories

1.   Many of Schulansky's interrogatories seek the identity of witnesses and records relevant to the action. Once Schulansky learns the names of relevant witnesses, they can be interviewed (if they are willing to be) or deposed (if they are not). The answers regarding records can be followed up with a Rule 34 Request for Production of Documents. As the Introduction explains, automatic disclosure of supporting witnesses and records is now required under Federal Rule 26(a).

Counsel often combine interrogatories with a request to produce the documents that are identified in the answers to interrogatories. For example, Schulansky's counsel could add a request after Interrogatories #5 and #6 that all records identified be produced for inspection and copying pursuant to Rule 34.

2.   The interrogatories are addressed to defendant Richard L. Ronan, not to both defendants together. Under Rule 33(a), court permission is required to serve more than 25 interrogatories on "any other party." Presumably, Ronan Construction Company is a different "party," even though it is Ronan's company, so Schulansky can presumably still serve 25 *more* interrogatories on it.

Placing a limit on the number of interrogatories may lead counsel to resort to questions with sub-parts. See, for example, Interrogatories #15 and #22. This can lead to tedious battles (at $150 an hour, no less) over whether such sub-questions are really separate questions that should count toward the limit.

3.   Interrogatories must be served on all other parties to the action (not just the responding party), and usually must be filed with the court.[11] See Rule 5(a), (d). This keeps all parties fully informed of what has occurred in the action.

4.   Interrogatory #19 seeks discovery on the issue of the court's jurisdiction to hear the case rather than the merits. Discovery on jurisdictional issues is proper, since they obviously pertain to the adjudication of the dispute. *Oppenheimer Fund, Inc. v. Sanders,* 437 U.S. 340, 351 n.13 (1978); Chapter 19, ex. 3.

5.   Interrogatories #18-20 ask Ronan to state all the facts upon which he bases various defenses raised in the answer. These are known as "contention

---

11. Some courts now *bar* the routine filing of most discovery materials, presumably because of the burden of filing and storing these materials. See, e.g., Local Rules of the Federal District Court for the District of Massachusetts, Rule 26.6(A).

interrogatories," because they ask the opponent to lay out the factual basis for contentions raised more generally in the pleadings.

For many years, the courts were split on whether contention interrogatories were permissible. In 1970, Rule 33(c) was added, which provides that an interrogatory is not objectionable "merely because an answer to the interrogatory involves an opinion or contention that relates to fact or the application of law to fact." This amendment clearly approves use of contention interrogatories to probe the factual basis for allegations, and also to narrow the issues by revealing what is *not* contended. Here, for example, Ronan's answer to Interrogatory #18 shows that he relies on the conversation at the worksite as the ground for his waiver argument. This will assist Schulansky in preparing to meet this defense at trial.

Sometimes parties will not be able to respond effectively to contention interrogatories until they have conducted most of their own discovery. To obviate this problem, Rule 33(c) allows the court to order that such interrogatories not be answered until other discovery is completed.

Comments on Ronan's Answers to Interrogatories

6.   Although Rule 33 does not require parties responding to interrogatories to restate each interrogatory before the response, this obviously makes the responses much easier for all parties to review. Some local rules require setting forth the interrogatory before each response.

7.   These interrogatories look so comprehensive and detailed that you would expect them to yield a great deal of useful information. When you compare the answers, however, the reality doesn't live up to their promise. Some answers are too general to be really helpful. Others seem to reflect stonewalling or laziness. Still others indicate that Ronan has no information on the matter. (This, it turns out, can be *very* helpful, since Ronan will be bound by this representation; he cannot later bring forth evidence at trial which he has denied having in answering the interrogatories.)

For example, Ronan's answer to Interrogatory #2 seems minimally responsive: It does not provide details of who said what, in what order, even to the best of Ronan's memory. Schulansky might move for further answers, but the court probably won't be impressed. Interrogatories like this tend to invite summary answers. To get precise details, counsel should ask very specific questions ("At your meeting on February 23, 1999, did you tell the plaintiff that you would tear out the old foundation and rebuild it?" or "State exactly what you told the plaintiff at the February 23, 1999, meeting that you would do to the old foundation."). Or, better still, she should depose Ronan so she can ask precise follow-up questions.

8.   Ronan has objected to Interrogatory #10 as burdensome and irrelevant. These details do seem pretty peripheral to the issue of the sinking foundation, so the objection is at least arguable. And Ronan has made his position

look more reasonable by providing the one item that Schulansky probably would press for, the agreement between Ronan and Jones, which is relevant on the question of whether Jones was a Ronan employee or an independent contractor. Schulansky's counsel probably won't press the point.

9.   Presumably Schulansky has included Interrogatories #12 and #13 to determine whether Ronan, who represented to her that he was an expert at working on historic houses, had had problems on other such jobs. This might, I suppose, lead to other admissible evidence (see Rule 26(b)(1)), but it is pretty much of a fishing expedition. By objecting, Ronan puts the burden on Schulansky to give up on this or move to compel production. And, by responding that he hasn't been sued on any jobs, Ronan lets her know that she at least won't find that if she pushes the point. (Notice that he did *not* say there had been no disputes, just that there had been no suits.)

It is common for parties to state an objection to an interrogatory, but then to provide some responsive information anyway, both to appear cooperative and to reduce the opponent's incentive to file a motion to compel further answers.

10. Schulansky's counsel asked for any reports of investigations by Ronan, but did not consider the possibility that he investigated but didn't write anything down. Now she will have to ask supplemental interrogatories as to his findings or explore this at Ronan's deposition.

11. Interrogatory #21 and #22, requesting information concerning expert witnesses, may not be appropriate. Rule 26(a)(2) requires automatic disclosure of information concerning the qualifications, compensation, and opinions of trial experts 90 days before trial. Here, Ronan has taken the position that Rule 26(a)(2) governs disclosure of experts, so that he does not have to provide information about them until that rule requires it.

12. As discussed in the examples, Ronan has signed the interrogatories, but Ronan's counsel has signed separately as to the objections, indicating that he has considered the objections raised and deems them legally justified.

21

Defective Allegation or Insufficient Proof?: Dismissal for Failure to State a Claim Compared to Summary Judgment

Introduction

One major theme of the civil procedure course is "The Perils of Plaintiff" or "all the ways you can bring a lawsuit and never get to trial." We have already explored a variety of purely *procedural* defects that may bring the suit to an untimely end, such as lack of jurisdiction, improper venue, and improper service of process. However, there are also several devices that defendants may use to challenge the *merits* of the plaintiff's case before trial, which may foreclose a trial if the court agrees with the defendant's objections. The principal devices for such pretrial resolution are the motion to dismiss for failure to state a claim upon which relief can be granted, or "12(b)(6) motion," and the motion for summary judgment under Rule 56. This chapter will examine these two motions in turn and offer some examples to help you distinguish them.

The Rule 12(b)(6) Motion

Under Rule 12(b)(6) of the Federal Rules (and the similar "demurrer" device in code pleading jurisdictions) a defendant may move to dismiss the plaintiff's complaint on the ground that it fails to state a claim that entitles the plaintiff to any form of relief. The gist of the defendant's objection in making the motion is that the "wrong" that the plaintiff describes in his complaint is not recognized as a violation of any legal rights. If that is true, the court would not be able to grant damages or other relief to the plaintiff even if he proved all the facts alleged.

Suppose, for example, that Ferraro sues Gramm for voting Republican, after he promised Ferraro that he wouldn't. The law does not currently recognize a right to have promises performed unless consideration, estoppel, or some other additional acts make the promise binding. Even if Ferraro proves that Gramm made the promise, a court could not grant her any relief for Gramm's failure to keep it. Since there is no right to relief on Ferraro's claim, it would simply place a pointless burden on the court and the parties to proceed with the action. On these facts Gramm could move to dismiss the complaint for failure to state a claim upon which relief can be granted.

Because the purpose of the Rule 12(b)(6) motion is to test whether the plaintiff's allegations (assuming they can be proved) state a claim for which a court might grant relief, the *only* question posed by the motion is whether the complaint itself states a legally sufficient claim. Consequently, the court does not consider any other pleadings or evidence in deciding the motion. Nor does the court consider or determine whether the facts alleged in the complaint are ture; for purposes of the motion, it assumes that the facts alleged *are* true. The motion only addresses a purely legal question: whether, if the plaintiff proves the allegations in the complaint, he will have established a cause of action entitling him to some form of relief from the court. In cases like Ferraro's, dismissal on the basis of the complaint alone is appropriate under this test. Since Ferraro's complaint does not state a legal wrong for which the court could grant her redress, allowing her to litigate the allegations through discovery and trial would be a waste of both the parties' and the court's time.

Dismissal of a suit for failure to state a claim is a drastic measure. If the court dismisses, the plaintiff will never have the opportunity to present his case to a jury, or to gather evidence through the discovery process that might demonstrate that he has suffered a legally cognizable injury. Consequently, courts give every benefit of the doubt to the plaintiff in deciding the motion. The Supreme Court has held that a complaint should not be dismissed under Rule 12(b)(6) "unless it appears beyond doubt that the plaintiff can prove no set of facts in support of his claim which would entitle him to relief." *Conley v. Gibson,* 355 U.S. 41, 45-46 (1957). The court may not consider the likelihood that the plaintiff will be able to prove his factual allegations; it must assume for purposes of deciding the motion that the plaintiff *will* prove them.

In considering the motion, the pleadings must be liberally construed in favor of sustaining the complaint. Thus, if the allegations in the complaint are susceptible of two constructions, one of which would support relief while the other would not, the court must construe the complaint in favor of the pleader. For example, a complaint that alleges that the defendant "swerved and ran into me on Bleecker Street" might be construed to allege either negligent driving or an unavoidable accident. The court, under *Conley,* would likely infer that the plaintiff (who is suing the defendant, after all) is alleging that the collision resulted from the defendant's negligence.

In cases like Ferraro's, a complaint will be vulnerable to dismissal under Rule 12(b)(6) because the plaintiff has sought relief for acts that are simply not proscribed under current law. In other cases, however, the complaint may be defective because the plaintiff (or his lawyer) has simply failed to allege the necessary elements of a claim that, if properly pleaded, would state a sufficient claim. Suppose, for example, that Berlin sues Porter for malicious prosecution, alleging that Porter filed a criminal complaint against him without cause, and that as a result he suffered damage to his reputation. To recover for malicious prosecution a plaintiff must prove that the original proceeding (in this example, the criminal case) was brought without probable cause, that it was terminated in his favor, that the defendant acted with an improper purpose, and that the plaintiff suffered resulting harm. See Restatement (Second) of Torts §653. If Berlin's complaint does not allege favorable termination, Porter may move to dismiss for failure to state a claim, on the ground that Berlin has failed to allege all the necessary elements of a claim for malicious prosecution.

Now, Berlin's failure to plead favorable termination may simply be an oversight. If so, the court will allow Berlin to amend the complaint to add this allegation, and the suit will proceed.[1] However, Berlin may not be able to allege favorable termination. For example, he may have been convicted, or entered into a plea bargain. If that is the case, his complaint is fatally defective and cannot be rescued by an amendment. Since an essential element of the complaint cannot be alleged, the claim may be dismissed under Rule 12(b)(6).

Before comparing the Rule 12(b)(6) motion with the motion for summary judgment, a few examples may help to clarify the function of the

---

1. When a complaint is dismissed, the court will ordinarily give the plaintiff at least one opportunity to amend to cure defects in the original complaint. See 3 Moore's at §12.34[5].

motion to dismiss for failure to state a claim. In considering the examples, assume that all actions are brought as diversity actions in federal court, that personal and subject matter jurisdiction are proper, and that state substantive law applies. (The explanations begin on page 398.)

EXAMPLES

Threshold Challenges

1.   While Gershwin and his wife, Comden, are jogging in Central Park in New York City, a car driven by Hart negligently careens off the road and hits Gershwin. Comden is not hit herself but suffers severe emotional distress from seeing Gershwin seriously injured. She sues Hart, alleging the above facts in her complaint and claiming a right to damages for negligent infliction of emotional distress. Hart moves to dismiss under Rule 12(b)(6).

    a. How would you phrase the issue posed by Hart's motion?

    b. Assume that New York law does not recognize a right to relief for negligent infliction of emotional distress unless the plaintiff also suffered direct physical injury from the defendant's negligence; that is, she was hit by the car too (or, perhaps, flying debris). Will Hart's motion be granted?

2.   Assume that Comden makes the same allegations but also includes in her complaint an allegation that there is a right to relief under New York law for negligent infliction of emotional distress even if the plaintiff suffered no physical injury. Hart moves to dismiss for failure to state a claim. Should the motion be granted?

3.   Assume, for purposes of this example only, that the right to recover for negligent infliction of emotional distress under New York law is not quite so clear. Early cases rejected such recovery, but recent appellate cases have allowed recovery for intentional infliction of emotional distress without physical injury. Comden can make a fair argument that the recent cases effectively overrule prior law and recognize a right to relief for negligently inflicted emotional injuries as well. Is a motion to dismiss for failure to state a claim a proper means for Hart to challenge the complaint?

Void for Vagueness?

4.   Assume that New York law bars recovery for emotional injuries without accompanying physical impact but that Comden words her complaint more generally. She alleges that Hart negligently drove his automobile in Central Park on the day in question and that Hart's negligence proximately caused personal injuries to her, for which she claims damages. Hart moves to dismiss for failure to state a claim. Will the motion be granted?

5.   Jones is arrested for vagrancy by Rogers, a police officer of the Town of Broadway. Rogers books Jones and places him in a cell. An hour later, Jones

is found hanging from the bars of the cell, an apparent suicide. Kern, the administrator of Jones's estate, sues Broadway for wrongful death, claiming that the town is liable for the failure of Rogers and other officers to take precautions to prevent Jones from taking his own life. Under applicable tort law, the Town would be liable if its employees, acting in the scope of employment, failed to take precautions to protect Jones from suicide, provided they knew or had reason to know of the particular risk that Jones might attempt suicide.

The complaint alleges that Rogers arrested and booked Jones, that neither he nor the other officers took any precautions to assure Jones's safety, that Jones committed suicide in the cell, and that the Town is therefore liable to the estate for damages. Broadway moves to dismiss the complaint for failure to state a claim upon which relief can be granted. Should the motion be granted?

6. Assume, on the facts of example 5, that Kern files an amended complaint, which properly alleges the necessary elements of the claim, including the requirement that the officers should have known of the risk that Jones would attempt suicide. Broadway answers the complaint, denying that its officers had any reason to know that Jones might attempt suicide. The Town then files a motion to dismiss for failure to state a claim, on the ground that its officers had no reason to know this risk.

   a. Can Broadway make the motion at this point?

   b. Will the motion be granted?

Summary Judgment Distinguished

The first part of this chapter suggests that the plaintiff does not bear a heavy burden in avoiding dismissal under Rule 12(b)(6). He need not prove any facts nor even allege them in detail so long as the court can infer that he is alleging the elements of a proper claim. The motion offers no assistance in weeding out cases in which a proper cause of action has been alleged but the plaintiff cannot prove his claim.

The motion for summary judgment under Fed. R. Civ. P. 56 is designed to allow early resolution of cases in which the plaintiff meets the minimal burden to plead the elements of a compensable claim, but cannot *prove* one or more of those elements. *Summary* judgment means entry of judgment by the court in favor of either the plaintiff or the defendant without trial. Such resolution of the case (or a part of it) by the judge is appropriate only if the evidence before the court demonstrates that there are no disputed issues of material fact to be tried and that the moving party is entitled to judgment on the undisputed facts. Fed. R. Civ. P. 56(c).

Suppose, for example, that Berlin, the malicious prosecution plaintiff introduced above, properly alleges that Porter brought a criminal action against him, that he had no probable cause, that it was brought without a proper purpose, and that it terminated in his favor. However, Porter knows that the case was "continued without a finding" by the court, rather than dismissed.[2] If this disposition does not constitute "favorable termination," Berlin cannot win his malicious prosecution case. Under Rule 56, Porter may challenge Berlin's ability to prove favorable termination by moving for summary judgment, supported by evidence to prove that the case was continued without a finding and a memorandum arguing that the continuance is insufficient to meet the "favorable termination" element of a malicious prosecution action.

Porter's motion challenges Berlin's ability to prove an essential element of his claim. Berlin cannot recover without showing that the criminal case was resolved in his favor; Porter has produced evidence that it was not. When the motion is made and adequately supported, Berlin must respond by producing admissible evidence that tends to prove the challenged element. Fed. R. Civ. P. 56(e). He might, for example, submit evidence that there were two charges against him and that one was continued but the one on which he relies was dismissed. He might submit evidence that the continuance the defendant relies on was simply to postpone the hearing and that the case was subsequently dismissed. Such evidence would demonstrate that there is a "genuine issue of material fact" as to whether the prior proceeding was terminated in Berlin's favor.

If Berlin produces such countervailing evidence, summary judgment must be denied. Summary judgment is not meant to try the facts but only to determine whether there are genuinely contested issues of material fact. Thus, the burden of the party opposing summary judgment is only to show that he has legally competent evidence upon which a jury could resolve the factual issues in his favor. If there is a genuine dispute as to the relevant facts, it is the jury's role to resolve it. The judge's role on summary judgment is only to determine whether the parties' evidence reveals such a factual dispute.

If Berlin does *not* produce countervailing evidence, he has not demonstrated that there is a factual dispute for the jury to try. If his action against Porter were allowed to go to a jury without any evidence to prove that the original action had terminated in his favor, the jury would have no legitimate basis upon which to find for Berlin. A verdict for him could only reflect irrational decision-making. Summary judgment avoids this risk, as well as the delay and expense of trying unprovable cases.

---

2. In some states, criminal cases may be "continued" for a period of time rather than dismissed or tried. Under this procedure the court can impose conditions on the defendant in exchange for suspending the prosecution, but the defendant does not plead guilty or acquire a criminal record. Since this practice is routinely used in cases in which the defendant's guilt is clear, it is doubtful that the court would hold that such a continuance constitutes "favorable termination" under the common law of malicious prosecution. At least one case has held that it does not. *Van Arsdale v. Caswell*, 311 S.W.2d 404 (Ky. 1958).

Some Interim Questions

7. Assume that Berlin has alleged that the prior suit was terminated in his favor but has no evidence to prove it. Could Porter obtain dismissal of Berlin's claim under Rule 12(b)(6) at the outset of the case?

8. Why might Berlin have filed the action if the case was continued indefinitely rather than dismissed? Isn't he wasting his time and money and flouting the ethical constraints on pleading in Rule 11?

Summary judgment provides a needed avenue for resolution of another category of cases, in which the parties agree on the underlying facts but disagree as to the legal implications of those facts. In Berlin's case, for example, the parties may agree that the case was decided by a continuance without a finding but disagree as to whether that disposition constitutes "favorable termination" for purposes of an action for malicious prosecution. If so, Porter might move for summary judgment, supported by evidence that the case was continued without a finding. If Berlin admits that the case was continued, he will not respond with countervailing evidence but instead make the legal argument that the continuance satisfies the "favorable termination" element of a malicious prosecution claim. On these facts, the motion has framed a single, dispositive legal issue for the court. If it concludes that the continuance suffices for favorable termination, it will deny summary judgment and allow the case to proceed. If it concludes that it does not satisfy the favorable termination requirement, it will enter judgment for Porter because he is "entitled to judgment as a matter of law."[3]

The motion can also be used to resolve individual claims in a multi-claim lawsuit. Fed. R. Civ. P. 56(c), (d). See, for example, the motion in the *Schulansky* case, infra p. 615, which sought summary judgment on one of the plaintiff's contract claims only. Or, claims by or against one party might be resolved on summary judgment, leaving others for trial. For example, Hart might get summary judgment on the emotional distress claim alleged by Comden in example 1, but still have to go to trial on Gershwin's physical injury claim.

Rule 56 provides that a motion for summary judgment may be supported by affidavits, depositions, answers to interrogatories, admissions, and admissible documents. Fed. R. Civ. P. 56(c), (e). These materials are not always admissible at trial themselves, but they demonstrate that the party has access to evidence that would be admissible. For example, an affidavit of Hart concerning the Central Park accident is a sworn evidentiary statement based upon personal knowledge. If the case went to trial, Hart could come into

---

3. Often the parties will stipulate to the relevant facts and submit the case for decision on "cross motions" for summary judgment, each arguing that he should get judgment as a matter of law on the undisputed facts.

court and give the same testimony. So the affidavit shows that Hart *has* admissible evidence to support his claim. The same is true for depositions, admissions, and answers to interrogatories, all of which represent sworn statements of parties or witnesses. Many documents, if shown to be authentic, are also admissible under the rules of evidence and therefore may also be used to support or oppose a summary judgment motion. In the Broadway case, for example, the police booking records would be admissible evidence. However, allegations in the pleadings, which represent the parties' *assertions* as to what they can prove, are not admissible evidence and therefore may not be used as supporting evidence on a summary judgment motion.

Another Interim Question

9.   Why must the evidence presented in support of or in opposition to a motion for summary judgment be evidence that would be admissible at trial?

The function of the summary judgment motion is similar to that of the Rule 12(b)(6) motion, but there are important differences. The following examples should help you to understand summary judgment and its relationship to the motion to dismiss for failure to state a claim.

EXAMPLES

No Genuine Issue

10.   Recall example 5, involving Comden's claim against Hart for negligent infliction of emotional distress. In that example Comden pleaded generally that she had suffered "personal injuries" and the complaint therefore survived a motion to dismiss.
- a. If New York law did not recognize a right to relief for negligent infliction of emotional distress without direct physical injury, could Hart obtain judgment on a motion for summary judgment?
- b. If he seeks summary judgment, what supporting materials might he submit?

11.   Suppose, on the same facts, that Hart moves for summary judgment on Comden's claim, supported by an excerpt from Comden's deposition in which she admits that she suffered no direct physical injury. Comden responds with an affidavit stating in detail the emotional injuries she sustained and the lost earnings that resulted from her emotional reaction to the accident. She also submits authenticated bills for resulting psychiatric care. Should the motion be granted?

12.   Consider again Berlin's case against Porter, in which he sought recovery for malicious prosecution. Assume that the original criminal action was tried, and Berlin was found not guilty. After suing Porter for malicious

prosecution, and alleging favorable termination, Berlin files a motion for summary judgment, attaching a copy of the court docket that shows the not-guilty finding and subsequent dismissal of the criminal case. If Porter produces no countervailing evidence, what order should the court enter?

13. In Kern's action against Broadway arising from the jail suicide, assume that Kern's complaint properly alleges the elements of the claim. Broadway answers, denying that Rogers or the other officers knew or should have known of Jones's suicidal tendencies. It then moves for summary judgment, supported by an affidavit of Rogers, the booking officer, in which he testifies that Jones was sullen and uncommunicative when arrested, that he never made any statement indicating an intent to take his life, and that Jones was strongly intoxicated and never said a word during the entire booking process. Kern opposes the motion, but does not submit any supporting materials. Should the motion be granted?

Point/Counterpoint

14. Broadway moves for summary judgment, supported by affidavits of all the police officers involved in the arrest and booking of Jones. Each testifies that Jones behaved normally during the process, cooperated with the officers, did not appear depressed, and made no statements suggesting he might attempt suicide.

    a. Assume that Kern submits no opposing affidavits or evidence. How does the judge know that the officers are telling the truth in their affidavits? If she doesn't, how could she grant summary judgment for Broadway?

    b. Kern submits no opposing evidence but argues in opposition to the motion that he has alleged in his complaint that the officers knew or should have known that Jones was suicidal, thus placing that fact in dispute. Should the motion be granted?

    c. Kern submits his own affidavit in opposition to the motion, in which he states under oath that Officer Rogers "knew or should have known from Jones's behavior that Jones was depressed and suicidal." Should the motion be granted?

    d. Kern submits an opposing affidavit that states that Jones called him shortly after his arrest and was crying and threatening suicide on the phone. He also submits an affidavit from a witness to Jones's arrest, who states that Jones was irrational and made suicidal statements when Officer Rogers arrested him. Should the motion be granted?

    e. In responding to the police officers' affidavits described in the beginning of the example, Kern submits an affidavit in opposition to the motion stating that the officers failed to take Jones's belt away from him, and that Jones hung himself with the belt. Broadway responds with a further affidavit of Rogers stating that Jones was not wearing a belt at the time of his arrest. Should the motion be granted?

Baring the Burden

15. Broadway moves for summary judgment. In support of the motion, it submits Kern's answer to an interrogatory asking him to "state all facts upon which you base your allegations that the police officers knew or should have known that Jones was suicidal." Kern's response to this interrogatory states that Jones had told him several days earlier that he wanted to die, and that Jones was in desperate financial circumstances and had just separated from his wife. Broadway also submits an excerpt from Kern's deposition, in which he is again asked what facts he relies on to establish the officers' knowledge that Jones might attempt suicide. Kern's response was, "It was obvious; he had been depressed for months, often talked of suicide, and was out of a job. Don't your officers have any common sense?" Broadway does not submit any evidence from its own witnesses but argues that this record demonstrates that Kern cannot support his claim that the officers knew of the risk of suicide. Kern offers no affidavits of his own. Should the motion be granted?

EXPLANATIONS

Threshold Challenges

1a. The issue posed by the motion is whether a party who suffers emotional distress from witnessing negligently caused injury to another, but suffers no direct physical injury himself, has a right to recover damages for emotional distress from the negligent party. Note that the issue is not whether Comden actually suffered the emotional distress or whether Hart was negligent but only whether, assuming all the pleaded facts to be true, the law authorizes an award of damages for such injuries.

  b. On the assumption given, this motion should be granted. It is clear from the allegations in Comden's complaint that she is claiming relief based solely on emotional distress. If New York law does not recognize a right to relief for acts that only cause emotional distress to a defendant, Comden has asked for relief that the court cannot grant. If the court allowed Comden to proceed to trial, and Comden proved at trial that Hart was negligent, that his negligence caused physical injuries to Gershwin, and that Comden suffered emotional distress as a result, the court would still be unable to grant Comden's demand for damages. The claim Comden has alleged is simply not recognized under the applicable law as a legal wrong entitling her to compensation. If that is true, there is no reason to proceed to trial. In such cases, the court can short-circuit the process by dismissing the case at the outset. That's what Rule 12(b)(6) is designed to do.

2. Comden's train of thought here is creative, though unavailing. If the court must assume the truth of the allegations in the complaint, why not allege that the law allows relief for emotional distress without physical injury? Unfortunately, Comden is singing the wrong tune. The court only accepts

the *factual* allegations of the complaint as true for purposes of the motion. The legal issue of whether her allegations state a claim is exactly what the motion is intended to resolve. Rule 12(b)(6) would be useless if the plaintiff could simply allege that he has stated a compensable claim and thereby prevent the court from deciding whether he has.

3.   In this example it is difficult to determine whether Comden has stated a claim for relief because the state of the law on the crucial issue in the case is not definitively settled by the cases. If the recent cases have effectively overruled the old doctrine, Comden has stated a compensable claim and must be allowed a chance to prove her allegations. If, on the other hand, the old rule remains valid (perhaps because the recent cases limited the right to recover to emotional distress caused by intentional acts) Comden has not stated a claim.

Although the motion here requires close analysis of the relevant case law, Hart's motion to dismiss is still a proper means to challenge the sufficiency of Comden's complaint. The Rule 12(b)(6) motion is available to resolve difficult issues of law as well as clear ones, and whether Comden has stated a claim depends on a question of law. If the court determines that the recent New York cases have established a right to recover for negligent infliction of emotional distress without physical injury, it should deny the motion and allow Comden to go to trial. On the other hand, if the court concludes that the recent cases are limited to intentional acts, it should dismiss since Comden's allegations are based solely on negligence.

Admittedly, some courts may be reluctant to grant motions to dismiss if the state of the law is unsettled. The court may sense that the issue is a close one that could be better decided on a full record after discovery or trial. The judge might therefore allow the case to proceed to trial and allow the appellate court to clarify the law on appeal after a verdict. But if the court is convinced that the case law does not allow recovery, it has the power to dismiss under Rule 12(b)(6) since the issue, though difficult, is one of law for the court.

Void for Vagueness?

4.   Comden has phrased her allegations so generally here that the court cannot tell from the complaint that the "personal injuries" she has suffered are solely emotional. You and I may know it from the facts described in example 1. Hart may know it since he knows that his car only hit Gershwin. But for purposes of the motion to dismiss, the court only "knows" what is in the complaint. Under *Conley v. Gibson,* the court must ask whether the plaintiff, on the allegations of the complaint, could prove any set of facts that would entitle her to relief. On these general allegations, Comden might prove that the "personal injuries" she suffered were direct physical injuries, clearly compensable under traditional negligence law. Thus, the complaint may state a claim upon which relief may be granted, and the motion must be denied.

If this tactic will avoid dismissal, and pleading this generally is sufficient under *Conley v. Gibson*, why would plaintiffs ever plead a questionable cause of action more specifically? One answer is that a more specific complaint is more helpful to the court and also will trigger more specific responses from the defendant in his answer. See Chapter 31, p. 573. In addition, the plaintiff may prefer to put the difficult legal issue on the table from the beginning. After all, if the case will ultimately turn on the legal question, it may be desirable to resolve it at the outset rather than vigorously litigating the truth of the factual allegations only to discover down the line that proving them will still leave the plaintiff without any right to relief.

On the other hand, in many cases plaintiffs *do* plead their claims very generally, as *Conley v. Gibson* allows, in order not to reveal weaknesses in their cases or simply to avoid giving the opposing party any "free discovery." In some cases such generality may at least postpone the day of reckoning, but as we shall see, the defendant will likely use the summary judgment motion to flush out such weaknesses anyway.

5. This complaint is insufficient for several reasons. To begin with, the Town is only liable if the police officers acted in the scope of employment, but Kern has not alleged that they did. However, most judges would not dismiss the complaint on this basis. Although the complaint does not explicitly include the scope-of-employment allegation, the complaint alleges that the police officers acted at the jail, performed acts that are part of ordinary police procedure, and that the Town is liable. It is a fair inference that the estate bases its claim on the fact that the officers acted in the scope of their employment for the Town. In ruling on the motion to dismiss, the court must resolve any ambiguities in the pleadings in favor of the nonmoving party. If the court, looking at the complaint, can reasonably infer that the plaintiff has stated a valid cause of action, it must deny the motion to dismiss. In this case, there is enough there for a court to conclude under the liberal pleading standard of *Conley v. Gibson* that the estate may have a compensable claim. Perhaps a judge who loves his rules will require the estate to amend to allege that the officers acted in the scope of employment, but the court should not dismiss the action on this ground.

The other defect, however, is substantive. Kern has not alleged that the officers had any reason to know that Jones was suicidal. Under the applicable tort law, the duty to take precautions arises once the officers in charge of Jones have reason to know that he might try to injure himself. If they didn't know or have reason to suspect that, the Town is not liable, even if they could have prevented the suicide by greater vigilance. Unless Kern alleges that they had reason to believe there was a risk of suicide, he has not alleged a necessary element of the cause of action.

It may be that Kern's counsel simply neglected to allege this element clearly in the complaint. If so, he will certainly be allowed to amend to cure the defect. However, if he didn't allege it because he has no reason to believe it is true, he will not be able to amend to make the allegation. If that is so, the complaint may be dismissed under Rule 12(b)(6) because, without such an allegation, there is no right to relief.

6a. The timing of Broadway's motion is procedurally proper. Rule 12(h)(2) authorizes the defendant to raise the objection of failure to state a claim in any pleading, by motion for judgment on the pleadings[4] or even at trial. The rules allow this objection to be raised throughout the suit because it is pointless for a court to proceed if it cannot ultimately provide the plaintiff with any relief for the claim he asserted.

b. Be careful to distinguish the issue of the legal sufficiency of the plaintiff's allegations from the factual issue of whether the allegations are true. Here, Broadway does not deny that Kern could recover, if he proved that its police officers should have known of the risk of Jones's suicide. Rather, Broadway denies that the officers had any reason to know of that risk. Broadway has really asked the judge to determine the truth of this allegation in the complaint, not its legal sufficiency.

At this stage of the case the court has no basis to determine whether the officers knew of the need to take precautions to protect Jones. Kern has alleged that they did, and Broadway has denied it. But at this point *there is absolutely no evidence before the court on the issue.* All it has before it is Kern's allegations and Broadway's denial. The motion to dismiss for failure to state a claim, whether made before or after the defendant answers the complaint, still challenges only the legal sufficiency of those allegations. Broadway's denial in its answer that the officers had reason to know that Jones might attempt suicide does not change the fact that Broadway may be liable if Kern proves that they did. Whether its officers should have realized the risk and taken precautions is a factual issue, which cannot be resolved on a 12(b)(6) motion.

Some Interim Questions

7. Even if he knows that Berlin cannot prove his claim for malicious prosecution, Porter will not be able to obtain dismissal under Rule 12(b)(6). On a 12(b)(6) motion the court only considers whether the plaintiff has alleged the elements necessary to state a claim. Here, Berlin alleged all the elements of malicious prosecution in his complaint, including that the original action terminated in his favor. The court cannot look beyond the plaintiff's allegations in deciding the Rule 12(b)(6) motion; therefore, such a motion would

---

4. A judgment on the pleadings is authorized by Fed. R. Civ. P. 12(c). It may be used either as a delayed motion to dismiss, that is, a challenge to the sufficiency of the complaint standing alone, or as a challenge to the sufficiency of the complaint in light of particular defenses raised in the answer. See generally 2A Moore's at §12, 38.

At this stage, the motion still challenges the legal sufficiency of the complaint, but it is technically not a "Rule 12(b)(6) motion"; that Rule applies to *pre*-answer motions only.

have been denied, since Berlin has alleged all the elements of the claim. Porter needs to "pierce the pleadings," that is, go beyond the allegations in the complaint in order to convince the court that although Berlin has *alleged* a proper claim for malicious prosecution, he cannot *prove* the favorable termination element of his claim.

8.   People file lawsuits for many reasons. Berlin may have been unclear as to the necessary elements of the claim, or he may have had grounds to believe that under the applicable law a continuance is sufficient to satisfy the favorable termination requirement. He may have hoped to induce Porter to settle the claim, despite doubt as to its legal sufficiency. He may even have had little hope of winning, yet filed suit as a means of venting his anger or embarrassing the defendant. In some cases such suits may violate the ethical limitations on pleading in Fed. R. Civ. P. 11 or the Code of Professional Responsibility, as a misuse of court process. In others, however, they may simply reflect the uncertainties inherent in the application of general legal principles to particular cases.

For whatever reason, many suits are filed that, when tested on the merits, prove fatally defective. Summary judgment provides a means to probe for such defects without going to trial on all issues in the case.

Another Interim Question

9.   When a party presents his case to the jury, he must place evidence before the jury on each element of his claim or defense. In order to present that evidence to the jury, it must be "admissible." Admissible evidence is evidence that is deemed sufficiently reliable, under established rules of evidence, for a jury to hear and consider in reaching its decision on the facts.

Since the point of the summary judgment motion is to see if there is any evidence on the challenged allegation for the jury to consider, it follows that the evidence used to support the motion should be evidence that the jury could hear at trial. If the party opposing summary judgment has no admissible evidence on one or more elements of his claim, the jury would have no evidentiary basis upon which to find that he had proved that element of his case. The summary judgment motion tests whether this is so by challenging the opposing party to produce such admissible evidence in opposition to the motion.

No Genuine Issue

10a. This is exactly the type of situation in which summary judgment allows parties to obtain judgment without trial, despite the fact that the plaintiff's complaint alleges a proper claim for relief. Here, Hart knows that Comden cannot prove a compensable claim under New York law, but Hart has to show the court that this is true by demonstrating that Comden cannot prove physical injury, an essential element of her claim. By moving for summary judgment supported by admissible evidence that Comden suffered no physical injuries, Hart will flush out the fatal weakness in Comden's case. Presumably, Comden will be unable to counter Hart's evidence since it is true. The motion will therefore demonstrate that there is "no genuine issue" (Fed. R. Civ. P. 56(c)) as to whether Comden suffered physical injuries and that Hart is entitled to judgment as a matter of law, since solely psychic injuries do not give rise to a right to recover under applicable law.

Note that here, as on the motion to dismiss under Rule 12(b)(6), the case ultimately boils down to a legal issue. However, in the procedural posture of this case, a 12(b)(6) motion would have been denied because Comden had alleged a compensable claim (due to the generality of her complaint), even though she cannot prove a crucial element of it. The summary judgment motion allows Hart to demonstrate this fatal weakness in Comden's case.

b. Hart may use any materials that demonstrate that he has admissible evidence to support his motion. A party's answers to interrogatories, for example, are sworn statements that the party could testify to at trial. Hart could send interrogatories to Comden asking whether she suffered direct physical injury in the accident. Comden would presumably answer "no," and that answer could be submitted in support of the motion. Hart could offer similar testimony from Comden's deposition or his own affidavit stating that his car did not hit Comden, that he observed Comden after the accident, and that she had no physical injuries. Sworn affidavits of other witnesses or a certified police report in which Comden stated that she suffered no physical injury would also constitute proper supporting evidence.

11. Assuming that New York law does not allow recovery for purely emotional injuries, Comden's claim will again end on a sour note. Hart has submitted admissible evidence in support of his motion that indicates that Comden did not suffer direct physical injury. Comden has filed an opposing affidavit, but the affidavit does not demonstrate that there is any issue as to whether she suffered physical injury. Her evidence goes to prove the severity of her psychic injury, but that is not enough to entitle her to take her case to a jury. She may be totally incapacitated and prove it by the testimony of 20 unimpeachable witnesses, but she will still not be entitled to relief if the law requires accompanying physical injury.

This example illustrates an important point. It is not enough to show that there is a dispute in the evidence on *some* fact; the dispute must be on an issue that is material to the right to recover. Here, Comden's opposing affidavits indicate that she can prove facts, but facts that are irrelevant under the governing law. Thus, there is no dispute of *material* fact (see Fed. R. Civ. P. 56(c)), and Hart is entitled to judgment as a matter of law.

Actually, Rule 56 is very confusing on this point. Rule 56(c) provides that summary judgment can only be granted if there is "no genuine issue as to any material fact," but in many cases summary judgment is granted even though there are many hotly disputed, clearly material issues in the case. Suppose, for example, that Simon sues Hammerstein for damages in an auto accident, and there is lots of contradictory evidence as to whether his injuries resulted from the accident or a pre-existing condition. However, Simon has no evidence that Hammerstein was negligent in causing the accident. Here, there is a genuine issue for trial as to damages, but Hammerstein would still be entitled to summary judgment if Simon has no evidence of negligence. In other words, the "no-dispute-of-material-fact" language means that there is no factual dispute concerning the *particular element of the claim that is challenged by the motion.* There may be genuine disputes in the evidence on every other element, but a chain is only as strong as its weakest link: If Simon has no proof of negligence, he must lose.

12. Since Porter has not shown the existence of any factual dispute concerning favorable termination, the judge should enter an order granting *partial* summary judgment for Berlin on his allegation that the criminal prosecution was terminated in his favor. However, this does not mean that Berlin automatically wins the case; it simply establishes one element of Berlin's claim. He will still have to prove all the other elements, including lack of probable cause, that Porter acted with an improper purpose, and damages.

Compare the converse situation, in which the judge grants summary judgment for Porter after Berlin produces no evidence of favorable termination. Berlin can only win if he proves each element of his claim; if the proof fails on any one of them, he cannot recover. So Porter's successful challenge on the favorable termination element will lead to summary judgment for him on the entire claim; the whole case will be dismissed. But summary judgment for the *plaintiff* may simply establish one element of the claim, leaving him to shoulder the burden on the other elements at trial.

13. You may have concluded that Brodway's motion should be granted on the purely procedural ground that Kern has filed no affidavits or other evidence in opposition to the motion. Rule 56(e) appears at first blush to require this result, since it provides that a party opposing summary judgment may not simply rest on the allegations in his pleading but is required to come forward with evidence in support of those allegations.

That conclusion, while understandable from an initial reading of Rule 56(e), is wrong. Summary judgment should only be granted under Rule 56(e) "if appropriate." It is never "appropriate" to grant the motion if the moving party's evidence itself raises doubts as to the relevant facts. It is only where the moving party's materials would suffice to establish that party's version of the facts that the burden shifts to the opposing party to introduce contrary evidence.

In this example, Roger's testimony indicates that Jones never stated that he intended to commit suicide, but surely that is not the only behavior that would put police officers on notice of such a risk. Maybe his sullenness, refusal to talk, and intoxication should be sufficient in themselves to suggest depression and reduced impulse control, factors commonly associated with suicide. This affidavit hardly suffices to eliminate the possibility that the officers were on notice of the risk. In deciding the summary judgment motion, the court will view the evidence submitted in the light most favorable to the party opposing the motion. If the evidence offered on the summary judgment motion could give rise to two inferences, one of which would support the opposing party's case, the court should assume that the jury would make that inference and deny summary judgment. *Anderson v. Liberty Lobby, Inc.,* 477 U.S. 242, 255 (1986). Thus, Broadway's supporting evidence does not demonstrate that there is no genuine issue of fact as to whether the officers knew of Jones's suicidal tendencies.[5] Since Broadway's own materials do not entitle it to summary judgment, the motion should be denied even if Kern does not file opposing materials.

Of course, it is hardly advisable for Kern to rest solely on the argument that there is ambiguity in Broadway's evidence. Kern should also respond with positive evidence to support his contention that the officers knew or should have known of the risk, rather than stake his case on the argument that Broadway has failed to meet its initial burden to adequately support the motion.

Point/Counterpoint

14a. The judge *doesn't* know that the officers are telling the truth; they may be lying through their teeth. But the purpose of the summary judgment motion is not to determine whether the officers are telling the truth: that would be finding the facts, a role reserved for the jury. Instead, the motion tests whether the party opposing summary judgment—Kern, in this case—has any meaningful evidence to prove her allegation that they were on notice of Jones's suicidal tendencies. The defendant has produced evidence that they weren't on notice; if Kern doesn't have any evidence that they were, how can she ever prove that essential allegation at trial? And if she can't prove an essential allegation, how can she win? If the case went to trial, and Kern submitted no credible proof on the knew-or-should-have-known allegation, the judge would have to direct a verdict for Broadway. The summary judgment motion thus tests whether the plaintiff has sufficient evidence on the challanged element of the claim to make a trial necessary. If she doesn't, the case must be dismissed on summary judgment, whether the officers are telling the truth or not.

b. Kern's response here is insufficient to keep the show on the road. Rule 56(e) specifically provides that a party may not avoid summary judgment

---

5. Similar ambiguities in their own evidence led Ronan's lawyers to decide not to file their motion for summary judgment in *Schulansky v. Ronan*. See Chapter 34.

by resting on contrary allegations in the complaint. All that Kern has done here is to say, "All right, you have evidence to prove that the officers didn't suspect that Jones was suicidal, but I say they did." This is mere persistence, not proof. The court knows that is Kern's position, but a summary judgment motion challenges him to show that he has evidence to prove it, not just allege it.

c. Once again, Kern is whistling Dixie. He has simply taken the knew-or-should-have-known allegation in his complaint and restated it in his affidavit. If Kern cannot avoid summary judgment by resting on the allegation in his complaint, it hardly seems appropriate to let him achieve the same result by simply repeating the same allegation in an affidavit. This is not admissible evidence as to facts, but simply the unsupported opinion of an interested party as to how the factual issue should be resolved. If parties could avoid summary judgment by this tactic, it would hardly be an effective device.

If a party moves for summary judgment and properly supports the motion with admissible evidence, the opposing party must respond with countervailing evidence in order to avoid the entry of judgment against him. Fed. R. Civ. P. 56(e). It is not sufficient for the opposing party to respond by simply reiterating that he disagrees with the evidence proferred by the moving party. At the summary judgment stage the court wants to see what evidence the parties have to put before the jury if a trial is held, not a rehash of their positions in the pleadings. See *Street v. J. C. Bradford and Co.*, 886 F.2d 1472, 1478 (6th Cir. 1989) (summary judgment motion challenges opponent to "put up or shut up" on a critical issue). Otherwise, the motion would simply occasion a renewed swearing match between the parties, which would not probe their ability to prove their cases.

d. This is an entirely different situation. Here Kern has offered admissible evidence, his own testimony and that of another witness to relevant events, as to *facts* that tend to prove that the officers should have been aware that Jones might attempt suicide. These affidavits do not absolutely establish that awareness, but they do raise a question of fact on the issue. Summary judgment should be denied here because the evidence is contradictory, thus posing a triable issue of fact as to whether the officers were on notice of Jones's suicidal tendencies. In this case, the show must go on.

e. The parties' affidavits here certainly raise a factual issue as to whether Jones was wearing a belt. But the issue is not *material* to the cause of action alleged by Kern. His claim is that they should have taken precautions to protect Jones because they were aware that he might attempt suicide. The duty to take such precautions is premised on knowledge of the risk; absent that knowledge, the fact that they didn't take appropriate precautions, such as taking the belt away, is irrelevant. Unless Kern can prove notice of the risk, failure to avert it is legally irrelevant.

As Kern's lawyer, you would probably argue (as my students do when we study the case on which these examples are based)[6] that it is negligent not to take belts away from *all* prisoners, regardless of any reason to anticipate a risk of suicide. Maybe it is (though it was not held to be in the actual case), but that is a different theory of the case than the one alleged in Kern's complaint. If Kern wants to argue this, he should plead that the officers were negligent in their general booking procedures, as well as in failing to take special precautions because of their awareness of Jones's condition. If he pleaded that theory, the conflict in the evidence on the belt issue *would* be material to that theory, and would keep his case alive even if his claim based on their knowledge of Jones's suicidal tendencies failed on summary judgment.

Baring the Burden

15. In this example, Broadway has not submitted any evidence to *disprove* Kern's allegation that its officers knew of Jones's suicidal tendencies. Instead, it has submitted materials to show that Kern cannot meet his burden to prove that they did. Broadway is saying, "Hey, Court, look at this record. I've used the discovery tools the way they're supposed to be used, to probe the other side's case, and look what he's got: nothing. His statements in his deposition and answers to interrogatories do not contain any evidence to show that the police officers knew or should have known that Jones was suicidal. On this record, it is clear that the plaintiff has nothing whatsoever to prove that we knew of Jones's suicidal tendencies. Kern cannot prove that element of his case, so we win. Throw this case out."

Broadway is right on this record. Kern's answers do not show that the officers had any reason to take special precautions to protect Jones. The facts that he was depressed, out of work, and separated tend to prove that he might be suicidal, but do not prove that the officers *knew or should have known it.* Whether the motion should be granted turns, then, on whether the moving party can get summary judgment by pointing out that the party with the burden of proof lacks adequate evidence to meet that burden, without producing any evidence of its own to disprove the alleged facts.

In *Celotex Corp. v. Catrett,* 477 U.S. 317 (1986), the Supreme Court held that a party can support a summary judgment motion with materials that show that the party who has the burden of proof on an essential fact cannot prove that fact. In *Celotex,* the issue was whether the plaintiff's decedent had been exposed to the defendant's asbestos products. The record suggested that the plaintiff had no proof of such exposure. The Court held that, if the defendant demonstrated that there was no evidence in the record to support the plaintiff's claim of exposure to its product, and the plaintiff did not

---

6. *Slaven v. Salem,* 386 Mass. 885 (1982).

produce evidence tending to prove exposure, the defendant could get summary judgment without presenting any evidence to show lack of exposure. Celotex would be "entitled to judgment as a matter of law" because the plaintiff, who held the burden of proof on the issue, had no evidence to carry that burden.

This holding makes some sense: You can't very well carry the burden of proof at trial without any evidence. At the same time, however, it puts plaintiffs like Kern in a very difficult position. Broadway can move for summary judgment, supported by the interrogatory showing that Kern has no evidence to prove that the officers knew or should have known of the risk. The burden would then fall on Kern, in opposing the motion, to produce some evidence of that knowledge. If he can't, he will lose, even if they knew of the risk all along.[7]

Thus, after *Celotex,* Kern must aggressively develop the evidence before the motion, perhaps by taking the depositions of the officers to determine what they knew or suspected. If he doesn't, he may lose, not because his claim lacks merit, but because he has not yet gathered the evidence necessary to prove it. The moving party, on the other hand, can force his opponent (usually the plaintiff) to this effort without tipping his own hand as to the contrary proof he will produce at trial if the plaintiff avoids summary judgment by producing admissible evidence on the issue.

Plaintiffs in this position will doubtless have recourse to Rule 56(f), which allows the court to grant continuances to allow the opposing party to develop his case. However, relief under Rule 56(f) is discretionary; the party seeking it should always be ready to specify exactly what further discovery is necessary in order to properly respond to the defendant's "*Celotex* motion."

---

7. It is sometimes said that summary judgment is not appropriate on issues involving state of mind, such as the officers' awareness of the risk of suicide in Kern's case, because they are subjective questions, which turn on credibility and difficult inferences about what people intend or know. However, summary judgment may be proper if there is no evidence from which those inferences can be made. In *Slaven,* for example, the court granted summary judgment because there was no evidence in the record to support the allegation that the officers were on notice of the decedent's suicidal tendencies.

22

The Judge and the Jury, Part One: Judgment as a Matter of Law (Directed Verdict)

Introduction

Every good citizen knows that the Constitution guarantees "the right to trial by jury." However, a good part of the civil procedure course is devoted to studying various hurdles that stand between the litigant who demands jury trial and actual jury decision of the merits of her case. As the last chapter demonstrates, the plaintiff's case may be cut short by a motion to dismiss under Rule 12(b)(6), which allows the judge to enter judgment for the defendant on the ground that the plaintiff's complaint does not state a legal claim for relief. If the plaintiff's case survives a Rule 12(b)(6) challenge, it may still meet an early demise on a motion for summary judgment if the judge concludes that there is "no genuine issue of material fact" for the jury to consider.

Although these two motions may preclude the parties from obtaining a jury trial, they are justifiable, since both are based on the premise that there is really nothing for the jury to do. It comes as more of a surprise to students to learn that even after the beginning of trial and the presentation of evidence the judge may still snatch the case from the jury or even more invasively, allow the jury to render a verdict and then enter judgment for the party who *lost* the jury verdict. This chapter and the one that follows are intended to help you understand several devices that the judge may use to control the jury's decision-making process: judgment as a matter of law and new trial.

The Plaintiff's Burden of Production

In order to understand these devices, it helps to have a preliminary understanding of the plaintiff's burden to produce evidence at trial in support of her claim. Figure 22-1[1] represents varying degrees of evidence in support of the plaintiff's claim. At the extreme left is the case in which the plaintiff produces no evidence to prove her claim; as you move to the right along the line the strength of the plaintiff's evidence increases. The X line on the diagram indicates the point at which the plaintiff has produced evidence that is sufficiently persuasive that a jury, acting rationally, could find that she has proved each element of her case. If the plaintiff's evidence crosses this line, she is said to have satisfied her *burden of production*. Even though the judge may consider the plaintiff's evidence weak or less persuasive than the defendant's, if the evidence is sufficient to cross the X line the case falls in the realm of legitimate difference of opinion and must go to the jury for decision.

The Z line on the diagram represents the point at which the evidence is evenly balanced; that is, evidence of equal probative value supports the plaintiff's position and the defendant's. In a civil case the plaintiff's *burden of proof* is to establish that her version of events is more probably true than the defendant's — that is, that a simple preponderance of the evidence favors the plaintiff's version of events. In terms of the diagram, her evidence must fall to the right of the Z line to carry her burden of proof. The Y line represents the point at which the plaintiff's proof becomes so strong that any reasonable jury would have to conclude that the plaintiff has proved her case.[2]

Between the X and Y lines lies the arena for legitimate differences of opinion as to the proper outcome — and hence the arena for jury decision. Even though the judge concludes that the evidence falls at point Q, well to the left of the point where the balance of the evidence favors the plaintiff, she must allow the jury to decide the outcome. If the judge could take the case from the jury when the proof lies between X and Y, she could essentially usurp the role of the jury by substituting her own judgment for that of the jury at any time. General practice (and the constitutional right to jury trial)

---

1. A similar diagram in Landers and Martin, Civil Procedure (1981) was used, with permission, as the basis for this diagram.

2. In a criminal case, the state's burden of proof falls near if not on the Y line since the state must prove the defendant's guilt beyond a reasonable doubt.

Figure 22-1

denies the judge such power: If reasonable minds can differ as to the result, the case is for the jury, not the judge.

Similarly, if the judge concludes that the balance of the evidence falls at point R on the spectrum, where the plaintiff's evidence substantially out-weighs the opposing evidence (but is not so persuasive that the only reason-able verdict is for the plaintiff), the case must also go to the jury. Even though the judge believes that the balance tips in the plaintiff's favor, at this point on the spectrum that conclusion is legitimately debatable, just as it is at point Q. If the jury could rationally find for the defendant, it must be given the opportunity to consider the case, even though the judge believes that the preponderance of the evidence favors the plaintiff.

Old Wine in New Bottles: The Motion for Judgment as a Matter of Law

The courts have long provided a procedural means for judges to take cases away from the jury if the plaintiff's evidence does not reach the magical X line. If the judge concludes that the plaintiff's case[3] is so weak that no jury, acting rationally on the evidence before it, could find for her, allowing the case to go to the jury simply invites irrational decision-making based on ir-relevant or prejudicial factors. The judge has traditionally had the authority to guard against such flawed verdicts by refusing to send cases to the jury if there is no legitimate doubt as to which side should prevail. See *Rutherford*

---

3. The motion may be granted for plaintiffs as well as defendants (if the plaintiff's ev-idence is so strong as to pass the hypothetical Y line), though for reasons discussed below this is much less common than directed verdicts for defendants.

v. Illinois Central R.R., 278 F.2d 310, 312 (5th Cir.) cert. denied, 364 U.S. 922 (1960) (court's power to take case from jury provides "a method for protecting neutral principles of law from powerful forces outside the scope of law — compassion and prejudice.")

The traditional device for taking the case from the jury has been the "motion for a directed verdict." Under early procedure, the judge actually did "direct" the verdict: If she concluded that the evidence was too weak to support a verdict for the plaintiff, she ordered the jury to go out and come back with a verdict for the defendant![4] Eventually, this pro forma (if not demeaning) procedure was dropped; instead, the judge would "direct the verdict" for the defendant herself, and the case would not go to the jury at all.

In truth, this practice does not involve a "verdict" at all, which connotes a jury's finding of facts. However, the motion is still called a motion for a "directed verdict" in most state courts. The "directed verdict" terminology was also used in the federal courts until 1991, when the federal rulemakers changed the name without altering the substance of the motion. Now, in the federal courts, a party seeking to have the judge take the case from the jury on the ground that the evidence is too weak to support a verdict makes a "motion for judgment as a matter of law." Fed. R. Civ. P. 50(a). This is a good name for the motion for several reasons. First, it eliminates any implication that the jury has a role in the decision: As under directed verdict practice, if the judge grants the motion, the jury is discharged without deliberating or deciding anything. Second, the new name emphasizes that the judge, in theory, does not resolve factual issues when he withdraws the case from the jury but makes a legal judgment that the evidence is so lopsided that there really is no meaningful factual dispute for a jury to consider.

However, the change in terminology will create some confusion. The federal courts have developed a good half-century of "directed verdict" case law. Lawyers — like you — who will practice under the current rule must understand that the motion for judgment as a matter of law really is old wine in a new bottle. The rulemakers have not changed the *substance* of Rule

---

4. See W. Blume, The Origin and Development of the Directed Verdict, 48 Mich. L. Rev. 555, 582 (1950). For a curious example of this practice, see *Cahill v. Chicago, Minneapolis & St. Paul Ry. Co.*, 74 F. 285 (7th Cir. 1896), in which the judge ordered the jury to return a verdict for the defendant and one juror refused to do it. The court of appeals was not pleased with such recalcitrance:

> The conduct of the juror in this instance was in the highest degree reprehensible, and might well have subjected him, and any who encouraged him to persist in this course, to punishment for contempt. His conduct was in violation of law, subversive of authority and obstructive of the orderly administration of justice.

74 F. at 290. (Really, court, lighten up a little!)

50(a). They did not change the fact that the judge makes the decision, rather than the jury. They did not change the *standard* for taking the case away from the jury. Thus, the case law under prior Rule 50(a) is still authoritative on most aspects of the motion. In addition, the change in terminology in Rule 50(a) only applies to the federal courts. State courts allow the judge similar latitude to control the jury, but most still use the "directed verdict" terminology. Thus, you will have to adjust to the schizophrenic need to make the same motion in federal court under one name and in state court under another. In this chapter I will generally use the term "judgment as a matter of law," since much of the discussion focuses on the federal rule, Fed. R. Civ. P. 50(a).

The Timing of the Motion

As Figure 22-2[5] indicates, the plaintiff in a civil case presents her evidence first at trial. She has the burden during her case-in-chief to produce enough evidence on each element of her claim to pass the X line and reach the jury. Typically, the defendant will move for judgment as a matter of law at the close of the plaintiff's evidence, on the ground that that evidence does not cross the X line, that is, it does not satisfy the plaintiff's burden to produce credible evidence in support of each element of her claim. If the judge agrees that the plaintiff has not produced enough evidence to support a rational verdict in her favor, she may withdraw the case from the jury by entering judgment as a matter of law for the defendant at this point.

If the judge denies the motion, the defendant will present her evidence to rebut the plaintiff's case or to establish affirmative defenses. After the defendant rests she may move again for judgment as a matter of law. When the motion is made at this point it challenges the sufficiency of all the evidence, both plaintiff's and defendant's, to support a verdict for the plaintiff. As the diagram indicates, the plaintiff may also move for judgment as a matter of law at this point, though not at the close of her own case.

Two Fundamental Questions

1.   Why may the defendant, but not the plaintiff, move for judgment as a matter of law at the close of the plaintiff's case?

2.   What will happen next if the judge grants the defendant's motion at the close of the plaintiff's case?

---

5. The diagram and the accompanying discussion are a bit oversimplified. For example, after the close of the defendant's case, the court will often allow the plaintiff to re-open her case to offer rebuttal testimony.

Opening
statements

Plaintiff presents
her evidence

Defendant presents
his evidence

Closing
statements

Judge
instructs Jury
jury

Jury
deliberates

Jury   Judge
renders enters
a   judg-
verdict ment
        on
        verdict

Defendant may
move for directed
verdict (judgment
as a matter of law)
here

Either party may
move for directed
verdict (judgment
as a matter of law)
here

Figure 22-2: Sequence of Trial

The Standard for Entering Judgment as a Matter of Law

Because the judge risks encroachment on the role of the jury in taking the case away from it, it is important to have a clear picture of just where the X and Y lines fall. Unfortunately, while it is easy to draw diagrams conceptualizing the parties' burdens of production, it is a great deal harder to articulate a clear and workable *standard* for deciding when the evidence crosses those lines. Federal Rule 50(a) specifies that judgment as a matter of law may be entered when "there is no legally sufficient evidentiary basis for a reasonable jury to find for" the nonmoving party. However, this really just poses the question of when the evidence is legally sufficient, rather than providing an answer.

A few state courts hold that the case must go to the jury if there is even "a scintilla" of evidence to support the opposing party's case. See, e.g., Ala. R. Civ. P. 50(e). Under this test, if the plaintiff has any evidence to support the elements of her claim, she will get to the jury. This standard places point X almost on top of point W in Figure 22-1. See, e.g., *Brown v. Turner,* 497 So. 2d 1119, 1120 (Ala. 1986) (case goes to jury if there is "'a mere gleam, glimmer, spark...or a scintilla'" in support of complaint). Obviously this stretches the area between X and Y, giving the greatest latitude to the jury but at the expense of effective judicial control of irrational jury decision-making.

Another suggested standard requires the judge to consider *only* the evidence that supports the nonmoving party (usually the plaintiff). Under this standard, the judge must assume the truth of all evidence offered by the nonmoving party (usually the plaintiff), take all the inferences from the evidence in the light most favorable to that party, and enter judgment as a matter of law only if that evidence would not support a verdict for the nonmoving party; *Reeves v. Sanderson Planting Products, Inc.* 120 S. Ct. 2097 2110 (2000). *Wilkerson v. McCarthy,* 336 U.S. 53, 57 (1949). In passing on the motion, the judge may not determine the credibility of witnesses; the issue of which witnesses to believe is classically a jury decision. The test is not whether the judge believes the plaintiff's witnesses, but whether the jury, if it chooses to believe those witnesses, would have sufficient evidence to support a verdict for the plaintiff.

Suppose, for example, that Pavarotti sues Sills for negligence after he is hit by a car on Maple Street in Cleveland, Ohio. He presents evidence that Sills lives three blocks from the scene of the accident and owns a red Chevrolet bearing the license number 301-LJM. One of Pavarotti's witnesses testifies that she saw a red Chevrolet leave the intersection after the accident, driven by a blonde woman (assume that Sills is blonde) and read the first three numbers of the license number as 311. Although this evidence is hardly overwhelming, it may be sufficient to allow a jury to make a rational inference that Sills was the driver. Under the "plaintiff's evidence" standard, the judge would probably allow this case to go to the jury, regardless of the evidence Sills presented in rebuttal.

A third standard for taking the case from the jury requires the judge to consider the nonmoving party's evidence in its most favorable light (just as in the second test) but also to consider any evidence put forward by the moving party that is not impeached or contradicted by the opposing party's evidence. *Reeves,* 120 S. Ct. At 2110. If, considering all of that evidence, "there can be but one reasonable conclusion as to the verdict" (Moore's Federal Practice, s 50.60[1]), the judge should enter judgment as a matter of law for the moving party. A frequent statement of the rule is as follows:

> [T]he court should consider all of the evidence — not just that evidence which supports the non-mover's case — but in the light and with all reasonable inferences most favorable to the party opposed to the motion. If the facts and inferences point so strongly and overwhelmingly in favor of one party that the Court believes that reasonable men could not arrive at a contrary verdict, grant of the motions is proper. On the other hand, if there is substantial evidence opposed to the motions, evidence of such quality and weight that reasonable and fair-minded men in the exercise of impartial judgment might reach different conclusions, the motions should be denied, and the case submitted to the jury.

Boeing Co. v. Shipman, 411 F.2d 365, 374 (5th Cir. 1969). The federal courts apply this standard under Fed. R. Civ. P. 50(a). For easy reference, I will call it the "federal standard," although this approach is very widely followed in state courts as well.

To illustrate the operation of this standard, assume that Sills (after the plaintiff, Pavarotti, presents the evidence described above) offers the undisputed testimony of two eyewitnesses to the accident that she was not the driver of the car and documentary evidence that indicates that she was performing in an opera in Minneapolis at the time of the accident. On this state of the evidence, her motion for judgment as a matter of law at the close of all the evidence should be granted under the federal standard. The plaintiff produced enough evidence to support a legitimate (but not compelling) inference that Sills had hit him. But that inference is negated by the defendant's uncontradicted, unimpeached evidence to the contrary and leaves the jury without a reasonable basis to conclude that Sills is liable. By contrast, if Sills's case consisted of her own testimony that she was having lunch at the time of the accident at a restaurant two miles away, issues of credibility would be posed, and judgment as a matter of law would be denied.

The examples that follow should help you to get a sense of the court's role in controlling jury action by entering judgement as a matter of law.

The examples are based on one of the classic cases on directed verdicts, *Pennsylvania R.R. Co. v. Chamberlain,* 288 U.S. 333 (1933). The relevant evidence in *Chamberlain* is set forth immediately below, but you may want to read *Chamberlain* before considering the examples.

The decedent in *Chamberlain* was killed when he fell from a train he was riding, while sorting groups of cars in a railroad yard.

> The lead track crossed a "hump," and the work of car distribution consisted of pushing a train of cars by means of a locomotive to the top of the "hump," and then allowing the cars, in separate strings, to descend by gravity, under the control of hand brakes, to their respective destinations in the various branch tracks. Deceased had charge of a string of two gondola cars, which he was piloting to track 14. Immediately ahead of him was a string of seven cars, and behind him a string of nine cars, both also destined for track 14. Soon after the cars ridden by the deceased had passed to track 14, his body was found on that track some distance beyond the switch. He had evidently fallen onto the track and been run over by a car or cars.

288 U.S. at 335-336. The plaintiff's theory was that the railroad's employees negligently caused the string of cars Chamberlain was riding to collide with the following string of nine cars, throwing him under the train.

EXAMPLES

The Plaintiff's Case

3.   In *Chamberlain* the plaintiff offered the following evidence as to the cause of the accident:

> The plaintiff's only witness to the event, one Bainbridge, then employed by the road, stood close to the yardmaster's office, near the "hump." He professed to have paid little attention to what went on, but he did see the deceased riding at the rear of his cars, whose speed when they passed him he took to be about eight or ten miles. Shortly thereafter a second string passed which was shunted into another track and this was followed by the nine, which according to the plaintiff's theory, collided with the deceased's. After the nine cars had passed at a somewhat greater speed than the deceased's, Bainbridge paid no more attention to either string for a while, but looked again when the deceased, who was still standing in his place, had passed the switch and onto the assorting track where he was bound. At that time his speed had been checked to about three miles, but the speed of the following nine cars had increased. They were just passing the switch, about four or five cars behind the deceased. Bainbridge looked away again and soon heard what he described as a "loud crash," not however an unusual event in a switching yard. Apparently this did not cause him at once to turn, but he did so shortly thereafter, and saw the two strings together, still moving, and the deceased no longer in sight.... Until he left to go the accident, he had stood

fifty feet to the north of the track where the accident happened, and about nine hundred feet from where the body was found.

288 U.S. at 336-337.

Assume that the plaintiff in *Chamberlain* presents this evidence as to the cause of the accident and rests her case. The defendant moves for judgment as a matter of law.

    a. If the court applies the "plaintiff's evidence" standard, should the motion be granted?

    b. Assume that the case is tried instead in a court that applies the federal standard, which also allows consideration of the moving party's uncontradicted, unimpeached evidence. Should the railroad's motion at the close of the plaintiff's case be granted?

4.   Suppose that Bainbridge was again the only witness and gave the same testimony but that he had made his observations while riding on a third string of cars following the nine-car string. If the railroad moved for judgment as a matter of law at the close of the plaintiff's case, should the court grant the motion? Assume that the "plaintiff's evidence" standard applies.

5.   Assume that the *Chamberlain* case involved extensive evidence on damages (such as pain and suffering, medical costs, and lost earnings), as well as on liability. At trial, the plaintiff's evidence for liability is the same, again based on Bainbridge's testimony. After she presents her case on liability, but before she offers her evidence on damages, the railroad moves for judgment as a matter of law. Is the motion proper?

The Defendant's Case

6.   If the federal standard applies, should the railroad be allowed to move for judgment as a matter of law at the close of all the evidence if it failed to do so at the close of the plaintiff's case?

7.   Suppose that the plaintiff in *Chamberlain* rests her case, and the railroad rests its case without offering any evidence. The plaintiff moves for judgment as a matter of law. Should it be granted?

8.   Assume that the court refuses to enter judgment for the defendant in *Chamberlain* at the close of the plaintiff's evidence. Therefore, the railroad proceeds to present its case. (See Figure 22-2 supra.) As the case report indicates, the railroad's case was as follows. "Three employees, riding the nine-car string, testified positively that no such collision occurred. They were corroborated by every other employee in a position to see, all testifying that there was no contact between the nine-car string and that of the deceased." 288 U.S. at 336.

    a. After presenting its case, the railroad moves for judgment as a matter of law. Should the motion be granted under the plaintiff's evidence standard?

    b. Should the motion be granted under the federal standard?

A Few Variations

9.   Suppose that Bainbridge offered the same testimony as above, but there were only two trains, the two-car string and the nine-car string, in the yard at the time. How should the court rule if the railroad offers the same evidence as above and then moves for judgment as a matter of law at the close of all the evidence? Assume that the federal standard applies.

10.   Suppose that Bainbridge's testimony was the same as that offered in the actual case, but that he testified that he actually saw the trains collide. Could the judge enter judgment for the railroad?

11.   Suppose again that Bainbridge's testimony was the same, but that there was only one witness for the defendant, the railroad yardmaster. Assume that he was standing near the spot where the decedent was found and testified unequivocally that no collision occurred. Could the judge enter judgment as a matter of law for the railroad?

12.   Assume once again that the plaintiff offered the same proof, through Bainbridge, and in rebuttal the railroad called only one witness, the brakeperson riding on the nine-car string following the decedent's. She testifies that she braked the nine-car string as it descended from the hump, followed the two-car string at a distance, and that the two strings never collided. At the close of the evidence, the railroad moves for judgment as a matter of law. Should the motion be granted under the federal standard?

Trial and Error

13.   Assume that the *Chamberlain* case was tried to the judge instead of a jury. The defendant's counsel rises at the close of the plaintiff's case and moves "for judgment as a matter of law under Rule 50(a), on the ground that no reasonable jury could find for the plaintiff." What two grievous errors did defendant's counsel make?[6] See Fed. R. Civ. P. 52(c).

A Retrospective

14.   Let's back up a minute and assume that the railroad moved for summary judgment before trial and submitted affidavits in support of the motion from its employees. The affidavits all state that no collision took place between the two strings. The plaintiff submits an opposing affidavit of Bainbridge, stating his testimony as it is given in example 3. Should the railroad's motion be granted?

---

6. Your humble author made both of these mistakes in a case involving a large Boston pothole. Learn from his mistakes!

EXPLANATIONS

Two Fundamental Questions

1.   Due process of law entitles every litigant to an opportunity to be heard before a court adjudicates her rights. If the court could enter judgment as a matter of law for the plaintiff at the close of her case, the defendant would be deprived of the opportunity to present evidence, either to refute the plaintiff's proof or to establish an affirmative defense. Even if the judge concludes that the plaintiff's evidence has crossed the Y line, the defendant may well produce countervailing evidence that would leave legitimate doubt as to the facts, making the case an appropriate one for the jury. Thus, no matter how strong the plaintiff's evidence may be, the defendant will be given a chance to rebut it.

2.   The judge may only grant judgment as a matter of law for the defendant if she concludes that the plaintiff has not produced enough evidence to support a rational verdict in her favor. If the judge concludes that the plaintiff has not produced adequate evidence on each of the elements of her "prima facie case," there is no need to go on and hear the defendant's evidence. The judge will enter judgment for the defendant on the basis of the insufficiency of plaintiff's proof.

The Plaintiff's Case

3a.   Under the plaintiff's evidence standard, the motion should be denied if the jury, considering only the evidence supporting the plaintiff's case, could reasonably infer that the accident resulted from the railroad's negligence. Although the plaintiff's evidence that the two strings collided (thus indicating negligence by the railroad) is less than compelling, it is probably sufficient to support a rational inference that a collision caused the accident. If the jury credits Bainbridge's testimony, it would have evidence that the sound of a crash was heard, that the nine-car string was moving considerably faster than the two-car string before the crash, and that the two strings subsequently were seen moving in tandem. In addition, the fact that the decedent had fallen from the train supports the inference that a collision had knocked him off. If such an inference could rationally be made, the jury should be allowed to make it (or reject it). The defendant's motion should probably be denied.

b.   The result at this stage of the case should be the same under the federal test. At the close of the plaintiff's case the only evidence before the court is that offered by the plaintiff. Thus, the defendant's motion at this point will usually be based on the position that the plaintiff's evidence is insufficient to cross the X line, that is, it does not satisfy her burden to produce evidence that would rationally support the conclusion that the accident resulted from the railroad's negligence. As indicated above, the plaintiff's evidence in *Chamberlain* was probably sufficient to defeat this motion.

It is conceivable that the railroad's attorney would elicit evidence from the *plaintiff's* witnesses that would foreclose a verdict in the plaintiff's favor. For example, the railroad might get Bainbridge to admit on cross-examination that he is unable to see farther than 25 feet without his glasses, which he was not wearing at the time. This evidence would be considered under the federal standard and, if not impeached or contradicted by other evidence for the plaintiff, it could force the plaintiff's case back over the X line and lead to a directed verdict (judgment as a matter of law) for the railroad even before it presents its own case. Absent such evidence, however, the result should be the same under either standard at this point.

4.   Although the judge is required to view the case in the light most favorable to the plaintiff, there comes a point where the unlikely fades into the impossible. As the case report indicates, Bainbridge apparently viewed the moving trains from a three-degree angle if he was standing *beside* the track. If he were actually on a train following the nine-car string (and there were no bend in the track) it would be impossible for him to observe a collision 900 feet in front of him on the same track. On this evidence the reasonable judge could reasonably conclude that only an unreasonable jury could find for the plaintiff.

It is true that the judge, by taking the case from the jury on these facts, exercises some judgment as to the strength of the plaintiff's case. In this sense, the term "judgment as a matter of law" is a bit of a misnomer because the judge has made a factual judgment here that the evidence is too far-fetched to justify a finding for the plaintiff. But a line must be drawn somewhere between the inherently incredible and the unlikely-but-possible. If the court abdicates the responsibility of doing so, the jury becomes the unrestrained arbiter of the parties' rights regardless of the inadequacy of their proof.

5.   The motion is proper. The railroad's position here is that the evidence on damages is legally irrelevant if Chamberlain has not proved liability. Why should the parties and the court waste their time on lengthy damage evidence if Chamberlain has not met her burden of production on the liability issue? To reach the jury, the plaintiff must present credible evidence on each element of her claim; if proof fails on *any one*, the defendant is entitled to judgment as a matter of law.

While motions for a directed verdict are usually made after the plaintiff presents her entire case (see Figure 22-2), it may sometimes be appropriate to try a dispositive issue first and determine the legal sufficiency of the evidence on that issue. If Chamberlain has not passed the X line on the liability element of her claim, there is no need to hear the damages evidence. The Advisory Committee notes to Rule 50(a) emphasize that a motion for judgment as a matter of law may be appropriate "as soon as a party has completed a presentation on a fact essential to that party's case." Advisory Committee note to the 1991 revisions to Rule 50(a), fifth paragraph. This suggestion is in line with the modern tendency to encourage judges to aggressively manage cases in order to speed their disposition. See, e.g., Fed. R. Civ. P. 16 (authorizing discovery and pretrial conferences to streamline the trial process).

Under this approach, a judge might even order that an affirmative defense be tried first, if it appeared that the defense might be decisive. For example, if a defendant in a negligence case claims that the plaintiff gave him a release of the claim, and the evidence on the issue is strong, the judge might order this issue tried first, to determine whether there is a jury question as to whether the claim was released. If she concludes that the release defense is established as a matter of law, the case will be dismissed without trying the plaintiff's basic negligence case at all.

Some lawyers feel that this managerial approach unfairly encroaches on their traditional prerogative to present their cases in their own way. In the example, Chamberlain's counsel would doubtless prefer to put in his entire case, hoping that the judge's decision on the motion would be colored by the compelling evidence of Chamberlain's damages. Many courts will still defer the decision to the end of the plaintiff's evidence, but there is a marked tendency, especially in the federal courts, to curtail counsel's autonomy in litigation procedure in the interest of efficient resolution of cases. The federal rulemakers, in revising Rule 50, have given judges a green light to extend this tendency to directed verdict practice as well.

The Defendant's Case

6.   Yes. There is no requirement that a defendant move for judgment as a matter of law at the close of the plaintiff's case in order to preserve her right to do so at the close of all the evidence. Nor should there be; as stated in the Introduction, the motion raises distinct issues depending upon when it is made. When the defendant makes this motion at the close of the plaintiff's case the issue is whether the plaintiff has produced so little evidence that no reasonable jury could conclude that she has carried her burden of proof. The defendant's motion at the close of all the evidence may, if the federal standard applies, be based on the argument that the plaintiff had initially presented a strong enough case to go to the jury, but the unimpeached and uncontradicted evidence that she has presented forces the case back to the left of the X line in Figure 22-1, where the judge must enter judgment for the defendant. If that is true, then it would be improper to take the case from the jury at the close of the plaintiff's case, but appropriate at the end of all the evidence under the federal standard.

7.   A plaintiff's motion for judgment as a matter of law at the close of the case asserts that the uncontradicted, unimpeached evidence in support of her case is so strong that the proof falls to the right of the Y line, where no reasonable jury could reach a verdict for the defendant. In passing on the plaintiff's motion, the court must assume that the jury would believe all of the

defendant's evidence and reject all evidence for the plaintiff that had been contradicted or impeached. If, upon these assumptions, the only rational conclusion is that the plaintiff has proved each element of her case, the verdict may be directed.

On the *Chamberlain* facts, the motion should be denied. Even though the railroad offered no evidence, it does not follow that the plaintiff has established her case beyond doubt. The jury would still have to infer from Bainbridge's circumstantial evidence that a crash occurred between the two-car string and the nine-car string. Reasonable jurors might make that inference, but they also might not. The evidence is strong enough to support a verdict for Chamberlain but not strong enough to compel it.

As a practical matter, the judge seldom orders judgment as a matter of law for plaintiffs because they bear the burden of proof as to each element of their claim. Most cases turn at least in part on the credibility of witnesses. If the credibility of the plaintiff's witnesses has been challenged, the court will have to assume for purposes of the motion that the jury will disbelieve them. If their testimony is necessary to establish any element of the plaintiff's claim, and there is any basis for doubting that testimony, the motion will be denied.

8a.   The analysis of example 3a suggests that the plaintiff's evidence, taken alone, was sufficient to place the *Chamberlain* case in the middle area of the diagram, between the X and Y lines, where the jury must decide the contested issues of fact. If the plaintiff's evidence standard is applied here, the court must disregard all of the railroad's opposing testimony, and the same result will follow in this case even though the defendant has introduced very strong contrary evidence.

b. If the federal standard is applied, the court must consider not only Bainbridge's testimony for the plaintiff but also the uncontradicted and unimpeached testimony for the defendant. The crucial question is whether the defendant's witnesses, who testify directly that no crash occurred (and therefore no negligence and no ground for recovery), are contradicted or impeached by the plaintiff's evidence.

The Court holds, and I think rightly, that Bainbridge's and the defendant's versions of the incident are not contradictory. Bainbridge's testimony indicates that there was a crash and that the trains were moving along at the same speed after the crash. A jury could infer from this that the nine-car string collided with the two-car string. Alternatively, they could infer that a collision took place someplace else in the yard, and that these two strings were moving at the same speed because each had been braked to the same speed. The defendant's witnesses do not contradict Bainbridge; their testimony that the nine-car and the two-car strings did not collide simply eliminates one of the two possible inferences from his testimony. Unless the jury has some rational basis for rejecting their testimony, it is no longer possible to infer from Bainbridge's circumstantial version of events that these two strings actually collided.

It might be argued that the jury could reject the testimony of the defendant's witnesses because they were all employed by the railroad and thus could be biased. The argument has some force, but the Court concluded in *Chamberlain* that the mere fact of employment by the defendant was insufficient to impeach their testimony. See also *Chesapeake & Ohio Railway Co. v. Martin*, 283 U.S. 209, 216-220 (1931). The case would likely be different if only one employee testified for the railroad and the evidence indicated that he was promoted the week after the accident.

Needless to say, application of these standards for taking the case from the jury is hardly scientifically precise. In *Chamberlain*, the trial judge directed a verdict for the railroad. The court of appeals reversed, in a two-to-one decision, on the ground that the case should have been left to the jury. The eminent Judge Learned Hand wrote for the majority, and Judge Swan, another respected jurist, registered a strong dissent. 59 F.2d 986 (1932). The Supreme Court then unanimously reversed the court of appeals. Clearly, reasonable judges may differ about when reasonable jurors may differ. Yet the fact that there are close cases does not change the fact that the motion provides needed control of irrational jury behavior.

A Few Variations

9.   This change in the facts introduces a direct contradiction between the plaintiff's and the defendant's evidence. Bainbridge testifies that he heard a crash of the type made by trains colliding, and there only were two in the yard. If you believe Bainbridge, the only possible inference is that those two strings of cars collided. Unlike the facts of the actual case, this testimony would directly contradict the testimony of the defendant's witnesses. Although there were six or seven witnesses for the defendant and only one, Bainbridge, for the plaintiff, the court may not pass on issues of credibility in ruling on a motion for judgment as a matter of law. If there is a legitimate conflict in the evidence, the jury must resolve it. If the jury believes Bainbridge over the railroad's employees, it could reasonably find for the plaintiff and should be given the opportunity to do so.

10. Here again Bainbridge's testimony directly contradicts that of the defendant's witnesses and should therefore raise a jury issue unless the Court concludes that his testimony is inherently incredible. The Supreme Court intimated that it may have been physically impossible for Bainbridge to actually see whether the two strings were in contact. *Chamberlain* at 342. Thus, it is not clear that direct testimony from Bainbridge of a collision would have changed the result. The court might have disregarded it as physically impossible and concluded that the plaintiff's case was built entirely on an inference, which was negated by the defendant's direct evidence to the contrary. Many judges, however, would conclude (as the court of appeals did in *Chamberlain*) that Bainbridge's acute angle of vision is a fact for the jury to

weigh in deciding whether to believe his testimony, rather than making that testimony inherently incredible.

11. As suggested above, practice in this area is heavily fact-specific and un-scientific. Consequently, distinctions that are conceptually clear do not al-ways dictate results. In this case, the state of the evidence has not changed much when evaluated under the federal standard for taking the case from the jury. The plaintiff's case is still built upon inference, and it is still directly contradicted by evidence that the jury has little or no reason to discredit.

Yet many courts would not direct the verdict on these facts. There is not the same level of certainty about the defendant's case as there was in the real case, in which six or seven witnesses unanimously denied a collision. A sin-gle witness might be unbiased but simply wrong. The argument for bias is stronger here as well since there is more incentive for a managerial employee of the railroad to testify falsely than for lower-level yard workers to do so.

12. Here, the motion should be denied. Not only is there only one witness who denies a collision, but that witness has a strong incentive to deny the collision even if it happened. No one wants to admit that she committed a negligent act, especially if it led to the death of a co-worker. Such an admis-sion would expose the railroad to substantial liability and the employee to likely dismissal. Thus, the jury could reasonably disbelieve her self-serving denials and infer from Bainbridge's testimony that the strings did in fact col-lide. Since the jury has a rational basis for disregarding the employee's testi-mony, they should be given the chance to decide whether or not to do so. See Wright and Miller §2527 p. 286 (jury may often disbelieve even unim-peached, uncontradicted testimony of interested witness).

Trial and Error

13. The railroad's attorney has made two mistakes here, one technical but the other substantial. *First,* he should not have sought judgment under Rule 50(a) at all. That rule addresses the judge's power to enter judgment in a case tried to a jury. See Rule 50(a)(1) ("If, during a trial by jury..."). Here, the case was tried to the judge, so Rule 50(a) is not relevant; the proper mo-tion would have been for judgment on partial findings by the court under Fed. R. Civ. P. 52(c).

Second, and more important, the railroad's attorney has inappropriately asked the judge to apply the standard for withdrawing a case from the jury to a case in which *the judge is the factfinder.* In a jury case the judge's role is to act as a gatekeeper, keeping obviously inadequate cases from the jury. However, when the defendant in a nonjury trial moves for judgment at the close of the plaintiff's case, the judge *is* the factfinder. The issue is not whether the evidence is strong enough that a reasonable jury could find for the plaintiff (i.e., whether it has passed the X line on the diagram), but rather whether the judge, as the factfinder, believes that the plaintiff has proved the elements of her cause of action by a preponderance of the evidence (i.e., whether the plaintiff's evidence has passed the Z line). If the plaintiff has not satisfied that standard, the judge may enter judgment without hearing the defendant's evidence, since the plaintiff has had a full opportunity to make her case and has not carried her burden of proof. See Fed. R. Civ. P. 52(c), as amended by the 1991 revisions to the Federal Rules, and the accompanying Advisory Committee note.

In determining whether the plaintiff has carried her burden of proof, the judge may also consider the credibility of the witnesses; she is not deciding whether the jury *could* believe plaintiff's witnesses but rather whether she, the judge acting as the factfinder, *does* believe them. In other words, in a judge-tried case, the motion for a finding allows the judge to determine whether the plaintiff has carried her burden of *proof,* while in a jury case the judge acts as a gatekeeper to prevent the jury from hearing insubstantial cases, and must confine herself to considering whether the plaintiff has carried her burden of *production.*[7]

A Retrospective

14. Summary judgment is only appropriate if there is "no genuine issue of material fact" to be resolved by the jury. It is often said that if the evidence is so one-sided that a judge would be required to enter judgment as a matter of law at trial, then no genuine factual issue exists and summary judgment is appropriate. See, e.g., *Anderson v. Liberty Lobby, Inc.,* 477 U.S. 242, 250 (1986). Under this analysis, the difference between the Rule 50(a) motion and the summary judgment motion under Rule 56 is essentially procedural: The Rule 50(a) motion is raised during the trial and decided on the basis of the testimony and documentary evidence offered at trial, while the summary judgment motion is made before trial and determined solely on the basis of documentary evidence such as depositions, interrogatories, and affidavits. See *Anderson,* 477 U.S. at 251.

While this is conceptually consistent, many courts are more reluctant to grant summary judgment than judgment as a matter of law under Rule

---

7. The analogy in a jury case would be if the judge sent the jury out after the plaintiff rested her case to determine whether the plaintiff's evidence had moved the case over the Z line (that is, satisfied the plaintiff's burden of proof) and dismissed the action if the jury concluded that the plaintiff had not. I suppose jury trials could be run that way: The jury would deliberate twice, once after the plaintiff's case to determine whether she had carried her initial burden of proof by a preponderance of the evidence; and a second time after the defendant's evidence to determine if she had pushed the case back over the Z line. Such a system would break the flow of the evidence and confuse the jury as well. But the judge *can* do this in a nonjury trial, since she is used to dealing with the concept of burdens of proof and can more easily break up the presentation of the evidence to consider the motion.

50(a). Although in theory the judge asks the same question in passing on both motions—whether the party opposing the motion has offered enough evidence that a reasonable factfinder could find in her favor—the context of the motions is strikingly different. In most cases summary judgment motions are decided on the basis of affidavits and other documentary evidence. The opposing party may submit her own evidentiary materials but will not have the benefit of cross-examination. In addition, the motion often comes fairly early in the litigation, before the parties have exhaustively developed their cases. If the judge senses that the case will turn on questions of fact that are not fully elucidated by the record, she will likely conclude that the parties should have a full opportunity to present their evidence at trial before a decision is made to withdraw the case from the jury.

> In considering a motion for summary judgment, the district court must give the benefit of the doubt to the party who asserts he can prove a dubious proposition at trial. In considering a motion for a directed verdict, in contrast, the district court has had the benefit of seeing what the parties alleged they could prove prior to trial tested in the crucible of open court. Accordingly, the district court is entitled to grant a directed verdict even though some evidence supports the opposite position.

Kim v. Coppin State College, 662 F.2d 1055, 1059 (4th Cir. 1981). Consequently, it is not unusual for the court to deny summary judgment but subsequently grant judgment as a matter of law at trial for the same party.

In the *Chamberlain* case there is ample ground for a court to conclude that full trial of the issues might reveal a submissible case for the plaintiff. The evidence was largely testimonial; cross-examination might have revealed inconsistencies in the defendant's witnesses' testimony, or impeached their credibility. In such cases judges tend to give the party opposing summary judgment the benefit of the doubt by allowing the case to proceed to trial. See Field, Kaplan, and Clermont, Civil Procedure (7th ed. 1997) at 698 (motion for directed verdict "comes at a later stage in the litigation with lesser worry of prematurely interceding, and it is decided upon a more complete and effective airing of the evidence. The result is a practical difference in standards, with the test for directed verdict being slightly easier to meet"). Even if (as here) the judge ultimately takes the case from the jury, such forbearance gives the parties the fullest opportunity to satisfy their burden of production (and thus get to the jury) in close cases.

23

The Judge and the Jury, Part Two: Whose Case Is This, Anyway?

Introduction

A misguided minority of law students think that civil procedure is dull, but in truth it is full of surprises. You may well have been surprised to learn from the last chapter that a judge may snatch a case from the jury in the middle of trial by entering judgment as a matter of law. It is perhaps even more surprising that the judge may actually allow the jury to deliberate and reach its verdict on the evidence but refuse to enter judgment on the verdict rendered. At first blush this seems the ultimate affront to the jury system, to allow the jury to go through the entire trial process and reach its decision, and then disregard or reverse it. Yet, as we shall see, there are good reasons to allow the judge to do so.

Traditionally, the judge has had the authority to displace the jury's verdict by entering a "judgment notwithstanding the verdict," or j.n.o.v.[1] The j.n.o.v. motion is essentially a delayed (or, more accurately, renewed) motion for a directed verdict. The standard for granting the j.n.o.v. motion is the

---

1. J.n.o.v., or judgment *non obstante veredicto*," is Latin for judgment notwithstanding the verdict. The two terms are used interchangeably in practice.

same as that for directing a verdict: Either motion will be granted if the opponent's evidence is so weak that no reasonable jury could have reached a verdict for him. Of course, when the losing party moves for j.n.o.v. after the jury's verdict, a jury *has* found for the opposing party. Thus, the j.n.o.v. motion asserts that the jury acted irrationally, in disregard of the evidence in reaching a verdict for the party opposing the motion.

The j.n.o.v. motion has long been a fixture of trial practice in both the state and federal courts. However, the 1991 amendments to the Federal Rules changed the name of the j.n.o.v. motion: It is now called a motion for judgment as a matter of law, the same as the Rule 50(a) motion made during trial to take the case away from the jury. See Fed. R. Civ. P. 50(b). Again, the change in the name makes sense because it emphasizes that the motion after verdict asks the judge to do exactly the same thing that the motion during trial does: take the case from the jury to prevent an irrational result. Again, as with the earlier motion, the new wine really is the same vintage as the old: The motion for judgment as a matter of law after verdict is the functional equivalent of a motion for j.n.o.v. And, again, the j.n.o.v. terminology persists in most state courts, so you will have to use both terms in practice. In this chapter, I will use the federal terminology. However, because the new name refers to both the pre-verdict and post-verdict motion, I will indicate in parentheses whether I am referring to a motion made before the case goes to the jury (d.v.) or after the verdict (j.n.o.v.).

You may well wonder what purpose is served by allowing the motion for judgment as a matter of law after the verdict (j.n.o.v.). If the standards for granting the motion before the jury deliberates (d.v.) and after (j.n.o.v.) are the same, why not simply grant the motion before the jury deliberates? This will save the jury the trouble of unnecessary deliberations and avoid the affront of having their findings disregarded.

If the decision to take the case from the jury was cut and dried, this argument would have considerable force. However, reasonable judges may differ — and often do — about whether a given case is strong enough to go to a jury. Because the decision that the evidence is too weak to go to the jury is often debatable, the judge's entry of judgment as a matter of law before the jury deliberates (d.v.) will frequently be appealed. If the appellate court concludes that the evidence *was* sufficient to send the case to the jury,[2] it will reverse the judge's entry of judgment and order a new trail. This will then require a wasteful repetition of the entire first trail. See scenario 1 in Figure 23-1.

If, on the other hand, the judge withholds decision on the sufficiency of the evidence by denying the motion for judgment as a matter of law (d.v.) at

---

2. Because the decision to grant a directed verdict motion is based on the conclusion that the evidence is too weak as a matter of law to support a verdict for the other party, it is reviewed de novo by the appellate court under the same standard used by the trial judge. See Moore's §50.92 [1].

Scenario 1	Scenario 2

D seeks judgment as a matter of law (d.v.) at close of evidence

↓

Judge grants, discharges jury, enters judgment for *D*

↓

P appeals

↓

Appellate court finds evidence legally sufficient to go to the jury, reverses, sends back to trial court

↓

Case must be retried from beginning

D seeks judgment as a matter of law (d.v.) at close of evidence

↓

Judge denies or defers decision on motion

↓

Case goes to jury, which renders verdict for *P*

↓

After verdict, *D* renews motion for judgment as a matter of law (j.n.o.v.)

↓

Judge grants renewed motion (j.n.o.v.)

↓

P appeals

↓

Appellate court finds evidence legally sufficient to go to the jury, reverses

↓

Appellate court orders judgment entered on jury verdict (no retrial needed)

Figure 23-1

the close of the evidence, this scenario can be avoided. In most cases, where the evidence is weak enough to lead the judge to consider directing the verdict, the jury will agree that the case is too weak and return a verdict for the moving party anyway. This is the best possible result: It avoids any apparent intrusion on the right to jury trial, leads to a verdict that the judge finds supportable on the evidence, and avoids the appeal that would likely have followed if the judge had taken the case from the jury.

If, on the other hand, the jury returns a verdict for the party (usually the plaintiff) against whom the judge considered directing the verdict, the judge can still enter judgment as a matter of law (j.n.o.v.) for the other party. Here again, the party whose verdict has been taken away will frequently appeal on the ground that the evidence was strong enough to support a rational verdict in his favor. If the appeals court agrees and reverses the judge's order for entry of judgment as a matter of law (j.n.o.v.), it can simply order judgment entered on the jury's verdict. Thus, the need to retry the case is avoided by waiting until after the verdict to decide whether the case is jury-worthy. See scenario 2 in Figure 23-1.

Prerequisites to the Renewed Motion

There are several important limitations on the right to seek judgment as a matter of law (j.n.o.v.) after the verdict. Under Fed. R. Civ. P. 50(b) (and many state rules modeled on it) the motion must be filed within ten days of the entry of judgment on the jury's verdict.[3] In addition, a party may only move for judgment as a matter of law (j.n.o.v.) after the verdict if he made the same motion (d.v.) before the verdict. See Fed. R. Civ. P. 50(b) (party who made motion for judgment as a matter of law at the close of all the evidence may "renew" motion after verdict).

There are two reasons for this second requirement, one historical and rather silly, the other policy-based and entirely sensible. The historical reason has to do with the seventh amendment to the United States Constitution, which provides that "no fact tried by a jury, shall be otherwise reexamined in any Court of the United States, than according to the rules of the common law." Early cases held that it was unconstitutional for the judge to allow the jury to decide the facts and then "reexamine" them through the j.n.o.v. motion. *Slocum v. New York Life Ins. Co.*, 228 U.S. 364 (1913). However, the Supreme Court retreated from this position in *Baltimore & Carolina Line, Inc. v. Redman*, 295 U.S. 654 (1935). In *Redman* the Court held that it was permissible for the trial court to grant judgment notwithstanding the verdict if the moving party had sought a directed verdict before the jury deliberated and the court had reserved decision on the motion.[4] The first sentence of Rule 50(b) embodies the *Redman* fiction that the judge who denies a directed verdict has simply delayed decision upon it, rather than "reexamined" the jury's findings.

The second reason for requiring a pre-verdict motion as a prerequisite for granting judgment as a matter of law (j.n.o.v.) after the verdict is more

---

3. Entry of judgment occurs when the court clerk enters a notation of the judgment on the case docket. See Fed. R. Civ. P. 58, 79(a). It is also permissible to seek j.n.o.v. after the verdict but before entry of judgment; Rule 50(b) merely requires that the motion be filed "no later than" ten days after entry of judgment.

4. This was regarded as permissible, despite the "reexamination" clause in the seventh amendment, because the court was deemed to have the power to direct the verdict for the defendant without ever sending the case to the jury. If the judge could do that, the *Redman* court reasoned, he should also be allowed to submit the case subject to a subsequent decision on the directed verdict motion. Instead of "reexamining" the jury's verdict, the judge is simply "examining" the sufficiency of the evidence for the first time, but a little late.

substantial. A party who moves for judgment as a matter of law at the close of the evidence must state his grounds for concluding that the case should not be submitted to the jury. Fed. R. Civ. P. 50(a)(2); see also Fed. R. Civ. P. 7(b). Thus, the motion will alert the court and the opposing party to the defects in that party's case before the jury has gone out, while there is still time to offer further evidence to cure the defect. Suppose, for example, that the plaintiff sues an employer for negligence of its employee, but fails to put on evidence that the employee was acting in the scope of employment at the time of the accident. If the employer moves for judgment as a matter of law, it will have to specify that the ground for the motion is the lack of evidence of scope of employment, a crucial element of the claim. Doubtless, the judge will then allow plaintiff to reopen her case to submit evidence on the scope-of-employment question. If the lack of evidence was due to inadvertence, plaintiff will cure it. If, however, it is because plaintiff has no such evidence, she won't, and the motion will be allowed, either before or after the case goes to the jury.

Thus, by requiring the motion before the jury goes out in order to preserve the right to move for judgment after the verdict, the rule prevents a party from "sandbagging" his opponent by raising defects in the opponent's evidence after the jury has been discharged, when it is too late to cure those defects. It may be frustrating to a careful lawyer to be forced to help a less perceptive opponent make his case by pointing out those defects. However, remember that the entire thrust of the Rules is to ensure that suits are determined on the merits, not on the procedural skills of counsel.[5]

New Trial Distinguished

The judge may also deprive a party of a verdict by granting a new trial under Fed. R. Civ. P. 59. Unlike the motion for judgment as a matter of law, which leads to a judgment for the moving party, the grant of a new trial does not end the case but leads to a second trial on all or part of the case.

There are two general categories of cases in which the courts have traditionally granted new trials. The first is for errors in the trial process. Every litigant is entitled to "due process of law," including a fair trial procedure before his rights are determined. Any number of mistakes may be made in the course of trial, such as the improper admission or exclusion of evidence, improper instructions by the judge as to the legal principles the jury must apply, or juror contacts with witnesses outside the courtroom. Errors of this sort may taint the jury's decision-making process, leading it to consider inappropriate information in reaching a verdict or to use the wrong rules of law

---

5. Despite this reasoning, many states do not follow the federal practice of requiring a directed verdict motion to preserve the right to seek j.n.o.v. See Friedenthal, Kane and Miller. p. 562.

in assessing liability or damages. See generally James, Hazard & Leubsdorf at §§7.25-7.27.

If the losing party moves for a new trial on the basis of such errors immediately after trial,[6] Rule 59 allows the judge to vacate the verdict and order the case retried in order to assure the parties a fair trial procedure. If the judge refused to grant a new trial despite substantial errors at the trial, the party prejudiced by the error would doubtless appeal, the appellate court would reverse, and a new trial would be ordered anyway, after much additional effort and expense. The judge can save this effort and expense by ordering the new trial himself if he is convinced that there was prejudicial error in the first trial.

In addition to new trials for procedural errors, the trial judge has traditionally had the power to grant a new trial if he believes the trial *process* was fair but the *result* is clearly wrong. The federal cases suggest various (but quite similar) standards for granting a new trial based on a dubious outcome. It is said that the judge may grant a new trial if the jury's verdict is "against the 'clear weight,' 'overwhelming weight,' or 'great weight' of the evidence" (*Goldsmith v. Diamond Shamrock Corp.*, 767 F.2d 411, 416 (8th Cir. 1985)); when it is "quite clear that the jury has reached a seriously erroneous result" (*Lind v. Schenley Industries, Inc.*, 278 F.2d 79, 89 (3d Cir. 1960)); or when a new trial "is necessary to prevent injustice" (*Whalen v. Roanoke County Board of Supervisors*, 769 F.2d 221, 226 (4th Cir. 1985)); see generally Wright & Miller §2806. Under such formulas the judge cannot displace the verdict simply because he disagrees with the jury. But he may order a new trial in cases in which the evidence is strong enough to rationally support the jury's verdict, but he believes that verdict is seriously erroneous (represented, perhaps, by point Q on the diagram in the last chapter, p. 411. The difference in the judge's role in passing on motions for new trial and motions for judgment as a matter of law is illustrated in Figure 23-2 on p. 435.

In passing on the new trial motion, the judge *may* consider the credibility of the witnesses. Compare the motion for judgment as a matter of law, which, in both its incarnations, requires the judge to assume the truth of the evidence for the nonmoving party, Thus, the judge in passing on the motion for a new trial acts to some extent as a "thirteenth juror," making an independent assessment of the evidence. The judgment to be made is not whether the verdict was totally irrational but whether the judge is convinced that it is so strongly suspect that it would serve the ends of justice to have another jury hear the case.

Arguably, the judge's power to grant a new trial on this ground is even more intrusive than the power to take the case away from the jury, since

---

6. The motion for new trial, like the Rule 50(b) motion for j.n.o.v., must be filed within ten days of entry of judgment. Fed. R. Civ. P. 59(b).

weaker evidence for plaintiff ← → stronger evidence for plaintiff

Evidence Evenly Balanced

	Judge's assessment of the evidence	Judge's disposition of the case
	Evidence too weak to support a rational verdict for plaintiff	Judge may enter directed verdict or j.n.o.v. for defendant
X	A verdict for plaintiff is supportable, but against clear weight of the evidence	Judge may order new trial
	Judge does not agree with jury, but cannot say verdict for plaintiff is against clear weight of the evidence	Judge will order entry of judgment on the jury's verdict
Z	Judge and jury concur that preponderance of the evidence favors plaintiff	Judge will order entry of judgment on the verdict for plaintiff
	A verdict for defendant is supportable but against clear weight of evidence	Judge may order new trial
Y	Judge concludes that evidence is so compelling that no reasonable jury could find for defendant (rare — see infra p.423)	Judge enters directed verdict or j.n.o.v. for plaintiff

Figure 23-2: The Judge's Power to Displace the Jury's Verdict: A Schematic

435

the standard for granting a new trial is less stringent than that for entering judgment as a matter of law. However, it may be defended on the ground that a new *jury,* not the judge, will reconsider the case if the motion is granted. In fact, if a new trial is granted, the next step in the case will be to hold the second trial, at least in federal court. Under federal procedure, the party who won the verdict may not immediately appeal the judge's new trial grant, since parties are only entitled to appeal when the case is over in the trial court. When the judge enters an order to retry the case, there is no "final decision" from which to take an appeal. See 28 U.S.C. §1291; Moore's at §59.50[1]. Some state systems, however, allow an "interlocutory" (i.e., immediate) appeal from the grant of a new trial. G. Shreve and P. Raven-Hansen, Understanding Civil Procedure (2d ed. 1994) p.410 n.74.

The judge may also grant partial new trials in appropriate cases. If, for example, the jury's verdict on liability is clearly supportable but the damages greatly exceed the losses reflected in the evidence, the judge may order a new trial as to damages only.[7] In other cases, the judge may find the verdict against one defendant clearly supported by the evidence but not against another and grant a new trial solely on the claims against the second defendant.

An important difference between new trials for trial error and for verdicts against the weight of evidence is the standard of appellate review. Questions concerning the admission or exclusion of evidence or the proper instructions to the jury often involve issues of law, which can be reviewed de novo by the courts of appeals. Appellate judges, after all, are specialists in such legal questions. However, whether the verdict goes against the great weight of the evidence is a delicate decision that requires a balancing of evidence, usually including live testimony, which only the trial judge has had a full opportunity to observe. Consequently, it is rare for appellate judges to second-guess the trial judge's on-the-spot judgment that a new trial is warranted on this ground. Early federal cases suggested that the grant of a new trial on this ground was "unreviewable," that is, committed completely to the discretion of the trial court. See *Fairmount Glass Works v. Cub Fork Coal Co.,* 287 U.S. 474, 481-482 (1933). The trend, however, has been for the courts of appeals to review new trial grants—rather gingerly—under an abuse of discretion standard. This trend was approved by the Supreme Court in *Gasperini v. Center for Humanities, Inc.,* 518 U.S. 415 (1996).

The first examples that follow illustrate the relationship between motions for judgment as a matter of law before the verdict (d.v.) and after the verdict (j.n.o.v.), and new trial. The second part of the chapter explores

---

7. In cases where the verdict is excessive, the judge may also offer the plaintiff a remittitur. Under remittitur practice, the court agrees to enter judgment for the plaintiff if he will accept a lesser sum than the jury's verdict. If the plaintiff refuses to accept the remittitur, the judge orders a new trial. See generally Wright and Miller §2815.

the procedural complexities of joint motions under Rule 50(c) and (d). Assume that all actions are brought in federal court.

EXAMPLES

Never Say Die

1.   Milne brings an action against Potter for infringement of a copyright Milne holds on a book about a bear. The case is tried to a jury. Potter moves for judgment as a matter of law (d.v) at the close of Milne's evidence. The motion is denied. Potter renews the motion after presenting her own evidence. The motion is denied again. The jury is instructed, deliberates, and returns a verdict for Milne. May Potter now move again for judgment as a matter of law (j.n.o.v.)?

2.   Potter, the defendant, moves for judgment as a matter of law (d.v.) at the close of the evidence. The motion is denied. The jury returns a verdict for Potter. Milne believes that the jury's verdict is completely unsupported by the evidence.
   a. May *Milne* now move for judgment as a matter of law (j.n.o.v.)?
   b. May he move for a new trial?

3.   Assume, as in example 1, that Potter (the defendant) moved for judgment as a matter of law (d.v.) at the close of Milne's evidence but did not renew her motion at the close of all the evidence. The verdict went for Milne, and Potter now moves again for judgment as a matter of law (j.n.o.v.). Is the motion proper under the Rule?

4.   Potter moves for judgment as a matter of law (d.v.) at the close of the evidence. The motion is denied, and the jury returns a verdict for Milne. Judgment is entered on the verdict. Potter believes that the verdict is completely unsupported by the evidence. Three days after judgment is entered, she renews her motion for judgment as a matter of law, under Rule 50(b). The judge denies the motion five weeks later. Potter now moves for a new trial, on the ground that the judge improperly excluded important evidence at trial and that the verdict is against the weight of the evidence. The judge, after research, agrees on the exclusion-of-evidence point but not on the weight-of-the-evidence point. What should the judge do?

Contingency Planning

5.   Assume the same basic facts as example 4, except that both parties have some complaints about the trial. The jury rendered a verdict for the plaintiff, Milne, but Potter believes that the judge should have granted her motion for judgment as a matter of law (d.v.). She also objects to the judge's instruction on the standard for liability. Milne is satisfied with the verdict but is also convinced that his case would have been stronger if the judge had not excluded important evidence that he offered at trial.

     a. How should Potter present her objections?

     b. What should Milne do about his objection to the exclusion of the evidence?

6.   Assume that Milne's case is tried to a jury, which returns a verdict for Potter. Milne moves for a new trial on the ground that the judge improperly instructed the jury on the standard for recovery under the copyright statute. Potter argues strenuously that the instructions were proper. The judge concludes that Milne is right and orders a new trial. What happens next?

7.   Assume that Potter moves for judgment as a matter of law at the close of the evidence on the ground that Milne's evidence is too weak to support a verdict. The motion is denied, and the jury returns a verdict for Milne. In frustration, Potter reviews her trial notes and recalls that the judge allowed Milne to introduce hearsay evidence that probably should have been excluded. Although she did not object at the time, Potter researches the evidentiary issue and concludes that the evidence was indeed improperly admitted. Within the ten-day period, she makes two motions, one for a new trial on the ground that the evidence should have been excluded, and a second motion for judgment as a matter of law (j.n.o.v.) on the ground that without the inadmissible evidence, Milne's case was too weak to go to the jury.

     a. Should the judge grant the motion for a new trial?

     b. Should he grant the motion for judgment as a matter of law?

8.   Assume that *Milne v. Potter* was tried before the judge, instead of a jury. After a full hearing, the judge finds for Milne and enters judgment accordingly. Potter believes that the judge improperly excluded important evidence she had offered on the liability issue.

     a. How should Potter present her objection before the trial court?

     b. What will the judge do if he agrees with Potter?

Combined Motions and Appellate Review

As the examples above suggest, counsel for both parties may have multiple objections to the course of the trial, which they will seek to raise after trial by combined post-trial motions. Subsections (c) and (d) of Rule 50 set forth the procedure for presenting such objections in motions for judgment as a matter of law (j.n.o.v.) and new trial, and for appellate review of such combined motions.

Under Rule 50(c)(1), the trial judge confronted with a combined motion for judgment as a matter of law (j.n.o.v.) and new trial must not only rule on the j.n.o.v. but must also make a conditional ruling on the alternative motion for new trial. The court of appeals can then address both issues at once in one consolidated appeal, if the case is appealed. A similar purpose lies behind Rule 50(d), which allows a party who won the verdict below, but has it taken away on appeal, to assert objections to the original trial process.

The examples that follow should help you to see how the use of combined motions under these two intimidating provisions facilitates the disposition of cases on appeal. For some very helpful background you may want to read *Montgomery Ward & Co. v. Duncan*, 311 U.S. 243 (1940), in which the Supreme Court established the broad outlines of the procedure later embodied in Rule 50(c) and (d). However, you should be able to analyze the examples from a careful reading of these parts of the rule alone.

EXAMPLES

No Stone Unturned

9. Carroll sues Alcott for breach of contract. Alcott moves for judgment as a matter of law (d.v.) at the close of all the evidence. After the motion is denied, the jury returns a verdict for Carroll and judgment is entered on the verdict. Alcott moves for judgment as a matter of law (j.n.o.v.) and, in the alternative, for a new trial on the ground that the verdict was against the weight of the evidence. The judge grants the j.n.o.v. motion and "conditionally" grants the new trial motion as well.
   a. May Carroll appeal at this point?
   b. Assume that the court of appeals holds that the evidence was sufficient to go to the jury, so that judgment as a matter of law (j.n.o.v.) should not have been granted. What will that court do next?

10. Alcott, the defendant, loses at trial and moves for judgment as a matter of law (j.n.o.v.) and for a new trial on the grounds that the verdict was against the weight of the evidence and that the judge's instructions to the jury were improper. The judge denies both motions. Alcott appeals. What will the court of appeals do if
   a. it concludes that judgment as a matter of law (j.n.o.v.) should have been granted?
   b. it concludes that j.n.o.v. was properly denied and that the verdict was not against the weight of the evidence but that the instructions were improper?

Delayed Reaction

11. Assume that both Alcott and Carroll are unhappy with the trial. The jury returned a verdict for Carroll, the plaintiff, but Alcott believes that the evidence was too weak to support the verdict. Carroll believes the verdict is proper but also believes that the judge improperly excluded evidence that would have strengthened his case. Alcott moves for judgment as a matter of law (j.n.o.v.); Carroll opposes the motion but makes none of his own. The

j.n.o.v. motion is denied. Alcott appeals on the ground that j.n.o.v. should have been granted, and the court of appeals agrees. Where does the case go from here?

Practice Makes Perfect

12. Consider the following possible outcomes at the trial and appellate level. Assume in each case that the plaintiff won the verdict, and that the defendant seeks judgment as a matter of law (j.n.o.v.) on the basis that the evidence was too weak to support a plaintiff's verdict, and, in the alternative, a new trial on the ground that the judge mistakenly excluded important evidence offered by the defendant.

What should the appellate court do in each case?

Trial court	Appellate court
a. grants *D*'s motion for j.n.o.v., and his conditional motion for new trial	agrees that j.n.o.v. proper, but not new trial
b. grants *D*'s motion for j.n.o.v. and grants his conditional motion for new trial	agrees with both decisions
c. denies *D*'s motion for j.n.o.v. and grants his conditional motion for new trial	agrees on j.n.o.v., disagrees on new trial
d. grants j.n.o.v. for *D*, denies *D*'s conditional motion for new trial	disagrees on both

EXPLANATIONS

Never Say Die

1. In this case Potter has already twice asked the judge to rule that Milne's evidence is too weak to go to the jury. Each time the judge has allowed the case to proceed. However, this does not bar Potter from renewing her challenge to the sufficiency of the evidence by seeking judgment as a matter of law (j.n.o.v.) after the verdict for Milne. As the Introduction indicates, the rule *requires* that the motion be made before verdict (d.v.) in order to preserve the right to make the motion after verdict (j.n.o.v.). Thus, every party who seeks judgment as a matter of law after the verdict will be renewing a similar motion made before the jury retires. The judge's denial of the pre-verdict motions does not necessarily indicate that he believes the evidence

poses a jury issue; he may simply wish to reserve judgment on the issue, so as to get the jury's verdict and save a complete retrial if the decision to grant judgment as a matter of law after verdict (j.n.o.v.) is reversed on appeal.

2a. Rule 50(b) only authorizes a party who has moved for judgment as a matter of law before the verdict (d.v.) to renew the motion after the verdict (j.n.o.v.), for the reasons discussed in the Introduction. Although Potter sought judgment as a matter of law (d.v.) at the close of the case, Milne did not. Thus, Milne's failure to make a similar motion will bar him from seeking judgment notwithstanding the verdict after the jury finds for Potter.

Milne may not argue that his motion is proper because *Potter* sought judgment as a matter of law (d.v.) before the case went to the jury. As discussed in the Introduction, the motion must be made before the verdict in order to alert the opposing party to weaknesses in that party's case. Potter's motion was obviously directed to the weaknesses in Milne's case, not her own.

b. Milne is barred from seeking entry of judgment in his favor under Rule 50(b), but Rule 59 contains no analogous requirement of a prior motion for judgment as a matter of law (d.v.) (or for a new trial) in order to move for a new trial on the ground that the verdict is against the weight of the evidence. Since Milne believes the evidence was too weak to support a rational verdict for Potter, he presumably also believes that the verdict is against the great weight of the evidence. Thus, Milne can at least ask the judge to vacate the verdict and grant a new trial on this ground. That will not get him the judgment but will at least give him the opportunity to convince another jury of the strength of his case.

3. A party must move for judgment as a matter of law (d.v.) before the case goes to the jury in order to preserve the right to renew the motion after the verdict. Here Potter did make such a motion at the close of the plaintiff's case but did not renew it at the close of all the evidence. This is probably not sufficient to preserve the right to seek judgment as a matter of law after the verdict. See Rule 50(b), first sentence (referring to a motion for judgment as a matter of law "at the close of all the evidence.")

Some cases have adopted a more flexible approach to this requirement and entertained motions for j.n.o.v. where the defendant had sought a directed verdict earlier in the trial but not at the close of all the evidence. See, e.g., *Bohrer v. Hanes Corp.*, 715 F.2d 213, 216-217 (5th Cir. 1983). Although these cases may have stretched the language of Rule 50, they are consistent with the purpose for requiring a preverdict motion: The motion, even when made at the close of the plaintiff's case, does put the plaintiff on notice of the alleged weakness in his case. For example, if Potter moves for judgment as a matter of law (d.v.) at the close of Milne's evidence, Milne will have already offered all the evidence he believes is necessary to make a prima facie case. Thus, the motion should alert Milne to the unproved elements in his case and prevent him from being "sandbagged" by a renewed motion after the verdict.

However, the language of Rule 50(b) suggests that the rulemakers have rejected this approach. See also the Advisory Committee note to the 1991 revisions to Rule 50(b), which repeatedly refers to the requirement of a motion "made at the close of all the evidence." The rule appears to require that the defects be raised after the whole case is in, in order to preserve the right to seek j.n.o.v. after the verdict. This requirement gives the court a chance to consider the sufficiency of the entire evidence before sending the case to the jury.[8]

4.   The judge must deny the motion despite his conclusion that Potter has a valid claim that the trial was unfair. Under Rule 59, as under Rule 50(b), the motion must be filed within ten days of the entry of judgment. Potter's Rule 50(b) motion (j.n.o.v.) was timely, but her subsequent new trial motion was not, and the making of one post-trial motion does not suspend the time for making the other. Potter should have made both motions together within ten days of entry of judgment in order to assert all her objections in a timely fashion. See Rule 50(b), second sentence, which authorizes combined motions for new trial and judgment as a matter of law (j.n.o.v.).

Nor may the judge relieve Potter of her procedural mistake by granting the motion for a new trial "sua sponte" (on his own initiative). Rule 59(d) authorizes the trial judge to grant a new trial sua sponte but requires him to do so within ten days of the entry of judgment. The implication is that he may not correct an error brought to his attention after this period has lapsed. This limitation seems unfortunate, at least where the judge becomes convinced of the error within the 30-day appeal period in Fed. R. App. P. 4(a)(1). If the judge is really convinced that he improperly excluded evidence that would have affected the result, it makes sense to allow him to grant the new trial. Otherwise, Potter will be forced to appeal, and the court of appeals will be forced to hear and decide an appeal that could have been avoided by the grant of a new trial as soon as the error became apparent.[9]

The strict limit on the time for granting a new trial reflects a strong policy in favor of finality of judgments. Parties must know at some point that the decision rendered in an action will not be revised, so they can order their affairs accordingly. If the judge could reconsider at any time, the outcome would still remain uncertain despite the entry of a "final" judgment.

---

8. Despite the tighter language in the revised rule, some courts have continued to interpret it somewhat loosely. See, e.g., *Taylor Publishsing Co v. Jostens, Inc.,* 216F 3d 465 (5th Cir. 2000).

9. The judge might achieve the same result by granting relief from the judgment under Fed. R. Civ. P. 60(b), at least before the period for appeal of the judgment has run.

Contingency Planning

5a. It is not unusual for both parties to have complaints about the conduct of a trial. Here, Potter believes that the outcome was unwarranted by the evidence, and, in addition, that the process was tainted due to improper instructions. Milne is content with the outcome but believes that he could have made an even stronger case if all his evidence had been placed before the jury.

Potter, of course, should renew her motion for judgment as a matter of law (seek j.n.o.v.), since she believes that the evidence was too weak to support a rational verdict for Milne. In addition, if she believes the evidence was too weak to go to the jury, she must also believe it was against the great weight of the evidence. Consequently, she should join a motion under Rule 59 for a new trial on this ground with her Rule 50(b) motion. Finally, she should assert the improper jury instruction as an alternative ground for a new trial. She may assert all three grounds in a combined motion, but must do so within ten days of entry of judgment.

b. Milne is in a slightly different position. Because he won the verdict, he has no cause to press his objection to the exclusion of evidence (unless, of course, the evidence went to the size of the verdict and he is unhappy with that). He prevailed without the evidence and presumably has no interest in trying the suit again just to have a perfect process. However, Milne is still somewhat at risk since Potter has asked the judge to displace the jury's verdict. If the judge grants judgment for Potter (j.n.o.v.) on the ground that Milne did not produce sufficient evidence to pose a jury issue, Milne will surely wish to argue that he *could* have made a submissible case if the judge had not excluded important evidence.

Of course, the rulemakers have provided for this contingency. If the judge deprives Milne of his victory by entering judgment as a matter of law (j.n.o.v.) for Potter, Rule 50(c)(2) allows Milne to move for a new trial within ten days after entry of *that* judgment, on the ground that the evidence was improperly excluded. Thus, he need not raise the objection until the verdict in his favor is taken away. At that point, it becomes apparent that the judge's evidentiary ruling has harmed Milne's case, and he may ask the court to grant a new trial on that ground.

6. If Potter believes that the instruction was proper, she would like to appeal immediately, in hopes that the court of appeals will agree with her, reverse the new trial grant, and enter judgment on the jury's verdict. However, when a new trial motion is granted, the judge will enter an order for the case to be retried. As the Introduction states, parties in Potter's position may not appeal the grant of a new trial until after the new trial is held because a new trial grant is not considered a final judgment under federal practice. See 28 U.S.C. §1291 (authorizing appeal from "final decisions" of the district courts).

Thus, Potter will have to go through the second trial before appealing. If she wins at the second trial, she will presumably be satisfied with the result (though not the elongated process to reach it) and have no incentive to appeal the grant of the new trial. However, if she loses at the second trial, Potter will be entitled to appeal the judge's earlier decision to grant the new trial since the court will render a final judgment for Milne on the second verdict (assuming no further motions for new trial are granted after the *second* trial). The court of appeals will then review the disputed instruction from the first trial. If it agrees with Potter that the original instruction was proper, it will enter judgment on the original verdict for her. If it concludes that the trial judge's initial instruction was wrong, it will uphold the grant of the new trial and (assuming no reversible error in the second trial) affirm the judgment for Milne.

Although there is logic to delaying review of the new trial grant in these cases, there is also much to be said for immediate appeal. If the case is reviewed before the new trial and the new trial order is reversed, it will save the considerable effort of trying the case a second time, perhaps to no purpose.[10] For this reason some state systems allow interlocutory review of new trial grants. See Friedenthal, Kane, and Miller at p.579.

7a. The example here indicates that Potter did not object to the judge's error in admitting the evidence at the time that the error was made. In most cases the failure to object to the ruling during trial will foreclose relief on a motion for new trial afterwards. See Wright and Miller at §2805 pp.57-59 (in absence of a timely objection, new trial will not be granted "unless the error was so fundamental that gross injustice would result"). Although this rule seems draconian, especially given the pressures of trial, it makes good sense. If the error is brought to the judge's attention immediately, he may exclude the evidence and avoid a reversible error. If it is only raised after trial on a new trial motion, it is too late to save the trial.

If Potter could raise such objections without having objected during trial, it would open the door to manipulation of the trial process. She might deliberately withhold objection to one or more arguably prejudicial decisions of the trial judge. Then if she lost the verdict, she could undermine the unfavorable verdict by pulling these objections out of her hat as grounds for a new trial.

---

10. In *Roy v. Volkswagen of America, Inc.*, 896 F.2d 1174 (1990), for example, the plaintiffs won a verdict of $3 million in a negligence action after a 21-day trial. The judge ordered a new trial. The Roys attempted an appeal, which was dismissed because the new trial order prevented a final judgment. At the new trial, the jury found for the defendant. On appeal by the Roys from this judgment, the court held that the evidence was "substantially balanced" (896 F.2d at 1179) so that the new trial should not have been granted in the first place. Consequently, the court ordered judgment entered on the original jury verdict for the Roys — some six years after that verdict was rendered.

b. The judge will also deny Potter's motion for judgment as a matter of law (j.n.o.v.). Her argument here is that the evidence would have been too weak to go to the jury if the disputed evidence had not been admitted. Here again Potter should have avoided the error by a timely objection, rather than invoking it later to overturn the jury's verdict. Note that, while Potter did make a motion for judgment as a matter of law (d.v.) before the case went to the jury, it was *not on the ground of admission of the improper evidence*. Thus, neither the court nor Milne was given a chance to cure that problem.

A Rule 50(a) motion at the close of all the evidence on one ground will not preserve the right to seek judgment as a matter of law (j.n.o.v.) on a different ground. The purpose for the prior motion is to point out the problem at a time when it can be cured. Here Potter raised the objection that the evidence before the jury was too weak to support a verdict but did not raise the hearsay problem. Thus, her motion did not alert the court or Milne to the other evidentiary problem at a time when it could have been cured. See *Lifshitz v. Walter Drake & Sons, Inc.*, 806 F.2d 1426, 1428-1429 (9th Cir. 1986) (directed verdict motion only preserves right to seek j.n.o.v. on the specific grounds raised in the motion).

8a. Parties have the same right to seek a new trial in cases tried to the judge as they do in jury cases. See Fed R. Civ. P. 59(a)(2). Potter should make her motion for a new trial (often called a "rehearing" in nonjury cases) within ten days of entry of judgment, stating as her ground the exclusion of the disputed evidence.

b. Although the procedure for presenting the motion is similar, a rehearing after a nonjury trial differs significantly from a new trial in a jury case. In a jury case, the jury is discharged after a verdict is reached. They cannot be called back after the new trial is granted to hear the additional evidence that had been wrongly excluded. Thus, the only way to provide both parties with a full opportunity to be heard is to start over and present all the evidence to a new jury in a complete new trial.

In a nonjury case the judge need not go back and start from square one. He has already heard all the evidence and decided the relevant legal rules to apply in reaching a decision. If Potter's only objection is that the judge failed to consider certain evidence (and if the judge concludes that she is right), the judge can reopen the hearing, hear that evidence, and reconsider the case, taking the additional evidence into account. Thus, the rehearing in such cases can be a relatively brief proceeding to simply augment the record with the additional evidence. See Fed. R. Civ. P. 59(a), second sentence.

If Potter's objection had been that the judge *admitted* evidence that should have been excluded, the "rehearing" might be even simpler. The judge could simply sustain the motion and reconsider the case without taking the inadmissible evidence into account. At least that's the theory. In practice it is obviously questionable whether the judge can really disregard persuasive evidence that he has already heard simply on the technical ground that it is inadmissible under the rules of evidence.[11]

No Stone Unturned

9a. Carroll may appeal the judge's combined ruling, even though the new trial was "conditionally" (Fed. R. Civ. P. 50(c)(1)) granted. The judge has ordered judgment as a matter of law (j.n.o.v.) for Alcott. Rule 50(c)(1), second sentence, clearly states that the decision on the new trial motion does not prevent this from being a final judgment. Alcott is the winner and if no one appeals the case is over. The purpose of requiring the judge to rule conditionally on Alcott's alternative motion for a new trial is to help the court of appeals to decide how to dispose of the case if it reverses the decision to enter judgment as a matter of law for Alcott. If the j.n.o.v. stands, the conditional grant of the new trial has no effect; Alcott won't have any interest in a new trial if the court upholds his j.n.o.v.

b. If Carroll appeals and the court reverses the entry of judgment as a matter of law for Alcott, the judge's conditional ruling on the new trial motion assists the appellate court in deciding what should happen next in the case. The court of appeals can now review the judge's conditional decision that a new trial should be granted. If it concludes that the judge did not abuse his discretion in concluding that the verdict went against the clear weight of the evidence, the court can uphold the grant of the new trial and remand the case to the trial court for retrial. See Fed. R. Civ. P. 50(c)(1), third sentence. If, on the other hand, the court concludes that even the new trial motion should not have been granted (an unlikely decision, given the broad discretion accorded the trial court in making the new trial decision), it may reverse both decisions and order entry of judgment for Carroll on the jury's verdict.

The good sense of this procedure is highlighted by considering the alternative. If the trial judge decided only the Rule 50(b) motion, and that was reversed, the court of appeals would have to remand for the judge to consider whether a new trial should be granted. If he granted it on remand, the new trial would proceed since the grant of a new trial is an interlocutory decision. Only after a second trial would Carroll be able to challenge the new trial grant, on a second appeal.

On the other hand, if the judge denied the motion for a new trial on remand after reversal of the judgment as a matter of law (j.n.o.v.), Alcott

---

11. If one party in a case has evidence that is extremely persuasive but probably inadmissible under the rules of evidence, this may be a strong tactical reason for the other party to seek a jury trial. The judge must often see the evidence that is offered in order to pass on its admissibility. If he is also the factfinder, it will be difficult for him to disregard what he has seen. If the case is tried to a jury, however, the judge will see such evidence, but the factfinder (the jury) will not.

could *appeal that denial,* and a second trip to the court of appeals would be needed to fully dispose of the case. The Rule 50(c) procedure for conditional rulings on both motions allows the appellate court to fully dispose of these rulings in a single appeal.

10a. If the court concludes that judgment should have been granted for Alcott because Carroll's evidence was too weak to go to the jury, it may enter judgment as a matter of law (j.n.o.v.) itself. Unlike the discretionary Rule 59 decision as to whether the verdict was contrary to the clear weight of the evidence, which involves consideration of the credibility of witnesses, the j.n.o.v. decision is a question of law that the appellate court reviews de novo. The court must review all the evidence, consider it in the light most favorable to the nonmoving party, and make its own judgment as to whether Carroll's case was legally sufficient to submit to the jury.

b. If the court of appeals concludes that judgment as a matter of law (j.n.o.v.) was properly denied and that the verdict is not against the weight of the evidence, it will then consider whether the new trial should have been granted due to legal error in the instructions. The issue of the proper rules for the jury to apply in deciding the case is a question of law, which the court of appeals decides de novo. If the court concludes that the jury was not properly instructed, it can remand for a new trial. If the instructions were correct, it can affirm the denial of the new trial and (since it had already ruled that j.n.o.v. was properly denied) affirm the entry of judgment for Carroll. Either way, the use of combined motions again allows the appellate court to consider all of the losing party's objections without remand for decision of further post-trial motions.

Delayed Reaction

11. The situation here is similar to that in example 5b, in which the plaintiff won the verdict but had the victory snatched away when the trial judge granted j.n.o.v. for the defendant. Here, the same thing happened, except that it was the court of appeals rather than the trial judge that displaced the verdict. Until judgment was granted for Alcott on appeal, Carroll was content with the result of the original trial. Although he believed his case would have been stronger if the excluded evidence had been admitted, it was already strong enough to win. Thus, Carroll had no reason to seek a new trial due to the exclusion of the evidence.

It is only after the court of appeals deprives him of his judgment by granting judgment as a matter of law (j.n.o.v.) for Alcott that Carroll will wish to raise his objection to the evidentiary ruling. At that point, he will want to argue that the original trial was flawed and that he is entitled to a new trial at which the excluded evidence is placed before the jury. After all, it may be that his case was too weak to reach the jury precisely because that evidence was excluded.

Under Rule 50(d) Carroll may raise this argument at the appeal stage even if he did not seek a new trial in the district court. (Of course, he would have had to object at the time the evidence was excluded. See the answer to example 7.) If Carroll raises the issue on appeal, and the court of appeals reverses the denial of j.n.o.v., that court will consider the evidentiary point as well. It may order a new trial on this ground or remand to allow the trial judge to address the motion. Fed R. Civ. P. 50(d). Or, of course, it may deny the new trial if the evidence was properly excluded and enter judgment for Alcott based on its conclusion that j.n.o.v. should have been granted for her.

Practice Makes Perfect

12a. The appellate court enters judgment for the defendant, since it concludes that the plaintiff's case was too weak to support a verdict. Although the decision that the defendant is entitled to a new trial due to the exclusion of the evidence was erroneous, the error is harmless. The defendant has now prevailed without the evidence; the last thing he wants is a new trial.

b. Judgment is entered for the defendant, since both trial and appellate courts agree that the plaintiff's case was too weak to support a verdict. Once again, the defendant has no further interest in a new trial, though both courts agree that he would be entitled to one if the plaintiff's case were strong enough to go to the jury.

c. Initially, the appellate court won't do anything at all. Since the trial judge denied the j.n.o.v. motion, but granted the new trial motion, the case will be scheduled for a new trial. (Remember that in the federal courts, the grant of a new trial motion is an "interlocutory" decision, since the case is not over in the trial court.) If the plaintiff wins at the second trial, she will presumably not appeal. However, if she loses at the second trial, she may then appeal the decision to grant a new trial. If, as the example suggests, the appeals court concludes that there was no ground for granting the new trial, it will reverse the entry of the order for a new trial and (since it agrees with the trial judge's decision to deny j.n.o.v.) order entry of judgment on the first jury's verdict.

d. Here, the case is immediately appealable, because the court has entered judgment as a matter of law for the defendant on the basis that the case was too weak to go to the jury. Because the appellate court disagrees with this conclusion, it should reverse the entry of judgment for the defendant. However, since it concludes that a new trial was warranted due to the exclusion of the evidence, it should remand the case to the trial court for a retrial at which the evidence will be admitted.

PART FIVE

The Effect of the Judgment

24

Res Judicata: The Limits of Procedural Liberality

Introduction

Perhaps you are thoroughly tired of hearing how *reasonable* the Federal Rules of Civil Procedure are. Certainly, one of the recurrent themes of the Rules is to create a flexible procedural system in order to prevent procedure from dominating substance, to assure that the merits of the parties' claims, not procedural missteps, determine the outcome of lawsuits.

For example, parties are given broad power to join claims and parties in a single suit. Fed. R. Civ. P. 13, 14, 18, 20, 24. They are given the latitude to plead all their possible claims against opposing parties, within the limits of proper pleading. Fed. R. Civ. P. 8(a), 8(e)(2), 11. Pleadings are liberally construed, Fed. R. Civ. P. 8(f); *Conley v. Gibson*, 355 U.S. 41 (1957), and amendments freely allowed. Fed. R. Civ. P. 15(a). Even if amendments are not offered, the court can treat the pleadings *as though* they had been amended, when justice so requires, Fed. R. Civ. P. 15(b), and may grant parties the relief to which they are entitled even though they never asked for it. Fed. R. Civ. P. 54(c). If the process still goes awry, despite all these opportunities to correct procedural errors, the court may grant relief from judgment under Fed. R. Civ. P. 60(b) or a new trial under Fed. R. Civ. P. 59.

Given all this procedural liberality, you might expect that the rules governing relitigation of claims would be correspondingly indulgent. However, the exact opposite is true. Once the parties have had a full and fair opportunity to be heard under the flexible rules reviewed above, all this paternalistic indulgence comes to an abrupt halt. Regardless of a party's reason for wishing to relitigate a dispute, the doctrine of res judicata stands like a brutish, unreflecting myrmidon, guarding the doors of the courthouse.[1] While the Rules are liberal, res judicata is strict and uncharitable. No matter how unfair the result in the first suit may seem or indeed, no matter how unfair it may actually have been, the myrmidon will not step aside.

For example, suppose that the plaintiff in the *Schulansky* case recovers $7,000 from Ronan for breach of contract. If Schulansky believes that the verdict was too low, she cannot bring a second action against Ronan for more. Or, if she discovers a statute that allows a more generous measure of damages, she cannot bring a new action based on that statute. If Schulansky loses but believes that her lawyer did not litigate the case energetically, she will be barred by res judicata from trying again with a new lawyer.

In the traditional terminology, Schulansky's claim was said to be "merged" into the judgment she had won. That is, the claim was extinguished and replaced by the judgment. Restatement (Second) of Judgments §§17, 18 (1982). Once the judgment was entered, a suit could be brought to enforce that judgment if necessary (see Chapter 3, pp. 44-46), but no further suit could be brought on the extinguished claim. Conversely, if Schulansky lost, her claim was said to be "barred" by the adverse judgment so that no further suit could be brought on the claim.

The rationale for the doctrine is ancient and fundamental. Litigation is burdensome enough the first time without redoing it again whenever one of the parties is unhappy with the result — as at least one will be in every case. Parties must also get on with their affairs; without the certainty provided by res judicata, parties would not be able to rely on court decisions in planning their future conduct. Finally, from the point of view of the system, there is no justification for multiplying the costs and delay of litigation by allowing parties to go at it again once they have had a full and fair opportunity to litigate a claim.

Of course, the efficiency of res judicata would not be justified if it were achieved at the expense of fairness to the parties in presenting meritorious claims. For example, it would be a hard system indeed that barred the plaintiff from amending her complaint in the first action to assert new theories for relief unearthed during discovery and also barred her from bringing a separate action based on those theories. But, if amendments are liberally allowed

---

1. A myrmidon is a servant who mindlessly but doggedly obeys his master's every command. The first myrmidons were ants, who were changed into men by Zeus to repopulate the island kingdom of Aegina. They were known for their loyalty and courage in following their leader, Achilles, in the Trojan War. See E. Hamilton, Mythology 296 (1969).

in the first suit, it is fair to bar a second action on theories left out of the first suit. Thus, it is precisely because the Rules of Civil Procedure are so liberal in facilitating presentation of claims in the first action that the res judicata myrmidon can so stubbornly bar a second try. Indeed, the specter of res judicata encourages parties to take full advantage of the Rules to present their claims initially, since they know that they will not get a second chance to try the suit, that there will be no "second bite at the apple."

In most jurisdictions, there are four prerequisites for res judicata: (1) there must be a final judgment; (2) the judgment must be "on the merits"; (3) the claims must be the same in the first and second suits; and (4) the parties in the second action must be the same as those in the first (or have been represented by a party to the prior action). Most of the interpretive issues in applying the doctrine concern the requirements that the claims be the same in both suits and that the original judgment be on the merits.

The "Same Claim" Requirement

The definition of a single "claim" for res judicata purposes varies from one jurisdiction to another. See generally Friedenthal, Kane, and Miller at §14.4. The federal courts and an increasing number of states have adopted the standard in the Restatement (Second) of Judgments §24 (1982), which essentially equates a party's claim for res judicata purposes with the "transaction or occurrence" test of the federal joinder rules. See 18 Wright and Miller at §4407, p.62. Under this approach, a party who has asserted a right to relief arising out of a particular transaction or occurrence must join all claims she has arising from it, or the omitted claims will be barred by res judicata.

There is good sense to a theory that makes the scope of preclusion mirror the test for allowing initial joinder under the Rules. If a party had the right to join two claims for relief arising from the same transaction in the first suit, it is reasonable to require her to do so, instead of bringing two suits that will rehash the same facts. Conversely, if the scope of preclusion is to mirror the scope of permissible joinder, res judicata should *not* bar claims that could not have been joined in the first action. For example, before the development of the unified civil action under the Rules, parties could not always seek legal and equitable relief in the same proceeding: They were often forced to split their claims between the law courts (for damage claims) and the equity courts (for claims to equitable relief, such as specific performance or injunctions). See generally James, Hazard, and Leubsdorf Civil Procedure (4th Ed. 1992) at 13-17. In such cases, a party who had sought damages in an action at law was not precluded from seeking injunctive relief based on the same transaction or occurrence from a court of equity because she could not have obtained an injunction in the prior action at law. Under the Federal Rules, however, parties may almost always assert all their claims in a single suit, and res judicata is correspondingly broad.[2]

Under the transaction or occurrence test, preclusion turns on the *right* to join the claim in the original action, not on whether the claim actually was asserted. Consequently, claims need not have actually been litigated to be barred in a later action; they need only have been *available* to the plaintiff in the first suit. For example, it is clear that Schulansky, after recovering $7,000 from Ronan in the contract action described in Part Six, could not sue Ronan again for this claim on a breach of contract theory. However, res judicata will also bar Schulansky from suing Ronan for fraud connected with the addition work, even though she had never pleaded fraud in her first suit, never tried the case on a fraud theory, and in fact never thought of it. Indeed, the message of res judicata is that Schulansky (or, more particularly, Schulansky's lawyer) had *better* think of it, sooner rather than later.

The Second Restatement of Judgments approach, which equates the scope of a "claim" with the scope of the underlying transaction or occurrence that gave rise to the suit, is followed in the federal courts and in many state courts. However, there are other approaches. Some courts bar a second action if allowing it might impair or contradict the judgment in the first, if the same evidence would support the claims in both actions, or if the same "primary right" is at issue in both suits. For a good discussion of these alternative—generally older—approaches to the definition of a single claim, see Friedenthal, Kane and Miller, s. 14.4. These earlier approaches have often proved frustratingly ambiguous. The same-underlying-transaction approach involves ambiguities of its own, but has the distinct advantage that it focuses the analysis on a single set of historical facts, regardless of what legal theories are asserted in the two actions or how much overlap there is in the evidence supporting the first and second actions.

Judgment "On the Merits"

Another res judicata prerequisite that has raised interpretive problems is the requirement of a decision "on the merits" in the first action. Clearly, a full trial followed by a verdict and judgment is the paradigm of a decision on the merits. At the other extreme, some dismissals, such as dismissals for improper venue or lack of personal jurisdiction, do not bar a second action, on the rationale that the court never reached the merits in the first action, much less decided it after a full opportunity to be heard. The very basis of such dismissals is that the court does not have the power to reach the merits because the plaintiff has chosen an improper court under the "three ring" analysis.

---

2. However, the right to join claims under the Rules does not automatically lead to the conclusion that res judicata will bar a separate suit on those claims. See Chapter 25.

The toughest cases fall between these extremes. For example, jurisdictions differ as to whether a dismissal for failure to state a claim (see Fed. R. Civ. P. 12(b)(6)) should bar a second action. The Second Restatement of Judgments concludes that such dismissals should bar relitigation, on the theory that a plaintiff whose complaint is dismissed for failure to state a claim is allowed liberal opportunities to amend. Restatement (Second) of Judgments §19, comment d (1982). If she cannot amend to state a compensable claim on a second or third try, it is presumably because she has no right to relief under the law. If that is true, there is no reason to allow her to harass the defendant with a new action. This is the rule applied in the federal courts. *Federated Department Stores v. Moitie*, 452 U.S.394, 399 n.3 (1981); Moore's §30.04[8]. However, some state courts allow a second action under these circumstances because comparatively little litigation effort goes into these preliminary dismissals, and hence a basic value underlying res judicata, preservation of scarce judicial resources, is not compromised by allowing a new action.

Actually, it is a bit of a misnomer to say that judgment must be "on the merits" to bar a second action. In fact, the court need not reach the merits at all for its judgment to have full res judicata effect. For example, if the plaintiff files suit, but does not pursue the case, it will eventually be dismissed for failure to prosecute. Clearly the parties have not litigated the merits in such cases; they haven't litigated anything at all. But such a dismissal is deemed "on the merits" in the sense that it will bar a subsequent action because the plaintiff had a full *opportunity* to litigate the merits in the first action. If she doesn't choose to take the opportunity, she must accept the res judicata consequences. Similarly, a defendant who defaults (that is, never answers to the merits and therefore loses by default), is also barred by res judicata on the same reasoning.

Final Judgment

A judgment must also be "final" before res judicata attaches. There is obviously little point in barring a second action on a claim that has not yet been fully resolved in the first. Suppose, for example, that Schulansky sues Ronan in federal court on breach of contract and fraud theories, and the court dismisses the fraud claim under Fed. R. Civ. P. 12(b)(6) but allows the contract claim to proceed. Generally, courts remain free to reexamine interlocutory rulings made in the course of suit, including a ruling dismissing one of the plaintiff's claims. See 18 Wright and Miller at §4478 pp. 789-90. Thus, the dismissal of the fraud claim might be reconsidered and vacated by the judge in the first action before the case is finally determined in the trial court. Thus, until final judgment is entered in the trial court, it remains too uncertain to support a res judicata plea in a separate action between the parties.

However, many courts give res judicata effect to a judgment once it has become final in the trial court, even if an appeal is pending. This is the

Restatement view. Restatement (Second) of Judgments §13, comment f (1982). Under this approach, a judgment may bar relitigation even though the original case is still being litigated and is not yet enforceable by execution or otherwise. Other courts, however, only give res judicata effect to judgments if the time for appeal has passed or the case has been finally resolved by the appellate court. James, Hazard, and Leubsdorf at §11.4.

In working through the examples that follow assume that all suits are brought in federal court and that the Restatement principles discussed above apply. If you want further background, Professor Wright has a good, short discussion of the doctrine. Wright, at pp.720-724. For more detail, I recommend the Second Restatement itself, which is replete with helpful examples and comments. Restatement (Second) of Judgments §§13-26 (1982). But keep in mind (not for the examples below but for those long lawyering years ahead) that the doctrine varies from one jurisdiction to another. Even if the Restatement principles are generally followed, each jurisdiction is likely to have its own quirks and quiddities that can only be learned from studying local practice.

EXAMPLES

Fielder's Choices

1.   Rizzuto's eye is injured when his baseball glove breaks while he is fielding a vicious grounder. He sues Allston Leather Company for negligent manufacture of the glove. The case is tried and judgment is entered for Allston. Later, Rizzuto sues again. He argues that the judge in the first suit erroneously excluded important evidence from Rizzuto's expert on baseball glove manufacturing standards and that he should have a chance to have a trial with all the admissible evidence properly before the jury. Allston pleads res judicata. Will the defense bar Rizzuto's second action?

2.   After the judgment for Allston in Rizzuto's case, Boyer tells Rizzuto that he was also injured using the same type of Allston glove and recovered judgment against Allston on a strict liability theory, which did not require proof that Allston was negligent. Rizzuto files a new action against Allston based on the original accident but asserting a right to recover only on the basis of strict liability. Will the claim be barred?

3.   Assume that Rizzuto won his first suit against Allston and recovered $3,000 in compensatory damages. Boyer subsequently tells him that he had claimed gross negligence by Allston in a prior suit based on the same defective glove and recovered punitive damages. Rizzuto brings a second action against Allston for punitive damages based on gross negligence. Can Allston plead res judicata?

4.   Assume that Rizzuto recovered $15,000 in an action against Allston, but Allston was in shaky financial condition and never paid. Rizzuto later

brings a new action against Allston after learning that its financial condition has improved. Does res judicata bar the second suit?

5.   Assume that Rizzuto presented evidence in the original action against Allston that he suffered impaired vision in his eye for several weeks as a result of the accident, missed two weeks of the baseball season, and had some pain from the injury. This is the only evidence he presented on damages. The jury finds for Rizzuto and awards him $10,000 damages. Three years later, after the judgment has been entered and paid, Rizzuto develops migraine headaches. His doctor tells him that these often result from an eye injury and are likely to continue indefinitely. Can Rizzuto sue Allston for damages for these headaches?

An Absurd Hypothetical

6.   Imagine that Rizzuto's vicious grounder breaks through his glove, whacks him in the eye, and bounces off Kubek, injuring him as well. Kubek sues Allston and recovers. Rizzuto testifies in Kubek's suit. Rizzuto now takes the cue and brings an action to recover for his injuries in the same accident. Allston pleads the inevitable res judicata. Is the suit barred?

7.   At the time Rizzuto was injured using Allston's glove, he had an endorsement contract with them to promote the glove in television commercials. He had made the ads but had not been paid by Allston.

Acting on the advice of his lawyers that asserting the contract claim in the negligence suit would confuse matters, Rizzuto did not assert his contract claim in the negligence suit against Allston. Instead, he sues separately on the contract claim after judgment in the negligence action. Allston pleads res judicata. Was the lawyers' advice sound?

8.   Assume that Rizzuto's contract calls for royalties (or "residuals" in the language of the trade) to be paid to Rizzuto for each year that the commercials are used. Allston pays the residuals in the first year at 5 percent, while Rizzuto claims it should be 10 percent. Rizzuto sues and wins. At the end of the next year, Allston pays Rizzuto again at the 5 percent rate. Rizzuto sues again and Allston pleads res judicata. Is the second action barred?

9.   Rizzuto sues Allston to collect under the endorsement contract. Allston defends the action and wins on the ground that Rizzuto had not performed his obligations under the contract because he abandoned filming after making several commercials. Allston subsequently brings a separate suit against Rizzuto for damages for *his* breach of the contract. Is Allston's suit precluded by res judicata?

Judgment on the Merits

10. Rizzuto sues Allston on the negligence claim in federal court. Allston moves to dismiss under Fed. R. Civ. P. 12(b)(1) for lack of subject matter

jurisdiction on the ground that complete diversity does not exist because its principal place of business is in New York (Rizzuto's home state). The court holds a full evidentiary hearing on the motion, including extensive testimony from officials of Allston as to the extent of Allston's business activities in New York and other states. After presentation of the evidence and briefs and argument by the parties, the court concludes that Allston's principal place of business is New York and therefore dismisses the suit. Rizzuto now sues in a New York state court, and Allston pleads res judicata. Will the defense prevail?

11. Assume that the court in the case described in example 10 concludes that it has subject matter jurisdiction. Allston therefore answers Rizzuto's negligence complaint and subsequently moves for summary judgment on the ground that Rizzuto cannot prove any negligence of Allston. It submits supporting affidavits of its employees, stating under oath that they had examined the glove after the accident and it was not damaged or defective in any way. Rizzuto submits no opposing affidavit, and summary judgment is entered for Allston. Subsequently, Rizzuto sues again. Is the second suit barred?

Pendent or Independent?

12. Koufax sues Throneberry in state court under a state unfair competition statute. He claims that Throneberry wrote a book about great baseball heroes of the 1950s, which plagiarized a similar book by Koufax. The court dismisses Koufax's claim on the ground that the statute of limitations on the unfair competition claim has run. Subsequently, he sues in federal court for violation of the federal copyright laws, based on the same acts. Is the second action barred by res judicata? Look at 28 U.S.C. §1338(a) before answering this example.

13. Suppose that Koufax sued first in federal court on the federal copyright claim, and the court held that Throneberry's book was sufficiently distinct that it did not violate Koufax's copyright. Koufax loses. Subsequently, Koufax sues Throneberry in state court under a state unfair competition statute, based on the same acts. Will the second action be barred?

14. Assume that Rizzuto brought his negligence case against Allston in a New York state court, and that New York law did not recognize strict liability claims under the circumstances of Rizzuto's injury. After losing on his negligence claim, Rizzuto brings a second action in Minnesota, where Allston manufactures its gloves. Minnesota recognizes strict liability, and Rizzuto sues solely on a strict liability theory. Is the suit barred by res judicata?

"The Game Ain't Over 'til It's Over"

15. Berra sues Durocher in a New York state court for intentional infliction of emotional distress, arising out of an altercation behind home plate at Yankee Stadium. The court dismisses the suit on the ground that New York case law bars recovery for infliction of emotional distress unless the plaintiff

also suffered physical injury. Judgment is entered for Durocher. Six months later, the New York Court of Appeals (New York's highest court) overrules this approach in another case, holding that a plaintiff may recover for intentional infliction of emotional distress without proof of physical injury. Berra brings a new action to recover for the same incident. Is the suit barred?

16. Assume that Berra sued Durocher for intentional infliction of emotional distress in a New York state court. The court dismissed the suit on the ground that the applicable law did not allow recovery for infliction of emotional distress unless the plaintiff also suffered physical injury. Berra appealed. While the appeal was pending, the New York Court of Appeals held in a separate case that plaintiffs may recover for infliction of emotional distress without accompanying physical injury. Which rule should apply to Berra's case?

17. Assume that Berra learns of the change in the law six months after the judgment in his original suit became final. Rather than bring a new action on the claim, Berra takes a different tack: He brings a motion for relief from the *original* judgment, under Fed. R. Civ. P. 60(b), asking the trial court to reopen the first case in light of the change in the applicable law. Should the court grant the motion?

18. Fred and Martha get a divorce. Fred gets custody of the children. As part of the decree the court orders Martha to pay $400 a week in child support. Three years later, after two years of high inflation, Fred moves to reopen the judgment and for an increase in the weekly support. Should the court deny the motion on the basis of res judicata?

Double Plays

19. Schulansky sues Ronan for negligence in constructing an addition to her antique home in New Hampshire. She claims that his negligence in doing the work caused the foundation of the main house to subside, resulting in damage to the older part of the house. The jury concludes that the damage was caused by natural subsidence, not by Ronan's negligence. Judgment is entered for Ronan.

Which of the following later suits would be precluded by the judgment in *Schulansky v. Ronan?*

    a. Schulansky sues Ronan for breach of contract, claiming that he agreed in his contract to conduct the work carefully and without causing damage to the main structure, and that he failed to do so.

    b. Schulansky sues Ronan for damages, claiming that he constructed the addition one hundred square feet smaller than the contract required.

    c. Schulansky sues Ronan for damage to plantings at her house in Massachusetts, caused when Ronan constructed an addition on her Massachusetts house before the New Hampshire job.

    d. Schulansky sues Ronan for the negligence of Jones, the backhoe contractor he hired to dig the foundation for the addition. She claims that Jones's digging undermined the foundation of the main house, causing the damage, and that Ronan is liable for Jones's negligence under respondeat superior.

e. Schulansky sues Ronan for fraud, claiming that in negotiating the contract for the construction of the addition at her house in Massachusetts, Ronan misrepresented his experience with older houses, and that the damage resulted from his lack of expertise in working on historic structures.

f. Schulansky sues Jones, claiming that his backhoe work undermined the foundation, causing the subsidence.

EXPLANATIONS
Fielder's Choices

1. Res judicata will bar Rizzuto's second action. A judgment need not be right to preclude further litigation; it need only be final and on the merits. "Decisions that plainly are wrong and that would be reversed on appeal, were that route available, are valid final judgments for res judicata purposes. After all, the policies of res judicata — finality of decision and protection from harassment — would be frustrated completely if a plaintiff could evade the doctrine simply by arguing that the original decision was wrong. Res judicata reflects the policy that sometimes it is more important that a judgment be stable than that it be correct." Friedenthal, Kane, and Miller at 636. Here, Rizzuto tried his case and lost, and final judgment was entered for Allston "on the merits," that is, based on a verdict by the jury that Allston was not negligent. That judgment bars a second suit by Rizzuto on the same claim even if evidence was wrongly excluded. If that exclusion was improper, Rizzuto should have appealed it in the first suit, not attempted to relitigate it in a second. See *Federated Department Stores, Inc. v. Moitie*, 452 U.S. 394, 398 (1981).

If Rizzuto could avoid the effect of the first judgment by claiming it was wrong, the res judicata doctrine would lose much of its value. A major purpose of the doctrine is to preserve judicial resources by barring rehearing of cases already litigated and decided. This purpose would be undermined if the evidence would have to be reheard in order to ascertain whether the first case was rightly decided. It would also place the judge in the second suit in the inappropriate position of reviewing the first trial to determine whether it was error-free in order to determine whether it should have res judicata effect.

2. Res judicata bars not only those claims that were asserted in the first suit, but also any others arising out of that transaction that could have been asserted but were not. Here, Rizzuto has simply switched theories of relief and sued again based on the same vicious grounder he complained of in the earlier suit. Since his suit arises out of the same occurrence as the first, it will be barred.

The rigidity of this rule forces parties to litigate their claims fully in their first suit. Lawyers, knowing they will get only one bite at the apple, must consider all possible grounds for relief raised by the underlying facts and plead them in the first action. This is one reason why complaints often contain numerous counts based on different legal theories. It is better to be comprehensive in the original action (subject, of course, to the ethical constraints of Rule 11) than to try to battle the res judicata myrmidon in a subsequent action.

3.   Allston will also prevail on his res judicata defense here. In example 2, Rizzuto tried to "split his claim" by asserting one theory of relief in the first action and another in the second. Here he has tried a different type of claim-splitting, seeking different types of damages in different actions. Here too, the myrmidon says no. The claim for punitive damages is based on the same incident as the prior suit. It could have been, and therefore should have been, asserted in the first action. No matter how clear Rizzuto's right to punitive damages, the court will not hear this claim.

In an earlier day many states allowed "claim-splitting" based on distinct types of damages. For example, plaintiffs in auto negligence cases were frequently allowed to seek recovery for their personal injuries and damage to their vehicles in separate actions, on the theory that these involved discrete rights protected by distinct causes of action. See, e.g., *Vasu v. Kohlers, Inc.*, 61 N.E.2d 707 (Ohio 1945). This rule has given way in many jurisdictions to the view that all damages from a single incident must be sought in a single suit. See *Rush v. City of Maple Heights*, 147 N.E.2d 599 (Ohio), cert. denied, 358 U.S. 814 (1958) (effectively overruling *Vasu*).

4.   Rizzuto's problem here is not dissatisfaction with the relief he obtained in the first action but difficulty in collecting it from the defendant. The fact that the defendant has not satisfied the judgment does not give the plaintiff the right to bring a second action on the original claim. Under res judicata theory, his claim is "merged into the judgment"; once he obtains the judgment, his right to sue on the original claim is replaced by a right to enforce the judgment. In most jurisdictions a judgment remains enforceable for many years, as long as an execution is issued promptly after judgment. See, e.g., Wis. Stat. Ann. §815.04 (20 years); S.D. Codified Laws Ann. §15-18-1 (20 years). There is no need for Rizzuto to bring a new suit and relitigate matters already settled in his favor. When Rizzuto learns that Allston is in a position to pay, he should seek execution on the original judgment or bring an action on the judgment in another state where Allston has assets that can be taken on execution. See Chapter 3, pp. 44-46.

5.   This is a hard case indeed. Here Rizzuto sought all his known damages in his original suit but did not seek recovery for a potential future consequence of the injury. Naturally when that consequence arises he feels entitled to compensation for it as well. And since res judicata only bars claims that could have been joined in the original action, he has a good argument for a new action.

Rizzuto's position is certainly sympathetic, but it has generally been rejected by the courts. Imagine the havoc that would result if plaintiffs could relitigate claims whenever their disabilities or medical expenses turned out to be more than expected at the time of trial. Judgments would never be final because they would be subject to revision in the light of future events. Defendants would be unable to rely on the finality of judgments in planning their future conduct and estimating their liabilities. In most cases the benefit of providing full relief based on subsequent evidence would be far outweighed by the burden of renewed litigation and the uncertainty that would result.

Consequently, the usual rule is that a plaintiff must recover for all her damages in the original action, including those suffered prior to trial and all future damages that are reasonably likely to ensue. Restatement (Second) of Judgments §25, comment c.[3] Here, for example, Rizzuto should have presented evidence in his original suit that victims of this type of eye injury are likely to develop headaches. The jury could then have assessed additional damages based on this probable consequence of the injury. Admittedly, this is a very rough measure of Rizzuto's actual damages, but it is the best that the system can do without retrying Rizzuto's case repeatedly in future years.

A related problem arises in many asbestos personal injury cases. Frequently, the plaintiff sues and recovers for asbestosis caused by exposure to asbestos, and later—often many years later—develops cancer. Under strict res judicata doctrine, a second suit for the cancer is barred. This is a hard result, in view of the long latency period for the cancer (often 30 to 35 years from date of exposure) and the uncertainty as to whether it will develop at all. Some courts have allowed the plaintiff to bring a second action in such circumstances, but there is no doubt that in doing so they are bending the traditional rules of claim preclusion.[4]

---

3. Rizzuto would have an alternative remedy if his headaches appeared within a year. See Fed. R. Civ. P. 60(b)(2), which allows a party to seek relief from the *original* judgment within one year on the ground that newly discovered evidence should be considered.

4. See, e.g., *Mauro v. Raymark Industries, Inc.*, 561 A.2d 257, 264-267 (N.J. 1989) (recognizing the right to bring a second action for cancer after prior recovery for asbestosis caused by the same exposure to asbestos); compare *Gideon v. Johns-Mansville Sales Corp.*, 761 F.2d 1129, 1136-1137 (5th Cir. 1985) (under Texas law asbestos victim must recover all resulting damages in a single action). See generally Note, Claim Preclusion in Modern Latent Disease Cases: A Proposal for Allowing Second Suits, 103 Harv. L. Rev. 1989 (1990).

This so-called "two-disease" rule, which allows an asbestos plaintiff to sue for later-developing cancer even if she was previously aware of a separate injury from exposure (such as asbestosis), is now clearly the majority approach. See, e.g., *Sopha v, Owens-Corning Fiberglas Corp.*, 601 N.W. 2d 627 (Wis. 1999); *Wilber v. Owens-Corning Fiberglass Corp.*, 476 N.W.2d 74 (Iowa 1991). It will be interesting to see whether this inroad on the traditional res judicata rules spreads to cases like Rizzuto's, where the later "injury" is not a separate disease, but simply an unexpected consequence of the first. Perhaps the myrmidon will turn out to be a cream puff after all.

An Absurd Hypothetical

6.   The four prerequisites for application of res judicata are not met here since the parties are not the same in the second action. Rizzuto was not a party in the first suit; though Allston was, *both* parties must be the same (or represented by the prior parties) for res judicata to apply. In addition, the "claim" is not the same in the second action. The rights of different plaintiffs to relief arising out of a single incident are not considered one "claim" simply because they arise out of one transaction or occurrence. Every potential plaintiff who suffers injury from a transaction or occurrence has a distinct claim for res judicata purposes. Here, for example, although Kubek's and Rizzuto's claims both arise out of the same incident, the two claims are distinct. The fact that Kubek has sued for his injuries does not bar Rizzuto from suing separately for his.

If res judicata barred a second suit in a situation like this, all plaintiffs with claims arising out of a single incident would be forced to sue together. The usual rule in American courts is to the contrary: The "plaintiff is master of her claim" and *may* sue jointly with other plaintiffs (see Fed. R. Civ. P. 20 (a)) but need not. Even though he knew of Kubek's suit and appeared as a witness, Rizzuto still has the right to sue separately.

7.   The advice that Rizzuto may sue separately on the contract claim without fear of the myrmidon is sound. Even though the contract claim had accrued at the time of the negligence suit (that is, the breach had occurred and Rizzuto had a right to sue on it), Rizzuto is not required to assert this claim in the negligence action. Under the Restatement definition of a single "claim," these are separate claims because they arise out of separate transactions. Restatement (Second) of Judgments §24. Rizzuto's first action was based on an accident on the playing field. His second is based on a separate transaction, the contract to promote Allston gloves on television.

This example highlights several important points. *First,* it is important to understand that Rizzuto's right to sue separately on these claims is not based on the fact that one action is for tort and the other for contract. In many cases a plaintiff has a right to recover under both tort and contract theories, based on a single incident. In the *Schulansky* case, for example, Schulansky asserts contract and tort claims against the defendants, which both arise out of the construction of the addition on her house. See the Schulansky complaint infra p.538. If either of these were left out, res judicata would bar Schulansky from suing on it separately. By contrast, Rizzuto may sue separately here because his contract claim arises from a different set of historical facts.

Second, note that Rizzuto *could* have joined both of these unrelated claims in a single action under Fed. R. Civ. P. 18(a). It does not always follow that you must join claims in a single action simply because the Rules allow you to do so. See Chapter 25, which explores in more detail the relationship between res judicata and the joinder rules.

8.   On these facts Rizzuto's second action will not be barred. At the time of his first suit Rizzuto did not have a claim for the second year's royalties. He can hardly be expected to predict future defaults and sue for them before they occur. Even though the two suits arise out of a single contract, the separate breaches in successive years are different occurrences that may be sued on separately.

That would not be true, however, if Rizzuto had waited until the end of the second year to sue. At that point, the royalties for both years had accrued, and the usual rule is that Rizzuto must sue for them all as a single debt due on an account. Friedenthal, Kane, and Miller at 650; Restatement (Second) of Judgments §24, comment d. Similarly, a landlord who sues a tenant for back rent must seek recovery for all months' rent due but not future defaults. This reflects the basic premise that res judicata bars all claims arising out of a single transaction or occurrence that could have been raised in the original action. But here, the claims for future nonpayment could not have been raised since the plaintiff has no right to sue for these claims until they accrue.

Although res judicata will not bar Rizzuto's second suit here, collateral estoppel will bar relitigation of issues that were litigated and decided in the first suit. For example, if the court held that the contract called for payment of all royalties at the 10 percent rate, Allston will be estopped from claiming that the rate should be 5 percent in the second action. See Chapter 26, 486-487.

9.   If you focused carefully on the prerequisites for res judicata discussed in the Introduction, you should have concluded that the myrmidon will not bar Allston's suit against Rizzuto. As example 6 suggests, every separate party has a separate claim for res judicata purposes even though their claims arise out of the same incident. Thus, Allston's claim against Rizzuto is not the "same claim" as Rizzuto's claim against Allston.

However, while traditional res judicata doctrine does not bar Allston's claim, many jurisdictions provide by court rule that counterclaims arising out of the same transaction or occurrence must be brought in the original action. See, e.g., Fed. R. Civ. P. 13(a) (counterclaim is compulsory if it arises out of same transaction or occurrence as the opposing party's claim). If the defendant fails to join a compulsory counterclaim, she will then be barred from bringing it later, not because the common law res judicata doctrine applies, but in order to enforce the compulsory counterclaim rule. See James, Hazard & Leubsdorf, p.604. Under this approach, Allston's suit would be barred.

In a jurisdiction that does not have a compulsory counterclaim rule, Allston would remain free to assert its claim in a separate action. However, the crucial issues underlying its claim may have been decided in the original suit anyway. In this case, for example, the earlier action determined that Rizzuto had breached his contract. In Allston's separate action, collateral estoppel would bar Rizzuto from relitigating that issue.

Judgment on the Merits

10. Res judicata does not apply here because the claim has never been decided on the merits. Although an actual hearing was held and testimony and argument heard, the issue under consideration was the power of the court to hear the action, not the substance of Rizzuto's claim. Since the court held that it lacked subject matter jurisdiction over the suit, it never reached the merits. Consequently, one of the prerequisites for res judicata is not met.

It would certainly be a hard rule if litigants in Rizzuto's position were barred from going to a second court after dismissal for lack of jurisdiction in the first. Under that approach, the second suit would be barred even though the first court never considered the merits of plaintiff's case and, in fact, never had the power to do so. To avoid this risk, the plaintiff would be forced to choose a court that definitely has jurisdiction, even though she would prefer to sue in another that *may* have it. The res judicata doctrine does not put the parties to such risks. The "on the merits" requirement assures that preliminary dismissals due to lack of jurisdiction or venue will not bar suit in another court that has the power to proceed.

11. In this case, although Rizzuto's claim has been resolved without trial, it has been decided on the merits. Summary judgment in Allston's favor was based on the court's conclusion that Rizzuto has no evidence to support his contention that his accident resulted from Allston's negligence, and therefore no jury could find for Rizzuto on the negligence issue. Because Rizzuto cannot prove an essential element of his claim, judgment for Allston is proper. This is "on the merits" because it represents an adjudication of Rizzuto's substantive claim for relief, not a preliminary issue. Similarly, a judgment as a matter of law under Rule 50 is given res judicata effect because it determines that the plaintiff's claim has so little "merit" that no reasonable jury could uphold it. Restatement (Second) of Judgements §19, comments g, h.

Pendent or Independent?

12. Under the four prerequisites Koufax's second action should be barred since he is suing the same defendant again on a claim arising out of the same events as the first suit. The procedural quirk here, however, is that Koufax could not have included the federal copyright claim in the state law action: The federal courts have exclusive jurisdiction over federal copyright claims under 28 U.S.C. §1338 (a).

Most courts have held in these circumstances that the second suit is not barred. If it were barred, it would force Koufax to sue in federal court to avoid losing his federal copyright claim by operation of res judicata. Consequently he would lose the chance to have the state court decide his state unfair competition claim. Most courts have concluded that it is better to allow the second action in such cases so as to avoid interfering with the authority of state courts to hear claims created by their own law. See Restatement (Second) of Judgments §26 (1)(c) and illustration 2; 18 Wright and Miller at §4412, pp.97-99 and 2000 Supp.

13. When the first suit is brought in federal court, the situation is somewhat different. The state unfair competition claim is a state law claim that would be within the court's supplemental jurisdiction in the federal copyright suit. See 28 U.S.C. §1367(a); Chapter 15, example 1. However, under §1367(c) the court has discretion to hear or dismiss the supplemental claims. It might not have heard Koufax's state law claim even if he had asserted it in his federal suit.

The general rule is that plaintiffs like Koufax who are in federal court must assert their supplemental claims or lose them by operation of res judicata. If the federal court entertains the state unfair competition claim, it will contribute to judicial efficiency and consistency of decisionmaking, two goals of the res judicata doctrine. If the court refuses to hear it, then Koufax will not be barred from suing separately on the claim in state court, since it could not be heard in the first action, and the plaintiff has therefore not had an opportunity to litigate that claim. All that Koufax can do is ask; if he does and the court refuses, he is protected. If he doesn't ask, the potential benefits of joint litigation are lost through his own neglect, and the myrmidon will be characteristically unsympathetic.

By the way, it is worth noting that res judicata is an affirmative defense that must be pleaded by the party asserting that the second action is barred. Fed. R. Civ. P. 8(c). If it is not pleaded, the case may go forward. Given the fact that claim preclusion protects not only the parties but the courts themselves, it seems appropriate that the court itself should have the authority to bar relitigation by raising the defense *sua sponte*. I haven't researched the point, but wouldn't be surprised to find cases supporting that view. Even if the court cannot dismiss *sua sponte* on res judicata grounds, judges are practical people who should have little trouble throwing a hint to the party with an incentive to assert the defense that she should do so.

14. It is easy to see the plaintiff's argument for allowing the second case here: Res judicata requires the plaintiff to assert in the first action all claims that were available to her in that action. In this case, the strict liability claim could not have been asserted in the New York suit because New York tort law does not recognize such claims. Thus, since he could not assert the strict liability claim in the first suit, he can bring a new one on it in another state that recognizes such claims. Right?

The argument has superficial appeal, but on closer examination it is inconsistent with the basic purposes of res judicata doctrine. If this second action were not barred, the plaintiff could give it a preliminary try in State A, with limited tort remedies, and then try again in a State B if he lost—and maybe even in State C with some further remedy not available in the first two. This would lead to wasteful relitigation, which would have been avoided had he sued in State B (or C) to begin with.

But (I can almost hear you protest) we didn't force Koufax to choose federal court first in example 12. To be consistent, shouldn't Rizzuto, as "master of his claim," be entitled to sue in New York first if he chooses without losing the remedy that only Minnesota will give? Well, I don't think so. The rule that a plaintiff can bring state claims in state court and not lose related claims within exclusive federal jurisdiction preserves the right to use the state courts for state law claims and the federal court for related federal remedies. But plaintiffs do not have the right to have tort cases decided under the inconsistent tort law of two different states. Rizzuto could have chosen to sue in Minnesota first if its law was more favorable. He also could have argued in the New York court that it should apply Minnesota tort law to the case. See Chapter 12, pp. 210-211. Having made his choice to bring the action in New York, the plaintiff must live with that choice. See Restatement (Second) of Judgments §18, comment d (states required to give full faith and credit to damage judgments from sister states).

"The Game Ain't Over 'til It's Over"

15. Assuming that the New York courts, like federal courts, give res judicata effect to dismissals for failure to state a claim, Berra's second action *will* be barred, unless the subsequent change in the substantive law provides a basis to avoid the usual effect of res judicata.

This subsequent change in the law will not allow Berra to start a new action. Parties are not entitled to have their cases decided under the law as it will be at some future time; each case must be decided under the law at the time it is considered. See Moore's at §30.04 [11]. Imagine the confusion that would ensue if parties could bring new suits if the law changed after they lost a case. Finality of judgments would be meaningless since cases might be reopened (or nullified by the results in a later suit) at some indeterminate time in the future. How long would parties have to reopen the judgment? How much later could the law change and still be applied to a previously decided case?

Clearly, such a principle, even if circumscribed by some form of statute of limitations, would undermine two goals of the res judicata doctrine: judicial economy and certainty of judgments. Besides, rules may be fair at the time they are applied even though they change later, when conditions have changed. See Chapter 10, pp. 167-168 (suggesting that Athenians of one generation may choose to live under different laws than those of their predecessors). Better to leave it at that than to undermine the finality of judgments by reconsidering them every time the underlying substantive law is reconsidered.

If Berra believed that the physical injury rule should be overruled, he should have appealed on that ground instead of waiting for a future plaintiff to carry the laboring oar. Perhaps the Court of Appeals would have changed the rule in his case instead of the next one six months down the line. See, for a case on point, *Federated Department Stores, Inc. v. Moitie,* 452 U.S. 394 (1981).

16. There is a crucial difference between this case and the last. Here, Berra's first action is still going on. Although he lost in the trial court under the old approach to intentional infliction, he has taken his appeal and asked the higher court to change the rule. If the court had not adopted the new rule in the other case raising the issue, it presumably would have done so in his. He should not be disadvantaged by the fact that the appeal in the other case was heard first. Consequently, the general rule is that the court will apply the law as it stands when the pending appeal is decided, not the law as it stood at the time of trial. The dismissal of Berra's case will be reversed, and it will be sent back for trial on the merits.

17. If Berra could get the trial judge to reopen the original action, it would undermine the finality of the judgment just as clearly as allowing a new action would in example 15. Instead of starting a new suit, he could simply revive the old one and ask the court to retry the case under the new state of the law. The majority rule in the federal courts, therefore, appears to be that the court may not grant relief from judgment due to a change in the substantive law once the period for appeal has passed. See, e.g., *Morris v. Adams-Millis Corp.,* 758 F.2d 1352, 1358-1359 (10th Cir. 1985); cf. *De Weerth v. Baldinger,* 38 F.3d 1266 (2d Cir. 1994) (reaching same result in diversity case after clarification of applicable state law). But see *Adams v. Merrill, Lynch, Pierce, Fenner & Smith,* 888 F.2d 696, 702 (10th Cir. 1989) (in Tenth Circuit, Supreme Court change in law warrants relief from judgment); *Sprou v. Union Texas Products Corp.,* 944 F.2d 911 (10th Cir. 1991).

18. Strictly speaking, res judicata doesn't apply here at all: Fred has not brought a new action based on the same claim as before. Instead, he has moved to reopen the judgment in the *first* action and get the decree in that action changed. However, the motion does compromise several of the values protected by res judicata. It requires the court to revisit a case previously settled by the judgment, and it unsettles the expectations of the parties.

As an equitable doctrine, however, res judicata must sometimes step aside in deference to other values. Where a judgment has prospective application (that is, it doesn't simply order payment of a dollar judgment but governs the ongoing future conduct of the parties), the court must retain authority to modify its orders in light of changed conditions. Here, for example, it may be entirely appropriate to adjust the child support payments in light of high inflation and resulting increases in Martha's income. The power to do so is quite generally recognized. See Restatement (Second) of Judgments s. 73 (power to modify judgment in light of "substantial change in the circumstances" that would make it unjust to continue the prior judgment in effect).

Double Plays

19a. This action is barred. It arises from the same transaction as the first—the construction of the addition. Schulansky has simply switched legal theories.

b. This one is barred too; again, it arises from the same construction work, but simply asserts a different type of damage caused by that work.

c. This one arises from a separate transaction, the work on her house in Massachusetts. Even though it had accrued at the time she brought her first action against Ronan, she was not required to assert it in that action, since it is not the "same claim" as her claim for damages for the New Hampshire job.

d. This claim is also barred by res judicata. It is a claim against Ronan for damages for the New Hampshire job. Schulansky has switched theories, but the underlying transaction for which she seeks a remedy is the same as in her first suit.

e. This one would be barred too. Schulansky will presumably argue that she bases her claim on Ronan's prior misrepresentations, not the addition work. But Schulansky's complaint is still based on the construction work on her New Hampshire house. Even though the transaction may have arisen because of earlier misrepresentations, the basic focus is the same set of events as the earlier claim. Res judicata forces Schulansky's lawyers to assert all claims arising from that work at the same time, to avoid multiple suits over the same events. The effect of the doctrine would be undermined (excuse the pun) if she could argue that this action was based on earlier acts of Ronan which *led to* the defective work on the house.

Consider the problem if this were not barred. A plaintiff could sue a defendant for injuries suffered in an auto accident, claiming that the defendant had failed to signal a turn. If she lost, she could sue her again for negligence in fixing her brakes a month before the accident. There would be as many "claims" as there were earlier acts which arguably contributed to the ultimate injury. Better to take a broader view of the meaning of a "transaction" to include prior acts that lead up to the accident than to open that can of worms.

f. Here the myrmidon steps aside. Jones is a different party whom Schulansky has not sued before; she is free to sue him in a separate action. However, collateral estoppel may bar her from proving that his backhoe work caused the subsidence since she litigated and lost on the issue before.

25

Res Judicata and the Rules of Joinder: When Does May Mean Must?

Introduction

In any reasonable civil procedure world, there ought to be a close relationship between the parties' right to join claims in their first lawsuit and the scope of res judicata in subsequent suits between them. If, for example, the rules of joinder did not allow plaintiffs to join counts for property damage and personal injury in a single lawsuit, it would be a rigid system indeed that barred the plaintiff who had sued for his property damage in one suit from bringing a separate action to recover for his personal injuries. Similarly, if the joinder rules limited a plaintiff to proceeding on a single theory, such as negligence, in his first suit, it would be unfair to bar him from starting a second action on a strict liability theory. One way or another, the system ought to offer parties a chance to have all of their claims heard, either through limited claims in multiple suits or multiple claims in a single suit.

The early English common law followed the first course, allowing multiple actions on different theories or seeking different relief. Under the common law system, the rigid limitations on joinder of claims frequently prevented plaintiffs from seeking full relief in a single action. For example, a plaintiff who sued at law for damages for trespass could not get an injunction against further trespasses in the same suit; he had to go to an equity court for that. Because the plaintiff was forced by these limitations to split his cause of action, the preclusion rules did not bar him from bringing the second action even though it arose out of the same occurrence as the first.

The federal courts (and many state systems as well) have chosen the second course, allowing many claims to be heard in a single action. This approach is implemented by extremely broad rules governing pleading and joinder. See Rules 8(a)(3), 8(e)(2), 13, 14, 18, 20. Under these liberal joinder rules, plaintiffs have broad power to join all their theories of recovery in their initial suit. Consequently, they will seldom be able to argue that they should be allowed to start a new action based on the same occurrence because they were unable to assert an omitted claim in the first suit.

For example, Fed. R. Civ. P. 18(a) allows the plaintiff to join virtually all possible theories of recovery in a single action. It is hardly unreasonable therefore to hold that res judicata bars him from suing later on any theory that is omitted from the first suit. In this situation the *may* of the rules clearly means *must* when the effects of res judicata are considered. If Elbers sues Doe Chemical Company for negligently manufacturing a drug, Rule 18(a) allows but does not require him to assert a separate strict liability claim against Doe based on the same events. See also Fed. R. Civ. P. 8(e)(2) (authorizing alternative or inconsistent pleading). However, if Elbers leaves out the strict liability claim, res judicata will bar him from asserting it in a later action. This is simply another theory of recovery for the same injuries already sued upon, and any claims arising from that occurrence that are not joined in Elber's first action will be barred by res judicata doctrine. See Chapter 24, example 453-454.

There are a few instances, despite Rule 18(a), when initial joinder of a particular claim is not available. In such cases the res judicata myrmidon[1] grudgingly steps aside to allow the plaintiff to reenter the courthouse door. Suppose, for example, that Allen sues Moser in state court under a state unfair competition statute. Suppose further that Allen might also recover against Moser for patent infringement, a federal claim over which the federal courts have exclusive jurisdiction. Here, Allen could not have included his federal theory in the first state court action because the federal courts have exclusive jurisdiction over patent claims. Consequently, he will not be barred from asserting the patent claim in a later suit. See generally Restatement (Second) of Judgments §26(1)(c).

It would make life a lot easier for civil procedure students, as well as for practicing lawyers, if it were invariably true that every claim that could have been joined in the initial action will be barred in a later action. Alas, though this would be neat and symmetrical, it just isn't so. Although *theories* that could have been joined are generally barred, the scope of permissible joinder

---

1. For a natural history of this creature, see Chapter 24, n.1.

of *parties* is much broader than the dimensions of a single "claim" for res judicata purposes. Thus, in many cases, claims against additional parties could be joined under the Rules but will not be barred by res judicata if they are not.

For example, if Fellows is involved in a three-car collision with Rich and Rontowski, he could sue them as codefendants in a single lawsuit. Fed. R. Civ. P. 20(a). However, he doesn't *have* to: If he sues Rich alone, he is not precluded from suing Rontowski later in a separate action. A plaintiff's rights to recover from separate defendants are considered distinct "claims" under res judicata analysis, even though they arise out of the same occurrence. In addition, the "same parties" requirement of res judicata is not met in such cases since the defendants differ in the two actions.

This is puzzling at first, but if it were not true, the res judicata rules would convert permissive joinder under the Rules into compulsory joinder. Rule 20(a) says that Fellows *may* choose to sue Rich and Rontowski together. Clearly, the rulemakers have chosen to allow him to sue them jointly but also have given him the option not to. This reflects the traditional precept that the "plaintiff is master of his claim," free to choose when and where to sue each potential defendant. But, if res judicata barred Fellows from suing Rontowski because he had previously sued Rich without joining Rontowski, the *may* of Rule 20(a) would be converted to *must* by the preclusion rules: Fellows would be forced to sue them both in the first action. Although such a compulsory joinder of parties rule might make sense from an efficiency point of view, the rulemakers have favored freedom of choice over efficiency.[2] And the res judicata rules should be crafted to protect that policy decision.

This principle that claims against different parties need not be joined even if the rules would allow it does not prevent the first action from having some preclusive effect, however. If Fellows loses his suit against Rich on the ground that he was contributorily negligent, Rontowski may be able to invoke collateral estoppel to establish Fellows's negligence if Fellows subsequently sues him. See *Blonder-Tongue Laboratories, Inc. v. University of Illinois Foundation,* 402 U.S. 313 (1971); Chapter 27, pp. 504-506. Certainly, this inhibits Fellows's freedom of choice to some extent, since he cannot start his action against Rontowski with a completely clean slate.

The following examples will help you sort out the relationship between the joinder and res judicata rules. Assume that all actions are brought in federal court, that subject matter jurisdiction is proper in each case, and that the broad "transactional" test of the Second Restatement of Judgment applies. Consider in each case whether the omitted claim could have been joined under the rules and, if so, whether res judicata will bar the second action.

---

2. Some of the reasons for that choice are discussed in Chapter 13, example 1.

EXAMPLES

A Few Warm-Ups

1.   Roosevelt is hit by a car while walking across Park Avenue in New York City. The only occupants of the car were Kefauver and Warren, but each denies that he was driving. Roosevelt sues Kefauver, a Tennessee citizen, in the federal court for the Middle District of Tennessee. She loses. Now Roosevelt sues Warren, a New Yorker, in the Southern District of New York.

    a. Could Roosevelt have joined Kefauver and Warren in the first action?

    b. Is Roosevelt's second suit barred?

2.   Roosevelt sues Kefauver in the Tennessee federal court for battery, based on the collision on Park Avenue. The jury finds that Kefauver did not hit Roosevelt intentionally, and judgment is entered for Kefauver. Subsequently, Roosevelt sues Kefauver in the Southern District of New York for negligently injuring her in the collision.

    a. Could Roosevelt have joined the negligence claim in the first suit?

    b. Is the second suit barred by res judicata?

3.   Roosevelt sues Kefauver for battery and for negligence based on the accident. She later sues Kefauver again in the same court for a breach of contract that took place before the accident.

    a. Could Roosevelt have joined the contract claim in the first action?

    b. Is the second suit precluded by res judicata?

4.   Stanton sues Anthony for her injuries in a two-car collision and recovers $17,000. Now, Blatch, a passenger in Stanton's car, sues Anthony for her injuries in the collision.

    a. Could Stanton and Blatch have joined as coplaintiffs in the first action?

    b. Could Blatch have intervened in Stanton's suit against Anthony? See Fed. R. Civ. P. 24.

    c. Is Blatch barred by res judicata from bringing her suit?

A Hybrid Case

5.   Grasso sues Adams for breach of contract, arising out of a contract for the delivery of livestock to Grasso. Grasso loses. Subsequently, Adams sues Grasso for breach of the contract, seeking to collect the balance due under the contract.

    a. Could Adams have joined his contract claim in the original action?

    b. Is Adams's action against Grasso barred by res judicata?

6.   After Grasso sues Adams for breach of the livestock contract, could Adams start a separate action against Grasso on an unrelated fraud claim that accrued before the contract dispute?

7.   Grasso sues Adams Pharmacy and Johnson Drug Co. for personal injuries suffered as a result of using a drug made by Johnson and sold to her

by Adams. She recovers judgment for $35,000 against each defendant. Adams pays the judgment and then sues Johnson for indemnification, claiming that since the negligent manufacture of the drug caused Grasso's injuries, Adams should be indemnified by Johnson for the damages it paid to Grasso.

    a. Could the claim have been asserted in the first action?

    b. Is Adams barred from bringing the second suit?

A Myrmidon in the Labyrinth

8.   Assume that Grasso sued Adams Pharmacy alone on the drug claim and recovered. Now Adams sues Johnson for indemnification.

    a. Could Adams have asserted this claim in the original action?

    b. Is its action against Johnson precluded?

9.   Smith, from South Dakota, sues Bryan, from Minnesota, for breach of a contract to construct a home for him. Smith claims that the foundation of the house was improperly poured. Bryan impleads Coolidge, a South Dakota subcontractor who poured the foundation, for indemnification. The court holds that the foundation meets the specifications, and therefore judgment is entered for Bryan on the main claim and for Coolidge on the third-party claim. Subsequently, Bryan sues Coolidge to collect the wages of five laborers Bryan had lent to Coolidge to help him perform the foundation work.

    a. Could Bryan have asserted the wage claim in the first action?

    b. Is the second suit barred by res judicata?

10. Assume the same facts as example 9, but that the claim Bryan asserted in the second action was for a previous breach of another contract between him and Coolidge.

    a. Could Bryan have asserted the second contract claim in the first action?

    b. Is he barred from bringing it in the second suit?

11. On the same facts as example 9, assume that Smith sues Bryan on the foundation claim, and that Bryan impleads Coolidge. The case is tried and Smith loses, since the jury finds that the work was properly done. Now, Coolidge sues Smith, the owner, seeking the price of his foundation work on a quantum meruit theory.

    a. Could Coolidge have asserted this claim in the first suit?

    b. Would the court have had subject matter jurisdiction over this claim in the first action?

    c. Is Coolidge's suit against Smith barred by res judicata?

When Does *May Not* Mean *Must?*

12. Suppose that Smith sued Bryan for breach of the contract, as a result of defects in the foundation. Three years into the suit, when the parties have completed discovery and trial is imminent, Smith moves to amend the complaint to assert a second claim against Bryan for negligence, on the

ground that the foundation was inadequately poured. The court denies the motion to amend on the ground that it is untimely, since it could have been asserted earlier in the suit, and allowance of the motion would delay the trial and prejudice Bryan's ability to prepare his defense. See *Foman v. Davis*, 371 U.S. 178, 181-182 (1962)(delay in seeking amendment and prejudice to opponent may justify denial of leave to amend).

The breach of contract claim is tried and Smith loses. He then brings a second action against Bryan, asserting only the negligence claim. (Assume that the applicable statute of limitations is six years, so that the action is not yet barred on this ground.) Bryan pleads res judicata.

a. If you represented Smith, how would you argue that the second action is not barred by res judicata?

b. How will the judge rule on the res judicata defense?

EXPLANATIONS

A Few Warm-Ups

1. Joinder: Yes   Res judicata: No

a. This is a simple case of one plaintiff who has claims against two defendants. Rule 20(a) allows Roosevelt to sue them together because the claims arise from the same accident and will involve the common issue of who was driving the car. However, Rule 20(a) does not require Roosevelt to sue the defendants together; the rule says *may* and means it. In this case Roosevelt might have been well advised to sue them jointly. As it is, the first jury may conclude that Warren was driving, and the second that Kefauver was, leaving Roosevelt a double loser. For one reason or another, Roosevelt has chosen to take that risk, as the joinder rules allow her to do.

b. Roosevelt's second action is not barred because her claim against Warren is distinct from her claim against Kefauver, and they are not the same parties. If res judicata did bar the second action, it would force Roosevelt to sue the two defendants together, thus undermining the choice given to Roosevelt by the rules. Consider the consequences that such a result would have for Roosevelt's case. It is unlikely that she could get personal jurisdiction over Warren in Tennessee for this New York accident. Consequently, if the res judicata rules forced her to sue the two together, Roosevelt would lose her choice of forum against Kefauver. She would be forced to sue in New York, where she could obtain personal jurisdiction over both defendants because the claim arose there.

This is another example of the intricate interrelations of various civil procedure doctrines. A change in this aspect of the res judicata rules would directly affect the joinder rules and the choice of forum rules. The rulemakers have chosen to preserve one value—the plaintiff's right to choose his forum against each defendant—and have had to mold the related joinder and preclusion rules accordingly.

As indicated in the Introduction, however, it is still possible that the first suit will affect the second if the court in the second action allows Warren to invoke nonmutual collateral estoppel to bar relitigation of any issues decided in the first.

2. Joinder: Yes   Res judicata: Yes

a. The issue here is joinder of "claims" (in the sense of theories of recovery) rather than joinder of parties. Rule 18(a), the epitome of liberality, allows a plaintiff to join any claims he has against a defending party. But again, the rule is permissive; under Rule 18(a) Roosevelt has the option but is not required to join the negligence claim in the first action.

b. The myrmidon[3] will stubbornly resist Roosevelt's efforts to bring this second action. Joinder of these "claims" may be permissive under the rules but is made mandatory by the res judicata principles applied in the federal courts. Under those principles, all theories for recovery arising out of a single transaction constitute a single "claim" for preclusion purposes. See Chapter 24, pp. 453-454. A party who seeks relief based on a particular set of historical facts must join all his grounds for recovery on those facts in the first action or face the res judicata defense if he tries to sue later on one of these grounds. Thus, Roosevelt's second suit for negligence will be barred even though Rule 18(a) appears to give her the option to join or withhold it in the first action. Here, unlike the joinder-of-parties situation in example 1, the preclusion doctrine demands what the rule merely permits.

It makes no difference that Roosevelt's second action is brought in a different court. Under full faith and credit principles, each court within the system will honor the judgments of its sister courts by giving them full res judicata effect. See Friedenthal, Kane, and Miller, 3rd. ed. §14.15.

3. Joinder: Yes   Res judicata: No

a. Rule 18(a) authorizes joinder of "claims," both in the sense of different theories arising out of the same events and also completely unrelated claims arising out of completely separate events. Thus, Roosevelt could have joined her contract claim with her other claims in the first action even though it arises from a separate transaction.

b. Roosevelt's second action is not barred. Unlike example 2, in which the omitted "claim" simply asserted a different theory of recovery for the same loss litigated in the first suit, the contract claim here arose out of a separate incident from the negligence and battery claims. Roosevelt's prior suit based on the accident will bar all future suits against Kefauver based on that accident but not other suits based on separate events.

Thus Roosevelt is free to bring a separate action on the contract claim even though she could have joined it in the first suit. Here, the *may* of the

---

3. I will drop this metaphor eventually. There's no point in beating a dead myrmidon.

rule does not mean *must* under res judicata because the claim does not satisfy the res judicata definition of a single "claim." See Restatement (Second) of Judgments §24 (single claim under res judicata analysis includes all grounds for relief arising out of a single transaction).

4.   Joinder: Yes   Intervention: Maybe   Res judicata: No

a. Rule 20(a) authorizes, but does not require, Stanton and Blatch to sue jointly since they seek relief arising from the same occurrence, and their claims will involve a number of common questions of law or fact, including the central question of the cause of the accident.

b. Blatch could at least have tried to intervene under Rule 24(b) since her claim and Stanton's will involve a common question of fact—whether Anthony's negligence caused the accident. But intervention under Rule 24(b) is permissive; the court might have declined to allow Blatch into the suit for a variety of reasons.

It is unlikely that Blatch could have intervened in Stanton's suit as a matter of right under Rule 24(a). She will not be prejudiced by the Stanton/Anthony litigation unless she will be barred from bringing her own action against Anthony. As explained immediately below, she will not be barred from doing so. In addition, even if Blatch meets the criteria for intervention as of right, she is still under no duty to intervene since Rule 24(a) authorizes intervention as of right but does not force parties to intervence even when they would have a right to do so. Last, there may be jurisdictional problems if there is not complete diversity among the parties. See 28 U.S.C. §1367(b) (barring supplemental jurisdiction over claims by intervening plaintiffs in diversity cases if inconsistent with requirements of §1332).

c. Blatch's suit against Anthony is not precluded by Stanton's because she is a different party from the original parties and because her claim against Anthony is not the same as Stanton's claim against Anthony. Thus, two of the prerequisites to res judicata are not met. While Blatch had several avenues for getting into the first action, they are both permissive, and *may* is not converted to *must* here because the separate requirements for preclusion are not met. See *Martin v. Wilkes*, 490 U.S. 755, (1989).

Blatch may obtain some benefit from Stanton's action, however: Because Stanton has proved Anthony's negligence, Blatch may be able to invoke offensive nonmutual collateral estoppel to bar Anthony from relitigating the issue. See Chapter 27, pp. 507-509.

A Hybrid Case

5.   Joinder: Yes   Res judicata: In a way

a. Adams's claim for the payments due under the contract was a compulsory counterclaim in the first action since it arose out of the same events as Grasso's original claim. Under Fed. R. Civ. P. 13(a), Adams was *required* to assert this claim in the original action. The drafters of Rule 13(a) decided that the gain in litigation efficiency from hearing a defendant's related claims in the original action outweighed the defendant's usual right to choose his own forum. Consequently, they required such related claims to be asserted in the original action.

b. The rulemakers' goal will only be achieved if Adams is barred from suing separately on the omitted counterclaim. Under traditional res judicata doctrine, however, Adams would not be precluded from suing separately on this claim because Adams's claim against Grasso is not the "same claim" as Grasso's claim against him. However, the courts have barred parties in Adams's position from suing separately on the omitted counterclaim, simply to enforce the policy underlying the compulsory counterclaim rule. This form of "rule-based res judicata" applies even though the same claim requirement of res judicata is not met. See Friedenthal, Kane, and Miller 3rd ed. §14.6.

In some state systems counterclaims are not compulsory, whether or not they arise out of the same transaction as the main claim. In those systems Adams would not be barred from starting a second action on the counterclaim. However, such jurisdictions sometimes hold that a party waives his right to sue separately on an omitted counterclaim if the same issues were raised defensively in the prior action. Id.

6.   In this example, Adams's claim was available at the time of the original action and could have been joined as a permissive counterclaim under Rule 13(b). However, Adams was not required to join it in the first suit, and it will not be barred by res judicata if he omits it. By definition, a permissive counterclaim arises out of a separate transaction from the main claim. See Fed. R. Civ. P. 13(b). Thus, it is not part of the "same claim" as the plaintiff's claim, nor is it barred by rule-based preclusion, as a compulsory counterclaim would be. Here, *may* really means *may;* Adams's fraud claim will not be barred.

If the claim were barred by res judicata if omitted from the first action, the preclusion rules would make permissive counterclaims compulsory, undermining the rulemakers' choice and raising serious jurisdictional problems in many federal cases.

7.   Joinder: Yes   Res judicata: No

a. Adams could have joined this indemnification claim as a cross-claim in the original action, under Rule 13(g), which authorizes but does not require a defendant to assert any related claim he has against a codefendant in the original action.

b. Res judicata will not bar Adams from seeking indemnification from Johnson in a second suit. Under the res judicata analysis, Adams's claim against Johnson is not the same as Grasso's claim against Adams, so that Grasso's suit does not bar Adams from suing Johnson separately. Again, this result is consistent with the policy of the Rules. The rulemakers have chosen to make cross-claims permissive; if res judicata barred subsequent assertion of omitted cross-claims they would effectively be compulsory.

Compulsory cross-claims actually might not be a bad idea. As long as all the parties are already in the case, why not force them to litigate all claims among them arising out of the same transaction? The Rules make defendants do it under Rule 13(a) but draw the line at forcing the assertion of other related claims such as cross-claims and third-party claims.

A Myrmidon in the Labyrinth

8.   Joinder: Yes   Res judicata: No

a. Adams could have impleaded Johnson for indemnification under Rule 14(a) since Adams seeks recovery from Johnson for the damages Grasso seeks from it.

b. If Adams is free to refrain from asserting this claim against Johnson in the last example, in which they are both already in the suit, it should similarly be free *not* to implead Johnson when sued by Grasso. Impleader is permissive, and Adams is free to sue Johnson separately for indemnification instead if it prefers. Res judicata will not bar the suit.

Tactically, it may be preferable to implead Johnson to prevent the risk of inconsistent judgments, but Adams may have reasons for failing to do so, such as lack of personal jurisdiction over Johnson. It would certainly be inappropriate to force Adams to join Johnson if it couldn't obtain personal jurisdiction over it. Such problems were undoubtedly in the minds of the rulemakers when they decided not to make Rule 14 impleader claims compulsory.

However, if Adams did implead Johnson, res judicata obviously would bar it from bringing a separate action against Johnson on the same claim. Further, Johnson may be able to invoke collateral estoppel in the second action on issues decided against Adams in the first.

9.   Joinder: Yes   Res judicata: Yes

a. Bryan could have asserted this claim against Coolidge under Rule 18(a), which provides that a party seeking relief from an opposing party may assert as many claims as he has against that opposing party. Granted, Bryan could not have impleaded Coolidge on the basis of this claim alone because it does not satisfy the Rule 14(a) requirement that Coolidge may be liable to Bryan for all or part of the plaintiff's claim. See Chapter 14, pp. 247-249. Once Bryan has properly impleaded Coolidge on the indemnification claim, however, he may assert whatever claims he has against Coolidge, related or unrelated.

Of course, there would also have to be a basis for subject matter jurisdiction over Bryan's additional claim for it to be asserted in the original action. The supplemental jurisdiction statute, 28 U.S.C. §1367, provides a basis for jurisdiction, since Bryan's wage claim arises from the same foundation work as the main claim brought by Smith. (There may not even be a need to invoke §1367, since the parties to the wage claim are diverse and Bryan may aggregate his claims against Coolidge. If Bryan sought more than $75,000 in damages on the combined claims the amount-in-controversy requirement would be met, and the court would have jurisdiction based on diversity.)

b. Assuming that there was subject matter jurisdiction over the wage claim in the original suit, res judicata will bar Bryan from suing on the claim later. Res judicata applies not only to a plaintiff who has asserted claims against a defendant, but to other parties in the suit who have asserted claims. Here, Bryan has asserted a claim against Coolidge by impleading him on the foundation claim. Having done so, the res judicata rules require him to assert all claims he has against Coolidge arising out of that transaction. Bryan omitted the wage claim, which also arose from the construction of the foundation, and he is therefore barred from asserting it in a new action.

Bryan had the option not to implead Coolidge at all, in which case he could have asserted the indemnification and wage claims in a separate suit (but *not* in two separate suits). However, once he has joined issue with Coolidge on claims arising out of the foundation work, he must assert all his claims arising from it in that suit. Although Rule 18(a) says he *may* assert his related wage claim, the res judicata rules convert that to *must* in this situation.[4]

10. Joinder: Maybe   Res judicata: No

a. As in example 9, Rule 18(a) authorizes Bryan to assert this claim along with his third-party indemnification claim. Here, of course, the claim is completely unrelated to the impleader claim, but Rule 18 doesn't seem to care. However, there would not be supplemental jurisdiction over this claim since it arises from an unrelated contract breach. Bryan would have to establish independent jurisdiction over the added claim based on diversity. He might have been able to do so, if the impleader claim and the unrelated claim together sought more than $75,000 in damages.

b. Bryan is not barred from suing separately on this claim, since the claim asserted in the second action does not arise out of the same transaction as the impleader claim against Coolidge in the first suit. Therefore, it does not satisfy the "same claim" requirement of res judicata, and Bryan was not required to assert it in the prior action.

If Bryan were forced to join this unrelated claim, the symmetry of the res judicata and jurisdiction rules would be lost. The court would not have

---

4. Of course, if jurisdiction were based on 28 U.S.C. §1367, the court might have declined to exercise jurisdiction, in its discretion, under §1367(c). If the first court had refused to hear the wage claim, then it would not be barred in a later suit. See Chapter 24, pp. 466.

supplemental jurisdiction over the unrelated claim, since it is not part of the same "case or controversy" under §1367(a). If there were no independent basis for subject matter jurisdiction, Bryan would be forced by the preclusion rules to join this claim but prevented by the jurisdiction rules from doing so.

11a. Yes. The sixth sentence of Rule 14(a) authorizes (but does not require) a third-party defendant to assert claims against the plaintiff if they arise out of the same transaction or occurrence as the main claim. Since Coolidge's claim arises from the foundation work this test is satisfied.

b. Yes. Although there is no diversity, §1367(a) would authorize supplemental jurisdiction over this claim, since it arises from the same dispute as the main claim. And §1367(b) does not bar the claim, since it is not a claim by a plaintiff. See Chapter 15, example 9a.

c. Coolidge's suit is not barred. Because he never asserted any claim against Smith in suit one, and assertion of the claim was permissive under Rule 14, he is free to save this claim and sue on it separately. Note that this claim was *not* a counterclaim in suit one, because he and Smith, while both parties in the first action, were not "opposing parties" in that action. So, Rule 13(a) did not require Coolidge to assert this claim against Smith in that suit. It might make sense to amend the Rules to force Coolidge to assert this claim in the initial action, but currently they don't. Consequently, it would be anomalous for the res judicata rules to bar the second action.

When Does *May Not* Mean *Must?*

12a. Ordinarily, Smith's negligence claim would be barred because it arose out of the same transaction as the breach of contract claim. However, Smith may argue that he should be allowed to bring a second action on the negligence claim because he tried to join it in the first action, but the court refused to hear it. The situation is roughly analogous to the case of supplemental claims, which must be asserted in the original action but will not be barred if the court refuses in its discretion to entertain them. See Chapter 24, example 13. Similarly, in this case Smith will argue that he sought but was denied the right to assert the claim in the original suit and should therefore be allowed to resurrect it here.

b. Smith's argument is clever, but the analogy is a bit too rough to carry the day. Here, the negligence claim was disallowed because it was asserted in an untimely manner. Once Smith brought suit against Bryan, Smith had to assert all his claims properly in that action. Although the amendment rules are liberal, Smith has no right to hold back some claims arising from the construction and spring them on Bryan just before trial. At some point the defendant has a right to focus his trial preparation on those issues that have been properly placed in dispute and let the others go. See *Northern Assurance Company of America v. Square & Co.*, 201 F.3d 84, 87-89 (2d Cir. 2000); 18 Wright and Miller §4412, p.105; and cases cited at 2000 Supp.

n. 28. This claim will be barred because it arose from the same transaction as the original claim and was available to Smith if timely asserted in the first suit.

The irony here, of course, is that if Smith had waited for three years to bring the entire suit, he could have asserted all of his claims, since the limitations period had not expired. But, once the suit has been commenced and the case approaches trial, fairness to the defendant and the need to expedite litigation may prevent the assertion of additional claims even though they would not be barred by the statute of limitations. In this case, the court's refusal to allow Smith to amend means that the omitted claim is lost.

26

Collateral Estoppel: Fine-Tuning the Preclusion Doctrine

Introduction

If law is a mysterious profession, it is partly because lawyers have such a knack for attaching intimidating names to relatively commonsense principles. Names such as "res judicata" and "collateral estoppel," for example; handles like these are enough to intimidate any client and most lawyers. But once you rub elbows with these related doctrines for a while, they will lose their power to intimidate, and you will recognize them for what they are, essential and sensible tools of the trade.

Although they serve related functions, these two tools are different in character. Res judicata acts like a bludgeon, indiscriminately smashing all efforts of a party to relitigate events that have already been litigated and decided in a prior suit. Collateral estoppel, by contrast, operates like a scalpel, dissecting a lawsuit into its various issues and surgically removing from reconsideration any that have been properly decided in a prior action.

Speaking less metaphorically, res judicata bars Smith from suing Jones for any kind of relief arising from a particular transaction or occurrence if Smith had previously brought an action against Jones based on that transaction or occurrence, and the prior action was decided on the merits. Restatement

(Second) of Judgments §24 (1982).[1] Res judicata bars any relitigation of Smith's rights against Jones based on those events, including not only the claims that Smith did raise the first time around but also any other claims arising out of the same set of facts that Smith could have raised (but did not) in the first action.

Collateral estoppel is more narrowly focused. It only precludes Smith from relitigating issues that were actually litigated and decided in a prior action with Jones. If an issue could have been raised in the first case but was not explicitly raised and decided, collateral estoppel will not bar Smith from litigating that issue in a subsequent action against Jones.

An example will help to distinguish the two. Smith sues Jones for trespass on her property. Jones defends on the ground that she holds an easement to enter on the land to cut firewood. The court concludes that the easement is valid and enters judgment for Jones. Res judicata would bar Smith from suing Jones again based on the same wood-cutting incident. For example, Smith could not bring a new action on the theory that an implied condition of the easement was that Jones pay fair value for the timber cut. Nor could she seek damages for property damage done to her land during the cutting. When Smith sues Jones for that occurrence, res judicata forces her to bring forth all claims she has arising from it in the original action, rather than plaguing Jones with successive suits based on the same incident but asserting new theories for recovery or seeking different types of relief.

Collateral estoppel, by contrast, would bar Smith from relitigating specific issues decided in the first action, such as the validity of Jones's easement. If Jones returns to cut wood again on Smith's land and Smith sues, this second suit will not be barred by res judicata because she is not suing for the same incident as the original action. However, Smith will be collaterally estopped from trying again to prove that Jones's easement is invalid because that issue was litigated and decided in the original action. But Smith would be free to litigate other issues not resolved in the earlier action. For example, Smith could still claim in the later suit based on the second incident that an implied condition of the easement required payment for the timber. This issue would not be barred by collateral estoppel because it was not raised and decided in the first action.

At this point you may be asking, "Well, who needs collateral estoppel?" If res judicata so broadly precludes relitigation, whether or not an issue was previously raised, what is the need for a separate doctrine with

---

1. The discussion in this chapter is based on the principles of the Second Restatement of Judgments. These principles have been widely applied in the federal court (see, e.g., *Montana v. United States,* 440 U.S. 147, 153, 162 (1979); *United States v. Stauffer Chemical Co.,* 464 U.S. 165, 171 (1984)) and have been increasingly adopted by state courts as well.

another mysterious name?[2] The answer is that collateral estoppel is needed because issues already litigated may come up again in later litigation based on separate events. Smith's second action against Jones for the second wood-cutting incident would not be barred by res judicata since this is a new "claim" that has not been litigated before. See Restatement (Second) of Judgments §24 (1982) (defining "claim" to include all rights arising out of a single transaction). But the issue of whether Smith has an easement to cut timber will arise again in the new action. Collateral estoppel will preclude litigation of that issue even though res judicata is inapplicable.

This example shows that collateral estoppel is both broader and narrower than res judicata. It is narrower in that it does not preclude all possible issues that might have been raised in a prior action but only those actually decided in that action. But it is also broader in that it can foreclose litigation of a particular issue in an entirely new context. Once the validity of Jones's easement has been determined between the parties, estoppel may preclude either party from relitigating that issue in suits arising out of completely different underlying facts. Suppose, for example, that Jones went to cut wood again on Smith's property and was injured when she fell in an abandoned well. Under common law negligence principles, the duty of care Smith owed to her might depend on whether she was a trespasser. In her negligence action Jones could estop Smith from defending on the ground that Jones was a trespasser, since the prior suit determined that the easement allowed her to enter the property. Although the context is different in the second action (in fact, the original plaintiff is now the defendant), Jones's right to be on the land is at issue in both suits and there is no reason to allow Smith to relitigate it.

Prerequisites for Estoppel

Collateral estoppel is a flexible doctrine, which varies in its application from one jurisdiction to another. However, the basic prerequisites are fairly uniform. *First*, the issue in the second case must be the same as the issue in the first. In the example above, the issue in both suits is whether Jones has a legal right to enter upon Smith's property to cut wood. But if Smith sues Jones for breach of a contract made in June of 1997, and Jones is held to have been incompetent to make the contract because she was a minor, it does not follow that Jones was incompetent to make another contract in October of 1999. Here, the issues are not the same, and the resolution of one should not preclude litigation on the other.

Second, the issue must have been actually litigated. Restatement (Second) of Judgments §27 (1982). This requirement will obviously not be satisfied

---

2. With *two* mysterious names, actually. Collateral estoppel is also frequently referred to as "issue preclusion," and res judicata as "claim preclusion."

when a party failed to raise an issue in a previous action, such as Smith failing to assert a right to be paid for the wood Jones cut in the first suit. But an issue may not have been "actually litigated" even though it *was* raised in a prior action. Suppose, for example, that Smith sues Jones for breach of contract and Jones admits in her answer that she made the contract but defends the action on another ground. Under the Restatement view, Jones may defend a second suit for a later breach of the same contract on the ground that she never made the contract, since she never actually litigated that issue in the original suit.

> There are many reasons why a party may choose not to raise an issue, or to contest an assertion, in a particular action. The action may involve so small an amount that litigation of the issue may cost more than the value of the lawsuit. Or the forum may be an inconvenient one in which to produce the necessary evidence or in which to litigate at all. The interests of conserving judicial resources, of maintaining consistency, and of avoiding oppression or harassment of the adverse party are less compelling when the issue on which preclusion is sought has not actually been litigated before. And if preclusive effect were given to issues not litigated, the result might serve to discourage compromise, to decrease the likelihood that the issues in an action would be narrowed by stipulation, and thus to intensify litigation.

Restatement (Second) of Judgments §27, comment e (1982).

Third, even if an issue was litigated in a prior action, collateral estoppel will not bar relitigation unless the issue was actually decided in that action. Restatement (Second) of Judgments §27 (1982). Suppose, for example, that Jones publishes a book that Smith claims to hold all rights to publish, and Smith sues Jones on copyright infringement and breach of contract theories. The case goes to trial on both issues. If the court finds for Smith on the ground that Jones breached the contract (and therefore does not decide the copyright issue), collateral estoppel will not bar relitigation of the copyright infringement issue in another context even though both sides fully presented their evidence on the copyright issue in the first case. The parties have fully litigated the issue, and it seems wasteful to have them relitigate it in another suit. However, it is a little hard to apply collateral estoppel without knowing which party to estop. Without a winner or loser on the copyright issue, the court in the later action has no choice but to rehear it.

Fourth, it is usually said that collateral estoppel will not apply unless the decision on the issue in the prior action was necessary to the court's judgment. Restatement (Second) of Judgments §27 (1982). In the course of a suit, the judge may decide a number of issues that do not ultimately determine the outcome of the case. Here's a nice example: In *Balcom v. Lynn Ladder and Scaffolding Co. Inc.,* 806 F.2d 1127 (1st Cir. 1986), the plaintiff sued a scaffolding company for injuries suffered on a ladder. The defendant impleaded a ladder manufacturer, claiming that it had made the defective ladder and should indemnify the defendant for any damages awarded. The jury found that the manufacturer had built the ladder, and that the ladder was defective, but that the defect had not caused the plaintiff's injury. The First Circuit held that collateral estoppel would not bar the manufacturer from relitigating the issue of who made the ladder, since that finding was not "necessary to the judgment." The finding that had led to the verdict in the manufacturer's favor was the finding that the ladder did not cause the injury, not the finding that the manufacturer made the ladder. Because this latter finding did not affect the outcome of the suit, the manufacturer could not appeal it. Consequently, it should not be barred from relitigating the issue in a later action.

In other cases, a court may find for a litigant on two independent, sufficient grounds. For example, suppose that the court in Smith's copyright and contract action finds that Jones breached her contract with Smith *and* that she infringed Smith's copyright. Each issue has been actually litigated and actually decided, but the Restatement would deny collateral estoppel effect to either decision since it is impossible to tell which decision was necessary to the judgment:

> First a determination in the alternative may not have been as carefully or rigorously considered as it would have been if it had been necessary to the result, and in that sense it has some of the characteristics of dicta. Second, and of critical importance, the losing party, although entitled to appeal from both determinations, might be dissuaded from doing so because of the likelihood that at least one of them would be upheld and the other not even reached. If he were to appeal solely for the purpose of avoiding the application of the rule of issue preclusion, then the rule might be responsible for increasing the burdens of litigation on the parties and the courts rather than lightening those burdens.

Restatement (Second) of Judgments §27, comment i (1982). See *Halpern v. Schwartz*, 426 F.2d 102, 105-106 (2d Cir. 1970). However, this rationale has not been universally accepted; some courts have given collateral estoppel effect to *both* alternative determinations in these circumstances. See, e.g., *Winters v. Levine*, 574 F.2d 46, 67 (2d Cir. 1978), in which the Second Circuit appeared to limit *Halpern* to bankruptcy cases. Other cases and commentators have suggested a flexible middle ground between these extremes, which would apply estoppel if the second court can determine from the record of the first that both holdings were given full consideration. See *Malloy v. Trombley*, 427 N.Y.S.2d 969 (1980); 18 Wright and Miller at §4421, p.208.[3]

There are further wrinkles to the collateral estoppel doctrine. In particular, the issue of nonmutual estoppel, considered in *Parklane Hosiery Co.*,

---

3. This issue continues to divide the courts. Compare *In re Carozza*, 167 B.R. 331, 338-340 (Bankr. E.D.N.Y. 1994) (following *Winters v. Levine*) with *York Ford, Inc. v. Building Inspector and Zoning Administrator of Saugus*, 338 Mass. App. Ct. 938, 940-942 (1995) (adopting Second Restatement view and characterizing it as "the trend").

Inc. v. Shore, 439 U.S. 322 (1979), adds an additional level of complexity to the analysis, which is explored in the following chapter. For the moment, however, we will focus on the basics. In analyzing the following examples, assume that all actions are brought in federal court and that the "modern" Second Restatement principles of collateral estoppel apply.

EXAMPLES

First Principles

1.   Vanderbilt enters into a contract with Fisk for the delivery of 50 tons of coal per week to Vanderbilt's power plant, for the period from January 1994 to December 1998. In 1995 Vanderbilt sues Fisk for breach of contract. He claims that the coal delivered from March to August 1994 was "grade AB" rather than "first quality" coal, as required by the contract. Fisk denies the allegation that he delivered grade AB coal instead of first quality coal and prevails in a jury trial.

Subsequently, Vanderbilt sues Fisk again for breach of contract on the ground that the coal delivered between February and June 1996 was grade AB. Fisk again denies that he delivered AB coal.

a. Why is Vanderbilt's second suit not barred by res judicata?

b. Does collateral estoppel bar relitigation of any issue decided in the first suit?

2.   Assume that Vanderbilt claims in the first suit that Fisk delivered grade AB coal from March to August of 1994, which did not comply with the contract specification for "first quality" coal. Fisk admits that he delivered grade AB coal during that period but defends on the ground that AB coal satisfies the contract specification. The case is tried to a jury, which finds for Vanderbilt and awards him damages.

a. Vanderbilt sues Fisk again for delivering grade AB coal from February to June 1996. Will collateral estoppel apply to any issue?

b. If Vanderbilt sues for the second (1996) breach, could Fisk defend on the ground that the contract is void because the parties entered into it on the basis of a mutual mistake as to the type of coal to be delivered?

c. Assume that in Vanderbilt's second action Fisk defends on the ground that AB coal satisfies the contract specifications. He offers expert testimony, not offered in the original action, that AB coal is universally accepted in the industry as "first quality" coal. Will the court bar him from relitigating the issue?

d. Assume that Vanderbilt's second suit against Fisk is for delivering grade AB coal from September to December 1998. Fisk defends on the ground that Vanderbilt had agreed to an oral modification of the contract allowing delivery of grade AB coal due to a national shortage of "first quality" coal during those months. Will collateral estoppel bar Fisk from relying on this defense?

3.   Vanderbilt sues Fisk for breach of the coal delivery contract, claiming that Fisk delivered AB coal from March to August 1994. Fisk defends on the ground that the contract was invalid due to mutual mistake and, in the alternative, that AB coal complies with the contract specifications. The jury renders a general verdict[4] for Fisk.

   a. Later, Vanderbilt sues Fisk for a subsequent breach of the contract by delivering AB coal from February to June 1996. Fisk again defends on the ground that AB coal satisfies the contract specifications. Does collateral estoppel bar relitigation of this issue?

   b. Assume that in the original suit described in this example Vanderbilt moved for judgment as a matter of law on Fisk's mutual mistake defense, and the court granted the motion, finding, as a matter of law, that there was no mutual mistake. The case went to the jury on the defense that AB coal was adequate under the contract, and the jury rendered a verdict for Fisk. Subsequently, Vanderbilt sues Fisk for the 1996 breach. Fisk raises the same defenses. May Fisk estop Vanderbilt from claiming that AB coal does not meet the contract specifications?

   c. On the preceding facts, may Vanderbilt bar Fisk from relitigating the mutual mistake defense?

   d. Assume that the first case went to the jury on both defenses, and the jury rendered a verdict for Vanderbilt in the first suit. Now Vanderbilt sues for the second breach during 1996, and Fisk defends on the ground that the parties entered into the contract under a mutual mistake. May Vanderbilt estop Fisk from relitigating the issue of mutual mistake?

4.   Consider again the facts of example 3d. In the first case Vanderbilt sued for delivering AB coal in 1994, and Fisk raised two defenses: that the contract had been based on a mutual mistake and that AB coal satisfies the contract specifications. Vanderbilt wins the case and recovers damages. Later, he sues Fisk for a 1996 breach of the contract, and Fisk tries to raise the defense that AB coal satisfies the specifications. Vanderbilt's counsel recognizes that collateral estoppel should bar Fisk from relitigating the defense (see the explanation to example 3d).

   a. What procedural motion should Vanderbilt make to present his collateral estoppel objection to the court?

   b. What evidence should Vanderbilt use to support his motion?

Isn't This Example in the Wrong Chapter?

5.   Morgan sues Gould for violation of the federal antitrust laws, in the federal district court for the Southern District of New York. Gould moves

---

4. A general verdict is a simple verdict for the plaintiff or defendant without specifying the ground upon which the decision is based.

to dismiss for lack of personal jurisdiction. The court allows discovery on the jurisdictional issue, takes evidence on the issue at a hearing, hears oral argument, and subsequently denies the motion. Gould defaults on the merits, and Morgan gets judgment. Morgan then brings an action to enforce the judgment in Florida. Gould opposes enforcement of the judgment on the ground that the New York court lacked personal jurisdiction over him.

   a. Will collateral estoppel bar relitigation of the personal jurisdiction issue?
   b. Will collateral estoppel bar relitigation of the merits of the antitrust claim?

6.   Carnegie sues Astor in California for manufacturing a type of railroad engine in that state. Carnegie bases his suit on two claims. First, he alleges that he has a patent on the engine under the federal patent laws and that Astor is infringing his patent by building the engine without his permission. Second, he claims that Astor is violating California's unfair competition statute by using Carnegie's engine design. The case is tried to a jury, which renders a general verdict for Carnegie and awards him damages.

   Subsequently, Astor resumes making the same engines in Nevada, which (we will assume) has no unfair competition statute. Carnegie sues him for patent infringement. Does collateral estoppel bar relitigation of the infringement issue?

A Brainteaser with a Commonsense Answer

7.   Assume the same facts as example 6, except that Astor resumed making the engines in California. Carnegie sues him there again. He seeks to enjoin Astor from making the engines and argues that the decision in the prior suit establishes his right to the injunction. Will collateral estoppel bar Astor from relitigating the legality of his conduct?

8.   Assume that Carnegie's first suit against Astor was tried to the court rather than the jury and that the judge's written decision expressly finds that Astor is liable on both theories. Astor then begins production of the engines in Nevada, and Carnegie brings a second action against him there. Will collateral estoppel bar Astor from claiming that he has not infringed Carnegie's patent?

Mega-Hypo: Exercise for the Enthusiast

9.   The examples above illustrate particular issues in the application of collateral estoppel. Often, though, cases are not so conceptually clean; it is necessary to cull through a long procedural history and voluminous record to prove that the requirements of collateral estoppel are met. Indeed, it may take as much litigation to prove that the issue is precluded as it would to

relitigate it, thus undermining one of the policy reasons for allowing issue preclusion. For a taste of these complexities, try the following example.

Hill buys two identical blast furnaces from Villard. One of them explodes, and Hill sues Villard for his injuries. He asserts claims for negligent design, breach of warranty, and strict liability. He seeks compensatory damages on all three counts and punitive damages, which are only available on the negligence claim. Villard admits that he made the furnace but denies that the design was negligent. He admits that a warranty of fitness for its intended use arose upon the sale but denies that he breached the warranty. He also denies that he is strictly liable for injuries resulting from the explosion. In addition, he raises contributory negligence as a defense on the negligence claim (a complete defense under applicable law) and claims that Hill's negligence claim is barred by the statute of limitations. The judge dismisses the strict liability claim under Rule 12(b)(6), on the ground that the applicable law does not allow recovery on a strict liability theory. Villard moves for summary judgment on the statute of limitations defense, but the judge denies the motion. At trial Hill moves for judgment as a matter of law on the negligent design issue. The judge denies it. The jury returns a verdict for the plaintiff and awards compensatory and punitive damages.

Two weeks after the judgment in the original suit, the second furnace explodes, and Hill sues Villard on the same theories. What issues will be precluded in the second action?

EXPLANATIONS

First Principles

1a. It is important at the outset to distinguish the relitigation of claims from the relitigation of issues. Res judicata only bars relitigation of the same claim, that is, the same transaction or occurrence that was the subject of the first suit. See Chapter 24, pp. 453-454. Vanderbilt is not seeking to relitigate his original claim for the breach of contract that took place in 1994. Rather, he is litigating a new claim for a later breach of the same contract. This second breach is not the same transaction or occurrence as the first, even though it involves the same contract. Indeed, since it had not occurred when Vanderbilt first sued Fisk, it obviously could not have been joined in the first action.

b. Collateral estoppel, in contrast to res judicata, precludes relitigation of issues in a second suit that have previously been litigated and decided in a prior action. Even though the second suit is for a separate claim, so that res judicata does not apply, a subsequent suit may involve issues already settled in an earlier suit between the same parties. If so, it makes no sense to allow the parties to relitigate those issues.

However, the first prerequisite for collateral estoppel is that the issues in the two suits must be the same. Therefore, analysis of collateral estoppel issues should always begin with a determination of what was decided in the first action. In this case the issue in the first suit was whether Fisk had delivered first-quality coal from March to August 1994. The issue in the second suit was whether Fisk delivered first-quality coal during a subsequent period. This is a different factual issue, which was not raised in the prior suit and must be litigated in the new one.

2a. In this example, the issue in the first suit was not whether Fisk actually delivered AB coal (he admits that he did), but whether AB coal was insufficient under the contract specifications. Since this was the basis for Vanderbilt's claim that Fisk breached the contract, and the jury found for Vanderbilt, they must have concluded that AB coal did not satisfy the specifications. Since that issue was litigated and decided in the first suit, the court in Vanderbilt's second action for a later breach will estop Fisk from defending the second suit on the ground that AB coal satisfies the specifications. Here, although the issue in the second suit arises from a later transaction (and thus would not be barred by res judicata), it will be barred by collateral estoppel since the issue was previously litigated and decided between the parties.

b. As indicated above, the issue that was raised and decided in the first suit was whether AB coal satisfied the contract specifications. Although the separate defense of mutual mistake at the time of entering into the contract was available to Fisk in the prior action, he failed to raise it. However, collateral estoppel does not bar him from doing so later in a second suit for a new breach of the contract. Collateral estoppel only bars issues that were litigated and decided in the prior action; it does not affect claims or defenses that *could have been* raised but were not.

Compare res judicata doctrine, which bars litigation of any issues that could have been raised in a prior suit on the same claim. Res judicata does not apply in this hypothetical because Vanderbilt's second suit is for a separate claim, the 1996 breach.

c. Essentially, Fisk's position here is that he should be able to relitigate the AB coal issue because, while he failed to prove his defense the first time, he can prove it now. As long as Fisk had a full chance to present his case in the first suit, this argument will fall on deaf ears. This testimony could presumably have been offered in the original suit and should have been. There is no reason why preclusion should operate against parties who litigated carefully the first time around but not against those who did not. Nor is there a requirement that the original finding has to be "right" to preclude relitigation. If that were true, the second court would have to rehear the issue to determine whether it was correctly decided the first time, thus completely undermining the purpose of the doctrine itself.

In limited situations, a party who discovers new evidence on an issue may move for relief from judgment under Fed. R. Civ. P. 60(b)(2). Under this rule, Fisk could seek to reopen the *original* action and overturn the finding that AB coal was insufficient. If he succeeded, of course, that original finding would no longer be entitled to collateral estoppel effect in subsequent suits.[5]

    d. In this case the original finding that AB coal did not comply with the specifications could not be relitigated. However, Fisk's defense is not that AB coal is sufficient under the original contract but that a subsequent modification of the contract allows him to deliver AB coal. This is a new issue, which was not raised in the original action, has never been litigated or decided, and is available to Fisk as a defense to the new action.

3a. Collateral estoppel does not apply unless the issue was decided in the prior suit. In this case Fisk raised two defenses to Vanderbilt's first claim. If the jury accepted either defense, they would have had to find for Fisk. Obviously, they did accept one of those defenses, but it is impossible to tell from the jury's general verdict for Fisk which one it was. When a case is submitted to a jury with a general verdict form, the jury is simply asked to find for the plaintiff or for the defendant (and if it finds for the plaintiff, to find the amount of the plaintiff's damages). In this case, the jury's general finding "for the defendant" does not indicate whether it found the contract void or, alternatively, that AB coal complied with the specifications. Because it is impossible to tell which issue was decided, Fisk will not be able to demonstrate that the issue of whether the coal was sufficient was actually decided or necessary to the judgment. Consequently, collateral estoppel will not bar relitigation of that issue.

    b. The result here is different because the procedural history of the suit clearly indicates what issues were decided. The judge's entry of judgment as a matter of law for Vanderbilt on the mutual mistake defense is a decision on that issue; it constitutes a finding that on the evidence produced by the parties no reasonable jury could find for Fisk on that issue. Thus, that issue was actually litigated and decided in Vanderbilt's favor. That left only one defense, that the AB coal complied with the contract specifications. The jury's verdict for Fisk must have been based on this defense.

    In this case, therefore, unlike example 3a, it is clear that the AB coal issue was decided in Fisk's favor in the previous action and that it was the basis for the jury's verdict for Fisk. Consequently, Vanderbilt will be estopped from relitigating that issue; the court will grant judgment for Fisk

---

5. Fisk will have an uphill fight in obtaining relief from judgment. First, Rule 60(b)(2) only allows the court to reopen the suit due to newly discovered evidence within one year after judgment. In addition, the moving party on such a motion must show that the new evidence could not have been discovered in the exercise of due diligence in time for presentation at the original trial.

    In a few cases, courts have refused to apply collateral estoppel because new scientific evidence on a complex issue has been developed since the prior action. See Madden, Issue Preclusion in Products Liability, 11 Pace L. Rev. 87, 117 (1990) (describing several complex medical causation cases which refused estoppel on this ground).

if Vanderbilt sues him for damages on the ground that AB coal was inadequate under the contract.

As this example indicates, collateral estoppel can work for either party. In example 2a, Vanderbilt used it to establish an issue crucial to obtaining relief. In this case Fisk uses it to establish a defense that had been previously litigated and decided in his favor.

c. If Fisk raises the defense of mutual mistake again, Vanderbilt will argue that Fisk should be estopped from relitigating the issue since it was litigated and decided adversely to Fisk in the first suit. Unfortunately for Vanderbilt, this will not work, since the finding for Vanderbilt that there was no mutual mistake was not necessary to support the original judgment. That judgment was for Fisk and was based on the jury's finding that Fisk had proved his defense that AB coal was adequate under the contract. Vanderbilt lost *even though* the contract was valid because the AB coal complied with it; the finding that there was no mutual mistake did not lead to the judgment. Thus, although the mistake issue was litigated and decided, the court will deny collateral estoppel effect on that issue since it was not essential to the decision of the case.

Although this seems artificial, consider Fisk's point of view. Even if he believes that the court wrongly decided the mistake issue, he has no incentive to appeal since he won the verdict. If he did appeal for fear that some future court might apply collateral estoppel on the mutual mistake issue, the appellate court would probably refuse to hear the appeal, since Fisk won below and review of the mutual mistake issue would therefore serve no purpose. In a sense, then, there has been no final decision on the issue; Fisk should not be estopped by a potentially erroneous decision that he has no opportunity or incentive to correct.

d. Here, Vanderbilt may invoke collateral estoppel to bar Fisk from relitigating the mutual mistake issue. In this example Fisk raised two defenses in the first suit. If the jury accepted either one they would have found for Fisk. Because they found for Vanderbilt, they must have considered each of the defenses and concluded that Fisk had not proved either one. In addition, the decision on each defense was necessary to the judgment since they had to consider and reject each defense raised by Fisk in order to find for Vanderbilt: If the jury had found either a mutual mistake in making the contract or that AB coal was sufficient, Fisk would have won.

4a. Vanderbilt should move for partial summary judgment under Fed. R. Civ. P. 56 on Fisk's defense that AB coal satisfies the contract specifications. His position is that Fisk is barred from asserting this defense, because he litigated and lost on the defense in the earlier lawsuit. If he can show that collateral estoppel applies, there is "no genuine issue as to any material fact" (Fed. R. Civ. P. 56(c)) on that defense, and he, Vanderbilt, is "entitled to judgment as a matter of law." Id. His position is that as a matter of law Fisk cannot prove the AB-coal-suffices defense, because he failed to prove it earlier and is not allowed (under collateral estoppel) to try to prove it again.

b. To prevail on his motion, Vanderbilt would have to establish that the issue was tried in the earlier suit, was decided in his favor, and led to the judgment in the prior suit. To show that it was raised, he could submit the pleadings from the prior suit, which would show that Fisk raised the AB-coal-suffices defense. He could also submit the judge's instructions to the jury, which would show that the issue had been litigated at trial and submitted to the jury for decision. Last, the jury's verdict slip finding in favor of Vanderbilt and the court's judgment on the verdict would demonstrate that the jury had rejected the defense (since they could not have found for Vanderbilt unless they did) and that rejection of the defense had led to the judgment for Vanderbilt.

Of course, if Vanderbilt moves for summary judgment on this issue, and prevails, the case will not be over. Vanderbilt will get partial summary judgment on the AB coal defense; that defense will be stricken, but he will still have to establish the basic elements of his breach of contract claim and prove his damages. However, he can at least use estoppel to avoid relitigating a major issue that was already disposed of in the earlier action.

Isn't This Example in the Wrong Chapter?

5a. This situation should sound familiar: It echoes example 5 from Chapter 3. If you look at that example, you will see that the defendant was barred from relitigating whether the rendering court had personal jurisdiction over him because he had already raised and litigated that issue in the rendering court. Now it should be clear to you that this result is a straightforward application of collateral estoppel principles: The personal jurisdiction issue was raised, litigated, and decided in the original action and was necessary to the judgment as well, since the court would not have taken jurisdiction and entered a default judgment for Morgan if it had concluded that it lacked jurisdiction over Gould. Thus, all the requirements for collateral estoppel are met, and Gould will be barred from relitigating the issue.

Note that in this case Morgan invokes collateral estoppel on an issue that has nothing to do with the merits of the lawsuit, indeed, in a situation where the merits were never litigated at all. But a decision "on the merits" of the plaintiff's substantive claim is not necessary before collateral estoppel applies: So long as the particular issue, be it procedural or substantive, was litigated and decided and necessary to the judgment, issue preclusion will bar relitigation of the issue. This result makes good sense. Gould should not be allowed to relitigate the personal jurisdiction question if it has been fully and fairly decided in another court.

Distinguish res judicata, however. That doctrine only bars relitigation of *claims* once they have been decided on the merits. When a case is dismissed on procedural grounds, the merits have never been litigated, and the plaintiff may sue again in a court that can properly reach the merits.

   b. Collateral estoppel will not bar relitigation of the antitrust claim. None of the substantive issues in the case were litigated on the merits in the New York court, so none were "actually litigated" or "actually decided" there. However, res judicata will bar Gould from litigating the merits in Florida. Under res judicata principles, the New York default judgment is a decision "on the merits" in favor of Morgan which bars relitigating any claims arising out of the underlying events giving rise to the case. (Note that, for res judicata to apply, there is no requirement that the substantive issues have been "actually litigated," as there is for collateral estoppel.) Under full faith and credit principles, the Florida court will give the New York default judgment the same res judicata effect it would have in New York.

6.   Carnegie will have to relitigate the patent infringement issue. Although he won the first suit, it is impossible to tell from the general verdict which claim prevailed before the jury. They may have decided that Astor infringed Carnegie's patent, or that he violated the state unfair competition statute (or both). Thus, it is not possible to tell whether the "actually decided" and "necessary to the judgment" requirements are met.

   Because a general verdict obscures the basis of the jury's decision, one or both of the parties may want to request use of a special verdict form, under Fed. R. Civ. P. 49, if they foresee the possibility of future litigation involving the same issues. A special verdict asks the jury to make findings on particular issues, rather than finding generally for the plaintiff or defendant. See Friedenthal, Kane, and Miller (2d ed. 1999) §12.1. In this case, for example, the jury could be asked specifically whether they find that Astor infringed Carnegie's patent and whether they find that he violated California's unfair competition laws. If they answered "yes" on the patent infringement issue but "no" on the unfair competition issue, then it would be possible to prove in subsequent actions that the patent question was actually decided and necessary to the decision of the original suit.

   The situation would be different if Carnegie had lost the first case. Then it would be clear — even with a general verdict — that the jury had rejected both Carnegie's theories, and collateral estoppel could prevent relitigation of either.

A Brainteaser with a Commonsense Answer

7.   At first glance, it seems that the answer here ought to be "no" in light of the answer to example 6. It is unclear whether the jury in the first suit found for Carnegie on the patent claim or the unfair competition claim. However, it is clear that they found that Astor's conduct infringed on Carnegie's rights on one ground or the other. This should be sufficient to preclude relitigation in some contexts, at least. Carnegie may invoke

collateral estoppel to bar relitigation of Astor's right to make the engines, on the ground that the original judgment necessarily decided that he had no right to do so. The court may not need to decide which of Carnegie's theories the jury accepted in the first action; it may be enough to support the injunction that they accepted one.

However, if Carnegie seeks damages from Astor in the second suit, it may not be possible for him to rely on the previous judgment. If the measure of damages under the two claims differs, it will be necessary to determine which theory of liability applies in order to assess the damages. Because Carnegie can only show that the first suit determined that Astor was barred from making the engines, but not which theory that determination was based on, the jury in a second damage action would have to decide anew whether Astor is liable and, if so, on which ground.

8.   This example raises the "alternative holdings" problem discussed in the Introduction. The judge's opinion leaves no doubt that both the patent and unfair competition issues were actually litigated and decided. However, there is a problem as to whether either is "necessary to the judgment" when each is sufficient to support the judgment: Presumably, if either of the alternative holdings had been left out, the outcome would have been the same anyway, based on the other ground.

The Second Restatement of Judgments takes the position that neither holding is entitled to preclusive effect because it is impossible to tell whether each received full consideration and because the losing party has no incentive to appeal on one arguably incorrect ground if the other would support the judgment. As indicated in the Introduction, however some courts take the opposite view, that *both* holdings are entitled to collateral estoppel effect.

Mega-Hypo: Exercise for the Enthusiast

9.   This is not a particularly unusual scenario for a products liability action, yet it takes some doing to unravel the procedural history and ascertain whether any issues will be barred in the second suit.

A good place to start is to determine what issues were decided in the original action. Villard admitted that he made the furnace and that a warranty of fitness for its intended use arose upon the sale. However, as the Introduction points out, these admissions do not satisfy the "actually litigated" requirement for collateral estoppel purposes.

The denial of the motion for summary judgment on the limitations issue does not "actually decide" that issue; it simply indicates that both parties have some evidence on that issue and therefore ought to have the opportunity to go to trial on it. See Chapter 21, p. 394. Similarly, the denial of the motion for judgment as a matter of law on negligent design does not satisfy the requirement that the issue be "actually decided." That denial simply indicates that there is enough evidence to support a rational verdict for Villard, the nonmoving party, on that issue.

By contrast, the judge's dismissal of the strict liability claim clearly indicates that he decided as a matter of law that there is no strict liability claim arising out of the sale. A dismissal under Rule 12(b)(6) does "actually decide" the issue of whether strict liability applies, so this could give rise to issue preclusion later.

How about the verdict; can we discern what the jury actually decided in reaching their verdict for Hill? The case went to trial on breach of warranty and negligence (but not on strict liability since the judge dismissed that claim), and the jury's general verdict does not expressly indicate whether the jury found for Hill on one or both theories. However, the jury awarded punitive damages, which were only available on the negligent design claim. Thus, the jury must have found for Hill on that claim. And in order to do so it must have rejected the defense that the negligence claim is barred by the statute of limitations and that Hill's contributory negligence bars relief.

The jury *may* have also found for Hill on the breach of warranty claim, but we can't tell, since compensatory damages are available on both theories. Even if the jury found for Hill on both theories, it would only award him his actual losses as compensatory damages: Thus, the amount of the compensatory damages does not reveal whether the jury accepted both theories or only one.

We have identified four issues as actually litigated and decided: whether the statute of limitations barred the negligence claim, whether Hill's contributory negligence barred the negligence claim, whether the furnace was negligently designed, and whether Villard is strictly liable for the injuries resulting from the explosion. The first three were necessary to the judgment since the jury could not have found for Hill on the negligence claim without rejecting the statute of limitations and contributory negligence defenses and finding that the design was negligent. The dismissal of the strict liability claim is not necessary to the judgment, however; Hill should be able to relitigate strict liability in the second suit. After all, he *won* the first action on other grounds, so he had no incentive to appeal the dismissal of his strict liability claim.

Only three issues, then, satisfy the prerequisites. But two of those, the statute of limitations and contributory negligence issues, are not likely to be the same in the two suits since the two explosions took place at different times and perhaps under different circumstances.[6] Only the negligent design

---

6. In some circumstances, the contributory negligence issue might be the same, so that the rejection of the defense in the first action would bar Villard from asserting it in the second. Suppose, for example, that Hill installed the two furnaces in the same way at the same time, and Villard claimed in the first suit that inadequate installation contributed to the explosion. On those facts the issue would be the same in the second suit, and Villard would be barred by collateral estoppel from raising the defense again. But Hill would still have to prove that the furnaces *were* installed in the same way in order to support estoppel.

issue remains. That issue will presumably be the same since the two furnaces are identical.

Even though Hill will have to go through all of that to show that collateral estoppel applies, he will still have a strong incentive to do so. If he can get the judge to travel this long road, at the end of it he will have established an issue crucial to his right to relief, without relitigating the merits of that issue and without the risk of losing on it before the second jury. For Hill, the value of invoking collateral estoppel is not merely to save litigation time, but to assure the same favorable result he obtained in the first suit. Ironically, he may be willing to spend as much litigation time to obtain that result as it would take to try the issue again.

The Obscure Kingdom: Nonmutual Collateral Estoppel

Introduction

We began this journey at the beginning (see p. 3), and we should end at the end...but nothing is quite that simple in civil procedure. A lawsuit "ends" when a final judgment is entered or an appeal of the trial court judgment is decided. But the suit may send out waves that break on very distant shores. Under collateral estoppel doctrine, issues decided in one lawsuit may have effects in another suit between the parties at a later time or in a different court. And, beyond this fairly well-mapped terrain lies the more obscure kingdom of nonmutual collateral estoppel.

Under traditional issue preclusion principles, a party may be estopped from relitigating an issue that he had litigated in a prior suit and lost. Restatement (Second) of Judgments §27 (1982); Chapter 26, p. 486. Assume, for example, that Cartier sues La Salle, a tenant in his shopping center, for breach of a provision in the standard lease signed by all Cartier's tenants. If the court finds that the lease provision is invalid, La Salle may estop Cartier in a future suit involving the same lease from claiming that the disputed provision is enforceable. Conversely, if the provision had been held valid, Cartier could estop La Salle from defending a future action based on the same lease on the ground that the provision was invalid.

Nonmutual collateral estoppel goes a step beyond this basic doctrine by allowing a new party to invoke collateral estoppel against a party who litigated and lost on an issue in a prior action. Suppose, for example, that Cartier, after losing his suit against La Salle on the ground that the lease provision was unenforceable, sues Cortez, another tenant who had signed the same standard lease. Under nonmutual preclusion principles, Cortez, the new defendant, could estop Cartier from claiming that the disputed provision was enforceable, since Cartier had previously litigated that issue against La Salle and lost.

For many years, this frontier concept remained, if not undiscovered, at least unexplored by most courts. The general rule was that estoppels must be mutual, that is, the only parties who could invoke collateral estoppel were those who were involved in the suit in which the issue was initially decided. This "doctrine of mutuality" allowed La Salle to estop Cartier on the issue of the validity of the lease provision but would not allow Cortez, a stranger to the first suit, to do so. The courts reasoned that La Salle had litigated in the first action; he took the risk that, if he lost on the issue, he would be bound by that finding in subsequent suits, under basic collateral estoppel doctrine, and therefore he—and only he—had earned the right to assert estoppel if he won. But Cortez was not a party to the first action; he took no risk of being bound by an adverse judgment if Cartier proved that the lease provision *was* valid. Consequently, since he would not be bound by an unfavorable finding, the mutuality doctrine barred Cortez from taking advantage of a favorable finding in the La Salle/Cartier suit.

A Fundamental Question

1.   Why is it true, whether or not the mutuality rule applies, that Cortez could not be bound by a finding in the original suit that the lease provision was valid?

Courts that applied the mutuality rule were also influenced by an additional reason in confining estoppel to the original parties. If the litigants know that findings will only affect other suits with the same adversaries, they can usually anticipate the future implications of an adverse decision in the original suit. However, if estoppel is available to new parties, the litigants may be forced to over-litigate issues in the original action for fear of unknown risks of estoppel in future actions involving new parties.

While the mutuality rule has had a respectable history and widespread acceptance, it has been abandoned in many jurisdictions since the landmark case of *Bernhard v. Bank of America National Trust & Savings Assn.*, 122

P.2d 892 (Cal. 1942). In *Bernhard,* Mrs. Bernhard claimed that certain funds held by Cook, the executor of an estate, belonged to the estate. Cook claimed they were a gift to him from the decedent, which he need not include in the assets of the estate. Bernhard challenged Cook's claim in a probate proceeding during the course of the settlement of the estate, and the court held that the funds were a gift to Cook. Bernhard then sued the bank that had been holding the funds and paid them to Cook, alleging again that the funds were assets of the estate that should have been paid to the estate rather than to Cook.

The bank pleaded collateral estoppel, arguing that Bernhard had already adjudicated the right to the funds in the probate proceeding, had lost, and should be precluded from relitigating the issue against the bank.

Who's Who?

2. Why was the bank's invocation of collateral estoppel in *Bernhard* "nonmutual"?

In *Bernhard,* Justice Traynor concluded that it was not categorically improper to allow a new party to take advantage of findings in an earlier suit to estop a party who had litigated the issue in the prior action. Instead of focusing on the "free ride" that the bank received by borrowing the favorable result achieved by Cook in the earlier case, Justice Traynor emphasized the fact that Bernhard, the party *against* whom the estoppel was asserted, had been a party to the first action and had had a full and fair opportunity to litigate the issue there. *Bernhard* at 895. In such circumstances, the court saw no reason to allow her to relitigate the decided issue by simply switching adversaries.

The United States Supreme Court first endorsed the use of nonmutual estoppel in the federal courts in *Blonder-Tongue Laboratories, Inc. v. University of Illinois Foundation,* 402 U.S. 313 (1971). The situation in *Blonder-Tongue* was analogous to *Bernhard.* The University of Illinois Foundation sued one defendant for infringing a patent but lost on the ground that its patent was invalid. It then "switched adversaries," bringing suit against another defendant for infringement of the same patent. The Supreme Court reversed its long-standing rule allowing such relitigation and approved use of nonmutual collateral estoppel against the university on the issue of the validity of the patent. The Court noted the unfairness and waste of judicial resources that flows from allowing "repeated litigation of the same issue as long as the supply of unrelated defendants holds out." *Blonder-Tongue* at 329.

Like the *Bernhard* court, the Court in *Blonder-Tongue* emphasized that preclusion was only appropriate if the precluded party had had a full and fair opportunity to litigate the issue in the first action. *Blonder-Tongue* at 332-334. In addition, the Court emphasized the unique burdens that patent infringement actions impose on the courts. However, the lower federal courts have not construed the Court's holding as limited to patent cases. Subsequent cases have applied nonmutual collateral estoppel in a wide variety of cases, at least when the posture of the parties in the successive actions is similar to that of the parties in *Blonder-Tongue* and *Bernhard*. See generally 18 Wright and Miller at §4464.

Defensive Nonmutual Estoppel

This matter of the posture of the parties introduces a further wrinkle to the nonmutual preclusion problem. In both *Blonder-Tongue* and *Bernhard,* the new party in the second action was a defendant who invoked estoppel to prevent the plaintiff from establishing a fact that the plaintiff had been unable to establish in the first suit. Bernhard, for example, had essentially been a plaintiff in the first probate proceeding, trying to establish the estate's right to the funds held by Cook. In the second action, she was again the plaintiff, attempting to prove the same issue in order to recover from the bank. The bank asserted estoppel "defensively," to prevent her from proving an essential element of her claim. Similarly, in *Blonder-Tongue,* the university foundation had brought the first suit and lost and was also the plaintiff in the second suit. The new defendant asserted defensive nonmutual estoppel to prevent the foundation from establishing the validity of a patent previously held invalid. See *Parklane Hosiery v. Shore,* 439 U.S. 322, 326 n.4 (1979) ("[d]efensive use occurs when a defendant seeks to prevent a plaintiff from asserting a claim the plaintiff has previously litigated and lost against another defendant"). This use of estoppel is "nonmutual" because the party asserting the estoppel on the issue was not a party to the action in which the issue was first litigated. Visually the sequence looks like this:

Suit 1:   P ————————→ D₁   (plaintiff loses on Issue A)

Suit 2:   P ————————→ D₂   (new defendant pleads
collateral estoppel to bar
plaintiff from relitigating
Issue A)

This defensive assertion of nonmutual estoppel is more easily justified than the offensive use of estoppel discussed in *Parklane*. In defensive estoppel cases, the party being estopped was usually the plaintiff in the original suit and chose the forum and the defendant against whom to litigate the issue. When that is true, it hardly seems unfair to bind the plaintiff to the first resolution of the recurring issue.

Offensive Nonmutual Estoppel

By contrast, offensive use of collateral estoppel usually involves a new plaintiff who seeks to borrow a finding from a prior action to impose liability on a party who was a defendant in the prior action. See *Parklane* at 326 n.4 ("offensive use of collateral estoppel occurs when the plaintiff seeks to foreclose the defendant from litigating an issue the defendant has previously litigated unsuccessfully in an action with another party"). For example, suppose that La Salle had brought suit against Cartier to enjoin him from enforcing the disputed provision of the standard lease, and the provision was held invalid. If Cortez now sued Cartier for damages resulting from the invalid provision and invoked collateral estoppel to prevent Cartier from relitigating the validity of the provision, that would be offensive, nonmutual estoppel. The new plaintiff, Cortez, would be taking advantage of the finding against Cartier, a defendant in the prior action, to help establish a claim against Cartier in a new suit.

This is exactly what the plaintiff did in *Parklane*. In the first case to go to judgment, the Securities and Exchange Commission had claimed—and the court had held—that Parklane Hosiery had issued a false and misleading proxy statement. Subsequently, the plaintiffs in a class action suit against Parklane, based on the same proxy statement, invoked collateral estoppel against Parklane on the question of whether the statement was false and misleading. Since Parklane had litigated and lost that issue in the S.E.C. suit, the class plaintiffs argued that it had had its day in court on the issue and should be barred from relitigating it. The plaintiffs' use of estoppel was "offensive," since they sought to use it to establish the defendant's liability in a new action. It was nonmutual, because they were not parties to the action in which the issue was first litigated. The sequence of suits looks like this:

In these offensive nonmutual estoppel situations, there are a number of reasons for the courts to exercise particular caution in deciding whether to apply nonmutual collateral estoppel. For one thing, the party against whom estoppel is asserted in the second action (i.e., Parklane in the *Parklane* case and Cartier in the preceding example) was a defendant in the first suit and did not choose the forum in which the issue was initially decided. While it is possible to say that the losing party in a defensive-use situation gave it his best shot in the original action, this is not so clear in the offensive-use situation, in which the estopped party did not choose the time and place of the first suit or the adversary against whom to try the issue.

The Supreme Court in *Parklane* noted several other risks posed by offensive use of estoppel. *First,* the prospect of taking advantage of another plaintiff's victory to establish crucial issues without trial may lead plaintiff's to "wait and see," that is, to hold back from joining in the first plaintiff's suit. After all, if La Salle lost the first action against Cartier because the lease provision was held valid, Cortez would not be barred from relitigating the issue because he has never litigated it, and no party can be estopped until he (or someone in privity with him) has had his day in court on the issue. But if La Salle wins and the court recognizes nonmutual collateral estoppel, Cortez may be able to establish this crucial issue without trial and the resulting risk of losing on the issue altogether.

Second, the *Parklane* Court recognized that a party might not have litigated the issue aggressively in the first action if the stakes were small or the forum inconvenient. It may be inappropriate to apply estoppel in a second suit if the estopped party did not have the incentive to litigate the issue fully in the first. *Third,* the Court noted that it may not have been possible for the losing party to litigate effectively in the first action if the procedural rules of the court that decided the first case were more restrictive than those of the court hearing the second.[1] *Last,* one or more prior inconsistent judgments on the issue may suggest that it would be unfair to give conclusive effect to any one of them.

In *Parklane* the Supreme Court did not categorically endorse or reject offensive nonmutual collateral estoppel. As modern courts are wont to do, the Court held that lower courts should exercise discretion in deciding whether to allow such offensive assertions of estoppel. The court should consider, on the unique facts of each case, all the factors described above and any other factors that may indicate that the issue was not fully and fairly decided in the first suit. If, considering all the circumstances, the court is con-

---

1. This could be true in a number of ways. For example, the second court's civil procedure rules might allow broader discovery. The rules of evidence might allow crucial evidence that was excluded in the first case. The long-arm statute might authorize personal jurisdiction over defendants who could not be brought into the first case. Or the rules governing the subpoena power might authorize the court to order the appearance of witnesses from a broader area.

vinced that the issue was fully adjudicated in the first action, then it may allow preclusion, including offensive nonmutual estoppel. If, on the other hand, the court is doubtful, for whatever reason, that the party being estopped had a full "bite at the apple" in the first action, it should deny estoppel.[2] See generally Restatement (Second) of Judgments §29 (detailing factors to consider in analyzing nonmutual estoppel).

Although the *Parklane* case goes into more detail than *Blonder-Tongue* concerning the risks of nonmutual collateral estoppel, the two cases are entirely consistent. The Court in *Blonder-Tongue* emphasized that the court in the second action must be convinced that the estopped party had a full opportunity to litigate the issue in the first case. *Parklane* emphasizes the same fundamental prerequisite but spells out in more detail the factors to be considered in making that determination. In fact, most of the cautionary factors discussed in *Parklane* are equally applicable to defensive use situations, such as whether the estopped party had a strong incentive to litigate in the first suit, whether the procedural opportunities to do so were as broad in that action, and whether there are any prior inconsistent judgments. Other factors, however, such as whether the plaintiff should have joined in an earlier action, are unique to offensive estoppel.

Let me end this introduction with a truism. Nonmutual collateral estoppel, whether of the offensive or defensive persuasion, *is* a form of collateral estoppel. As such, it must meet all of the basic prerequisites for application of estoppel discussed in the previous chapter. In every case, mutual or nonmutual, the court must find that the issue is the same, that it was actually litigated and decided in the prior action, and that it was necessary to the judgment in the first action before it can apply estoppel in a second action. However, in nonmutual preclusion situations, the court must consider not only these basic requirements for estoppel but also the additional factors discussed above in order to determine whether it would be fair to preclude relitigation of findings from the prior action in a new suit involving a new party. Remember, too, that while mutuality has been abandoned in the federal courts, some states still apply the doctrine.

---

2. When the Supreme Court takes cases in which to adopt a new principle, they often take ones that present good facts for application of the new principle. *Parklane* is an example. On the facts of the case, all of the factors the court discussed argued for estoppel: There were no prior inconsistent judgments; the procedural opportunities available in the two cases were the same, since both were filed in federal court; and the plaintiffs in the second action could not have joined in the first, since private litigants are not able to join in securities actions brought by the government. See *Parklane* at 332 n.17. Finally, Parklane had every incentive to litigate aggressively in the first suit: Corporations can expect shareholder suits in the wake of a government action for securities violations, and in this case the class action against Parklane was filed *before* the government's suit, though the latter went to judgment first.

In analyzing the following examples, assume that contributory negligence constitutes a complete defense if it is proved. Also, assume that all actions are brought in state court unless otherwise specified.

EXAMPLES

Charting the Terrain

3. Lewis sues Clark for trespassing on his property. Clark denies that Lewis owns the land. The court determines that Lewis owns the land and awards him damages for the trespass.

Subsequently, Lewis sues Fremont for trespass on the same piece of land.
   a. Who would be likely to invoke collateral estoppel in the second action?
   b. Would estoppel be allowed in a mutuality jurisdiction?
   c. Would estoppel be allowed in a jurisdiction that allows nonmutual estoppel?

4. Suppose that Lewis sued Clark for the trespass, and the court found for Clark on the ground that Lewis does not own the land. Subsequently, Lewis sues Fremont for trespassing on the same property.
   a. Who would be likely to invoke collateral estoppel?
   b. Would this be mutual or nonmutual use of collateral estoppel?
   c. Would it be defensive or offensive use of estoppel?
   d. Could the court apply collateral estoppel in the second suit if the suits were brought in a jurisdiction that has abandoned the mutuality doctrine?

5. Earhart brings a negligence action against Lindbergh for serious injuries suffered when a plane Lindbergh was piloting crashed. The jury finds for Earhart and awards her damages. Subsequently, Wright, another passenger in Lindbergh's plane, brings a separate action against Lindbergh for his injuries in the same accident. Wright invokes collateral estoppel to prevent Lindbergh from relitigating the issue of his negligence.
   a. Is this offensive or defensive collateral estoppel?
   b. Is it mutual or nonmutual?
   c. Could the court apply collateral estoppel in the second action if both suits were brought in federal court?

New Frontiers

6. Mr. and Mrs. Byrd sue Da Gama for serious injuries suffered in a collision involving three cars: the Byrds', Da Gama's, and Vespucci's. Da Gama pleads contributory negligence as a defense against Mr. Byrd, who was driving the Byrd car, but not against Mrs. Byrd. (Assume that any contributory negligence by Mr. Byrd would bar his recovery.) The jury returns a verdict

for Da Gama on Mr. Byrd's claim but for Mrs. Byrd on her claim for her own injuries.

Mr. Byrd now sues Vespucci, the third driver involved in the collision, to recover for his injuries. Vespucci pleads contributory negligence.

    a. Who would seek to invoke collateral estoppel in the second action? On what issue?

    b. Would this be offensive or defensive use?

    c. Would it be permissible in a jurisdiction that requires mutuality?

    d. Would it be permissible in a jurisdiction that has abandoned the mutuality doctrine?

7.   In 1981 Carol Burnett brought a libel suit in California against the *National Enquirer*, arising out of a story in the *Enquirer* about her behavior in a Washington restaurant. One of the *Enquirer's* defenses was that it had printed a retraction of the story; under a California statute a newspaper can avoid substantial liability by printing a timely retraction. See Cal. Civ. Code §48(a). A major issue in the case was whether the *Enquirer* was a newspaper, which enjoys the protection of the statute, or a magazine, which would not. The court held that the *Enquirer* was a magazine and thus not entitled to the protection of the retraction statute. Burnett recovered a very substantial verdict.

The *Boston Globe* reported the verdict in a story on March 27, 1981, and went on to state:

> Burnett's case has been watched closely by other celebrities who have sued, or want to sue, the tabloid and other gossip publications over items they consider fiction and harmful to their careers.
>
>   Singer Helen Reddy and her manager-husband Jeff Wald were the most recent to sue the *National Enquirer*, asking $30 million this week for a March 3 article about them.

Boston Globe, March 27, 1981, p.4.

Assume that the *Enquirer* printed a similar retraction of the Reddy/Wald article. After the decision in the Burnett case, Reddy and Wald bring suit against the *Enquirer*, and assert collateral estoppel on the issue of whether the *Enquirer* is a magazine or a newspaper.

    a. Would this be offensive or defensive use of estoppel?

    b. Would this be allowed if both actions were brought in courts that applied the mutuality doctrine?

    c. Would it be allowed if both suits were brought in courts that have abandoned the mutuality approach?

Outer Space

8.   Armstrong sues Ride and Gagarin in federal court for injuries arising out of a three-car auto accident. Each defendant denies negligence and claims that Armstrong was negligent. After trial, the jury finds for Armstrong against Ride but finds Gagarin not liable.

Subsequently, Gagarin sues Ride for his injuries in the accident. Ride pleads contributory negligence (a complete defense). Visually, the two cases look like this:

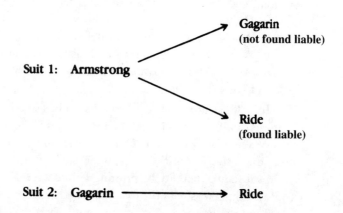

a. Could Gagarin have joined his claim against Ride in the first suit?
b. Who would seek to invoke collateral estoppel in the second action? On what issues?
c. Is this mutual or nonmutual estoppel?
d. Which party would invoke defensive estoppel and which would invoke offensive estoppel?
e. Will the court allow use of estoppel on any issues?

EXPLANATIONS

A Fundamental Question

1. We began this voyage by emphasizing that every litigant is entitled to due process of law before a court adjudicates his rights. See Chapter 1, p. 3. The very essence of due process is an opportunity for the parties to be heard, to litigate the issues before those issues are resolved for or against them. If Cartier won his suit against La Salle and then sued Cortez for violating the same lease provision, Cortez would be a new party who has never had an opportunity to litigate the validity of the provision. It would come as quite a surprise to Cortez to learn that he had effectively lost his action (because the crucial issue was already decided in Cartier's favor) before he had even reached the courthouse, simply because La Salle had previously lost *his* suit. Cortez may well believe that he can litigate the lease question more effectively than La Salle, who may not have had the resources to litigate the issue aggressively or may have made a tactical decision to focus his defense on other grounds. Maybe Cortez won't do better but under the due process

clause every party gets one chance to try, and Cortez has not yet had his "bite at the apple."

Although it would promote efficiency to estop Cortez from relitigating decided issues (just as it promotes efficiency to bar La Salle from doing so under traditional estoppel doctrine), efficiency is only one goal of the procedural system. In this case it is outweighed by the countervailing value of fairness to new parties.

Who's Who?

2.   The *Bernhard* case is an example of nonmutual collateral estoppel because the party seeking to invoke estoppel was not a party to the suit in which the issue was initially decided. That action was between the heirs (including Bernhard) and Cook. Under mutuality doctrine, only these original parties could use or be barred by estoppel in subsequent cases; the bank, a new party, would not be entitled to assert estoppel because it was not a party to the original suit and hence took no risk of being estopped on the issue if it were decided in Bernhard's favor. Since the bank could not be burdened by the result in the original case (see the explanation above for example 1), courts that adhered to the mutuality rule concluded that it should not be able to benefit from the prior decision if Bernhard lost.

Charting the Terrain

3a.   The issue that is common to both actions is whether Lewis owns the land. Lewis won on this issue in the first suit and is therefore the party likely to assert estoppel in the second to establish his ownership of the property.

b.   Lewis will not be allowed to estop Fremont on the ownership issue because Fremont, like Cortez in the earlier example, has never had his day in court on the question of Lewis's title, and no court will estop him from litigating that issue until he has had a full and fair opportunity to do so. Besides, Fremont was not a party to the original action, and the mutuality doctrine confines estoppel to the parties to the original suit or those in privity with the original parties.

c.   It is crucial to understand that estoppel would also be denied on these facts in a nonmutuality jurisdiction. As indicated above, Fremont has never had an opportunity to litigate the issue of Lewis's title to the land; due process entitles Fremont to an opportunity to do so. The abandonment of mutuality has *not* changed this basic tenet of the system. In every nonmutual estoppel situation, the estopped party must have been a party in the first suit and therefore had his chance to litigate the issue. Thus, the crucial question in such cases is the one emphasized in *Bernhard:* whether the party being estopped litigated the issue in the prior action. Because Fremont was not a party in the first suit and did not litigate and lose on the issue, estoppel would not bar him from litigating the issue in the second action.

4a. In this case, Fremont would seek to take advantage of the finding in the prior action that Lewis did not own the land. If Fremont can estop Lewis from trying to prove that he owns the land, Fremont will defeat Lewis's claim, since a plaintiff must prove that he has an interest in the property to recover for trespass.

b. Fremont would be invoking nonmutual collateral estoppel since he was not a party to the prior action. The only parties who could use mutual collateral estoppel are Lewis and Clark, the parties to the first suit. Here estoppel is invoked against a prior party by a stranger to the original action.

c. This would be defensive collateral estoppel since Fremont, the defendant, would invoke estoppel to prevent Lewis, the plaintiff in the first suit, from relitigating the ownership issue that he had previously litigated and lost. Lewis is analogous to the university foundation in *Blonder-Tongue*, which was barred from relitigating the validity of its patent against a second defendant after failing to prove it in a prior action. See the diagram on p.506.

d. In a jurisdiction that has abandoned mutuality, the court would have the authority to apply defensive nonmutual collateral estoppel to bar Lewis from relitigating the ownership issue. Under *Bernhard* and *Blonder-Tongue*, a court may allow the use of defensive estoppel by a new party, so long as the party being estopped was a party to the prior action and litigated the issue there. Those criteria are met here because Lewis was a party to the prior suit against Clark and litigated and lost on the ownership issue in that action.

However, the court would not automatically apply defensive estoppel to bar Lewis from relitigating. As the *Bernhard* court pointed out, and the Supreme Court reiterated in *Blonder-Tongue*, a party who has already litigated an issue should not be estopped from relitigating it unless he had a full and fair opportunity to contest the issue in the first action. Thus, the court will only apply estoppel if it is convinced, after review of the proceedings in the first suit, that Lewis had the incentive and opportunity to litigate the ownership issue tenaciously against Clark.

The burden to establish that the issue was fully litigated falls on Fremont, the party invoking estoppel. Friedenthal, Kane, and Miller at §14.11. Thus, the abandonment of mutuality opens the door to preclusion in situations like this, but the court must exercise caution in deciding who to let in.

5a. This is an example of offensive estoppel. Here, Wright invokes the negligence finding from the first action to *establish* an issue necessary for recovery against Lindbergh, the defendant in both the first and second suits. Wright seeks to use estoppel "as a sword," to establish a fact necessary to recovery, rather than as a "shield" against liability, as in example 4. See the diagram on p.507 supra.

b. Because estoppel is invoked by Wright, a new party who did not litigate the negligence issue in the first action, this is nonmutual estoppel. Of course, Lindbergh *was* a party to the first suit; in every nonmutual estoppel case *one* of the parties in the second suit will have been a party (or in privity with a party) to the first, since estoppel may only be invoked against a party who litigated and lost on the issue before.

c. The Supreme Court held in *Parklane* that the federal courts may apply offensive nonmutual collateral estoppel in situations such as this in which a new plaintiff invokes estoppel to establish an issue that was decided against the defendant in a prior suit. Although Wright, the new party invoking estoppel, was not a party to the original action, the party against whom it was invoked (in this case Lindbergh) was there and litigated the issue in the first suit. Lindbergh has had an opportunity to be heard on the issue, the fundamental prerequisite to barring relitigation.

However, as in the defensive estoppel cases, the court will not automatically bar Lindbergh from relitigating. The court must examine the circumstances of the first case to determine whether Lindbergh had an adequate opportunity to litigate and whether other cautionary factors (such as whether Wright sat out the first suit to see how Earhart would fare) counsel against application of estoppel.

In this case, several of these factors favor application of estoppel. *First,* since Earhart's injuries were serious, Lindbergh presumably had a strong incentive to defend her action vigorously to avoid paying substantial damages. In addition, Wright was a passenger in the same plane; surely Lindbergh would foresee that he would sue as well. *Second,* the example indicates that both suits were brought in federal court. Thus, there are not likely to be procedural advantages available to Lindbergh in the second suit that were not available in the first; both will governed by the Federal Rules of Civil Procedure. Absent other factors suggesting unfairness to Lindbergh, this case looks like a good candidate for application of nonmutual offensive collateral estoppel.[3]

New Frontiers

6a. The first step in analyzing this case, as in every collateral estoppel case, mutual or otherwise, is to determine what issues were decided in the first action that may recur in the second. In this case the verdict for Mrs. Byrd indicates that the jury found Da Gama negligent. However, their verdict for Da Gama against Mr. Byrd indicates that they also found Mr. Byrd contributorily negligent.[4] It is this finding that is relevant to the second action: If Vespucci pleads contributory negligence as a defense to Mr. Byrd's suit and is able to invoke collateral estoppel to establish it, he will escape liability regardless of his own negligence.

---

3. The four factors discussed in *Parklane* are not exclusive. Other factors may also counsel against giving the prior determination preclusive effect. See Restatement (Second) of Judgments §29.

4. This assumes that the evidence of Mr. Byrd's injuries eliminates the possibility that the jury found that he had suffered no damages. Compare *Illinois Central Gulf R.R. Co. v. Parks,* 390 N.E.2d 1078 (Ind. App. 1979).

b. This example looks partly like offensive estoppel and partly like defensive estoppel. It is like defensive use because the defendant in the second action invokes estoppel to preclude Byrd, a plaintiff in both the first and second suits, from relitigating an issue that he litigated and lost upon in the prior suit.

However, the case is like offensive use in that Vespucci uses estoppel to establish a fact—in this case, the *affirmative defense* of Byrd's negligence—that Byrd lost on in the first case. In cases such as *Blonder-Tongue*, the plaintiff lost on an issue that was an element of his prima facie case and was precluded in a later action from proving that element. In this case, Vespucci is not trying to use estoppel to prevent Byrd from proving an element of his case; he is using it to establish a defense against the claim based on Byrd's contributory negligence. In one sense he uses it as a "sword" to establish a fact, Byrd's negligence. In another, he uses it as a "shield," to prevent Byrd from proving that he is liable by borrowing the finding from an earlier suit in which Byrd lost on the same issue. Thus, it is a hybrid case, not quite like the classic defensive or offensive situation. Most courts would probably call this defensive estoppel, based on the fact that the party invoking estoppel is a defendant, as in *Bernhard* and *Blonder-Tongue*, and that the defendant invokes estoppel to avoid liability.[5]

c. Vespucci would not be able to assert collateral estoppel in a mutuality jurisdiction since he was not a party to the first suit and therefore was not allowed to take advantage of favorable findings in that action.

d. A court in a nonmutuality jurisdiction could allow Vespucci to invoke collateral estoppel even though he was not a party to the Byrd/Da Gama suit in which Byrd's negligence was initially established. As in all nonmutual estoppel cases, however, estoppel would be discretionary. The court will only apply estoppel if it is convinced that Byrd had a full opportunity and incentive to litigate the issue of his negligence in the first action.

7a. The *Enquirer* was the defendant in the first action, and lost on the issue of whether it is a newspaper within the meaning of the California statute. In the second action, two new plaintiffs try to use the finding from the first case to help establish their case against the *Enquirer*, a defendant in each suit. Based on the configuration of the parties, this would likely be classified as offensive collateral estoppel.

Just as example 6 represents a twist on the typical defensive estoppel case, this is not quite the classic example of offensive nonmutual estoppel. Here the new plaintiff asserts estoppel to preclude the defendant from proving a defense that failed in the first action. In the more typical offensive use situation, the plaintiff asserts collateral estoppel to establish an element of his prima facie case (such as the defendant's negligence) after another plaintiff proved that element against the same defendant in a prior action.

---

5. This is not entirely a matter of semantics. The characterization can make a difference, since some courts are more receptive to defensive nonmutual estoppel than to offensive nonmutual estoppel.

In *Parklane,* for example, the plaintiffs in the second suit had to prove that the proxy statement was false and misleading in order to recover. They sought to do so by borrowing the court's finding to that effect in the earlier action.

b. Estoppel would be denied in a mutuality jurisdiction since Reddy and Wald were not parties to the prior action or in privity with the plaintiff in that action.

c. The answer to this example is a cautious "maybe." The analysis must start with the truism at the end of the Introduction. Nonmutual estoppel is a species of collateral estoppel; as such, it is only applicable if the basic prerequisites for estoppel are satisfied. Before collateral estoppel can ever be applied, the court must determine that the issue in the first and second actions is the same. Here, it is clear that the issue of the *Enquirer's* status as a magazine or newspaper under the California statute was litigated and decided in the first action. But obviously, estoppel will only apply if the issue in the Reddy/Wald suit is the same, that is, if the California statute applies. If Reddy and Wald reside in Virginia and suffered most of their damages there, a court might not apply the California statute to their suit at all; it might apply Virginia law, which might authorize magazines as well as newspapers to escape liability by printing a retraction or not allow the retraction defense at all. Thus, the issue may be different in the second suit or irrelevant to it.

Assuming that the California statute would apply in the Reddy/Wald suit, the court would still have to consider the various factors that may make offensive nonmutual estoppel inappropriate. Although it certainly appears that the *Enquirer* had a strong incentive to litigate the issue in the Burnett case, it might not be fair to apply estoppel if the procedural system in which the second suit was brought was more flexible, or if important witnesses were unavailable to the *Enquirer* in the first case but can be produced in the second. Or the court could deny preclusion if it determined that Reddy and Wald had deliberately decided *not* to join in the Burnett case in order to get the advantage of nonmutual estoppel without taking the risk of losing on the issue in the first action. (This would not be a problem on the facts here because the incident involving Reddy and Wald took place long after the Burnett case was filed.) Once again, the point is that the abandonment of mutuality opens the door to case-by-case consideration of whether estoppel should be available to the new party; it does not automatically lead to preclusion.

Outer Space

8a. Gagarin could have cross-claimed against Ride for his injuries in the first action, under Fed. R. Civ. P. 13(g), but was not required to do so, since Rule 13(g) is permissive. Thus, he may bring the claim separately. Res judicata does not bar the separate suit because Gagarin's claim against Ride was never adjudicated in the first suit; he never asserted a right to relief against her. See Chapter 25, example 7.

b. The verdicts in the first action indicate that the jury found Ride negligent, but not Gagarin or Armstrong. If Armstrong was negligent, he would have lost against Ride. If Gagarin was negligent, he would have been held liable along with Ride. In the second action, Gagarin would assert collateral estoppel to estop Ride from relitigating both her own negligence and Gagarin's.

c. This could be either mutual or nonmutual estoppel, depending on what Ride and Gagarin actually attempted to prove in the first action. Although they were both parties to the prior suit, they were not adversaries, and neither had to try to prove the other's negligence. Ride, for example, may have defended by trying to show that she acted with due care and that Armstrong's negligence caused the accident. If that is true, then she has not litigated the issue of Gagarin's negligence. Similarly, Gagarin may have simply tried to show that he was careful and Armstrong was not. If that is true, then he has not litigated the question of Ride's negligence. On these assumptions, use of estoppel in the second action would be nonmutual, since (while Ride and Gagarin were both parties to the first suit) neither has litigated the other's negligence. Consequently, they would not be able to assert preclusion against each other in a mutuality jurisdiction. The key to "mutuality" is not just having been a party to a prior suit but actually having litigated issues against one another.

Suppose, however, that Ride and Gagarin had each defended against Armstrong by trying to show that the other was negligent. Then they *would* have litigated each other's negligence in the prior suit, even though they did not assert claims for relief against each other. On this assumption, they would each be bound by the decision on those issues, even in a mutuality jurisdiction.

d. Gagarin's assertion of estoppel on the issue of Ride's negligence is an offensive use of estoppel: He invokes estoppel as a "sword" to establish Ride's negligence, a fact necessary to impose liability on Ride, which was established in the prior action. Assuming that Gagarin had not tried to prove Ride's negligence in the prior action, this would be nonmutual offensive collateral estoppel since he would be seeking to establish Ride's negligence on the basis of the fact that Armstrong had proved it in the first case.

Gagarin might also invoke defensive estoppel to defeat Ride's contributory negligence defense. That is, he would claim that since he was found free of negligence in the first action, estoppel should bar relitigation of the issue. Assuming again that Gagarin and Ride did not try to prove each other negligent in the first suit, this would be nonmutual estoppel. Gagarin would be trying to estop Ride from proving his negligence because Armstrong (the plaintiff in the prior action) had failed to prove it.

e. First, let's consider Gagarin's use of defensive estoppel against Ride. If Ride and Gagarin did not attempt to prove each other's negligence in the prior action, the court will not allow Gagarin to estop Ride from relitigating Gagarin's negligence. Ride was under no duty to litigate Gagarin's negligence to defend the first suit, and she chose not to do so. Although they were both parties to the suit, they were not adversaries and were not required under the procedural rules to assert claims against each other. Although Armstrong was unable to prove Gagarin's negligence, Ride will be entitled to her opportunity to do so unless it is clear from the record of the first action that she tried to in that suit.

The situation is different as to Gagarin's use of offensive estoppel on the issue of Ride's negligence. Ride did fully litigate that question in the prior action and lost. Gagarin now seeks to use offensive estoppel to establish Ride's negligence in his own action for damages. The court will have to review the proceedings in the first action to determine whether it would be appropriate, under the *Parklane* analysis, to apply collateral estoppel based on it.

Ride will no doubt argue that Gagarin decided to "wait and see" whether Ride was found negligent in the first action, in hopes of using offensive collateral estoppel in the second. See *Parklane* at 330. Gagarin could have asserted his claim for damages as a cross-claim in the prior action and the court would have had supplemental jurisdiction over it. See Chapter 15, example 3. Although he had the right to withhold the claim in the first action, since cross-claims under Fed. R. Civ. P. 13(g) are permissive, the court (Ride will argue) should deny him the further benefit of offensive collateral estoppel since he chose this less efficient course.

Few cases address whether a party will be barred from using offensive collateral estoppel because he failed to assert a claim in a prior action. This seems like a particularly strong case for denying estoppel, since Gagarin was already in the suit and the negligence issues were already being litigated against another party. See Restatement (Second) of Judgments, §29(3) (ability to join claim in prior suit supports denial of nonmutual estoppel). However, refusing to apply estoppel in this case, in order to deprive Gagarin of the benefit of holding back his claim, also burdens the court system with additional litigation on an issue already resolved. If all the other prudential factors favor preclusion, it seems doubtful that the court will refuse to apply it simply because Gagarin exercised his right under the rules to bring his own action against Ride. See, however, *Nanninga v. Three Rivers Electric Co-op.*, 203 F.3d 529 (8th Cir. 2000) (relying on *Parklane* in refusing to allow party who could have joined prior action to assert offensive nonmutual collateral estoppel).

PART SIX

Thinking Procedurally: The Rules in Action

28

An Introduction to the Pretrial Litigation Process: Setting the Stage for the Schulansky Case

The first five parts of this book have dealt with the "substance" of civil procedure, that is, the various judicial rules and doctrines that govern the litigation process. The chapters that follow are intended to give you a sense of how the process actually works by chronicling the early stages of a typical (though hypothetical) civil case, *Schulansky v. Ronan*. Each chapter includes the court papers filed at one stage of the *Schulansky* suit, including typical pleadings, motions, and supporting documents. In addition, the materials provide a look at the legal and tactical questions that the attorneys considered in drafting those documents. This chapter is intended to help you to place the ones that follow in context, by providing a brief description of the process of litigating a civil suit, from the beginning up until trial.

Preparation for Filing Suit

In most cases the litigation process begins well before the parties get to court. Obviously, the first step is for the client to bring a dispute to a lawyer.

The plaintiff's lawyer will obtain as much information as possible from the client. On the basis of this information, some investigation, and her assessment of the client, the lawyer must make a judgment as to whether to take the case. If she does agree to take it, she will propose a fee arrangement, and if the client accepts, a contract for services will be signed. In personal injury actions the agreement will frequently provide for a contingent fee, that is, an attorney's fee based on a percentage of any eventual recovery, frequently set at one-third of the amount recovered. The expenses of the action, such as deposition costs, expert witness fees, and other out-of-pocket expenditures, will also be paid out of the recovery.

Once the plaintiff's lawyer has agreed to handle the case, she will conduct a preliminary investigation of the events giving rise to the claim. She will obtain as much information as possible from her client and from other witnesses who are willing to discuss the case. She will gather and review documentary evidence, such as accident reports, correspondence, business records, government reports, or other available materials. She will also do preliminary legal research if the case involves novel theories of recovery or other critical issues of law, in order to ascertain whether her client's injuries give rise to a right to relief.

On the basis of this preliminary development of the case, the plaintiff's attorney will usually send a claim letter to the defendant or her insurer, or discuss the claim with the defendant's counsel in order to explore the possibility of settling the claim without bringing suit. Many claims can be settled without the expense of litigation, particularly if there is little question as to liability and the only issue is the extent of the plaintiff's damages. However, in other cases the settlement value of a claim will depend on facts that have not yet been fully explored at this early stage. In the *Schulansky* case, for example, the defendant's judgment of the settlement value of the claim will turn in part on the parties' testimony as to their negotiations before the construction work began. The plaintiff's testimony as to those negotiations will only be available to the defendant through court-supervised "discovery" in the course of litigation. In such cases the parties will be less likely to reach an agreement until suit is brought and the facts are more fully developed.

The plaintiff's attorney must also consider a number of tactical issues in deciding whether to file suit. She must consider whether the case is strong enough and the value of a potential judgment high enough to justify the considerable expense of litigation. She must assess whether the client is patient enough and financially solvent enough to await a judgment several years down the road. She must consider possible alternative means of obtaining a remedy, such as invoking the assistance of a public agency, seeking an administrative remedy, or agreeing to mediation or arbitration.

Drafting the Complaint

Assuming that informal settlement efforts fail, and the plaintiff's attorney concludes that it makes sense to file suit on the claim, she will begin the lawsuit by filing a complaint, the first "pleading" required under the Federal Rules (and many similar state rules). Pleadings are the papers filed by the parties at the beginning of the action, in which they set forth their positions as to the facts in issue. Pleadings are not evidence; they are not even sworn testimony by the parties or their attorneys. They are simply statements of the parties' positions on the factual and legal issues in dispute.

In the simplest two-party suit the only pleadings required will be a complaint, in which the plaintiff sets forth her claim, and an answer, in which the defendant responds by stating her position as to each of the allegations in the complaint and asserting any other defenses she may have to the plaintiff's claim. See the plaintiff's complaint in the *Schulansky* case, infra p. 538, and Ronan's answer, infra p. 568. But further pleadings may be necessary if additional parties are brought into the suit or if counterclaims are asserted. See, e.g., Chapter 32, which includes a third-party complaint; see also Fed. R. Civ. P. 7(a), which describes the various pleadings that may be filed in appropriate circumstances.

Both the form and the content of the complaint are governed by the rules of procedure applicable in the court where the suit is filed. Because the *Schulansky* case was filed in the Massachusetts Superior Court, it must comply with the Massachusetts Rules of Civil Procedure, which are quite similar to the Federal Rules. Chapter 29 illustrates in detail how the complaint was drafted to comply with those rules. In addition, most courts have local rules of procedure that supplement the general civil rules. For example, the Massachusetts Superior Court has its own supplementary rules that cover numerous details of practice before that court. Thus, all applicable local rules must be checked in order to comply with any additional requirements.

In drafting the complaint, counsel must also consider whether the procedural rules allow joinder of all the desired parties as plaintiffs or defendants. (The joinder rules are analyzed in Chapters 13-16.) The substantive law governing the plaintiff's claims must also be analyzed to ascertain whether there is good ground to file suit on the claims asserted in the complaint. A large part of the attorneys' memos in the following chapters is devoted to considering whether the law of contracts and negligence will support the claims for relief in the *Schulansky* case, and, if so, how those claims should be asserted in the pleadings.

Tactical Considerations in Choosing the Forum

The plaintiff's counsel faces a number of "real world" tactical issues in deciding where to bring a lawsuit. To begin with, she must choose a court that has subject matter jurisdiction, personal jurisdiction over the defendant, and satisfies the applicable rules of venue. See Part One for a detailed analysis of those requirements. It may not always be clear from the facts whether jurisdiction and venue are proper in a particular court. (In *Schulansky,* for example, there is some doubt as to whether the Massachusetts court has personal jurisdiction over the defendants.) If so, the attorney will have to make a judgment as to whether the advantages of litigating in her chosen forum are outweighed by the risk that the suit will be dismissed on one of these grounds, causing additional expense to the client and possible statute of limitations problems.

The plaintiff's counsel must also decide whether to file suit in federal or state court, assuming, as will frequently be the case, that jurisdiction and venue are satisfied in both. Numerous factors may be important in making that choice. For example, the scope of pretrial discovery may be broader in federal court. Federal courts also have broader power to tranfer cases than do state courts. On the other hand, the scope of interlocutory review may be broader in state court than federal court. (See Chapter 3, example 9, concerning interlocutory appeal of decisions on motions to dismiss for lack of personal jurisdiction.) The right to join additional parties may differ, as may the court's power to exercise personal jurisdiction over them.

Differences involving the trial process itself may also be important in a case. For example, the rules of evidence in the state and federal courts may differ in crucial respects. The power of the court to subpoena witnesses will differ. The ethnic and economic characteristics of the jury will differ because a federal court jury will be drawn from a broader geographical area. The judges in one system may be more familiar with the type of case in suit. It may be possible to get to trial a good deal more quickly in one system than another (or in one state than another).

Convenience may also play an important role in the decision. The plaintiff's lawyer may be more familiar with practice in one system. One court may be more conveniently located for the plaintiff (or her attorney) or more inconvenient for the defendant (or her attorney). Attorney Slater's initial memo in the *Schulansky* case does not reveal all of the factors she considered in deciding to go to state court, but proximity to her client's home and her own office was undoubtedly an important one in such a relatively small case. Innumerable other such factors may also be significant in a particular case.[1]

Filing the Complaint

In view of all these considerations, the attorney will draft the complaint, file it with the clerk of the appropriate court, and serve it on the defendant. (As

---

1. For a more detailed discussion of the tactical reasons for choosing state or federal court, see S. Steinglass, The Emerging State Court §1983 Action: A Procedural Review, 38 U. Miami L. Rev. 381, 412-424 (1984).

to the proper methods of service, see Chapter 17.) If the defendant is already represented by counsel, the plaintiff's lawyer may as a matter of courtesy call the defendant's lawyer to let her know that suit is being filed. In turn, the defendant's counsel may agree to accept service of the complaint and summons without compliance with the formal service rules. (As Chapter 18 indicates, the defendant may waive any objection to the manner of service by failing to object to it.)

It is only upon the filing of the complaint that the court gets involved in the case. At least initially, its involvement will be minimal. The clerk will assign a docket number to the case and establish a case file. All subsequent pleadings and other papers filed in the case will be "docketed," that is, entered on a docket sheet kept with the case file, and added to the file. (Not surprisingly, case dockets are increasingly computerized, and courts are experimenting with electronic access to court dockets and other records.) In federal courts, the case will usually be assigned to a judge when the complaint is filed; that judge will then preside over the case for the duration.

In some state courts, however, the case is not permanently assigned; different proceedings will be heard by different judges depending on which judge is "sitting" at the time a motion comes up for hearing or when the case is reached on the trial list. For example, if the *Schulansky* case had remained in Massachusetts state court, the motion to dismiss might have been heard by Judge A, but the motion for summary judgment by Judge B. Judge B would have no previous knowledge of the case but would have to review the pleadings and other papers before or during the hearing to familiarize herself with the suit. When the case reached trial, it might be tried before Judge C, who was assigned to the civil jury session at the time the case was reached on the trial list. By contrast, in federal court the same judge would preside over the suit from the outset and would develop a "feel" for the case through hearings on motions, discovery conferences, and other pretrial proceedings. As Chapter 34 indicates (see infra p. 613), knowing which judge will preside over the case can have an important effect on the attorneys' tactical decisions.

Responding to the Complaint

Once the defendant or her counsel receives the complaint, she must respond. In most cases, the defendant will answer the complaint. If the defendant has certain preliminary objections to the suit, however, she may move to dismiss instead. See the motion to dismiss for lack of personal jurisdiction filed by Jones, the third-party defendant in the *Schulansky* case, infra p. 597. Chapter 18 reviews in detail the circumstances in which a motion to dismiss may be filed instead of an answer.

It is important to understand the difference between a pleading and a motion. A motion is not a pleading. See Fed. R. Civ. P. 7(a) and (b), which provide separately for pleadings and motions. The pleadings set forth the positions of the parties on the claim. A motion, by contrast, is a direct application to the court for an order. Whenever a party seeks action from the court, a motion is the appropriate way to do so. For example, a defendant's motion to dismiss for lack of personal jurisdiction is a direct request to the court to dismiss the case.

Although many types of motions are specifically provided for in the Rules (see, e.g., Fed. R. Civ. P. 12(b), (e); 56), the motion is a flexible device for seeking any type of action from the court. Other common examples are motions for further discovery, motions to place a case on the trial list, to convene a discovery conference, to implead a third party, to amend the complaint or answer, to extend the time to answer, or for any other assistance in the litigation process. (One well-known pro se litigant in Massachusetts is rumored to have filed a "Motion for a Landmark Decision"!)

If the defendant answers the complaint instead of moving to dismiss, her answer must set forth her position on the allegations in the complaint. As Chapter 29 demonstrates, the Federal Rules of Civil Procedure require the plaintiff in federal suits to set forth her allegations in numbered paragraphs. The defendant's answer must respond to each allegation, paragraph by paragraph. The defendant may also assert affirmative defenses or counterclaims in the answer, as Ronan has done. The answer must be filed with the court and served on the plaintiff. The rules require the answer or motion to dismiss to be filed within 20 days, but extensions of time to answer are frequently granted, often with the consent of the opposing party.

Discovery

Once the pleadings are complete, the case will move into the *discovery phase*. Discovery is the process by which the parties obtain information from each other and outside witnesses through several commonsense devices authorized by the rules of procedure. In the federal courts, four primary discovery devices are used to develop factual evidence in preparation for trial. *Interrogatories,* authorized by Fed. R. Civ. P. 33, are written questions sent by one party to another, which must be answered under oath. *Requests for production of documents,* under Fed. R. Civ. P. 34, are requests from a party for an opposing party to produce documents that may be relevant to the issues in suit, for inspection or copying by the requesting party. The third basic discovery tool is the *oral deposition,* authorized by Fed. R. Civ. P. 30. A deposition is a procedure for taking oral testimony from a witness. Fourth, the federal discovery rules require parties to make automatic disclosure of certain information regarding the case. See generally Chapter 19 on these tools of discovery.

Usually counsel will take the depositions of crucial witnesses for the other party, in order to prepare for trial and to get the witness's testimony "on the record." The deposition is taken before a licensed court reporter, usually at the office of one of the parties' attorneys. The witness testifies under oath and may be represented by counsel. Counsel for opposing parties are entitled to cross-examine but usually do not do so extensively. Chapter 34 contains an excerpt from the plaintiff's deposition in the *Schulansky* case.

Many cases involve complex technical issues, sophisticated reconstruction of accidents, complex statistical or economic projections, or specialized knowledge of medical procedures. In such cases, a crucial aspect of trial preparation is the hiring and preparation of expert witnesses. Both sides will retain, often at considerable expense, recognized experts in the relevant discipline to testify on issues like causation, proper technique for industrial or medical procedures, accident reconstruction, or probable future damages. Both sides will seek discovery of the other side's experts. Much time will also be spent educating their own experts about the case, conducting experiments or calculations, and preparing them for direct and cross-examination.

Despite the emphasis in this book on procedural rules and doctrines, the most crucial phase of a lawsuit is the development of the evidence through the discovery process and investigation by the attorneys. Most cases are won, lost, or settled on the basis of the strength of the facts, and it is through discovery that the facts and the credibility of the crucial witnesses can be evaluated. Typically, the discovery phase will take at least a year in a reasonably substantial case, but it may take considerably longer.

Attorney Cooperation in the Discovery Process

Throughout this period, it is the attorneys who conduct the litigation by using the discovery tools provided in the rules, reponding to discovery requests from the other side, and developing the evidence to support their cases at trial. In many cases judicial involvement may be minimal right down to the time of trial. The attorneys carry the laboring oar by filing their pleadings, sending and responding to requests for discovery, scheduling and conducting depositions, meeting to discuss settlement, and, where possible, agreeing to stipulations of the undisputed facts to shorten the trial.

Because discovery is conducted primarily by the attorneys, it is important for opposing counsel to cooperate in the discovery process. The formality of the civil procedure rules and the adversary nature of litigation practice frequently lead beginning attorneys to conclude that they are not serving their clients unless they resist every request of opposing counsel. In the long run, however, unrestrained belligerence is counter-productive. It is entirely feasible for counsel to work together to facilitate moving a case to trial without in any way compromising their clients' substantive rights.

For example, many questions will arise during the pleading and discovery phases of the suit that can be resolved by agreements of counsel.

Extensions of time to file pleadings can be agreed to, saving the need to argue a contested motion for an extension. Stipulations of agreed facts can be drawn up to obviate the need to prove those facts at trial. Disagreements as to the scope or timing of discovery, claims of attorney-client privilege, or limits imposed by a preliminary injunction may often be worked out by counsel instead of taking court time. In addition, scheduling of depositions and hearings on pretrial motions can be arranged with opposing counsel. In these and other ways, the process will run much more smoothly (and inexpensively) for all concerned if the attorneys cooperate.

The Changing Judicial Role in Litigation

Under the traditional model (still followed to a degree in many state courts) the court itself plays a largely passive role in litigation. The parties file the pleadings, conduct discovery, initiate settlement discussions, and seek a trial when ready. Under this system, there is no active, periodic judicial review of pending cases. For example, a judge will not review complaints as they are filed to determine whether the court has personal jurisdiction over the defendant or the complaint states a claim upon which relief can be granted. It is up to the attorneys to raise such questions by filing an appropriate motion. The court is simply there as a referee to respond to motions by the parties if the pleading or discovery process goes awry and to supply a judge to preside over the trial when and if a trial is necessary. If the attorneys choose to litigate at a leisurely pace, the court under this model does little to force them to trial.

However, the litigation process is moving away from this "hands off" model as the volume of litigation increasingly strains court resources. Particularly in the federal courts, judges are taking an activist role in managing cases by monitoring the discovery and disclosure process, limiting the issues in pretrial conferences, and setting deadlines for discovery and trial. For example, the court in federal cases is now required to enter a scheduling order in many cases, setting deadlines for the joinder of additional parties, amendment of pleadings, and completion of discovery. See Fed. R. Civ. P. 16(b). The court may also schedule discovery conferences with the attorneys to monitor the progress of discovery, to narrow the issues, and to encourage settlement discussions. See Fed. R. Civ. P. 16(a), (c).

Moving Towards Trial

As discussed in Chapter 19, lawsuits may be cut short by pretrial dismissal or summary judgment. However, most cases survive these hurdles and, if not settled during the discovery phase, continue on track toward the culmination of the litigation process: a trial on the merits. As the discovery process nears completion, the court will usually hold a pretrial conference to resolve pending motions, address evidentiary issues, encourage stipulations as to undisputed facts, determine the issues and witnesses for trial, explore the possibility of settlement, and set a final schedule for trial. See Fed. R. Civ. P. 16. In some systems, trials may be fairly prompt, but in others the court's caseload forces long delays before the case is reached on the trial list. Such delays may lead counsel to agree to various alternative dispute resolution mechanisms—such as mediation, arbitration, or a summary trial—to try to resolve the case without waiting for a formal trial. If the parties persevere, they will eventually get a trial, but it is almost impossible in many systems to predict or control exactly when that will be.

Most cases, even if they are actively litigated through the discovery phase and are set down for trial, are never tried. More than 90 percent of all civil actions are ultimately settled, many on the eve of trial. However, the considerable effort that goes into discovery and pretrial preparation in such cases is not wasted. It is the intensive development of the facts and the parties' increasingly sophisticated understanding of the strengths and weaknesses of their positions that make an equitable settlement possible. As trial approaches, settlement discussions become more focused, and the parties usually begin to move toward an acceptable middle ground. In addition, the incentive to settle increases markedly as trial becomes an impending reality rather than a distant possibility.

The Attorney's Experience of Litigation

All of this is very well, but it still gives little impression of what the experience of litigation is like for the lawyers who conduct it. In practice, litigation is episodic. A lawyer may have anywhere from 20 to 50 or more active cases at a time, at various stages from pre-filing investigation to post-trial motions. At any given time, there will not be much happening in many of those cases: The lawyer might be awaiting responses to discovery requests in one, awaiting judicial action on a motion to dismiss in another, discussing responses to interrogatories with her client in another, drafting an answer in another, awaiting a trial date in another, conducting settlement negotiations, and so on.

Much of the average litigator's time is spent in detailed factual investigation: reviewing depositions and documents produced under discovery requests, interviewing witnesses, meeting with clients or experts, tracking down other sources of proof, and preparing and organizing testimony for trial. The work requires a painstaking attention to detail; a good memory and a methodical approach to trial preparation helps. In addition, a good deal of time is spent drafting pleadings and motions, supporting affidavits, and other materials. There is frequently legal research to be done (especially by junior attorneys in the office) and memoranda to be written in support of or in opposition to pending motions.

A litigator's cases have a way of "acting up" unexpectedly. The morning mail may bring a motion for summary judgment in a case that has been sitting on the back burner, a motion for sanctions in a case based on an allegedly inadequate response to a request for production of documents, notice of a deposition of an important witness, or an order from the court to appear for a pretrial conference. The phone rings a lot, often with calls from opposing counsel or a frantic client. Often these litigation events require a prompt response — a memorandum in opposition to a motion, an appearance in court to argue a motion, a conference with a client to draw up answers to interrogatories, or preparation for and attendance at a deposition.

Thus, a litigator is constantly juggling a number of cases, trying to keep all the balls in the air at once. The unexpected happens frequently, and a constant procession of deadlines beckons. Periodically, the process is punctuated by trials, which usually involve intensive periods of long hours and single-minded attention to one case (with consequent reshuffling of commitments in other cases). However, for most litigators, trials are infrequent; litigation practice resembles continuously preparing for exams, most of which are then called off at the last minute. Some lawyers find it exhilarating; others, simply nerve-wracking. Few find it dull.

29

First Moves: Schulansky Goes to Court

The Drafting Request

MEMORANDUM

TO: David E. Howard
             Associate

FROM: Phyllis Slater

RE: Schulansky construction dispute
             Our file No. 99-1248

DATE: November 20, 1999

- -

Deborah Schulansky, a client of ours, has consulted me concerning a dispute that has arisen between her and a contractor who recently built an addition to her vacation home. It appears that this problem cannot be resolved without filing suit. I would like you to help me with the case.

Although Schulansky lives here in Plymouth, Massachusetts, she also owns an antique colonial home in Alton, New Hampshire, which she uses as a vacation home. The house dates from 1782 and is listed in the National Register of Historic Places. Last spring, Ms. Schulansky met Richard Ronan, a New Hampshire contractor, while he was restoring a house in Plymouth. After some negotiations at her home in Plymouth, the parties agreed that

Ronan would build an addition on the back of the Alton house. Ronan mailed a "Proposal and Estimate" to Schulansky in Plymouth, and she signed and returned it. I have attached a copy of the Proposal and Estimate for the job, signed by both parties. [See p. 542—ED.]

The work involved taking out part of the back wall of the house and building an 18' × 25' addition behind the living room, with a full cellar under the addition. The contractor was to excavate the earth from the original foundation, excavate the adjacent area to be occupied by the addition, lay a cellar floor and foundation walls in the excavated area to support the addition, and build the addition above the new cellar area. In order to provide access to the new cellar, the contractor was to break a doorway through the original foundation of the main house adjacent to the addition.

There were problems from the beginning of the construction work. Ronan hired a backhoe operator named Jones to do the excavation work, as he had told Schulansky he would. When Jones excavated the earth from the original foundation with his backhoe, he discovered that the lower part of the foundation was simply loose rubble. Evidently, in colonial days it was fairly common to simply pile large rocks around the perimeter of the house site and build brick and mortar foundations on top of the rocks. These rubble foundations apparently last remarkably well as long as they are undisturbed, but are less stable if exposed, as was necessary here to construct the cellar for the new addition.

Apparently, there was some discussion during the negotiations about possible problems with the old foundation. Schulansky asked Ronan if he anticipated any problems due to disturbance of the foundation. He responded that he doubted that it would be a problem, but if anything was loose he would do whatever was needed to provide adequate support for the addition. When Schulansky visited the site during construction and observed the excavation, she became concerned about the stability of the original foundation. For one thing, she could see that the foundation was just loose rubble, with no mortar or other support except the surrounding earth. For another, the backhoe had repeatedly ploughed into the old foundation in the course of excavating the new cellar, and loose rocks from the foundation were lying in the ditch next to the foundation. Schulansky asked Ronan several times if the old foundation was adequate and asked him to reinforce or rebuild it. Ronan refused to do any major reconstruction, on the ground that he had not agreed to do so and that it was unnecessary. Instead, he simply poured some cement in between the rocks and left it at that.

In May, when the job was virtually complete, Schulansky began to notice cracks in the plaster walls of the living room, in the bedroom above it, and in the addition itself. She also observed some sagging in the floor at the joint between the main house and the addition. She had a friend who is a structural engineer come and look at the house. He concluded that the cracks resulted from settling of the old foundation, evidently due to shifting of the rubble after exposure during the excavation. He is unsure whether the settling resulted from negligent excavation (that is, the rubble being disturbed by the backhoe), or from the removal of the supporting earth on the outside of the old foundation.

In either case, his opinion is that the settling will continue, causing major structural damage, unless the foundation is rebuilt. Because the addition is now completed, that reconstruction will be substantially more expensive than it would have been if it had been done during construction of the addition. He estimates that it could cost as much as $25,000 to jack up the house and reconstruct the foundation, and another $60,000 to repair the damage to the house due to the settlement of the foundation.

Schulansky has tried to work this out with Ronan, but he denies any responsibility. Consequently, she refused to make the final payment under the contract. I have talked to Ronan myself, and written him a demand letter, but it is clear that he will refuse to provide any satisfaction to our client. Instead, he has threatened to file suit himself if Schulansky does not pay him the last progress payment under the contract.

I intend to initiate suit against Ronan personally and against Ronan Construction Company for breach of contract and negligence. Although we could probably bring suit in federal court on the basis of diversity (Ronan lives in Nashua, Ronan Construction is incorporated in New Hampshire, and its principal place of business is probably in New Hampshire), I would prefer to litigate here in Plymouth Superior Court.

I realize that we may have a claim against Jones as well. At the moment, however, I am not even sure of Jones's full name, much less where he lives, whether he is insured, and whether he is subject to personal jurisdiction here. We will have to learn more about Jones through discovery and amend to add him if necessary. But I have some hope that this can be settled quickly without the expense of lengthy, multi-party litigation.

Please draft a complaint and summons to initiate this suit in the Superior Court for Plymouth County. If you need further information, talk to me or call Ms. Schulansky directly. As you know, Rules 8-11 of the Massachusetts Rules of Civil Procedure are similar to Rules 8-11 of the Federal Rules of Civil Procedure. One important distinction for our purposes is that it is unnecessary under the Massachusetts version of Rule 8 to allege the basis for subject matter jurisdiction. Compare Fed. R. Civ. P. 8(a)(1).

We will also want to assert our right to a jury trial. See Mass. R. Civ. P. 38(b) (identical in relevant part to Fed. R. Civ. P. 38(b)).

The Associate's Response

MEMORANDUM

TO: Phyllis Slater

FROM: David E. Howard

RE: Complaint in *Schulansky v. Ronan*
          Our file No. 99-1248

DATE: December 1, 1999

- -

I have attached a draft complaint and summons in the Schulansky matter. Please note that I have made both Richard Ronan and Ronan Construction Company defendants in the suit. (I refer to them collectively as "Ronan" in this memo.) The contract is signed by Richard Ronan, but on the stationery of Ronan Construction Company. At this stage, it is not clear whether Ronan signed on behalf of the corporation or individually, or both. Since either or both may be liable, I have named both as defendants.

As my draft complaint indicates, Schulansky may be entitled to relief on two separate theories, breach of contract and negligence. Ronan may have breached the contract in several ways. First, Ronan may have agreed to reconstruct the foundation if necessary, but failed to do so. The Proposal and Estimate is hardly clear on this; the only relevant provision is paragraph two, which requires construction of "...foundation walls to support 18' × 25' addition." However, an argument can be made that the old foundation wall at the juncture of the house and the addition is part of the foundation of the addition, and therefore the contractor had a duty to make sure that that part of the foundation was solid as well. Paragraphs 23 and 24 of the draft complaint assert this basis for recovery for breach of contract.

Our argument that paragraph two required Ronan to reconstruct the foundation is bolstered by the negotiations between Ronan and Schulansky concerning possible reconstruction of the foundation if it turned out to be inadequate. The potential problem here is that these discussions took place before the Proposal and Estimate was signed. The defendants will no doubt argue that the written contract embodies the entire agreement between the parties, that on its face it does not include any obligation to reconstruct the old foundation, and that the parol evidence rule bars evidence of prior negotiations to vary the terms of the contract. See generally, Farnsworth on Contracts §7.12 (1998). We will have to argue that paragraph two is ambiguous, so that evidence of the prior negotiations is proper to demonstrate the intent of the parties.

Alternatively, it may turn out that the settling resulted from damage done to the foundation by Jones in the course of excavating the cellar. If this is true, Ronan would still be liable on a breach of contract theory. Certainly, an implied term of the contract between Ronan and Schulansky is that the work will be carried out in a careful manner, including the work that Ronan chooses to delegate to his employees or agents. See Restatement (Second) of Contracts §318(3) (1981) (delegation of duties under contract does not discharge delegating party from its duty to perform those duties). Even if it was Jones who damaged the foundation with the backhoe, this would constitute a breach of Ronan's duty to perform the contract work carefully. Thus, even if we cannot prove that Ronan had agreed to rebuild the foundation, this would constitute a separate breach of the contract, which gives rise to a claim for whatever subsidence resulted from the damage. I have included this allegation in paragraph 25 of the draft.

The second claim for relief in my draft complaint asserts a tort claim for negligence, based on the allegation that the negligent excavation by Jones led to the subsidence. If Jones acted as Ronan's employee in performing the excavation work, Ronan will be liable for Jones's negligent acts, since employers are liable for the torts of their employees in the scope of employment. Restatement (Second) of Agency §219 (1958). It is not clear at this stage whether Jones operated as an employee or independent sub-contractor in performing the excavation work. The legal distinction between an employee and independent contractor turns on the employer's right to control the details of the work. *Cowan v. Eastern Racing Assn.*, 330 Mass. 135, 141-142 (1953); see generally J. Glannon, The Law of Torts; Examples and Explanations, 2d ed. 397-399; Restatement (Second) of Agency §220 (1958). If Ronan exercised detailed control over Jones in the manner of digging the new cellar, Jones acted as Ronan's employee, and Ronan would be liable for Jones's negligence. However, if Ronan simply hired Jones to complete the excavation work in his own manner for an agreed price, Jones may have acted as an independent subcontractor.

There is some reason to believe that Jones acted as Ronan's employee, since (according to Schulansky) Ronan appeared to direct him in the course of the excavation work. Thus, I have drafted the second claim for relief on this theory. An important goal of discovery on our second claim for relief will be to ascertain the exact course of dealing between Ronan and Jones, to determine whether Jones acted as Ronan's employee or as an independent contractor.

Once you have reviewed the draft and made any changes, I will arrange for filing of the complaint and service on the defendants in New Hampshire.

The Resulting Documents

1.

COMMONWEALTH OF MASSACHUSETTS

PLYMOUTH COUNTY

SUPERIOR COURT
DEPARTMENT CIVIL
ACTION NO.

DEBORAH SCHULANSKY

Plaintiff

v.

RICHARD L. RONAN
RONAN CONSTRUCTION CO.

Defendants

COMPLAINT AND
DEMAND FOR
JURY TRIAL

2. ⟶ <u>PARTIES</u>

1. The plaintiff, Deborah Schulansky, is an individual residing at 219 Parker Street, Plymouth, Plymouth County, Massachusetts.

3.

2. The defendant Ronan Construction Company is a corporation incorporated in New Hampshire with offices at 1124 Newark Road, Nashua, New Hampshire.

3. The defendant Richard L. Ronan is an individual residing at 3 Carleton Drive, Nashua, New Hampshire, and the president of Ronan Construction Company.

4. At all relevant times, the defendant Richard L. Ronan acted as the authorized agent of Ronan Construction Company.

4. ⟶ <u>FACTS</u>

5.

5. The plaintiff owns an antique colonial house located at 53 School Street, Alton, New Hampshire. The house was built in 1782, and is listed in the National Register of Historic Places.

6. In February, 1999, the plaintiff met the defendant, Richard L. Ronan, while Ronan was working on a restoration project in Plymouth, Massachusetts.

7. At this first meeting, Ronan represented to the plaintiff that he was experienced at restoration of historic houses in New Hampshire and Massachusetts.

8. In early March, 1999, the plaintiff met with Ronan at her home in Plymouth, Massachusetts, to discuss the possibility of hiring him to build an addition on her house in Alton, New Hampshire.

9. During that meeting, the parties discussed the need for extensive rebuilding of the foundation of the main house adjacent to the planned addition.

10. During that meeting, the defendant Richard L. Ronan agreed that any necessary reconstruction of the old foundation would be included as part of the construction of an adequate foundation for the addition.

6. ⟶ 11. After the March meeting, Richard L. Ronan sent a Proposal and Estimate to the plaintiff in Plymouth, Massachusetts, describing the work to be done and offering to perform the work for $40,000. A copy of the Proposal and Estimate is attached to this complaint as Exhibit A.

12. The plaintiff accepted the defendants' offer by signing and mailing the Proposal and Estimate and mailing it to the defendants, at their office in Nashua, New Hampshire, on April 3, 1999.

13. The defendants commenced work on the addition on April 15, 1999, and continued until June 3, 1999.

14. In the course of the work, the defendants or their agents excavated the earth from the outside of the foundation of the main house to a depth of approximately seven feet.

15. This excavation revealed that the base of the foundation consisted of loose rocks piled on top of each other and held in place by the surrounding earth.

16. In the process of excavation, the defendants or their agents damaged the foundation of the main house by digging up and displacing large boulders, which formed part of that foundation.

17. As a result of the removal of the supporting earth outside the foundation, or the damage done to it during the excavation, or both, it became necessary to reconstruct this part of the foundation to adequately support the main house and the addition.

18. Despite their agreement to do so, the defendants failed to reconstruct the original foundation to provide adequate support for the house and the addition.

19. Even after the plaintiff brought the problem to the defendants' attention during construction, and demanded that they reconstruct the foundation in accordance with their agreement, the defendants refused to do so.

20. As a result of the inadequate foundation work, the main house and the addition have sustained major

structural damage, including cracks in the walls and sagging of the first floor immediately above the affected area.

7. ⟶ <u>FIRST</u> <u>CLAIM</u> <u>FOR</u> <u>RELIEF</u>:

<u>BREACH</u> <u>OF</u> <u>CONTRACT</u>

8. ⟶ 21. The plaintiff repeats and realleges the allegations in paragraphs 1-20 of the complaint.

22. The Proposal and Estimate signed by the defendant Richard L. Ronan and the plaintiff constitutes a written contract for a valuable consideration between the defendants and the plaintiff.

23. Under paragraph two of the contract, the defendants agreed to construct an adequate foundation to support the addition and adjacent portion of the main house.

24. The defendants breached the contract by failing to perform their obligation to construct an adequate foundation for the addition.

25. The defendants also breached the contract by failing to perform the excavation work required by the contract in a careful manner, which resulted in damage to the existing foundation of the house.

26. The plaintiff made all progress payments under the contract in a timely manner, until she became aware of the defendants' breach.

27. As a result of the defendants' breach, both the main house and the addition have sustained severe structural damage, which will require extensive repair and reconstruction.

<u>SECOND</u> <u>CLAIM</u> <u>FOR</u> <u>RELIEF</u>:

<u>NEGLIGENCE</u>

28. The plaintiff repeats and realleges the allegations in paragraphs 1-20 of the complaint.

29. In the course of the construction of the addition, the defendants or their employees negligently excavated the area adjacent to the foundation of the main house.

30. As a result of this negligent excavation, the foundation of the main house was displaced and damaged, causing subsidence of the foundation and structural damage to the main house and the addition.

9. ————————————————————▶   <u>DEMAND</u> <u>FOR</u> <u>RELIEF</u>

WHEREFORE, the plaintiff demands judgment in the
amount of her actual damages plus interest and costs, and
such other relief as the court finds just and equitable.

10. ——————————————————▶   <u>DEMAND</u> <u>FOR</u> <u>JURY</u> <u>TRIAL</u>

Pursuant to Mass. R. Civ. P. 38(b), the plaintiff demands
jury trial of all issues triable of right by a jury.

11. ——————————————————————————▶ *Phyllis Slater*
Phyllis Slater
Gomez, Robbins and Slater
Attorney for Plaintiff
322 Puritan Road
Plymouth, MA 02360
(508) 293-7024

RONAN CONSTRUCTION CO.
1124 Newark Road
Nashua, New Hampshire 03061

TO: Deborah Schulansky
         219 Parker Street
         Plymouth, MA 02360

RE: Addition to premises at 53 School Street,
         Alton, New Hampshire

DATE: March 15, 1999

PROPOSAL AND ESTIMATE

1. Excavate 18' × 25' × 7' deep area at right rear of house; remove fill.

2. Construct footings, cellar floor, and foundation walls to support 18' × 25' addition.

3. Cut doorway through present foundation into new cellar area.

4. Construct one-story addition with peaked roof and unfinished attic crawl space—standard frame construction, including cedar clapboard siding and asphalt shingle roof.

5. Two standard double-hung windows each side (west and east), and two 6' bay windows (double glazed) on main south wall.

6. Interior walls standard drywall construction; clear maple finish floor and baseboards.

7. Remove wall where addition abuts house; support upper floors with steel beam spanning opening.

8. Clean-up of site; broom clean, no seeding or planting.

9. Electrical work to be done by separate contractor hired by owner.

10. Contractor reserves the right to sub-contract excavating and concrete work.

11. Work to be completed by June 20, 1999.

Estimated Cost: $40,000

Payment schedule: $5,000 on completion of excavation
                       $5,000 on completion of foundation
                       $5,000 on completion of framing
                       $10,000 on completion of exterior
                       Finish work
                       Balance upon completion of job.

                       Richard L. Ronan
                       Richard L. Ronan

Bid accepted: *Deborah Schulansky*
                       Deborah Schulansky

COMMONWEALTH OF MASSACHUSETTS

PLYMOUTH, ss.   SUPERIOR COURT DEPARTMENT OF THE
                                                 TRIAL COURT OF THE COMMONWEALTH
                                                 CIVIL ACTION NO.

Deborah Schulansky...................., Plaintiff(s)

                vs.

Richard L.Ronan,
Ronan Construction Company
...., Defendant(s)

SUMMONS

To the above-named defendant:

You are hereby summoned and required to serve upon ....Phyllis Slater Gomez, Robbins & Slater...... plaintiff attorney, whose address is 322 Puritan Rd. Plymouth, MA 02360...., an answer to the complaint which is herewith served upon you, within 20 days after service of this summons upon you, exclusive of the day of service. If you fail to do so, judgment by default will be taken against you for the relief demanded in the complaint. You are also required to file your answer to the complaint in the office of the Clerk of this court at Plymouth either before service upon plaintiff   attorney or within a reasonable time thereafter.

Unless otherwise provided by Rule 13(a), your answer must state as a counterclaim any claim which you may have against the plaintiff   which arises out of the transaction or occurrence that is the subject matter of the plaintiff   claim or you will thereafter be barred from making such claim in any other action.

Witness, SUZANNE V. DELVECCHIO Esquire, at Plymouth the .....Eighth.............................day of

...December.................................., in the year of our Lord one thousand nine hundred and Ninety-nine.

Frank R. Powers

CLERK.

NOTES
1.   This summons is issued pursuant to Rule 4 of the Massachusetts Rules of Civil Procedure.
2.   When more than one defendant is involved, the names of all defendants should appear in the caption. If a separate summons is used for each defendant, each should be addressed to the particular defendant.
3.   To the plaintiff's attorney: please circle type of action involved-Tort-Motor Vehicle Tort-Contract-Equitable Relief-Other.

PROOF OF SERVICE OF PROCESS

I hereby certify and return that on ....,   , I served a copy of the within summons together with a copy of the complaint in this action, upon the within-named defendant, in the following manner(See Mass. R. Civ. P. 4(d)(1-5)):...

....

....

Dated: , ...

N.B.   TO PROCESS SERVER:-
                PLEASE PLACE DATE YOU MAKE SERVICE ON DEFENDANT IN THIS BOX ON THE ORIGINAL
AND ON COPY SERVED ON DEFENDANT.

Comments on the Schulansky Complaint

Although Schulansky's complaint has been drafted to comply with the pleading requirements of the Massachusetts Rules of Civil Procedure (Mass. R. Civ. P. 8-11), those rules are very similar to Rules 8-11 of the Federal Rules of Civil Procedure. The following comments therefore refer to the rules generically unless the federal and state versions differ on the particular point under discussion.

1.   While some of the contents of pleadings are a matter of custom in a particular court or personal preference of the drafting attorney, the Rules specifically govern many aspects of pleading. For example, Rule 10(a) requires every pleading to have a caption such as that in Schulansky's complaint. Under Rule 10(a), the caption must include the name of the court *(Commonwealth of Massachusetts, Plymouth County, Superior Court Department)*, the docket number of the action *(Civil Action No.)*, the names of the parties, and a designation of the pleading *(Complaint and Demand for Jury Trial)*.

The docket number is a number assigned to each case by the court clerk, for administrative purposes. On Schulansky's complaint, the docket number is left blank because the case will not be assigned a docket number until the complaint is filed with the clerk.

2.   Note that Howard has included a number of subheadings in the complaint. While these are not required by the Rules, such subheadings are frequently included for the sake of clarity. Particularly in a lengthy complaint that asserts a number of claims, or where the factual allegations are complex, separate sections for *Parties, Facts,* and *Claims for Relief* make it easy for the court and the parties to quickly find and review parts of the complaint during motion arguments and other proceedings.

In federal actions, a *Jurisdiction* subheading is frequently added because Fed. R. Civ. P. 8(a)(1) specifically requires the plaintiff to allege the basis for subject matter jurisdiction over the action. Such an allegation is not required under Massachusetts Rule 8 because, unlike the federal district courts, the Superior Court is a court of general jurisdiction.

For many simple cases, such as an action on a note or a straightforward motor vehicle tort case, the complaint may be so brief that subheadings are unnecessary. See the Appendix of Forms accompanying the Federal Rules of Civil Procedure, Forms 3-18 for examples of such complaints.

3.   The Federal Rules do not explicitly require separate paragraphs identifying the parties to the action.[1] However, it is customary to begin the complaint with descriptions of the plaintiff(s) and the defendant(s). This information is important to various issues, including personal jurisdiction,

---

1. The Massachusetts rules do, however, require that the residence or place of business of the parties be specified. Mass. R. Civ. P. 10(d).

venue, capacity to sue and be sued, and (particularly in federal diversity actions) subject matter jurisdiction. In Schulansky's complaint, for example, the allegation that Schulansky resides in Plymouth County indicates the plaintiff's basis under state law for laying venue there. See Mass. Gen. L. ch.223, §1 (venue proper in county where plaintiff lives).

4.   Many complaints will include a subheading entitled *Facts,* or *Factual Allegations,* setting forth a brief description of the events that gave rise to the plaintiff's claim for relief. This type of breakdown is useful, particularly in complex cases, to distinguish the underlying facts giving rise to the claim from the plaintiff's asserted claims arising out of those facts.

In Schulansky's case, for example, there is enough factual background that a separate facts section facilitates a clear understanding of her claims. It is true that Rule 8 (a)(2) only requires a "short and plain statement of the claim," and that very brief, general allegations will suffice to avoid dismissal. *Conley v. Gibson,* 355 U.S. 41, 47-48 (1957). But a little more detail than the absolute minimum needed under the pleading rules will give the court a clearer picture of the case, from the plaintiff's point of view. And since Rule 8(b) requires the defendant to respond paragraph by paragraph to the allegations in the complaint, a more detailed complaint will elicit more specific denials or admissions in the defendant's answer.

5.   The Rules require all allegations in the body of the complaint to be set forth in numbered paragraphs. Rule 10(b). This facilitates quick reference to the allegations in the complaint. It also allows defendants to respond to each of the plaintiff's allegations by number and allows the plaintiff to incorporate allegations by number in later parts of the complaint, as Howard has done in paragraphs 21 and 28 of the Schulansky complaint.

Rule 10(b) also provides that the allegations in each paragraph of the complaint "shall be limited as far as practicable to a statement of a single set of circumstances. . . ." However, reducing specificity to the atomic level (for example, by breaking Schulansky's paragraph five into three paragraphs), would make the complaint unduly tedious. The allegations in paragraph five all relate closely to the issue of the age and value of the house and form a logical grouping for a single paragraph. The Rule does not limit each paragraph to a single fact, but to a single "set of circumstances," and calls for a commonsense breakdown of allegations "as far as practicable."

6.   The Rules authorize parties to attach exhibits to their pleadings, as Schulansky has done here. Rule 10(c). Parties should exercise care in incorporating documents in the complaint, however, since doing so may constitute an admission at least of the authenticity of the documents, if not their accuracy. Here, for example, Schulansky's inclusion of the Proposal and Estimate, together with her allegation that it constitutes the contract between her and Ronan, may weaken her argument that Ronan had an additional duty, arising from their prior discussions, to repair the old foundation. See the Third Defense in Ronan's answer p. 571.

7. In paragraphs 21-27 and 28-30, Howard has recast the factual allegations in terms of claims for relief for breach of contract and negligence. These sections of the complaint are intended to show the court that the facts alleged satisfy the elements of legally recognized claims that, if proved, entitle Schulansky to relief.[2] The subheading *Claim for Relief* tracks the language of Rule 8 (a)(2), which requires the complaint to include a "short and plain statement of the claim showing that the pleader is entitled to relief." Here, Schulansky has asserted a right to relief under two distinct theories. If the court concludes that she has proved a right to recovery on either her contract theory or her tort theory, it will grant her whatever relief is proper under that claim. This "pleading in the alternative" is expressly authorized by Rule 8 (e)(2).

The rules do not require the pleader to state the legal theory on which he claims a right to relief. A brief description of the "claim," that is, the events giving rise to the action, is sufficient. See Friedenthal, Kane & Miller, §5.7, 3rd ed. 1999. However, it is certainly appropriate and helpful to allege the elements of each claim clearly, especially in cases involving multiple theories of relief based on the same underlying facts. See *O'Donnell v. Elgin, J & E. Ry. Co.*, 338 U.S. 384, 392 (1949) ("We no longer insist upon technical rules of pleading, but it will ever be difficult in a jury trial to segregate issues which counsel do not separate in their pleading, preparation or thinking.").

Separate pleading theories are often labeled as different "counts" instead of Claims for Relief. In simple complaints, such subdivisions are unnecessary. See, e.g., Appendix of Forms accompanying Federal Rules of Civil Procedure, Form 17, which asserts two theories of relief quite clearly without separate counts or subheadings.

Students sometimes ask why Schulansky's counsel assert two theories of relief. If they have a viable claim for breach of contract, why take on the extra burden of alleging and proving the negligence claim as well? Well, Schulansky's lawyers would do their client a serious disservice by omitting the negligence claim from their complaint. After all, they may *not* recover on the breach of contract claim. Perhaps they missed the limitations period, or the jury will find that Schulansky had waived the rebuilding of the foundation, or for some other reason the contract theory may fall by the wayside. If so, Schulansky's counsel will clearly want to preserve their options, by asserting any other viable theories of relief based on the defendants' conduct. Indeed, they would likely be liable for malpractice if they put all their eggs in one

---

2. Schulansky might have other claims for relief in addition to the two asserted in the complaint. For example, other claims might be based on the failure of Ronan to properly supervise Jones or negligent selection of Jones as the subcontractor. For illustration purposes, however, I have tried to keep the complaint to a manageable length.

basket, by leaving out a viable negligence claim, only later to lose on the contract claim. Clients expect their lawyers to assert all supportable rights they may have, not pick and choose among them based on which they think has the best chance of success.

Thus, lawyers feel considerable pressure to include any supportable theory of recovery in their complaints. Better to assert it and lose on it rather than leave it out and explain to the client later why they abandoned a claim that might have provided her some relief. At the same time, lawyers are under considerable pressure under Rule 11 of the Rules of Civil Procedure *not* to assert theories for which they lack support. See note 12 below. Such conflicting pressures, among other things, make a litigator's life interesting.

8.   Rule 10(c) authorizes a pleader to incorporate prior allegations by reference in later parts of his pleading. Here Howard has done so in order to make clear that the breach of contract claim is based on the facts alleged in the cited paragraphs.

9.   At the end of the complaint, Howard includes a demand for the relief Schulansky seeks on both claims, as required by Rule 8(a)(3). In this case, the relief sought is damages, but in other actions different types of relief are also commonly sought, such as specific performance, an injunction, or a declaration of the rights of the parties.

Attorneys differ as to whether to put a demand for relief after each claim for relief, or to place a single demand at the end of the complaint. Clearly, if the relief requested differs on the different claims, separate demands for relief are appropriate. For example, if Schulansky were seeking specific performance of the contract with Ronan, inserting separate demands for relief after each claim for relief would help to make it clear that specific performance is sought under the contract claim rather than the negligence claim (which would not support a demand for specific performance). Because she seeks only damages on each claim, however, and the measure of damages on each theory is apparently the same, either a single demand at the end of the complaint or demands after each claim would be appropriate. Compare the separate demands for relief in Ronan's third-party complaint, infra pp. 584-587.

Note that the demand for relief in the Schulansky complaint does not state a specific dollar amount requested. This is because a Massachusetts statute bars plaintiffs from stating a specific dollar demand. Mass. Gen. L. ch. 231, §13B. Several states have enacted such statutes, to avoid adverse publicity and possible jury prejudice from inflated damage figures in pleadings.

10. Rule 38(b) provides that a demand for jury trial "may be indorsed upon a pleading," which means, in plain English, that it may be put at the end of the complaint (or answer). Because the right to trial by jury is waived if not demanded within ten days of the close of the pleadings (see Rule 38(b)), it is wise to insert the demand for jury trial in the complaint. Otherwise,

plaintiff's counsel may forget about it, and the period for seeking jury trial may slip by unnoticed.

11. Rule 11 governs signature of the complaint and other pleadings.[3] It requires the attorney to sign the complaint and state his address. The rule also imposes important ethical duties on attorneys who sign complaints and other court papers. Under Federal Rule 11, an attorney's signature on a complaint certifies to the court that the attorney believes, after reasonable inquiry, that the factual allegations in the complaint "have evidentiary support," or (for specifically identified allegations) "are likely to have evidentiary support after a reasonable opportunity for further investigation or discovery." The attorney's signature also certifies that the legal positions taken in the complaint (in the *Schulansky* case, for example, that the plaintiff has the right to sue for breach of contract, or that Ronan is liable for the acts of Jones) "are warranted by existing law or by a nonfrivolous argument for the extension, modification, or reversal of existing law or the establishment of new law." Rule 11 (b) (2). Last, the signing attorney certifies that the pleading or motion is not filed for any improper purpose. Rule 11 (b) (1).

The "reasonable inquiry" requirement was added to Federal Rule 11 in 1983 to strengthen the attorney's obligation to the court to avoid frivolous or unethical pleadings. This language does not require Slater and Howard to complete their research or investigation before filing suit against Ronan, but it does require them to have a factual basis beyond mere opinion or speculation to support the pleaded facts, as well as a colorable argument for the legal positions asserted in the complaint.

The factual standard in Rule 11 would be met by the information Schulansky gave her attorneys about the construction problem before they drafted the complaint. They knew that the damage appeared shortly after the construction work began, in the area where the work was being done. They also knew that an engineer had viewed the damage and concluded that it resulted from the inadequate construction work. This provides "evidentiary support" for the factual allegations in the *Schulansky* complaint. The rule does not require certainty or admissible evidence at this early stage of the suit, only a reasonable pre-filing inquiry.

The legal standard in Rule 11 would also be satisfied in the *Schulansky* case. Howard and Slater had a copy of the contract, which required Ronan to construct walls to support the addition. If the damage to the house resulted from inadequate support, that would arguably constitute a breach of the contract. In addition, the discussions between Ronan and Schulansky during the negotiations may well support a claim that Ronan had agreed to

---

3. The complaint is shown here with the attorney's signature affixed. Subsequent pleadings and motions have not been signed because they are suggested pleadings for the partner's review and have not yet been filed in court.

reinforce or rebuild the foundation. Similarly, if the engineer's alternative conclusion that the backhoe damaged the foundation is accurate, that would certainly constitute actionable negligence.

Interestingly, the pleading requirement in Massachusetts Rule 11 are less stringent than those in Federal Rule 11. Under Massachusetts Rule 11, the attorney's signature certifies that "to the best of his knowledge, information and belief there is good ground to support" the pleading, and that it is not interposed for delay. It does not impose a requirement of pre-filing inquiry and does not make reference to improper purposes other than delay (as, for example, escalating the expense of litigation to the point where the opponent cannot sustain it). In addition, the Massachusetts version only authorizes sanctions for "wilful violations." The Massachusetts rulemakers have been unwilling to impose the stricter requirements of Federal Rule 11. Consequently, sanctions for improper pleading are invoked less frequently in the Massachusetts state courts than in the federal courts.

Comments on the Summons

Rule 4 requires both a summons and complaint to be served on the defendant. The complaint is written by the plaintiff or his attorney, setting out the allegations against the defendant. The summons, by contrast, is an official order from the court requiring the defendant to respond to the complaint. Hence, Rule 4 requires that the summons bear the seal of the court and be signed by the clerk.

In many courts printed summonses like the one used here, already signed and sealed, may be obtained in blank from the clerk's office. The plaintiff's attorney fills in the blanks and arranges for service of the summons with the complaint. Compare the printed summons with the detailed requirements of Federal Rule 4(a). (Mass. R. Civ. P. 4(b) closely parallels Federal Rule 4(a).) The summons includes the seal of the court,[4] the name of the court, space for the names of the parties, and the name and address of the plaintiff's attorney. It also warns the defendant, as required by Massachusetts Rule 4(b), that he must answer within 20 days or default judgment will be entered against him. See Rule 55, which authorizes entry of a default judgment if the defendant fails to respond to the complaint.

The first paragraph of the summons quire properly distinguishes between service and filing of the defendant's answer. Rule 12(a) requires the defendant to *serve* his answer on the plaintiff within 20 days of service of the complaint. See Chapter 17 for a discussion of methods of service of process.

---

4. In some courts, the seal is actually printed on the summons; in others, the court clerk embosses the seal on the summons by hand. The Plymouth County clerk's office uses an embossed seal, so it does not show up on the form illustrated here.

As the summons states, the answer must also be filed with the court before it is served or within a reasonable time thereafter.

Nothing in Rule 4(b) requires inclusion of the second paragraph of the summons, warning defendants that they must assert compulsory counterclaims under Rule 13(a). The purpose of the warning is obviously to remind defendants, who must respond within a short time, that they must assert any compulsory counterclaims in their answer or risk loss of those claims.

The printed summons usually includes space (here, at the bottom of the page) for the sheriff, constable, or other process server to provide proof of service. See Federal Rule 4(1). The server fills out the form, indicating the date and manner in which service was made, and files it with the court.

If service is made directly by the plaintiff's attorney (for example, in a case such as this one, where service on the out-of-state defendants will likely be made by mail), a separate, sworn affidavit must be filed setting forth the time and manner in which service was made. Federal Rule 4(1).

30

A Change of Forum: Ronan Removes to Federal Court

The Drafting Request

MEMORANDUM

TO: Marcia Losordo
           Associate

FROM: Arthur Ackerman

RE: *Schulansky v. Ronan*
           Plymouth Superior Court No. 99-2982

DATE: December 19, 1999

As you know, this office frequently handles litigation for Federal Security Insurance Company, a large insurer specializing in construction accounts. Federal Security has just asked us to represent one of their insureds, a New Hampshire contractor named Richard Ronan. On December 10 Ronan was served with process in a suit commenced against him and Ronan Construction Company in the Plymouth Superior Court. Copies of the complaint and summons are attached.

Ronan was in this morning for an initial interview on the case. (I would have asked you to sit in, but you were in court.) Although I didn't have much time, I did get the relevant background information on the case. The suit arises out of some work Ronan did for the plaintiff, Deborah Schulansky, on her second home in Alton, New Hampshire. Schulansky claims that Ronan agreed to build an addition to the house but failed to reinforce the foundation adequately, causing the main part of the house to settle. Ronan denies that the house has settled or, if it has, that it resulted from his work.

My initial reaction was that it seems doubtful that Ronan is subject to personal jurisdiction in Massachusetts for this claim, since the work was done out of state and Ronan is from New Hampshire. However, he did negotiate the contract with the plaintiff in Massachusetts, so he does at least have some relevant contacts here.

If Ronan is subject to jurisdiction in Massachusetts, I would prefer to litigate in federal district court here in Boston rather than down in Plymouth. Ronan lives in Nashua, New Hampshire, and Ronan Construction Company is incorporated in New Hampshire with its principal place of business in Nashua, so the case is removable on diversity grounds.

I need some quick information on removal of this case. Could you please write me a short memo answering the following questions:

1. Should the notice of removal be filed in the state or federal court?

2. What documents must be filed with the notice of removal?

3. Can we file our motion to dismiss for lack of personal jurisdiction in the state court and wait for a decision on that motion before removing the suit?

4. Do we have to answer or move to dismiss before removing? If not, when is our response due in federal court?

5. The plaintiff has demanded trial by jury in her state court complaint. If we also want a jury, do we have to request it again in the federal court after removal?

If we have to remove right away, rather than waiting for the state court to resolve the personal jurisdiction issue, please draft a notice of removal as well. Even though the holidays are imminent, please get to this during the next week; I believe there is a 30-day limit on removal, and we've already lost nine of them.

The Associate's Response

MEMORANDUM

TO: Arthur Ackerman

FROM: Marcia Losordo

RE: Removal of *Schulansky v. Ronan*
          Plymouth Superior Court No. 99-2982

DATE: December 23, 1999

I have researched your questions on removal of the *Schulansky* case. In addition, since I conclude that we must remove the case within 30 days even if the state court lacks personal jurisdiction, I have also drafted a notice of removal and other required documents, which I attach for your review.

The answers to your questions are as follows:

1. Should the notice be filed in the state or federal court?

The notice of removal must be filed in the federal district court "for the district and division within which such action is pending." 28 U.S.C. §1446(a). A copy of the notice must then be filed in the state court. 28 U.S.C. §1446(d). The case is only properly removed when the state court and the other parties to the action have been notified. Id.

2. What must be filed with the notice of removal?

Under 28 U.S.C. §1446(a), copies of "all process, pleadings, and orders" served upon the defendants must be filed with the notice of removal. In this case that includes only the summons and complaint served on each defendant.

A party who removes to federal court must give written notice of the filing to all other parties to the action "promptly after the filing of such notice." 28 U.S.C. §1446(d). I have prepared a notification form, as well as copies of the notice of removal for service on the plaintiff and filing in the state court.

3. Can I file my motion to dismiss for lack of personal jurisdiction in the state court and wait for a decision on that motion before removing the suit?

It is certainly permissible to file the motion to dismiss before removing. Until removal is sought, the case is governed by the state court rules, which require a response to the complaint within 20 days. Mass. R. Civ. P. 12(a).

However, §1446(b) provides that the notice of removal must be filed within 30 days after the defendant is served with the complaint. Nothing in the statute suggests that the 30-day period is suspended by any pending motions, and it is very unlikely that the motion to dismiss would be acted on before the 30 days elapse. Therefore, we cannot await decision on the motion before removing the case. We should remove the case now; the federal court will then decide whether to grant the motion to dismiss.

4. Do I have to answer or move to dismiss before removing? If not, when is my response due in federal court?

As indicated in the previous answer, the Massachusetts rules require a response within 20 days after service of the complaint and summons. If we do not remove within the first 20 days, a response to the complaint will be due, and we will have to file one or be in default. We should either remove before the response is due or file an answer or motion to dismiss in the state court. If we do answer before removing, the answer will stand as the answer in federal court, unless that court orders a further answer. Fed R. Civ. P. 81(c).

One reason why we might wish to remove before answering is that some authorities suggest that a defendant may waive the right to remove by taking some actions in state court, such as filing a counterclaim. See Friedenthal, Kane, and Miller, Civil Procedure, p. 64. The rationale for this view is that the defendant has demonstrated her willingness to have the state court adjudicate the case by taking affirmative steps in the state court. Removing and then answering in federal court will avoid any risk of raising the waiver issue.

If we remove before responding to the complaint, Fed. R. Civ. P. 81(c) provides that we must answer within 20 days of service of the complaint or 5 days after the notice of removal is filed, whichever is longer. Thus, we had better begin preparing an answer immediately or move for an extension of time in which to answer, under Fed. R. Civ. P. 6(b).

5. The plaintiff has demanded trial by jury in her state court complaint. If we also want a jury, do we have to request it again in the federal court after removal?

Rule 81 (c) provides that a party who has properly requested jury trial prior to removal need not renew the request in the federal court. Once the case is removed, the federal rules will govern the action (Fed. R. Civ. P. 81(c)), including Fed. R. Civ. P. 38(d), which provides that a jury trial demand cannot be withdrawn without the consent of the parties. Therefore, this action will be tried to a jury unless both sides later consent to trial before the court.

However, I am not sure whether the plaintiff's general demand for jury trial would apply to any counterclaim we may assert in our answer. If the case reaches the point of filing an answer, and we decide to assert any counterclaims, a separate demand for jury trial should be made as to them.

The Resulting Documents

1.

UNITED STATES DISTRICT COURT

DISTRICT OF MASSACHUSETTS

2.

DEBORAH SCHULANSKY	CIVIL ACTION NO. _____
Plaintiff	
v.	NOTICE OF REMOVAL **3.**
RICHARD L. RONAN RONAN CONSTRUCTION CO.	
Defendants	

4.   Richard L. Ronan and Ronan Construction Company, the defendants in the above entitled action, respectfully state:

1. On December 7, 1999 a civil action was commenced against the defendants in the Superior Court Department of the Trial Court for Plymouth County, Massachusetts entitled Deborah Schulansky v. Richard L. Ronan and Ronan Construction Company, Civil Action No. 99-2982.

5.   2. The defendants received service of copies of the summons and complaint in this action on December 10, 1999. Copies of the summons and complaint are attached hereto, and constitute the only process, pleadings, and orders that have been filed in this action.

6.   3. This action is a civil action for damages between the petitioners, citizens of New Hampshire, and the plaintiff, a citizen of Massachusetts. At the time the action was commenced, the defendant Richard L. Ronan was, and now is, a citizen of New Hampshire. At the time the action was commenced, the defendant Ronan Construction Company was, and now is, a corporation incorporated under the laws of New Hampshire, with its principal place of business at Nashua, New Hampshire. At the time the action was commenced, the plaintiff was, and now is, a citizen of Massachusetts.

4. This action arises from the construction of an addition to the plaintiff's home in Alton, New Hampshire. The complaint alleges that the defendants performed the work improperly, causing major structural damage to the house and requiring extensive repairs. Complaint, par: 16-20. The amount in controversy in the action exceeds seventy-five thousand dollars, exclusive of interest and costs.

7.

→ 5. This court has original jurisdiction of this action on the basis of diversity of citizenship, under 28 U.S.C. §1332, and removal jurisdiction under 28 U.S.C. §1441(a).

8.

6. The defendants will give written notice of the filing of this notice to the plaintiff, as required by 28 U.S.C. §1446(d).

7. A copy of this notice will be filed with the clerk of the Superior Court Department for Plymouth County, Massachusetts, as required by 28 U.S.C. §1446(d).

WHEREFORE, the defendants request that this action proceed in this Court as an action properly removed hereto.

9.

Arthur Ackerman
Ackerman, Sloan and Cariotis
Attorney for the Defendants
59 State Street
Boston, MA 02114
(617) 228-6301

UNITED STATES DISTRICT COURT

DISTRICT OF MASSACHUSETTS

DEBORAH SCHULANSKY	CIVIL ACTION NO._____
Plaintiff	
v.	NOTIFICATION OF FILING OF NOTICE OF REMOVAL ← ——— **10.**
RICHARD L. RONAN RONAN CONSTRUCTION CO.	
Defendants	

TO: Phyllis Slater
Gomez, Robbins and Slater
Attorney for Plaintiff
322 Puritan Road
Plymouth, MA 02360

Please take notice that the defendants in the above-entitled action have this date filed their notice of removal of this action in the Office of the Clerk of the United States District Court for the District of Massachusetts. A copy of the notice is attached hereto.

You are further advised that the defendants, upon filing of the notice of removal, also filed a copy of the notice with the Clerk of the Superior Court Department for Plymouth County, thus effecting removal under 28 U.S.C. §1446(d).

Date: _____

_____
Arthur Ackerman
Ackerman, Sloan and Cariotis
Attorney for the Defendants
59 State Street
Boston, MA 02114
(617) 228-6301

Comments on the Notice of Removal

1.   The heading of the notice of removal reflects the fact that the notice is filed in the federal district court, not in the state court in which Schulansky filed suit.

2.   Although Fed. R. Civ. P. 10(a) only governs the caption for pleadings, and a notice of removal is not a pleading (see Fed. R. Civ. P. 7(a)), it is customary to use the same type of caption in all papers filed in the suit. (Indeed, this may be required by local rules of the federal district, as it is in Massachusetts. See United States District Court, District of Massachusetts, Local Rule 5.1(a).) Of course, the title of the paper will change, but the court, names of the parties, and docket number will appear on all filed papers. Note again that the docket number has not been filled in since the case will receive a new federal court docket number when the notice of removal is filed.

3.   Until 1988, a defendant filed a "petition to remove" a case to federal court rather than a notice of removal. The change in the statute to the term "notice" reflects the fact that removal is not at the discretion of the federal court: If the federal court has jurisdiction over the action, it must hear it upon removal. The "petition" terminology suggested that the defendant was requesting the federal court to hear the case, and that it might choose to grant or refuse that request. The substituted term, "notice," reflects the fact that the defendant has a right to remove if the case falls within the federal court's removal jurisdiction and is "notifying" the court that she is exercising that option.

4.   Although the removal statutes are not entirely clear on the point, the courts have held that all defendants must agree to the removal. See Chapter 7, example 7. This requirement is met here since both Ronan and Ronan Construction Company file the notice of removal.

5.   The allegation as to the date of service of the complaint indicates to the court that removal is timely, since the 30-day removal period begins to run on the date of service of the summons and complaint on the defendants. 28 U.S.C. §1446(b). This paragraph of the notice also indicates that the defendants have complied with the requirement of 28 U.S.C. §1446(a), that "a copy of all process, pleadings, and orders served upon such defendant or defendants" be filed with the notice.

6.   It will not always be clear from the plaintiff's complaint that a case meets the requirements for original or removal jurisdiction of the federal court. For example, Schulansky's state court complaint did not allege where Ronan Construction Company's principal place of business was, since it was not necessary to do so to invoke the state court's jurisdiction over the action.

Section 1446(a) authorizes the removing defendant to state facts in the notice of removal that are necessary to demonstrate that the federal court has jurisdiction. The information in paragraphs three and four of the notice of removal is intended to show the court that this is a proper diversity case, which could have been brought originally in federal court. These paragraphs also demonstrate that none of the defendants is a citizen of the forum state, a separate requirement in 28 U.S.C. §1441(b) for removal of diversity cases.

As was noted in Chapter 29, the Demand for Relief in Schulansky's complaint does not state a specific dollar demand—in fact, a statute barred her from including a dollar figure in the demand. This poses an awkward situation for the defendants. *First*, how is Ronan to know if the amount in controversy exceeds $75,000, as required by 28 U.S.C. §1332(a), when he contends that Schulansky hasn't suffered any damages at all from his work? Ronan is an experienced construction contractor, and he is familiar with the house and the work he did on it. In addition, he has the factual allegations as to the nature of damages and the type of repair needed, so he should have a factual basis for roughly estimating the possible damages. Naturally, he can't be very accurate about it, but the *St. Paul Mercury* rule doesn't require him to be. So long as there is a possible basis for damages in excess of $75,000, the requirement is met. Section 1446(a) requires Ronan to put in the notice of removal a statement of the grounds for believing that the amount-in-controversy requirement has been met, as he has done in paragraph four.

Including this statement is also awkward for Ronan for another reason. By alleging that the amount requirement is satisfied, he in some sense lends credibility to the argument that the plaintiff has suffered extensive damages, an allegation he will presumably deny in his answer. But again, remember that the amount-in-controversy requirement refers to the amount that is in dispute between the parties, not to the actual damages the plaintiff has suffered. See Chapter 5, p. 90. Ronan does not concede, by asserting in the notice of removal that the dispute concerns more than $75,000, that the plaintiff has actually suffered that great a loss, or any loss at all. Nor will the jury likely be aware of the amount-in-controversy requirement or that Ronan has invoked federal jurisdiction on the basis that a particular amount is disputed.

7.   The fundamental requirement for removal is that the case could have been brought initially in federal court. 28 U.S.C. §1441(a). In paragraph five, the defendants state that original jurisdiction existed and that removal is therefore proper under §1441(a).

8.   Paragraphs six and seven indicate that the removing defendants will comply with the requirements of 28 U.S.C. §1446(d), that the plaintiff be notified of the removal, and that a copy of the notice be filed in the state court.

9.   Section 1446(a) now explicitly states that the representations made in the notice of removal are subject to the ethical requirements of Rule 11. Thus, as with Slater's signature on the complaint, Ackerman's signature certifies to the court that he has made a preliminary inquiry both as to the

supporting facts and legal right to remove and concluded that he has support for the positions taken in the notice of removal.

10. The Notification of Filing of Notice of Removal is a fairly commonsensical document drawn up to comply with the requirement of 28 U.S.C. §1446(d), that the defendant give notice to the adverse parties of the filing of the notice. As with the notice itself, it is intended to demonstrate to the court and the plaintiff that the defendants have complied with the removal requirements.

The third question Ackerman asks in his memo is interesting. It seems like an unnecessary hassle to go through the formalities of removal if the action is likely to be dismissed for lack of personal jurisdiction anyway. However, as the answer indicates, the removal statute does not allow the defendants to litigate preliminary objections in the state court before exercising their right to remove; removal must take place within 30 days, regardless of objections the plaintiff may have to jurisdiction, venue, or other matters relating to the state court's competence to entertain the action.

Thus, even if Ackerman believes that he might fare better on some issues in the case in state court, he does not have the choice to litigate some issues there and then remove to federal court. Removal must be done immediately and brings the entire action into the federal court. Thus, he must make a quick decision as to whether the overall advantages of litigating in federal court outweigh those of staying in state court. (Some of the many considerations that may influence that decision are discussed in Chapter 28, pp. 525-526) This is a difficult position to be in, particularly if the suit was not expected. When the case came into Ackerman's office nine days of the removal period had already elapsed, leaving little time to research all of the strategic ramifications of removal. Thus, the decision will be based on a preliminary understanding of the case, and may be regretted later on as counsel develop a fuller appreciation of these strategic considerations.

The Defendants' Perspective: Ronan's Answer and Counterclaim

The Drafting Request

MEMORANDUM

TO: Marcia Losordo
Associate

FROM: Arthur Ackerman

RE: Answer and counterclaim in *Schulansky v. Ronan*
U.S. District Court No. 99-6719

DATE: December 28, 1999

Thank you for your informative memo and removal documents in this case. I have filed the notice of removal today and notified the plaintiff and the state court, so we are officially in federal court.

I have decided to file an answer to the complaint (instead of a Rule 12(b) motion) and would appreciate your assistance in drafting it. I realize that you have not yet had any Christmas vacation, but as your memo indicates, we are under the gun because Fed. R. Civ. P. 81(c) requires us to respond to the complaint within five days of removing the case.

Not surprisingly, Dick Ronan's version of the facts in this case differs significantly from the allegations in Schulansky's complaint. First of all, although there was some discussion about the old foundation during their negotiations, Ronan's position is that he never assumed responsibility for any extensive reconstruction work. He never said anything about rebuilding the foundation, except that he doubted it would be necessary. He did say he would pour cement into any gaps in the exposed boulders but definitely did not agree to anything more than that. He points out that reconstructing the foundation on a house that old is a very substantial job; he could never have quoted her the price he did if such reconstruction were included in the work.

Second, according to Ronan, he and Schulansky discussed the problem again after the old foundation had been exposed. She asked him whether it ought to be rebuilt, and Ronan said that he did not think it was necessary and that it was beyond the scope of the contract. He specifically recalls telling her at that time that he thought the foundation would be sufficient if he filled in the gaps with concrete, but "you can never be 100 percent sure — old houses are unpredictable." She agreed to his suggestion, and that is what he did.

Ronan also denies any negligence in excavating the foundation. There were some loose boulders in the excavated area near the foundation, which Schulansky assumed had been knocked out by the backhoe. Ronan admits that the backhoe hit the foundation a number of times, but he thinks those rocks were probably excavated from the new cellar area instead. He also states that digging the earth away from the foundation did not weaken it. According to him, it is the direct downward pressure of the structure on top of the rocks in the foundation, not the surrounding earth, that keeps the foundation — and the house itself — in place.

Last, Ronan denies that Schulansky's house has settled as a result of his construction work or any defect in the old foundation. He claims that most of the cracks she refers to were already there when he inspected the house before he bid on the job; after all, the house is over 200 years old, and there is evidence of settling in every room of the house. While he does not doubt the good faith of the plaintiff, he thinks she simply had not noticed these problems until the construction work caused her to take a close look at the structure of the house.

Please draft an answer to the Schulansky complaint, based on Ronan's understanding of the facts outlined above. Please contact Ronan directly for any further information you need.

Our answer should not only respond to the individual allegations in Schulansky's complaint, but also raise several additional defenses. First, I think we should take the position that the Proposal and Estimate constitutes the entire agreement between the parties and that Ronan is under no duty to rebuild the foundation if the Proposal and Estimate does not require it. Even if there was some prior discussion in which Ronan arguably agreed to rebuild the foundation, it is the contract itself, not the discussions leading up to it, that defines the parties' obligations. As you know, where a contract is clear and complete on its face, the parol evidence rule bars either party from varying or contradicting the terms of the contract by evidence of prior inconsistent negotiations. Here, the contract is clear: Paragraph two requires Ronan to build a foundation for the addition, not to rebuild the preexisting foundation.

Second, Ronan states (and the plaintiff's complaint admits) that Schulansky was present when the foundation was exposed. Ronan told her what he planned to do, and she evidently accepted his proposal to reinforce it rather than rebuild it. Thus, I think we can make a strong argument that Schulansky has waived any right to reconstruction of the old foundation.

Our answer should also raise the objection that the court lacks personal jurisdiction over both defendants. I realize that we could postpone answering by filing a motion to dismiss on this ground, but I have decided to answer instead. I am somewhat doubtful that the court will dismiss on this ground. If the court postpones decision on the motion (as it may under Fed. R. Civ. P.12(d), I would rather have our answer to the complaint, setting forth our position on the merits, before the court from the beginning of the litigation.

Please also include a counterclaim for the final payment under the contract, which Schulansky has never made. In addition, it is our position that Richard Ronan signed the contract as an agent of Ronan Construction Company, not on his own behalf. Consequently, he was not a party to the contract and is not personally liable for any breach of that contract. Please be careful in drafting the answer to observe this distinction in responding to the allegations in the complaint and in drafting the counterclaim.

We may also wish to file a third-party complaint against the excavation subcontractor, Arlen Jones. Please let me know whether this must be filed with the answer. I certainly would prefer to have more time to decide whether to file a third-party claim and, if so, whether there will be any jurisdictional problems involved. (Jones is apparently from New Hampshire, but I am not sure whether he may be subject to personal jurisdiction here on some ground.)

The Associate's Response

MEMORANDUM

TO: Arthur Ackerman

FROM: Marcia Losordo

RE: Answer and Counterclaim in *Schulansky v. Ronan*
            U.S. District Court No. 99-6719

DATE: December 28, 1999

I have attached a proposed answer and counterclaim in the Schulansky case.

I have based my responses to the plaintiff's allegations on the facts as you set them out in your memo and on direct conversations with Dick Ronan. In responding to the plaintiff's first claim for relief, for breach of contract, I have consistently taken the position that Ronan's only obligation was to construct foundation walls for the addition, not for any part of the main house.

The plaintiff's second claim for relief on a negligence theory is evidently premised on the assumption that Jones was an employee of either Ronan personally or Ronan Construction Company, so that one or the other would be liable for his negligence. However, it is not at all clear that Jones was an employee, as opposed to an independent contractor with Ronan. The decision turns on whether Ronan had the right of control over Jones in the detailed performance of the work. Restatement (Second) of Agency §220 (1958). If he did, Jones was an employee; if not, he acted as an independent contractor.

From what Ronan tells me, it is unclear whether the court would characterize Jones as an employee of Ronan or as an independent contractor. On the one hand, Jones was paid a flat fee for the job and used his own backhoe, factors that suggest that he was independent. Restatement (Second) of Agency §227 (1958). On the other, Jones worked for Ronan on a regular basis, did not have any written agreement for the work, and generally did whatever Ronan told him to do. These facts would support a finding that Jones was an employee. Where the facts could reasonably support the conclusion that Jones was independent, I conclude that it is proper under Fed. R. Civ. P. 11 to deny that he was Ronan's employee, and I have done so. See paragraph 29 of the First Defense and the Sixth Defense.

If you decide to file a third-party complaint against Jones, it need not be filed with the answer. You may serve a third-party complaint without leave of court within ten days of serving the answer in the original action. Fed. R. Civ. P. 14(a). After that you will need leave of court, after notice to the plaintiff, to assert any third-party claims. Id. However, even if we file within the ten-day period for filing as of right, the court does not have to entertain the third-party claim. The decision to allow or dismiss a third-party claim is a discretionary one in each case. Wright at 548. If the court concludes that entertaining the additional claim would not advance the efficient and fair resolution of the entire dispute, it may dismiss it at any time.

As I read the technicalities of Fed. R. Civ. P. 6(a), our answer is due on January 4: We have to answer within five days. Tuesday the 28th, the day on which the case was removed, does not count under the rule, but the 29th, 30th, and 31st do. Saturday, the 1st, and Sunday, the 2nd don't count because weekend days don't count when the period is less than eleven days. See Rule 6(a), fourth sentence. So Monday, the 3rd is the fourth day, and our answer is due on Tuesday, the 4th. Even though the holiday is coming up, please remember to save time to review the documents before that date.

One last point you may wish to consider. Is it possible that, by seeking affirmative relief from Schulansky in our counterclaim, we will waive our objection to personal jurisdiction? I have not researched this point but will do so if you think this is a possible problem.

The Resulting Documents

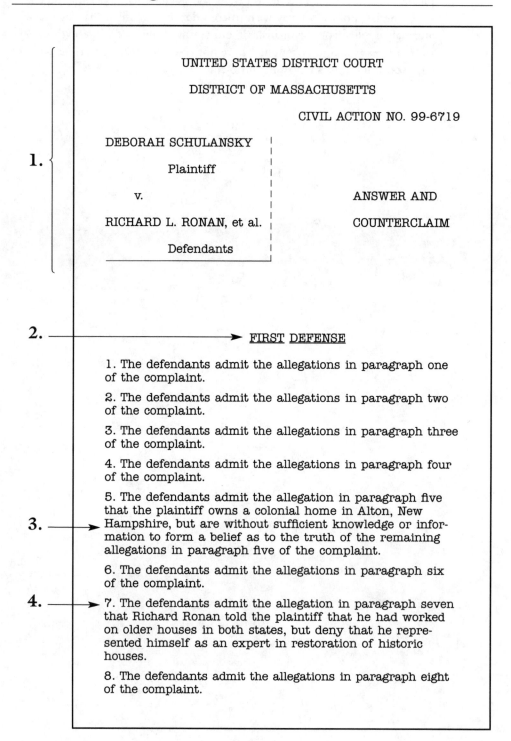

1.

UNITED STATES DISTRICT COURT

DISTRICT OF MASSACHUSETTS

CIVIL ACTION NO. 99-6719

DEBORAH SCHULANSKY

Plaintiff

v.

RICHARD L. RONAN, et al.

Defendants

ANSWER AND

COUNTERCLAIM

2. ⟶ FIRST DEFENSE

1. The defendants admit the allegations in paragraph one of the complaint.

2. The defendants admit the allegations in paragraph two of the complaint.

3. The defendants admit the allegations in paragraph three of the complaint.

4. The defendants admit the allegations in paragraph four of the complaint.

3. ⟶ 5. The defendants admit the allegation in paragraph five that the plaintiff owns a colonial home in Alton, New Hampshire, but are without sufficient knowledge or information to form a belief as to the truth of the remaining allegations in paragraph five of the complaint.

6. The defendants admit the allegations in paragraph six of the complaint.

4. ⟶ 7. The defendants admit the allegation in paragraph seven that Richard Ronan told the plaintiff that he had worked on older houses in both states, but deny that he represented himself as an expert in restoration of historic houses.

8. The defendants admit the allegations in paragraph eight of the complaint.

9. The defendants admit the allegation in paragraph nine that the parties discussed the condition of the old foundation at the March meeting, but deny that there was any discussion of a possible need for extensive reconstruction of the foundation.

10. The defendants deny the allegations in paragraph ten that they, or either one of them, agreed to reconstruct the foundation, or that such reconstruction was part of the construction of the foundation for the addition agreed to in the contract between the plaintiff and Ronan Construction Company.

11. The defendants admit the allegation in paragraph eleven that the defendant Richard Ronan sent a Proposal and Estimate to the plaintiff. The defendants further state that the Proposal and Estimate constituted an offer by the Ronan Construction Company, not by the defendant Richard Ronan individually.

12. The defendants admit the allegation in paragraph twelve that the plaintiff signed and returned the Proposal and Estimate on or around April 3, 1999, but further state that the Proposal and Estimate constituted an offer solely by Ronan Construction Company.

13. The defendants admit the allegations in paragraph thirteen of the complaint.

14. The defendants admit the allegations in paragraph fourteen of the complaint.

15. The defendants admit the allegation in paragraph fifteen that the foundation consisted of loose boulders without mortar, but deny that they were held together by the surrounding earth.

16. The defendants deny the allegations in paragraph sixteen of the complaint.

17. The defendants deny the allegations in paragraph seventeen of the complaint.

18. The defendants admit the allegation in paragraph eighteen that they did not completely reconstruct the preexisting foundation, but deny that they had agreed to do so, or that such reconstruction was necessary to provide adequate support for the house or the addition. The defendants did heavily reinforce the preexisting foundation with concrete in the course of constructing the addition.

19. The defendants deny the allegation in paragraph nineteen that the plaintiff demanded that they reconstruct the foundation or that the contract required them to do so.

20. The defendants deny the allegations of paragraph twenty of the complaint.

5. ➤ 21. The defendants repeat and reallege their responses to the allegations in paragraphs one to twenty of the complaint.

22. The defendants admit the allegation in paragraph twenty-two that the Proposal and Estimate constitutes a contract between Ronan Construction Company and the plaintiff. The defendants deny that Richard L. Ronan is a party to the contract.

23. The defendants admit the allegation in paragraph twenty-three that, under the contract, the defendant Ronan Construction Company agreed to construct an adequate foundation for the addition. They deny that the contract imposed any obligation upon Ronan Construction Company to reconstruct the foundation of the main house. They deny that Richard L. Ronan personally undertook any obligations under the contract.

24. The defendants deny the allegations in paragraph twenty-four of the complaint.

25. The defendants deny the allegations in paragraph twenty-five of the complaint.

26. The defendants admit the allegation in paragraph twenty-six that the plaintiff made the first four progress payments under the contract, but deny that they breached the contract. The defendants further state that the plaintiff has refused to make the final payment due under the contract, in the amount of $15,000, although the defendant Ronan Construction Company has performed all of its obligations under the contract in a timely and satisfactory manner and has demanded payment of the balance due under the contract.

27. The defendants deny the allegations in paragraph twenty-seven of the complaint.

28. The defendants repeat and reallege their responses to paragraphs one to twenty of the complaint.

29. The defendants deny the allegation in paragraph twenty-nine that the area adjacent to the foundation of the main house was negligently excavated. They further deny that the excavation was performed by employees of either defendant.

30. The defendants deny the allegations of paragraph thirty of the complaint.

6. ➤ ### SECOND DEFENSE

This action must be dismissed because the court lacks personal jurisdiction over the defendants under the Fourteenth Amendment and the Massachusetts Long-Arm Statute, Mass. G.L. c. 223A, §3.

THIRD DEFENSE

The plaintiff's first claim for relief fails to state a claim upon which relief can be granted, because the Proposal and Estimate constitutes the entire agreement between the parties, and does not require any reconstruction of the original foundation.

7. ———————————————▶

FOURTH DEFENSE

If the defendants had any obligation under the contract to reconstruct the preexisting foundation, the plaintiff waived performance of that obligation on or about April 17, 1999, when she agreed that the defendants could fulfill their obligations under the contract by reinforcing the preexisting foundation with cement.

FIFTH DEFENSE

The plaintiff's first claim for relief fails to state a claim upon which relief can be granted against the defendant Richard L. Ronan, because he was not a party to the contract.

SIXTH DEFENSE

If there was any negligence in the excavation of the foundation, that negligence was solely the act of Arlen Jones, an independent contractor for whose negligence the defendants cannot be held liable.

8. ———————▶ WHEREFORE, the defendants request that the court dismiss the plaintiff's complaint and award the defendants their costs, together with such other relief as the court finds just and equitable.

9. ———————▶

COUNTERCLAIM OF RONAN CONSTRUCTION COMPANY—BREACH OF CONTRACT

The defendant Ronan Construction Company counterclaims against the plaintiff as follows:

10. ———————▶ 1. This court has subject matter jurisdiction of this action under Article III, §2 of the United States Constitution and 28 U.S.C. §1332. This counterclaim is a compulsory counterclaim under Fed. R. Civ. P. 13(a). This court has supplemental jurisdiction over the counterclaim under 28 U.S.C. §1367(a).

11.

2. The signed Proposal and Estimate attached to the plaintiff's complaint constitutes a valid contract between the plaintiff and the defendant Ronan Construction Company.

3. Under that contract, the plaintiff agreed to pay Ronan Construction Company $40,000 for the construction of an addition to her home at 53 School Street, Alton, New Hampshire.

4. The defendant Ronan Construction Company has fully performed all of its obligations under the contract.

5. Although the defendant Ronan Construction Company has demanded payment of the final balance due under the contract, the plaintiff has failed to pay Ronan Construction Company the final progress payment of $15,000.

WHEREFORE, the defendant Ronan Construction Company demands judgment from the plaintiff in the amount of $15,000 and interest and costs and such other relief as the court finds just and equitable.

DEMAND FOR JURY TRIAL

12.

Under Fed. R. Civ. P. 38(b), the defendants demand jury trial of all issues raised by the plaintiff's complaint and the defendant Ronan Construction Company's counterclaim.

13.

Arthur Ackerman
Ackerman, Sloan and Cariotis
Attorney for the Defendants
59 State Street
Boston, MA 02114
(617) 228-6301

14.

CERTIFICATE OF SERVICE

I hereby certify that on this date I served a true copy of the above answer and counterclaim upon Phyllis Slater, Gomez, Robbins and Slater, 322 Puritan Road, Plymouth, MA 02360, by First Class mail, postage prepaid.

Date: _____

Arther Ackerman
Ackerman, Sloan and Cariotis
59 State Street
Boston, MA 02114
(617) 228-6301

Comments on the Answer and Counterclaim

1.   Rule 10(a) governs the caption of the answer as well as the complaint and all other pleadings. Note that the federal docket number is now known and will be used in all subsequent pleadings and other papers.

2.   Rule 8(b) specifically requires the defendant to respond to each allegation in the complaint by admitting or denying the allegations, stating the parts that are true and denying the remainder, or stating that the defendant does not have enough information to assess the truth of the allegation. In his First Defense, Ronan complies with this requirement by responding, paragraph by paragraph, to the allegations in the plaintiff's complaint. Rule 10(b) requires these responses to be set forth in numbered paragraphs, and the drafting attorney here has numbered her admissions and denials to correspond to the appropriate paragraphs in the complaint. This will make it easy for the parties and the court to compare the pleadings during the course of the suit, in order to quickly ascertain the positions of the parties on the various issues.

In some cases, the defendant may group his responses to parts of the complaint in a single sentence. For example, the answer might state that "the defendant admits the allegations in paragraphs one to eleven and sixteen to twenty-one of the complaint." See, e.g., Official Form 20, accompanying the Federal Rules of Civil Procedure. This saves space and time, but in cases with a large number of paragraphs and varied responses it is less helpful for quick reference in comparing the complaint and the answer.

3.   It is permissible for a party to respond by stating that he lacks sufficient information to admit or deny an allegation. Fed. R. Civ. P. 8(b). The defendants here probably have no particular knowledge of the National Register of Historic Places and are under no duty to scurry around and verify this allegation in order to answer the complaint.

4.   Rule 8(b) requires the defendant to respond clearly and forthrightly to the allegations of the complaint. ("Denials shall fairly meet the substance of the averments denied. When a pleader intends in good faith to deny only a part or a qualification of an averment, the pleader shall specify so much of it as is true and material and shall deny only the remainder.") It would not be proper for the defendants here to simply deny the entire allegation in paragraph seven, because Ronan had told the plaintiff that he had worked on old houses. However, the defendants do not accept the plaintiff's characterization of Ronan's statements and have therefore crafted their response to paragraph seven to negate any inference that Ronan represented himself as an expert in this area. A number of the defendants' other responses also admit some parts of the allegations but deny other parts or recharacterize allegations in the complaint. See, e.g., paragraphs 11, 15, 18, and 26.

5.   Rule 10(c) authorizes adoption by reference of parts of a pleading in another part of the pleading. The language of the rule is general, so it is clear that a defendant—or any other pleader—may do so as well as a plaintiff. Because Schulansky incorporated all of her factual allegations by reference into her First Claim for Relief, Ronan has similarly incorporated his answers to the earlier paragraphs in his answer to her First Claim for Relief.

6.   As you are probably aware, defending parties will frequently have further defenses to the plaintiff's claims, in addition to denials of the allegations in the complaint. After responding in the First Defense to each of the allegations of the complaint, the answer goes on to set forth several further defenses. This breakdown is proper under Rule 10(b), which provides in part that "each defense other than denials shall be stated in a separate count or defense whenever a separation facilitates the clear presentation of the matters set forth."

The defendants' Second Defense here is an objection to the court's power to adjudicate, on the ground that it lacks personal jurisdiction over the defendants. This objection could be raised by pre-answer motion under Rule 12(b), but it does not have to be. It is always proper to include this objection in the answer instead of raising it by pre-answer motion, so long as no pre-answer motion is made. See Chapter 18, p. 313. As Ackerman's memo indicates, the decision to answer rather than move to dismiss is a tactical one.

Careful counsel should be aware, however, that inserting an objection to personal jurisdiction in the answer, as the defendants have done here, may not be enough to preserve the defense. Some courts have held that defendants who assert the personal jurisdiction defense in the answer must subsequently take the initiative to seek a ruling on the issue, by moving to dismiss the case or asking for a hearing on the defense, or else forfeit the defense for failure to pursue it. See, e.g., *Hamilton v. Atlas Turner, Inc.*, 197 F.3d 58, 61-62 (2nd Cir. 1999). This is a serious trap for the unwary lawyer who raises the defense in the answer and assumes that the court will eventually get around to doing something about it.

7.   The defendants' Fourth Defense raises an affirmative defense. The defendants take the position that, even if the contract required reconstruction of the foundation and the defendants failed to do so, the plaintiff waived performance of this obligation by her assent to Ronan's alternative suggestion. An affirmative defense asserts new facts that avoid liability even if the plaintiff proves her basic allegations. It is akin to the old common law "confession and avoidance" device, except that the defendant need not admit the plaintiff's allegations ("confess") in order to allege additional facts that avoid liability.

Under Rule 8(e)(2), a defendant may plead inconsistently, and the *Schulansky* defendants have done so in their answer. In their First Defense, they deny that they agreed to reconstruct the foundation. In their Fourth Defense, they assert that, even if they did agree to do so, the plaintiff waived performance of that obligation.

The order of the various defenses is not prescribed by the rules. On occasion, you will see an answer that begins with objections and affirmative defenses and leaves the admissions and denials until later. Of paramount importance, of course, is that all defenses be raised in the answer, to avoid waiving any by omission.

8.   Defendants frequently include a paragraph like this at the end of the answer, asking the court, on the basis of the defenses and denials in the answer, to dismiss the complaint. In the federal courts (and state systems as well) a prevailing party is entitled to recover certain costs of suit, such as witness fees and the cost of transcripts. See 28 U.S.C. §1920. It is customary to ask for these in the answer and, in a lawyerly excess of caution, to append a request for any other relief the court finds "just and equitable" as well.

9.   It is entirely proper to include a counterclaim within the answer. It should be set apart from the rest of the answer, however, and clearly labeled as a counterclaim. If a counterclaim is not clearly labeled as such, it may look a good deal like an affirmative defense. (Compare, for example, paragraph 26 of the answer, which could be construed to seek relief from Schulansky for the unpaid balance under the contract.) Unless it is clearly labeled as a counterclaim and set apart from the various defenses, it may be unclear whether Ronan is defending on the basis of Schulansky's failure to fulfill her obligations under the contract or seeking independent, affirmative relief by way of counterclaim.

Note that Losordo has consistently taken the position in drafting the answer that the contract is between Ronan Construction Company and Schulansky. See paragraphs 10, 11, 12, 22, 23, and 26 of the First Defense. Thus, the company is the proper party to assert the counterclaim for breach of the contract. Indeed, Losordo might have chosen to emphasize the difference in the positions of Ronan and Ronan Construction Company by filing completely separate answers for them. The rules do not require the defendants to file a joint answer, and in cases where their interests are clearly divergent, they will not do so.

10.   Federal Rule 8(a) requires "a pleading which sets forth a claim for relief" to include a statement of the grounds for the court's jurisdiction. A counterclaim is such a pleading, and Losordo has accordingly asserted here that the court has supplemental jurisdiction over it. Supplemental jurisdiction is proper for this claim because it is a compulsory counterclaim. See Chapter 15, example 4.

Strictly speaking, this is probably overpleading. Rule 8(a)(1) does not require a jurisdictional allegation if the court already has jurisdiction (i.e., if an earlier pleading has already provided a basis for jurisdiction over the action), and the new pleading does not require "new grounds" for jurisdiction. In this case, the court has jurisdiction over the main claim based on diversity, and supplemental jurisdiction over the related counterclaim is arguably not a "new ground." However, since Schulansky's complaint was originally filed in state court, it contained no explicit allegation as to the basis of jurisdiction, and it is certainly appropriate, even if not required, to assert the ground of jurisdiction in the counterclaim.

The Rule 8(a)(1) requirement to state the ground of the court's jurisdiction refers to subject matter jurisdiction, not personal jurisdiction. *Sterling Homex Corp. v. Homasote Co.*, 437 F.2d 87, 88 (2d Cir. 1971). It is not necessary to assert in a pleading that the court has personal jurisdiction over the defendant, but, of course, the court must have it in order to proceed.

11. The general rules of pleading govern the allegations in a counterclaim, including the use of numbered paragraphs and inclusion of a demand for relief.[1] Like an original complaint, a counterclaim may include a number of claims for relief based on different theories. It is even permissible to assert completely unrelated counterclaims (see Fed R. Civ. P. 13(b)), although there will not be supplemental jurisdiction over such claims.

Unlike the common law, where the parties might plead back and forth a number of times before a single issue is reached, the answer usually ends the pleadings under the Federal Rules. However, Fed. R. Civ. P. 7(a) does require the plaintiff to reply to a counterclaim if it is "denominated as such." This means that if the defendant does not clearly label the counterclaim in the answer, the plaintiff need not file a reply. Thus, he need not guess whether vague allegations in an answer are affirmative defenses, denials, or counterclaims. Schulansky would be required to file a reply to this counterclaim, since Ronan's counsel has clearly labeled it as such, putting Schulansky on notice that Ronan is claiming affirmative relief from her.

The plaintiff's reply is governed by the same pleading requirements as Ronan's answer and should include responses to each of the paragraphs in the counterclaim as well as affirmative defenses. Of course, the reply will only address the allegations in the counterclaim itself, since the parties' positions on the main claim are already established by the complaint and the answer. The reply must be served within 20 days after service of the answer. Fed. R. Civ. P. 12(a)(2).

12. Losordo has followed her own suggestion in her memo on removal (see infra p. 556) and included a demand for jury trial on the counterclaim. It may be that the jury demand is unneccessary, but at most it is redundant. Rather than invest substantial research time (and the client's money) in

---

1. In putting a dollar demand in his counterclaim, Ronan has not ignored Mass. Gen. L. ch. 231, §13B, the statute that bars putting a dollar demand in some complaints. That statute only bars a dollar demand in cases of unliquidated damages, that is, damages that cannot easily be calculated. In cases where the damages can be easily ascertained by calculation, a specific demand is proper. Here, all Ronan has to do to ascertain the damages is to subtract the earlier progress payments from the contract price.

finding a definitive answer to this question, Losordo has simply erred on the side of caution by including it in the answer. Just to cover all the bases, she has also demanded jury trial on the main claim as well.

13.   The answer, like the complaint and all other pleadings and motions, must be signed by the attorney and is subject to the ethical constraints and sanctions set forth in Fed. R. Civ. P. 11.

14.   The elaborate service provisions of Fed. R. Civ. P. 4 only govern service of the complaint. Subsequent papers may be served under the simpler provisions of Fed. R. Civ. P. 5(b), which authorizes service by personal delivery or regular mail to the attorney for the opposing party. Once properly notified that the suit has been commenced, the parties should be in contact and should watch the docket for subsequent filings. But a party who never receives initial notice of a suit cannot take such precautions.

The certificate of service constitutes a representation by the serving attorney that he has complied with the service requirements of Rule 5(b). It is often drafted as a separate document, but the local rules for the District of Massachusetts provide that the certificate of service must appear on the pleading or motion itself, rather than on a separate sheet. Local Rule 5.2(b)(2).

Losordo raises an interesting question at the end of her memo, concerning the possibility that asserting the counterclaim might waive the defendant's objection to personal jurisdiction. In fact, if Ronan's attorneys look into this issue, they will find that the courts are split on this question. Some cases have held that a defendant waives his objection to personal jurisdiction by asking the court to adjudicate a counterclaim. Others, however, have recognized that this puts the defendant in an awkward position, because Fed. R. Civ. P. 13(a) *requires* him to assert any counterclaim that arises out of the same events as the plaintiff's claim. (Of course, the defendant could present the personal jurisdiction issue by pre-answer motion, thus obtaining resolution of that issue before answering.) See generally 5A Wright and Miller at §1397, which reviews this issue and suggests that assertion of a compulsory counterclaim should not waive the personal jurisdiction defense.

One of the things that makes a litigation practice unnerving is the number of uncertainties that arise in the course of a case, in circumstances that make it impossible to give those issues the full attention they deserve. Here, the attorneys are under the gun to get their responsive pleading in and are doubtless handling many other matters as well. Many lawyers would never even have thought of this rather subtle ramification of the counterclaim. Even if their client could afford to have exhaustive research done on this point, it would have been hard for Ronan's lawyers to find the time to do it before answering. They probably would not have found a definitive answer even if they had researched the point.

It is also interesting to compare the facts as stated in the Slater memo (pp. 533-535) and Ackerman's memo in this chapter. The dispute looks quite different from the two parties' points of view. It is unlikely that either is lying or deliberately distorting the facts; they just see things from different perspectives, like Republicans and Democrats, or Mainers and Californians. The truth, if there is such a thing in a case like this, is likely to be ambiguous and elusive. If there is a trial, the system will resolve the dispute one way or the other, but it is unlikely that it will definitely determine who is "right" or leave either party feeling fully satisfied for the effort and emotional stress it engenders.

Naturally, the attorneys' job in drafting the pleadings, and in representing the parties generally, is to state the case most strongly from their clients' viewpoints. Hopefully, providing vigorous advocacy will not prevent them from seeing the facts as they are likely to play out at trial and advising their clients accordingly. But even if they keep some perspective on the case, there is little doubt that the lawyer's duty in an adversary system tends to accentuate the differences in the parties' views rather than the search for common ground. This has spawned an increasing emphasis on alternatives to litigation, such as mediation, which try to educate the parties about each others' views and bring the parties together rather than focus, as the litigation system tends to, on the differences in their points of view.

Chain Reaction:
Ronan Brings
In Jones

The Drafting Request

MEMORANDUM

TO: Marcia Losordo
 Associate

FROM: Arthur Ackerman

RE: Third-party complaint in *Schulansky v. Ronan* U.S. District
 Court No. 99-6719

DATE: January 4, 2000

- -

  I have reviewed and filed your answer and counterclaim in the Schulansky case. I have also discussed with Dick Ronan the possibility of filing a third-party complaint against Arlen Jones, the backhoe operator who did the excavation work on the job. On the basis of that discussion, I have decided to proceed with the third-party complaint.

  As you are no doubt aware, Fed. R. Civ. P. 14(a) allows us to implead Jones if he "is or may be liable to [our clients] for all or part of the plaintiff's claim" against them. In other words, we can implead Jones if we have a right to reimbursement from him for any damages Schulansky recovers from us. In my judgment, we may be able to obtain indemnification from Jones if

Schulansky recovers on either her breach of contract claim or her negligence claim. Please let me know if you agree with the following line of reasoning, which leads me to that conclusion.

As you suggested in your earlier memo, it is not clear whether Jones acted as a subcontractor to Ronan or as Ronan's employee in doing the excavation work. The accepted test is the extent of control Ronan could exercise over Jones in the course of the work, and the facts on this are ambiguous. On the one hand, Ronan apparently did not have a written contract with Jones for the excavation work; he simply called Jones up and asked him to do the work for $3,000. The facts that Jones worked for a flat price and used his own equipment support the argument that he acted as an independent contractor. On the other hand, according to Ronan, he consistently directed Jones in the course of the work and considered Jones (who worked quite regularly for Ronan) an employee, even though he usually paid him by the job. In addition, the informality of their arrangement suggests an employment relationship more than a contract. Given the ambiguity in the evidence, it will likely be a jury question whether Jones should be characterized as an employee or independent contractor. Restatement (Second) of Agency §220, comment c (1958).

If the jury were to find that Jones was Ronan's employee, Ronan would be liable for his negligence, under respondeat superior principles (Restatement (Second) of Agency §219 (1958)), but would have a right to indemnification from Jones. Thus, if Schulansky proves that Jones negligently disturbed the existing foundation during the excavation, and the jury concludes that Jones acted as an employee in doing the work, Schulansky will recover judgment from us, but Jones will be liable to indemnify us for the entire judgment.

Alternatively, if the jury finds that Jones was not directly under Ronan's control and therefore acted as a subcontractor to Ronan, Ronan should still have a right of indemnification from him under contract principles. If Jones's negligent excavation caused a breach of the main contract between Ronan and Schulansky, Ronan would be liable directly to Schulansky for the breach by his subcontractor. However, Jones would have breached his subcontract with Ronan by failing to perform the work properly, so Ronan would have a cause of action against him for breach of the subcontract. The damages for this breach would include the judgment Ronan incurred to Schulansky, as well as any attorneys' fees Ronan pays us for defending the claim. Thus, if Schulansky recovers on her breach of contract claim, we should be entitled to recover from Jones both the damages we pay to Schulansky and our fees for defending the main action.

If you agree with my reasoning, please draft a third-party complaint against Jones for indemnification on both of the plaintiff's claims. I realize that our theories for indemnification are based on inconsistent allegations, since we will allege on the negligence claim that Jones was an employee, but on the contract claim that he was a subcontractor. However, Rule 8(e)(2) expressly allows us to plead inconsistent versions of our claim. Nor do I view this as inappropriate under the ethical pleading requirements in Rule 11, since there is factual support for characterizing Jones either as an employee or an independent contractor. Where the jury could properly reach either conclusion, it is appropriate to assert whatever rights we may have against Jones based on either theory.

As you pointed out in our discussions, it is a little awkward to deny that the foundation was damaged at all during the excavation (as we did in our answer) but to turn around and implead Jones for causing that damage. Ronan tells me that he is not convinced that Jones's excavation work destabilized the foundation, or that anything did. But there is some evidence to support a finding that Jones was negligent. Apparently Jones did hit the foundation a number of times with his backhoe, and the excavation turned up some loose rocks along the edge of the foundation. Schulansky was present at the time, and this is probably what is behind her negligence claim.

I do not think the Rules require us to disregard our possible rights against Jones just because we denied in our answer that any negligence took place. As indicated above, the Rules specifically authorize inconsistent pleading. Of course, we must have evidentiary support for the allegations under Rule 11, but I believe Ronan's observations about Jones's encounters with the foundation during the excavation meet this test, since they suggest that Jones may have damaged the foundation in the course of the excavation. We shouldn't have to abandon a possible right to indemnification against Jones just because we think the stronger argument is that there was no negligence in the first place.

We may have a serious problem obtaining personal jurisdiction over Jones in Massachusetts. Jones lives in New Hampshire, agreed to do the work in a telephone conversation with Ronan, and performed all the work in New Hampshire. According to Ronan, Jones does work occasionally in Massachusetts, but I doubt that this occasional work in the state is sufficient to support personal jurisdiction over Jones for a claim unrelated to his work here in the state. On the other hand, since Jones occasionally works for contractors here in Massachusetts perhaps we can serve process on him while he is working here and obtain jurisdiction based on in-state service. Please do a little research to determine whether this would establish personal jurisdiction over Jones here.

I realize you have not yet had a chance to open your Christmas presents, but please get on this right away. I would like to file this within the ten-day limit for filing the third-party complaint without leave of court.

The Associate's Response

MEMORANDUM

TO: Arthur Ackerman

FROM: Marcia Losordo

RE: Third-party complaint in *Schulansky v. Ronan*
            U.S. District Court No. 99-6719

DATE: January 7, 2000

- -

I have attached a draft third-party complaint against Jones in the Schulansky case. I agree with your analysis of Jones's potential liability to us, but I have several additional observations. First, it is conceivable that Schulansky would recover from us for breach of contract on both grounds alleged in her complaint. It may turn out that the structural damage resulted in part from Ronan's failure to rebuild the foundation, and in part from damage caused by Jones's backhoe. If the jury finds that both causes contributed to the settling, we would have a right to partial indemnification from Jones: Presumably the court would apportion the damages between the two causes, and Jones only contributed to one of them.

It is proper to implead a third party for partial as well as full indemnification; Rule 14(a) authorizes impleader of a party who "is or may be liable to the third-party plaintiff for all *or part* of the plaintiff's claim..." (emphasis supplied). Thus, I have asserted two claims for relief based on the theory that Jones breached his subcontract with Ronan, one for full indemnification and a separate claim for partial indemnification.

Second, note that our claim against Jones for any attorneys' fees Ronan pays us to defend Schulansky's claim against him does not satisfy the Rule 14 requirement, since this is not reimbursement for damages Ronan must pay Schulansky. These fees represent separate consequential damages Ronan has suffered as a result of Jones's breach of the subcontract, and the resulting need to defend Schulansky's lawsuit. However, it is proper to assert this additional claim in the third-party complaint. Once a defendant has asserted a proper impleader claim under Rule 14(a), she may also assert independent claims against the third-party defendant under Fed. R. Civ. P. 18(a). Since the claim arises from the same events as the main claim, the court will have supplemental jurisdiction over it under 28 U.S.C. §1367(a).

As you suggest, the fact that Jones does occasional business in Massachusetts is not sufficient under the *International Shoe* minimum contacts test to support personal jurisdiction over him for a claim unrelated to the in-state business. See *Helicopteros Nacionales de Columbia, S.A. v. Hall*,

466 U.S. 408, 414-415 (1984) (where claim does not arise out of contacts with forum state, the defendant must have continuous and systematic contacts there to support jurisdiction). Since Jones only works in Massachusetts occasionally, it is doubtful that he would be subject to general in personam jurisdiction here. However, personal jurisdiction can be obtained over Jones by serving process on him here in Massachusetts, under the hoary doctrine of *Pennoyer v. Neff*. The Supreme Court reaffirmed the sufficiency of such "transient personal service" in *Burnham v. Superior Court of California*, 495 U.S. 604 (1990). Of course, this requires us to keep track of Jones's movements, locate him on the job site in Massachusetts, and actually serve him in person in the state.

Alternatively, we may be able to serve Jones in New Hampshire under Fed. R. Civ. P. 4(k)(1)(B), the "100-mile bulge" provision for service on certain additional parties to actions in federal court. Under Rule 4(k)(1)(B), a third-party defendant may be served with process outside the forum state but within 100 miles of the courthouse. This provision authorizes service on Jones in New Hampshire, as long as he is served within 100 miles of the courthouse in Boston. Evidently, Rule 4(k)(1)(B) not only authorizes service of process on Jones within the bulge area, but also *makes him subject to personal jurisdiction in Massachusetts,* even if he would not be subject to jurisdiction under fourteenth amendment due process analysis. In other words, even if a Massachusetts state court could not subject Jones to personal jurisdiction, because he lacks minimum contacts with Massachusetts, the federal court here could apparently require Jones to defend in Massachusetts under Rule 4(k)(1)(B). See the title of Rule 4(k) ("Territorial Limits of Effective Service").

However, Rule 4 clearly cannot confer jurisdiction if it would be unconstitutional to exercise it: Neither the rulemakers nor Congress can repeal the restrictions of the due process clause. (I am not even clear as to what due process restrictions actually apply here — state standards under the fourteenth amendment or federal standards under the fifth?) Thus, there is some question as to whether serving Jones under Rule 4(k)(1)(B) will force him to defend in Massachusetts.

This is a very sophisticated personal jurisdiction issue, which could require extensive research and briefing if it is contested. But the issue won't arise if we serve Jones in Massachusetts, or if we serve him in New Hampshire under Rule 4(k)(1)(B), and he does not raise an objection to personal jurisdiction. I suggest that we serve him on the job in Massachusetts if possible, and if not, within the 100-mile bulge. (Please note that the third-party complaint and summons must be served on Jones under the provisions of Fed. R. Civ. P. 4, not under Rule 5.) If he submits to jurisdiction, we will save our clients a good deal of expense in a relatively small-stakes case.

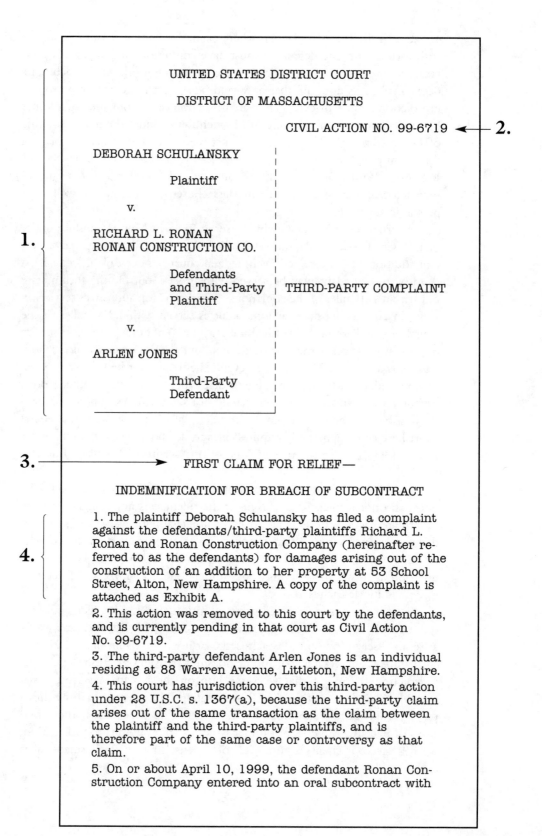

UNITED STATES DISTRICT COURT

DISTRICT OF MASSACHUSETTS

CIVIL ACTION NO. 99-6719 ◄——— **2.**

DEBORAH SCHULANSKY

Plaintiff

v.

RICHARD L. RONAN
RONAN CONSTRUCTION CO.

Defendants
and Third-Party   THIRD-PARTY COMPLAINT
Plaintiff

v.

ARLEN JONES

Third-Party
Defendant

3. ————————►   FIRST CLAIM FOR RELIEF—

INDEMNIFICATION FOR BREACH OF SUBCONTRACT

1. The plaintiff Deborah Schulansky has filed a complaint against the defendants/third-party plaintiffs Richard L. Ronan and Ronan Construction Company (hereinafter referred to as the defendants) for damages arising out of the construction of an addition to her property at 53 School Street, Alton, New Hampshire. A copy of the complaint is attached as Exhibit A.

2. This action was removed to this court by the defendants, and is currently pending in that court as Civil Action No. 99-6719.

3. The third-party defendant Arlen Jones is an individual residing at 88 Warren Avenue, Littleton, New Hampshire.

4. This court has jurisdiction over this third-party action under 28 U.S.C. s. 1367(a), because the third-party claim arises out of the same transaction as the claim between the plaintiff and the third-party plaintiffs, and is therefore part of the same case or controversy as that claim.

5. On or about April 10, 1999, the defendant Ronan Construction Company entered into an oral subcontract with

the third-party defendant, Arlen Jones, for performance of the excavation work on the addition.

6. Under the contract, the third-party defendant agreed to perform all the excavation work required by the main contract, using his own labor and equipment, and the defendants agreed to pay the third-party defendant the sum of $3,000 upon completion of the work.

7. The excavation work was performed entirely by the third-party defendant, on or about April 15-18, 1999.

8. The First Claim for Relief in the plaintiff's complaint alleges a right to relief for breach of contract, on the ground that the defendants breached their contract with her by failing to perform the excavation work in a careful manner, resulting in damage to the existing foundation of the house.

9. If defendants breached their contract with the plaintiff by failing to perform the excavation work in a careful manner, that breach and any resulting damage was caused solely by the acts of the third-party defendant.

10. If the third-party defendant failed to perform the excavation work in a careful manner, that failure constituted a breach of the contract between the defendants and the third-party defendant.

5. ⟶ 11. If the plaintiff recovers against the defendants on the ground that the damage to the foundation in the course of excavation constituted a breach of their contract, the third-party defendant is liable to the defendants for any damages adjudged against them in the main action described in paragraph one.

6. ⟶ WHEREFORE, the defendants demand judgment against the third-party defendant as follows:

    a. For any and all sums that may be adjudged against them in the plaintiff's main action against them.

7. ⟶   b. For all costs, including attorneys' fees, incurred in defense of this action.

    c. For such other relief as the court deems just and proper.

SECOND CLAIM FOR RELIEF—

PARTIAL INDEMNIFICATION FOR BREACH OF SUBCONTRACT

12. The defendants repeat and reallege the allegations in paragraphs one to ten of the third-party complaint.

13. If the plaintiff recovers from the defendants both on the ground that they breached their contract with the plaintiff by negligently excavating the foundation and on the ground that they failed to rebuild it, the third-party defendant is liable to the defendants under the subcontract for that part of the damages resulting from the negligent excavation.

WHEREFORE, the defendants demand judgment from the third-party defendant as follows:

a. For any and all sums that may be adjudged against them for breach of contract resulting from the third-party defendant's negligent excavation.

b. For that part of the defendants' attorneys' fees and costs in defending this action attributable to the plaintiff's claim for negligent excavation.

c. For such other relief as the court deems just and proper.

THIRD CLAIM FOR RELIEF—

INDEMNIFICATION FOR NEGLIGENCE

14. The defendants repeat and reallege the allegations in paragraph one of the third-party complaint.

15. The Second Claim for Relief in the plaintiff's complaint alleges a right to recover from the defendants on the ground that the defendants were negligent in excavating the area in which the addition was to be constructed.

8. 16. On or about April 10, 1999, the defendants employed the third-party defendant Jones to perform the excavation work for the addition.

17. The excavation work was done entirely by the third-party defendant in the course of his employment for the defendants.

18. If the excavation work was negligently performed, any negligence in the work was due solely to acts of the third-party defendant.

19. If the plaintiff recovers from the defendant on her Second Claim for Relief, the defendants are entitled to indemnification from the third-party defendant for any and all damages that they are ordered to pay to the plaintiff on that claim.

WHEREFORE, the defendants demand judgment from the third-party defendant as follows:

a. For all damages that the defendants are ordered to pay to the plaintiff on her second claim for relief.

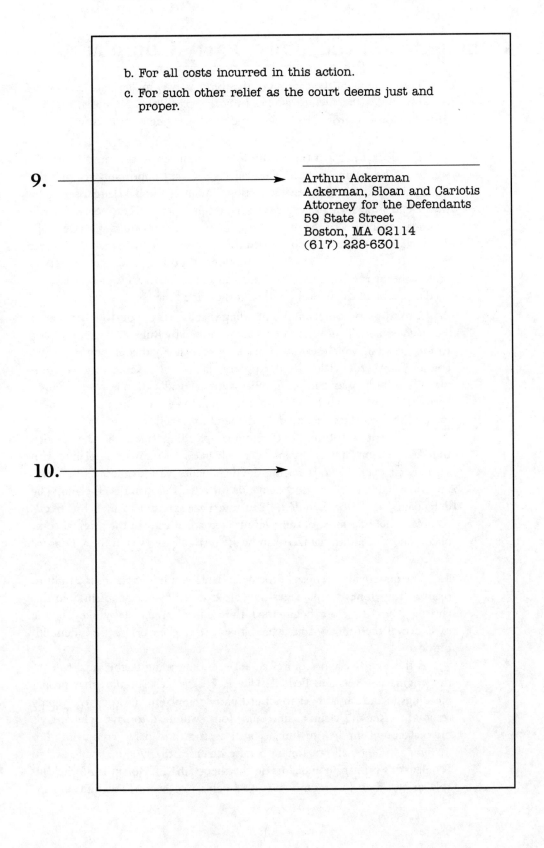

b. For all costs incurred in this action.

c. For such other relief as the court deems just and proper.

9. ──────────────────────────▶
Arthur Ackerman
Ackerman, Sloan and Cariotis
Attorney for the Defendants
59 State Street
Boston, MA 02114
(617) 228-6301

10. ──────────────────────────▶

Comments on the Third-Party Complaint

1.   The contents of the caption of the third-party complaint are again governed by Rule 10(a), which applies to "every pleading." Note that the title of the action has grown to include the third-party defendant as well as the original parties.

2.   The docket number on the third-party complaint is the same as that assigned to the original action. This reflects the very important fact that the third-party action is *not* a separate action, but an additional claim asserted by the defendant against a new party in the original action. This new claim will be litigated along with the main claim unless the court orders separate trials. Thus, all three parties will be entitled to seek discovery from each other (see, e.g., Fed. R. Civ. P. 33, 34, 36), all motions and other papers will be served on all other parties, all parties will participate in any hearings or pretrial proceedings, and all claims will be tried at the same time.

3.   A third-party complaint is a pleading that asserts a right to relief against a new defendant. Thus, its contents are governed by Rule 8(a), which applies to any "pleading which sets forth a claim for relief, whether an original claim, counterclaim, cross-claim, or third-party claim...." Like an original complaint, the third-party complaint must contain an allegation as to the court's basis for subject matter jurisdiction (see paragraph 4), a short and plain statement of the plaintiff's claim, and a demand for relief.

Because it is subject to the regular pleading rules, the defendants' third-party complaint is organized much like an original complaint, with separate claims for relief asserting the defendants' various theories for holding Jones liable to them, and demands for relief following each claim. The defendants have not included a separate Facts section as in Schulansky's complaint because most of the relevant facts are already in the original complaint, and the additional facts can be set forth clearly within the *Claim for Relief* sections.

4.   The underlying premise of the defendants' impleader claims is a right to recover from Jones for damages they are ordered to pay Schulansky in this lawsuit. They therefore begin their third-party complaint by alleging the existence of the primary suit, which gives rise to their claims for indemnification.

A third-party claim requires an answer conforming to the same rules as the original answer. See Fed. R. Civ. P. 7(a), which specifies that proper pleadings include an answer to a third-party complaint. In order to properly respond to Ronan's claim against him, Jones will need to have Schulansky's original complaint before him as well as the third-party complaint. For example, Rule 14 allows Jones to raise defenses that *Ronan* may have to Schulansky's primary complaint, on the theory that, if Ronan is not held liable to her, then Jones cannot be held liable to Ronan. Jones can only do this if he has the original complaint to work with in formulating an answer. The defendants should therefore append a copy of the original complaint to the third-party complaint.

5.   The defendants may bring in Jones if he is or may be liable to them for all or part of Schulansky's claim against them. The third-party complaint properly seeks recovery from Jones for those damages that the defendants are ordered to pay Schulansky.

6.   Since the third-party complaint is governed by the pleading requirements of Rule 8(a), it must include a demand for relief. Again, since Ronan seeks recovery over against Jones, their main demand for relief (subsection a) is for the damages they must pay Schulansky. Here the defendants have included separate demands for damages after each claim for relief. Since the potential damages differ under at least the first two claims, including separate demands after each claim makes it easier to understand each claim. Compare the original complaint, supra p. 538, which includes a single demand at the end of the entire complaint, and comment 10 following it.

7.   The associate's point about the right to attorneys' fees is a perceptive one. While Ronan's claim to recover from Jones any damages he pays to Schulansky is derivative under Rule 14, his claim for fees is for a separate loss he suffered as a result of Jones's acts. Essentially, Ronan's fees claim is based on the theory that he would not have had to defend Schulansky's suit if Jones had done his job properly. Thus, the fees expended in the defense are a consequential loss resulting from Jones's breach, although they are paid to Ronan's lawyer, not to Schulansky. They constitute a distinct claim that does not satisfy Rule 14 but may be asserted along with the idemnnification claim under Fed. R. Civ. P. 18(a). Compare Chapter 14, example 6. It is quite likely that the court would have jurisdiction over this related claim under the supplemental jurisdiction statute, 28 U.S.C. §1367(a).

Actually, it is unlikely that Ronan would directly incur attorneys' fees for the defense of this action. His liability insurance coverage almost certainly would include the costs of defense as well as coverage for any liability that results from the action. However, his coverage might not cover claims for breach of contract; if that is true, the insurer might disavow the duty to defend on this claim, or make some arrangement for Ronan Construction to cover part of the costs of defense. If so, then Ronan could seek those from Jones on an indemnification theory.

8.   In paragraphs 16 and 17 of the third claim for relief, Ronan alleges that Jones acted in the scope of his employment for Ronan. Compare paragraphs five and six of his first claim for relief against Jones, which allege a contractual relationship. As Ackerman's memo indicates, the two theories of relief are premised on differing underlying factual conclusions that the jury might reach. Consequently, the factual allegations in the two claims for relief reflect these inconsistent positions.

9.   The attorney's signature on the third-party complaint, as on any other pleading or motion, is subject to the ethical requirements of Rule 11. As Ackerman's memo indicates, he gave considerable thought to those requirements before including inconsistent allegations concerning Jones's status in the third-party complaint.

10.   Note that there is no attorney's certificate of service at the end of the third-party complaint. The reason is that the third-party complaint must be served on Jones, a new party who has no prior notice of the action, under the more exacting provisions of Rule 4, not Rule 5. Proof of service will thus be made in the manner provided by Rule 4(1), not by a simple attorney's certificate. (However, the third-party complaint would be served on *Schulansky* under the provisions of Rule 5.)

Losordo's suggestion in her memo that they postpone research on the issue of personal jurisdiction over Jones is a good one. Any practicing lawyer will attest that innumerable complex issues arise in the practice of law. Sometimes it is evident from the outset that a case will turn on such an issue. Often, however, issues arise that may turn out to be important or may not, depending on the course of the suit, the evidence turned up in discovery, whether the opposing party raises the issue, and whether the case goes to trial. Attorneys constantly make pragmatic judgments about which issues to spend their time and their clients' money researching. Frequently, those complex issues just go away for one reason or another.

In this case, for example, the issue of Jones's amenability to jurisdiction under Fed. R. Civ. P. 4(k)(1)(B) could be a complicated one. But it may never need to be decided, if Jones is served in Massachusetts, or if he does not object to jurisdiction, or if he does but the case settles before the issue is litigated. Here, Losordo has noted the potential problem but quite sensibly delayed extensive research on the issue until it becomes clear that it will have to be resolved.

33

Preliminary Objections: Jones Seeks a Way Out

The Drafting Request

MEMORANDUM

TO: Phillip Torres

FROM: Don Philbrook

RE: Arlen Jones Construction Case

DATE: January 21, 2000

- -

I represent Arlen Jones, a neighbor of mine who is in the excavation business. He has just been served with process in a federal court suit down in Boston, arising out of some work he did on a house over in Alton. I have attached the original complaint in the action and the third-party complaint against Jones. He is surprised and puzzled by the suit, since he thought the job went fine and the owner was happy. He is also concerned about defending an action down in Boston. Arlen is a local guy with a small business; he is hardly in a position to pay big city legal fees. (I'm not even sure he'll be able to manage mine ... I'll probably have to put in a pool so he can pay me off by doing the excavation!)

Naturally, Jones would rather litigate up here than down in Boston, or, better still, get out of this suit entirely. It seems to me that we may have several grounds for dismissal of this action by motion. First, it seems dubious to me that Jones should be subject to personal jurisdiction in Massachusetts on this claim. He negotiated with the general contractor, Ronan Construction Company, here in New Hampshire. He did the work in New Hampshire. The job was a small one at that, only a few days' work for something like $3,000. Whatever damages the owner suffered were suffered here. Thus, this claim does not arise out of any "minimum contacts" Jones has with Massachusetts. Nor is he subject to general in personam jurisdiction there—he lives next door to me here in Littleton, and though he works in Massachusetts once in a while, he does not do business there regularly.

Jones wasn't even served with process in the suit in Massachusetts; Ronan had the summons and complaint served on Jones while he was working on a job down in Dover. Now, I'm just an old country lawyer, and you young fellas may know more about these things than I do, but it seems dubious to me that Jones could be served with process here in New Hampshire, and dragged down to defend a federal court case in Massachusetts, if he lacks minimum contacts with that state. Please do a little research on this issue. Don't go overboard on it—we're not talking million dollar damages here, and Jones can't afford to pay for overkill—but give it a few hours to see if we may have grounds for filing a Rule 12(b) motion to dismiss based on lack of personal jurisdiction and draft an appropriate motion for my signature if there is reasonable support for it.

We may also be able to move to dismiss for lack of subject matter jurisdiction, since we are from the same state as Ronan, the third-party plaintiff, and this is a state law claim. I believe there is a statute now that governs such ancillary claims in federal court. I just looked at it briefly when it was enacted, but I thought it barred claims brought under Rule 14. Please research and advise me on this as well.

If we can't get the claim against Jones dismissed under Fed. R. Civ. P. 12(b)(1) or (2), perhaps we can convince the court to transfer this action to the District of New Hampshire under 28 U.S.C. §1404(a). It seems to me that it makes much more sense to litigate this case here than in Boston. The work was done here, both of the defendants and the third-party defendant live and do business here, and any damages resulting from the job were suffered here. I assume that most of the witnesses other than Schulansky will be from New Hampshire, since Jones tells me that all of Ronan's employees are also local.

Please take a quick look at the case law on the grounds for transfer of venue. If the cases support our argument for transfer, please draft a separate motion to transfer this action to the District of New Hampshire and advise me as to whether you think we should file it along with our motion to dismiss or hold off until decision of that motion. Be sure to check the local rules of the District of Massachusetts for any special requirements pertaining to motions filed in that court. Feel free to call Jones directly if you need further information from him.

Our response is due within 10 days (the 20-day period under the rule minus the 10 days it took Jones to come to me), so please take care of this right away.

The Associate's Response

MEMORANDUM

TO: Donald Philbrook

FROM: Phillip Torres

RE: Preliminary Motions in *Ronan v. Jones*
            Ma. Federal Dist. Ct. Civil Action No. 99-6719

DATE: January 24, 2000

- -

I have done preliminary research on the three issues you raised in your memo. I conclude that we do not have grounds to move to dismiss for lack of subject matter jurisdiction. On the personal jurisdiction issue, I conclude that there is a slim argument for dismissal but that we are very unlikely to prevail. The strongest argument is for transfer under 28 U.S.C. §1404(a). I recommend making a motion to transfer only.

1. Subject Matter Jurisdiction

It appears that we do not have a valid objection to subject matter jurisdiction over Ronan's claim against Jones. Before the passage of 28 U.S.C. §1367, governing "supplemental jurisdiction," it was clear that the citizenship of an impleaded third party was not relevant to establishing diversity jurisdiction. Several distinguished authorities supported the proposition that, if the original action was a proper diversity action, the addition of a third party did not affect the court's jurisdiction. See C. Wright, Federal Courts 515 (4th ed. 1983), J. Glannon, Civil Procedure: Examples and Explanations 152 (1st ed. 1987). Jurisdiction over such claims was based on "ancillary jurisdiction." *Owen Equipment & Erection Co. v. Kroger,* 437 U.S. 365, 375-376 (1978).

Under §1367, however, which now governs "supplemental jurisdiction," state law claims that are related to a case properly before the federal court may also be heard by the court. See 28 U.S.C. §1367(a), which provides that claims that are part of the same "case or controversy" as the main claim may be brought in federal court along with it. There is little question that the statute authorizes supplemental jurisdiction over third-party claims where there is no independent basis for subject matter jurisdiction. See now J. Glannon, Civil Procedure: Examples and Explanations p. 275 (4th ed. 2001). Consequently, I have not included this defense in the motion to dismiss.

Your memory is correct that the statute contains a special provision governing certain Rule 14 claims. See §1367(b). This provision bars supplemental jurisdiction over claims by *plaintiffs* against persons made parties under Rule 14 (and other rules), but it does not apply to claims by a defendant against an impleaded party.

2. Personal Jurisdiction

I spent several hours researching whether Jones is subject to personal jurisdiction in the Massachusetts federal court on the basis of personal service in New Hampshire. My preliminary analysis is as follows:

In *Burnham v. Superior Court of California*, 495 U.S. 604 (1990), the Supreme Court reaffirmed that personal jurisdiction may be based on service of process within the forum state, but *Burnham* does not authorize personal jurisdiction in Massachusetts based on service in New Hampshire. However, service in this case may be proper under Fed. R. Civ. P. 4(k)(1)(b), the "100-mile bulge" provision of Rule 4. Frankly, I had never heard of Rule 4(k)(1)(b) until I started to research this issue. It provides that certain parties (including parties like Jones who are brought in under Rule 14) may be served anywhere within 100 miles of the courthouse. Dover, where Jones was served, is well within that limit. So it is clear that Ronan was authorized to *serve* Jones in this manner.

It is not absolutely clear, however, that Jones can be forced to defend in Massachusetts just because he is served in New Hampshire under the 100-mile bulge provision, since he has no minimum contacts with the state where he is being forced to appear. Rule 4(k) is clearly intended to be a federal long-arm provision as well as a service-of-process provision; that is, it is intended not only to authorize service of process within the bulge area but also to authorize the exercise of personal jurisdiction over parties served there. See Fed. R. Civ. P. 4(k)(1) ("[s]ervice of a summons . . . is effective to establish jurisdiction over the person of the defendant [who fits into one of the categories in the rule]"); see also Advisory Committee note to 1993 revisions of Rule 4, subdivison k.

Even though the rulemakers explicitly sought to extend personal jurisdiction to parties served under Rule 4(k), the rule still must not exceed the bounds of due process. Under the old rule, there was some authority that suggested that it would exceed due process limits to exercise personal jurisdiction over a bulge defendant if he had no contacts with the forum state. See *Karlsen v. Hauff*, 278 F. Supp. 864 (S.D.N.Y. 1967) (overruled by *Coleman v. American Export Isbrandtsen Lines, Inc.*, 405 F.2d 250, 251-253 (2d Cir. 1968). Most of the cases under earlier versions of this rule, however, allowed personal jurisdiction if the bulge defendant had relevant minimum contacts *with the bulge area itself*, which Jones clearly does—he did the work in Alton, which is within 100 miles of Boston. Even though

this is a diversity case, the federal courts' power to exercise personal jurisdiction is probably limited by the fifth amendment due process clause, not
the fourteenth. Cf. *Trans-Asiatic Oil, Ltd. S.A. v. Apex Oil Co.,* 743 F.2d
956, 959 (1st Cir. 1984) (in admiralty cases, contacts with United States
as a whole support jurisdiction; state limits on personal jurisdiction do not
apply.) Thus, while there may still be a colorable argument for the *Karlsen*
result (at least in a diversity case like this one), the weight of authority—
plus the clear view of the rulemakers that they *could* assert jurisdiction over
bulge defendants—argues strongly to the contrary. See L. Teply and
R. Whitten, Civil Procedure (2nd ed.) 310-311. I think we are very unlikely
to get out on this basis, and it is not worth the expense to the client of
pursuing it.[1]

I have drafted a motion to dismiss for lack of personal jurisdiction for
your consideration. If you want to pursue this objection, I will research it
more fully.

3. Transfer under 28 U.S.C. §1404(a)

Our strongest argument is for transfer of the case under 28 U.S.C.
§1404(a). Under §1404(a), the court may transfer cases "for the convenience of parties and witnesses, in the interest of justice." The primary factors to be considered are those established in *Gulf Oil Corp. v. Gilbert,*
330 U.S. 501 (1947) (decided under the related doctrine of forum non
conveniens), including the plaintiff's choice of a forum, relative ease of
access to sources of proof, availability of compulsory process, convenience
of the parties and witnesses, possibility of a view, and advantages of
enforceability of a judgment. See generally Moore's Federal Practice,
§111.13[1][b].

Many of these factors support an argument for transfer of this action.
As you indicate, the events that gave rise to the suit took place in New
Hampshire, and all witnesses and parties except for Schulansky live here. In
fact, it will not be possible to compel all of Ronan's employees to testify in
Massachusetts because several of them are not subject to the subpoena power
of the Massachusetts court and Jones tells me that they no longer work for

---

1. There is another argument we could make here. Even if jurisdiction is proper if the
defendant has minimum contacts with the "bulge" area, Jones's contacts, which gave
rise to this claim, are with Alton, New Hampshire. A quick look at the atlas indicates
that Alton is about 75-80 *air miles* from Boston, but probably over a hundred by
road. We could argue that the miles should be measured by road, since this is how
people usually get from place to place.

Believe it or not, this esoteric issue has also been litigated. See, e.g., *Sprow v. Hartford Ins. Co.,* 594 F.2d 412, 417-418 (5th Cir. 1979), which concluded that the better approach is to measure the hundred miles "as the crow flies." Wright and Miller
also advocate this approach. 4A Wright and Miller §1127 n.1. So I think this argument is also likely to be a loser.

Ronan. It may also be necessary for the court and the jury to view the house, which would obviously make trial here more appropriate.

In addition, while I have not yet had the time to research the issue, it seems likely that the Massachusetts federal court, applying Massachusetts conflicts of law doctrine (see *Klaxon Co. v. Stentor Electric Mfg. Co.*, 313 U.S. 487 (1941)) would apply the contract and tort law of New Hampshire to this case, since most of the events giving rise to the action took place here, the property is located here, and the damage was suffered here. A number of cases have concluded that the need to apply the law of another state is a factor in favor of transfer. See, e.g., *Laumann Mfg. Corp. v. Castings U.S.A, Inc.*, 913 F. Supp. 712, 721-722 (E.D.N.Y. 1996); *Gundle Lining Constr. Corp. v. Fireman's Fund Ins. Co.*, 844 F. Supp. 1163, 1165 (S.D. Tex 1994); but cf. *Houk v. Kimberley-Clark Corp.*, 613 F. Supp. 923, 932 (W.D. Mo. 1985) (applicable law not given great weight unless it is complex or unsettled).

Because a major reason for transfer under §1404(a) is for the convenience of the parties, it would certainly bolster our position if the defendants were willing to join in the motion to transfer. You may wish to call Ronan's counsel to see if he is willing to do so. Ironically, while it would be more convenient for Ronan personally to litigate up here, it would be less so for his lawyers because Ackerman, Sloan and Cariotis only have offices in Boston. You might get a more enthusiastic reception if you could suggest this directly to Ronan. However, I realize this would be improper under the Code of Professional Responsibility.

I have attached draft motions to dismiss and to transfer, along with supporting affidavits from Jones. Tactically, we could file the motion to dismiss under Fed. R. Civ. P. 12(b)(2) and hold our motion to transfer, as there is no requirement that the transfer motion be filed before answering the complaint. However, since the argument based on lack of personal jurisdiction looks doubtful, we may want to file both motions together. Perhaps the judge will latch on to the transfer motion as a means of avoiding the more complicated personal jurisdiction question. Last, since we will have to participate in discovery while the motions are pending, we should present both motions in hopes of getting out of the Massachusetts court as soon as possible.

Thank you for reminding me to check the local district court rules. Rule 7.1(B)(1) of the Local Rules of the District of Massachusetts provides that affidavits and other supporting materials, including supporting memoranda, must be filed with the motion. Otherwise, they may only be filed with leave of court. In view of this rule, I suggest that we file a motion for an extension of time to file a responsive pleading under Fed. R. Civ. P. 6(b) or ask Ronan's counsel to assent to an extension, to give us adequate time to prepare a supporting memorandum of law to file with these motions. Alternatively, I have included a request in each motion for leave to file supporting memos at a time specified by the court.

The Resulting Documents

UNITED STATES DISTRICT COURT

DISTRICT OF MASSACHUSETTS

CIVIL ACTION NO. 99-6719

DEBORAH SCHULANSKY

    Plaintiff

    v.

RICHARD L. RONAN   THIRD-PARTY DEFENDANT'S
RONAN CONSTRUCTION CO.
                                    MOTION TO DISMISS THE
    Defendants   THIRD-PARTY COMPLAINT

    v.   FOR LACK OF PERSONAL

ARLEN JONES   JURISDICTION

    Third-Party
    Defendant

       The third-party defendant, Arlen Jones, moves to dismiss the third-party complaint under Fed. R. Civ. P. 12(b)(2) on the ground that the court lacks personal jurisdiction over him on this claim. In support of the motion the third-party defendant states as follows:

1. The third-party defendant is not domiciled in Massachusetts or doing business in Massachusetts on a regular basis, as more fully appears from the Affidavit of Arlen Jones, paragraphs one and three, attached as Exhibit A to this motion.

2. This claim arises out of construction work performed by the third-party defendant in Alton, New Hampshire, as more fully appears from paragraphs one to four of the Third-Party Complaint, and paragraphs four and five of the attached Affidavit of Arlen Jones.

3. The third-party defendant has no contacts with Massachusetts that are related to this claim, as further appears from the Affidavit of Arlen Jones.

4. The exercise of personal jurisdiction over the third-party defendant in these circumstances exceeds the limits of due process under the United States Constitution.

REQUEST FOR ORAL ARGUMENT

The third-party defendant requests twenty minutes for oral argument on this motion, pursuant to Local Rule 7.1(D), and leave to file a supporting memorandum at a time specified by the court.

Donald R. Philbrook
Attorney for Third-Party Defendant
11A Grove Street
Littleton, New Hampshire 03561
(603) 471-8200

UNITED STATES DISTRICT COURT

DISTRICT OF MASSACHUSETTS

CIVIL ACTION NO. 99-6719

DEBORAH SCHULANSKY

    Plaintiff

    v.

RICHARD L. RONAN
RONAN CONSTRUCTION CO.

    Defendants

    v.

ARLEN JONES

    Third-Party
    Defendant

AFFIDAVIT OF ARLEN JONES

IN SUPPORT OF MOTION TO

DISMISS THIRD-PARTY

COMPLAINT

State of New Hampshire

County of Littleton

ss.:

Arlen Jones, being first duly sworn, states as follows:

1. On January 11, 2000, I was personally served with a summons and Third-Party Complaint in the above-captioned action. Service was made at Dover, New Hampshire, while I was engaged in a small excavating project for a condominium complex there.

2. At the time of service and at all other times relevant to this action I resided at 88 Warner Avenue, Littleton, New Hampshire, and conducted a small excavating business from that address as a sole proprietor.

3. Although I occasionally (approximately once per year) do small excavation jobs in Massachusetts, I am not licensed to do business in Massachusetts, do not conduct business there on a regular basis, and receive less than 5% of my income from Massachusetts business.

4. This action arises out of renovation work performed by Richard Ronan on the plaintiff's house in Alton, New Hampshire. The third-party complaint alleges a right to relief for faulty excavation work performed as part of the renovation work at the Alton site.

5. All negotiations, agreements, preparation, and performance of the work giving rise to this claim took place in New Hampshire. I did not solicit this job in Massachusetts nor perform any act related to the events in suit in Massachusetts, nor was I aware until I received process in this action that the plaintiff resided there.

6. I have never consented to suit in Massachusetts on this claim.

                                            _____
                                            Arlen Jones

Subscribed and sworn to before me this ___ day of _____, 2000.

                                              _____
                                            Notary Public

My commission expires:

_____

UNITED STATES DISTRICT COURT

DISTRICT OF MASSACHUSETTS

CIVIL ACTION NO. 99-6719

DEBORAH SCHULANSKY

    Plaintiff

v.

    THIRD-PARTY DEFENDANT'S

RICHARD L. RONAN
RONAN CONSTRUCTION CO.   MOTION TO TRANSFER

    Defendants   UNDER 28 U.S.C. §1404(a)

v.

ARLEN JONES

    Third-Party
    Defendant

The third-party defendant, Arlen Jones, moves to transfer this action to the federal district court for the District of New Hampshire, under 28 U.S.C. §1404(a), for the convenience of the parties and in the interest of justice. In support of the motion, the third-party defendant states as follows:

1. This action arises out of construction work performed on the plaintiff's home in Alton, New Hampshire, as more fully appears from paragraphs 5 and 14-20 of the plaintiff's complaint and paragraphs 7-9 of the Affidavit of Arlen Jones, attached hereto as Exhibit A.

2. The defendants on the main claim are a New Hampshire resident and a New Hampshire corporation, as more fully appears from paragraphs 2-3 of the plaintiff's complaint.

3. All negotiations between the defendant and the third-party defendant concerning the excavation work took place in New Hampshire, as more fully appears from the Affidavit of Arlen Jones, paragraph 8.

4. All of the construction work giving rise to both the plaintiff's claims against the defendants and the defendants' claims against the third-party defendant took place in Alton, New Hampshire, as more fully appears from the Affidavit of Arlen Jones, paragraph 9.

5. Any damages suffered by the plaintiff or the defendants were suffered in New Hampshire, where the premises involved in this action are located and the defendants are located.

6. All potential witnesses who worked on the construction of the addition reside in New Hampshire, as more fully appears from the Affidavit of Arlen Jones, paragraph 10.

7. At least some of the potential witnesses in this action are beyond the subpoena power of this court, as more fully appears from the Affidavit of Arlen Jones, paragraph 10.

8. This claim could have been brought in the District of New Hampshire because the events giving rise to the claim took place there and all defendants are subject to service of process in that district.

REQUEST FOR ORAL ARGUMENT

The third-party defendant requests one half hour for oral argument of this motion, and leave to file a supporting memorandum at a time specified by the court.

Donald R. Philbrook
Attorney for Third-Party Defendant
11A Grove Street
Littleton, New Hampshire 03561
(603) 471-8200

UNITED STATES DISTRICT COURT

DISTRICT OF MASSACHUSETTS

CIVIL ACTION NO. 99-6719

DEBORAH SCHULANSKY

Plaintiff

v.

RICHARD L. RONAN
RONAN CONSTRUCTION CO.

Defendants

v.

ARLEN JONES

Third-Party
Defendant

AFFIDAVIT OF ARLEN JONES

IN SUPPORT OF MOTION TO

TRANSFER UNDER

28 U.S.C. §1404(a)

State of New Hampshire ⎫
                        ⎬ ss.:
County of Littleton   ⎭

Arlen Jones, being first duly sworn, states as follows:

1. I reside at 88 Warner Avenue, Littleton, New Hampshire, approximately 125 miles from Boston, and have resided there at all times relevant to the events involved in this action.

2. I operate a small excavation business, as a sole proprietor. The business is operated out of my home and grosses about $60,000 per year.

3. Over 90% of my business is done in New Hampshire, most of it in the Littleton area of northern New Hampshire. While I occasionally do small jobs in Massachusetts, I do not work there more than approximately once a year. I do not currently have any orders for future jobs in Massachusetts.

4. I am currently booked solid for the new construction season with jobs all over New Hampshire. Since I am a small proprietor, and must attend to my business every day, it would seriously inconvenience me to litigate this action, which arises out of one of the smallest jobs I did last year, in Massachusetts.

5. At no time did I have any direct negotiations with the plaintiff in this action, nor was I apprised of the fact that she lives in Massachusetts or of any other facts that would have led me to expect to have to defend this claim in a Massachusetts court.

6. On information and belief, the defendants Richard Ronan and Ronan Construction Company are primarily engaged in residential construction in New Hampshire.

7. Sometime during the first week of April 1999, Richard Ronan called me in Littleton concerning an excavation job on the Schulansky house in Alton, New Hampshire.

8. After several phone calls between Ronan and me, all of which took place in New Hampshire, I agreed to do the excavation work on the Alton job, for $3,000.

9. I commenced work on the Schulansky job on April 15, 1999, and completed the work on April 17. All preparation and performance of the work took place in either Littleton, New Hampshire or Alton, New Hampshire.

10. I have done at least twenty excavation jobs for Ronan and/or Ronan Construction Company during the past three years. I am acquainted with all of Ronan's employees who worked on the Schulansky job. All of those employees live in New Hampshire, and at least four of them in the Littleton area, more than 100 miles from Boston.

11. Since the Schulansky job in April 1999, several of the carpenters who worked on the job have left Ronan's employ.

_____
Arlen Jones

Subscribed and sworn to before me this ___ day of _____, 2000.

_____
Notary Public

My commission expires:

_____

Comments on the Third-Party Motions

1.   The same formal rules that govern captions for pleadings also apply to motions and to affidavits as well. See Fed. R. Civ. P. 7(b)(2). In addition, the ethical constraints on pleadings in Rule 11 also apply to motions. Fed. R. Civ. P. 7(b)(3). Under Rule 11, attorneys must investigate both the factual and legal bases for filing motions before doing so. Under earlier practice, defense counsel would frequently respond to a complaint with a motion to dismiss, including a long laundry list of dubious objections. Such habits, while they die slowly, are now clearly inconsistent with the Rule 11 requirements for reasonable inquiry and evidentiary support for such objections.

2.   Rule 7(b)(1) provides that a motion shall "state with particularity the grounds therefor." In both the motion to dismiss and the motion to transfer, Jones's counsel has set forth briefly the reasons that support the particular order sought in the motion. This satisfies the requirement of "particularity" and assists the court in understanding the basis of the motions. A motion must also "set forth the relief or order sought." Id. Torres's draft motions do this as well: The first seeks dismissal and the second, transfer. See the first paragraph of each motion.

However, the motion itself is not the right place to *argue* the merits of the motion, or to set forth in detail the facts that support the motion. The supporting arguments and discussion of authority should be set forth in an accompanying memorandum of law. Any facts necessary to support the motion should be provided in accompanying affidavits, deposition transcripts, interrogatories, business records, or other evidentiary documents.

3.   An affidavit is a sworn statement by a witness. It is usually notarized and is signed subject to the penalties of perjury. The "ss." in the heading is a legal formalism frequently found in affidavits. It stands for "silicet," which roughly means "to wit" or "let it be known," and simply indicates that the affiant publicly asserts the facts in the affidavit.

It is entirely proper to submit affidavits in support of a motion, to establish the facts necessary for the court to rule on the motion. See Fed. R. Civ. P. 43(e). In the case of Jones's motion to dismiss for lack of personal jurisdiction, for example, the earlier pleadings do not indicate whether Jones has sufficient contacts with Massachusetts to support jurisdiction over him for this claim. Jones's affidavit provides the court with admissible evidence (since it is sworn personal testimony of the affiant), which supports the position taken in his motion.

If the other parties have countervailing evidence, they may submit their own affidavits or other materials in opposition to the motion. The court may decide the motion on the basis of the facts presented or, if issues of credibility are involved or further evidence needed, may take testimony from the witnesses in a full evidentiary hearing on the motion.

4.   You may have been puzzled as to why Jones's lawyers have included a paragraph in the affidavit stating that several potential witnesses no longer work for Ronan and do not live within 100 miles of Boston. These facts are relevant to the motion to transfer: If these witnesses still worked for Ronan they would presumably be subject to his control and therefore would appear to testify at a trial in Massachusetts. If they no longer work for Ronan, however, and are outside the subpoena power of the Massachusetts federal court, they will probably not be available to testify at a trial in Boston. See Fed. R. Civ. P. 45(b)(2) (authorizing service of subpoenas within the judicial district where suit is pending or within 100 miles of the place of trial). The New Hampshire federal court, however, could subpoena witnesses from any place within New Hampshire, thus supporting the argument for transfer.

5.   It is entirely proper to file combined motions for more than one form of action by the court. Jones's lawyers could, for example, decide to file a combined "Motion to Dismiss for Lack of Personal Jurisdiction, or in the Alternative to Transfer Venue under 28 U.S.C. §1404(a)." Torres drafted the two separately because the tactical decision whether to file them together or separately had not yet been made.

6.   Torres's suggestion that Philbrook contact Ronan's counsel is interesting. It would certainly lend credence to the motion if the original defendants also sought transfer. Although Jones and Ronan are adversaries on the merits, their interests may coincide on this issue or others in the suit. As Chapter 28 indicates (supra p. 529-530), it is appropriate to contact Ronan's counsel to discuss a possible joint motion or any other such issues that arise in the course of the litigation.

Further, the point that Torres makes about the potential difference in interests between Ronan and his attorneys is a delicate and interesting one. If the case is transferred, Ronan's insurance company may retain local counsel in New Hampshire to handle it, and the Boston firm may lose the case. However, Ronan's counsel is there to represent his clients' interests, not his own, and should join in the motion to transfer if Ronan prefers to litigate in New Hampshire, or if other tactical considerations point to New Hampshire as the preferable forum.

7.   This book writing business is frustrating. I started out to create a fairly straightforward case for illustration purposes, but like all lawsuits, *Schulansky v. Ronan* refuses to be simple. The motion to transfer presents a good example. There is some authority for the proposition that the third-party defendant has no standing to object to venue or, apparently, to move to transfer. Instead, the court should consider any inconvenience to the third-party defendant in deciding whether to allow him to be impleaded in the first place. See *Gundle Lining Constr. Co. v. Adams County Asphalt*, 85 F.3d 201, 209-210 (5th Cir. 1996); see also *Pelinski v. Goodyear Tire & Rubber Co.*, 499 F. Supp. 1092, 1095 (N.D. Ill. 1980) ("some question" whether a third-party defendant can seek transfer under §1404(a)).

To be truthful, your humble author never knew this arcane bit of procedural lore until his research assistant stumbled on the point in researching the standards for transfer. It is hardly surprising that Jones's attorneys have not yet discovered it. They well may when they reach the stage of briefing the transfer issue. Or they may not. If they don't, the issue may be raised by one of the other parties or the judge. Or it may not. If the court decides that Jones lacks standing to seek a transfer (or that transfer is not warranted, since the plaintiff and defendants are happy with the forum), he could still dismiss the third-party claim in his discretion under Rule 14(a). Or, Jones can try to convince Ronan to sponsor the motion, since Ronan clearly has standing to seek a transfer.

8. An important limitation on transfer is the requirement that the suit "might have been brought" in the transferee district. 28 U.S.C. §1404(a). In *Hoffman v. Blaski*, 363 U.S. 335, 342-343 (1960), the Supreme Court held that this phrase limits transfer to districts in which venue is proper and service could have been made on the defendant. This requirement is obviously met here, since venue in the initial action would be proper under 28 U.S.C. §1391(a)(1) or (a)(2) and all defendants would be subject to personal jurisdiction in New Hampshire. In paragraph eight of his motion, Torres represents that this requirement for transfer is satisfied.

9. It is fortunate that Philbrook, a New Hampshire practitioner,[2] remembered to have Torres check the local rules for the District of Massachusetts. Most federal districts have their own rules, in addition to the Federal Rules of Civil Procedure, and they frequently cover important aspects of local practice. In this case, Rule 7.1(B)(1) of the Local Rules for the District of Massachusetts specifically requires that supporting affidavits and memoranda be filed with the motion, or else only with leave of court. One effect of this requirement is to discourage "shotgun" motions raising a long laundry list of possible objections. Since counsel must brief all the issues at the outset, they are much more likely to separate the wheat from the chaff in raising preliminary objections. If there is no viable argument for an objection, that will become clear to counsel when he tries to support the argument in a brief. Thus, the need to brief the question right off will often lead counsel to drop the objection instead.

Rule 7.1(D) further requires that a request for a hearing be included in the motion if the moving party wants one and that the party seeking a hearing indicate in the motion the amount of time needed for oral argument, as Torres has done at the end of each motion.

---

2. Philbrook will not automatically have the right to appear on behalf of Jones in the Massachusetts Federal District Court, unless he is a member of the Massachusetts bar. However, Rule 83.5.3 of the Massachusetts District Court Local Rules authorizes the district court to allow an attorney admitted to practice in another state to appear in particular cases.

Rule 7.1(B)(2) of the local district court Rules imposes another requirement that may trap the unwary litigant. Under that Rule, a party who *opposes* a motion must file an opposition to the motion within fourteen days. There is nothing in the Federal Rules of Civil Procedure that requires that an opposition be filed. It is thus essential for counsel to be familiar with the local rules as well as the Federal Rules themselves, which apply generally to *all* federal district courts.

10. Note that the draft motion to dismiss for lack of personal jurisdiction says nothing about Rule 4(k)(1)(B) or the line of cases Torres unearthed in his research. It simply asserts the position that there is no jurisdiction because Jones lacks minimum contacts with Massachusetts. However, because the local rule requires a supporting memorandum of law, Jones would have to set out his argument as to why such contacts are necessary. Thus, he would have to cite the few cases in support of his argument, and this would doubtless trigger a response from Ronan with a wealth of contrary cases. Torres is probably right to suggest that, given the strength of the opposing case law and the expense of the motion, it is better to let this one go. While the lawyer's job is to raise arguments that benefit his clients, that does not require him to abandon good judgment in tilting at litigation windmills. Such unrestrained aggressiveness will simply raise the cost of litigation and provoke similar unproductive conduct from the opposition.

34

A Tactical Dilemma: Ronan's Motion for Summary Judgment

The Drafting Request

MEMORANDUM

TO: Marcia Losordo

FROM: Arthur Ackerman

RE: Summary judgment in *Schulansky v. Ronan*
U.S. District Court No. 99-6719

DATE: September 8, 2000

- -

Now that the judge has denied Jones's motion to transfer this action (somewhat to my surprise, actually), I think we should review the file to determine whether we might be able to get at least some of the claims in this case dismissed on a motion for summary judgment.

In particular, it seems to me that we may be able to get summary judgment on Schulansky's claim (see Complaint, paragraphs 23 and 24) that Ronan agreed to rebuild the old foundation wall. Schulansky virtually admits in her complaint (paragraphs 11-12, 22-23) that the Proposal and Estimate is the entire contract between the parties. If that is true, Schulansky will have to prove that the terms of the Proposal and Estimate itself required Ronan to rebuild the old foundation. The only provision of the contract that arguably addresses this issue is paragraph two. We may be able to convince the court that the interpretation of that paragraph is a question of law for the court and that the only reasonable reading of the paragraph is that it required Ronan to build supporting foundation walls for the three walls of the addition itself, but not to rebuild the original foundation as well.

Schulansky will probably argue that the Proposal and Estimate did not embody the entire agreement between the parties and that she and Ronan had a separate understanding about the scope of the work to be done on the old foundation wall. However, as I recall, Schulansky's deposition testimony strongly supports our position that there were no other agreements or implied terms of the agreement apart from the written terms of the contract.

If the court agrees that the contract is complete on its face, won't the parol evidence rule bar Schulansky from introducing evidence of any prior representations by Ronan concerning rebuilding the foundation? And if such evidence is inadmissible, shouldn't we be entitled to summary judgment based on the language of paragraph two, which only requires Ronan to build walls to support the new addition itself?

In order to determine whether this motion has a reasonable chance of success, I think we should go over the evidence relevant to this issue in detail. Please review the Schulansky deposition and pull out her testimony concerning the negotiations on the foundation problem. Also, talk to Ronan and draw up an affidavit that we could submit in support of our motion, setting out his testimony as to the course of their discussions. Last, please draw up a draft motion for summary judgment and briefly give me your assessment of the likelihood of prevailing on the motion, based on the evidence set forth in the affidavit and deposition. Please do not draft a memorandum in support of the motion at this time, in case we decide not to file the motion.

The Associate's Response

MEMORANDUM

TO: Arthur Ackerman

FROM: Marcia Losordo

RE: Partial Summary Judgment in *Schulansky v. Ronan*
          U.S. District Court No. 99-6719

DATE: September 16, 2000

As you requested, I have reviewed Deborah Schulansky's deposition and pulled out her testimony concerning the negotiations on the reconstruction of the old foundation and the signing of the Ronan contract. (The relevant pages of the deposition are attached to this memo.) I have also discussed this aspect of the case in detail with Richard Ronan and drawn up an affidavit for his signature that sets forth his version of the facts. I also attach a draft motion for partial summary judgment on the issue of Ronan's contractual duty to rebuild the foundation.

After reviewing the documents and spending about three hours researching Massachusetts law on the parol evidence rule and contract interpretation, my preliminary conclusion is that the court will probably deny our motion for summary judgment in this case. Summary judgment will only be granted if our evidence demonstrates that there is no disputed issue of fact for the jury to resolve and that, on the undisputed facts, we are entitled to judgment as a matter of law. Fed. R. Civ. P. 56(c). I doubt that we will be able to make that showing in this case. Given the expense to the client, it may not be worth litigating the motion in a case of this size.

You are correct in stating that Schulansky would be barred from proving any separate agreement with Ronan if the Proposal and Estimate is "fully integrated," that is, constitutes the complete and final agreement of the parties. *Shain Investment Co. v. Cohen*, 15 Mass. App. Ct. 4, 13 (1982); Restatement (Second) of Contracts §215 (1981). A fully integrated contract is one that includes "all the matters agreed upon." Restatement (Second) of Contracts §210, comment a (1981). If a contract is fully integrated, prior negotiations (like the March discussion in this case) are irrelevant, since they have been superseded by the contract, which includes all the rights and obligations of the parties. *Thomas v. Christenson*, 12 Mass. App. Ct. 169, 176 (1981); Restatement (Second) of Contracts §215 (1981). If the contract is not fully integrated, evidence of other agreements would be admissible.

The fact that the contract in issue here is so short, and obviously drafted by Ronan himself rather than counsel, will weaken the argument that it was intended as a fully integrated contract. In addition, the court may hear evidence of prior negotiations to determine whether a contract was meant to comprehensively set forth the obligations of the parties. Restatement (Second) of Contracts §214 (1981); see *Wang Laboratories Inc. v. Docktor Pet Centers, Inc.*, 12 Mass. App. Ct. 213, 219-220 (1981). Thus, (somewhat ironically) the court will hear the evidence as to the negotiations between Ronan and Schulansky about the old foundation, if only to determine whether a separate agreement existed that covered additional matters not addressed in the written contract.

In deciding whether the Proposal and Estimate constitutes the complete agreement of the parties, the court will probably not give too much weight to Schulansky's answers to your questions in the deposition (pp. 9-10) about the existence of additional agreements. Although she does appear to concede that there was no separate agreement about the foundation, her answers indicate some confusion as to exactly what you were asking. She probably was not aware of the legal significance of your questions; she may have thought you were asking whether there were any other formal contracts, rather than an oral understanding between the parties. Slater's objections suggest that she is aware that the issue of a possible separate agreement regarding the foundation is crucial. If we file our motion, supported by the deposition testimony, Slater will doubtless file a counter-affidavit of Schulansky stating that she did not fully understand your questions, that she did not mean that there was no separate understanding about rebuilding the old foundation, and that such a separate oral agreement did in fact exist.

Our strongest argument for summary judgment is that the plaintiff's complaint itself relies exclusively on the Proposal and Estimate as the source of the contractual duty to rebuild the old foundation. See paragraphs 22 and 23. Frankly, I don't understand why her counsel wrote the complaint so narrowly. If the court does not allow an amendment, Schulansky may effectively be barred from proving that she and Ronan had a separate agreement about the old foundation, since she has based her right to relief exclusively on the terms of the Proposal and Estimate. We can argue that any proof of collateral agreements is outside the scope of the complaint. Therefore, if no obligation is created by the terms of the written contract, Ronan is entitled to judgment on the contract claim.

However, this argument may still not carry the day. First, Slater is likely to move to amend the complaint, to add an allegation that the parties had an additional oral agreement concerning the old foundation. At this stage of the case, the court is likely to allow the motion. (Indeed, Schulansky's deposition itself indicates that we are already litigating the issue of possible additional agreements; thus it will be hard to argue that the amendment should be denied due to surprise or prejudice to us.)

Second, even if the court accepts our argument that it is solely the Proposal and Estimate that governs the work, there is still a question as to the interpretation of the second paragraph, requiring Ronan to build foundation walls "to support the addition." This might mean only the three new walls, or it could be construed to include the fourth wall, the old foundation wall adjoining the addition. If the term is ambiguous, and there is conflicting evidence as to the intended meaning, the issue is for the jury, and summary judgment will be denied. Restatement (Second) of Contracts §212(2) (1981).

After review of the deposition, I think that Judge Meliotis would likely find that there is a genuine issue of material fact as to the meaning of paragraph two. Although Schulansky did not testify that Ronan explicitly agreed to rebuild the old foundation, if the jury believed her testimony they could find that Ronan agreed to do whatever was necessary to make the foundation solid. Schulansky understood him to say that he would do whatever had to be done to stabilize the old foundation. See Schulansky deposition at 12 (Ronan "would take care of it"); pp. 12-13 (she got the impression that "he would rebuild it if it had to be done"). Ronan himself admits that they discussed the subject, although he has a very different view of their understanding on it. See Ronan affidavit, paras. 4-8. Thus, I conclude that the judge will find issues of fact as to what Ronan agreed to here—even under the Proposal and Estimate itself—which have to be resolved at trial.

I agree with you that Ronan's testimony is more precise and is supported by the fact that he did exactly what he says he agreed to do, stabilize the foundation with concrete. See Affidavit of Ronan, paragraphs 7, 12. In addition, Schulansky's own testimony tends to support Ronan's version of their discussions. Deposition, p. 12 (Ronan said he would "use concrete to fix" the foundation). This suggests that we may prevail on this factual issue at trial, but it does not make the issue a question of law appropriate for summary judgment. As long as a reasonable jury *could* infer from Schulansky's testimony that Ronan had agreed to do more, a factual issue is posed and summary judgment must be denied. See Fed. R. Civ. P. 56(c) (summary judgment appropriate where there is "no genuine issue of material fact").

Please let me know whether you intend to file the motion; I assume you will want me to write a memorandum in support of the motion if you do.

MEMORANDUM

TO: Marcia Losordo

FROM: Arthur Ackerman

RE: Summary judgment in *Schulansky v. Ronan*
U.S. District Court No. 99-6719

DATE: September 19, 2000

- -

Thank you for your memo on the complexities of contract interpretation in this case. Given the expense of briefing and arguing the motion and the obstacles to prevailing on it, I have decided not to seek summary judgment at this time. Although I think we have a very strong case for our interpretation of the contract, I reluctantly agree that getting a judge to say as a matter of law that there was no separate agreement on the foundation, or that paragraph two of the Proposal and Estimate *must* carry our meaning, is unlikely.

Several other points in your memo also suggest that we might be better advised not to file the motion, at least at this stage of the case. Your memo reminded me that Judge Meliotis has this case. Judge Meliotis is affectionately referred to as "Try It" Meliotis among experienced members of the local bar, for her well-known propensity to give plaintiffs their "day in court" by denying pretrial motions under Rule 12 or Rule 56.

In addition, I agree that the plaintiff's allegations in the complaint may ultimately limit her right to prove a collateral agreement at trial. She has not alleged a separate oral agreement to rebuild the foundation in the complaint as it stands. If we move for a summary judgment this early in the case, you quite rightly point out that the court is likely to allow an amendment. However, if the plaintiff does not amend before trial, the court might refuse to allow her to do so at trial. At that point, we will be able to argue that the motion is unduly delayed and that our trial preparation has been shaped by the original pleadings. Under the circumstances, we should probably not educate the plaintiff now about possible defects in those pleadings.

Since the Parnell case has just settled unexpectedly, and we will not be filing the summary judgment motion in the Schulansky case, maybe you should try to catch a few days off. Don't we owe you some time from last Christmas?

The Resulting Documents

UNITED STATES DISTRICT COURT

DISTRICT OF MASSACHUSETTS

	CIVIL ACTION NO. 99-6719
DEBORAH SCHULANSKY	
Plaintiff	
v.	
RICHARD L. RONAN et al.	DEFENDANTS' MOTION FOR
Defendants	PARTIAL SUMMARY
v.	JUDGMENT
ARLEN JONES	
Third-Party Defendant	

The defendants move for summary judgment under Fed. R. Civ. P. 56 on the plaintiff's Claim for Relief for breach of contract set forth in paragraphs twenty-one through twenty-four of the complaint. Based on the complaint (including the Proposal and Estimate, attached as Exhibit A to the complaint), the answer, the attached excerpt from the deposition of Deborah Schulansky, and the attached affidavit of Richard L. Ronan, there is no genuine issue of material fact as to this claim and the defendants are entitled to judgment as a matter of law.

In support of this motion, the defendants state:

1. The plaintiff's complaint alleges a right to relief for breach of a contract between her and the defendants, dated March 15, 1999, and entitled "Proposal and Estimate."

2. The plaintiff admits that she signed the Proposal and Estimate (see complaint, paragraphs eleven, twelve) and that it constitutes the final and complete contract between the parties for the work to be done on the Alton house. Complaint, paragraph twenty-two; Deposition of Deborah Schulansky, pp. 9-10.

3. Paragraph two is the only provision of the Proposal and Estimate that covers foundation work to be done under the contract.

4. Paragraph two does not create any obligation on the part of the defendants to rebuild the foundation of the main house.

REQUEST FOR ORAL ARGUMENT

Pursuant to Rule 7.1(D) of the Local Rules of the District Court of Massachusetts, the defendant requests one half hour for oral argument on this motion.

_____
Arthur Ackerman
Ackerman, Sloan and Cariotis
Attorney for the Defendants
59 State Street
Boston, MA 02114
(617) 228-6301

UNITED STATES DISTRICT COURT

DISTRICT OF MASSACHUSETTS

CIVIL ACTION NO. 99-6719

DEBORAH SCHULANSKY

    Plaintiff

  v.

RICHARD L. RONAN et al.

    Defendants

  v.

ARLEN JONES

    Third-Party
    Defendant

DEPOSITION OF DEBORAH SCHULANSKY, taken on behalf of the defendants Richard Ronan and Ronan Construction Company, pursuant to notice under the Federal Rules of Civil Procedure, before Alexander Barlow, a Registered Professional Reporter and Notary Public in and for the Commonwealth of Massachusetts, at the office of Ackerman, Sloan and Cariotis, 59 State Street, Boston, Massachusetts, on Wednesday, May 10, 2000, commencing at 10:00 a.m.

Q. Now, Mrs. Schulansky, I show you this document, headed "Proposal and Estimate," which is attached to your complaint and marked Exhibit A. Are you familiar with that document?

A. Yes, that's the paper Richard Ronan sent me to sign about the job.

Q. Is this the contract between you and Ronan Construction Company for the construction of the addition?

A. Yes, that's it.

Q. Did you make any additions or changes to this agreement before you signed it and returned it to Ronan?

A. No, I didn't change anything on it.

Q. Did you make any written changes or modifications in the agreement _after_ it was signed, either before the work commenced or while it was being done?

A. No.

Q. Is this the only contract you had with Ronan or Ronan Construction Company relating to the construction of the addition?

A. Yes.

Q. You didn't enter into any other agreements with Ronan concerning the work?

A. I'm not sure just what you mean...

Q. Did you sign any other documents describing the work to be done or other terms of the agreement?

A. No, that was the only thing I signed.

Q. Did you have any other oral agreements about the job, apart from the Proposal and Estimate?

-9-

Ms. Slater: Objection. You are asking for a legal characterization of the negotiations between the parties.

Q. Well, I think the plaintiff is qualified to testify to her own understanding of what happened. Let me rephrase the question.

Was it your understanding that there were other agreements between you and Ronan Construction Company, or between you and Richard Ronan, governing the work to be done on the addition?

A. No, I didn't have any other agreements with him. Just that contract you have there that I signed in March. But I'm still not sure I know what you mean.

Q. So this Exhibit A, the Proposal and Estimate, was the only agreement you had for the construction?

A. Yes, it was the only thing I signed.

Q. And it represents the complete agreement between you as to how much you would pay, the work to be done, the timing, all the terms of the contract?

Ms. Slater: Objection. The question calls for a legal conclusion.

A. That's the only agreement I signed, if that's what you're getting at.

Q. Now, Mrs. Schulansky, could you tell us what was the first time that you discussed the foundation of the house with Richard Ronan?

A. It was the second time we talked. He came to my house—the one in Plymouth, that is—to go over the details of the project.

After we met the first time, he went over and took a look at the house in Alton so we could talk more specifically about what had to be done. Then we sat down in Plymouth to go over the details.

Q. Who brought up the subject of the foundation at that time?

A. Well, I don't really remember. I remember that it was a concern of mine, and I planned to ask him about it, but I can't say whether I brought it up or he did. I think probably I did, but I'm not sure.

Q. Could you tell me as accurately as you can recall just what the sequence of the conversation was about the foundation?

A. Well, I think I asked him whether he thought there would be any problem with the foundation, and he said he didn't think so.

Q. Did you specify problems with the old foundation, as opposed to the foundation to support the addition?

A. Well, I don't think I was as specific as that, but I'm sure he knew what I was talking about. In fact, I remember saying that one reason I had some concerns about it was that we were going to cut a door through it into the new cellar.

Q. Exactly what did you ask him about the foundation?

A. As I said, I asked him whether it would be O.K., whether it would be disturbed by the construction and whether it would have to be rebuilt when he dug a new cellar.

-11-

Q. Did you use the word "rebuilt"?

A. I really couldn't say what words I used, but that was the gist of what I was asking.

Q. And what did Ronan answer?

A. Well, he said that he didn't think it would be a problem, that it had been there for 200 years and would probably be there for 200 more, something like that. But if there was a problem he would take care of it.

Q. Were those his exact words?

A. I really don't remember exactly what he said, but it was something about if anything was loose he would take care of it, or fix it, or something like that.

Q. Did he say he would rebuild the foundation?

A. I don't remember whether he used those exact words, but I do remember him saying he would use concrete to fix it. He definitely said he would use concrete, he would fix it with concrete, which I assume means the same thing as rebuilding it.

Q. But he didn't use the word "rebuild"?

Ms. Slater: Objection as to the form of the question.

A. I can't swear that he used that exact word, but that was the impression I got, that he would rebuild it if it had to be done.

Q. Did he say he would "reinforce" the foundation?

A. Again, I just can't say, it was over a year ago and I didn't expect to get in a law suit over this thing. I can't say he said "rebuild" or "reinforce" but it was clear to me that he was going to take care of any problems with the foundation, because that was part of the job.

Q. Was there any discussion about the type of foundation that was there, what it was made up of or how it was put together?

A. I think he said he couldn't tell for sure until it was exposed during the excavation, but that it was probably stones and cement, or I guess they called it mortar back then.

Q. Did Ronan say that he would fix it no matter what he found when he got in there?

A. I already told you, he said he didn't think it would be a problem, but he would take care of it.

Q. Did he discuss any different methods he would use to fix it, depending on what he found when it was exposed?

A. Well, he said he would reinforce it, fix it with concrete.

Q. But he didn't make any distinction between what he would do if it was a mortar foundation or a rock foundation, anything like that?

Ms. Slater: Objection as to the form.

A. No, he just assured me it would be all right.

Q. Was that all of the discussion you had concerning the old foundation?

A. At that time, yes.

Q. Did you discuss it again later?

-13-

A. Yes, when they were doing the excavating and that guy with the backhoe started tearing it to pieces...

Q. But you didn't discuss it again at any time before the job started, before you signed the Proposal and Estimate?

A. No, just the one time. I thought we had a clear understanding on it; I didn't bring it up again.

Q. Was there anything in the Proposal and Estimate about rebuilding the foundation?

Ms. Slater: Objection, the question calls for a legal interpretation.

Q. I will withdraw the question. When you got the Proposal and Estimate from Ronan did you have any question about whether the proposal covered rebuilding the foundation?

A. No, it seemed to me to cover the ground ... he was going to build the addition as we discussed and I was going to pay him $40,000, or whatever it was.

Q. Did you contact Ronan with any questions about the Proposal and Estimate?

A. No, I just looked it over and signed it. It looked all right to me, but I'm a stockbroker, not a lawyer. I wasn't planning on getting into a lawsuit over this thing. He seemed like he knew what he was talking about, and he did a good job for my neighbor, so I assumed he would do the job right.

Q. Now, Mrs. Schulansky, moving on, when was the next time, after your March meeting, that you discussed possible problems with the old foundation with Ronan, or any other employee of Ronan Construction Company?

A. Well, I guess it was when I drove up to Alton, when they started the work, in mid-April.

Q. You didn't discuss it with Ronan between signing the Proposal and Estimate and the time the work started?

A. No, I didn't see him again until then.

Q. No phone discussions prior to the beginning of the work?

A. No.

Q. Could you tell me how the subject arose when you went to the job site?

A. Well, I went there when they started the job, to check out any last minute problems and see how the excavation went. When I arrived the backhoe man was already in there digging out the new cellar, and I started to get nervous about the foundation problem. So I stayed to see what the foundation was like. It wasn't until after lunch that he really started to excavate around the foundation, but as soon as he did I could see there were going to be problems.

Q. Did you talk to Ronan at that point about the foundation?

A. Yes. I was upset because the backhoe kept smashing into the rock foundation, and I could see he was loosening up the rocks that hold up the house. So I spoke to Ronan about it.

UNITED STATES DISTRICT COURT

DISTRICT OF MASSACHUSETTS

CIVIL ACTION NO. 99-6719

DEBORAH SCHULANSKY

Plaintiff

v.

RICHARD L. RONAN et al.   AFFIDAVIT OF RICHARD

Defendants   L. RONAN IN SUPPORT OF

v.   MOTION FOR SUMMARY

ARLEN JONES   JUDGMENT

Third-Party
Defendant

Commonwealth of Massachusetts   }ss:

Suffolk County

I, Richard L. Ronan, being first duly sworn, depose and say:

1. I am the president of Ronan Construction Company, a New Hampshire corporation with offices at 1124 Newark Road, Nashua, New Hampshire.

2. Ronan Construction Company is engaged in residential construction work in New Hampshire and Massachusetts.

3. In March of 1999, I entered into negotiations, on behalf of Ronan Construction Company, with Deborah Schulansky, the plaintiff in this case, concerning an addition that she wished to build onto the back of her home in Alton, New Hampshire.

4. During one of the meetings I had with the plaintiff concerning the work to be done as part of the construction of the addition, the plaintiff asked me about possible reconstruction of the old house foundation, where the addition adjoined the living room of the main house.

5. At that time, I stated that such reconstruction would probably not be necessary, because the foundation

appeared to be stable, had been there for many years and was unlikely to shift.

6. However, I further stated that you can never be sure about a foundation that old, and that it was impossible to tell for sure what the foundation was like until we uncovered it in the process of excavating the new cellar.

7. I further stated that it was likely that it was a rock and mortar foundation, or a plain rock foundation, and that if there were holes in it I would fill them in with cement.

8. At no time during this conversation did I indicate that I would completely rebuild the foundation, or that I could guarantee that the foundation would last for any period of time or never be subject to subsidence.

9. This was the only discussion that I or anyone else on behalf of Ronan Construction Company had with the plaintiff concerning the old foundation until the actual excavation began.

10. Complete reconstruction of even a small part of the original foundation, without disturbing the structure above it, is a delicate and expensive job, that could easily cost as much as the entire bid I made on the Schulansky job.

11. Such reconstruction would normally be done separately, by a masonry contractor, not as part of a construction job such as the one in issue in this case.

12. After exposure of the foundation, it became clear that the foundation was stable, although no mortar had been used in the original construction. In accordance with my earlier statements to the plaintiff, I had the mason pour cement into the holes among the rocks.

13. At no time did I state that I would rebuild the old foundation, or do anything more than add small amounts of concrete to the existing foundation.

_____
Richard L. Ronan

Subscribed and sworn to before me this _____ day of _____, 2000.

_____
Notary Public

My commission expires:

_____

Comments on the Motion for Summary Judgment

1.   A motion for summary judgment, like any other motion, is governed by Rule 7(b) of the Federal Rules of Civil Procedure. It must be in writing and must state "with particularity" the grounds of the motion. The four numbered paragraphs of Ronan's motion briefly state the supporting reasons for the motion.

2.   As the motion indicates, the defendants only seek summary judgment on part of Schulansky's first claim for relief. Even if they prevail on their argument that Ronan had no duty to rebuild the old foundation, Schulansky also seeks relief for breach of contract on the ground that Jones, acting on behalf of the defendants in performing the contract work, damaged the foundation with the backhoe. See Complaint, paragraph 25, supra p. 540. That issue (and, of course, the negligence claim in the second claim for relief) would still have to be litigated, even if summary judgment were granted on the duty-to-rebuild issue.

3.   As Chapter 21 indicates, a motion for summary judgment is based on the assertion that there is no "genuine issue" as to the material facts. To support that position, the moving party must submit admissible evidence that supports its version of the facts.[1] In this case, Losordo has reviewed the deposition, pulled out those pages that contain relevant testimony, and attached them to the motion. The defendants' position, if they file the motion, is that Schulansky's testimony (at pp. 9-10), when read together with the Ronan affidavit, demonstrates that the Proposal and Estimate constitutes the complete agreement of the parties and that, as a matter of law, it cannot be construed to require Ronan to rebuild the foundation.

4.   As the Introduction to these materials indicates, depositions are arranged by the parties. The evidence is taken under oath by a licensed court reporter. After the deposition, the reporter prepares a transcript and sends it to the party who scheduled the deposition, with a copy to opposing counsel if requested. The parties usually agree that the deposition will not be filed with the court.

Depositions are an extremely effective means of discovery, since they provide the opportunity to examine the witness in person and to follow up immediately on issues that arise from the deponent's answers. However, they are also expensive. A typical deposition might run anywhere from 50 to 200

---

1. In cases in which summary judgment is sought against the party who bears the burden of proof, the moving party may rely on the absence from the record of any admissible evidence to support the opposing party's case. See *Celotex Corp. v. Catrett,* 477 U.S. 317 (1986). But in most cases the moving party will submit evidence to establish its own version of the facts.

pages or more. The court reporter may charge $3.00 per page or more for recording the deposition and providing the transcript to the attorney who took the deposition. Preparation for taking the deposition takes time, and of course the lawyer charges for her time during the deposition. In view of the expense involved, counsel must exercise judgment in deciding whether the size of the case and the likelihood that the deposition will be productive justify such expense.

5.   Tactically, the defendants should probably submit only that part of the Schulansky deposition (pp.9-10) that deals with the existence of other agreements. They would probably not submit the following pages (pp.11-14) of the deposition, since the testimony about the March negotiations may raise a question of fact as to whether the parties had a separate agreement about the old foundation or, if not, about the meaning of paragraph two of the Proposal and Estimate.

Of course, if the defendants did not submit this part of the testimony, Schulansky's lawyers probably would. When a motion for summary judgment is made and supported by evidence that tends to establish the movant's version of the facts, the party opposing summary judgment must come forward with evidence that shows that there is a factual dispute for the jury. As Losordo's memo suggests, Schulansky's testimony about the March discussions probably is sufficient to raise a factual question as to whether a separate agreement existed and, if so, what it required Ronan to do.

6.   Losordo's memo points out a real problem with the plaintiff's complaint. Paragraphs 22-24 of the complaint allege that Ronan had a duty under the Proposal and Estimate to rebuild the foundation. No mention is made of a possible separate understanding regarding this part of the work. Ackerman's questions in the Schulansky deposition have undoubtedly alerted Schulansky's counsel to the fact that the defendants will argue that any obligation to rebuild must be based on the Proposal and Estimate. Slater might well seek to amend the complaint to assert, in the alternative, that the parties had a separate oral agreement regarding reconstruction of the foundation.

Such an amendment would likely be granted at this stage of the case. The spirit of the federal "notice pleading" system is to have the parties set forth their positions at the outset but to allow them to clarify those positions as the discovery process provides more detailed information about their claims and defenses. That is precisely what has happened here. As the parties proceed with discovery and focus in on the pivotal issue of the exact terms of the agreement between the parties, Schulansky's counsel will refine their understanding of both the facts and the (somewhat amorphous) law of contract formation.

Absent undue delay or other demonstrable prejudice to the defendants, they should be allowed to amend their pleadings to reflect that clearer understanding of the case. However, as Ackerman's second memo suggests, the likelihood that such an amendment will be allowed decreases as trial approaches. If Schulansky's attorneys do not seek an amendment promptly, they risk the possibility that the court will deny a motion to amend later on. If that happens, they could be precluded from proving that a separate understanding required Ronan to rebuild the foundation, because they failed to give the defendants timely notice that the issue would be raised.

7. Ackerman's comment about Judge Meliotis raises an interesting tactical point. As the Introduction indicates, cases in federal court in Massachusetts are assigned to one judge, who presides over the case from start to finish. Thus, Ronan's attorneys know who will hear their motion for summary judgment and will naturally take into account whatever they know about that judge's predilections.

While ours is supposedly "a government of laws, not of men [and women]," any practicing lawyer will tell you that it makes a difference which judge hears your case. If Judge Meliotis is conservative in interpreting the rules of procedure, she may be less likely to grant summary judgment. Or, if she is particularly sensitive to reversal on appeal, she may see denial of the motion as the safest course, since denial of the motion is much less likely to be reversed than a grant of summary judgment. These and many other considerations may influence a judge's decision, and hence must be taken into account (to the extent they are known) by the parties litigating before that judge.

8. Obviously, an essential component of the defendants' motion for summary judgment will be an accompanying memorandum of law, explaining why there are no material facts in dispute and why, as a matter of law, the court should enter judgment in their favor. See Local Rule 7.1(B)(1) of the District of Massachusetts, which requires that a supporting memorandum be filed along with the motion.

Although *Schulansky* is a relatively low-stakes case, the legal issues involved are not correspondingly simple. For example, Losordo's memo demonstrates that the summary judgment motion raises complex issues of contract interpretation. In addition, an even more complex issue may be lurking: Which state's contract law should apply to this case?

Under *Erie Railroad Co. v. Tompkins,* 304 U.S. 64 (1938), the federal court must apply state law to this diversity case — but which state's law, Massachusetts's or New Hampshire's? In *Klaxon Co. v. Stentor Electric Mfg. Co.,* 313 U.S. 487 (1941), the Supreme Court held that the court must apply the law that the state court would apply if the case were in state court. Under *Klaxon,* the federal judge must determine whether a Massachusetts State court would apply Massachusetts or New Hampshire law to this case, under "choice of law" principles. See Chapter 12, pp. 213-215. The defendants' lawyers might spend a good deal of their clients' money to research that issue and still only come up with an educated guess. The plaintiff's counsel will also have to research these issues and write a memorandum in opposition to the motion for summary judgment.

One of the difficult calls lawyers make all the time is how much time to put into particular issues, given the client's ability to pay, the likelihood that the issue will arise, the likelihood that research will yield helpful results, and the amount at stake in the case. Losordo could easily spend 15 hours researching the contract issues raised above and drafting an effective memorandum in support of the motion. At $75 per hour, that amounts to $1,500 just to file the motion. Additional time will have to be spent preparing to argue the motion, arguing it in court, and writing a reply to the plaintiff's memorandum in opposition to the motion.

Obviously, this is only one stage in the case; trial will doubtless involve substantially more hours (often billed at a higher rate), and other time has already gone into the pleadings and discovery. As every lawyer knows, litigation provides a means for resolving disputes, but it is neither simple nor fast in most cases.

Index